SUPPLEMENT II, Part 1
W. H. Auden to O. Henry

AMERICAN WRITERS

A Collection of Literary Biographies

A. WALTON LITZ
Editor in Chief

SUPPLEMENT II, Part 1
W. H. Auden to O. Henry

Charles Scribner's Sons, New York

Copyright © 1981 Charles Scribner's Sons

Library of Congress Cataloging in Publication Data   (Revised)
Main entry under title:

American writers.

The 4-vol. main set consists of 97 of the pamphlets originally published
as the University of Minnesota pamphlets on American writers;
some have been rev. and updated. The supplements cover writers
not included in the original series.
    Includes bibliographies.
    CONTENTS: v.1. Henry Adams to T. S. Eliot.—v.2. Ralph Waldo Emerson
to Carson McCullers. —v.3. Archibald MacLeish to George Santayana.—[etc.]
    1. American literature—History and criticism.
2. American literature—Bio-bibliography. 3. Authors, American—Biography.
I. Unger, Leonard, ed.   II. Minnesota. University. Pamphlets on American writers.
PS129.A55   810′.9 [B]   73-1759
ISBN 0-684-16482-5

35791113151719   QD/C   201816141210864

Printed in the United States of America

Acknowledgment is gratefully made to those publishers and individuals who have permitted the use of the following materials in copyright.

"W. H. Auden"
from W. H. Auden's previously unpublished letter to his father, by permission of Edward Mendelson, copyright © 1981 by Edward Mendelson, William Meredith and Monroe K. Spears, Executors of the Estate of W. H. Auden. From William Butler Yeats, "To a Friend Whose Work Has Come to Nothing." Reprinted with permission of Macmillan Publishing Co., Inc. from *Collected Poems of William Butler Yeats.* Copyright 1916 by Macmillan Publishing Co., Inc., renewed 1944 by Bertha Georgie Yeats. Also used by permission of A. P. Watt & Sons. Acknowledgment is made to Random House, Inc. for permission to quote from the following copyrighted works of W. H. Auden: *W. H. Auden: Collected Poems* and *The English Auden: Poems, Essays, and Dramatic Writings, 1927–1939,* both by W. H. Auden and edited by Edward Mendelson. Selected quotations reprinted by permission of Faber and Faber Ltd. from *Collected Poems* by W. H. Auden.

"Amiri Baraka"
from *The Dead Lecturer.* Copyright © 1964 by LeRoi Jones. From *Black Magic: Collected Poetry 1961–1967.* Copyright © 1969 by LeRoi Jones (Amiri Baraka). From *Dutchman and the Slave.* Copyright © 1964 by LeRoi Jones (Amiri Baraka). From *Preface to a Twenty Volume Suicide Note.* Copyright © 1961 by LeRoi Jones (Amiri Baraka). From *In Our Terribleness (Some Elements and Meaning in Black Style).* Copyright © 1970

by LeRoi Jones. Lines from "A Poem for Anna Russ and Fanny Jones," "Reprise of One of A.G.'s Best Poems," "Like This Is What I Meant," "Afro-American Lyric," "Pres Spoke in a Language," "Am/Trak," "Spring Song," "Child of the Thirties," "Afrika Revolution," "Dictatorship of the Proletariat," "A Poem for Deep Thinkers," "Race Line," in *Selected Poetry of Amiri Baraka/LeRoi Jones.* Copyright © 1979 by Amiri Baraka. By permission of William Morrow & Company.

"R. P. Blackmur"
from unpublished material by R. P. Blackmur, by permission of Joseph Frank, Literary Executor of the Estate of R. P. Blackmur.

"Malcolm Cowley"
"Prayer on All Saints' Day" was first published in the *Sewanee Review* 86, 4 (Fall 1978), copyright © 1978 by Malcolm Cowley. Reprinted with the permission of Malcolm Cowley. From "Blue Juniata," in *Blue Juniata,* copyright © 1968 by Malcolm Cowley. From *And I Worked at the Writer's Trade* by Malcolm Cowley. Copyright © 1978 by Malcolm Cowley. Reprinted by permission of Viking Penguin Inc.

"Ralph Ellison"
Portions of this essay are used here with the permission of the publishers from *The Craft of Ralph Ellison,* by Robert G. O'Meally, Cambridge, Mass.: Harvard University Press. Copyright © 1980 by the President and Fellows of Harvard College. From *The Invisible Man* by Ralph Ellison. Copyright 1952 by Ralph Ellison. Reprinted by permission of Random House, Inc. Also used

Introduction

Like the essays in the first Supplement to *American Writers* (2 vols., 1979), the essays in this second Supplement follow the pattern set in *American Writers: A Collection of Literary Biographies* (4 vols., 1974). The ninety-seven essays in the original four volumes first appeared as the University of Minnesota Pamphlets on American Writers, a distinguished series published between 1959 and 1972. (For a history of this enterprise the reader should consult the Introduction to the first four volumes.) When the Minnesota series was started, the pamphlets were described as "introductory essays . . . aimed at people (general readers here and abroad, college students, etc.) who are interested in the writers concerned, but not highly familiar with their work," and the present Supplement was edited with the same audience in mind. From the beginning, however, the authors of the *American Writers* pamphlets managed to combine a balanced account of basic issues with the results of original research and criticism. The essays in Supplement II, all written by recognized experts and published here for the first time, carry on this tradition of writing for the general reader in a way that the specialist will also find interesting and informative. In several instances—most notably the essays on R. P. Blackmur, Malcolm Cowley, and W. E. B. Du Bois—the authors have produced the fullest account to date of the writer's life and work.

While the essays in Supplement II embody the original aims of the *American Writers* series, they have inevitably been affected by the radical changes in literary taste and critical perspective of the past quarter-century. The first *American Writers* essays were conceived at a time when a New Critical emphasis on formal literary analysis and the autonomy of the art-work dominated American criticism: as a result, biographical and cultural discussions were sometimes subordinated to close analyses of individual works. The essays in Supplement II, many written by young scholars, reflect a renewed interest in literary biography and cultural history, although they still provide detailed examinations of major works.

The essays in Supplement II also reflect the important changes in the canon of American literature that have occurred since the post-World War II scholarly and critical consensus began to break down in the early 1960's. As in the first Supplement, greater attention has been given to women writers, among them Joyce Carol Oates, Anne Sexton, and Margaret Fuller. Supplement II is especially rich in essays on black writers: Amiri Baraka (LeRoi Jones), W. E. B. Du Bois, Paul Laurence Dunbar, Ralph Ellison, and Robert Hayden. Our enlarged sense of what constitutes a literary text has led to the inclusion of social critics and historians, among them Du Bois, Lewis Mumford, and Francis Parkman. The major critics of the generation that came to maturity between the two world wars are given full treatment as literary artists. Writers from the earlier periods who have recently gained in reputation, such as Cotton Mather and Philip Freneau, are now included; but Supplement II follows its predecessor in placing emphasis on contemporary writers who have attained wide recognition in recent years, such as Allen Ginsberg and Thomas Pynchon. In their chronological range (from Cotton Mather to Joyce Carol Oates) and their variety of critical and scholarly approaches, the essays in Supplement II remind us that our native literary tradition is reviewed by every generation of readers, and that it must be constantly revised and augmented if it is to remain alive.

—*A. WALTON LITZ*

Editorial Staff

List of Subjects

List of Contributors

Listed below are the contributors to *American Writers*, Supplement II. Authors' names are followed by institutional affiliations at the time of publication, titles of books written or edited, and titles of essays written for this Supplement.

MAXINE OLIAN APSEL. Instructor of Humanities and Interdisciplinary Studies, Bloomfield College. Author of essays on Charles Olson in *boundary 2* and the *Markham Review*. **Charles Olson.**

HERBERT APTHEKER. Director of the American Institute for Marxist Studies. Author of *American Slave Revolts*; *A History of the People of the United States* (3 volumes to date); and *The Urgency of Marxist-Christian Dialogue*. Compiler of *An Annotated Bibliography of the Published Writings of W. E. B. Du Bois*. Editor of *A Documentary History of the Negro People in the United States* (3 volumes); *The Autobiography of W. E. B. Du Bois*; and *The Collected Published Writings of W. E. B. Du Bois* (23 of the projected 40 volumes have been published). **W. E. B. Du Bois.**

KENT BALES. Associate Professor of English, University of Minnesota. **O. Henry.**

PAUL BRESLIN. Assistant Professor of English, Northwestern University. **Delmore Schwartz.**

R. W. BUTTERFIELD. Reader in Literature, University of Essex. Author of *The Broken Arc: A Study of Hart Crane*. **Robinson Jeffers.**

BELL GALE CHEVIGNY. Associate Professor of Literature, State University of New York at Purchase. Author of *The Woman and the Myth: Margaret Fuller's Life and Writings*. Editor of *Twentieth Century Interpretations of Endgame*. **Margaret Fuller.**

GEORGE CORE. Editor of the *Sewanee Review*. Author of *The Literalists of the Imagination: Southern Letters and the New Criticism*; and of various essays and reviews in the *Virginia Quarterly*, *Southern Review*, *Wall Street Journal*, and elsewhere. Editor of *Southern Fiction Today*. **Malcolm Cowley.**

FRANK R. CUNNINGHAM. Associate Professor of English, University of South Dakota. Author of articles and reviews in various journals. **Clifford Odets.**

CHARLES T. DAVIS. Musser Professor of English and Afro-American Studies, Yale University. Author, with Gay Wilson Allen, of *Walt Whitman's Poems*. Editor of *E. A. Robinson: Selected Early Poems and Letters* and Lucy Larcom's *A New England Girlhood*. **Paul Laurence Dunbar.**

PAUL A. DOYLE. Professor of English, Nassau Community College, State University of New York. Author of *A Concordance to the Collected Poems of James Joyce*; *Liam O'Flaherty: A Critical Introduction*; *Sean O'Faolain*; *Pearl S. Buck*; *Evelyn Waugh: A Checklist of Primary and Secondary Material*; *Liam O'Flaherty: An Annotated Bibliography*; *Paul Vincent Carroll: An Introduction*; *Henry David Thoreau: Studies and Commentaries*; *Guide to Basic Information Sources in English Literature*. **Pearl S. Buck.**

WILTON ECKLEY. Professor of English, Drake University. Author of *Harriette Arnow*; *T. S. Stribling*; *Guide to e. e. cummings*; *Herbert Hoover*; and numerous articles on short fiction and science fiction. **Bret Harte.**

PETER FIRCHOW. Professor of English and Comparative Literature, University of Minnesota. Author of *Aldous Huxley, Satirist and Novelist*; *Friedrich Schlegel's "Lucinde" and the Fragments*; *The Writer's Place*. Co-editor, with E. S. Firchow, of *East German Short Stories: An Introductory Anthology*. **Lewis Mumford.**

WILLIAM C. FISCHER. Associate Professor of English, State University of New York at Buffalo. **Amiri Baraka.**

RUSSELL A. FRASER. Professor of English, University of Michigan. Author of *The Court of Venus*; *The Court of Virtue*; *Shakespeare's Poetics*; *The War Against Poetry*; *An Essential Shakespeare*; *The Dark Ages and the Age of Gold*; and *The Language of Adam on the Limits and Systems of Discourse*. Editor of *Selected Writings of Oscar Wilde*; *Essays Presented to Frank Livingston Huntley, Michigan Quarterly Review*; and, with Norman Rabkin, *Drama of the English Renaissance*. **R. P. Blackmur.**

MAUREEN GOLDMAN. Assistant Professor of English, Bentley College. Author of numerous conference papers on writing and literature. **Philip Freneau.**

ROBERT M. GREENBERG. Visiting Assistant Professor of English, Temple University. **Robert Hayden.**

BRUCE KELLNER. Professor of English, Millersville State College. Author of *Carl Van Vechten and the Irreverent Decades*. Editor of *"Keep A-Inchin' Along": Selected Writings of Carl Van Vechten About Black Arts and Letters*. Compiler of *A Bibliography of the Work of Carl Van Vechten*. **Carl Van Vechten.**

VERLYN KLINKENBORG. Assistant, Department of Autograph Manuscripts, The Pierpont Morgan Library. Author of *British Literary Manuscripts: 800–1914* (2 volumes). **Francis Parkman.**

EDWARD MENDELSON. Visiting Associate Professor of English, Columbia University. Author of *Early Auden*. Editor of *Homer to Brecht*; *Pynchon: A Collection of Critical Essays*; *Collected Poems of W. H. Auden*; and *The English Auden*. **W. H. Auden.**

JAMES MERSMANN. Associate Professor of English, University of Alabama. Author of *Out of the Vietnam Vortex: A Study of Poets and Poetry Against the War.* **Allen Ginsberg.**

ROBERT O'MEALLY. Visiting Professor of Afro-American Studies, Yale University. Author of *The Craft of Ralph Ellison.* **Ralph Ellison.**

SUSAN RESNECK PARR. Associate Professor of English, Ithaca College. Author of numerous articles and conference papers. **Anne Sexton.**

RICHARD PEARCE. Professor of English, Wheaton College, Massachusetts. Author of *Stages of the Clown: Perspectives on Modern Fiction from Dostoyevsky to Beckett; William Styron;* and *The Novel in Motion: An Approach to Modern Fiction.* Editor of *Critical Essays on Thomas Pynchon.* **Thomas Pynchon.**

PETER J. REED. Professor of English, University of Minnesota. Author of *Kurt Vonnegut, Jr.,* and numerous articles. **Kurt Vonnegut.**

ORMOND SEAVEY. Assistant Professor of English, George Washington University. Managing Editor of the *Little Magazine.* **Cotton Mather.**

DIANE TOLOMEO. Assistant Professor of English, University of Victoria. Author of articles on James Joyce and Flannery O'Connor. **Joyce Carol Oates.**

MICHAEL TRUE. Professor of English, Assumption College. Author of *Worcester Poets, With Notes Toward a Literary History* and *Poets in the Schools: A Handbook;* and various articles in *Commonweal, America,* and the *Progressive.* **Karl Shapiro.**

ROBERT VON HALLBERG. Associate Professor of English and Humanities, University of Chicago. Author of *Charles Olson: The Scholar's Art* and numerous articles. **Yvor Winters.**

JEFFREY WALKER. Assistant Professor of English, Oklahoma State University. Author of various articles and reviews in *Early American Literature, Seventeenth-Century News,* and *Rocky Mountain Review.* **Joel Barlow.**

SUPPLEMENT II, Part 1
W. H. Auden to O. Henry

W. H. Auden
1907–1973

"TRUE Love," W. H. Auden wrote, "enjoys twenty-twenty vision, but talks like a myopic." As a poet his central task was truthtelling, but he knew that his art obliged him to translate even the most painful and difficult truths into verbal artifacts of great complexity and beauty. The drama of his career grew out of the unresolvable conflict between his craftsman's impulse to construct memorable patterns of sound and feeling, and the ethical impulse to draw attention to the uglier world of fact. An artist who was constantly aware of the dangers of art, he knew that the potential danger of a work was often in direct proportion to its artistic excellence. The most beautiful and compelling works always invited their audience to conclude (he wrote) "that, since all is well in the work of art, all is well in history. But all is not well there."

The truth Auden was concerned to tell was neither the autonomous "truth of art" nor the inner psychological truths proclaimed by various poets and painters during the nineteenth and twentieth centuries. However moving, however personally authentic these "truths" might be, they could not be of much use to anyone other than the artists who originated them. What Auden was concerned with (after the first few years of his career) were truths that might be communicated and shared. He had no wish to limit access to his work to a sophisticated avant-garde audience, and he made no claim that he plumbed depths accessible only to poets.

These were democratic attitudes, but he had to teach them to himself, because his poetic predecessors held very different and more aristocratic views. The modernist poetic revolution of the early twentieth century, brought about by W. B. Yeats, T. S. Eliot, Ezra Pound, and D. H. Lawrence, was largely a revolution in poetic language. Its purpose (in the words of Stéphane Mallarmé translated by Eliot in *Four Quartets*) was "To purify the dialect of the tribe," to free language from tired conventions and trivialities, to give it clarity, directness, sincerity. But these admirable goals had certain limits. In the view of the modernists, poetry did not refer to a common world of shared experience, accessible to anyone who looked. Poetry and poetic language served as its own authority. What mattered was its intensity and clarity, and it was taken for granted that truthfulness would follow.

In fact something very different happened. When Auden began writing in the late 1920's, and began his efforts at truthtelling a few years later, the older generation offered little help in what he was trying to do. Eliot was struggling to break out of the isolation of his inner life; Lawrence was refusing to believe anything he couldn't feel in his solar plexus; Pound was arguing that the books Ezra Pound happened to have read constituted the true liberal education on which society must be based; and Yeats was communicating with spirits—or wasn't, depending on how he chose to talk about it that day.

In the eyes of most modern critics and teachers of literature there is nothing wrong with any of this. Every literary period devises sets of critical theories and unexamined assumptions that will justify its poetic practice. The literary theory that rose in the wake of the great modernists—a theory that has an ancient and venerable ancestry—held that art was independent of what is ordinarily called truth. A poem was at best a "pseudo-statement," a model of what a true statement might be like. It did not have to be true to experience. Yeats wrote a poem to a friend whose hopes to bring art to the Dublin public had come to nothing, and advised her to find strength and confidence in her own self:

> Amid a place of stone,
> Be secret and exult,
> Because of all things known
> That is most difficult.

No one would question the rhetorical magnificence of these lines, and to anyone who has ever found consolation in the thought that the world fails to recognize one's secret inner merits—a thought that has consoled everyone who ever lived—the lines provide a thrill of self-congratulation. As poetry is taught in most classrooms or discussed by most critics, it doesn't matter at all that the lines are simply untrue, that exulting in secret is not the most difficult of all things known but the easiest, the most banal, and the most universal of self-delusions.

To Auden it did matter. Where Vladimir Nabokov, one of the last of the great modernists, wrote that "art is an intricate game of deception and enchantment," Auden disagreed: "In so far as poetry, or any of the other arts,

can be said to have an ulterior purpose, it is, by telling the truth, to disenchant and disintoxicate." Auden found himself in the curious position of taking art more seriously than did those for whom art was the be-all and end-all, an independent realm with laws of its own. Auden saw that art could never be independent, because it persuades its readers to accept the attitudes it presents so beautifully—attitudes about relations and responsibility that are eventually translated into personal and political action, with results far less beautiful than any poem.

If the danger for the autonomous artist is the danger of losing touch with the real world, the danger for the truthtelling artist is that he will grow so concerned with the plain fact that he forgets about art, and becomes too boring for anyone to read. Auden survived this danger through his love of (in his words) "Riddles and all other ways of not calling a spade a spade ... Complicated verse forms of great technical difficulty, such as Englyns, Drott-Kvaetts, Sestinas, even if their content is trivial ... Conscious theatrical exaggeration. ..." He packed his longer poems with as many complex verse forms as he could fit in—fifty-five in *The Age of Anxiety* alone—and then ended each long poem by, in effect, snapping his fingers to wake his readers from their aesthetic fascination. At the end of *For the Time Being* the narrator says of the poem's Christmas pageantry: "Well, so that is that. Now we must dismantle the tree, ..." The end of *The Sea and the Mirror* admits that in this as in all other works of art the "effects" can never entirely succeed in persuading us of art's reality: "no piece of business, however unimportant, came off." The last pages of *The Age of Anxiety* echo the conclusion of *Finnegans Wake,* but where Joyce returns his reader to the start of the book in an endless insomniac cycle of reading and rereading, Auden restores his reader to "the actual world where time is real."

Auden's passion for truthtelling was a commitment to public service—a commitment not unlike that held generally by artists and writers up to the eighteenth century. It was only with the romantic revolution that artists began taking it for granted that they were necessarily opposed to society in all its forms, that personal integrity required the individual to reject all institutions. It is a law of intellectual history that a condition which one era regards as a rare calamity, a later era will accept as the norm. Thus the anxious isolation of Hamlet in a rotten society—for William Shakespeare a unique tragedy—becomes, a few centuries later, the conventional self-image of every well-to-do adolescent.

Like every young writer since the romantic era, Auden began by rebelling against his personal and literary ancestors, and he spent most of his adult life in voluntary exile from his native England. But through all his years of revolt and exile he remained a product of the English professional middle class, and he embodied its values in his poetry. Only in his late adolescence and early twenties did he think of his art in terms similar to those used by his modernist predecessors. If they were isolated, he felt, he would be even more isolated; such was the necessary course of history. But around the age of twenty-five, when his revolt changed character and became less personal than socialist, he made no effort to renounce his bourgeois upbringing. He read Karl Marx, he said later, in order to become a better bourgeois, not to destroy his society but to save it from destroying itself by its own injustice. The great modernists, when they thought politically at all, also held radical politics, but a radically nostalgic politics of the right, which denounced democracy in favor of the secure aristocracy of an idealized or imaginary past. Auden's whole career, in contrast, was shaped by his sense of continuity between past and present, by his respect for his literary tradition and personal roots. Where the modernists saw all around them fragments and isolation and longed for some distant wholeness, Auden saw a complex and finally coherent present, with responsibilities that could not be deferred for the sake of an artist's beautiful dreams.

Wystan Hugh Auden was born on February 21, 1907, in the medieval city of York in the north of England, where his doctor father worked as a general practitioner. The following year the family moved to the industrial city of Birmingham, where Dr. Auden was appointed to the newly established post of school medical officer; later he became professor of public health at Birmingham University. Auden's mother had been among the first women to take an honors degree (in French) at London University. She then studied to be a nurse, intending to serve with missionaries in Africa, but gave up this plan when she met and married Dr. Auden. She and her husband were both children of Anglican clergymen. Dr. Auden held a detached intellectual attitude to religion, while Mrs. Auden held intense religious convictions and raised her children in the rituals of the High Church.

From his father, who was widely read in history, archaeology, and the classics, the young Auden learned the elements of science. From his mother he learned music, emotion, and religion. In later years he traced his homosexuality partly to his strong identification with his mother, an identification strengthened when his father was away from England with the Army Medical Corps during World War I. Isolated from other children by his mental precociousness and physical clumsiness, Auden devoted much of his childhood from the ages of six to twelve to constructing an imaginary private world. His fantasy was, however, made up from very real objects: "a limestone landscape mainly derived from the Pennine Moors in the North of England, and . . . an industry—lead mining." The character of his adult poetry was already implicit in the nature of his childhood imaginary world. His concern was not simply with the symbolic depths of the mines or the personal nostalgia of the lonely moors but also with the practical details of mining machinery, with the ways in which real means led to plausible ends. Later, as a poet, he would differ from predecessors like Thomas Hardy, Yeats, and Eliot in caring less for the intensities of solitary vision or the emotional power of rhetoric than for the ethical complexities of the world in which he and everyone else must choose and act. Once, he recalled of his childhood fantasy, "I had to choose between two types of a certain machine. . . . One type I found more sacred or 'beautiful,' but the other type was, as I knew from my reading, the more efficient. At this point I realized that it was my moral duty to sacrifice my aesthetic preference for reality or truth."

His adolescence brought a conventional adolescent rebellion. He discovered that he had lost the religious faith his mother had taught him and discovered his homosexuality (which his father eventually accepted, although his mother remained baffled and antagonistic). At school he had fewer difficulties than at home. He showed an aptitude for science and mathematics, but no more interest in literature than might be expected of any intelligent pupil. Until he was fifteen, he saw himself moving toward a career as a mining engineer, or something equally technical and scientific. Then a school friend, filling an awkward silence during a country walk, casually asked if he wrote poetry. He had never thought of doing so, but at that moment he recognized his vocation. Three years

later, at Oxford, when he introduced himself to Nevill Coghill, his English tutor, he explained that he intended to be a poet. The tutor observed that this would help with his English studies, by giving him insights into the technical side of the subject. "You don't understand at all," Auden replied. "I mean a great poet."

Both at school and at Oxford, Auden was an awesome if slightly comic figure to his contemporaries. His father's library had provided him with arcane knowledge of sex and psychoanalysis, and his intellectual assurance completed the effect. The saving comedy emerged in the extravagance with which he advanced his opinions, opinions liable to change at any moment. Poetically, though, he was little more than a highly competent provincial while he was at school and in his first year at Oxford. At fifteen he had pastiched William Wordsworth, then Walter de la Mare and other twentieth-century traditionalists. At sixteen he discovered Hardy and for more than a year read and imitated no one else. At seventeen he added Edward Thomas, then A. E. Housman, Robert Frost, and Emily Dickinson. Then, at nineteen, in 1926, he discovered T. S. Eliot's *The Waste Land* and discarded everything he had written earlier. For a few heady months he produced nothing but distilled Eliot. In spring, in his verse, "The itching lover weighed himself / At stations on august machines"; sunlight became "Inexorable Rembrandt rays, which stab / Through clouds as through a rotting factory floor." He proclaimed a severely "classical" poetic dogma to his friends: poetry, he said, must be austere, must ignore public issues and shared meanings, must virtually ignore its own subject, because the subject of a poem was merely the peg on which to hang the poetry.

It was another year before he began writing poems in a voice that he recognized as his own. In the summer of 1927, after his second year at

Oxford, when he was twenty, he wrote a poem he later titled "The Watershed." It marked the watershed between his juvenilia and his adult work and was the earliest poem he preserved between hard covers in his published volumes.

"Who stands, the crux left of the watershed," it opens, in radical ambiguity. Are the first two words interrogative or declarative? What is the missing word replaced by the comma? Is the crux a crossroads or a dilemma? And which of its two possible and antithetical meanings is expressed by "watershed"—a dividing line on high ground or a field on low ground? The poem makes all these matters clear in the lines that follow, but the obscurity of the opening, the way it seems to exclude the reader from the poem, proves, in effect, to be the subject of the lines that follow. The poem concerns a "stranger" who stands indecisively at a crossroads looking down over a ruined landscape, one who can never enter the land he observes, can never find the satisfaction he vaguely seeks. "Stranger, turn back again, frustrate and vexed:" commands the voice of the poem:

This land, cut off, will not communicate,
Be no accessory content to one
Aimless for faces rather there than here.
Beams from your car may cross a bedroom
   wall,
They wake no sleeper. . . .

In "The Watershed" and the poems of the next year or two, Auden entered the extreme psychological isolation Eliot had explored in "The Love Song of J. Alfred Prufrock" and went ever deeper, to the point where the observing mind and the observed world were not merely isolated but antagonistic. Guarded borders cross the landscape of these early poems, as in "No Change of Place," "Where gaitered gamekeeper with dog and gun / Will shout 'Turn back'." Even the features on a face, the mouth and eyes, seem "Sentries between inner and outer." Any movement toward erotic satisfaction (in his early twenties Auden had little hope for any deeper love) is the act of a doomed spy or secret agent:

Control of the passes was, he saw, the key
To this new district, but who would get it?
He, the trained spy, had walked into the trap
For a bogus guide, seduced by the old tricks.

. . .

. . . They would shoot, of course,
Parting easily who were never joined.

Auden's style developed rapidly in these early years, but certain basic elements remained constant. A whole repertory of techniques preserved his isolation from his readers. Few poets have made so many threatening noises: "The game is up for you . . . It is later than you think"; "Before you reach the frontier you are caught." His obscurity became notorious, but it was only partly deliberate; in a journal entry he blamed it on his own laziness. What was entirely deliberate, however, was the baffling instability of his tone. He would shift within a few lines from lyric intensity to slapstick comedy, from solemn echoes of ancient epics to transient contemporary slang. There were superficial parallels between this style and the modernist styles of Eliot and Pound, but Auden's purposes were entirely different from theirs. Where *The Waste Land* and *The Cantos* echoed older forms to make an ironic contrast between a splendid hierarchical past and a depleted chaotic present, Auden emphasized the continuity between the anxiety and violence of ancient times and of today. Auden found in the past, not a better world, but disasters like those of the present: "The pillar dug from the desert recorded only / the sack of a city." Where Eliot and Pound tended to quote ostentatiously from the high style of the European renaissance, Auden moved further back into the past, to the sad dangerous world of Old English poetry and the

Old Icelandic sagas. And where Eliot and Pound always drew attention to their learned quotations, Auden, whose reading was wider than theirs, made no fuss about his use of earlier literature, no show of erudition. For example, a line quoted above, "Parting easily [two] who were never joined," is translated from an Old English poem "Wulf and Eadwacer." A phrase from "1929," another early poem, "love . . . gives less than he expects," is from Anton Chekhov's notebooks; a line about the "restlessness of intercepted growth" is from a book on psychology by Trigant Burrow; and there are hundreds of other examples. If a reader recognizes the source, all well and good; but however else Auden's earliest poems exclude their readers, they never do so by implying that the poet who wrote them is a learned sage whose knowledge lesser mortals can never share. For Auden throughout his career, a poet is one who handles words and poetic forms better than others do, never one whose vision and emotions are stronger or better than anyone else's.

Auden collected his earliest short poems in a book titled simply *Poems* (1930; second edition with slightly different contents, 1933; American edition, 1934). His longer works in this period were the brief play *Paid on Both Sides: A Charade* (printed in the various editions of *Poems*) and the long poem in prose and verse *The Orators* (1932; revised edition, 1934; included in the American edition of *Poems*). These books quickly established Auden as the major poet of his generation. No poet since Lord Byron achieved such wide fame so early in his career, but his work was widely misunderstood. Early reviewers and critics tended to read Auden's first books in light of the political concerns that entered his work only after 1932, concerns almost absent from his earliest poems, whose concerns were almost wholly psychological.

Paid on Both Sides is a compressed psychological tragedy, an expressionistic *Romeo and Juliet.* Two families in the north of England have been feuding for generations. The origins of the feud have long been forgotten, but as each generation transmits its hatreds to its children the cycle of murder and revenge continues. Abruptly, the son of one family breaks out of the cycle. He is cured of his hatred by a self-revealing dream that makes clear to him his willing complicity in the feud. Now he rides to the house of his enemies and proposes marriage to their daughter. Up to this point the play reflects the teachings of an American psychologist, Homer Lane, whose work Auden learned about during a year in Berlin (1928–1929) after finishing at Oxford. Lane taught the romantic doctrine that man was naturally good and that neurosis and disease could therefore be cured if one would only obey one's inner impulses. (Freud, in sharp contrast, distrusted the violent impulses of the id and welcomed the civilizing effects of sublimation.) The hero of *Paid on Both Sides* rejects parental repression and obeys his inner impulse to love. But although Auden briefly allowed his friends to believe he had embraced the optimism of Homer Lane, his play presents a darker and lonelier vision. The hero is murdered on his wedding day, to avenge a killing that he himself had committed before his cure, and the feud resumes.

The theme of *Paid on Both Sides* is the persistence of ancient hatreds into the present. Its style and setting evoke a comparable persistence of the past. The language ranges from the laconic manner and alliterative meters of Old English poetry to modern telegraphese and schoolboy slang. The hero's curative dream mixes patriotic speeches from World War I with passages from a psychology textbook and scraps of the traditional Christmas mummers' play of rural England. The title *Paid on Both Sides* is a scraping from *Beowulf,* from a line about a hard bargain, paid on both sides with the lives of friends.

The Orators, three years later, uses similar methods on a more elaborate scale. As in *Paid,* the setting often seems to shift even within a single sentence. As if in an optical illusion, the book's action takes place simultaneously in a boarding school, a primitive tribe, a suburban home, and a military airfield. This strange *sui generis* work, subtitled "An English Study," amounts to an anthropological survey of English society. As in more straightforward anthropology, Auden treats his subject apolitically, regarding his society not as the product of deliberate moral and practical choices (as its apologists would claim) but as the unconscious product of myth and ritual, a society powerless to understand itself or to change. The book's focus is the world of school, where the ruling bourgeois learn the rites and customs they will follow in later life. In the first of the book's three parts, "The Initiates," different prose voices record the initiation of a group of schoolboys into their tribal codes of behavior and belief; then into adolescent combativeness and sexuality; finally into middle-aged nostalgia for the lost glories of youth. The initiates are followers of a neurotic hero, whose thoughts, recorded in a "Journal of an Airman," make up the book's second part. The airman tries to organize society around hero worship but is destroyed by his own paranoia. What is especially unsettling about his journal is that it mixes Auden's own verses and opinions with passages designed to indicate the madness of its fictitious "author." (Auden later wrote that *The Orators* reads like the work of "someone talented but near the border of sanity" and guessed that his reason for writing it was partly therapeutic, "to exorcise certain tendencies in myself by allowing them to run riot in phantasy.") The third part of the book is a series of odes on various aspects of group life and hero worship, ending in a confession of frustration and defeat, and a mock prayer for change. A brief epilogue abandons the whole world described in the book for some unspecified other place that Auden can identify only by saying it is somewhere else:

"O where are you going" said reader to rider,

. . .

"Out of this house"—said rider to reader . . .

Around the time *The Orators* was published (1932), Auden began to think of this reader's destination in political terms. For a few months he thought he was in the process of what he called a "conversion to communism"—which never in fact took place. He wrote a few poems that adopted the voice of a communist (this was in the deepest phase of the great economic depression of the 1930's), but a communist of a very idiosyncratic kind, more concerned with a visionary community of love than with basic economic change. Auden was now working as a schoolmaster, but he found education, much as he enjoyed the work, a paradoxical task. "You cannot train children to be good citizens of a state which you despise." When he tried to write an epic poem that would portray the communist struggle for a different and better state, he abandoned it before it was half-finished. "No, I am a bourgeois. I shall not join the C[ommunist] P[arty]," he wrote in a letter to a friend. Yet the sense of isolation in which he began his career was growing intolerable, and he urgently needed a way out.

The lonely vigil of Auden's early years, his youthful contempt for the public realm, ended on a warm night in June 1933. That evening, he recalled, he was sitting on a lawn after dinner with three colleagues at the Downs School in Colwall, where he taught, when " . . . something happened. I felt myself invaded by a power which, though I consented to it, was irresistible and certainly not mine. For the first time in my life I knew exactly—because, thanks to the power, I was doing it—what it means to love one's neighbor as oneself." Thirty years later he identified the event as a "vision of agape," of religious charity and love. At the time, he thought he was finished with Christianity forever, and he said almost nothing about the experience—beyond asking one of his colleagues on that evening if the feeling had been shared, and learning that it was.

He was silent on the details or the cause, but for a short time his writings were suffused with a tone of exaltation unlike anything he had done before. In a poem written within days of the event, "A Summer Night" ("Out on the lawn I lie in bed, . . ."), he evoked the scene of some peaceable kingdom:

> Equal with colleagues in a ring
> I sit on each calm evening,
>   Enchanted as the flowers
> The opening light draws out of hiding
> From leaves with all its dove-like pleading
>   Its logic and its powers.
>
> That later we, though parted then
> May still recall these evenings when
>   Fear gave his watch no look;
> The lion griefs loped from the shade
> And on our knees their muzzles laid,
>   And Death put down his book.

As in his first political writings, he felt his class was doomed, that revolution was imminent—

> Soon through the dykes of our content
> The crumpling flood will force a rent

—but now he hoped that the love he felt on these evenings might survive as one of the strengths of the new order,

> As through a child's rash happy cries
> The drowned voices of his parents rise
>   In unlamenting song.

What is especially striking about this poem is its use of regular, almost jaunty meters in a tone of celebration and joy. The modernist poets, especially Eliot and Pound, had reserved serious subjects almost exclusively for free verse. Regular meters, if they could be used at all, were strictly for the purpose of satire or nostalgia, standing as a formal rebuke to the disorder of the modern world. Eliot wrote in 1917 that formal rhymed verse could now have only a limited role; it would not lose its place entirely, but "we need the coming of Satirist . . . to prove that the heroic couplet has lost none of its edge. . . . As for the sonnet I am not so sure." In the same 1933 summer when Auden began writing nonsatiric rhymed verse he also began writing not merely sonnets but whole sequences of sonnets. At first these preserved their conventional status as love poetry, but within a few years Auden was using sonnets for historical and mythical subjects on the largest possible scale; the sequence "In Time of War" (1938) extends without implausibility from the creation of the world to the present moment of crisis.

The whole character of Auden's work changed drastically after his vision of agape in 1933. Earlier he had assumed that his work must take the next logical step in the modernist revolution, extending the line laid down by Yeats, Pound, and Eliot. This early sense that he must work according to historical necessity, not by personal choice, had been encouraged by modernism itself, which took far more interest in the aesthetic intensity of the unique moment or the large determined cycles of history than it did in personal choice and the consequences of choice. Modernism emphasized formal innovation in art, but determined necessity in human affairs. Auden, in the mid-1930's, broke with modernism by restoring traditional meters in his art and by emphasizing freedom and choice in his vision of mankind.

When he wrote a love poem, such as the untitled one that begins "Fish in the unruffled lakes," the lover's beauty was important, but not as important as the lover's personal decision to love:

> . . . I must bless, I must praise
> That you, my swan, who have
> All gifts that to the swan
> Impulsive Nature gave,
> The majesty and pride,
> Last night should add
> Your voluntary love.

"Swan," "majesty," "pride," and the poetic diction in which Auden sets these words—all derive from the love poetry of Yeats. But in acknowledging Yeats's preeminence as a love poet Auden corrected a crucial fault in Yeats's vision, his failure to take account of the voluntary quality of human relations. Elsewhere in the same poem Auden makes comparable references to "goodness *carefully* worn" and "Duty's *conscious* wrong" (italics added).

Because modernist poetry took little interest in choice and its consequences, the art to which it was most closely allied was the relatively static art of painting. In Yeats, Lawrence, Pound, William Carlos Williams, and Wallace Stevens, reality is most strikingly evoked by means of visual images. Auden deliberately broke this entangling alliance between poetry and painting, almost to the point of banishing visual images from his poetry entirely and replacing them with terms from the fields of ethics and morals, as in "Lullaby" (italics added):

> Lay your sleeping head, my love,
> *Human* on my *faithless* arm;
> Time and fevers burn away
> *Individual* beauty from
> *Thoughtful* children, and the grave
> Proves the child *ephemeral*:
> But in my arms till break of day
> Let the *living* creature lie,
> *Mortal*, *guilty*, but to me
> The *entirely* beautiful.

In all his writings from the mid-1930's Auden reiterated that the human world is the product of choices, not necessity. Where Yeats and Eliot dreamed in different ways of escaping from the world of time into the serenity of timelessness, Auden constantly turned back to the immediate problems of love and politics. Almost everything he wrote referred at some point to the difference between the world of nature and that of humanity. Both derived their energies from the life force that Auden called, after Freud's example, Eros. But in nature Eros made all the decisions for its creatures; animals and plants "knew their station and were good for ever." In individual men and women Eros has abdicated its authority to the individual will. Each of us is free to choose whether to "build the Just City" or to seek "the suicide pact, the romantic / Death." The instinctive powers of Eros insisted only on finding expression; in the human world they did not insist on any special kind of expression. If they were denied expression as love or art, they would emerge in distorted forms instead, as psychosomatic disease or the collective hatred of war.

So although Auden wrote more love poems during the 1930's than at any other time in his career, they were poems from which the shadow of political or personal disaster was seldom distant. "A Bride in the 30's," which began in the luxuriant erotic rhythms of a line like "Easily, my dear, you move, easily, your head," quickened, only a few stanzas later, to the martial beat of "Ten thousand of the desperate marching by / Five feet, six feet, seven feet high." It was not enough to withdraw from politics to the pleasures of the bed: "Hitler and Mussolini in their wooing poses" made an appeal not unlike the poet's to his love, and the poet knew it. Personal Eros could be as possessive and damaging as the political one. In another poem he recognized "How insufficient is / The endearment and the look" "Before the evil and the good."

The same kinds of choice that set the course of a personal life also set the course of nations. As on one hand the Great Depression exposed the weakness of capitalist society, and on the other the rise of fascism threatened to put an end to democracy, it seemed crucial to Auden and many of his contemporaries to become didactic artists, to educate their audience in the ways of responsible choice. Although Auden's sympathies were clearly socialist, he knew that he would violate his didactic purposes if he tried to dictate the choices others should make:

Poetry is not concerned with telling people what to do, but with extending our knowledge of good and evil, perhaps making the necessity for action more urgent and its nature more clear, but only leading us to the point where it is possible for us to make a rational and moral choice.

This principle was easier, at first, to enunciate than to follow. In the 1930's, too often for his own comfort, his sense of political urgency led him to try to tell people what to do, even when he was by no means certain what he ought to do himself.

His most important political works in the 1930's were commissioned by the Group Theatre of London. The Group had been founded in 1932 to pioneer modern stage techniques in England, and only later added political purposes to its aesthetic ones. Auden's first work for the Group was the playlet *The Dance of Death* (1933). On paper this seems a perfunctory trifle, but on stage, with music and dancing, it had a notable success. Auden had no use for the conventionally realistic theater of his day but did not wish to follow Yeats's withdrawal of poetic drama into the symbolic intensities of drawing-room theater. Instead, arriving independently at many of the techniques used by Bertolt Brecht, he adopted the styles of the cabaret, music hall, and revue in an attempt to establish a popular poetic drama, without the

archaism or pomposity that damaged most of the recent efforts in that form. The ostensible subject of *The Dance of Death* is the decline of the middle classes, whose death wish and death throes are mimed by a dancer. The dancer and a chorus of singers and actors illustrate various bourgeois evasions of social change—romantic fantasy, mysticism, nationalism, fads in health and sex, with songs appropriate to each—until the dancer collapses. Karl Marx strides on stage to the tune of Mendelssohn's wedding march and pronounces the dancer dead of economic causes; and the play ends. The conclusion is a bit too abrupt and absurd to give much comfort to any committed Marxist, and Auden later called the play "a nihilist leg-pull." Through much of this period, when critics generally regarded Auden as a communist sympathizer, the newspaper of the Communist party, the *Daily Worker,* kept complaining about his severe lapses from party orthodoxy.

His next play, *The Dog Beneath the Skin* (1935), was the first of three written in collaboration with the novelist Christopher Isherwood. Again using techniques from music hall and cabaret, Auden now adopted a more straightforward didactic purpose. An improbable plot about a naive young hero's search for his village's missing heir (who is in fact disguised as the dog who tags along on the search) serves largely as an excuse for a satiric tour of Europe, modeled loosely on Voltaire's *Candide.* The play is designed to be an easy lesson in history. The village England of the opening scene is comfortably Edwardian, its characters singing in the rhythms of Gilbert and Sullivan. The hero's travels take him from Europe's tired old monarchies to its new lunatic fascism, introducing him along the way to decadent sexuality, the power of wealth and privilege, and a few hints of socialist revolution offstage. Finally he returns to his village, able at last to see the reactionary viciousness behind its innocent facade. As the play ends he and the village heir—now out of the dogskin—leave to join "the army of the other side." A chorus, which from the start has been explaining the action to the audience, now urges us to "Repent ... Unite ... Act." This triad of commands derives less from any political sympathy than from the closing exhortations in *The Waste Land* to give, sympathize, and control. The "army of the other side" and its purposes have never appeared on stage, except for one sympathizer who dies to the tune of a comic Wagnerian pastiche. The future liberator of English society, as Stephen Spender observed, is someone "whom the writers have not put in the picture because they do not know what he looks like, although they thoroughly support him."

Despite such ambiguities and cross-purposes, Auden was now generally accepted as a propaganda poet, a spokesman for his literary generation. He did his best to sabotage this impression in the next play that he and Isherwood wrote, but almost no one, possibly not even Isherwood, fully understood what he was doing. The play was *The Ascent of F6* (1936), a parable of the self-destructiveness of the pursuit of fame. Now the political satire has diminished to perfunctory gestures. The focus is on the psychology of the hero, superficially based on Lawrence of Arabia but ultimately a metaphoric self-portrait of Auden himself. The hero, Michael Ransom, is a mountaineer (metaphorically, an artist) who climbs mountains for the challenge of it but also partly as a neurotic release. Denied his mother's love in childhood, he is constantly seeking admiration as an adult. When the British government asks him to climb a peak on a colonial border for the sake of a propaganda victory, Ransom, despite his dreams of conquering that very peak, refuses to make his art serve a political cause. But when his mother adds her voice to those who insist he make the climb, his resistance fails. As he as-

cends the peak he is taken for a hero by the masses, who follow his efforts on radio and in newspapers; and he begins to dream of himself as a savior for mankind. But in conquering the mountain he destroys himself. His companions are seized with the nationalistic excitement of the race to the top, and he accedes to their wish to make the last part of the climb in a dangerous blizzard. He dies at the summit. Behind the story is Auden's conviction that the fame he had won for his political writing was a fatal temptation, that his propagandistic work, however much it delighted his audience, betrayed his art. When he wrote the play he was at the height of his fame, but he decided at that moment that he must someday leave England if he were to escape the temptations that he could not resist if he stayed.

In the months after finishing *F6* Auden kept away from direct political statements. He collected his poems of 1932–1936—toning down some of the politics of the earlier ones—in a volume that his British publishers titled *Look, Stranger!* (1936). Auden disliked the buttonholing tone of this and had the American edition titled *On This Island.* (He dedicated the book to Erika Mann, Thomas Mann's daughter, whom he married in 1935 in order to provide her with a British passport when the Nazis took away her German citizenship.) In a long poem written during the summer of 1936, *Letter to Lord Byron,* he adopted an urbanely ironic tone on politics, poetry, and himself—a comic tone but one entirely unlike the slapstick of *The Orators.* The poem keeps emphasizing the very real problems of society and art, both of which it discusses in materialist terms derived from Marx, but emphasizes also that artists are not the most likely source for solutions to these problems. Against the romantic and modernist dogma of the artist-hero, inspired by a deeper and sharper vision than his fellowmen, Auden's poem traces the artist's isolation to the rise of the *rentier* class in the eighteenth century, which made it possible for artists to devote their lives to writing what they wished, as they lived on their dividends—or starved heroically. Against the heroic stature he himself had begun to achieve among his contemporaries, Auden offers many stanzas of self-deflating autobiography—for example, about his Oxford days under the influence of Eliot and Eliot's quarterly magazine the *Criterion:*

All youth's intolerant certainty was mine as
    I faced life in a double-breasted suit;
I bought and praised but did not read
    Aquinas,
    At the *Criterion*'s verdict I was mute,
    Though Arnold's I was ready to refute;
And through the quads dogmatic words rang
    clear,
"Good poetry is classic and austere."

So much for Art. Of course Life had its
    passions too;
    The student's flesh like his imagination
Makes facts fit theories and has fashions too.

He wrote much of this poem in Iceland, where he spent a summer, partly as a holiday from European politics, partly to seek out the country of his distant ancestors. Auden's sense of the past tended to focus, not on the renaissance grandeurs or vague arcadias that modernism sought by the Mediterranean, but on the colder clarity and sanity of the North. To visit Iceland was to find a place where historical nostalgia was impossible, where the landscapes of the sagas remained unaltered. It was a cure, he hoped, for the political madness further south.

But while he was there he heard the first news of the Spanish Civil War. He had no doubt that Francisco Franco's invasion of Republican Spain was a trial run for a fascist war on the whole of Europe. There could be no es-

cape. Now political themes reentered his work, no longer with the old jokey ambiguities but in a tone of urgency and even despair. The great forces of history seemed to call everyone to action. Early in 1937 he went to Spain. He intended to drive an ambulance for the Republican forces but was instead put to work broadcasting propaganda. After two months he cut his journey short and returned to England. Only later did his friends realize that he had been profoundly disillusioned. Like many others who went to Spain hoping to serve an ideal, he found instead that the Republicans had divided into vindictive factions and the Stalinists were taking charge. He still regarded fascism as an absolute evil, but it was no longer possible to deceive himself that those who opposed one form of evil might not prefer another one instead. When he returned to England he wrote "Spain," a poem with grand rhetorical gestures and a concluding summons to action—one that he felt the urgency of the times demanded but in which he no longer believed:

The stars are dead; the animals will not look:
We are left alone with our day, and the time
    is short and
        History to the defeated
May say Alas but cannot help or pardon.

These lines are based on Auden's characteristic distinction between nature and man, and on his equally characteristic insistence on choice. But they also affirm that history will not pardon those who lose. If the final phrases are read metaphorically, they seem innocuous enough: history, they seem to argue, gives no second chance; we must act now. But Auden was not writing metaphorically when he used the word "pardon." This word and its fraternal twin "forgiveness" were gradually to become the crucial words in his poetic vocabulary. Both words pointed to that voluntary acceptance of another's imperfection, which, in both the personal and political realms, is essential to sympathy and love. To deny pardon to the defeated is, as Auden later charged against his own poem, "to equate goodness with success." In a ballad written about a year after "Spain," "As I Walked Out One Evening," he portrayed lovers who fantasized about their perfect loyalty to each other and their loved one's perfection—a fantasy that denied the need for forgiveness. But in answer to these doomed fantasies, the chiming clocks warn instead: "You shall love your crooked neighbour / With your crooked heart." The addition of the word "crooked" is not a denial of the biblical injunction but an explanation of what it means and how it must be obeyed.

Yet in his political writings in the late 1930's what Auden said was still often in conflict with his beliefs. *On the Frontier* (1938), the last of the Auden-Isherwood plays, is a tragedy of war and separation, ending with dying lovers reciting verses that sound very much like a Christian hymn to a better world, but Auden felt obliged to add some passages of versified propaganda. It scarcely mattered; the whole play was too tired and sketchy to mean much to its authors or audience. But a much finer book, Auden and Isherwood's *Journey to a War* (1939), a report in prose and verse on their visit to the Sino-Japanese War, is marked by a similar contradiction. Auden devoted all his skills to the sonnet sequence "In Time of War," tracing the whole history of mankind and the moral causes and effects of war but he then tacked on a verse "Commentary" that included propagandistic fantasies of civic unity in the face of a common enemy. The real state of "unity" in China between the Nationalists and the Communists was very different.

And when World War II finally began, "September 1, 1939" (a throwback to a manner he had otherwise abandoned earlier that year) included yet another denial of his convictions about the voluntary aspects of love:

> Hunger allows no choice
> To the citizen or the police;
> We must love one another or die.

This, like the conclusion of "Spain," seems perfectly reasonable, and when Auden discarded this stanza and then the whole poem he puzzled his critics. But the point behind the lines is that love is a hunger that must be satisfied, not a voluntary gift of mutual forgiveness. The equation of love with hunger struck Auden as a lie—memorable, stirring, but still a lie. He ended a poem of the 1950's, "First Things First," with the line: "Thousands have lived without love, not one without water."

By the start of 1939 Auden no longer found tolerable his public role as court poet to the English Left. He still made political gestures, but more from a wish to support his left-wing friends than from any deep convictions. Since writing *The Ascent of F6* he had spent much of his time traveling around Europe and then the world, as if searching for someplace other than England in which to live. When he and Isherwood were on the way back from the war in China, in the summer of 1938, they spent two weeks in America. They decided to return there permanently.

They sailed for New York in January 1939. In England their departure was widely felt as the end of an era. In America their arrival was hardly noticed—which was precisely what Auden hoped for. He later said that in England he always felt as if he were living among his family, and it was this sense of family obligation that led him to write in ways he considered dishonest and inauthentic. Even his politically charged writing fulfilled the expectations of his audience that a bright young man must be a rebel; and Auden knew furthermore that his political writings largely served as preaching to the converted and made no practical difference. In America, a nation that has never taken its writers as seriously as England takes its, he would be free from all temptation to please an audience that wanted to hear his familiar formulas.

A few weeks before he left for New York he was staying in Brussels, where he saw the Brueghels in the art museum. What he learned from these paintings was a rebuke to his own resonant calls to action. He realized that the most important events never occurred under a historical spotlight, never enjoyed the thrilling benefit of Yeatsian heroicizing rhetoric. The truth was less beautiful, more disturbing. Brueghel, in paintings like *The Massacre of the Innocents* and *The Fall of Icarus,* made this point quietly and exactly ("Musée des Beaux Arts"):

About suffering they were never wrong,
The Old Masters: how well they understood
Its human position; how it takes place
While someone else is eating or opening a
      window or just walking dully along;
                  . . .
They never forgot
That even the dreadful martyrdom must run
      its course
Anyhow in a corner, some untidy spot . . .

In Brueghel's *Icarus,* for instance: how
      everything turns away
Quite leisurely from the disaster; the
      ploughman may
Have heard the splash, the forsaken cry,
But for him it was not an important failure;
                  . . .
. . . and the expensive delicate ship that must
      have seen

Something amazing, a boy falling out of the
      sky,
Had somewhere to get to and sailed calmly
      on.

Earlier he had written about opposing ideological armies, with their pure causes. In "Spain," in stanzas dropped soon after he reached America, Franco's Nationalists were the manifestations of neurosis and fear, the People's Army the flower of tenderness and love. Now Auden could not be so self-congratulatory. Brueghel showed how we all turn away from suffering. The next step was to understand that we all cause it. In "Herman Melville," one of the first poems he wrote in America, Auden saw that "Evil is unspectacular and always human, / And shares our bed and eats at our own table. . . ."

Auden was beginning to immerse himself in American literature and the American language. Within a few months, in the long poem *New Year Letter*, although he wrote that "England to me is my own tongue," he could present this sweeping survey of American history and landscape as a backdrop for his continuing focus on the problem of choice:

A long time since it seems to-day
The Saints in Massachusetts Bay
Heard theocratic COTTON preach
And legal WINTHROP'S Little Speech;
Since MISTRESS HUTCHINSON was tried
By those her Inner Light defied,
And WILLIAMS questioned Moses' law
                  . . .
Long since inventive JEFFERSON
Fought realistic HAMILTON,
Pelagian versus Jansenist;
But the same heresies exist.
Time makes old formulas look strange,
Our properties and symbols change,
But round the freedom of the Will

Our disagreements center still,

    . . .

Here, as in Europe, is dissent,
This raw untidy continent
Where the Commuter can't forget
The Pioneer; and even yet
A *Völkerwanderung* occurs:
Resourceful manufacturers
Trek southward by progressive stages
For sites with no floor under wages,
No ceiling over hours; and by
Artistic souls in towns that lie
Out in the weed and pollen belt
The need for sympathy is felt,
And east to hard New York they come;
And self-respect drives Negroes from
The one-crop and race-hating delta
To northern cities helter-skelter;
And in jalopies there migrates
A rootless tribe from windblown states
To suffer further westward where
The tolerant Pacific air
Makes logic seem so silly, pain
Subjective, what he seeks so vain
The wanderer may die; and kids,
When their imagination bids,
Hitch-hike a thousand miles to find
The Hesperides that's on their mind.

Auden's early months in America, both in New York and on the travels that produced these lines, seemed filled with exhilarating renewals and also a calm sense of purposeful serenity. He gathered the poems he had written since 1936 in a volume entitled *Another Time* (1940), as if signaling that he had begun something new. "For the first time," he wrote a friend, "I am leading a life which remotely approximates to the way I think I ought to live."

Most important, perhaps, was that he had fallen in love. His earlier affairs had been, he knew, temporary and had done little to break through his personal isolation. In the spring of 1939 he met a college student named Chester Kallman, a young poet who offered the right mixture of personal similarities and differences that seemed to Auden essential for a faithful love. Auden had always disapproved of his own homosexuality on the grounds that it resulted in a species of narcissism, in which the loved object was a version of the lover himself. To counter this he had tried to love people who were different from himself, less intellectual and introspective, more physically confident. Now he recognized in Kallman someone who shared his passion for language, his wit, but who was different enough in class and background (American Jewish petit bourgeois) to prevent narcissism from taking hold. Auden thought of their relationship as a marriage, and the story of a marriage began to emerge in his poetry. In 1940 he wrote "In Sickness and in Health," a meditation on marriage that takes its title from the wedding service. Two years later he wrote "Mundus et Infans," about the birth of a baby, and "Many Happy Returns," about the upbringing of a young child. About twenty-five years later it was time for an "Epithalamium" written in a parental tone for the younger generation as it began its own marriages.

He also began, in 1939–1940, a slow return to the religion he thought he had abandoned. In Spain, in 1937, he had been surprised by his own disturbed feelings at the sight of churches closed or destroyed by the Republicans. "The feeling was far too intense to be the result of a mere liberal dislike of intolerance," he wrote later. Soon after his return from Spain he met the writer Charles Williams, who seemed to him, as to many others, an example of saintliness. The liberal tenets that Auden had taken largely for granted as the basis for progress and morals seemed almost overthrown by the rise of Hitler, who had come to power in one of the best-educated and intellectually sophisticated countries of Europe—despite the liberal assumption that education led directly to right actions. By what standards could he affirm that Hitler was absolutely wrong, that to oppose him was right? The answer seemed inevitably to have something to do with the moral absolutes of religion and the religious sense of original sin that made the lure of fascism comprehensible, not some strange violation of human nature beyond understanding. Religion proposed an ultimate moral truth that was real and absolute even if no human intelligence could fully encompass it.

Auden returned to Christianity largely by an intellectual process that involved matters like these, but he was helped along the way by his memories of the emotional beliefs of his childhood and by the personal example of figures like Charles Williams. His religious beliefs had almost nothing of the supernatural to them. Instead he found in religion an intellectual sense of the coherence of things, especially the relation of actions and consequences, a relation that is the basis of ethics. The moral law, he said, was not like a flawed human legal code but like the laws of physics or chemistry. Just as one did not violate the laws of physics by jumping out the window, one did not violate the moral law by committing murder. What the law determined in each case was the necessary consequence of a free action: the jumper lands with a thud, the murderer isolates himself from the human community, from all opportunity for trust and peace.

In the midst of his reconversion Auden wrote *New Year Letter* (published with other poems in *The Double Man*, 1941), the American passages of which were quoted above. This is a 1,700-line philosophical poem, moving, as Auden did in his conversion, from abstract speculation to personal prayer. By any standards, it is an astonishingly powerful and important poem. That the heir to Eliot's free-verse fragments should have said good-bye to all that

and written a poem in eighteenth-century couplets that included—without Joycean irony—the styles of history, criticism, and philosophy that modern poetry had mostly banished from its pages, and that he made it all work, seemed the most unlikely of all possible literary events. Yet the Augustan style of *New Year Letter* is consistent with a central aspect of Auden's earliest, most modern-sounding poems. It makes explicit the assumptions hidden in his earlier borrowings from Old English. In both cases he treated the past as something useful to the present, not as something lost or destroyed that now must be mourned. The poem joins romantic energy to Augustan decorum and is, in effect, Auden's *Faust*. Like Johann Wolfgang von Goethe's enormous drama, Auden's poem begins with a restless search among alternative ways of action and understanding; follows this with the temptations offered by "Poor cheated Mephistopheles"; then moves through vast ranges of history and myth (even versions of *Faust*'s "die Mütter," the source of all forms, in Auden's "The Terrible, the Merciful, the Mothers"); and ends with a hymn to the eternal feminine in the person of Auden's friend Elizabeth Mayer:

> Dear friend Elizabeth, dear friend
> These days have brought me, may the end
> I bring to the grave's dead-line be
> More worthy of your sympathy
> Than the beginning;
>
> . . .
>
> We fall down in the dance, we make
> The old ridiculous mistake,
> But always there are such as you
> Forgiving, helping what we do.

Or, in Goethe's concluding words: "Das Ewig-Weibliche zieht uns hinan."

Auden's politics had changed with his religion. In his first reaction against his 1930's work he briefly espoused pacifism during the summer of 1939. But by early 1940 he wrote in a letter that he had "absolutely no patience with Pacifism as a political movement, as if one could do all the things in one's personal life that create wars and then pretend that to refuse to fight is a sacrifice and not a luxury." Although some English writers loudly charged him with fleeing the war by staying in America, Auden quietly went to the British embassy and volunteered to return. (He was told that only technically skilled people were needed.)

In New York, with no family to live among, Auden established a household of his own. Around 1940–1941 he lived in a large house in Brooklyn populated by artists and writers—at various times Carson McCullers, Louis MacNeice, Benjamin Britten, Richard Wright, Paul Bowles—where, in the midst of bohemian chaos, he took the role of bourgeois paterfamilias, banning politics from the dinner table, seeing to it that the rent was collected and paid. Much as he enjoyed New York, he decided that it was time to learn more of America and arranged to teach at the University of Michigan during 1941–1942, where the atmosphere might be more quiet.

In the summer before he left, the growing difficulties in his relationship with Kallman reached the point of crisis. While Auden had committed himself to sexual loyalty and faithfulness, Kallman was constitutionally unable to accept such domesticity, and in 1941 he began an affair with someone else. Auden was almost certainly alluding to his feelings about this when he wrote some years later that "providentially—for the occupational disease of poets is frivolity—I was forced to know in person what it is like to feel oneself in the prey of demonic powers, in both the Greek and Christian sense, stripped of self-control and self-pity, behaving like a ham actor in a Strindberg play." When the crisis abated he and Kallman agreed to have no further sexual relations with each other but to continue in many respects living as if in a marriage. For most of the rest of their lives they shared the same household, and in later years they developed the domestic habits of long-married couples, routinely sharing errands, finishing each other's sentences.

The crisis left Auden's poetry with a new depth of feeling, less showy than much of his earlier work, more wise and self-aware. In Michigan, in 1941–1942, he wrote a Christmas oratorio, *For the Time Being,* intended for setting by Benjamin Britten. It was animated by popular styles and contemporary satire, but its Christmas celebration was shadowed by its "apprehension at the thought / Of Lent and Good Friday which cannot, after all, now / Be very far off." Auden once again used his technique of conflating, rather than contrasting, present and past in his version of the Christmas story. He explained the technique in a letter to his father:

Sorry you are puzzled by the Oratorio. Perhaps you were expecting a purely historical account as one might give of the battle of Waterloo, whereas I was trying to treat it as a religious event which eternally recurs every time it is accepted. Thus the historical fact that the shepherds were *shepherds* is religiously accidental—the religious fact is that they were the poor and humble of this world for whom at this moment the historical expression is the city-proletariat, and so on with all the other figures. . . . I am not the first to treat the Christian data in this way; until the 18th Cent. it was always done, in the Mystery Plays for instance or any Italian paintings. It is only in the last two centuries that religion has been "humanized," and therefore treated historically as something that happened a long time ago; hence the nursery picture of Jesus in a nightgown and a Parsifal beard.

After his year at Michigan Auden expected to join the U.S. Army but was rejected by the draft board for medical reasons in September 1942. He spent the rest of the war teaching at

Swarthmore College, where he wrote another long poem, *The Sea and the Mirror: A Commentary on Shakespeare's "The Tempest"* (this and his previous long poem were collected in book form as *For the Time Being,* 1944). The events of the poem occur after the end of Shakespeare's play, as Prospero makes a farewell speech to Ariel while packing to leave the island, and the other characters then report, as they sail home, what they learned there. The poem is Auden's most elaborate study in the range and powers of his art, a rebuke to the romantic idea of the autonomy of poetic imagination. Prospero, in his long opening poem, is the type of artist who cannot see anything except in terms of art (perhaps without intending to, Auden made Prospero into a poet like Wallace Stevens: "On walks through winter woods, a bird's dry carcass / Agitates the retina with novel images, / A stranger's quiet collapse in a noisy street / Is the beginning of much lively speculation"), and when he comments tartly on the other characters in the play he can see in them none of the depths he casually attributes to himself. Prospero sounds persuasive—the portrait is so vivid that more than one critic was trapped into reading it as Auden's self-portrait—but the rest of the poem shows how limited and ignorant his faith in the imagination has left him. In the middle section the other characters make their own speeches, culminating in a triumphantly beautiful villanelle for Miranda. But once we have been persuaded of the depths of this splendid sequence of poems, Auden brushes it aside as it had earlier brushed aside Prospero. In the third section Caliban speaks to the audience, reminding us at the start that the play we have seen, and the poem we have read, was all make-believe, all fiction: "If now," he begins, "having dismissed your hired impersonators with verdicts ranging from the laudatory orchid to the disgusted and disgusting egg, . . ." Auden's Caliban is the voice

of nature, of the energy and variety of life, of Eros itself. And since nature—as Auden emphasized in earlier years—has no personal voice of its own, it must speak in a borrowed one; hence Caliban's adoption of the most mannered of all English styles, the prose of the late novels of Henry James. This style allows for the greatest possible range of content and manner, from the vulgarly proverbial to the aristocratically ornate. Caliban uses his all-inclusive voice to record the failures not only of art but of all secular ambition and hope. He pictures us at the end in a moment of existential urgency, when "we do at least see ourselves as we are, neither cosy nor playful, but swaying out on the ultimate wind-whipped cornice that overhangs the unabiding void." Only at this moment (the idea derives from the New Testament via Kierkegaard) can the choice of religious faith be made and solid ground again rest under our feet. Only now can the ultimate order and coherence of the universe be acknowleged—and so "the sounded note is the restored relation." *The Sea and the Mirror* concludes with a love song spoken by Ariel, the disembodied voice of art, to Caliban, the solid disorder of life, as Ariel reminds Caliban that art has no real wish to be autonomous or self-sufficient, but knows that it depends on the flawed sad variety of mortal life for its very existence.

In 1945 Auden's *Collected Poetry* appeared. Critics had begun to charge that his earliest work was his best, so he arranged the book not chronologically or thematically, but by alphabetical order of first lines. This was an implicit challenge to critics to see whether they could tell by style alone whether one of his poems was early or late. Auden disliked the book's title— "collected" implied finality, which at thirty-eight he hoped was untrue—but the publisher insisted. Among the changes Auden made for this volume were wholesale deletions of political work, the breaking-up of *Paid on Both Sides* and *The Orators* into disconnected short poems (in later years, feeling less irritated by his younger self, he restored both works to their complete forms), and the addition of ironic, sometimes flippant titles to poems that had been untitled in earlier books. The volume eventually sold more than fifty thousand copies.

At the end of the war Auden left his Swarthmore job and worked for a few months with the U.S. Strategic Bombing Survey, in a unit of civilians and soldiers studying the effect of bombing on civilian morale in Germany. At first Auden thought the work a "statistical boondoggle" ("We asked them if they minded being bombed."). But his unit learned that morale increased as bombing did—a conclusion ignored by the military, who had to relearn it twenty years later in Vietnam.

Back from Germany, Auden settled again in New York, in Greenwich Village. There he worked at editing and reviewing, gave occasional lectures and, in the 1960's, went out across America on an annual reading tour. He and Robert Frost were the only poets able to make a living from their writing. Auden came to regard himself as one of a vanishing breed, the Man of Letters, who wrote not because he was devoted to the lonely discipline of his art but because his writing served a public function; Edmund Wilson was the closest parallel. In a late poem he referred to the audience of poets as "our clients"—in the same way doctors or lawyers have clients, who come to them for professional services they are trained to provide.

In New York, Auden finished the last of his long poems, *The Age of Anxiety* (1947). A "baroque eclogue" set in a Third Avenue bar, it records the intersecting thoughts of four characters—loosely embodying the four Jungian faculties of thought, intuition, feeling, and sensation—through an All Souls' Night that ends in varieties of religious negation and affirmation. The verse is Old English alliterative, but with

modern idioms and adapted into a wide range of lyrical, narrative, and epigrammatic forms. This modification of the Old Icelandic drottkvaett is characteristic:

> Hushed is the lake of hawks
> Bright with our excitement,
> And all the sky of skulls
> Glows with scarlet roses;
> The melter of men and salt
> Admires the drinker of iron:
> Bold banners of meaning
> Blaze o'er the host of days.

As in the Welsh model, this identifies the four traditional elements by way of riddles: the lake of hawks is the air; the sky of skulls, earth; the melter of men, fire; and the drinker of iron, water, which rusts it.

Nineteen forty-eight through 1957 were the Mediterranean years of this least Mediterranean of poets. Every spring he closed his apartment in New York and spent about six months on the island of Ischia, near Naples. He deliberately chose a climate and culture with as little as possible in common with the Nordic landscapes he found most congenial. In "Good-Bye to the Mezzogiorno" (1958) he came "Out of a gothic North"

> In middle-age hoping to twig from
> What we are not what we might be next. . . .

He was too much the product of his English roots ever to settle in:

> If we try
> To "go southern," we spoil in no time, we grow
>   Flabby, dingily lecherous, and
> Forget to pay bills: . . .

but his years in Ischia altered the character of his poetry and his beliefs.

In his early years in America he had focused virtually all his attention on the solitary choices of the individual mind. Now he wrote about the world of the flesh and about the world of the citizen, of mankind in landscapes and cities. The great personal questions of faith and doubt he had largely resolved. It was now time to write the poetry needed by an age in which the heroic vision of the romantic artist, alone with his imagination, had grown trivial. It was

> in which the heroic image is not the nomad
> wanderer through the desert or over the
>   ocean,
> but the less exciting figure of the builder,
> who renews the ruined walls of the city.

And to give a local habitation and a name to this solid and rooted figure, he began writing poems about the unheroic body. Poets in the romantic and modernist tradition had always found the body difficult to write about in any plausible way, probably because they were embarrassed by an aspect of themselves that—unlike the works of their imagination—they clearly did not make by themselves and that shared so many qualities with the common run of mankind. Eliot, until the last years of his life, hated the flesh and all it did. Lawrence, dying of consumption, fantasized the body as a repository of sacred energies that no real human body could ever have contained. Yeats found the body interesting only if ideally and impossibly beautiful or grotesquely ugly. Pound, until he was locked up, scarcely noticed the body at all. In contrast to all these, Auden saw that the body had rights of its own, that it was also an object which everyone put to use—"my accomplice now, / My assassin to be"—yet despite the isolating acts of the individual will the body does its best to recover, "restoring / The order we try to destroy, the rhythm / We spoil out of spite." It is "The flesh we die but it is death to pity" (to look down on as inferior to the mind) the one aspect of ourselves that sees through every lie we try to tell and suffers the strain of

our mental disorder. At the close of Auden's long historical meditation "Memorial for the City" (1949), the flesh itself speaks:

> Without me Adam would have fallen
>   irrevocably
>   with Lucifer; he would never have been
>   able
>   to cry *O felix culpa.*
>
>   . . .
> I fell asleep when Diotima spoke of love; . . .
>
>   . . .
> I was the just impediment to the marriage of
>   Faustus with Helen; I know a ghost when I
>   see one.
>
>   . . .
> I was innocent of the sin of the Ancient
>   Mariner; time after time I warned Captain
>   Ahab to accept happiness.
> As for Metropolis, that too-great city; her
>   delusions are not mine.
> Her speeches impress me little, her statistics
>   less; . . .
> At the place of my passion her photographers
>   are gathered together; but I shall rise again
>   to hear her judged.

Auden's one article of religious faith that stood beyond the world visible to science was his belief in the resurrection of the body at the end of time, a belief that took the body seriously and on the body's own terms.

"In Praise of Limestone" (1948) is Auden's calm hymn to a landscape that "dissolves in water," which in its pliability and change is an image for the body itself. It is a personal landscape as well, the Pennine Hills of his English childhood and the hills of northern Italy. He makes no spectacular claims for this small and local setting, which he knows has neither grandeur nor historical importance to recommend it. (Neither, of course, has the body.) What both limestone landscape and human flesh do, however, is rebuke the romantic poet's celebration of his mind and the scientific observer's concern for the inhuman spaces of atoms or galaxies. The scientist is right, his distant places are important. The poem recalls only that there is also a human landscape of responsibility and love.

The negative image of the human landscape of "In Praise of Limestone" is the "plain without a feature, bare and brown," of "The Shield of Achilles." This is a place—or a nonplace—where all identity and sympathy are absent, where nameless children grow who

> . . . never heard
> Of any world where promises were kept,
> Or one could weep because another wept.

Auden's verse form in much of his late work is largely a twentieth-century invention but one that stands outside the mainstream of modernism. He uses lines arranged by the number of syllables, without regular rhymes or regular patterns of stress. The form of "In Praise of Limestone" is alternating lines of thirteen and eleven syllables, with adjacent vowels (and vowels and *h*) arbitrarily counted as a single vowel, so that *the in-* or *-ly home* each count as one syllable only—a practice with a long classical ancestry. Thus:

> If it form the one landscape that we, the
>   inconstant ones,
>   Are consistently homesick for, this is chiefly
> Because it dissolves in water. Mark these
>   rounded slopes
>   With their surface fragrance of thyme and,
>   beneath. . . .

Auden learned syllabic verse from Marianne Moore, and it was also used by Robert Bridges and other poets earlier in the century but without Auden's range or depth. What syllabics made possible was a form that had all the regularity and order of traditional meters without in any way sounding archaic or anachronistic.

They permitted the formal pleasures of older poetry, but the understatement with which they asserted their formal properties allowed them to accommodate what Auden called the characteristic style of modern poetry, "an intimate tone of voice, the speech of one person addressing another person, not a large audience." When a poem required a relaxed tone of voice, long-lined syllabics provided room for expansiveness. When more intensity was needed, Auden tightened the form by using shorter lines and extensive internal rhyming:

> Simultaneously, as soundlessly,
>   Spontaneously, suddenly
> As, at the vaunt of the dawn, the kind
>   Gates of the body fly open
> To its world beyond, the gates of the mind,
>   The horn gate and the ivory gate
> Swing to, swing shut, instantaneously. . . .

These lines open a sequence of poems titled *Horae Canonicae*—canonical hours, the hours of daily prayer. After *The Age of Anxiety* Auden turned from long poems to connected sequences of shorter poems. The seven *Bucolics* of 1952–1953 concern different ways of life appropriate to different landscapes. The seven *Horae Canonicae* poems of 1949–1954 have a larger and more ambitious subject, the relation of individuals and their personal acts to the life of the city, and the necessary connection between civilized order and the violence needed to maintain it. (Auden published these and his other poems from his Mediterranean years in *Nones*, 1951, and *The Shield of Achilles*, 1955.)

Horae Canonicae is one of the great masterpieces of twentieth-century poetry. It has received little critical attention because it demands to be read in ways very different from those appropriate to the modernist tradition from Yeats to Wallace Stevens. Its concern is not the imposition of imaginative order on a passive world but the discovery of order that already exists in the world. In its disturbing emphasis on the price that must be paid for civilization, on the murderous violence that defends civil order, it is in the direct line of Vergil's *Aeneid* and Shakespeare's history plays. Aeneas, the hero who makes possible the peace and order of imperial Rome, yields at the end to the violent furor he is dedicated to oppose. In Auden's sequence the great civilizers—those with vocations for the arts and sciences, those who command laws and buildings to come into existence—are also those who provide the instruments and authority for the murder of the scapegoat victim, the banished outsider, without whose exclusion no community has ever constituted itself. Where Auden had earlier emphasized the element of choice that led to acts of love, now he examines the role of choice in murderous acts of will.

The sequence extends over an epic range. The first six poems cover the events of a single day—a Good Friday in the present that is simultaneously the day of the historical crucifixion, like the Christmas of *For the Time Being*—but extend also from the poet's birth to his death, from the rise to the fall of his city, from the evolution of man to the end of the species, and from the creation to the apocalypse.

All the beginnings occur in "Prime." This opening poem also establishes the theme of the isolating will. To draw breath—to choose to draw breath on first waking—is

> . . . to wish
> No matter what, to be wise,
> To be different, to die and the cost,
> No matter how, is Paradise
> Lost of course and myself owing a death. . . .

(The pun on "owing a debt" is originally Falstaff's.) In "Prime" the "I" of the sequence is still solitary. In "Terce" he is in transition between privacy and a public role. At this moment the hangman shakes paws with his dog and sets

out to work; the judge gently closes his wife's bedroom door and descends with a weary sigh. It is a neutral moment when our only wish is to get through the day without being called upon to do or choose anything in particular, to be left alone. But that modest wish has its fatal consequences, because someone always gets in the way, and there will be the wish to move him out of it.

The third poem, "Sext," opens with awed praise for those more devoted to vocation than themselves, "the first flaker of flints / who forgot his dinner, / the first collector of sea-shells / to remain celibate." Then it grimly acknowledges the city's need for those in authority, "very great scoundrels," but without whom "how squalid existence would be." It ends in a devastatingly level tone, describing the common crowd who gather at any scene of destruction, the crowd whom everyone can join ("Only because of that can we say / all men are our brothers,") and that worships only the brute fact of force. With all three groups in place, the crucifixion can happen. Those with vocation provide the instruments of murder; those in authority give the command; the crowd assents.

The fourth poem, "Nones," shows an emotional range and force, an ethical intelligence and depth, scarcely equaled in modern verse. It deserves more than the brief explication that is possible here.

A reader need have no interest at all in religion to feel the power of "Nones." Its emotional focus is the abrupt sinking realization—which occurs at some point in all human relationships—that one has done harm to another, perhaps inadvertently, that cannot now be undone. Whether it is a hurtful word thoughtlessly spoken or an angry act of violence, the act and its consequences are irrevocably *there*:

> What we know to be not possible,
> Though time after time foretold

By wild hermits, by shaman and sybil
  Gibbering in their trances,
Or revealed to a child in some chance rhyme
  Like *will* and *kill*, comes to pass
Before we realize it. . . .

The shouting crowd that called for the victim's death has dissolved; each of those in it can blame the crowd, not himself. Nature, the realm of repetition and return, looks on in bewilderment at an act that, unlike the cyclical events of nature, cannot be repeated or reversed. (The modernist emphasis on cyclical history, as in Yeats or Joyce, or on the immediate moment, as in Williams or Stevens, or in a realm outside time, as in Eliot, excludes the whole subject of this poem from the world of modernist literature.) Every willed action seems to lead up to this definitive act of will. Every playful, apparently harmless, game of children or adults reveals its potentially fatal ending. We shall now,

      . . . under
  The mock chase and mock capture,
  The racing and tussling and splashing,
    The panting and the laughter,
  Be listening for the cry and stillness
    To follow after. . . .

Burdened by our own knowledge, we still "have time / To misrepresent, excuse, deny, / Mythify, use this event"; but its historical uniqueness, the real fact of murder, remains. "Its meaning / Waits for our lives." Meanwhile, "It would be best to go home, if we have a home"—all our fixities are in question—"In any case good to rest." And as we sleep "our dreaming wills" move through an ominous dream landscape of symbolic guilt and accusation:

  Through gates that will not relatch
  And doors marked *Private*, pursued by
    Moors
  And watched by latent robbers,

To hostile villages at the heads of fjords,
  To dark chateaux where wind sobs
In the pine-trees and telephones ring,
    Inviting trouble. . . .

And, at the same time, the sleeping body works undisturbed to restore order and wholeness to "our own wronged flesh." The language of the poem, up to this point rich in metaphor, for a moment becomes a language of plain fact as it describes the unpoetical workings of the body:

    . . . valves close
  And open exactly, glands secrete,
    Vessels contract and expand
  At the right moment. . . .

And the poem ends by rushing cinematically outward to the natural creatures, the unblinking hawk, the "bug whose view is balked by grass," the smug hens and shy deer, all awed by the fact of death, that sign of their own future which they, unlike man, cannot understand.

After the intensities of "Nones," the sequence relaxes somewhat. "Vespers," in prose, compares two fantasies of the ideal society, the innocent arcadia and ordered utopia, between which all real societies are built. "Compline" records the returns and endings of nightfall, of personal death and the end of the city, in a calm elegiac tone. And the sequence ends with the new dawn, in the early morning of "Lauds." After the encyclopedic range and intellectual rigor of the six preceding poems, it offers a simple musical promise of renewal and community:

The dripping mill-wheel is again turning;
Among the leaves the small birds sing:
In solitude, for company.

Auden intended to keep his summer house in Ischia at least until 1960, but when he won an Italian literary prize in 1957 his landlord tried to double his rent and Auden decided it was time to leave. He bought an eighteenth-century farmhouse in Kirchstetten, a small village thirty miles west of Vienna, and moved there the following year. He chose Austria, he said, because he loved the German language, because he wanted to be in a wine-drinking country, and because he wanted to be near an opera house. Opera was a taste he acquired from Chester Kallman, and in 1947 the two wrote the libretto for Igor Stravinsky's *The Rake's Progress*; later they wrote further libretti for Hans Werner Henze.

Auden's first years in Austria were among the happiest of his life. Once he stood in his garden and wept with joy at owning a home of his own. He wrote in 1958–1964 a sequence of twelve poems in celebration, *Thanksgiving for a Habitat*, the scale and exuberance of which suggests a house larger and grander than the rural domesticity of the Kirchstetten farmhouse with its low ceilings and dark rooms. Each room received a poem of its own, together with some general poems about the house itself, and each room is characterized, as in his earlier *Bucolics*, by special kinds of relationships, history, and rhetoric. In the study he recalls a dead friend, the poet Louis MacNeice, one of the many dead whose work survives in their influence on living writers; in the dining room he thinks of friends still very much alive; the cellar and attic evoke childhood memories; and so on through the living room, the guest room, the kitchen, the bath, and—the last and most difficult to write—the toilet. After the urban moralities of *Horae Canonicae* Auden narrowed his focus to the domestic and personal, but always in a historical and ethical context. Auden called *Thanksgiving for a Habitat* his first happy poems, the first he was able to write in the first person—that is, with all the quirks and details of his private existence on the visible surface of the poetry.

In the 1930's Auden had tried on the role of propagandist, had urged his readers to action. But he knew even then a poet had no more au-

thority to recommend one or another course of action than anyone else did, and he renounced that role as false when he moved to America. In the 1950's and 1960's he again adopted a public role, but without a partisan label. As a poet he was in "loyal opposition," affirming the importance of personal choice in a mass society, but never, unlike his modernist predecessors, condemning his society as irredeemably corrupt or hopelessly inferior to some imagined past. He wrote as a democratic counterpart to the court poet of earlier times. With no pretense of writing as a leader or guide—he preferred to think of himself as a craftsman rather than as a bard—he commented on public events, bringing to light their historical and moral aspects. Much of his later poetry—in *Homage to Clio* (1960), *About the House* (1965), *City Without Walls* (1969), *Epistle to a Godson* (1972), and the posthumous *Thank You, Fog* (1974)—is deliberately "occasional," prompted by events ranging in scale from international invasions, political assassinations, and moon landings, to retirements, birthdays, and marriages.

Whatever their occasions, all these poems took as their central subject the use and misuse of personal relations and responsibility. What made love and responsibility possible, he suggested, was an awareness of the real outline and nature of things; the means by which love and responsibility were brought into being was personal speech. He distinguished between impersonal "linguistic codes," which may be found among birds and insects as well as man, and "speech," the conscious statement of personal choice, found only among individual people. To use speech is to use the first person, to take responsibility for what one says. Speech is the language of an "I" with a personal name, linguistic codes the language of an anonymous "he" or "she." Since all individuals are at the same time biological organisms with needs and functions common to all mankind, and unique persons differing from all others, everyone is capable of using both kinds of language. If I ask you the way to the train station, you will (I hope) answer in a linguistic code, giving me the same answer anyone else would give. But if I ask you what emotional associations the station has for *you*, you may (if you choose) answer in personal speech, telling me feelings and memories that no one else could possibly tell.

So—to return to a poem from the early 1950's—in "The Shield of Achilles," the barren warlike landscape is a place without responsibility or personal names:

> . . . congregated on its blankness, stood
>   An unintelligible multitude,
> A million eyes, a million boots in line,
> Without expression, waiting for a sign.
>
> Out of the air a voice without a face
>   Proved by statistics that some cause was
>   just
> In tones as dry and level as the place:
>   No one was cheered and nothing was
>   discussed. . . .

This is a scene on a twentieth-century version of the shield that Hephaestos, in the *Iliad*, casts at the request of Thetis, mother of the warrior Achilles. But in Auden's poem the names of the god and goddess are replaced by the anonymous "he" and "she" because they do not act, and it is their impersonality that brings about the barren impersonality on the shield's images:

> She looked over his shoulder
>   For vines and olive trees,
>
>   . . .
>
> But there on the shining metal
>   His hands had put instead
> An artificial wilderness
>   And a sky like lead.

Only in the final stanza do the proper names appear, together with the personal characteristics of their owners; but now it is too late. The smith god walks away from his creation; the goddess finally speaks, but in horror and revulsion; and the hero in whose name the shield was made has already chosen his death:

> The thin-lipped armorer,
>   Hephaestos, hobbled away;
> Thetis of the shining breasts
>   Cried out in dismay
> At what the god had wrought
>   To please her son, the strong
> Iron-hearted man-slaying Achilles
>   Who would not live long.

The ideas of language implicit in "The Shield of Achilles" became explicit in later poems. Writing on the occasion of the Soviet invasion of Czechoslovakia in "August 1968," Auden, whose home in Austria was only a few miles away, made a linguistic parable. He responded to the event in the terms that, as a poet, he understood best, and the point he makes is stronger than any direct propaganda:

> The Ogre does what ogres can,
> Deeds quite impossible for Man,
> But one prize is beyond his reach,
> The Ogre cannot master Speech.
> About a subjugated plain,
> Among its desperate and slain,
> The Ogre stalks with hands on hips,
> While drivel gushes from his lips.

The relation of personal speech to impersonal code, the contrast between the scale of the individual body and the inhuman scale of nature's remoter aspects, the importance of unique unrepeatable events in history as contrasted with the cycles of nature—it was this framework of ideas that made possible the special personal tone of Auden's later years. He wrote more and more directly about his personal experience, but unlike the younger confessional poets then emerging in America, he never suggested his experience was important because it was his.

He always made didactic use of it, as an example or warning. And he wrote about it in the deliberately unheroic miniature forms of haiku or haiku-sequences that he learned about by translating similar poems in Dag Hammarskjöld's *Markings*:

> Money cannot buy
> The fuel of Love:
> But is excellent kindling.
>
> Our bodies cannot love:
> But, without one,
> What works of Love could we do?
>
> Thoughts of his own death,
> like the distant roll
> of thunder at a picnic.

A frequent topic in his later poems was his own aging, which was almost startlingly rapid in his late fifties and early sixties. "River Profile," written when he was fifty-nine, is a terrifying allegory of the growth and decline of the body in terms of a river's progress and an example of the great poetry of which he was still capable. The river's origin is a sexual storm ("head-on collisions of cloud and rock in an / up-thrust, crevasse-and-avalanche"); it first appears as a nameless stream; then it grows larger and stronger, until its middle age:

Polluted, bridged by girders, banked by
    concrete,
now it bisects a polyglot metropolis,
ticker-tape, taxi, brothel, foot-lights country,
à-la-mode always.

Broadening or burrowing to the moon's
    phases,
turbid with pulverized wastemantle, on
    through
flatter, duller, hotter, cotton-gin country
it scours, approaching

the tidal mark where it puts off majesty,

disintegrates, and through swamps of a delta,
punting-pole, fowling-piece, oyster-tongs
    country,
wearies to its final

act of surrender, effacement, atonement
in a huge amorphous aggregate no cuddled
attractive child ever dreams of, non-country. . . .

As the world of his poems drew inward from history and the city to the rooms of his house, and then to his aging body, Auden returned to the privacy of his beginnings. In 1972 he left his winter home in New York for a cottage provided by his old Oxford college, where he had been professor of poetry since 1956 (although he taught only three weeks of each year). He seemed to know he was near death: one of his last poems is ambiguously titled "Posthumous Letter to Gilbert White"; he wrote it only a month or two before he died. At the end his work took on a tone of elegiac gratitude as he recalled the culture and family that nurtured him. "A Thanksgiving" listed his debts to his literary ancestors, reviewing the whole course of his career. He named Hardy and Frost as his early masters, until

> Falling in love altered that,
> now Someone, at least, was important:
> *Yeats* was a help, so was *Graves*.
>
> Then, without warning, the whole
> Economy suddenly crumbled:
> there, to instruct me, was *Brecht*.

And onward until the last poet named, Goethe, whose poem *"Gegenwart"* provided Auden with the meter for his.

Auden spent only one winter in Oxford. He found it lonely and provincial after his years in New York. Then, in 1973, he spent his usual summer with Kallman in Austria. When the time came to return to Oxford, he closed up his house and left for a weekend in Vienna before his flight. He died there in his sleep in the early hours of September 29, 1973. He was buried in the village cemetery of Kirchstetten.

A memorial plaque in the poets' corner at Westminster Abbey is engraved with the lines with which, in 1939, he concluded his elegy for Yeats. Writing less to Yeats than to the living poets of whom he was one, Auden celebrated the didactic powers of his art. In the world of time and of physical necessity, in the world of impersonal language, the poet still preserved the responsible freedom of personal speech. His task was to offer that spoken freedom to others:

> In the prison of his days
> Teach the free man how to praise.

Selected Bibliography

WORKS OF W. H. AUDEN

COLLECTED EDITIONS

The Collected Poetry of W. H. Auden. New York: Random House, 1945. British edition: *Collected Shorter Poems, 1930–1944.* London: Faber and Faber, 1950. (Revised versions of most of Auden's earlier poems, with excisions.)

W. H. Auden. A Selection by the Author. Harmondsworth: Penguin/ Faber and Faber, 1958. American edition: *Selected Poetry of W. H. Auden.* New York: Modern Library, 1959. 2nd ed., New York: Vintage Books, 1971.

Collected Shorter Poems 1927–1957. London: Faber and Faber, 1966; New York: Random House, 1967. (Further revisions and excisions of earlier work, arranged chronologically.)

Collected Longer Poems. London: Faber and Faber, 1968; New York: Random House, 1969.

Collected Poems. London: Faber and Faber, 1976; New York: Random House, 1976. (Includes the two volumes listed immediately above, with some additional poems restored by Auden in later years and with the contents of his later volumes of short poems. Auden's final revised texts, with many early poems omitted.)

The English Auden. Poems, Essays, and Dramatic Writings, 1927–1939. London: Faber and Faber, 1977; New York: Random House, 1978. (Reprints the original versions, including all the poems that Auden printed in book form during his lifetime but omitted from his late collections.)

Selected Poems, New Edition. New York: Vintage Books, 1979; London: Faber and Faber, 1979. (Reprinted from the original versions, often differing from those in the *Collected Poems*, and including some omitted from the late collections.)

PROSE

The Dyer's Hand. New York: Random House, 1962; London: Faber and Faber, 1963.

Forewords and Afterwords. New York: Random House, 1973; London: Faber and Faber, 1973.

BIBLIOGRAPHY

Bloomfield, Barry C., and Edward Mendelson. *W. H. Auden: A Bibliography, 1924–1969.* Charlottesville: University Press of Virginia, 1972. (A full list of writings by and about Auden.)

BIOGRAPHICAL AND CRITICAL STUDIES

Blair, John G. *The Poetic Art of W. H. Auden.* Princeton, N. J.: Princeton University Press, 1965.

Carpenter, Humphrey. *W. H. Auden: A Biography.* New York: Harcourt Brace Jovanovich (in press).

Duchene, François. *The Case of the Helmeted Airman: A Study of W. H. Auden's Poetry.* London: Chatto and Windus, 1972.

Fuller, John L. *A Reader's Guide to W. H. Auden.* London: Thames and Hudson, 1970.

Greenberg, Herbert M. *Quest for the Necessary: W. H. Auden and the Dilemma of Divided Consciousness.* Cambridge: Harvard University Press, 1968.

Hynes, Samuel L. *The Auden Generation.* New York: Viking, 1977.

Johnson, Richard. *Man's Place: An Essay on Auden.* Ithaca, N. Y.: Cornell University Press, 1973.

Mendelson, Edward. *Early Auden.* New York: Viking (in press).

Spears, Monroe K. *The Poetry of W. H. Auden: The Disenchanted Island.* New York: Oxford University Press, 1963.

Spears, Monroe K., ed. *Auden: A Collection of Critical Essays.* Englewood Cliffs, N. J.: Prentice-Hall, 1964.

Spender, Stephen, ed. *W. H. Auden: A Tribute.* London: Weidenfeld and Nicolson, 1975.

Wright, George T. *W. H. Auden.* New York: Twayne, 1969.

—*EDWARD MENDELSON*

Amiri Baraka

1934 —

Born Everett LeRoi Jones, on October 7, 1934, in Newark, New Jersey, Amiri Baraka is in 1980 a man whose literary and political growth is in midlife. However inaccessible and unpopular his work has been from a conventional standpoint, he has established himself as a writer of significant stature. With the vantage point of the racial outsider, he has passed through a series of painful and searching stages of growth. Strenuously resisting the artistic and cultural ideals of what he has called "mainstream" and "bourgeois" America, he offers in their stead radical social analysis, new cultural values, and a boldly innovative literature. In the process he has experienced a series of simultaneously disruptive and healing transformations—adjustments of major personal, artistic, and political importance.

From this perspective his writings can be usefully understood as the record of intense and ongoing changes. They began in the late 1950's with a confused but determined movement away from what he perceived as white-dominated lyric egotism, continued into the 1960's in the form of an emotional and cultural reintegration with the black world, and emerged in the 1970's as a complete ideological dedication to worldwide revolution. Through each phase Baraka has had to question closely his role as a writer and to find ways of making literary art an effective instrument for defining his personal, cultural, and political goals. His remarkable achievements as a writer and activist—he came to regard the two roles as inseparable—bespeak a temperament marked by uncompromising energy and risk-taking modulated by intellectual and emotional resilience.

The son of Coyt LeRoi and Anna Lois Russ Jones, young LeRoi was raised in an urban black family with middle-class aspirations. Passing through the Newark public schools, he briefly attended Rutgers University on a science scholarship and then shifted to the more hospitable, if decidedly assimilationist, atmosphere of Howard University, majoring in English with a minor in philosophy and leaving in 1954 to join the Air Force. After nearly three years in the service, most of that time spent in Puerto Rico, he gravitated to New York City with certain distinct perceptions registered in his consciousness. "The Howard thing," he said in a 1964 interview with Judy Stone, "let me understand the Negro sickness. They teach you how to pretend to be white. But the Air Force made me understand the white sickness. It shocked me into realizing what was happening to me and others. By oppressing Negroes, the whites have become oppressors, . . . convincing themselves they are right, as people have always convinced themselves."

Finding the intellectual and artistic atmosphere of the East Village section of the city to his liking, he took graduate courses in comparative literature at Columbia, worked for *Record Changer* magazine, and was generally absorbed into the Bohemian life-style. At a time when the advanced politics of race was distinctly antibourgeois and integrationist, Jones found the countercultural posture of the predominantly white "beat" community initially supportive.

In that congenial atmosphere he began to acknowledge the first impulses leading into his early poetry. In the reachable past were such established older-generation moderns as Ezra Pound, William Carlos Williams, and even T. S. Eliot, whom Jones subsequently dismissed as a "lovely . . . rhetorician." At the same time several groups of the new poets, for an interval, furnished a sustaining poetics: the Black Mountain School of Robert Creeley and Charles Olson offered workable poetic theories and techniques while the New York coterie of Allen Ginsberg, Gregory Corso, and others fostered useful social attitudes and emotional strategies. He participated in two of the numerous "little magazines" then proliferating in the East Village community, evanescent mimeographed issues with small circulation designed to promulgate the work of his literary friends: *Yügen,* founded and coedited with Hettie Cohen; and *Floating Bear,* coedited with Diane DiPrima. Jones married Hettie, a young Jewish coworker at the *Record Changer,* in October 1958, marking his furthest incursion into the white world. He was on the threshold of an arduous artistic and political struggle.

Although Jones needed to pull away from what he soon came to recognize as certain debilitating aspects of his "beat" identity, there were also strands in his early literary experiences that later tied up with his nationalist writings. In a 1960 radio interview with David Ossman he tells how William Carlos Williams alerted him to the importance of the spoken word: "how to write the way I *speak* rather than the way I *think* a poem ought to be written—to write just the way it comes to me, in my own speech, utilizing the rhythms of speech rather than any kind of metrical concept. To talk verse." While he learned about crafting verse from Pound's example, "how a poem should be made, what a poem ought to *look* like," it was Williams, he said, who showed him "how to get it in my own language." Just as meaningful were Charles Olson's pronouncements in *Projective Verse* (1959), stressing the efficacy of sound in poetry, letting the poetic line follow the dictates of breath, which, Olson says, "allows *all* the speech-force of language back in."

Jones pointedly entitled his own brief statement on poetics "How You Sound??" (1959). He emphasized the need for a voice that will recreate the sound of his private experience:

MY POETRY is whatever I think I am. (Can I be light & weightless as a sail?? Heavy & clunking like 8 black boots.) I CAN BE ANYTHING I CAN. I make a poetry with what I feel is useful & can be saved out of all the garbage of our lives. What I see, am touched by (CAN HEAR). . . . "Who knows what a poem ought to sound like? Until it's thar." Says Charles Olson . . . & I follow closely with that.

Such dicta anticipated the extraliterary modes of black music and speech at the center of the nascent black aesthetic that Jones began to delineate in the early 1960's as he wrote *Blues People.* For the time being, though, his attention to poetic voice was almost entirely self-directed, there being as yet no sense of his singular voice in relation to the collective voice of the black community.

Initially inviting, too, must have been the extent to which the "beat" subculture drew unabashedly upon black culture, canonizing bebop musicians like Dizzy Gillespie and Charlie Parker and making the socially estranged world of black music a conspicuous image for its own consciously chosen alienation. The black perspective, as understood by the white poets, was an appealing metaphor for disenchantment, as with Ginsberg's typical assertion in *Howl* that the best minds of his generation were "dragging themselves through the negro streets at dawn." As much as Ginsberg and others were touched by images of black culture, they were unable to appropriate black style as a workable model for poetic form.

Nor could Jones do so effectively until he freed himself from the influence of the moderns and the "new" poets. His first formulations of himself as a writer did not exclude the pressing awareness that he was black, but they did restrict the manifestation of blackness in his poetry of the late 1950's and early 1960's. When asked why the sense of "being a Negro" one finds in the poetry of Langston Hughes did not occur in his own work, Jones, in his "beat" guise, demurred: "I'm fully conscious all the time that I am an American Negro, because it's part of my life. But I know also that if I want to say, 'I see a bus full of people,' I don't have to say, 'I am a Negro seeing a bus full of people.'" In the poetry of *Preface to a Twenty Volume Suicide Note....* (1961) and *The Dead Lecturer* (1964), as well as in *Blues People* (1963), his incisive social-historical interpretation of Afro-American music, Jones began a painstaking reassessment and slow moving out toward black self-identification as Amiri Baraka.

Preface to a Twenty Volume Suicide Note.... includes poems written between 1957 and 1961. The title suggests a posture common to much of the new poetry: that people are pressed to the brink of suicide by the internalization of popular myths and symbols that the poet must exorcise by a determined artistic in-

dividualism. With his own radio-prone youth much in mind, Jones typically assails the media heroes beamed into the American imagination—the inflated fictions of Tom Mix, Captain Midnight, and the Lone Ranger—along with the irrelevant serious art also produced by the same culture, "Great poets dying / with their strophes on." Such intrusions, damaging enough to acquiescent white perceptions, impinged even more menacingly on the mind of the vulnerable black artist. Jones's predicament was that he found himself beginning to question the efficacy of the new poetry, the vanguard literature of the very culture whose fantasies he was attempting to dissipate. Unlike Ginsberg, Jack Kerouac, and Creeley, he was much less certain that literary statement was an effective assertion of his integrity. So we see Jones at the beginning, laden with a cumbersome literary apparatus—prefaces and volumes bearing down heavily on his fragile "note."

"HYMN FOR LANIE POO," the second piece in the collection, satirically cuts into middle-class black pretensions fed by white-imposed stereotypes, fads, and beliefs. The ulterior responsibility, though, is identified in the final lines of the poem by an image that becomes a significant interpretive marker throughout *Suicide Note*:

> the huge & loveless
> white-anglo sun/of
> benevolent step
> mother America.

Throughout the poem the diffuse motioning toward whiteness is associated with the sun's penetrating light. By inverting this traditional life-giving symbol, Jones practices a strategy common to the black perspective: reversing the destructive meanings and values projected by the white world in order to buffer the besieged black psyche. The poem also implies that the values embodied in literary convention are part of the malign influence. A soothing aubade invites the poet into a lyrical acceptance of the sun as his ultimate genealogical source:

> Each morning
> I go down
> to Gansevoort St.
> and stand on the docks.
> I stare out
> at the horizon
> until it gets up
> and comes to embrace
> me. I
> make believe
> it is my father.
> This is known
> as genealogy

The permeating image violates the poet's deepest privacies, seducing his sister ("Lanie Poo" was the nickname of Sandra Elaine, Jones's sister) into a "generation of fictitious / Ofays." The ironic hymn sets the general tone for the recurring condemnation of the insinuating American sun culture. In "ONE NIGHT STAND," dedicated to Allen Ginsberg, the poets are "foreign seeming persons" visiting the decaying city with their "Hats flopped so the sun / can't scald our beards. . . ."

Jones toys with other clever inversions to undermine popular sentimentalism, as in demonstrating that love can be "an evil word . . ." by turning it backward: "see, see what I mean? / An evol word. . . ." Two poems about his wife Hettie, which Baraka now understandably withholds from republication, propose a more painful romantic inversion by commenting wryly on the poet's interracial marriage. "FOR HETTIE" describes not only a woman who happens to be left-handed but one who has reversed the prevailing social order by taking a black husband and carrying a child whose paternity the poet questions. He impatiently mocks Hettie's left-handedness by accusing her of seeming to write backward, a style ironically

suggestive of his own literary countertactics. But the most telling reversal is genealogical, the poet's uneasy anticipation of their mixed-blood child. In "FOR HETTIE IN HER FIFTH MONTH" he observes his pregnant wife basking her womb in the sun's fading rays, foreseeing in the birth his complicity in the emergence of an absurd Hebrew-"beat" legacy.

Beyond the interracial quandary is an even more deeply felt emotional displacement in "THE BRIDGE." Under the inscription "(# for wieners and mcclure)," this lyric of disorientation and suicide is structured by musical metaphors into a sharp message for two of Jones's fellow poets, John Wieners and Michael McClure. Unable to return to his and their familiar melodies, the beginning or "head" of his song, he finds himself in disruptive motion along the bridging phrase where harmonic "changes" are unfamiliar:

> you find yourself in its length
> strung out along its breadth, waiting
> for the cold sun to tear out your eyes.
>   Enamoured
> of its blues, spread out in the silk clubs of
> this autumn tune. The changes are difficult,
>   when
> you hear them, & know they are all in you,
>   the chords
>
> of your disorder meddle with your would be
>   disguises.

The old poetic values, Jones seems to assert to his friends, no longer apply: "& I have forgotten, / all the things, you told me to love, to try to understand, . . ." With the bridge leading only to the unknown and the song running out, he jumps into the "unmentionable black"—the territory to be charted in subsequent writings.

A crucial turning point for Jones was his 1960 visit to Cuba with a group of black writers, to attend a commemoration of the revolutionary attack by Fidel Castro against President

Fulgencio Batista in 1953. It was Jones's first direct contact with Marxism—his own conversion would not occur for a decade. The political nature of the event awakened Jones to a new social and artistic sense of himself, an awareness recorded in the poem "BETANCOURT," dated July 30, 1960.

In the 1960 essay "Cuba Libre," reprinted in *Home* (1966), Jones describes his encounter with Señora Betancourt, a Mexican delegate to the celebration. An ardent Communist, she had attacked Jones as a "cowardly bourgeois individualist" when he defended his political neutrality on artistic grounds: "I'm a poet. . . . I'm not even interested in politics." The encounter deeply affected him, pointing up the inadequacy of his old poetic ways in the context of newly perceived Third World politics. The result is "BETANCOURT," his first politically informed self-criticism as a poet.

The poem repudiates his former work as the buffered perceptions of "some old man's poems" rotting in the "heavy sun, pure / distance. . . ." Using an image of poetic abnegation often repeated in *Suicide Note* and later in *The Dead Lecturer,* he dismisses the old poetic conventions: "Our gestures / are silence." Implicit is the sense that the new avant-garde poetry is now old and useless, leading Jones to conclude with a tenuous poetics of rejection:

> . . . (I mean I think
> I know now
> what a poem
> is) A
> turning away . . .
> from what
> it was
> had moved
> us . . .

Not yet perceiving aesthetic or political alternatives, Jones closes "Cuba Libre" by indicting himself and the "beats" as impotent old rebels:

"Even the vitality of our art is like bright flowers growing up through a rotting carcass." The last two poems in *Suicide Note* affirm this rejection of the old self while tentatively pointing to new but unrealized directions. The title "DON JUAN IN HELL" suggests that the poet's genealogy is still inclusive, a Europeanized man under an "unfamiliar sun." He is without a progenitor, "like / some son / lost his old dead father" and unable to actualize the "new man" trapped in his "old self." The poet concludes with notes not quite so suicidal that leave open the possibility of rebirth and future utterance. While "NOTES FOR A SPEECH" posits alienation—" . . . You are / as any other sad man here / american."—it is alienation from a new native land: "African blues / does not know me. . . . / Does / not feel / what I am."

Blues People and *The Dead Lecturer* were written in the early 1960's during approximately the same period of time, the tough-minded prose and expostulating poetry each representing in its own way Jones's thrusting past ineffectual suicide and mere rejection. *Blues People,* a lucid retrieval of Afro-American and African culture, traces through black music "the *path* the slave took to 'citizenship,'" delineating a usable heritage distinct from the European-American mainstream. Generally speaking, Jones was working within a well-established posture in black letters.

Early writers like W. E. B. Du Bois in *The Souls of Black Folk* (1903) and James Weldon Johnson in *The Autobiography of an Ex-Colored Man* (1912) had made concerted attempts to bring to light the particulars of Afro-American history and culture. Closer to Jones's time, Langston Hughes, Zora Neale Hurston, and Ralph Ellison had consciously sought ways to shape their writings in accordance with stylistic modes and symbols particular to the black tradition. In a more contemporary sense, though, Jones's strict commitment to the integrity of an

African genealogy linked him with the surge of cultural nationalism in the 1960's.

Blues People established Jones's seminal presence among such writers of the Black Arts Movement as Haki R. Madhubuti (Don L. Lee), Ed Bullins, Sonia Sanchez, and Ishmael Reed. Introducing the study as a "strictly *theoretical* endeavor," Jones fervently argues the premise of a sharp dichotomy between the African/ Afro-American and Western/European-American culture families. Within this dialectic he pursues the thesis that music, if properly interpreted, is central to an accurate understanding of black American reality:

... I am saying that if the music of the Negro in America, in all its permutations, is subjected to a socio-anthropological as well as musical scrutiny, something about the essential nature of the Negro's existence in this country ought to be revealed, as well as something about the essential nature of this country, *i.e.,* society as a whole.

Jones goes on to show how Afro-American modes of communication have been nurtured within a fluent non-Western tradition of improvised music, one markedly different from the prevailing scores and scripts of the media-oriented culture discredited in *Suicide Note.*

The important contribution of *Blues People* lies not only in its insistence on a clarifying cultural dialectic but also in the detailed presentation of African cultural values and musical styles transformed by the particular pressures of Afro-American experience. One concept articulated by Jones became a chief criterion of the new black aesthetics: African music, like all stylized African expression, is "functional." Because it grows out of commonplace social and religious circumstances in which all members of the community participate, music exists to fulfill a specific secular or spiritual function. Jones claimed that when viewed comparatively, the

tradition of Western fine arts, especially since the humanist Renaissance, is basically one of individual achievement—the inactive majority passively appreciating the artifacts created by a select few. If, as in *Suicide Note,* art and life had become disjunct, Jones had found the rationale for a restorative:

If we think of African music as regards its intent, we must see that it differed from Western music in that it was a purely *functional* music. . . . : songs used by young men to influence young women (courtship, challenge, scorn); songs used by workers to make their tasks easier; songs used by older men to prepare the adolescent boys for manhood, and so on. "Serious" Western music, except for early religious music, has been strictly an "art" music. One would not think of any particular *use* for Haydn's symphonies, except perhaps the "cultivation of the soul." . . . It was, and is, inconceivable in the African culture to make a separation between music, dancing, song, the artifact, and a man's life or his worship of his gods.

This was the beginning of a serviceable aesthetic that went beyond the nearly dysfunctional statement in "BETANCOURT" of what a poem was not, a "turning away . . . / from what / it was." If art comes directly from the experience of a people, and if, as *Blues People* clearly shows, that experience has obvious social implication, then the expression issuing from that experience will by definition have social—indeed, political—content. Thus armed with an intellectual basis for freeing himself from his apolitical "beat" pose, Jones in subsequent writings increasingly embodied the politics of cultural nationalism.

Blues People also identifies the important elements in African music and speech from which blues and jazz derive. Jones gives special emphasis to such stylistic features of vocal in-

terpretation as polyrhythms, complex alterations in pitch and tone quality, improvisational
rather than written expressions, and communal
antiphony or call and response. These African-
isms survive in Afro-American music and
speech, providing a particular expressive interpretation of the experience of the African being
tested in the New World that was as valid for
the black artist of the 1960's as for the slave
three hundred years earlier.

From these African beginnings *Blues People*
goes on to identify the generic forms and social
meanings of Afro-American music as it has
evolved to the present—shouts, field hollers,
work songs, spirituals, blues, early jazz, swing,
bebop, and rhythm and blues. These musical
responses each represent "definite *stages* in the
Negro's transmutation from African to American," and lead Jones to understand that
"change," both social and stylistic, was a constant in both the historical fact of black reality
and the expression of it: "there are certain very
apparent changes in the Negro's reactions to
America . . . and again, I insist that these
changes are most graphic in music." After
Blues People the concept of change became
central to Jones's life and art. In accordance
with the stages of growth and change in his personal consciousness, the personae in his poetry
and drama shifted in posture from rage and victimization to the willful enactment of change.

The challenge for Jones was to find modes of
expression as responsive to the representation of
change as he understood black music to be. As
a writer initially using the forms of written
English, he must have felt at a distinct disadvantage in comparison with the fluent musicians and their music-related uses of Afro-
American speech. In a chapter entitled "Enter
the Middle Class," he deprecates the black literary tradition as not being informed with the
same "legitimacy of emotional concern" one
finds in coon shouts, the blues of Bessie Smith,

or bebop. With his own middle-class origins and
recent literary allegiances no doubt weighing
heavily, he sees the main function of literature
as that of having eased the black writer into the
bourgeois aspects of Western culture. Jones the
poet was in the process of discovering that
music was the primary black mode of expression, while the literature of black America was
"essentially undistinguished." Although *Blues
People* does not directly investigate the inadequacies of literary form, it validates in historical
and aesthetic terms Jones's rejection of himself
as a traditional poet. The implications of *Blues
People* were apparent in *The Dead Lecturer*
mostly through the poet's continuing struggle to
escape Western literary formalism.

Although there are no sudden ideological or
stylistic changes, the poems in *The Dead Lecturer,* written for the most part while *Blues People* was in the making, do represent forceful
emotional siftings. As the title suggests, the
poet, suffering the consequences of his attempted suicide, retains in many of the poems
the degenerative images of sun, old age, and silence from *Suicide Note.* But from the vantage
point of *Blues People* he can at least begin to
acknowledge the potent artists—the makers of
sound pictured in "SHORT SPEECH TO MY
FRIENDS":

> . . . these others, saxophones whining
> through the wooden doors of their less than
>   gracious homes.
> The poor have become our creators. The
>   black. . . .

Not yet able to incorporate flexible musical
stylings into the contained print of his verse,
Jones presented the old, fixed tradition as a parody of the very ideas and attitudes it embodies:

> . . . the proper placement
> of verbs and nouns. To freeze the spit
> in mid-air, as it aims itself
> at some valiant intellectual's face.

This defiant frustration is evident in a number of poems in *The Dead Lecturer*.

From this equivocal stance Jones began to challenge more directly the prevailing notion of the poem as a sanctuary of self-expression. Having tested the possibilities for isolated confession in such pieces as "THE BRIDGE," he now disclaimed such personalism even as he continued to indulge the lyric. Confronting the issue squarely in "Green Lantern's Solo," Jones broadly equates lyric egocentrism with a dangerously insular individualism. His intellectual acquaintances, he charges, are disconnected from the world of the living: "My friend, the lyric poet, / who has never had an orgasm. My friend, / the social critic, who has never known society...." Launching into their puerile solo performances, the Bohemian poets and liberal thinkers represent for Jones the real evil, pursuing a convoluted sense of the truth that is indistinguishable from the lie:

What we have created, is ourselves
as heroes, as lovers, as disgustingly
evil. As Dialogues with the soul, with
the self, Selves, screaming furiously
to each other. As the same fingers
touch the same faces, as the same
mouths close on each other. The killed
is the killer, the loved the lover
and the islands of mankind have grown huge
  to include all life,
all lust, all commerce and beauty. Each idea
  a reflection of itself
and all the ideas men have ever had. Truth,
  Lie, so close they defy
inspection, and are built into autonomy by
  naive fools,
who have no wish for wholeness or
    strength....

Writing in this unwholesome mode, the self-conscious poet is "The Liar," as Jones indicates in the title of the last poem in *The Dead Lecturer*: "... Publically redefining / each change in my soul, as if I had predicted / them." In the final sardonic lines, the dead lecturer serves notice that his poetry has merely falsified his character: "When they say, 'It is Roi / who is dead?' I wonder / who will they mean?"

Lacking a cohesive ideology and aesthetic, one of the tentative strategies of *The Dead Lecturer* is to discredit the tradition of Western art. Jones's only "political" recourse is to strike directly against the pernicious individualism of the lyric, to use the form against itself because it serves no positive social function. In "A Guerilla Handbook," egocentric poets "Convinced / of the lyric" are reflexively trapped within the form, "knowing no way out / except description...." In "Political Poem," near the end of the collection, Jones sees the poem as "undone" by its own irrelevance. Enshrouded in the lyric, he is left with only a "polite truth" and his ill-fated title role: "... like my dead lecturer / lamenting thru gipsies his fast suicide."

If *The Dead Lecturer* winds down in a series of politicized rejections of lyric individualism, there are several poems, conspicuous for their intensity, that move well beyond isolated self-accusations, toward a determined identification with the collective feelings of Afro-America. Taken together, they represent an important shift in focus that anticipates the eruptive dramatizations and terse explanatory preachings of the emerging nationalism in the plays soon to come.

This engaged sensibility first emerges in "A Poem For Willie Best," a substantial piece in eight sections. By ascribing a mythic stature to the suppressed feelings of the black victim, Jones breathes a drama of large dimension into the Hollywood character actor Sleep'n'Eat, who, along with Mantan Moreland in the 1930's, inherited the comic mantle of Stepin Fetchit. He sees in Best nothing less than the extreme racial distortion of all black men as deplorably fantasized and crucified by the "obscene invention" of the white imagination: "... The top / of a head, seen from Christ's / heaven, stripped of history / or desire." Restoring to Best an emotional and fleshly reality, Jones in effect proposes him as one of the valorous Blues People, seeking intimacy with his plight rather than stepping back to the safe satiric distance of such earlier poems as "HYMN FOR LANIE POO." The last two sections of the poem widen the scope of emotional possibilities even further, dignifying the victim's pain by revealing him as a "renegade / behind the mask." The tormented actor, "tired of losing," finally forces his vernacular anger through the habitual dialect: "'I *got* ta cut'cha.'" This is the germ of a new poetic voice, one already flexed in the play script for *The Toilet* (1967), that was intermittently tested in *The Dead Lecturer*.

The voice is strengthened by the mythic intensification of black music in "Rhythm & Blues," a poem that taps a deeper and more aggressive collective feeling. Although dedicated to Robert Williams, a Marine veteran who had been suspended as president of the Monroe, North Carolina, NAACP in 1959 for espousing militant self-defense (Jones had met him during the 1960 trip to Cuba), the poem addresses the response of a community rather than the predicament of an individual. At the center of that response is the percussive sound of rhythm and blues that forcefully expresses "a legitimacy of emotional concern," as he says in *Blues People,* not to be found in the silent passivity of written verse.

Jones imagines that the immediacy of musical statement not only gives form to feeling but also has the potential to heighten social awareness, perhaps even to the extent of moving people actively to resist their oppression, as Williams had done. As he makes this point through the poem itself, he questions the power of his own poetic art to have a similar effect:

> ... If I see past what I feel, and call
> music simply "Art" and will
> not take it to its logical end. For the
> death by hanging, for
> the death by the hooded political murderer,
> for the old man dead in his
> tired factory; ...

Unlike the retrospective, page-bound verses of the poet, the improvised formulations of the musician are a projection of emotions as they occur, an unflinching, expressive reaction tantalizingly close to active retaliation:

> ... There is no
> "melody." Only the foot stomped, the roaring
> harmonies of need.
> The
> hand banged on the table, waved in the air.
> The teeth pushed
> against
> the lip. The face and fingers sweating. "Let
> me alone," is praise enough
> for these musicians.

By comparison, the poet feels his impotence: "I am deaf and blind and lost and will not again sing your quiet / verse. I have lost / even the act of poetry. ...."

In the throes of this inadequacy, Jones begins to vent his suppressed energies through the penetrating image of the scream, an imposing sound he increasingly associated with the emotional and expressive fluency at the core of black life: " ... our screams. / Of the dozens, the razor, the cloth, the sheen, all speed adventure locked / in my eyes." As amply illustrated in *Blues People,* it is a stylistic element central to the musical tradition (in shouts, hollers, work songs). It was especially developed by postwar rhythm and blues performers who "literally had to shout to be heard above the ... electrified instruments." As a matter of survival, "the human voice itself had to struggle, to scream, to be heard."

In "The Screamers," a 1963 sketch reprinted in *Tales* (1967), Jones portrays "the screamed riff" of rhythm and blues saxophonist Lynn Hope—heroicized by Jones as an ethnic historian and priest of the unconscious—pushing his listeners to the verge of active protest in the Newark streets. The scream is proposed as a fantastic mode of self-realization that anticipates political change: "We screamed and screamed at the clear image of ourselves as we should always be. . . . It would be the form of the sweetest revolution, to hucklebuck into the fallen capital, and let the oppressors lindy hop out."

Music takes on the same generative power in "Rhythm & Blues," but the ineffectual poetry is seen as distinctly subordinate to the amplified sounds:

> The
> shake and chant, bulled electric motion,
>   figure of what there will
>   be
> as it sits beside me waiting to live past my
>   own meekness. . . .

The ideal poetic voice, the poem implies, would be the impossible re-creation of music itself in printed form.

Two other poems address the broad issue of the creative force behind the security of black expression toward which Jones is working. Both are couched in strongly anti-white terms and both culminate in an appeal to Damballah, the loa of fertility—the first positive evocations in Jones's poetry of a revitalizing African genealogy.

"Crow Jane," in part an inverted parody of William Butler Yeats's "Crazy Jane," is the more traditional of the two. It is an all-out attack on what had become for Jones a pernicious social and racial presence—the white woman. The contained anxiety expressed toward the pregnancy of his white wife in "FOR HETTIE IN HER FIFTH MONTH" has grown here to the repudiation of an entire culture. Crow Jane is nothing less than the seductive force of white sexual and artistic supremacy that deflects the procreative and creative power of the black artist. Her capacity for destruction is fully realized in the character of Lula in the play *Dutchman* (1964).

The poem is a terse statement of liberation from "Mama Death," whose romantic allure no longer deceives Jones: " . . . Cold stuff / to tempt a lover. Old Lady / of flaking eyes. Moon lady / of useless thighs." Her patronizing reverse racism, the female counterpart of an attitude known as Jim Crow, is merely a ploy to flatter his intellectual vanity on " . . . some pilgrimage / to thought. Where she goes, in fairness, / 'nobody knows'. . . ." He is now sufficiently possessed of his black emotive power to define, and thereby control, her emasculating character: "Now / I am her teller."

In a closing ceremony entitled "The dead lady canonized," the poet celebrates in grim fleshly terms the passing of Crow Jane's influence. To ensure that her womb will no longer incubate "dead nouns" and "rotted faces," the stillborn progeny of his past, he calls upon Damballah to administer the healing benediction:

> . . . The lady is dead, may the Gods,
>
>   (those others
> beg our forgiveness. And Damballah, kind
>   father,
> sew up
> her bleeding hole.

A precarious balance of controlled nuance and roiling emotion, "Crow Jane" bristles with ironic interplay between the Western poetic style that Jones is trying to shuck off and the motif of Afro-American separatism that he is in the process of embracing.

A second poem, "BLACK DADA NIHIL-ISMUS," although not following in exact sequence, can be read as a counter piece to "Crow Jane." Released from its self-destructive fantasy of the white woman, the poetic voice now concentrates the psychosexual distortions of whites into an aggregate black male antagonist who converts these lurid stereotypes into a frontal assault on the "grey hideous space" that is the West. In what is perhaps Jones's most pungent cultural inversion, the absurd artistic and philosophical legacy of the white culture is conjured into a threatening black weaponry. In a later essay entitled "Philistinism and the Negro Writer" (1966) he contended that one way black people might confront "the denial of reality . . . institutionalized in America" would be to "turn crazy, to bring out a little American Dada, Ornette Coleman style, and chase those perverts into the ocean where they belong."

Accordingly, Jones forgoes the mincing intricacy one finds in the structure of "Crow Jane" and speaks in the hammering post-bebop voice of the musician-priest, challenging a collective black manhood to shake off its lethargy and enact into reality the preposterous racial mythicizing of whites. If still somewhat formal, the voice is flagrant, exerting through Afro-American tones a pressure that transcends conventional usage and literal meaning:

> . . . why you stay, where they can
> reach? Why you sit, or stand, or walk
> in this place, . . .
>
> . . . Come up, black dada

nihilismus. Rape the white girls. Rape their fathers. Cut the mothers' throats. Black dada nihilismus, choke my
friends

And then, as if invoking the very style he cannot yet adequately express, he starkly incants the enriching aural images that will give black definition and coherence to the destruction: "Black scream / and chant, scream, / and dull, un / earthly / hollering. . . ." Jones resolves the poem stylistically and culturally in a chanted appeal to Damballah, reaching for the still-distant but now retrievable African past through a ritual naming of victims and heroes of color (including his grandfather Tom Russ) who struggled in the New World:

> For tambo, willie best, dubois, patrice,
>   mantan, the
>   bronze buckaroos.
>
>   For Jack Johnson, asbestos, tonto,
>   buckwheat,
>   billie holiday.
>
>   For tom russ, l'overture,
>   vesey, beau jack,
>
> (may a lost god damballah, rest or save us
> against the murders we intend
> against his lost white children
> black dada nihilismus

"BLACK DADA NIHILISMUS" best encapsulates the racial anger welling up through the lyric self-confusion of the early poetry, an emotional force that Jones's sense of restricted poetic form could no longer adequately contain. The lyric would not be totally abandoned; rather, it would appear in later nationalist poetry in a more sparing and emotionally positive form.

Although Jones's next significant body of work was in the drama, where the impulses of his expanding racial consciousness could be given scope in proportion to their intensity, some of the emotional current was diverted into the less restricted space of the prose narrative. The quasi-autobiographical fiction of the early stories in *Tales,* and especially of the novel *The System of Dante's Hell* (1965), can in part be seen as a transition to the more cohesive development of black character in the plays. In fact, some of the figures briefly glimpsed in the novel—Ora, Skippy, Knowles, Love, and James Karolis ("He died in a bathroom of old age & segregation")—spurted to fuller growth in *The Toilet*.

The first portion of the novel, published as "The System of Dante's Inferno" in the magazine *The Trembling Lamb* (1959), not surprisingly reflects many of the stylistic and emotional contours of the early poetry. In a first-person voice cluttered with images of decay, silence, and death reminiscent of Ginsberg's cityscapes in *Howl*, Jones strings together fragmentary impressions of his youth in Newark: "The breakup of my sensibility.... Vegetables rotting in the neighbors' minds.... Drowning city of silence.... All dead." In a brief afterword he says he intended to create "association complexes" of sound and image that would interpret the "Hell in the head" of his growing up.

With its underground allegory, Dante's inferno provides a classic Christian veneer for the organization of Jones's version of Hell into various circles, ditches, and transgressors (heathen, wrathful, seducers) that lend ready identity to the chapter headings. The emotional impulses veer away from Dante's mythic intentions, though, to draw upon the particular Afro-American sense of the underground as the psychic hell of invisibility. A condition imposed by white myopia and dangerously internalized by the black victim, it is the "torture of being the unseen object," as Jones puts it, "and, the constantly observed subject." In this sense the novelist's vision is largely determined by symbolic perceptions long established in the black writing tradition: from the veil of the color line in Du Bois' *The Souls of Black Folk* to Richard Wright's subterranean guilt in *The Man Who Lived Underground*, Ralph Ellison's ambivalent anger in *Invisible Man* (with its own Dantean

descent into rhythmic emotional depths), and James Baldwin's relentlessly exposed psychosexual afflictions in *Another Country*. These works all deal with the anguish of native sons having to balance precariously the tensions of the "lower frequencies," as Ellison put it, and as Jones himself masterfully dramatized through the hurtling subway setting of *Dutchman*.

The portion of *Dante's Hell* written after 1959 takes on greater narrative continuity, pulling the expansive yet difficult prose into more coherent interludes of experience. Language intensity, sexual motifs, and the probing into feelings specifically black all predict important elements in Jones's early drama. "The Eighth Ditch" is in effect a self-contained play, an episode of homosexual seduction in which the protagonist in his naive Boy Scout guise is stimulated by a streetwise companion into an indiscriminate desire for the blues. Ambivalent representations of homosexuality (a sexual and emotional alternative widely accepted in the "beat" culture) briefly occurred in *The Toilet* and *The Baptism* before emergent black nationhood and manhood rhetorically equated the "faggot" with feckless white impotence.

In the last two sections the prose resolves into what Jones terms "fast narrative," quick-moving fusions of violent action and troubled self-consciousness. Appearing in roles Jones knew all too well, the protagonist is presented successively as a college boy and a young Air Force man whose enfeebled middle-class psyche is assailed and finally impregnated by surges of blackness that he uneasily begins to comprehend as his birthright. In "The Rape" he coolly leads on his buddies to attempt the rape of a drunken prostitute, only to have his puerile bravado shattered by her powerful curses: "She screamed, and screamed, her voice almost shearing off our tender heads. The scream of an actual damned soul."

In the final section, sporting his uniform with "bright wings" and secretly harboring his pretentious literary elegance ("I'm beautiful. Stephen Dedalus"), he visits The Bottom—the poor black outskirts of a southern town where he expects easy women and a good time. Instead, he finds himself descending into the deepest region of the black underground, into a "culture of violence and foodsmells" where the drinking, dancing, screaming denizens abuse him as an "imitation white boy." The Bottom is the Purgatory where the redemption of his blackness will begin in earnest. After an initiation of vivid cursing and sexual humiliation at the hands of a challenging young prostitute, he can slip out into the night and begin to recognize The Bottom as his own legacy: "The place was so still, so black and full of violence. I felt myself." But he soon finds that he has made only partial expiation. On his ascent he is accosted by three "tall strong black boys" in the menacing spirit of "BLACK DADA NIHILISMUS." To them he is still "Mr. Half-white muthafucka," an interloper in their world, and they proceed to beat him into a limbo of unconsciousness. In this condition he has a mixed vision of reading books and weeping followed by "negroes" dancing around his body, leaving him to continue the struggle for the blackness revealed in him in The Bottom.

Jones told Kimberly Benston in a 1977 interview that in *Dante's Hell* he was "writing defensively," trying to escape the white literary influences of Creeley, Olson, and Ginsberg through a consciously improvisational prose impelled by both stream-of-consciousness and jazz techniques, but that the content, in Marxist retrospect, was now to be criticized "for celebrating the subjective and the idealistic."

Celebration of black feelings and black values, though, was precisely what the confluence of cultural and political forces required and brought about in the 1960's. Not only were Third World nations of color in the process of radical change—the Cultural Revolution in China, the struggles for national independence in Africa, and, closer to home, the examples of Fidel Castro and Che Guevara—but black liberation was being irresistibly preached in the United States itself, first by Malcolm X on behalf of Elijah Muhammad and the Nation of Islam, and subsequently through the open paramilitary posture of the Black Panthers.

In this turbulent atmosphere Jones came of age as a strikingly innovative dramatist, discovering the voice of the play as far more appropriate, at least at the time, than the poetry for his burgeoning sense of cultural and political need. The play, after all, was itself a public and social occasion of sorts, offering up a usually willing audience for immediate interaction with the instructive ideas and feelings of the playwright—potentially an instrument of political influence. Furthermore, in accordance with the aesthetics defined in *Blues People,* the play was far more hospitable than the silence of poetry to the extraliterary modes of black expression. As Jones progressed from the somewhat conventional strategies of his first plays into the more ritual and communal theater of his nationalist period, he increasingly integrated vocal strategies, performed music, and the motions of dance into the representation of black experience.

Jones's first one-act efforts, *The Toilet* and *The Baptism* (both produced in 1964), were tentative gropings away from the concerns of the poetry, *The Toilet* being more provocative and successful for its concentrated speech force and realistic setting. The action is structured through energetic vernacular dialogue and assertive physical gestures exchanged by nine black youths who, in the aggregate, constitute the voice of the play. They are preparing to beat up a white boy, James Karolis, in the high school bathroom because they suspect him of making homosexual overtures to their leader, Ray Foots. The combination of racial animosity and aggressive speech vigorously dramatizes the black dada strain, causing some viewers to resent the language as overly obscene, the action as excessively stark. Ed Bullins, on the other hand, saw the play's "radical . . . depiction of Black people" as fitting and precise "in a deep and profoundly revolutionary sense," affirming his own first uncompromising efforts to dramatize the intensities of black life in *Clara's Ole Man* (1965). If the style of *The Toilet* is exemplary, the presentation of Ray's confused feelings—he returns to cradle Karolis' bloodied head after his buddies have left—does not, in Jones's opinion, sufficiently clarify the black youth's entrapment by white sentimentality.

The Baptism, although set in a pretentious Baptist church, with the action taking place around an altar rather than a urinal, proposes similar themes and ambivalences in the form of a somewhat attenuated allegory. Both plays, for all their differences, are about the precarious struggles of black youth toward manhood in white America. Percy, a sincere young boy, naively tries to assert values of "humanity" and "charity" in the face of tangled sexual motivations and religious ideals as represented by the Minister and his deluded flock. Ironically, the presence of the Homosexual, whose cynical insights constitute the sanest voice in the play, at times threatens to overshadow the parable of Percy's thwarted manhood. Even though the knightly young protagonist is able to slay the Minister and congregation with his "silver sword," thereby signifying the promise of wholesome manhood, he is summarily whisked away by the laconic Messenger from the white world (on whose jacket is stenciled "The Man"). At the play's end, Jones pointedly resurrects the black Homosexual from Percy's carnage, leaving him casually to drift off to "cruise Bickford's," the sole emasculated survivor of

Christian hypocrisy and "The Man's" destruction.

Dutchman and *The Slave* (both produced in 1964) are more extensive dramas that crystallize the confused boyhood feelings of Ray and Percy into the full-blown rage of Clay and Walker, adult men conscious of the nature of their victimization. With these two plays Jones in effect broke from the tyranny of individualism implicit in white cultural values and began to place his art in the service of a collective black freedom. From an artistic standpoint this is nowhere more clearly noted than in a 1964 essay entitled "The Revolutionary Theatre" (reprinted in *Home*), in which the African-derived aesthetic of *Blues People* is catalyzed by the mounting pressure of political necessity. Change, as a social and stylistic process reflected in the development of black music, is now transformed into a conception to be willfully embodied and actively asserted by the black playwright: "The Revolutionary Theatre," Jones begins, "should force change; it should be change." The first phase, the essay makes clear, will necessarily involve alterations of consciousness in white, but especially in black, audiences, exposing the hatred inside "black skulls" so that "White men will cower," while at the same time moving the black victims "to look at the strength in their minds and their bodies."

If Clay in *Dutchman,* along with Walker in *The Slave,* and Ray in *The Toilet,* "are all victims," as Jones rightfully contends, they are portrayed at different stages of self-realization. Clay, the malleable college boy and would-be "black Baudelaire," hardens into a fiery preacher who reveals the relationship of sane black truths to absurd white illusions—a condition that the manic and fearful Ray can only intuit, or that the dazed initiate of The Bottom can only begin to grasp.

Dutchman, like *Dante's Hell,* melds Western

myth and legend into a usable black logic, creating a psychodrama that is unquestionably the most lucid and powerful of Jones's early plays. The portentous overtones are established before the dialogue begins, Jones introducing the nether-world setting as an ironic contemporary inversion of the Flying Dutchman: "In the flying underbelly of the city. . . . Underground. The subway heaped in modern myth."

Well-dressed and bookish, Clay is the doomed passenger on the rushing underground railroad, guilty of no crime but his blackness. He is destined, despite his respectable appearance, to be the repeated victim of America's most infamous social ritual—the lynching. Lula, the keeper of the ritual, is his white seductress and executioner, a perverse Eve who boards the train "eating an apple, very daintily." At heart she is the dramatic realization of Crow Jane, the tawdry purveyor of a hip Western rationalism calculated to prevent the suppressed rage of black manhood from bursting into insurrection. Having dispatched Clay and ordered his body thrown off the car, she makes an appropriate notation in her "notebook" and prepares to begin the ritual anew with another unsuspecting victim. Resonant with the psychosexual tension that motivates racial fear, she is a far more effective agent of white destruction than the Messenger in *The Baptism*.

While the deterministic ritual frame gives the play a solemn weight, the process of Clay's emotional awakening and climactic self-possession creates the dominant impression. Throughout the first scene Lula is clearly in charge, characterizing Clay to his face as "a well-known type" and easily manipulating him into feeling both flattered by her sexual attention and vaguely uncomfortable at taunts about his spurious middle-class aspirations. He is surprised when, at the end of the scene, she knowingly jokes that beneath his three-button suit and striped tie there lurks a murderer.

At the beginning of scene 2, as Lula becomes graphically suggestive about a rendezvous at her apartment ("I lead you in, holding your wet hand gently in my hand . . ."), it is revealed that her central concern—and Jones's—has all along been the question of Clay's "manhood." Impatient with his self-control, she finally draws his latent aggressions into the open by viciously insulting him with racial slurs and stereotypes. His response, a tirade addressed to both Lula and the whites in the audience, is a classic example of the "theatre of assault" Jones calls for in the essay. Clay's rage and capacity for retaliation are no longer deflected into subregions of feeling or coded into lies and devices, but consciously savored and directly expressed. Slapping Lula twice, he reveals himself to be the murderer she predicted:

I could murder you now. Such a tiny ugly throat. I could squeeze it flat, and watch you turn blue, on a humble. For dull kicks. And all those weak-faced ofays squatting around here, staring over their papers at me. Murder them too. Even if they expected it. That man there . . . (POINTS TO WELL-DRESSED MAN) I could rip that *Times* right out of his hand, as skinny and middle-classed as I am, I could rip that paper out of his hand and just as easily rip out his throat. It takes no great effort. . . . You don't know anything except what's there for you to see. An act. Lies. Device. Not the pure heart, the pumping black heart. You don't even know that. And I sit here, in this buttoned-up suit, to keep myself from cutting all your throats. . . .

But in the final analysis he cannot murder, it seems—and, ironically, because his pretensions as a poet make him vulnerable to the seduction of language. Through Clay, Jones states the predicament of the artist-activist, presenting in its most reductive form the conflict between the ineffective rhetorical gesture and the extreme revolutionary act. If the Charlie Parkers and the Bessie Smiths could have "killed some white people," Clay asserts, they "wouldn't have needed that music." At the same time he dismisses his own poetry as "Some kind of bastard literature . . . all it needs is a simple knife thrust. Just let me bleed you, you loud whore, and one poem vanished."

Here Jones has found, in substance, a representative black voice that the early poetry could not authenticate, a voice convincing by its intentions and intensities more than by its manner. (Clay's middle-American speech has only intermittent Afro-American nuances, as in the opening "hi're you?" to Lula, his class status setting him considerably apart from the collective voice in *The Toilet*.) And here, also, the voice suddenly wearies. Unable to assume the full responsibility for action that his explosion into consciousness dictates, Clay fatally lapses into his false intellectual security: "Ahhh. Shit. But who needs it? I'd rather be a fool. Insane. Safe with my words, and no deaths, and clean, hard thoughts, urging me to new conquests."

The visceral dramatization of racial conflict did not prevent *Dutchman* from being widely acclaimed or from winning the 1964 Obie Award for best off-Broadway play. It is undeniably good theater in the best conventional sense, with fast-paced dialogue, superb emotional timing, and compelling interaction between the two antagonists.

The Slave, although less engaging as theater, marks a transition from the intense but indecisive aggression of Clay to a more explicit radical consciousness in the character of Walker Vessels, one-time poet turned insurrectionary. As the black antagonist confronts his white ex-wife, Grace, in her tastefully furnished living room, he is a leader of the black revolution already in progress. His credentials are established at the very start: He is Lula's fantasy realized, having already killed whites and now appearing to Grace simply as a "nigger mur-

derer"; and he has adopted a militant pragmatism of "use," akin to the functionalism described in *Blues People,* in place of the safe words of Yeatsian poetry and romantic idealism. Essentially, even though Walker admits the possibility "that we might not win," the political act has triumphed over the aesthetic statement, symbolizing his freedom from enslavement to Western civilization. The longish first act is mostly an ironic exchange of revolutionary ideology and liberal platitudes between Walker and his white adversaries, projecting more the sense of a play of ideas rather than of characters.

Although Walker's basic function seems to be the clear articulation of political freedom, his visit to Grace is motivated by the additional and unresolved question of what to do about the children of their interracial marriage. The end of the short second act focuses almost entirely on the destiny of his two half-white daughters, to whom he is tied emotionally and biologically. Amid the explosions and rubble of the race war he tells the dying Grace that he has killed them, even keeps shouting it after she dies, as if to convince himself it is so; yet the play ends ambivalently as the wounded rebel stumbles offstage to the sounds of a child "crying and screaming as loud as it can." Even as a dedicated revolutionary Walker is still a victim, still bearing the legacy of Crow Jane through the painful reminder of his and her mixed-blood children. Walker's appearance in the prologue "dressed as an old field slave," and his return to that identity when the play closes, suggest that the forces of racial determinism are very much at work and that slavery is still claiming its victims. Indeed Walker is the epitome of Jones's belief, as stated in "Philistinism and the Negro Writer," that his works ought to "identify and delineate the slave, the black man—the man who remains separate from the mainstream."

Jones had for some time been on the verge of

leaving Hettie and their two daughters, the inevitable divorce coming in August 1965 after a period of mounting pressure and change of the sort autobiographically reflected in *Dutchman* and *The Slave*. The separation was also cultural. Jones cut all ties with the East Village by moving to Harlem (where he briefly took charge of the Black Arts Repertory Theatre/School) and then back to New Ark—as he renamed it—in late 1965. He had indeed come home, as the title of his 1966 social essays attests, completing his transformation from literary assimilationist to black separatist. Including pieces written between 1961 and 1966, *Home* is a graphic exposition of Jones's changing perspective, what he calls "the sense of movement—the struggle, in myself, to understand where and who I am, and to move with that understanding." The final essay, "The Legacy of Malcolm X" (1965), perhaps best summarizes his arrival at a nationalist sense of politics and art:

. . . we know for certain that the solution of the Black Man's problems will come only through Black National Consciousness. We also know that the focus of change will be racial. (If we *feel* differently, we have different *ideas*. Race is feeling. Where the body, and the organs come in. Culture is the preservation of these feelings in superrational to rational form. Art is one method of expressing these feelings and identifying the form, as an emotional phenomenon.) In order for the Black Man in the West to absolutely know himself it is necessary for him to see himself first as culturally separate from the white man.

Jones completed his personal reintegration into the black world by marrying a black woman, Sylvia Robinson, in August 1966 and subsequently taking the name Imamu Amiri Baraka—meaning spiritual leader, prince, and blessed one—an affirmation of his religious dedication to black nationhood. He founded Spirit House, a community center for political and educational activities, and launched himself vigorously into the political destiny of black Newark, including experiences as varied as his trumped-up arrest and conviction (overturned in a retrial) during the 1967 Newark insurrections and his later extensive assistance in the 1970 election of Kenneth Gibson as the city's first black mayor.

Baraka remained artistically productive despite the increased demands of his political and community activities. The plays collected in *Four Black Revolutionary Plays* (1969) and the late poems in *Black Magic* (1969) represent the major thematic and stylistic changes brought about by nationalism. Baraka's most succinct statement of the radical aesthetic embodied in these works is in a 1964 essay entitled "Hunting Is Not Those Heads on the Wall" (reprinted in *Home*). It crystallizes for literary use many of the stylistic implications of music suggested in *Blues People*. In contrast with the static art product of the Western tradition (the artifact, musical score, book), black art prizes the "lightning awareness of the art process" (any given instance or interval of creating), for which he coins the term "Art-ing." The hunter-artist is fulfilled by the experience of hunting-creating, not by the mounted trophy or the completed poem. To capture the immediacy and motion implied in Art-ing, the writer must favor the participle, as opposed to the nouns and object images of Western literature: "The clearest description of now is the present participle, . . . Walking is not past or future. Be-ing, the most complex, since it goes on as itself, as adjective-verb, and at the moment of."

This predicate concept is consistent with both the politics of revolutionary change and the improvisational flow of Afro-American music: "I speak of the *verb process,* the doing, the coming into being, the at-the-time-of. Which is why we think there is particular value in live music, contemplating the artifact as it arrives, listening to it emerge." As an instance of spoken language in process, the play itself was the closest literary approximation of Art-ing, while ritual structure—the sense of mythic inevitability and ceremonial ongoingness as conveyed in *Dutchman*—was one of the effective Art-ing strategies within the play. *Experimental Death Unit #1* (1964), in *Four Black Revolutionary Plays,* aptly reflects the head-hunting metaphor through the ritual appearance of black soldiers marching in cadence to drums. The play closes as they sever the heads of Duff and Loco, two perverted white artists in the "beat" mold who lust after blackness, and mount them on pikes. They do not covet the bloody members as trophies but display them as symbols of the execution that must be ceremonially repeated until all whiteness is destroyed. Unlike Clay and Walker, the disciplined soldiers firmly control their own fate as we see them in the process of collectively defining their history.

The significant work in *Four . . . Plays,* though, is *A Black Mass.* Written in 1965 and first performed in Newark in 1966, it is addressed to black audiences, as all his subsequent nationalist drama would be. It is, in effect, a play about Art-ing and is appropriately dedicated to "the brothers and sisters of the Black Arts." Unlike *Dutchman* its mythic structure is exclusively black, taking for its source Yacub's History, the demonology of the Nation of Islam (fully narrated in *The Autobiography of Malcolm X*), which openly attributes black suffering to the white Beast. Jacoub, a somewhat altered version of the original Yacub, is the type of the black artist, and his error is in misunderstanding the nature and function of creativity.

The first half of the one-act play expostulates the basic conflict between the humane and spiritual tenets of black art through the black magicians Nasafi and Tanzil, as opposed to the de-humanizing aesthetics of the West practiced by the thoughtless renegade Jacoub. He compulsively channels his creative powers into the production of what he egotistically perceives as original form rather than honoring the inherent value of the creative process itself; the end product is a beast he falsely believes can be educated to serve black mankind. Through the questionings of his fellow magicians, Jacoub is revealed to favor the principles of fixed time instead of prediction and ongoingness, of rational abstractions rather than emotional and spiritual energy, and of personal aggrandizement rather than a concern for the collective welfare of the black world. He is, for all intents and purposes, a black artist brought down by the self-serving values of Western individualism.

With the appearance of the inarticulate and soulless white Beast itself, the play shifts abruptly from a forum of aesthetic ideas to a vivid theatrical. Though sexless and sterile, the Beast paradoxically unleashes its destructiveness through a kind of rape by contamination, perpetuating itself by transforming black victims into white Beasts through mere touch. True to the tradition of the lustful incursions of white slave masters, the first victim is a woman, Tiila, whose metamorphosis into a "deadly cross between black and white" strongly suggests the biological-sexual quality of the Beast's violation. Just before he is himself assaulted, Jacoub acknowledges his hideous error and consigns the Beast and its cohorts to "the evil diseased caves of the cold," as they are in Yacub's History. The narrator concludes the play by asserting that the beasts "are still loose in the world" and instructing that they must be exterminated by the Jihad, a holy war to be waged against the white world.

As the title implies, the play itself partakes of ritual, opening as the three magicians conclude a mass celebrating the black arts. The action then unfolds to expose the betrayal of this ritual, the revolutionary message being that black art has been, and is, vulnerable to destructive white influences. The artistic integrity of the play itself is preserved, though, by an infusion of music throughout the entire production. The stage directions particularly call for a performance by Sun-Ra, whose music is the essence of predicate motion, "the flow of *is*," says Baraka in "The Changing Same," a 1966 essay in *Black Music* (1967). At first the soothing "Music of eternal concentration and wisdom" as the mass is in progress, the sounds modulate to the more familiar rhythmic tensions of contemporary black music as Jacoub's treachery begins, "swelling, making sudden downward swoops, screeching." The ongoing music is powerfully present, not as mere background but as an integral part of the play's ritual quality. Music and language are fused, the formal intonations of speech enriched by Afro-American tonalities as the musicians punctuate the spoken lines in call-and-response fashion with their improvised phrasings. Upon the entry of the Beast, the script calls for "Sun-Ra music of shattering dimension," the screeching instruments and screams of the victims eliding into an amalgam of sound. This responsive interweaving of music and language splendidly epitomizes the predicate quality of Art-ing that the bare play script could not by itself achieve, an aesthetic strategy Baraka applied with even greater effect in *Slave Ship* two years later.

Two other plays, *Great Goodness of Life* (1966) and *Madheart* (1966), are instructional allegories without the informing musical cotext, although background music fades intermittently in and out of the dialogue in *Madheart*. Subtitled *A Coon Show, Great Goodness of Life* is a convoluted psychodrama about a bourgeois black father, Court Royal, who acquiesces in the execution of his insurrectionary son. The play confronts the audience's racial integrity with the emotional impact of this be-

trayal. More and more the plays took on this sort of didactic purpose, not simply showing victims but teaching black audiences the precise and often painful nature of their condition. "Art must serve to illuminate and educate," Baraka says in "Work Notes—'66," in *Raise Race Rays Raze: Essays Since 1965* (1971). The anatomy of Court Royal's buffered consciousness and the harsh exposure of the flawed Mother and Sister in *Madheart* typify Baraka's educational intentions, however disturbing to the playgoer: "Each aspect of black life must have light shed on it, must be analyzed must make the pain of recognizing the exact place of our crucifixion, the exact sloth and cowardliness, the precise ugliness and ignorance."

J-E-L-L-O (written in 1965), a ribald satire of the Jack Benny show in which Rochester instructively comes into possession of his blackness, was to have been a fifth play in the collection but was suppressed by the publisher as potentially libelous. In other plays of the late 1960's Baraka heeds his own call, stated in "What the Arts Need Now" (1967), in *Raise Race,* for "plays of all instance. Filling in and extending so-called 'reality.' . . . a post-American form. An afterwhiteness . . . where history is absolutely meaningful and contemporary." The plays have moved away almost entirely from any focus on palpable character, as witnessed in the figures of Clay and Walker, to key in on conditions and issues dramatically reified as Jacoub and Court Royal. *Police* (1968), *Home on the Range* (1968), and *The Death of Malcolm X* (1969) all deal with specific local and national black circumstances, unequivocally drawing racial-emotional lines in their explanation and interpretation of black reality.

Baraka's quintessential nationalist play, though, is *Slave Ship,* first published in *Negro Digest* in 1967, then separately in 1969, and reprinted in *The Motion of History and Other Plays* (1978). It is a powerful instance of what he defines in a 1967 essay entitled "The Need for a Cultural Base to Civil Rites & Bpower Mooments," published in *Raise Race,* as the prime function of black art: " . . . to get people into a consciousness of black power, what it is, by emotional example" rather than by "dialectical lecture." This is achieved in the play by an almost complete subordination of individual character and spoken dialogue to an irresistible vocal-musical rendering of the collective black presence. Subtitled *A Historical Pageant, Slave Ship* has as its ritual basis the intensity of expression and feeling born of the horrifying Middle Passage. African drum rhythms are combined with the screams of people torturously pressed into the hold of a ship, an experience of pure sound conveyed in total darkness during the first third of the pageant—the portentous historical beginnings of the Afro-American underworld vision. The audience is prepared at the onset to feel the pressing reality by hearing it, not by seeing it. Baraka orchestrates the sounds of Africa's abduction and bondage in the elaborate stage directions:

African Drums like the worship of some Orisha. Obatala. Mbwanga rattles of the priests. BamBam BamBamBoom BoomBoom BamBam.

Rocking of the slave ship, in darkness, without sound. But smells. Then sound. Now slowly, out of blackness with smells and drums staccato, the hideous screams. All the women together, scream. AAAAAIIIIIEEEEEEEEEEEE.

The fragmentary expressions of fear, cursing, and appeals to African deities are bonded into emotional coherence by the ritualized screaming that marks the emergence of the black voice in the New World. The screaming then gives way to a "deathly patient" humming followed by strains of spirituals as the play shifts to its second phase, depicting slavery in America.

Here, lighting and dialogue are more pronounced, revealing the split consciousness of slave victims, some of whom shuffle and dance for their masters while others, like Nat Turner, plot uncompromising revolt against the white "Beast." In the final and contemporary phase of the pageant, the predominant sound is the aggressively clear screaming of a "new-sound" saxophone overriding the garbled nonsense speech of an integrationist preacher. Throughout, the African screams and voicings, especially through the recurrent motif of a mother calling for her lost child, Moshake, intersect the shifting sounds and historical changes as a persistent reminder of the enduring African spirit.

The pageant, in essence a processional of emotions, closes by celebrating the power of a unified black consciousness. All the members of the cast come together in a triumphant communion of Afro-American singing ("When We Gonna Rise") and dancing ("a new-old dance, Boogalooyoruba line") in a prelude to the eradication of whiteness. As a community in the fullest command of its expressive powers, they converge upon and kill the integrationist preacher and his white "boss," as if the political act could be accomplished by the very sounds and motions of Art-ing itself. In a final gesture of communal instruction, Baraka plays to the participatory expectations of his black audience by having them join with the cast in a continuation of the dance. When "the party reaches some loose improvisation," he jars the relaxed consciousness by throwing the severed head of the preacher onto the dance floor and dousing the lights. The final interruption and abrupt immersion in blackness force the playgoer to be aware that the struggle continues beyond the bounds of the play. In its fusion of terse speech fragments and vocal-musical improvisation into a unified play script, *Slave Ship* is significantly advanced in conception over the interacting dialogue text and musical performance of *A Black*

Mass. With the added dimensions of dance and audience participation, it stands as Baraka's most sustained and effective work of Art-ing.

"Sabotage," "Target Study," and "Black Art," the three books that make up *Black Magic* (1969), represent Baraka's continuing poetic activity between 1961 and 1967, while he was writing plays and flexing into nationalism. These poems begin (thematically if not chronologically) where *The Dead Lecturer* leaves off, developing toward predicate formulations of black spiritual integrity of the sort symbolized by the magicians Nasafi and Tanzil in *A Black Mass.* In the introduction Baraka dismisses his early poetry as preoccupied with suicide and death, "a cloud of abstraction and disjointedness, that was just whiteness." In contrast the poems of *Black Magic,* especially in the third book, strive for the "willpower to build" beyond whiteness in order to "force this issue," as he puts it, of transcendent black spirituality.

"Sabotage" (1961–1963), the first book, is a slow recovery from the old moribund misperceptions, the poet gathering his energies for the final breaking of all ties to the "superstructure of filth Americans call their way of life." In the third poem, "A POEM SOME PEOPLE WILL HAVE TO UNDERSTAND," the necessity for blotting out his "Watercolor ego" and "All the pitifully intelligent citizens / I've forced myself to love" is crisply stated: "Will the machinegunners please step forward?" His poetry still feels inert, though, and the actual breaking away is not easy. In "Citizen Cain" Baraka must prod himself: "Roi, finish this poem, . . . / . . . Your time is up / in this particular feeling. In this particular throb of meaning. / Roi, baby, you blew the whole thing." Although in "Letter to E. Franklin Frazier" he is isolated in a room ". . . where memory / stifles the present," he nevertheless sees himself, as he says in "THE PEOPLE BURNING," at a decisive and energizing turning point: " . . . It is

choice, now, and / the weight is specific and personal." He must turn the old death fixations into new life motions, the whiteness into blackness. The decadent white world and its hapless literature are virulently focused in "Sabotage" through metaphors of sexuality, tastelessness, and increasing anti-Semitic innuendo—"poets imagining / they are Shakespeare's hardon, . . . / . . . eating / into the strophe yard huge like empty Dachau. . . ."

There are indexes of wholesome change, though, the signs of personal and artistic rebirth parallel to the insights gleaned from *Blues People.* In "LEADBELLY GIVES AN AUTOGRAPH," music is exact and nurturing, opening up avenues of poetic expression. The poet is now assured by "The possibilities of music. . . . / . . . that scripture of rhythms," his voice no longer meek as it was in "Rhythm & Blues":

A strength to be handled by giants.

The possibilities of statement. I am saying,
   now,
what my father could not remember
to say. What my grandfather
was killed
for believing.

Foremost among the possibilities of poetic statement would be the bridging of personal feeling and broader social understanding. In a white-dominated world where everything is owned and objectified—God, people, time, language, as Baraka says in "Square Business"—his function would be to seek wholeness through subjectivity, through the expression of black feelings and spirit. In "The Bronze Buckaroo," at the end of "Sabotage," he is one of the "mutineers" in motion toward a more complete blackness, "Half way up the hill . . . / . . . and standing."

"Target Study" (1963–1965), Baraka says in the introduction, is in a more active mode, "trying to really study, like bomber crews do the soon to be destroyed cities. Less passive now, less uselessly 'literary.'" A twelve-line poem entitled "Ration" succinctly captures the spirit: "Banks must be robbed, / ... / The money must be taken / and used to buy weapons." As in "Sabotage," much energy is spent perverting shopworn symbols of American whiteness. The response here is more specifically keyed to avenge Jim Crowism, as opposed to the earlier exclusive repudiations of Crow Jane. Homosexual epithets abound (art is a "hairy" phallus, old artist friends "white drifting fairies," Uncle Sam "a queer," God "the baldhead faggot"), blatantly offensive sexual missiles aimed by the bombardier-poet to obliterate the presumption of white male omnipotence, establishing in its place a vision of manhood in accordance with the masculine dynamics of Black Power in the 1960's. Baraka's attitude reflects nothing more or less than the narrow sexual politics of the time, a racial rivalry perceived largely as a crisis of manhood. The opening poem, "Numbers, Letters," features the lean voice of a new man no longer " ... freakin' off / with white women, hangin' out / with Queens, ..." Unencumbered, he can speak straightforwardly, " ... Say what you mean, ... / ... and be strong / about it." The hesitations of "Sabotage" are all but gone:

I'm Everett LeRoi Jones, 30 yrs old.
A black nigger in the universe. A long breath
    singer,
wouldbe dancer, strong from years of fantasy
and study. All this time then, for what's
    happening
now. . . .

With this renewed sense of self, the poet urges the underground feelings of black manhood into visible realization. In "Ready Or Not," the bold print screams "BLACK MAN DREAMING OF MURDER / GET THE SHIT AND MEET ME / SOMEPLACE," as though addressing the Clays and Walkers of the 1964 plays. More and more reading his poems before receptive black audiences, Baraka had scant concern for the survival of "Ready Or Not" as a printed artifact. He implies in the final lines that the poem's chief function is the creation of consciousness at the moment of utterance: "This poem now has said / what it means, left off / life gone seconds ago". Some of the poems near the end of "Target Study" carp against the limits of written form. "Blank" states the ideal alternative of "live sound and image," formulations more readily embodied in the voices and gestures of the play. "THREE MOVEMENTS AND A CODA" exhorts open insurrection, the final lines defining the poem as an incomplete word-song awaiting its consummate formation through the extraliterary participation of the reader-listener: "These are the words of lovers. / Of dancers, of dynamite singers / These are songs if you have the / music"—no end punctuation but, rather, the expectation of the poem merging into whatever action might be induced in the responsive listener.

Such appeals to the essence of black manner and feeling culminate in "A Poem for Black Hearts." The poet elevates black self-identification and potential for action to mythic proportions in the name of Malcolm X, a contemporary black hero already a legend: "For Great Malcolm a prince of the earth, let nothing in us rest / until we avenge ourselves for his death. ..."

In "Black Art" (1965–1966), the final and most substantial book in *Black Magic,* the reach toward a black spiritual essence is even more pronounced—the white madness almost fully displaced by the new black magic. The opening poem, "SOS," sets the prescriptive tone for collective integrity: "calling all black people, come in, black people, come / on in." Having summoned his audience, the poet-teacher firmly establishes in "Black Art"—one of Baraka's most often quoted poem-manifestos—the principle of what one might call the living poem, the poem indistinguishable from the natural world and, especially, from the live gesture of black assertion: "Poems are bullshit unless they are / teeth or trees or lemons piled / on a step.... / words of the hip world live flesh & / coursing blood...." Clay's imprecation to Lula, that drawing her blood would cause one poem to vanish, is now the imperative aesthetic: " ... We want 'poems that kill.' / Assassin poems, Poems that shoot / guns...." In this terroristic manner, the poem represents the height of Baraka's anti-Semitism (" ... dagger poems in the slimey bellies / of the owner-jews ..."), with ethnocentric scattershot aimed at "wops," Irish cops, and non-black Negroes (" ... girdlemamma mulatto bitches") as well. These are to be poems of exorcism, the purging of whiteness stated in literal terms in order to restructure black consciousness.

Ideally, the people themselves are the self-affirming artists, their lives the Art-ing:

> ... Let Black People understand
> that they are the lovers and the sons
> of lovers and warriors and sons
> of warriors Are poems & poets &
> all the loveliness here in the world

Black statement is not to be an arty, individuated fact, but a collective participatory expression of poet and audience alike: "And Let All Black People Speak This Poem / Silently / or LOUD," he concludes.

The power Baraka wants to draw upon is perhaps best characterized in the essay "The Changing Same," in *Black Music*. As always, music is the exemplary medium, evidencing what the poet calls "the will of the expression." The musician-artist is in effect a priest whose sacred duty is to evoke spirituality: "This phe-nomenon is always at the root in Black Art, the worship of spirit—or at least the summoning of or by such force." In "Little Brown Jug" Baraka expresses the absolute equation of black selfhood, the song, and divinity—himself and all black people as the instrument (the little brown jug), the song, and the spirit force: " ... Companion, of melody / rhythm / turned around heart runs / climbed & jumped scream-ing / WE ARE GODS, ..." Several of the poems in "Black Art" are conceived as chants, invocations of spiritual energy—for example, "Sacred Chant for the Return of Black Spirit and Power." Where once "White evil" had pre-vailed (like the love once intellectually conceived as twisted to "evol" in *Suicide Note*), now the poet conjures positive spiritual inversions through the magical word power of the chant: "To turn their evil backwards / is to / live." So too has the once-evil Anglo-sun been restored and deified in the new righteous way of life, the poet proclaiming to his wife in "Stirling Street September" that " ... for the sake of, at the lust of / pure life, WE WORSHIP THE SUN."

Some poems, like the aptly titled "Form Is Emptiness," press poetic convention to the limit in attempting to force the issue of spirituality. After a monotonous printed extension of chanted vowel sounds to evoke the gods of color (Rah, Damballah, Allah), the poet can only affirm the total inadequacy of the fixed poem to represent infinite deity: "is not word / is no lines / no meanings." In "Vowels 2," though, the extended chant is invigorated with images of motion and sound that simulate the ecstatic freedom of spiritual consummation, "the energy / the force" of godhead percussively summoned into emotional and bodily sensation by the preacher-poet. Difficult to read silently, the lines can be effectively sung out to project the rhythmic spell of a sermon whose text is black freedom. The poem that perhaps most gracefully captures the predicate principles of "Hunting Is Not Those Heads on the Wall" is "Death is the beginning of a new form." Black selfhood is offered in the ultimate form—the "new form"—of infinite motion working timelessly toward complete self-possession and spiritual freedom. Participial forms combine with music images to create a flowing predicate style:

> of doing thinking feeling being
> forever endless in the instant
> we lean transformed into energy
> transformed into blurrd motion
> all that is transformed specks of fire
>
> . . .
>
> resolved in the silent beating of forever
>   divinity
> you are a portion of this
> you are the total jazzman
> a note on the horn
>
> . . .
>
> the universe is close to your lips
> blow it out

The poem collections following *Black Magic* show an intensification of spiritual concern and an emphasis on African origins rather than any further evolution in style. Baraka had come under the influence of Maulana Karanga's Kawaida doctrine in 1967, the full effects of which can be seen in the poetry of *In Our Terribleness* (1970) and *It's Nation Time* (1970). Carefully outlined in *Raise Race,* Kawaida is a program for black nationhood rooted in a seven-point African value system (unity, self-determination, collective work and responsibility, cooperative economics, purpose, creativity, and faith) that constitutes for Baraka a "religious creed." Although he soon abandoned Kawaida for Marxism, he saw its organizational features then as a distinct advance over the inspirational but unstructured teachings of Malcolm X. *In Our Terribleness* acknowledges Karanga as

"the master teacher" and at one point specifically directs that the "change" to nationhood take place by adhering to the seven principles. The main thrust of the poetry is toward a prophetic black future, sweeping the reader along in surges of black talk and preachment that make only occasional pro forma references to the white Beast—a romantic fusion of secular style and holy revelation extolling blackness.

The physical characteristics of *In Our Terribleness* as a book-artifact are in curious static tension with Baraka's predicate aesthetics. The title page is a hard, reflective silver, the 145 glossy leaves conspicuously unpaginated and black-bordered, the text in large, bold print and generously spaced. The poetry is combined with forty-three photographs by Fundi (Billy Abernathy), sometimes to caption the pictures but mostly unfolding as a dominant and independent sermon on *Some elements and meaning in black style,* as the book is subtitled. Baraka strains a bit to introduce the fixed images as Art-ing—"PAPERMOTION / PITCHAS . . ." he calls them—perhaps a tentative expression of his interest in cinematic techniques that influenced the plays of his Marxist period. The title itself symbolizes in poetic black language the integrity of style and culture that distinguishes black life for Baraka, an expansion of the Afro-American sense of the word "bad" as meaning good in the tested tradition of inverting white values: "Since there is a 'good' we know is bullshit, . . . / . . . We will be, / definitely, bad, bad, as a mother-fucker." Terribleness, then, is the ultimate goodness: "Our terribleness is our survival as beautiful beings." It is the essence of black life-style as expressed in the poem "LECTURE PAST DEAD CATS," the people exalted as a " . . . nation of super hip swift motional creation / . . . tone carriers of glowing magic" and the poet himself honored to be "one of the priests."

In "PRAYER FOR SAVING" Baraka exhorts the people to "Survive and Defend" the entire black tradition, evoking heroes and artists from Ray Robinson and Huey Newton to Claude McKay and John Coltrane, images to be immortalized in the collective black consciousness as "the together revelation of humanhood." He is most self-consciously Imamu (the title of Muslim priest or imam conferred upon him by Karanga) in the visionary poem "ALL IN THE STREET," where Allah speaks through the agency of the poet: " ... I am a / vessel, a black priest interpreting / the present and future for my people."

The same role is more confidently fulfilled in *It's Nation Time,* a compact, three-part service proclaiming the path to black nationhood. The first part, "The Nation Is Like Ourselves," is a litany urging unconverted "assimilados" to return to their blackness, preparatory to the inspirational message in "Sermon for Our Maturity." His congregation is now "the suns children / Black creatures of grace-" growing and expanding into an "Afro" space of "angelic definition." Baraka closes in the title poem, "It's Nation Time," by pressing the people to translate their newfound spiritual maturity into the necessary actions for building the black nation in the here and now.

This was the literary culmination of Baraka's nationalism, the final measure of the distance traveled from insurgent son to spiritual father—from Clay and Walker to the impassioned collective voice of *Slave Ship* and *In Our Terribleness.* As one of the prophet-teachers, Baraka also had a major hand in preparing the book that has become the primer of the Black Arts Movement, coediting *Black Fire: An Anthology of Afro-American Writing* (1968) with Larry Neal. A selection of essays, poetry, short fiction, and drama, it is a chronicle of 1960's nationalism comparable in importance with Alain Locke's documentation of the Harlem Renaissance in *The New Negro* (1925).

Abrupt as it might seem, Baraka's move to Marxism in the early 1970's was by no means a sudden turnabout. It was, rather, a continuation as well as an abandonment of certain facets of black ideology consistent with his sense of art and life as "The Changing Same." He is the same Amiri Baraka, but changed in discarding the religious pretense of the title Imamu; still a fervent spokesman for black people, but now with a worldwide revolutionary vision for all oppressed people; still an insurrectionary, but organizing against the international evils of capitalism and imperialism rather than the national tyranny of racism; still an artist of intensity, but keyed to structured gestures of political fact rather than the spiraling imagination of spirituality; still deeply committed, but to the discipline demanded by the "science of Marxism-Leninism-Mao Tse-tung Thought" rather than the program of Kawaida.

Although in the poem "HEGEL," from "Sabotage," he belittled the tedium of " ... trying to understand / the nightmare of economics," he subsequently described (in a published chapter from his unpublished 1973 autobiography "Six Persons") his own political conversion in hip Afro-Hegelian-Marxist terms: "But the class struggle yeh, then suddenly in 1971, and 2, and 3, fat gibber lip skunky funky declare the opening of the nigro pseudobourgeois hot foots. . . . Yeh its called, a 'qualitative leap.'" Although as late as 1969, Baraka was rejecting Marxist-Leninist "white ideology" as merely a violent form of integration, by 1973, under the influence of such African Marxists as Amilcar Cabral and Sekou Touré, we see his first distinctly postnationalist poem in "Afrika Revolution." The mother culture is no longer mythologized—made a "static absolute," as he would say self-critically of *Blues People.* Instead he enjoins African people all over the world "to make Revolution" against capitalism and imperialism. He sees change in political rather than metaphysical or aesthetic terms, the poetic voice frequently spare and didactically earnest: "The world must be changed, split open & changed / Transformed, turned upside down."

Baraka had altered his role from that of priest to the Leninist concept of the advanced worker, the socialist poet-instructor dedicated to "the education and organization of the proletariat." His literary subject is henceforth to be *Hard Facts,* as the poetry written during 1973–1975 is titled, not the ritual celebration of black magic. Instead of the former concern with "how you sound," he now stresses content, what you say. "Poetry," the introduction to *Hard Facts* begins, "is saying something about reality. It reflects the sayer's place in the production process, his or her material life and values." Following fundamental Marxism, Baraka conceives of himself as an artist-worker raising his audience's political and historical understanding of material reality. Moving from the concentrated if narrow sense of responsibility to black nationalism, he now accepts the broad premise of "a dynamic coalition of forces" against all forms of oppression. The keynote struck in most of his socialist poetry and drama is the pressing need to organize "a new revolutionary Marxist-Leninist party."

In the aggregate, *Hard Facts*—along with most of Baraka's subsequent Marxist poetry—addresses a black audience more than a multinational proletariat, his main concern continuing to be the political readjustment of black sensibilities. "WHEN WE'LL WORSHIP JESUS" speaks in a distinctly black voice charged with the energy of a preacher's rhetorical emphasis. It is a simple call to replace the anodyne of religion with a belief in science, knowledge, and revolution. Some poems isolate singular instances of black political regression, the prostitution of black integrity to bourgeois materialism and power by progressive people who in fact only represent the illusion of

change. These "attack pieces," as Baraka calls them in the introduction, are reminiscent of the corrosive voice in "Target Study." The satirical obscenities directed at poet Nikki Giovanni in "NIGGY THE HO" (transparently "Nikki the Whore") and the flaying of the mayor of Newark in "GIBSON" are exemplary. Even the hero of *Dutchman,* "Killed / by a white woman / on a subway / in 1964," is not allowed to rest in martyred peace. In "CLAY," that hero is derisively revived and then dispatched as "the first negro congressman" from Missouri: "we're not saying / that being dead / is the pre / requisite / for this honor / but it certainly helped make him / what he is / today"—an allusion to Congressman William Clay from St. Louis as well as a wry comment, no doubt, on the bourgeois acclaim accorded the play.

The most inventive piece of political instruction, one focused more on ideology than attitude, is "THE DICTATORSHIP OF THE PROLETARIAT." The poem is structured to desensitize the capitalist worker to the negative propaganda associated with the title phrase: "you hear that, the dictatorship / of the proletariat, and be scared / think somebody gonna hold you back / hold you down, . . ." The poem then encourages a correct resensitizing through clarification and gentle but firm repetition—" . . . Speak / of / the dictatorship until you understand it . . ."—concluding:

This is the dictatorship of the proletariat
the total domination of society by the working
    class

you need to hear that
you need to talk about that
you gonna have to fight for that

the dictatorship of the proletariat
think about that
the dictatorship of the proletariat

A lengthy explanatory passage near the end of the poem perhaps best exemplifies what Baraka called (in the 1977 interview with Benston) the "struggle form" he was attempting to realize in his poetry. An arhythmic discourse on proletariat rule, the unadorned lines in effect constitute a prose commentary patterned after the "short essay form" of the Chinese revolutionary democrat Lu Hsün—a form Baraka describes as a combination of "poetry and revolutionary observation."

Already a prolific essayist, as *Home* and *Raise Race* attest, Baraka feels more strongly than ever that the latitude of the essay and its emphasis on content are particularly suited, as he says, "to the kind of daily struggle I'm engaged in." And he is fully aware that this preference implies a relinquishing of at least some predicate quality in the rhythms of his poetry: "—I think the essay form could correspond to music *in places,* at a given moment. But I think it's less interested in the overall *sound* of words and more interested in *what* it's saying." This conscious tendency toward what might be called selected moments of expository poetry, however repressive it might seem to some of Baraka's more aesthetic-minded critics, is in some ways but a reversal of an earlier stylistic current one can observe in the infusion of poetry into the prose of *Dante's Hell, Tales,* and *Raise Race.*

Other poems have ideologically suggestive titles like "DAS KAPITAL" and "CLASS STRUGGLE," but concentrate on satiric description or poetic narrative to convey impressions of political reality rather than the clarification of doctrine. Instances of struggle form are limited to brief rhetorical calls for a revolutionary consciousness, as in "TODAY" and "RED AUTUMN." A central image is transformed yet again in "A POEM FOR DEEP THINKERS," the sun spiritualized in "Black Art" now but a symbol of romantic dissociation. Depicted as "Skymen," the nationalists are " . . . blinded by / sun, and their own images of things. . . . / . . . a buncha skies bought the loop-

dieloop program from the elegant babble of / the ancient minorities"—a sharp reassessment of his own Afro-American elegance. Baraka wants instead to write a "song of the skytribe walking the earth." The poem closes with a political revision of the salutation "hey my man, what's happening," the correct rejoinder hereafter to be: "meet you on the battlefield / . . . meet you on the battlefield." *Hard Facts* ends with a predicate call "FOR THE REVOLUTIONARY OUTBURST BY BLACK PEOPLE." Here the energies of black style and political expression converge in revolutionary climax: " . . . a spectrum of motion, . . . / We are poised in gradual ascendence to that rising" which is to be, as the poem concludes, "The violent birth process / of Socialism!"

Baraka's main dramatic work of the 1970's, a full-length play called *The Motion of History* (1975–1976), also conceptualizes motion as the political process leading inevitably to revolution. The play appears in *The Motion of History and Other Plays* (1978) with a shorter piece entitled *S-1* (1976)—after the abbreviated designation for the Criminal Justification, Revision and Reform Act, legislation Baraka interprets as dangerously repressive—and the previously published *Slave Ship.* In the introduction to the collection he mentions two earlier and still unpublished plays important to his development as a dramatist: *A Recent Killing* (1964), "about the U.S. Air Force," and *The Sidnee Poet Heroical* (subsequently published in 1979), which he says is "characterized by much petty bourgeois cultural nationalism." The two postnationalist plays in the volume, like the new poetry, "are vehicles for a simple message" aimed at the worker audience: "viz., the only solution to our problems . . . is revolution! And that revolution, socialist revolution, is inevitable."

Baraka is now concerned, as he told Benston, with a "theatre of ideas" that emphasizes an understanding of history rather than the "ahistorical worldview" fostered by his ritual drama, although in varying degrees such plays as *Dutchman* and, especially, *The Slave* and *A Black Mass* show an earlier need to deal with ideas as well. He acknowledges the influence of Bertolt Brecht, whose concept of "epic theatre" as a narrative social process arousing recognition and action is hospitable to both the nationalist plays and Baraka's present Marxist theater. Baraka sees the major change, as he says in the introduction, to be one from "the perceptual to the rational," from "the feeling and rage against oppression to the beginnings of actual scientific analysis of this oppression. . . ."

The Motion of History presents an analysis of two issues: the deliberate fostering of hostility between black and white workers by capitalism (an issue explored at length in the socialist writings of W. E. B. Du Bois) and the "recurrent rebellion" endemic to the history of the United States. Both the title and the action reflect Baraka's renewed sense of historical change through his engagement with dialectical materialism. "I began to understand very clearly," he explains to Benston, "that change is constant . . . that ultimately the motion of society and humanity is always onward and upward, from ignorance to knowledge, from the superficial to the in-depth and the detailed."

This is precisely dramatized in the play by the transformation of two apolitical emblematic characters, blandly designated Black and White, whose hedonism and ignorance buffer them from social injustice. In a quick montage of opening scenes (incorporating a movie screen and cinematic images, a technique used throughout the play), they suddenly merge into the stream of history by becoming James E. Chaney and Andrew Goodman, two of the three civil rights workers lynched in Mississippi in 1964. Act II moves back in time to the Hayes-Tilden compromise of 1876 that ended the Reconstruction, and from there to Bacon's Re-

bellion of 1676 in Jamestown, Virginia (represented as a spontaneous coalition of white indentured servants and black slaves rising up against the colonial ruling class). Curving forward toward the present in a kaleidoscope of episodes portraying black rebels in the 1800's (Nat Turner, Gabriel Prosser, Denmark Vesey, Harriett Tubman), Act III culminates in John Brown's insurrection at Harper's Ferry.

In the final and lengthy fourth act, the characters Black and White resurface to undergo their final changes in the strife-torn motions of the twentieth century. Their former bourgeois indifference is now a confused but earnest concern as they retrieve their different yet related heritages as Afro-American slave and Irish-American immigrant. The ultimate motion is their qualitative leap, embracing Marxism and fully clarifying the meaning of their common history of oppression under capitalism. Thus they assume a completely formed identity and naming as Lenny Nichols and Richie Moriarty, socialist factory workers united in the organization of a revolutionary Marxist party.

Baraka has moved from historical pageantry in *Slave Ship* to historical interpretation in *The Motion of History,* stressing that destiny is to be controlled by actions based on disciplined understanding rather than by confrontive rage. He now displaces separatism with a call for political unity among workers who understand that racism, black or white, is a capitalist strategy of control—not an acceptable rationale for determining human values. There is much explanatory monologue mixed with the dialogue, a play text more important for its content than for its style. The ultimate purpose is to clarify, through the example of Lenny and Richie, the need for a socialist revolution.

To this didactic end Baraka intercedes with the audience during the intermission after Act III to ask what they have learned from the play so far. His firm political hand always in evidence now, the stage directions call for "at least one plant in the audience" to guarantee the "correct" answers—that is, that the ruling class attempts "to keep the working-class people divided along national and racial lines," and that change will only come from "violent revolution" by the people. More structured than the participation improvised at the end of *Slave Ship,* this exchange is designed to raise consciousness through intellectual pressure rather than emotional shock. In the final scene, a meeting of the Red Congress, Baraka wants the audience to distinguish between the work of the artist and the work of the party activist, between the simulated reality of the play and the material reality in which they actually live:

RICHIE. . . . you know there's people like we was . . . looking at this like it was on a screen or on a stage. Got reality draped around them and won't step down into it and grab it up whole.

LENNY. That's what the party's for, to mobilize the great masses of people, to be a guide, a mobilizer, a leader, a clarifier, a fighter . . .

The strong voice of a woman concludes *The Motion of History,* anticipating an increasingly significant female dimension in Baraka's plays. The opening address to the Red Congress, delivered by Juanita Martinez, delegate from Puerto Rico (who otherwise has no role in the play), is the closing summons to the play viewer. In the struggle form of a short essay, her speech is Baraka's unabashed call for a "revolutionary party" based on "the correct political line" of "Marxism-Leninism-Mao Tse-tung Thought."

While *The Motion of History* interprets American rebellion as a precedent for accepting revolution, *S-1* (1976) is a more compact and somewhat slow one-act play that presents characters with a fully realized historical consciousness. Lil and Red Hall, black members of the Revolutionary People's Union (RPU), pick up where Lenny and Richie leave off, analyzing and actively resisting capitalist oppression in 1976. Numerous scenes take the form of party-line speeches, formal political debates, informal discussions, media interviews, and news broadcasts—a kind of running theatrical struggle form, a dialectic whose main purpose is to interpret the Criminal Justification, Revision and Reform Act as a fascist instrument of repression. The play ends with Red in jail (charged with treason under the deliberately vague provisions of the bill), proselytizing his fellow prisoners to accept "the formation of the party," while Lil and the RPU cadre attend a secret meeting of Marxist-Leninists preparing to unite as one central "Revolutionary Marxist-Leninist Communist Party." The pro forma presence of Juanita Martinez in *The Motion of History* is extended into the characterization of Lil Hall, who is equal with her husband as party strategist and political interpreter of events throughout *S-1.* She also provides the political theme song "America" that opens and threads through *S-1* (subtitled *A Play with Music in 26 Scenes*).

In a theater of ideas, music must supplement the play script "as background, to heighten the emotions . . . which is old, classic theater," Baraka now believes. It can no longer predominate as the direct expression of feeling inextricably linked to the text, as in *A Black Mass* or *Slave Ship.* The Liberation Singers in *S-1* who perform Lil's song are no doubt patterned after the Advanced Workers, a Newark group Baraka had recently been providing with political lyrics.

The protagonists of Baraka's Marxist plays are advanced workers like Lenny and Richie or Lil and Red. They function not as singular personalities but as representative commentators to enlighten the audience according to the discipline of Marxist-Leninist thought. Donna, the featured advanced worker of *What Was the Re-*

lationship of the Lone Ranger to the Means of Production? (1978), first printed in *Selected Plays and Prose of Amiri Baraka/LeRoi Jones* (1979), represents in part Baraka's acknowledgment of the issue of women's oppression in the larger context of the struggle against capitalism. A short satire set in a factory, the play is built around a continuous one-scene dialectical exchange between Donna, the no-nonsense voice of clarity, and the Masked Man and his chauvinist underling Tuffy, burlesques of the capitalist factory owner and his conspiratorial ally, the union bureaucrat.

This theatrical Lone Ranger is a culmination of the cowboy satirized throughout Baraka's works, the western hero who represents the extreme distortion of American values—"a butcher in a cowboy suit," as one poem puts it. While Donna serves mainly to interpret the madness of cowboy capitalism into sane political fact, she also directly confronts its offensive sexism. Resisting the masked owner's slick, wheedling efforts to co-opt the workers' political sensibility, she succeeds, like Lula in *Dutchman* but with a constructive motive, in drawing out her antagonist's real malevolence: the quick and easy readiness of the owner to murder in order to maintain control over the assembly line. The play ends with the striking workers going off to organize the party that will eventually put them in charge of the means of production.

Baraka's most recent poems are collected under the title "Poetry for the Advanced," poems written between 1976 and 1978 and published for the first time in *Selected Poetry of Amiri Baraka/LeRoi Jones* (1979). The poet begins by momentarily yielding his own voice, the entire introduction consisting of a quoted passage from Lenin that defines the advanced worker as the vanguard of the proletariat—as a representative of the "working-class intelligentsia." The voice of the worker-artist in the poetry, though, is confidently Baraka's own.

The elements of struggle form are inevitably there, but crafted so that on the whole they blend into a poetry that is stylistically, if not politically, advanced beyond *Hard Facts* (1976). There is more expressive power and less ideological self-consciousness—not less ideological intensity—as if some of the pressure of extended political exposition had been released into the plays. Predicate phrasings and musical motifs are much in evidence, and there is a firmer sense of the poet's personal place in the larger politicized scheme of reality.

The opening piece, "A POEM FOR ANNA RUSS AND FANNY JONES," equates his grandmothers' belief in a heavenly afterlife with the respectful concurrence that " . . . all society will / be raised to higher ground, a more advanced life" in this world. Their most natural humanity—and his—is lyrically shared by the masses of people: " . . . Your skin scraped off so the moonlight stings, so the swish of bird's wings / brings a message to the brain. . . . / . . . A link with the billions. . . ." Yet the "clear message" of crushing the "rule of the rich" by violent means " . . . cannot be hidden with lyricality / and mysticism. . . ." And so he concludes by gently and insistently implicating the traditional pacifism of his kinfolk in the people's revolution against the ruling class:

>   . . . They huddle and plot
>   our repression and pain. But
> just like the old stories grandmama, that ain't
>   no big thing, we learned how evil wd act in
> Sunday School, and how the people, the
>   righteous,
>   wd always win!

Baraka is less than gentle in alluding to Allen Ginsberg as a "blind & crazy / metaphysical" prophet. Yet he acknowledges that his old "petty bourgeois" friend (himself no stranger to Marxism) had made a point back in 1956, when in the poem "America" Ginsberg said, "Go fuck yourself with your atom bomb." Baraka rejuvenates the protest, composing around the quoted line his own poem about America entitled "REPRISE OF ONE OF A. G.'S BEST POEMS," with Marxist variations on the repeated theme word "America."

Rendered somewhat in the manner of a popular song lyric, one imagines parts of the poem as suitable for performance by the Liberation Singers who in *S-1* sing Lil's socialist song "America." Baraka offers "REPRISE" as a "Hymn-poem," a thrust at the patriotic hymn "America" brightly animated at the end by Latin-accented snatches from the "America" of Leonard Bernstein's *West Side Story*. Where Ginsberg mainly gestures with lyric confusion and ironic nostalgia—"America I used to be a communist when I was a kid I'm not sorry"—Baraka flings out struggle taunts: "I'm a red pinko Commie / ... a Marxist-Leninist / Whose ideology is / Marxism-Leninism-Mao Tse-tung Thought!" The repetitions and assertive refrains are similar to the song style of several other poems in the collection, making "REPRISE" more effective as a popular piece of music directed at worker audiences than as a fixed-print poem suitable for aesthetic analysis.

Baraka's musical intention in this regard is most evident in "LIKE, THIS IS WHAT I MEANT!," a song-manifesto defining the function of the poem for Marxist political purposes just as "Black Art" had earlier demarcated the poem from a strict nationalist view. The refrain "So that even in our verse" is used to unfold a series of short struggle quotations from Mao enlivened by a surge of interpolation and clarification from Baraka. Not only must poetry " ... sing, laugh & fight," but, as with the message of the plays, "Poetry must see as its central task / building / a Marxist-Leninist / Communist Party / in the USA."

Carried along in the musical flow, the diction of political advance ("raging mass," "struggle erupts," "sweep forward," "human explosion") resolves in proposing the poem as a revolutionary song. Baraka parenthetically instructs the reader to "repeat as song" the final rallying refrain: "So that even / in our / verse / even in / our dancing / even in / our song / yeh / in our pure lover song / REVOLUTION!!!"

Song refrain and the back-up style of vocal groups typify "ALL REACTION IS DOOMED!!!," a poem weakened by hackneyed political invective (Nikita Khrushchev a "Fat bald head traitor," Trotskyites "those bedbugs made of vomit"), intrusions that would not stir all advanced readers. "AFRO-AMERICAN LYRIC" is the most stylized song-poem, utilizing refrains that encourage the listeners to "think" about and "study" revolution. Unlike the other song lyrics, it conspicuously features the manipulation of vowel sounds as rhythmically stretched and fondled by an urban soul singer. Pithy denunciation is wrapped in Afro-American predicate sound:

> society's ugly is the graspingclass
> its simple
> shit uh
> see-imm-pull
> see-im-pull
> Seeeeeeeeeeeee-immmmmmmmmm
>   pull
> Some See   -   im   -   pull
>   shit

As the sounds are turned over and given intense vocal inflection, the stylistic process presumably will crystallize political meaning for the singer-listener: that understanding material reality and the need for revolution is basically simple. As with some of the chant poems in "Black Art," these worker songs—political heirs to the earliest Afro-American work songs—are for the ear, not the eye. They suggest Baraka's increased willingness to accommodate the impulses of Art-ing to Marxist content, the augmenting of a spare poetic lyricism by the song lyric.

A number of poems work in more conventional ways to focus the expected political themes. "MALCOLM REMEMBERED (FEB. 77)" eulogizes Malcolm X in a montage of recent black nationalist history, presenting him as the "comrade" who was killed before his "final motion" into socialist revolution. In the short poem "PRES SPOKE IN A LANGUAGE," Baraka withholds direct ideological statement, poetizing the collective black sounds of saxophonist Lester Young—" . . . in the teeming whole of us he lived"—as an exemplary history of survival: "translating frankie trumbauer into / Bird's feathers / Tranes sinewy tracks / the slickster walking through the crowd / surviving on a terrifying wit." The poem fulfills its revolutionary obligation, and then only by implication, in the final line: "Save all that comrades, we need it."

If nationalism has been discarded, the pertinence of black culture has not. John Coltrane's "sinewy tracks" become "AM/TRAK," an ambitious poem whose rush of Art-ing almost overtakes the political conclusion. The poem is probably a subjective offshoot of "John Coltrane: Where Does Art Come From?," an unpublished Marxist analysis of black music that Baraka was writing in the late 1970's (a chapter of which appears in *Selected Plays and Prose*). The poetic expression of Coltrane's history and art is reminiscent of verse from "Black Art": "nigger absolute super-sane screams against reality / course through him / . . . / . . . the precise saying / all of it in it afire aflame talking saying being doing meaning." The political harnessing of this energy comes at the end, the music of Coltrane's "Meditations" touching the poet as a metaphor of struggle and study: "& it told me what to do / . . . / Live! / & organize / yr shit / as rightly / burning!"

This forceful emergence of Coltrane, a major

inspiration for black poets in the 1960's, indicates that Marxism had not significantly displaced black culture in Baraka's art. It had only altered his interpretation of that culture. In "SPRING SONG," a recurrent symbol is once again changed in accord with Baraka's shifting perception of reality—the nationalist " . . . sun behind us, the day turned red,"—with musical pulsations reinforcing the political conceit at the end of the poem. The athletic "strides" of the advancing "black comrade" toward "the next hurdle," the qualitative leap, are likened to Coltrane's improvisations in the music of "Giant Steps":

> . . . the mass of people surging
> forward too, remind
> him of Trane—yeh Trane—you know that
> solo—Bee Dooo Bee Dooo Dooooo
> Dooo dooo   (Giant Steps)

The leap is completed in the autobiographical gesture of the last poem, "CHILD OF THE THIRTIES." Baraka stretches the child's game Red Rover into the same political image of the hurdle figured in "Spring Song," a motion that flows smoothly from the blues-blowing horn of the black musician:

> Red Rover, Red Rover, can you understand
> class struggle
>
>   . . .
> like the way your hand would reach your toe
> with the wood hurdle
> passing an 8th of an inch
> under your outstretched leg
> pass swift comrade, pass swift
> the way the everything do
> the way the all the things do
> the way the world is blew
> blue
> bluessssss

The musical note is ultimately political, the poem closing in a balance of metaphor and classic struggle statement: "Long Live Marx, Engels, Lenin, Stalin, Mao Tse-tung / Red Rover / Red Rover / You're over". This may or may not be LeRoi Jones's final motion. As he said many poems ago in *Suicide Note,* "the changes are difficult, when / you hear them, & know they are all in you." But as Amiri Baraka's subsequent experience has clearly shown, change is inevitable—indeed, is everything, as he says in "THE 'RACE LINE' IS A PRODUCT OF CAPITALISM": "all is, the only constant / is, / yeh yeh yeh, change!"

With Baraka's career as yet incomplete, summary is difficult. Comparable with Langston Hughes in stylistic finesse and with W. E. B. Du Bois in historical vision, Baraka is incomparably himself in creative scope and intellectual intensity. Always a hard critic of Western culture and the American way, he has wrenched from the bourgeois fine arts tradition—in the very process of rejecting much of its manner and many of its values—a commitment to the written word as a means of recording the personal and political struggles of one man: first speaking for himself, then for black people, and now for the proletariat. Most of all as a poet and playwright, but also as a writer of fiction and essays, his literary efforts have in common the quality of piercing inquiry—whether directed at himself or the world at large.

His questionable reputation with the critics is of little concern to Baraka. He measures his own achievement by the changes his writings have brought about in others. One reviewer has typically commented that in the Marxist poetry Baraka has "sacrificed artistic vitality on the altar of his political faith." Nothing could be further from the truth. In all the phases of his writing—whether "beat," nationalist, or Marxist—Baraka has shown a deep concern not only for attitudes and ideas but also for the effective adjustment of his aesthetics to the changing realities he tirelessly inscribes. Indeed, he is one of the important literary innovators working in the United States.

Selected Bibliography

WORKS OF AMIRI BARAKA (LEROI JONES)

BOOKS, PLAYS, PAMPHLETS

Preface to a Twenty Volume Suicide Note. . . . New York: Totem Press, 1961.

Blues People: Negro Music in White America. New York: William Morrow, 1963.

The Dead Lecturer. New York: Grove Press, 1964.

Dutchman and The Slave. New York: William Morrow, 1964.

The System of Dante's Hell. New York: Grove Press, 1965.

Home: Social Essays. New York: William Morrow, 1966.

The Baptism and The Toilet. New York: Grove Press, 1967.

Arm Yrself or Harm Yrself. Newark, N. J.: Jihad Productions, 1967.

Black Music. New York: William Morrow, 1967.

Slave Ship: A Historical Pageant. Negro Digest, 16, no. 6: 62–74 (April 1967). Reprinted Newark, N. J.: Jihad Productions, 1969.

Tales. New York: Grove Press, 1967.

Home on the Range. Drama Review, 12:106–11 (Summer 1968).

Police. Drama Review, 12:112–15 (Summer 1968).

Black Magic: Collected Poetry 1961–1967. Indianapolis–New York: Bobbs-Merrill, 1969. (Includes "Sabotage," "Target Study," and "Black Art.")

The Death of Malcolm X. In *New Plays from the Black Theatre,* edited by Ed Bullins. New York: Bantam Books, 1969. Pp. 1–20.

Four Black Revolutionary Plays. Indianapolis–New York: Bobbs-Merrill, 1969. (Includes *Experimental Death Unit #1, A Black Mass, Great Goodness of Life,* and *Madheart.*)

A Black Value System. Newark, N. J.: Jihad Productions, 1970.

In Our Terribleness (Some elements and meaning in black style). Indianapolis–New York: Bobbs-Merrill, 1970. (With Fundi/Billy Abernathy.)

It's Nation Time. Chicago: Third World Press, 1970.

J-E-L-L-O. Chicago: Third World Press, 1970.

Junkies Are Full of (SHHH . . .). In *Black Drama Anthology,* edited by Woodie King and Ron Milner. New York: New American Library, 1971. Pp. 11–23.

Bloodrites. In *Black Drama Anthology* (see immediately above). Pp. 25–31.

Raise Race Rays Raze: Essays Since 1965. New York: Random House, 1971.

Kawaida Studies: The New Nationalism. Chicago: Third World Press, 1972.

Spirit Reach. Newark, N. J.: Jihad Productions, 1972.

Hard Facts. Newark, N. J.: People's War, 1975.

The Motion of History. In *The Motion of History and Other Plays.* New York: William Morrow, 1978. Pp. 19–127.

The Motion of History and Other Plays. New York: William Morrow, 1978. (Includes *The Motion of History, Slave Ship,* and *S-1.*)

S-1. In *The Motion of History and Other Plays.* New York: William Morrow, 1978. Pp. 151–225.

"Poetry for the Advanced." In *Selected Poetry of Amiri Baraka/LeRoi Jones.* New York: William Morrow, 1979. Pp. 275–340.

Selected Plays and Prose of Amiri Baraka/LeRoi Jones. New York: William Morrow, 1979. (Includes the following previously unpublished prose: "I" [1973]; "National Liberation Movements" [1977]; "War/Philly Blues/Deeper Bop" [1978]; "The Revolutionary Tradition in Afro-American Literature" [1978].)

Selected Poetry of Amiri Baraka/LeRoi Jones. New York: William Morrow, 1979.

The Sidnee Poet Heroical. Berkeley, Calif.: Reed and Cannon, 1979.

What Was the Relationship of the Lone Ranger to the Means of Production? In *Selected Plays and Prose of Amiri Baraka/LeRoi Jones.* New York: William Morrow, 1979. Pp. 252–76.

WORKS EDITED BY BARAKA

Four Young Lady Poets. New York: Totem Press, 1962.

The Moderns: An Anthology of New Writing in America. New York: Corinth Books, 1963.

Black Fire: An Anthology of Afro-American Writing. New York: William Morrow, 1968. (With Larry Neal.)

UNCOLLECTED ESSAYS

"How You Sound??" In *The New American Poetry: 1945–1960,* edited by Donald M. Allen. New York: Grove Press, 1960. Pp. 424–25.

"Philistinism and the Negro Writer." In *Anger, and Beyond: The Negro Writer in the United States,* edited by Herbert Hill. New York: Harper and Row, 1966. Pp. 51–61.

BIBLIOGRAPHIES

There is no single completely up-to-date bibliography of Baraka's works or of criticism about Baraka. The best available sources are listed below.

Benston, Kimberly W. *Baraka: The Renegade and the Mask.* New Haven: Yale University Press, 1976. Pp. 278–83.

———, ed. *Imamu Amiri Baraka (LeRoi Jones): A Collection of Critical Essays.* Twentieth Century Views. Englewood Cliffs, N. J.: Prentice-Hall, 1978. Pp. 191–95.

Dace, Letitia. *LeRoi Jones: A Checklist of Works by and About Him.* London: Nether Press, 1971.

Hudson, Theodore. *From LeRoi Jones to Amiri Baraka: The Literary Works.* Durham, N. C.: Duke University Press, 1973. Pp. 198–209.

Sollors, Werner. *Amiri Baraka/LeRoi Jones: The Quest for a "Populist Modernism."* New York: Columbia University Press, 1978. Pp. 301–28.

BIOGRAPHICAL AND CRITICAL STUDIES

Baker, Houston A., Jr. "'These Are Songs if You Have The/Music': An Essay on Imamu Baraka." *Minority Voices,* 1:1–18 (1977).

Benston, Kimberly W. *Baraka: The Renegade and the Mask.* New Haven: Yale University Press, 1976.

———. "Amiri Baraka: An Interview." *Boundary 2,* 6:303–16 (Winter 1978).

———, ed. *Imamu Amiri Baraka (LeRoi Jones): A Collection of Critical Essays.* Twentieth Century Views. Englewood Cliffs, N. J.: Prentice-Hall, 1978.

Brady, Owen E. "Great Goodness of Life: Baraka's Black Bourgeoisie Blues." In *Imamu Amiri Baraka (LeRoi Jones),* edited by Kimberly W. Benston. Pp. 157–66.

Brecht, Stefan. "LeRoi Jones' *Slave Ship.*" *Drama Review,* 14:212–19 (Winter 1970).

Brown, Cecil M. "Black Literature and LeRoi Jones." *Black World,* 19, no. 8:24–31 (June 1970).

Brown, Lloyd W. "Comic-Strip Heroes: LeRoi Jones and the Myth of American Innocence." *Journal of Popular Culture,* 3:191–204 (Fall 1969).

———. "Jones (Baraka) and His Literary Heritage in *The System of Dante's Hell.*" *Obsidian,* 1:5–17 (Spring 1975).

Coleman, Larry G. "LeRoi Jones' *Tales*: Sketches of the Artist as a Young Man Moving Toward a Blacker Art." *Black Lines,* 1:17–26 (Winter 1970).

Costello, Donald P. "Black Man as Victim." *Commonweal,* 88:436–40 (June 28, 1968).

Cruse, Harold. *The Crisis of the Negro Intellectual.* New York: William Morrow, 1967. Pp. 355–68.

Dennison, George. "The Demagogy of LeRoi Jones." *Commentary,* 39:67–70 (February 1965).

Ellison, Ralph. *Shadow and Act.* New York: Random House, 1964. Pp. 247–58.

Fischer, William C. "The Pre-Revolutionary Writings of Imamu Amiri Baraka." *Massachusetts Review,* 14:259–305 (Spring 1973).

Hudson, Theodore R. *From LeRoi Jones to Amiri Baraka: The Literary Works.* Durham, N. C.: Duke University Press, 1973.

Hughes, Langston. "That Boy LeRoi." *Chicago Defender,* January 11, 1965, p. 38.

Jackson, Esther M. "LeRoi Jones (Imamu Amiri Baraka): Form and the Progression of Consciousness." *CLA Journal,* 17:33–56 (September 1973).

Jacobus, Lee A. "Imamu Amiri Baraka: The Quest for Moral Order." In *Modern Black Poets,* edited by Donald B. Gibson. Englewood Cliffs, N. J.: Prentice-Hall, 1973. Pp. 112–26.

Jeffers, Lance. "Bullins, Baraka, and Elder: The Dawn of Grandeur in Black Drama." *CLA Journal,* 16:32–48 (September 1972).

Lederer, Richard. "The Language of LeRoi Jones'

The Slave." *Studies in Black Literature,* 4:14–16 (Spring 1973).

Llorens, Davis. "Ameer (LeRoi Jones) Baraka." *Ebony,* 24:75–78, 80–83 (August 1969).

Mackey, Nathaniel. "The Changing Same: Black Music in the Poetry of Amiri Baraka." *boundary 2,* 6:355–86 (Winter 1978).

Margolies, Edward. *Native Sons: A Critical Study of Twentieth-Century Negro American Authors.* Philadelphia: J. P. Lippincott, 1968. Pp. 190–99.

Munro, C. Lynn. "LeRoi Jones: A Man in Transition." *CLA Journal,* 17:57–78 (September 1973).

Neal, Larry. "The Development of LeRoi Jones." *Liberator,* 6:4–5 (January 1966) and 18–19 (February 1966).

Ossman, David. *The Sullen Art.* New York: Corinth Books, 1963. Pp. 77–81.

Otten, Charlotte. "LeRoi Jones: Napalm Poet." *Concerning Poetry,* 3:5–11 (1970).

Phillips, Louis. "LeRoi Jones and Contemporary Black Drama." In *The Black American Writer,* vol. II, edited by C. W. E. Bigsby. Baltimore: Penguin Books, 1971. Pp. 204–19.

Pickney, Darryl. "The Changes of Amiri Baraka." *New York Times Book Review,* December 16, 1979, p. 9.

Schneck, Stephen. "LeRoi Jones, or, Poetics & Policemen, or, Trying Heart, Bleeding Heart." *Ramparts,* 6:14–19 (June 29, 1968).

Sollors, Werner. *Amiri Baraka/LeRoi Jones: The Quest for a "Populist Modernism."* New York: Columbia University Press, 1978.

Stone, Judy. "If It's Anger ... Maybe That's Good." *San Francisco Chronicle,* August 23, 1964, pp. 39, 42.

Taylor, Clyde. "Baraka as Poet." In *Modern Black Poets,* edited by Donald B. Gibson. Englewood Cliffs, N. J.: Prentice Hall, 1973. Pp. 127–34.

Tener, Robert L. "The Corrupted Warrior Heroes: Amiri Baraka's *The Toilet.*" *Modern Drama,* 17:207–15 (June 1974).

Williams, Sherley A. "The Search for Identity in Baraka's *Dutchman.*" In *Imamu Amiri Baraka (LeRoi Jones),* edited by Kimberly W. Benston. Englewood Cliffs, N. J.: Prentice-Hall, 1978. Pp. 135–40.

—WILLIAM C. FISCHER

Joel Barlow

1754—1812

IN December 1812, after a year of chasing Napoleon across the plains of Europe as special envoy from President James Madison, Joel Barlow found time to compose "Advice to a Raven in Russia," a bitter invective against the emperor's destructive and wasteful campaign. In this, Barlow's last and probably best poem, the poet asks his fabled bird, "Black fool, why winter here?" Observing that "These frozen skies, / Worn by your wings and deafen'd by your cries, / Should warn you hence, where milder suns invite" Barlow notes that Napoleon's "human carnage, that delicious fare, / That lured you hither" is as frozen as the Russian frontier. The poet's advice to the raven paints a bleak picture of the European landscape:

Go back and winter in the wilds of Spain;
Feast there awhile, and in the next campaign
Rejoin your master; for you'll find him then,
With his new million of the race of men,
Clothed in his thunders, all his flags unfurl'd,
Raging and storming o'er the prostrate
    world!

Barlow's anger bristles in this poem, and his satire is probably the bitterest condemnation of mankind written by an American at that time. And that condemnation is ironic, for Barlow, in most of his prose and poetry, gave advice that he felt would help mankind realize its vision of a near-perfect society. In "Advice to a Raven in Russia," though, his advice was not directed to the savior of mankind, but to the agent of its destruction. On the eve of his death, as he viewed the shambles Napoleon had made of his dream, Barlow was justifiably disillusioned.

Despite his anguish, caused more, it seems, by his frustrating and fruitless ambassadorial adventures than by a radical and permanent change in his outlook, Barlow remains, on the basis of his early work, the most articulate spokesman for the development of a national literature and the progress of America. In the tradition of a generation of writers like Philip Freneau, Hugh Henry Brackenridge, Charles Brockden Brown, and his fellow "Hartford Wits," John Trumbull, David Humphreys, and Timothy Dwight, who in their nationalistic zeal spoke out for a native American literature and for the future greatness of America, Barlow responded to the challenge of a new age and devoted his work to the declaration of American promises and ideals.

Born on March 24, 1754, in a farmhouse at Redding, Connecticut, Barlow was the son of Samuel and Esther Hull Barlow. Farm life seemed to agree with him, and he spent his first nineteen years in Redding, attending the village school and helping his father on the farm. During these early years Barlow showed great promise as a student and especially as a poet. In his free time he had composed several poems that his minister, the Reverend Nathaniel Bartlett, recognized for their promise. Bartlett showed Joel's poems to the boy's father and suggested that the young man prepare for college. Barlow's father agreed, and soon Joel was mastering both Greek and Latin. As his interest and skill increased, his teacher decided that young Barlow should be surrounded by a more academic environment.

In 1773, consequently, he entered Moor's School in Hanover, New Hampshire, then a preparatory school for Dartmouth, and the following year he enrolled at Dartmouth. Three months later his father died, leaving Barlow not only a small inheritance but also a decision to make: Should he continue at Dartmouth or take advantage of an opportunity to study at Yale? At the death of his father, his finances, despite the inheritance, were strained. For Barlow his education was of great importance, and Yale would provide him not only with a broader educational base but also with the financial advantages of being nearer home. So, in November 1774, he left the rural atmosphere of Hanover and traveled to the sophisticated world of New Haven.

Founded in 1701 by Harvard alumni disturbed by Harvard's liberal curriculum, Yale was at that time very conservative, especially in its religion. Jonathan Edwards' *Inquiry into the Freedom of the Will,* for example, was the standard text for religious studies at Yale. A typical New Englander, Barlow rebelled at some of these restrictions. For example, every morning he and his classmates were required to listen to the president or one of the tutors read a portion of the Bible in the college chapel. He also learned that he was not permitted to roam the grounds of the campus freely, and that such indiscretions as blasphemy, insubordination, profanity, and playing cards were grounds for immediate expulsion. For him, liberal thinking and intellectual exercise were important, though these practices were discouraged by a college that insisted upon order and regulation. Yet it was at Yale that Barlow met Joseph Buckminster, the new tutor to the freshman class, who convinced him that he might become a good poet. Buckminster became Barlow's closest friend and followed his career for many years.

Those early Yale years, though, were soon to lose that unwanted sense of order and regulation. During Barlow's first year of studies, the sounds of war were heard throughout the colonies. Students broke out of their lethargy and organized a militia company of their own; and when George Washington passed through New Haven, Barlow and his fellow students turned out to greet him. This excitement continued to increase, eventually forcing President Naphtali Daggett to dismiss the college two weeks earlier than usual.

During the summer of 1775, as news of the bloody battle of Bunker Hill reverberated across the colonies, Barlow and his classmates were once again immersed in their studies. But Barlow's second year was interrupted when word of his mother's death reached him. After going home to serve as executor of her estate, Barlow returned to Yale to complete his sophomore year. During this time he began to write poetry that he hoped might establish his reputation.

Meanwhile, still more important events were occurring in the colonies. Thomas Paine's *Common Sense* had been published and applauded, and the Declaration of Independence had been adopted. Despite the growing revolutionary fervor, the British were making advances into the colonies, and a call for men was issued. Among the Connecticut men who responded to that call was Barlow. But illness made his participation in the fighting brief: he enlisted in August 1776, and by autumn he was again enrolled at Yale and studying with Joseph Buckminster. No doubt his experiences in the New York campaign prompted his later praise of Revolutionary soldiers in both *The Vision of Columbus* (1787) and *The Columbiad* (1807). In spite of the war Barlow finished his program at Yale and graduated on September 9, 1778.

On graduation day Barlow, as class president, read his first ambitious poem, *The Prospect of Peace*. Written in heroic couplets, the poem begins with a hymn to the American struggle for independence:

> The closing scenes of Tyrants' fruitless
>   rage,
> The opening prospects of a golden age,
> The dread events that crown th' important
>   year,
> Wake the glad song, and claim th'
>   attentive ear.
>   Long has Columbia rung with dire
>   alarms,
> While Freedom call'd her injur'd sons to
>   arms;
> While various fortune fir'd th' embattled
>   field,
> Conquest delay'd, and victory stood
>   conceal'd;
> While closing legions mark'd their dreadful
>   way,
> And Millions trembled for the dubious
>   day.

Like others of its genre, *The Prospect of Peace* was a patriotic poem, singing forth the future greatness of America. Its emphasis on the need for a reformed American landscape was a theme that would be a constant in Barlow's career. Throughout the poem Barlow prophesies the achievement of American scientists ("Fair Science then her laurel'd beauty rears, / And soars with Genius to the radiant stars"); the creation of a great American philosophy ("Here, rap't in tho't, the philosophic soul / Shall look thro' Nature's parts and grasp the whole"); and the beginning of an American religious poetry ("Unnumber'd bards shall string the heavenly lyre, / To those blest strains which heavenly themes inspire").

Like Freneau and Brackenridge's *The Rising Glory of America,* read at their commencement exercises at Princeton in 1771, Barlow's verse announced what appeared to be a great opportunity for men of all talents in the new American republic. With the prospect of peace very possible in 1778, he concludes:

> THEN Love shall rule, and Innocence
>   adore,
> Discord shall cease, and Tyrants be no
>   more;
> 'Till yon bright orb, and those celestial
>   spheres,
> In radiant circles, mark a thousand years;
> 'Till the grand *fiat* burst th' etherial
>   frames;
> Worlds crush on worlds, and Nature sink
>   in flames!
> The Church elect, from smouldering ruins,
>   rise,
> And sail triumphant thro' the yielding
>   skies,
> Hail'd by the Bridegroom! to the Father
>   given,
> The Joy of Angels, and the Queen of
>   Heaven!

Barlow's Calvinist sentiments, coupled with the revolutionary ardor he raised, made the poem a great success, one that mirrored the rise of optimism and progress in America. In fact, the poem was so popular that a New Haven printer published it in pamphlet form.

Three years later, as a speaker at the first public commencement at Yale in seven years, Barlow repeated the performance. In his preface to *A Poem, Spoken at the Public Com-*

mencement at Yale College, in New-Haven; September 1, 1781, Barlow states that the "following performance" is taken from a "larger work [*The Vision of Columbus*]," and that his newest commencement poem reflects the "affairs of America at large, and the future progress of Society." Like *The Prospect of Peace, A Poem* is a prophecy of the march of the young republic toward the millennium. Barlow begins with a lament over the war years and the threat that war poses to education in America:

> Thro' seven long years hath war's terrific
>   power
> Rang'd every town and crimson'd every shore,
> Pursu'd fair Science from each happy seat,
> Rav'd in her domes and forc'd her last retreat,
> And oft, Yalensia, doom'd thy final fall,
> While thy sad Genius trembled for thy wall.

After this opening section the poet sees a strange form take shape:

> Now a calm splendor burst the saddening
>   gloom,
> And gales etherial breath'd a glad perfume,
> Mild in the midst a form celestial shone,
> Rob'd in the vestments of the rising sun;
> Tall rose his stature, dignity and grace
> Mov'd in his limbs and wanton'd in his face,
> His folding mantle flow'd in easy pride,
> His harp divine lay useless by his side,
> His locks in curls from myrtle chaplets
>   hung
> And sounds melodious melted from his
>   tongue.

This celestial vision imparts to Barlow some advice for the graduates:

> Tell them the wild commotions soon shall
>   cease,
> And blest Columbia hail the charms of
>   peace,
> Where rest the future deeds on earth design'd
> To raise, to dignify and bless mankind.

In *A Poem* Barlow's vision is an optimistic one, and he suggests throughout much of it that young America will develop into a society superior to any yet seen on earth. This superiority will be a product of the progress of mankind, a progress aided in large measure by the abundance of natural resources, resources by "nature's hand o'er all bestow'd, / The last pure polish of the forming God."

Numbered among those future glories will be the development of a great American poetry, the appearance of sculpture and painting, architecture, landscape gardening, and music. Of these the poet will contribute most significantly to the progress of America:

> His soul awakes the peace inspiring song,
> And life and happiness the strain
>   prolong.
> To moral beauties bids the world attend,
> And jarring realms in social compact
>   blend;
> Bids laws extend and commerce stretch
>   the wing,
> Far distant shores then barter'd tributes
>   bring;
> He sees the nations join, their bliss
>   increase,
> (League'd in his lays) and sings them
>   into peace.

Like *The Prospect of Peace, A Poem* was very successful, for it not only blended references to the expected victory for independence in the Revolution with typical allusions to Yale College but also, and most important, sang of the future greatness of America. Barlow's effectiveness in continuing the tradition of singing the American path to glory is due to his ability to sum up the meaning of American experience. Brimming with optimism, overflowing with the prevailing attitude of progress in America, Barlow's patriotic effusions were characteristic of the poetry being written in the new republic.

Yet Barlow, more than any other of his fellow "Hartford Wits," had the knack of orchestrating his poetry in such an effective way as to capture his audience's fancy.

For Barlow, the vision described in his commencement poems was just the beginning of the philosophy he would develop in his future epics. At the time of his graduation in 1778, Barlow's independent and inquiring mind began to assert itself in ways that went against established thinking. After a brief and unsuccessful stint of teaching school in New Haven, he returned to his alma mater to work on his master's degree. It was then that he began to conceive his great epic poem. Casting aside such ideas as a poem about Cyrus the Great or one dealing with biblical heroes, Barlow finally chose Columbus and the discovery of America as his subject. He felt that the discovery of the New World was a subject especially well suited to his plan, and his friends agreed. But as for the means to support himself and his epic poem, Barlow found little help. No one—businessman or politician— would agree to serve as patron for the bold venture.

Finally, after having little success, Barlow in 1779 considered the ministry, on the advice of his old tutor and friend, Joseph Buckminster. But this plan was unsuitable, for Barlow could not see himself as a preacher. He was convinced he could better serve mankind in some other capacity. In 1780, with no other alternative in sight, he compromised and accepted an appointment as chaplain of the Fourth Massachusetts Brigade. The choice proved to be a good one.

As an army chaplain Barlow was required to do little except deliver the Sunday sermon and conduct an occasional funeral or wedding. Most important, the post offered him time to write. Three weeks after his appointment, Barlow and his brigade were stunned by the discovery of Benedict Arnold's treason. The act raised Bar-

low's ire, and the result was a sermon. His sermon was so successful that he was invited to dinner by General George Washington. At the dinner he met Colonel David Humphreys, a future "Hartford Wit" and champion of Barlow's verse. His decision to accept the chaplaincy had already begun to promise rewards.

During those three years Barlow also found time, despite his continuing work on *The Vision of Columbus* and his duties as army chaplain, to marry Ruth Baldwin, sister of Barlow's former roommate and friend, Abraham Baldwin. They were married on January 26, 1781, amid a cloud of secrecy—her father did not learn of the union until nearly a year afterward. Barlow continued his duties with the army until the end of 1782, when he left the soldier's life and established his residence in Hartford.

Hartford was an ideal site for Barlow to continue his work. Many of his friends lived there, including Dwight, Trumbull, and Humphreys. Though those early years in Hartford were filled with the excitement of close friendships and the satisfaction that Barlow must have felt with his work on *The Vision of Columbus,* they were financially lean. With most of *The Vision* completed, his plan was to find a publisher for his long poem. All efforts failed until 1784, when Barlow agreed to go into partnership with Elisha Babcock, a Springfield, Massachusetts, printer, to publish the *American Mercury,* a weekly newspaper. He hoped that this venture would provide him with the funds necessary to publish *The Vision.* Barlow did most of the writing, and as the paper flourished, the money provided the partners a chance to start a small publishing house. They were successful, but the income was not nearly enough to support Barlow's plans. Thus, in 1785 the partnership was dissolved and Barlow looked for another way to help finance his poem.

The law seemed to promise a career in which he could not only shine but also support himself quite handsomely. In 1786, Barlow passed the law examination and was admitted to the bar. Although his early law career was undistinguished, in two years it paid dividends by enabling him to travel to Europe, a trip that was a turning point in Barlow's career.

Before that trip, one significant publication enhanced Barlow's reputation as a writer. Starting on October 26, 1786, and continuing through September 13, 1787, *The Anarchiad, A Poem on the Restoration of Chaos and Substantial Night, in Twenty Four Books,* appeared in the *New Haven Gazette.*

The Anarchiad appeared under the heading "American Antiquities," which created a context for the satire. According to the headnote, the manuscript had been discovered among the ruins of a buried civilization on the banks of the Muskingum River in Ohio. Its discoverers announced that certain portions of the epic would appear as regular installments in the *Gazette.* The ruse worked well, for *The Anarchiad* soon became the topic of conversation as readers eagerly awaited each new number with much the same fervor that American readers less than a century later awaited the next chapters of Charles Dickens' story of Little Nell.

The satire was truly a model of its time. In fact, at the end of the first number, the authors paid tribute to their inspiration: "I know not whether it is necessary to remark, in this place, what the critical reader will probably have already observed, that the celebrated poet, Mr. Pope, has proven himself a noted plagiarist, by copying the preceding ideas, and even couplets almost entire into the famous poem called 'The Dunciad.'" Penned by Barlow and his friends Humphreys, Trumbull, and Lemuel Hopkins, *The Anarchiad* establishes a familiar theme in book 8:

> In visions fair the scenes of fate unroll.
> And Massachusetts opens on my soul.

> There Chaos, Anarch old, asserts his sway,
> And mobs in myriads blacken all the way:
> See Day's stern port, behold the martial
>   frame,
> Of Shays' and Shattuck's mob-compelling
>   name.

Initiated at the same time as Shays's Rebellion—an insurrection of Massachusetts farmers to prevent imprisonment for debts incurred from high land taxes and foreclosures of mortgages, led by Daniel Shays, a Revolutionary War captain—*The Anarchiad* announced that chaos was the order of the day and predicted a gloomy picture for Americans: "Thy hand unbars th' unfathom'd gulph of fate, / And deep in darkness whelms the new-born state." Despite the public interest, the poem achieved little reform, although it produced great fury. But it did lay the path for political satire as the predominant form for verse in the 1790's, and it established the reputation of the "Hartford Wits."

While readers were still buzzing over the barbs thrown at them in *The Anarchiad,* Barlow finally realized his goal: *The Vision of Columbus* appeared. Advertised in the January 8, 1787, edition of the *Connecticut Courant* as a poem in nine books, "Dedicated, by permission, to the KING OF FRANCE," Barlow's *Vision* was to be finished in six weeks, "bound, gilt and lettered by an Artist equal to any in America, and perhaps not inferior to any workman in London." The price was announced as "ONE DOLLAR and a THIRD: A Price not higher than imported Books, of this size have commonly borne in America."

Eight years had passed since Barlow had begun the plan for his epic poem, but the response to *The Vision of Columbus* was astonishing and undoubtedly gratifying. Within a short time a second edition was printed. Subscribers to the book included the famous and soon-to-be-famous: Benjamin Franklin, Thomas Paine, and George Washington were among the more noteworthy, though the general public bought a generous number of copies. Barlow's *Vision* was a best-seller in its day and provided the tonic needed in the colonies to establish a sense of national pride and unity.

The plan for *The Vision of Columbus* was ambitious but simple: to present the history of America—past, present, and future—and to inculcate, as the preface states, "the love of national liberty, and to discountenance the deleterious passion for violence and war; to show that on the basis of republican principle all good morals, as well as good government and hopes of permanent peace, must be founded."

The Vision begins with Columbus, an old man dying in prison, traveling to the Mount of Vision with a "radiant seraph" who hopes to assuage his fears with a prospect of the future glories of America. Barlow traces their voyage across the ocean and provides the reader with a bird's-eye view of the geography of North and South America. His description of his own bailiwick, for instance, is typical of the scenery he paints:

> Now round the coast, where other floods
>   invite,
> He fondly turn'd; they fill'd his eager sight:
> Here Del'ware's waves the yielding shores
>   invade,
> And here bold Hudson oped a glassy
>   glade;
> Thy parent stream, fair Hartford, met his
>   eye,
> Far lessening upward to the northern sky.

After cataloging the flora and fauna of the American landscape in book 1, Barlow turns in book 2 to a dissertation on the early settlers of America. After discussing "from what dire sons of earth / The brutal people drew their ancient

birth," and the reasons for the dissimilarities of nations, he discusses in book 3 the history of the Inca empire and its legendary ruler, Manco Capac. Barlow's attempt to trace the roots of civilization is a fascinating approach to the creation of an epic poem, but the result is terribly bland and tedious. His turgid style and monotonous couplets lull the reader to sleep. Little of Alexander Pope's skill and deftness in handling the intricacies of the heroic couplet surfaces, here or elsewhere, in his description:

> When o'er the mountain flamed the
>   sun's broad ray,
> He call'd the host his sacred rites t' essay;
> Then took the loaves of maize, the
>   bounties brake,
> Gave to the chief and bade them all
>   partake;
> The hallowed relics on the pile he placed,
> With tufts of flowers the simple offering
>   graced,
> Held to the sun the image from his breast,
> Whose glowing concave all the God
>   exprest;
> O'er the dry'd leaves, the trembling lustre
>   flies,
> And thus his voice ascends the listening
>   skies.

Here, Barlow's mechanical use of the couplet reveals his too often plodding style. Unlike Pope, Barlow was not a master of the rhythms and nuances of sound often present in the heroic couplet. His lines tend to roll along without the startling effects that could be produced by careful attention to the use of caesura and the balanced phrase. In short, Barlow possessed an epic vision but lacked a poetic vision.

Throughout these early books Barlow's angel tries to show Columbus that much good has resulted from his discovery of America. His principal evidence—the colonization of America—originates in book 4, where Barlow argues that the new American state will be greater than any other:

> A new creation waits the western shore,
> And reason triumphs o'er the pride of
>   power,
> As the glad coast, by Heaven's supreme
>   command,
> Won from the wave, presents a new-form'd
>   land;
> Yields richer fruits and spreads a kinder soil,
> And pays with greater stores the hand of
>   toil; . . .

Finally, Barlow catalogs the early Americans: "the noble Baltimore"; "heaven-taught Penn"; and others whom "tyrants press and waves oppose in vain" and who "from their different shores, their sails unfurl'd, / Point their glad streamers to the western world." These are the men who will not only settle the New World, but will also make from that new land a world more ideal than any other seen on earth.

Books 5 and 6 trace the colonization from the French and Indian War through the American Revolution, while book 7 points to the accomplishments of Americans in the arts and sciences. Benjamin Franklin, for instance, is characterized as "bold Franklin," whose lightning rod "Curbs the fierce blaze and holds the imprison'd fire"; John Singleton Copley, as one who "Fair in his tints unfold[s] the scenes of state"; Benjamin West, as a man who "boldly bursts the former bounds of Art"; and Timothy Dwight, as an "Epic Muse sublime" who, like the others Barlow catalogs, "Hails her new empire on the western clime." Certainly Columbus' view is of the "promised land."

In book 8, Barlow prepares his readers for book 9—the final vision of the country America can become—by discussing such philosophical questions as the relationship between man and God, the excesses of passion and reason, and the discovery of truth from an understanding and careful recognition of the two. He concludes thus:

> Here the last flights of science shall ascend,
> To look thro' heaven, and sense with
>   reason blend;
> View the great source of love, that flows
>   abroad,
> Spreads to all creatures, centres still in
>   God,
> Lives thro' the whole, from nature's
>   compact springs,
> Orders, reverses, fills the sum of things;
> In law constrains, in gospel reconciles,
> In judgment frowns, in gentle mercy
>   smiles,
> Commands all sense to feel, all life to
>   prove
> The attracting force of universal love.

For Barlow "universal love" will solve problems and provide a better world.

The final book becomes Barlow's self-styled pulpit. If mankind responds to his charge in book 8 that "universal love" is the key to a great nation, then science, technology, government, and the arts can flourish. Barlow continues the seraph's narrative and describes the panorama as one that extends "over the whole earth." Through commercial, scientific, political, philosophical, and technological reform, the assimilation and final harmony of all languages, the "harmony of mankind" can be realized:

> Bid one great empire, with extensive sway,
> Spread with the sun and bound the walks
>   of day,
> One centred system, one all-ruling soul,
> Live thro' the parts, and regulate the
>   whole.

Although Barlow develops this theme in more detail and in more articulate fashion in *The Columbiad,* his emphasis in *The Vision of*

Columbus on technological and environmental reform is unmistakable. Because he sees the progress of America as depending on a society that is commercially and spiritually united, Barlow emphasizes the technological advances necessary to achieve such reform. Since his college days he had been interested in mechanical gadgetry. During his first trip to Europe in 1788, for example, he had been amazed by such devices as the steam engine, in which he saw great possibilities for unifying the young nation. His observations on these inventions appear in his notebooks and letters, and they reappear in his later work, especially in *The Columbiad.* In fact, Barlow had met and become friends with Robert Fulton. Together they decided to write a poem—Barlow would provide the philosophy; Fulton, the technology—on the feasibility of canal travel. Although the poem was never completed—only 290 lines of the projected first book were written before the plan was abandoned—"The Canal: A Poem on the Application of Physical Science to Political Economy," as it was to be titled, was epic in scope.

Like *The Vision of Columbus,* "The Canal" emphasizes the importance of science and technology. In a hymn to science early in the poem, Barlow suggests:

Science, celestial Priestess from thy birth,
Thy Charms are slighted by the Powers
    of earth,
Since proud Saturnalia, queen of Power,
    survey'd
Thy form burst forth from Jove's prolific
    head.
A form so pure, conceived without her
    love,
The unmingled essence of the mind of
    Jove.

Later, Barlow hopes to prove that "The Powers of State, *that 'tis no harm to know; /* And prove

how Science with these Powers combined, / May raise, improve, & harmonize mankind."

In "The Canal" Barlow demonstrates how science can "raise, improve, & harmonize mankind" by using as his metaphor for this projected unity the canal system carved out of the American waterways. To Barlow "Canals careering" across the "sunburnt hills" will "plant new ports in every midland mound."

Seeing the Mississippi as the American Nile, Barlow charts the results of such a harnessing of water resources: "Labor's land" will be "repaired"; "fruitful soil" will be spread over the land; "signs of fecundity" will fast appear. In all, "The Canal" presents a picture not unlike *The Vision of Columbus* or the later *Columbiad.* Technology, Barlow's "machine in the garden," holds the key to the future glory and greatness of America.

The Vision of Columbus, then, was important in continuing Barlow's theme of a materially reformed landscape. Although the unfinished "Canal" and the later *Columbiad* more clearly represent his mature prospect for America, *The Vision* represents his first ambitious undertaking along those lines.

But this first edition, although revealing the power of the later Barlow—especially in portions of book 9—fails as a poetic endeavor. Lacking the power of a John Milton, Barlow failed because his epic was simply too ambitious an undertaking for him. His *Vision* demanded both a narrative base to trace the history of America and a philosophical argument to explain its glories. To combine philosophy and narrative was beyond Barlow's skills at this stage of his literary development. The narrative sections in the poem are better than the philosophical portions, if only because they more closely align themselves with Barlow's talent at the time and enable him to show off his knowledge of the great literary epics and standard histories he had read at Yale. But they also lack originality and vitality. The philosophical portions, on the other hand, are colorful. These passages mirror Barlow's energy, but they often suffer from an excess of enthusiasm and a naiveté characteristic of the early Barlow.

Despite these problems the critical reception in America was largely favorable, and the sales of the book were quite surprising for the time. Few brave souls probably read *The Vision of Columbus* from cover to cover, but its influence and presence were felt. Notwithstanding the relatively unsophisticated nature of the American reading public in 1787, the opinion of the average reader was positive and the poem was much discussed and well known. In one of America's earliest novels, William Hill Brown's *The Power of Sympathy* (1789), for example, Barlow's epic is mentioned: "WHAT books do you read my dear? We are now finishing *Barlow's* Vision of *Columbus,* and shall begin upon *Dwight's* Conquest of Canaan in a few days."

But Barlow and his work were also the object of scorn. Peter Markoe, for example, penned in *The Times, A Poem,* published in Philadelphia in 1788, the following critique:

> That laurel'd Homer nodded, some
>   avow;
> Let poppies grace our dreaming poet's
>   brow,
> Who drowsily pursues his drowsy theme,
> And to a gallant chief ascribes his
>   dream.
> Thick mists of dulness on his readers
>   fall,
> Who sleep so soundly—they ne'er dream
>   at all.

Despite this somewhat lukewarm and uncharacteristic reception, Barlow's *Vision* was important in establishing the beginning of a national literature; and that, at least in part, softens the blow of his "drowsy theme." It was not until his later work, especially *The Hasty-Pudding* and "Advice to a Raven in Russia," that the power of Barlow's verse established his talents. In his early work, best exemplified by *The Vision of Columbus,* the poetry is derivative, like most verse in eighteenth-century America. Barlow recognized the polished wit of Pope and his circle, but he was never quite able to capture the skill inherent in that verse.

Barlow's changes in later editions of *The Vision of Columbus,* especially the fifth edition in 1793, represent his steadily growing sense of poetic development, although most of these changes are in philosophy rather than in form. In the fifth edition, printed in Paris, Barlow demonstrates his embrace of deistic doctrine by suggesting that man, and not God, as he had stated in the first edition, is largely responsible for the development of man and society. There is little emphasis on the "last pure polish of the forming God," found in *A Poem,* in this later version of *The Vision:* God is distinctly relegated to a secondary role. Barlow suggests that man, not God, will promote the greatness of America. In other changes Barlow charges that the French were less responsible than earlier thought for the success of the colonies in the war (a sign of his increasing disenchantment with the ideals of the French Revolution), and that French motives for entering the war were far less noble than he had originally conceived them to be. Most of these changes resulted from Barlow's growing maturity in matters of politics and theology, and they reflect the further changes that he would make in *The Columbiad.*

In *The Columbiad,* published in 1807, Barlow strikes out to write his final version of the American epic poem. Seeing himself in the role of poet as social reformer, he rewrites *The Vision of Columbus* as an epic, complete with the introduction of standard epic machinery, and including many of the ideas and motifs from

The Prospect of Peace and *A Poem.* Hesper replaces the "radiant seraph," and Potowmac, the river god, emerges as a new character. Barlow also adds a completely new book on the American Revolution, chronicling the noble adventures of the heroes of that war, and a section on Lucinda and Heartly, a melodramatic rendering of the eternal conflict between honor and love. The seriousness that marks *The Columbiad* is evident in the preface:

My object is altogether of a moral and political nature. I wish to encourage and strengthen, in the rising generation, a sense of the importance of republican institutions; as being the great foundation of public and private happiness, the necessary aliment of future and permanent meliorations in the condition of human nature.

This is the moment in America to give such direction to poetry, painting and the other fine arts, that true and useful ideas of glory may be implanted in the minds of men here, to take place of the false and destructive ones that have degraded the species in other countries; impressions which have become so wrought into their most sacred institutions, that it is there thought impious to detect them and dangerous to root them out, tho acknowledged to be false. Wo be to the republican principle and to all the institutions it supports, when once the pernicious doctrine of the holiness of error shall creep into the creed of our schools and distort the intellect of our citizens.

Clearly, Barlow's didactic charge in the preface echoes his glorification of America in the final version of *The Vision of Columbus.* For not only did he wish to continue his poetic description of the American past, present, and future, but he also sought to update that earlier vision with political reality.

If readers felt *The Vision of Columbus* to be didactic and pretentious, then *The Columbiad* was even more so. Epic in both scope and length (the poem is over 7,400 lines), the poem opens appropriately:

> I SING the Mariner who first unfurl'd
> An eastern banner o'er the western
>   world,
> And taught mankind where future
>   empires lay
> In these fair confines of descending
>   day.

Mirroring the initial sections of *The Vision of Columbus,* the opening books of *The Columbiad* detail the history of the West from the Inca empire to the present and describe the "wide regions" of America. Like the "radiant seraph" in *The Vision,* in *The Columbiad,* Hesper, the spirit of the Western world, transports Columbus from his prison at Valladolid to a mountaintop to view the broad panorama of history: "Land after land his passing notice claim, / And hills and mountains rise without a name."

But what Columbus sees in these early books, in his view of the world from the crow's nest, differs markedly from those similar scenes in *The Vision of Columbus.* Because Barlow insists upon man's responsibility for controlling his own destiny, Columbus' observations are tempered by the poet's increased didacticism. In book 4, Barlow sings a hymn to freedom:

> Yes! righteous Freedom, heaven and earth
>   and sea
> Yield or withhold their various gifts for thee;
> Protected Industry beneath thy reign
> Leads all the virtues in her filial train;
> Courageous Probity with brow serene
> And temperance calm presents her placid
>   mien;
> Contentment, Moderation, Labor, Art

Mold the new man and humanize his heart;
To public plenty private ease dilates,
Domestic peace to harmony of states.
Protected Industry, careering far,
Detects the cause and cures the rage of war
And sweeps with forceful arm to their last
    graves
Kings from the earth and pirates from the
    waves.
    But slow proceeds the work. Long toils,
      my son,
Must base the fabric of so vast a throne;
Where Freedom founds her everlasting
    reign,
And earth's whole empires form the fair
    domain.
That great coloniarch, whose exalted soul
Pervades all scenes that future years unrol,
Must yield the palm and at a courtier's
    shrine
His plans relinquish and his life resign;
His life that brightens, as his death shall
    stain
The fair, foul annals of his master's reign.

For Barlow, moral, social, and political improvement are possible only if freedom rules, and only if man can establish a world that takes advantage of the progress that technological reform can provide. This technology, according to Barlow's view, will enable man to control the elements and make the land cater to his wishes. With the advent of the machine age, Barlow's garden becomes a mechanized one that will not only improve man's life but also unite both the country and the two continents.

The major change from *The Vision of Columbus* to *The Columbiad* occurs in books 6 and 7. Here Barlow expands his history of the American Revolution by describing in more detail and with greater pomp the heroes of the War of Independence. These books are the most interesting and probably the most successful, for they have genuine epic proportions and portray much more vividly the heroic nature of the Americans and the villainous actions of the British. One of the new sections that Barlow adds to accomplish this is his melodrama of Lucinda and Heartly. Using the traditional conflict between honor and love as his basis for the inclusion of this episode, he recounts the story of two lovers who are separated because Heartly, the young hero, must answer the call to arms. When Lucinda, tearful at his imminent departure, follows him and is captured by the Indians, Barlow uses her suffering and death to contrast the innocence of the heroine with the demonic nature of the British hirelings (book 6):

    With calculating pause and demon
      grin,
They seize her hands and thro her face
    divine
Drive the descending ax; the shriek she
    sent
Attain'd her lover's ear; he thither bent
With all the speed his wearied limbs
    could yield,
Whirl'd his keen blade and stretcht
    upon the field
The yelling fiends; who there disputing
    stood
Her gory scalp, their horrid prize of
    blood.
He sunk delirious on her lifeless clay
And past, in starts of sense, the
    dreadful day.

Barlow's purpose in rendering this tearful scene is, of course, to protest the scourge of war and the destruction it produces. Only through peace can man hope to build a great nation.

Elsewhere, Barlow demonstrates his well-oiled epic machine by invoking Hesper to aid the army in its battle against flood and frost. In this scene Washington and his men are valiantly attempting to cross the Delaware, only to discover that the frozen river is not hospitable to their efforts. Hesper appears, "not to insult the brave, [but to] teach the proud stream more peaceful tides to roll." As in most of the poetry written at the turn of the century, the theme of moral and spiritual instruction pervades almost all the books of *The Columbiad.*

In book 8, which in part parallels book 7 of *The Vision of Columbus,* Barlow includes his hymn to peace, and adds a section on the survivors of the Revolution. In this homiletic ode to liberty, he reminds the patriots that they must preserve the liberty they so successfully fought for and won, and warns them that their task is not yet completed:

> Unnumber'd foes, far different arms that
> wield,
> Wait the weak moment when she quits
> her shield,
> To plunge in her bold breast the
> insidious dart
> Or pour keen poison round her
> thoughtless heart.

For Barlow the battle for freedom and progress was never-ending.

In book 9 the differences between *The Vision* and *The Columbiad* become even clearer. Because his philosophical and political ideas had matured rather radically over the years, especially in his version of the story of the Creation, Barlow revised his outlook and updated the explanation of the evolution of the earth. The world that Columbus sees is much more rational and utilitarian; nature, rather than God, is responsible for its development:

> Nature herself (whose grasp of time and place
> Deals out duration and impalms all space)
> Moves in progressive march; but where to
> tend,

> What course to compass, how the march must
> end,
> Her sons decide not; yet her works we greet
> Imperfect in their parts, but in their whole
> complete.

Barlow's last book reinforces this completeness as he reveals a unified world of men and nations. The process for this unification has been historically based, and his world is one that binds

> . . . all regions in the leagues of peace;
> Till one confederate, condependent
> sway
> Spread with the sun and bound the
> walks of day,
> One centred system, one all ruling soul
> Live thro the parts and regulate the
> whole.

With these lines Barlow's epic poem was complete. What he had written several times over was certainly not novel to his friends, but it was something with which most of them agreed. Their support was laudatory and exhaustive. But for the anti-Jeffersonians the poem became an opportunity for criticism. The Federalists damned it profusely. Characterized as generally devoid of interest, *The Columbiad* was attacked as tedious, discordant, redundant, and pretentious. Even Barlow's old college chum, Noah Webster, attacked what he saw as the "atheistical principles it contains." The stinging criticism eventually subsided, but Barlow was never able to cast off the atheist label.

Despite Barlow's celebration of the new American republic in *The Vision of Columbus* and *The Columbiad,* his mock-heroic and mock-pastoral poem on the growth and use of a favorite New England dish, *The Hasty-Pudding,* remains his most popular, most anthologized, and most readable work. Written in 1793, in the middle of his political and visionary work, *The Hasty-Pudding,* as Barlow suggests in the first stanza, is a poem written on a "softer theme," a "virgin theme, unconscious of the Muse, / But fruitful, rich, well suited to inspire / The purest frenzy of poetic fire."

Barlow begins his most popular poem by soft-pedaling his patriotic epics and calling forth the Muses to aid him in his first poetic inspiration (canto 1):

> Oh! could the smooth, the emblematic song
> Flow like thy genial juices o'er my tongue,
> Could those mild morsels in my numbers chime,
> And, as they roll in substance, roll in rhyme,
> No more thy aukward, unpoetic name
> Should shun the Muse, or prejudice thy fame;
> But rising grateful to the accustom'd ear,
> All Bards should catch it, and all realms revere!
> Assist me first with pious toil to trace
> Thro' wrecks of time thy lineage and thy race;
> Declare what lovely squaw, in days of yore,
> (Ere great Columbus sought thy native shore).

After dedicating his poem to an Indian maiden, "Some tawny Ceres, goddess of her days, / First learn'd with stones to crack the well-dry'd maize," Barlow explains "with logic clear" why the New England name of the pudding describes it best (canto 1):

> "In *haste* the boiling cauldron o'er the blaze,
> "Receives and cooks the ready-powder'd maize;
> "In *haste* 'tis serv'd, and then in equal *haste,*

"With cooling milk, we make the sweet repast.
> "No carving to be done, no knife to grate
> "The tender ear, and wound the stony plate;
> "But the smooth spoon, just fitted to the lip,
> "And taught with art the yielding mass to dip,
> "By frequent journies to the bowl well stor'd,
> "Performs the hasty honors of the board."

Barlow concludes the first canto by recognizing that other dishes—"green Succatash," "beans and corn," "rich Johnny-cake," for example—are not tempting: "You tempt me not, my fav'rite greets my eyes, / To that lov'd bowl my spoon by instinct flies."

Canto 2 details the rules and regulations necessary for creating a dish such as hasty pudding—a dish, he admits, "May still be bad, indifferent, or good, / As sage experience the short process guides, / Or want of skill, or want of care presides."

At this point in the poem, Barlow allows his epic strain to take over briefly, as he describes in majestic terms the growth of the corn:

> Slow springs the blade, while check'd by chilling rains,
> Ere yet the sun the seat of Cancer gains;
> But when his fiercest fires emblaze the land,
> Then start the juices, then the roots expand;
> Then, like a column of Corinthian mold,
> The stalk struts upward, and the leaves unfold;
> The busy branches all the ridges fill,
> Entwine their arms, and kiss from hill to hill.

This may seem mildly reminiscent of those melodramatic and discordant lines in *The Vision of Columbus* and *The Columbiad,* but the mock nature of *The Hasty-Pudding* enables Barlow's epic description to work for, rather than against, him. The very exaggeration present in these lines allows Barlow to poke fun at the epic vehicle, while at the same time it provides his readers with a chance to chuckle along with him. The context of the poem is serious, but its methods evoke good-natured humor.

Most amusing is the third and last canto, which emphasizes the rules governing the consumption of the pudding. Here Barlow parodies much of the machinery of American folklore as he describes the husking of the corn:

> For each red ear a general kiss he gains,
> With each smut ear he smuts the luckless
>   swains;
> But when to some sweet maid a prize is cast,
> Red as her lips, and taper as her waist,
> She walks the round, and culls one favor'd
>   beau,
> Who leaps, the luscious tribute to bestow.

Similarly amusing is Barlow's ode to a cow, which follows shortly thereafter:

> Blest cow! thy praise shall still my notes
>   employ,
> Great sources of health, the only source of
>   joy;
> How oft thy teats these pious hands have
>   prest!
> How oft thy bounties proved my only feast!
> How oft I've fed thee with my fav'rite
>   grain!
> And roar'd, like thee, to see thy children
>   slain!

The whimsical nature of these lines is very different from the seriousness Barlow displays in his epics. In recalling many of the pleasures of a simpler life he knew as a boy on the farm in Redding, Barlow takes a nostalgic look at his past and that of America. The future is temporarily shelved. To be sure, the progress of mankind has its place in *The Hasty-Pudding,* but it is treated with far less of the millennial fervor found in his longer poems.

The effect of this choice is both ironic and satiric. In *The Vision of Columbus* and *The Columbiad,* Barlow chose to display the benefits of progress by parading the development of American culture across the panorama of history. In this march through history, he foresaw something better for society. In *The Hasty-Pudding,* though, Barlow pokes fun at the result of progress by describing the trivial in the mock-epic tradition, as though it were of momentous importance. In the last canto, for instance, he describes in terms of exaggerated importance the process for selecting the proper spoons and bowls for eating hasty pudding:

> . . . The shape, the size,
> A secret rests unknown to vulgar eyes.
> Experienc'd feeders can alone impart
> A rule so much above the lore of art.

By suggesting that such trivial choices are the product of progress and a highly civilized and sophisticated society, Barlow at once satirizes that society and its artificial cultivation of good breeding. In fact, the entire poem moves in this direction.

In tracing the acquisition of good manners from the most primitive times in America, when an Indian maiden prepared this dish, to its preparation and consumption in this cultured era, Barlow achieves an effect he was never able to achieve in his longer epic poems. In those the level of seriousness and didacticism was so elevated that, ironically, his message became almost trivial. But in *The Hasty-Pudding* there is never any question of Barlow's tone. Unlike *The Vision of Columbus* and *The Columbiad,* the success of *The Hasty-Pudding* results from his use of a distinctive portion of American folklore treated in such a way as to appeal to an American-born audience. There is no attempt to chronicle world history, no use of unfamiliar exempla to illustrate the way to glory and greatness. What was vague and unimportant to an American audience in his epic poems becomes, in *The Hasty-Pudding,* clear and distinctly American. Probably for that reason, it is as the poet of cornmeal mush that Barlow achieved popularity.

Although *The Hasty-Pudding* and "Advice to a Raven in Russia" are Barlow's most popular and polished works, it is doubtful that he intended them to become his legacy. Surely Barlow saw *The Vision of Columbus* and *The Columbiad,* which occupied the majority of his creative energies, as his greatest works and those from which he derived the greatest satisfaction. They were symbolic of his foresight, and certainly represented for him the relationship he felt was necessary between Europe and America. But in a critical sense Barlow's greatest prose essays, remembered by few in the shadow of Thomas Paine's *The Rights of Man* and *Common Sense,* Thomas Jefferson's *Federalist* papers, and Franklin's prose satires, remain his most articulate expression of the progress of mankind in the late eighteenth century. Because these essays are not encumbered with the grandiose language and imagery of his epic poems or with the naiveté of a visionary, they provide the modern reader with a more concrete and accurate assessment of Barlow's abilities and prospect for America. Unlike *The Vision of Columbus* and *The Columbiad,* which display in Homeric and Miltonic epithets an exciting but generalized glimpse of the future of America and of mankind, Barlow's essays articulate, through very logical and concrete examples, his advice for a better world.

The best of Barlow's essays treat a variety of issues important to his prospect of the world at the turn of the century: the value of revolution (*Advice to the Privileged Orders, Part I,* 1792); advice to the leaders of Europe (*A Letter,*

Addressed to the People of Piedmont, on the Advantages of the French Revolution, and the Necessity of Adopting Its Principles in Italy, 1792) and of America (*Two Letters to the Citizens of the United States, and One to General Washington,* 1799); the importance of a national university (*Prospectus of a National Institution, to Be Established in the United States,* 1806); and an oration that smoothly blended many of Barlow's earlier ideas *(Oration Delivered at Washington, July Fourth, 1809).* Of these *Advice to the Privileged Orders* is probably his best.

In 1792, during his revision of *The Vision of Columbus,* Barlow was struck by Edmund Burke's contention that social change was unwise and harmful because it disturbed the status quo. That same year he had attacked Burke's ideas in a heavy-handed satiric poem, *The Conspiracy of Kings.* In it he had called Burke a "degenerate slave" who "leads you wrong, [for] the world is not his own." Portraying the Englishman as a "fool" and a "madman," he had urged his readers not to indulge the "vapory dream," the "thread-bare theme" that Burke espoused. It is not surprising, then, to see Barlow attack Burke's *Reflections on the Revolution in France* as propagating authoritarianism.

In *Advice to the Privileged Orders, Part I,* Barlow argues that the French Revolution was both necessary and desirable. He was convinced that tyranny was destructive, and that it not only violated the equal rights of men but also prevented them from taking part in their own government and determining their own future happiness. Taking a page or two from *The Vision of Columbus,* he advocates in strong and forceful language that the "example of America would have had great weight in producing this conviction." He believed that when Europeans recognized this, authoritarianism would be eliminated and man would become free. To explain his point, Barlow examines the "principal objects which make up the affairs of nations in the present state of Europe."

Of these, Barlow most strongly attacks the church and the military, two institutions he sees as guilty of perpetuating a social caste. Religion, he suggests in chapter 2, dupes the "community at large" in order "to conceal the strength of the many, and magnify that of the few." Using Europe as his example, he argues that the "pretence of extirpating the idolatries of ancient establishments and the innumerable heresies of the new, has been the never-failing argument of princes as well as pontiffs," and that "the extending and purifying of the Christian faith" has been their excuse for war. In short, when church and state are allied and man is made to believe "he is doing the immediate work of God, he divests himself of the feelings of a man." For these reasons the American government is best, because it continues "public instruction in the science of liberty and happiness, and promises a long duration to the representative government."

Likewise, Barlow states in chapter 3, the military keeps man in bondage. Suggesting that the code of honor that governs the military mind is also capable of "total perversion, of losing sight of its own original nature, and still retaining its name," Barlow concludes that the "principle of honor" works because it is "*convenient for the governing power.*" The military system, like the church, is corrupt because it places one man above another and destroys freedom and equality.

In other chapters Barlow explains the responsibility that government has for the individual, discusses the various theories of justice and the penal code, and carries on a disquisition against unfair taxes on the ground that taxation can easily lead to inequality among people. His arguments are well supported and very convincing, and his carefully constructed reasoning helps him establish the rational necessity for the progress of society toward independence.

Independence is also the subject, in part, of Barlow's advice to European leaders, especially the French and Italians. In *A Letter, Addressed to the People of Piedmont,* he encourages the Italians of the Piedmont to welcome the French army into their province so that freedom can be achieved. Believing that the French would invade Italy anyway, Barlow hoped to avoid bloodshed through his essay. Restating the principles of the French Revolution that he so ardently embraced, he appeals to reason by establishing the principles (paraphrased below) by which a majority can rule:

1. Because property requirement is a vestige of the monarchy, base representation solely on population.
2. Reduce the minimum age for a voter to twenty years, thus increasing the total number of voters.
3. Do not restrict citizenship by national boundaries. Give French citizenship to all who settle in France and allow those who move to other countries to retain their French citizenship.
4. Hold annual elections in order to keep representatives in touch with their constituents, and prohibit anyone from serving more than two years in every four, in order to ensure a larger number of active participants.
5. Keep salaries at a minimum, so that no one will pursue an office for monetary reward or the possibility of graft.
6. Make certain that representatives represent the people of the regions that chose them and not the nation as a whole.
7. Eliminate imprisonment for debt.

8. Reform penal practices and abolish the death penalty.
9. Require the government to undertake public instruction.
10. Eliminate public lotteries.
11. Reject colonies.
12. Eliminate the standing army, because if it is weak, it will fail to defend the country, and if it is strong, it will be a threat to the liberty of the people. Develop instead a militia.
13. Make provisions for amendments.

Barlow's ideas were culled in part from his earlier writings, and certainly represent many of the Jeffersonian ideals he espoused. Although that advice was unnecessary—the political turmoil in France prevented the conflict from occurring—it again established Barlow as a practical and reasonable man whose principles, although sometimes too idealistic, were reflected in the spirit and philosophy of his young republic.

Barlow also provided wisdom to his own government. With Napoleon on the move in Europe, he saw the political relationship between France and America in danger. In his letters to the American citizenry and to George Washington, he suggested a number of ways to avoid war between the two allies.

In the first letter to his fellow Americans, "On the System of Policy Hitherto Pursued by Their Government," dated from Paris, March 4, 1799, Barlow corrects several misconceptions concerning his statements regarding the American attitude toward Europe. These had been misquoted when that letter, sent to General Washington on October 2, 1798, had been published without Barlow's permission. In the second letter, "On Certain Political Measures Proposed to Their Consideration," dated from Paris, December 20, 1799, Barlow advocates complete freedom of the seas to ensure free trade. In both letters he urges restraint and argues that conflict would hinder, even destroy, rather than keep the peace and cooperation that had taken so long to establish. Always the practical man, he shows how a new war would divert the already dwindling funds of both nations into an unprofitable and unnecessary war. Barlow especially stresses cooperation among nations as the keystone to increased economic solidity.

Several years later, as the final draft of *The Columbiad* was nearing its conclusion, Barlow spoke to the public on the necessity of a national university (*Prospectus of a National Institution, to Be Established in the United States,* 1806). He saw education as a vital part of the development of the young American democracy, and he strongly advised the organization of such a system based on research and instruction, much like the educational plan the French supported. Barlow's theories of education were clear:

To explore the natural productions of our country, give an enlightened direction to the labors of industry, explain the advantages of interior tranquility, of moderation and justice in the pursuits of self interest, and to promote, as far as circumstances will admit, an assimilation of civil regulations, political principles and modes of education, must engage the solicitude of every patriotic citizen; as he must perceive in them the necessary means of securing good morals and every republican virtue; a wholesome jealousy of right and a clear understanding of duty; without which, no people can be expected to enjoy the one or perform the other for any number of years.

Education was important to the future of America, Barlow felt, and throughout his literary career he based his theories of the future of mankind on man's right and ability to make choices that would be a product of knowledge, of freedom, and of education. Barlow hoped that through a federally directed and funded educational system, those principles he had articulated so forcefully in his writings could be realized. And only through education, he stated, could man make those decisions.

In one of Barlow's last tracts, composed before he left America to chase Napoleon across the European continent and delivered to a Fourth of July crowd *(Oration Delivered at Washington, July Fourth, 1809)*, he articulated these ideas once more. Barlow believed that the preceding thirty-three years of national existence had merely prepared "this gigantic infant of a nation to begin its own development. They are only the prelude to the greater events that seem to unfold themselves before us, and call for the highest wisdom to give them proper direction." For America in the early nineteenth century, progress could best be continued if the nation could find ways of uniting itself. The answer, Barlow says, lies in creating mass transportation, "public improvements, such as roads, bridges, and canals." Rather than view them in a "commercial and economical . . . light," Americans should regard them in a "moral and political light."

In the same tract, mirroring a speech of Hesper's in *The Columbiad,* Barlow instructs his audience to "Cast your eyes over the surface of our dominion, with a view to its vast extent; with a view to its present and approaching state of population; with a view to the different habits, manners, languages, origins, morals, maxims of the people; with a view to the nature of those ties. . . ." Echoing the advice given to Columbus, this oration reiterates Barlow's insistence that future glory and greatness are possible for America only if its people work conscientiously toward them through a dedication to education and a recognition of the importance of technological and environmental reform.

Barlow's life and literary accomplishments were devoted unquestionably and unequivocally to a proclamation of the future of mankind. It seems ironic, then, that on the eve of his death in 1812, just three years after his stirring oration to a Washington gathering celebrating the birthday of America, he could pen a poem that seemed so contrary to the philosophy of freedom and progress he had articulated in his epic poetry and in his prose. Barlow must have shouted his condemnation of mankind in a moment of utter despair, for his vilification, rather than vivification, of society is an angry voice coming out of the frozen wilderness. For him to see the chaos he had so long warned against in the world Napoleon had created must have contributed to Barlow's frustration.

Nowhere else in his work is the irony so heavy, so bitter, as in "Advice to a Raven in Russia." His description of the frozen corpses as "Mere trunks of ice, tho limb'd like human frames" who "cannot taint the air, the world impest" paints a Dantean portrait of the world and questions even the intentions of a God he had come to ask "In what curst hands he leaves his world below."

Barlow's life had come full circle. No longer a naive singer of hymns to the freedom he found in the ideas of the French Revolution, Barlow now vehemently condemned in his bitterest jeremiad what that revolution and its precepts had produced:

> Each land lie reeking with its peoples slain
> And not a stream run bloodless to the
>   main.
> Till men resume their souls, and dare to
>   shed
> Earth's total vengeance on the monster's
>   head,
> Hurl from his blood-built throne this king
>   of woes,
> Dash him to dust, and let the world
>   repose.

Barlow's limitations as a poet are real, but his influence and role in American letters cannot be ignored. He is not a major American writer, but he is a very important one. He remains a vital figure in the history of American ideals, for his vision of America is vivid and accurate. Without question Barlow was a significant contributor to the American literary and cultural tradition. He should not be forgotten.

Selected Bibliography

WORKS OF JOEL BARLOW

POETRY

The Prospect of Peace. A Poetical Composition, Delivered in Yale-College, at the Public Examination, of the Candidates for the Degree of Bachelor of Arts: July 23, 1778. New Haven, Conn.: Thomas and Samuel Green, 1778.

A Poem, Spoken at the Public Commencement at Yale College, in New-Haven; September 12, 1781. Hartford, Conn.: Hudson and Goodwin, n.d. [1781].

An Elegy on the Late Honorable Titus Hosmer, Esq; One of the Counsellors of the State of Connecticut, a Member of Congress, and a Judge of the Maritime Court of Appeals for the United States of America. Hartford, Conn.: Hudson and Goodwin, n.d. [1782].

"The Anarchiad—A Poem on the Restoration of Chaos and Substantial Night." *The New Haven Gazette and Connecticut Magazine* (October 26, 1786–September 13, 1787).

The Anarchiad—A New England Poem, edited by Luther G. Riggs. New Haven, Conn.: Thomas H. Pease, 1861.

The Anarchiad—A Poem on the Restoration of Chaos and Substantial Night, edited by William Bottorff. Gainesville, Fla.: Scholars' Facsimiles and Reprints, 1967.

The Vision of Columbus; a Poem in Nine Books. Hartford, Conn.: Hudson and Goodwin, 1787.

The Vision of Columbus . . . the Fifth Edition, Corrected . . . to Which Is Added, The Conspiracy of Kings. Paris: English Press, 1793.

The Conspiracy of Kings. London: J. Johnson, St. Paul's Church Yard, 1792.

The Hasty-Pudding: A Poem in Three Cantos. Written at Chambery, in Savoy, January, 1793. New Haven, Conn.: n.p., 1796.

The Columbiad a Poem. Philadelphia: C. and A. Conrad and Co., 1807.

The Columbiad . . . with the Last Corrections of the Author. . . . Paris: Printed for F. Schoell, Booksellev [*sic*], 1813.

The Columbiad. A Poem, with the Last Corrections of the Author. . . . Washington, D. C.: Joseph Milligan, 1825.

Howard, Leon. "Joel Barlow and Napoleon." *Huntington Library Quarterly,* 2:32–51 (1938). Contains "Advice to a Raven in Russia."

Zunder, Theodore. "A New Barlow Poem." *American Literature,* 11:206–09 (1939).

PROSE

An Oration, Delivered at the North Church in Hartford, at the Meeting of the Connecticut Society of the Cincinnati, July 4th, 1787. In Commemoration of the Independence of the United States. Hartford, Conn.: Hudson and Goodwin, n.d. [1787].

Advice to the Privileged Orders, in the Several States of Europe, Resulting from the Necessity and Propriety of a General Revolution in the Principle of Government. New York: Childs and Swaine, 1792.

A Letter to the National Convention of France, on the Defects in the Constitution of 1791, and the Extent of the Amendments Which Ought to Be Applied. To Which Is Added the Conspiracy of Kings, a Poem. New York: Thomas Greenleaf, n.d. [ca. 1793].

A Letter, Addressed to the People of Piedmont, on the Advantages of the French Revolution, and the Necessity of Adopting Its Principles in Italy . . . Translated from the French by the Author. London: Daniel Isaac Eaton, 1795.

Letters from Paris, to the Citizens of the United States of America, on the System of Policy Hith-

erto Pursued by Their Government Relative to Their Commercial Intercourse with England and France, etc.* London: A Wilson, 1800.

Prospectus of a National Institution, to Be Established in the United States. Washington, D. C.: Samuel H. Smith, 1806.

Letter to Henry Gregoire, Bishop, Senator, Compte of the Empire and Member of the Institute of France, in Reply to His Letter on the Columbiad. Washington, D. C.: Roger Chew Weightman, 1809.

Oration Delivered at Washington, July Fourth, 1809; at the Request of the Democratic Citizens of the District of Columbia. Washington, D. C.: Roger Chew Weightman, 1809.

A Review of Robert Smith's Address to the People of the United States. Originally Published in the National Intelligencer. Philadelphia: John Binns, 1811.

Cantor, Milton. "A Connecticut Yankee in a Barbary Court: Joel Barlow's Algerian Letters to His Wife." *William and Mary Quarterly,* 19:86–109 (1962).

COLLECTED WORKS

Bottorff, William, and Arthur Ford, eds. *The Works of Joel Barlow.* 2 vols. Gainesville, Fla.: Scholars' Facsimiles and Reprints, 1970.

BIBLIOGRAPHIES

Blanck, Jacob. "Joel Barlow." In *Bibliography of American Literature,* vol. I. New Haven: Yale University Press, 1955. Pp. 169–84.

Spiller, Robert E. et al. *Literary History of the United States: Bibliography.* New York and London: Macmillan, 1974. Pp. 396–98.

BIOGRAPHICAL AND CRITICAL STUDIES

Adams, M. Ray. "Joel Barlow, Political Romanticist." *American Literature,* 9:113–52 (1937).

Arner, Robert D. "Joel Barlow's Poetics: 'Advice to a Raven in Russia.'" *Connecticut Review,* 5, no. 2:38–43 (1972).

———. "The Smooth and Emblematic Song: Joel Barlow's *The Hasty Pudding." Early American Literature,* 7:76–91 (1972).

———. "The Connecticut Wits." In *American Literature, 1764–1789, the Revolutionary Years,* edited by Everett Emerson. Madison: University of Wisconsin Press, 1977. Pp. 233–52.

Ball, Kenneth R. "Joel Barlow's 'Canal' and Natural Religion." *Eighteenth-Century Studies,* 2:225–39 (1969).

———. "American Nationalism and Esthetics in Joel Barlow's Unpublished 'Diary—1788.'" *Tennessee Studies in Literature,* 15:49–60 (1970).

Blau, Joseph L. "Joel Barlow, Enlightened Religionist." *Journal of the History of Ideas,* 10:430–44 (1949).

Boynton, P. H. "Joel Barlow Advises the Privileged Orders." *New England Quarterly,* 12:477–99 (1939).

Brant, Irving. "Joel Barlow, Madison's Stubborn Minister." *William and Mary Quarterly,* 15:438–51 (1958).

Christensen, Merton A. "Deism in Joel Barlow's Early Work: Heterodox Passages in *The Vision of Columbus." American Literature,* 27:509–20 (1956).

Durden, Robert F. "Joel Barlow in the French Revolution." *William and Mary Quarterly,* 8:327–54 (1951).

Ford, Arthur L. *Joel Barlow.* New York: Twayne Publishers, 1971.

Griffith, John. "*The Columbiad* and *Greenfield Hill:* History, Poetry, and Ideology in the Late Eighteenth Century." *Early American Literature,* 10:235–50 (1975).

Howard, Leon. *The Vision of Joel Barlow.* Los Angeles: Grey Bow Press, 1937.

———. "Joel Barlow and Napoleon." *Huntington Library Quarterly,* 2:37–51 (1938).

———. *The Connecticut Wits.* Chicago: University of Chicago Press, 1943.

Leary, Lewis. "Joel Barlow and William Hayley." *American Literature,* 21:325–34 (1949).

Lizanich, Christine M. "'The March of This Government': Joel Barlow's Unwritten History of the United States." *William and Mary Quarterly,* 33:315–30 (1976).

Parrington, Vernon Louis, ed. *The Connecticut Wits.* Hamden, Conn.: Archon, 1926.

Pearce, Roy Harvey. "Toward an American Epic." *Hudson Review,* 12:362–77 (1959).

———. *The Continuity of American Poetry.* Princeton, N.J.: Princeton University Press, 1961.

Richardson, Robert D., Jr. "The Enlightenment View of Myth and Joel Barlow's *Vision of Columbus.*" *Early American Literature,* 13:34–44 (1978).

Tichi, Cecelia. *New World, New Earth: Environmental Reform in American Literature from the Puritans Through Whitman.* New Haven: Yale University Press, 1979.

Todd, Charles B. *Life and Letters of Joel Barlow.* New York: G. P. Putnam, 1886.

Tyler, Moses Coit. *Three Men of Letters.* New York: G. P. Putnam, 1895.

Woodress, James. *A Yankee's Odyssey: The Life of Joel Barlow.* Philadelphia: J. B. Lippincott, 1958.

Zunder, Theodore. *The Early Days of Joel Barlow.* New Haven: Yale University Press, 1934.

BACKGROUND READING

Howard, Leon. "The Late Eighteenth Century: An Age of Contradictions." In *Transitions in American Literary History,* edited by Harry Hayden Clark. Durham, N.C.: Octagon Books, 1954. Pp. 51–89.

Nye, Russell B. *The Cultural Life of the New Nation, 1776–1830.* New York: Harper and Brothers, 1960.

Parrington, Vernon Louis. *Main Currents in American Thought.* 3 vols. New York: Harcourt Brace, 1927–30.

Silverman, Kenneth. *A Cultural History of the American Revolution.* New York.: T. Y. Crowell, 1976.

Simpson, Lewis P., ed. *The Federalist Literary Mind.* Baton Rouge: Louisiana State University Press, 1962.

Spencer, Benjamin T. *The Quest for Nationality.* Syracuse, N.Y.: Syracuse University Press, 1957.

—JEFFREY WALKER

R. P. Blackmur

1904—1965

IN 1937 the poet John Holmes put a question to his friend R. P. Blackmur. Holmes wanted to know "was there always a close relation between what a man makes of his own life and what he writes?" This question is central for Blackmur's achievement. He himself was at pains to obscure the relation between his life and work. "Whatever the lack" in Samuel Butler, he conceded in an early review for *Hound & Horn,* "we should not have had Butler without it." But the lack remained mysterious, and the reviewer was satisfied to leave it at that. Echoing Oscar Wilde, he said more than once how the artist is interesting only in what he makes, being totally uninteresting in what he is. Blackmur's devotion went to art for its own sake. He was in spirit a man of the Yellow Nineties, and that is the appropriate matrix in which to locate the New Critical method he sponsored.

His distrust of biography rose from more than aesthetic conviction, however. He did not know how you got to the heart of the matter. Behind what he called "the indurated New England exterior," he maintained an impenetrable reserve. This was by choice and from personal need. "In men of reticent habit," he wrote, comparing Blaise Pascal and Henry Adams, "it is the spiritual that is reserved even more closely than the emotional. Mere temper,

any of the products of irritation, might be permitted freely to air, but spirit and emotion had to be forced out and through channels that offered the look of remoteness." For Blackmur these channels were poetry, criticism, and fiction, where fiction means the aura in which he dressed himself no less than the words he put on paper. The most scrupulous exegete among the New Critics, he made his life into myth. The compelling fictions he created were the yield and the condition of his own impairment.

As a young man, Blackmur had wanted to go to Harvard. His unhappy childhood pushed him in other directions, however, and he never got through high school. This was a source of continuing disappointment, and characteristically he turned it to his credit. Having in himself (as he wrote of William Butler Yeats) a coldness or remoteness at the core, he warmed himself or discovered a center by dramatizing types as if they were individuals. He was the type of the scapegrace who has made an unexpected success, and friends took his dramatic version of the life at face value. Leslie Fiedler in a short story pictured Blackmur as having been thrown out of school "into the lap of literature" because he had written a term paper on self-abuse in the Old Testament. The crime of Onan, he had his Blackmurian hero insist, wasn't masturbation but simple birth control by withholding. On

Blackmur's own account, his high school principal had caught him reading Tobias Smollett, a "vulgar" novelist, and forbade him to return. He was remembering and outdoing his friend John Brooks Wheelwright, who liked to tell how he himself had been dismissed from Harvard for misspelling a word. Blackmur thought he could spin a better yarn than this.

In fact Blackmur had quarreled bitterly with the headmaster of the Cambridge High and Latin School, which would not take him back unless he apologized. He did not apologize, and his formal education ended in the fall term of his junior year. He was failing all his subjects at the time of his expulsion. This was not from want of interest in books, but rather from the things his instructors said about the books he was reading. From early childhood, he had haunted the public library in Cambridge. He had all the time he wanted to read on his own. Until he was almost nine, his mother kept him from school. She was his instructor, in cosseting ways his protector, and the close relation between them lasted until she died in old age, only two years before he died. Often she dressed him like a little girl, and she saw that his hair was cut long, like a girl's. He was the oldest of her five children and the one she loved best.

Already marriage had begun to go sour for Helen Palmer Blackmur when her first child was born, in Springfield, Massachusetts, on January 21, 1904. A career in medicine was what she had hoped for, and she prepared for this career at the Cambridge High and Latin School and after that at the Sargent School of Physical Education. She was just into her twenties and full of great expectations when she met and married George Edward Blackmur, an Englishman by birth and a rebellious but faltering kind of man more than twice her age. Helen Palmer's family tree went back to the Revolution, with roots in Fairfield, Maine. The family was in the Blue Book. Both her father

and her grandfather were celebrated Episcopal preachers, and her father's pastoral life reflected an unswerving commitment to duty. The man she chose for a husband followed the promptings of his wayward spirit. This made for a corrosive marriage and left an enduring stain on young Richard Blackmur.

About 1905, Blackmur's father took his wife and infant son to New York City. There he worked as a stockbroker on Wall Street, and there Ted and George, Richard's younger brothers, were born. After five years the move turned out abortive, and the family went back to Cambridge. In the dreary years that followed, Richard's mother was pretty much the sole support of the family. She ran a boardinghouse on Irving Street, near the Harvard Yard, while Richard's father failed successively as a wool broker and manufacturer's salesman specializing in children's toys. The birth of two daughters, Helen and Elizabeth, kept the marriage going. But having children did not make a marriage. It didn't make a family either, except in name's sake. Richard quarreled early with his dignified and reclusive father, and the two remained at swords' points all his young life. When George Edward Blackmur died in 1940, his embittered son declined to go to the funeral. Early stories, only thinly disguised as stories, tell of the bitterness. To the friends of his maturity, Blackmur said nothing of his childhood. For all they knew, he might have been an airborne spore. You can make out in this, obscurely but suggestively, the impinging of the life on the work. The artist, as the New Critic conceived him, was like the God of the Creation, knowable only in what he created.

In the fourth grade, Blackmur entered the Peabody Grammar School. He did not cut much of a figure there or later at his mother's old high school. After his expulsion in 1918 he lived at home, keeping himself in pocket by stirring sodas and clerking for bookstores in

Cambridge and for the Widener Library at Harvard. He did this for seven years, cherishing the genius he was sure he possessed but that only a few friends suspected. It does not seem fanciful to see him as like young John Milton in the six years' apprenticeship at Horton.

Blackmur was poor in all the visible marks of success. His life was rich in fantasy, though, and he covered the walls of his attic room on Irving Street with lurid scenes from Dante's *Inferno*. In his own eyes he figured as a Byronic hero who has sampled every vicious pleasure and has the taste of dust and ashes in his mouth. (It never left him.) Or he saw himself, being so poor as to want blankets for his bed, as the indolent scion of a wealthy Cambridge family. Sometimes he was Percy Bysshe Shelley the would-be tyrannicide (with his Harvard friend Jorge Mañach he planned to go to Cuba to blow up Machado's dictatorship), and in the attic room he constructed a chemistry lab and amused himself by setting off explosions. Often alone, he went for weeks without speaking. Long letters to his closest friend and cousin-by-adoption, George Anthony Palmer, dwell on the loneliness and tell how he entertained it by writing poems and stories and by courting Tessa Gilbert, the daughter of the composer Henry Gilbert. In 1922 Richard's favorite uncle, George Munroe Palmer, who had married George Anthony's mother, killed himself. For Blackmur this event was cataclysmic. It shrouded the last years of his boyhood in a melancholy whose source he never divulged (except in private journals) and never shook off altogether.

Here is a version of Blackmur in these years: "Born poor . . . he got just enough education to raise him from one state of society, and not enough—or not enough wealth to go with it—to adapt him to another state of society. Socially . . . he hung all his life suspended."

(Blackmur in his twenties was reflecting on D. H. Lawrence, a writer he detested, finding in him at a guess a disquieting version of himself.) "As economic society could not accept him, so neither church nor chapel was of much use to a mind self-trained in an age of liberalism stultified by wealth." By temperament Lawrence was profoundly religious, but formal religion left him an outsider. Sick all his life, he was an outsider in his body, too. Blackmur concluded his brief character of Lawrence: "He was not only an outsider but a fugitive. . . . Genius was his agonized resource."

Blackmur's luck took a turn for the better in 1925. With his future brother-in-law Wallace Dickson, he opened a bookstore in Cambridge. Although the partnership of Dickson & Blackmur, Sellers of New and Used Books, lasted only a year, it had important consequences. Selling books put the young man in the way of Maurice Firuski, the proprietor of the Dunster House Book Shop in Cambridge. When Blackmur's venture failed, he caught on with Firuski. He learned shorthand and how to keep the books, and for two years he clerked for Firuski and served him as secretary. He read incessantly in these years, making his soul; he filled notebooks with poetry; and he developed his taste in music under the tutelage of Robert Donaldson Darrell, the creator in 1926 of the *Phonograph Monthly Review*. The small body of essays that Blackmur contributed to this periodical—they range in subject from Igor Stravinsky to the makers of Gregorian chant—adumbrate faithfully his lifelong preoccupation with form.

Chaos was the milieu in which Blackmur lived. Unlike his model failures among the poets, D. H. Lawrence and Hart Crane (as he presented them later), he did not give himself to chaos. He stretched his reason to include it, so brought chaos to heel. Rational intent was what he wanted to evangelize in the arts, he said: " . . . rational statement, and rational technique; and I want to do it through technical judgment, and the judgment of discovery, which together I call rational judgment." You hear him protesting too much. But he had something in him to fear.

In 1928 his friends Lincoln Kirstein and Bernard Bandler appointed him editor of the *Hound & Horn,* which became the best and most successful of the little magazines, after the demise of the *Dial* the following year. Blackmur lost this job in 1930 but continued to appear frequently in the *Hound & Horn* until it ceased publication in 1934. His literary essays of the late 1920's and early 1930's—notably on T. S. Eliot, Wallace Stevens, E. E. Cummings, and Henry James—established his reputation as among the foremost American critics. Nobody has ever done more handsomely by these writers than Blackmur. He was not swelling the chorus of praise either. He began the chorus.

So he had his foot on the ladder. Ambition consumed him, said his fellow editor A. Hyatt Mayor, and he did not live much except in the mind. But his body, a sort of appendage, clamored for attention. He put it like that in letters to his cousin, and on June 14, 1930—after much backing and filling—he hearkened to his body and married the painter Helen Dickson. For most of the next ten years they spent winters in the West End of Boston and summers in the Dickson farmhouse near Harrington, Maine. The experience of Maine changed Blackmur's life. He became an expert gardener and subsisted largely on what he grew and what he took from the sea. He cultivated an ear for country speech and country pieties, and this shows in his poetry, as in his fiction and his critical prose. You would never guess that the self-anointed State-of-Maine man had grown up on city streets and had never plucked a flower or put his hand to the soil until he was well into

his twenties. The taxonomy of flowers, Latin names included, absorbed him, and his urban past receded and finally disappeared from view. Friends like Edmund Wilson thought him a lobster fisherman in his beginnings, or a backwoods carpenter who had educated himself by reading prodigiously in his spare time. Blackmur did not make it his business to correct these impressions.

Fame but not fortune was just over the horizon. In 1935 Blackmur's first book appeared. This was a gathering of twelve critical essays, mostly on modern poets, and was called, appropriately, *The Double Agent.* The title signifies the neutral critic who is neither fish nor flesh but partakes of them both. He has no "views," his allegiance does not go to theories or to causes, only to the matter in hand. With this book, said Allen Tate, Blackmur "invented" the New Criticism in America. The New Critical method meant essentially sitting down before a text with absolute patience and humility, so encouraging the words to give up their sense. The critic, Blackmur said, "treats of nothing in literature except in its capacity of reduction to literary fact." Biographical and social contexts were not scanted exactly—the ideal New Critic was, like John Crowe Ransom, Allen Tate, and Blackmur, a deep scholar—only the work itself got primary consideration. Blackmur did not read the work as "an elongation of the poet's self." It was independent of the poet, having within itself "a rational structure which controls, orders, and composes in external or objective form the material of which it is made." In this collection, as in *The Expense of Greatness* (1940), the unblinking eye, backed by the dictionary, was Blackmur's instrument for elucidating the figure a poem makes. He made them part of the critic's paraphernalia.

An almost obsessive preoccupation with language and its meaning enlivens his first book of poetry, *From Jordan's Delight* (1937). Not the self, but the world, represented by the rocky island off the Maine coast that gave Blackmur his exotic title, functions as his point of departure in these poems, and that is all to the good. His early masters in poetry were T. S. Eliot and Ezra Pound, and in his juvenilia he imitated them slavishly. Blackmur became a poet as imitation gave way to expropriation. In these poems he speaks not in his own voice but in the Down East idiom he had practiced and made his own; and the result, said Tate, was "the best American poetry of the decade." Looking back, this seems a tenable judgment. Most readers have not been inclined to look back, or perhaps the makers of anthologies have neglected their business, and Blackmur's poetry is little noticed today. That is an oversight that time will put right. The level of quality goes up and down in Blackmur's three volumes of poetry, but the proportion of good things is very high.

Blackmur made at least half a dozen permanent poems. In execution and by intention, his best poems are modest. He liked the short line. He was a formalist, writing in a time when many poets (as his friend John Crowe Ransom has it) were taking free verse as the inevitable form of the flux of the matter. Blackmur disputed the inevitability of this. In his poems, as he wrote of the medieval mystics, "reason was stretched to include disorder and achieved mystery." The achievement depended, at least for him, on projecting or ordering "the chaos of private experience . . . in a form external to the consciousness that entertained it in flux." (It did not occur to him that free verse might offer a projection of this form.) Mostly he wins your suffrage as he appeals to the ear—paradoxically the source of his "rational structure." But never mind the paradox, Blackmur's ear was infallible. In the peculiar excellence of his poetry, and in its limitation, he harks back to early

poets like Charles Sedley, Richard Lovelace, Charles Cotton, and Henry King. This is the company he keeps.

Ideas were a will-o'-the-wisp for the autodidact, however, and as he got older he chased them, to his mortification. You see this in his poetry of the 1940's—in *The Second World* (1942) and *The Good European* (1947), where a growing dependence upon abstraction displaces the concreteness that validates the poems of *From Jordan's Delight*. The swapping of the lowercase for the capital-letter "Thing" weakens the later criticism too. With the outbreak of World War II and increasingly in the postwar period, Blackmur began to cultivate the prophetic and evangelizing mode. Criticism of fiction was not his strongest suit, but the great European fiction of the nineteenth and twentieth centuries attracted him irresistibly and with mounting force, as it constituted a vast "censorium" of ideas. From the eighteenth century on, he wrote, the novel "has had the charge of organizing all our disorders into theoretic forms of life." The novel fulfilled this charge not as it was theoretic but, rather, as it was parochial. Blackmur did not say this; and when he gave his attention to the great organizing genre, as in *Eleven Essays in the European Novel* (1964), he committed a sin that was unpardonable for him: he considered his material in translation. Inevitably his patented adherence to the text was a casualty of this reading-at-a-remove. Perhaps he thought that the social and political bias of his later writing and the amplifying in it of what he called the "heuristic" voice offered adequate compensation. But the loss was greater than the gain. In *The Lion and the Honeycomb* (1955) and *A Primer of Ignorance* (1967) the disappearance of the old "myopic" fixity (as hostile readers saw it) makes you feel how a great critic is losing his way. There is plenty of luminous writing in these books but not much meticulous analysis. You could say that late Blackmur suffers not from a dearth but a plenitude of inspiration, where inspiration works out to self-indulgence.

Blackmur, in his own view, was destined for greatness not only as a poet but also as a novelist and playwright. In the 1920's and 1930's he worked heroically at short stories, novels, and plays. He failed at this labor and it isn't hard to see why. Many years later he and W. H. Auden shared a radio talk at the University of Massachusetts. The subject was Henry James, the novelist Blackmur loved above all others. "There is a sense," he said, speaking of James, "in which the heroes of a man's work are himself." This is certainly true. But the more important truth—throughout his career Blackmur insisted on it almost hysterically— says how the artist, in his heroes and villains, estranges himself from himself. Gilbert Osmond, the neutered expatriate of *The Portrait of a Lady* (1881), who treats people as things, is Henry James—but at art's length, what this writer might have been. Blackmur in his fiction dispenses with art's length. He looks in the mirror, and what he sees is merely personal—so in the extreme case, nobody's business but his. Philosophizing, the fatal attending on ideas, came more easily to Blackmur than making the truth incarnate. In the achieved work of art, he said—his point was to the poetry of Emily Dickinson—you had to translate ideas "to the terms and modes of the imagination." Prescribing was not the same as achieving, however.

Blackmur had high hopes for two of his plays—one a funny and rancorous version of life in the boardinghouse on Irving Street, the other an account of Charles Lindbergh, the hero as fugitive whose fabulous success turns to dust and ashes. Blackmur's characters in these plays dance about each other without ever taking hands. This mimics the isolation that enveloped their creator. Writers who are locked in

the prison of themselves do not find the theater congenial, and usually what they write declares their skeptical view of the chance for personal communion. Blackmur at theater dramatized this view, and the result was predictable. Attempts to secure a Broadway production for his mordant essays-in-autobiography came to nothing.

At fiction also, Blackmur made a valorous failure. His first novel, "King Pandar," was rejected by fifteen publishers before he stopped sending it around. In the equivocal hero whom the title stigmatizes he presented himself; and friends like Florence Codman, who had published his first critical books, shifted uneasily when they read him in manuscript. Blackmur's surrogate, the Boston lawyer, Henry King, uses his words "with a deep piety of demeanor, as a man uses the long-sought sight of the sea." Blackmur was rusticating in Maine when he wrote this; the eminent years at Princeton were still remote in time, but already his hero makes you think of the Princeton professor. "He yawned, and, always a public figure in his own eyes, caught himself up, stroking his chin." Entering court, he "felt his face grow vitally public, and he could not help putting on the manner and mask of a personage." The critical verdict on "King Pandar" said it was "a bad book well written."

Blackmur's inability to escape from himself persists and deepens in his second novel. He called it "The Greater Torment," intending the comparative to speak of love surfeited as against love unfulfilled. In the misadventures, mostly sexual, of the rarefied physician who is all there is for hero, the life and hard times of Richard Blackmur are replicated. Blackmur's failing marriage is everywhere apparent and too painful to contemplate, not least for him. Having blocked out three books—he describes them in a lengthy synopsis—he broke off with only a first book completed. Friends found even this first book stronger medicine than they wanted to swallow. Florence Codman had no quarrel with romans à thèse so long as the thesis stayed in the background and you could say at the end, "There's a humaneness, a richness of interest, a pleasure." She heard herself saying, when she got to the end: "Neither moon, nor sun, nor any stars shone there."

Perhaps failure looks inevitable only in retrospect, and that is partly true for Blackmur at fiction. In his novels, as in the surviving short stories, the ear for dialogue is often sharp and the eye for prosaic detail acute. He saw the world clearly and he got it down on paper (when ideas do not blot out the palpable world). But the essential stuff in which he was trading, being personal, shows as fictitious. Mere reality will always come home as fictitious, and commands assent only as it makes an artistic coherence in which the author's life plays no evident part. Blackmur the critic did not have to be told. His comment on a bad novel of the 1920's sums up his own partial success: "The small jewels are real, the big are glass."

Blackmur did better when he went afield for his subject. The great labor of the 1930's and after was his projected life of Henry Adams. To write this book, he received a Guggenheim Fellowship in 1938, which was renewed a year later. During the Princeton years Blackmur continued to work on the book, and from time to time he plundered his manuscript for publication in the little magazines. At his death he left a huge fragment of more than six hundred pages. This fragment lacks both a formal beginning and the coda Blackmur kept promising to write. But it makes a great book, also a finished book, except as the author designed it.

Blackmur's evocation of the High Middle Ages is the living heart of the book, and in eloquence and passion is unsurpassed—perhaps unequaled—elsewhere in his prose. In the essay he entitled sourly "A Feather-Bed for Critics,"

he said how the writer requires a deep collaboration between himself and society. This, for once only, Blackmur achieved. The collaboration, recorded in the life of Adams, "is marked by the unity . . . [that the writer and society] make together, and by the culture which the individual, by the act of his convicted imagination, brings to light." Medieval culture is Blackmur's ideal subject because it is unassuming, impersonal, and catholic. So with rare force it "convicted" him where he lived. He wrote in his Japanese lectures: "When you get maturity of imagination and of intellect . . . balance without loss of passion or vitality, you get great literature and great criticism, or let us say, criticism that has become a part of literature." This phrase defines what he made.

Himself a bifurcated man always in danger of coming apart, Blackmur celebrated in the medieval period a perfect stasis that held for a little while, then disappeared forever. Like Adams, he saw how the radiant energy or emotion that aspiring minds must feel toward the universe is expressed in some periods as intellectual understanding and in others as sexual love. This preferring of alternative modes of expression meant that the human equation was almost always imperfect. There were, however, those rare periods "when there is no clear dominance on either side, when, rather, a double effort is made with such intensity that a kind of vital, shaking balance is struck where both imaginative and rational faith make a single, and full—if perilous—equilibrium." The vital, shaking balance of which Blackmur wrote and which he located in the art, religion, and philosophy of the twelfth and thirteenth centuries is persuasive because aloof from himself. Finding his point of purchase, he was able to move the world. In this book the double agent transacts his proper business. Working both sides of the street, he pays homage to both, and the sum of what he honors is greater than the parts that compose it. Blackmur's best criticism is like the best of the book, objective or impersonal, hence ascending to art. What is a critic's business? he asked inferentially, and answered: to see "with supreme attention not only the actual but also . . . the values that enlighten the actual as the actual grounds the values. This is critical labour."

Subjective feeling taints the biography of Adams, however. Its intrusion made the book a cross for the biographer to bear as well as a crowning glory. For half his life, Blackmur sought to come to terms with his ambiguous hero. He identified with Adams the indurated man—in the words of his wife Marian Adams just before she killed herself, "such a man as God might envy." Struggle as he might, Blackmur could not get free from his personal involvement with the guilty husband and the stricken wife in whom he saw his own wife. The involvement, extending to complicity in Marian Adams' suicide, determined his inability to bring the book to conclusion. He was like Daedalus as Vergil tells of him, grieving for the death of Icarus and trying, unsuccessfully, to work the fall in gold. The failure envelops the life of Adams in mystery. What is missing from the book is what the artificer wanted most of all to record. Along the way, though, he found an unexpected success, and this is emblematic of the incidental nature of his craft.

Only slightly less ambitious was Blackmur's endeavor to write the definitive study of Henry James. In 1940 he signed a contract for the James book with New Directions, but doubt began to assail him almost at once. "You see," he wrote to his publisher Jay Laughlin, "James is a man I feel at home with." This meant that he was troubled by "NOT saying too much, NOT making out the wonderful problems I feel in him always." He had intended a "shortish book," but he wrote in 1943 how the book "grows in prospect." Not seeing how to keep it short, he let it run into the sand.

Part of the book got written as essays on the ghost stories and on the artist in James's fiction—not for Laughlin but for little magazines like *Accent* and the *Kenyon Review*. But even the essays made Blackmur climb the wall. He feared they were too long for magazine publication. "But I cannot do anything about cutting them," he said, and he was unwilling for anyone else to cut them. The amputation he dreaded seemed almost physical, and James an extension of himself. When James spoke slightingly of Leo Tolstoy's "loose and baggy monsters," Blackmur showed in an essay how to turn this phrase back on its maker. But that did not argue a fault, or else the fault hinted at virtue. Reading over what he had written, he felt "both the warmth and distrust that go with affection rise" in him, "two tides at once." Importunate editors, appealing to the affection, could almost always rely on "the Jacobean visible sign" of assent. (Laughlin was the unlucky exception.) Blackmur's health was failing when he agreed to edit a collection of American short novels for the Crowell series—*Washington Square* being one—but he finished the job "despite my talent for the dilatory, and the processional squallings of my liver." By then he was nearing sixty, and his youthful enthusiasm had not abated but strengthened with years.

James was one of the twin stars in Blackmur's firmament from the early 1920's until he died. (Adams was the other.) Already in the 1930's he told Morton Zabel at *Poetry* magazine that he had enjoyed "more than any criticism I have written" the piece he did for *Hound & Horn* on James's prefaces. He thought it "also my most useful piece." The novels and tales had begun to absorb him when he was only a boy. On a summer evening in 1922, having finished his first reading of *The Wings of the Dove,* he sat down "in an obscure richness of emotion" and tried to say what he had learned or what his reading corroborated, as the problems James canvassed met his sense of his own problems. Style came first and last—"the soft voices . . . [James] so well composed"; the murmured but perfected conversations "one can never hope, in any society, to hear"; the beautiful voice "impressed on the, we admit, somewhat strained, audition." The syntax was what he learned and unconsciously parodied. It remained a lifelong addiction. The sense of James—his own anguished sense—Blackmur already had by heart. This was "the sure necessity, before sentient life, of despair." The book, charged with cumulative authority ("vraie vérité"), convicted him of emptiness, "a void in the heart . . . all that the roll of surf reveals." His cousin George Anthony Palmer, to whom he was writing, knew that mournful sound: he and young Richard had heard it often as they sat together, watching the sun rise over the ocean at Lynn, Massachusetts. It said that, in the core, "victory is no more than defeat." James's novel constituted a long gloss on this saying. "The novel is a growth—a change from a surety and a hope to frustration and despair."

The change for the worse did not preclude elation, and this is worth emphasizing. Blackmur was not a sentimentalist, but got much satisfaction from despair. In 1962, in an inspired piece of hack writing, he remembered his first encounter with James. Alimony payments and then his new house in Princeton kept him short in the purse; and he took commissions he had no time for, sometimes staying up all night to fulfill them. This essay was the product of one of those times. "When I was first told, in 1921, to read something of Henry James," he began—characteristically, he moved the date back a year; it made him younger, so more prodigious:

I went to the Cambridge Public Library looking, I think, for *The Portrait of a Lady*. It was out. The day was hot and muggy, so that from the card catalogue I selected as the most cooling

title *The Wings of the Dove,* and on the following morning, a Sunday, even hotter and muggier, I began, and by the stifling midnight had finished my first elated reading of that novel. Long before the end I knew a master had laid hands on me. The beauty of the book bore me up; I was both cool and waking; excited and effortless; nothing was any longer worth while and everything had become necessary. A little later, there came outside the patter and the cooling of a shower of rain and I was able to go to sleep, both confident and desperate in the force of art.

Exhilaration marks the tone of this essay. Its burden, however, is "the dumb part of despair," which Blackmur defined elsewhere as "the menace of life itself." These are nebulous terms, though doubtless felt by the writer, and you can see how they make trouble for fiction. The great advantage of plot, Blackmur said, especially when you mean "to mirror or represent the ultimate conflicts of the spirit," is that the words released or precipitated by the crises of your story will, "however ordinary in themselves, gather from the plot an extraordinary or maximum force of meaning." He himself was mostly innocent of plot, so when he turns to fiction, his words live only in air. In 1961, Blackmur got a letter from a doctor in Grand Rapids, Michigan, who addressed him as an "authority" on James. The doctor wanted to know what ailed Milly Theale, the heroine of *The Wings of the Dove.* "I believe that she died of leukemia," he said. "But why didn't James ever say that she had a real illness?" Blackmur answered, ". . . about the leukemia: in James, people are ill of life." James would likely have assented to this. But the answer, for the purposes of fiction or medical practice, does not take us very far.

Blackmur had earlier allowed himself another go at the question. In the long essay he wrote for Robert Spiller's *Literary History of the United States* (1948), he saw the mysterious illness that destroyed James's heroine as having crippled the author as well. This illness, attacking James in his youth, wrought "a deep central damage . . . never repaired and never forgotten." You have the sense that Blackmur is the distressful subject here. The illness originated, he said, in "the experience of the immanence of overwhelming evil—the final menace to the self," and it barred the afflicted man not only from love and war but also from religion and history. So life remained "always perilous" for James. No need, perhaps, to draw the parallels fine.

Blackmur at this point took refuge in a cloud of unknowing. Forensic medicine did not have a name for the affliction he was describing. He allowed that it was virulent in James's villains, though, and he called it "the thing, whatever it is, that ruins loyalty, prevents love, sullies innocence—the morass in which some part of every human being is in a nameless mortal combat." Your identity was forfeit as you sank in this morass; Blackmur did not care to particularize further. It was right that James's injury should remain obscure, he said, "for it was only the outward sign of the inward mystery of his character, the sign of his having been barred from the direct experience . . . of human passion." The injury remained obscure, but so did the passion. Blackmur knew that we live by this passion, and always he saw it as corrosive. But it offered the only chance for escape from the prison of the self. The passion comes and goes—remembering Eliot in *The Waste Land*—and we think of the key, each confirmed in his prison. The question for Blackmur in his life and art is all but put in these reflections on the life of Henry James, shading as they do to autobiography. To what degree did he escape the prison of the self?

Blackmur's years as a free-lance critic and poet, living—often barely—by his wits, came to an end in 1940, when he accepted an appointment at Princeton University as assistant to Allen Tate in a newly constituted program in the creative arts. He took the job, he said, only to secure "the minimum necessities," and he expected to move on within a year. But the man who came to town as if he were passing through came at last to dwell in the sanctum sanctorum. Twenty-five years later he died in Princeton, on February 2, 1965.

It is easy to say that the university destroyed him. This is partly true. The harder truth is that Blackmur collaborated in his own destruction. Princeton was his fate and his desire. He was still a young man, thirty-six years old, when he joined the faculty, but his life was already more than half over and much of his best work was done. On the rest of his life the university put its seal. It offered him a rostrum; he used it and became a famous literary person. His fame depended mostly on the sibylline style that grew in him in the later years. This dark muttering describes Blackmur in Princeton, not the early Blackmur, and is not only his hallmark but his vice. To distinguish between them is not exactly to winnow the chaff. There is plenty of chaff in Blackmur, but the good and great things are inseparable from it. In his life and work he is a parti-colored man. His sin is patched with virtue and his virtue patched with sin.

In the beginning Blackmur jibbed at the unvaried routine of academic life, so different from the helter-skelter of his own life. He liked his informal sessions with the Princeton students and seeing Allen Tate and Caroline Gordon. He said he didn't like anything else. Tate, the first director of the creative arts program, had engineered his appointment. Later Tate came to regret this. He saw Blackmur as a cuckoo who had flown into his nest and fouled it, then taken the nest for himself. But Blackmur the ingratiating presence does not bear scrutiny. He got too much obvious pleasure from poking fun at the academic mind, "putting an inch rule on it," he said to Tate, "by way of amusement." One colleague recalled an evening when they played the dictionary game. "You open the book at random and consider the word on which your finger falls." On this occasion the word was "tenesmus," a medical term denoting the urgent need to urinate or defecate, with a straining but unsuccessful effort to do so. Great hilarity as Blackmur and friends identified various members of the faculty who, from their pinched facial expressions, must have suffered from this disease.

On his students Blackmur was less severe, though he wrote in his journal how they ate him alive. Except to himself, he did not remonstrate. Lincoln Kirstein, remembering how Blackmur used to play professor to the Harvard boys when he was clerking in the Dunster House Book Shop, thought him a born teacher. But Blackmur found formal teaching "a queer and monstrous thing." Here at Princeton, he complained to Delmore Schwartz—mistakenly he supposed that Delmore was happier at Harvard—"I get dipped so deep in the adolescent bath all week that I begin to sweat behind my ears." He was obliged to be "professionally stimulating, habitually seminal," so "the chances of masturbation ... [were] overwhelming." What was he going to say "about Shelley's West Wind or Crane's Melville's Tomb at two thirty tomorrow to make both those poems ring and wring, too, as they both should?"

After a while, Blackmur found things to say:

His speech was elliptical, inclining toward the runic, but his lectures were legendary—Poetics in the fall and Aesthetics in the spring, the same course, what he happened to bring to class in his Harvard bookbag—and once an hour he would come awake as from a private reverie with a dazzling penetration of text or motive.

To have him as a weekly presence in your life was everything, said Geoffrey Wolff in *The Duke of Deception* (1979). Not unexpectedly, his special province was diction. Words to him were "rubies, emeralds, diamonds, dogshit." Each possessed its own weight. The reality of language, he said, "is superior and anterior to the reality of the uses to which it is put." He was prodigal with words but jealous of them too, venerating their anterior power, and his students loved and feared him for this. "We find ourselves closer to you than anyone," two of them confessed in a letter of the 1950's, "perhaps closer than you yourself realize." But they had to struggle hard "to find a form or adjustment for even starting to talk" to the imperious presence.

Blackmur did not mean to be imperious. Detesting authority, he gave the students free rein. Perhaps his own bitter experience of school underlay the permissive manner and the insistence that you had to do it all on your own. Easy judgments were beneath him, though, and he made a tough critic of the fiction that his students submitted. Wolff was one of these students. Having completed his first novel, he went to Blackmur for sympathetic counsel. "Put it in your desk drawer," Blackmur said. This, Wolff supposed, was the old Horatian chestnut: leave the manuscript alone for a while, then come back to it fresh? "No," Blackmur said, "that is not my advice to you. My advice is to put it in your desk drawer, lock your desk drawer, lose the key to your desk drawer. However, keys are sometimes found, returned to their owners. This could happen, so I would set fire to your desk."

The rigor was real enough, partly the tough-guy pose was just that. If you sought out Blackmur not from weakness but from strength, you did not find it all that hard to get behind the indurated exterior. Strength in Blackmur answered to strength in his students. He liked them because their minds had not yet closed—always he felt drawn to what he called the "hospitable intellect"—and also because with young people he did not have to be on stage. He resented the compulsion "to act a series of caricatures of oneself, and then, in self-defense, to add to the series: it is as if one had always to keep the *extracted* promise and were never permitted to keep the *given* promise." On a lecture trip to the Middle West, he looked up a former student who had gone on to graduate school at Minnesota. They spent three hours together. They sat on the grass and talked about dogs— "dogs he had known—dogs I had known as a child." Later, at parties given for him by the faculty, who were there to kiss his hem, he said practically nothing. What on earth had he and his former student to say to each other, his frustrated colleagues wanted to know. The student was hard put to answer.

The newly minted academic remained an alien presence in the academy. Some colleagues took him up, and some of them became his close friends. This failed to appease Blackmur's sense of alienation. In his letters he said how distasteful it was to cater to the social whims of the faculty, buy evening clothes, entertain people he didn't want to know. He made them aware that he did not want to know them in that Calvin Coolidge way he had, the taciturnity that complemented the monologues. The "wonderfully expansive" man, said William S. Merwin, was also a man "wonderfully Yankee reserved."

Princeton stimulated both sides of Blackmur's nature. He thought "you'd have to live here to like it." He did not want to live in Princeton; neither did Pomfret, his cat. The receptions and the lectures induced boredom, so did the "flat, Polish" terrain of Mercer County. He himself presented New England; and Irving Howe recalled how he played "the role of small-town feller" to his cosmopolitan associates. He liked to highlight the contrast between his own education, a crazy quilt made anyhow, and that starchier thing dispensed at Old Nassau. He

was Ben Franklin, the type of the autodidact, who had got on despite the absence of the usual advantages—maybe because of their absence. Along the way, to hear him tell it, he had been blowing up the neighborhood with his chemistry set.

Blackmur played this role more easily since, on one side, he remained a provincial all his life. Confronting "the sharp abysmal difference that Princeton shows," he felt like a transient set down in a hotel. "You can have it," he wrote to the musicologist Robert Darrell. He looked back with regret to his three-story apartment on Chambers Street in the West End of Boston— dirty but palatial compared to Linden Lane with its bedbug-brown furniture veneered with boxwood on pulp—and his footloose life as a poet and critic. He had rather—"not starving"—live as he and his wife had lived in the 1930's. "I shall hope to return to doing so." That was how he ended his morose reflections on the new life.

The trouble was starving. Blackmur's early poverty left him profoundly respectful of money. In the boardinghouse in Cambridge, there was not always enough to eat. His mother in her youth was a beautiful woman, emaciated as she got older. She suffered from malnutrition, and so did he. Matthew Josephson remembered the brilliant youngster of nineteen or twenty to whom John Wheelwright introduced him—"skinny, emaciated-looking, very poor." Blackmur got through the Great Depression thanks partly to his wife and the paintings she did for the WPA. The 1940's had "looked very bad" to him, failing the help of Allen Tate. So he was grateful to Tate for "the wonderful title" of associate in creative arts at Princeton, and nervous when he heard that the English department had considered replacing them both with T. S. Eliot. Never mind his scorn for the academy, he wanted to be reappointed; he even played politics a little to that end, and after one semester he thought he could stand the "lone-liness and academic gossip" for "one more year." He got the reappointment, and he never left Princeton.

In some respects it was the perfect job. The faculty of the English department would not have put up with him had they considered him "just like themselves." But they were willing to put up with a man who was merely a writer. Blackmur said to his cousin George how this expressed their indifference to writing. He cared for little else, and cared terribly. In his lonely dedication he defined the outsider—in Irving Howe's phrase, a man "gallant, passion-ate, strange." The scruple of his mind drove him outside, at the same time gave value to his ec-centricity. His colleagues dwelt on the eccen-tricity, missing the rest. So he became their butt and they cautioned their students against him. A Ph.D., they supposed, "gave them a special place in the world." Blackmur had no Ph.D. and his place was a mystery. But as they de-spised him, they did not fear him, so left him alone. He saw the beauty of it, "that no one like me can be considered a professor au carrière." No matter how long he stayed in Princeton, he knew it would always be on a temporary basis. He called that a very good arrangement—"not because it diminishes responsibility but because it concentrates . . . [responsibility] entirely on what I teach." He was not vexed with the busywork that preoccupied the rest of the de-partment. "I am able, if I want," he told his cousin, "to keep myself on my toes precisely for my own work."

The sense of one's work takes color from the environment in which it is performed. No envi-ronment is more seductive than Princeton's, not least for those who feel themselves an alien presence. Albert Einstein, living across town from Blackmur at 112 Mercer Street, felt equally "estranged from the society here." Un-like Blackmur, he had no yearning for it, being more nearly secure in himself. Princeton he thought "a wonderful little spot, a quaint and ceremonious village of puny demigods on stilts." That is not what Blackmur's colleagues were saying when, in the mid-1940's, they gathered to discuss the relationship of the writer and the academy. "Why assume that life in a university is necessarily stultifying?" one of them asked. The question was rhetorical. "Princeton," said Professor X, "with its east end, west end, Italian section, negro section, etc. . . . could provide a Trollope with material for a life time of work." Blackmur, unhappily, put in his oar. "Or a Balzac!" he said.

Balzac and Blackmur's approbation notwith-standing, he had a difficult time catching on. Isolated among "the bland and heavy scholars" who ran the department to which he was only nominally attached (that is how his young friend A. Alvarez remembered him), he found his cronies mostly among sports like himself. Often they were Jewish—this, though you could say that Blackmur was anti-Semitic, not a particularly illuminating thing to say in the context of his own time. Almost "everyone" from Sheridan to Hemingway was unreflec-tively like him in this. Partly in his occasional *bêtises* he was aping the snobbish talk of his early friend March Wheelwright (as filtered through his reading of the archsnob Henry Adams), partly he was having on his liberal friends. They might have hooted him down, and they didn't. Anyway, some of his best friends were Jews. "You and I have a lot in common," he said to Philip Roth. "I'm a Maine Yankee and you're a New York Jew." Roth said, "New-ark Jew." But Blackmur meant seriously the asserting of a tie between them. Different him-self, he cultivated difference in others. He liked Irving Howe, "this odd bird with a radical background who aspired to literary things" and suffered from the chilliness of academic Prince-ton when he lived there in the 1940's and

1950's. The professors of English who gave him the back of their hand had their reasons, Howe thought. "I was a New Yorker. I was connected with the *Partisan Review* group, which made them uneasy. . . . And I was Jewish."

Professor X, on the Princeton that Trollope might have described, does not distinguish a Jewish community. Still, Princeton had always accommodated Jews. One of them—he came from New York—lived in "12 Univee" with Amory Blaine, the hero of F. Scott Fitzgerald's *This Side of Paradise* (1920). Blaine recalled how one night "they filled the Jewish youth's bed with lemon pie." This was fun. The Princeton Jew, like Robert Cohn in *The Sun Also Rises* (1926), was a figure of fun, sometimes a boor, by definition a little outré. The sprinkling of Jews who went to Princeton in Blackmur's time were left high and dry by the annual Bicker or fraternity rush, which denied them a bid to join the eating clubs on Prospect Street. Some became angry young men, like Ralph Schoenman, subsequently Bertrand Russell's private secretary, parading with his picket in front of Nassau Hall. No picket line formed behind him. Others, more or less fortunate, merged with the Princeton society that scorned them, effacing from their personality every trace of the nice Jewish boy from Bayonne. Blackmur, who was Anglo-Saxon all the way through, was also this nice Jewish boy. Later, in his essay on James Joyce's *Ulysses,* he told how the Jew is Everyman the outsider and how, "in each of us, in the exiled part, sits a Jew." He was thinking of himself.

To palliate the life of the exile, Blackmur made himself an ultramontanist, more papist than the pope or more zealous "in the nation's service" (a motto of the university) than Woodrow Wilson, who coined the phrase during his tenure as president of Princeton. This misapplied zeal—it denotes the man who is looking over his shoulder—accounts partly for the shift in Blackmur's writing from the meticulous criticism of the 1930's to the vatic pronouncements that characterize the Old Pretender.

In the small community to which he came in the middle of his life, there was more intelligence per square foot than anywhere else in America. Intelligence argues laissez-faire. John Wheeler the physicist, speaking into his portable Dictaphone as he walked along Springdale Road, was an unselfconscious figure. Nobody marked him—or Wigner or Oppenheimer or Panofsky. This was Princeton on its democratic side. Another side was Presbyterian, and on that side everyone marked you, like the colleague who got divorced and was sent away to Philadelphia—he was Ovid among the Goths. Time passed and the scandal cooled, and they let him come back again.

But Princeton was not exhausted in its dour morality. There was the bibulous Princeton, of which Blackmur was a mainstay, "the pleasantest country club in America." One of his former students, having it dinned into him that the university epitomized the life of the mind, believed at first that "student" derived from *studeo.* This proved a piece of simplicity. However, he wrote to Blackmur, "if you want a wife, a home, a car, a lot of names for cocktail parties (what a job Art 303 does), fine food at a Princeton eating club, it is still one of the top two or three universities." President Patton saw this Princeton, in an inspired gaffe, as dedicated to high living and plain thinking.

In Blackmur's Princeton, aesthetics and morality declared their connection. "Learning without piety is pernicious," said President Witherspoon when the university was mewing its youth. No one used just those words to Blackmur the novitiate. In the imagery of official pronouncements their sense was residual, though. Blackmur was not offered a teaching job at Princeton. He was "called," as to a clerical cure. His vocation, unsuspected by himself, was charismatic; it was like the accession of grace. Other men were not so lucky. Edmund Wilson, the favorite candidate of his old teacher Christian Gauss, never heard the call. Blackmur's associates found Wilson contentious. Francis Fergusson didn't suit them, so they sent him away. Erich Auerbach was lost to Yale. It was a wonder, thought Robert Fitzgerald, "that Princeton didn't hang on to him." But Princeton was a small pond, so looked mistrustfully on the exotic species.

You wonder, then, how Richard Blackmur made the grade. He had no formal credentials. In appearance he struck no sparks except for his dandyism, and that counted against him. An acquaintance of his in Cambridge would not have put him on a list of the hundred persons he thought most likely to succeed. The young man Seán O'Faoláin first encountered as an editor of the *Hound & Horn* was substantially the man who came to Princeton, "slight, slim, reticent, patient, rather romantic looking." O'Faoláin looked around for his Keatsian or Rossettian mistress. There wasn't one.

At social functions the young man didn't circulate, he sat because "he was too thin to circulate, too thin in the rear, being but a flat bag under the coattails." This description, from an unpublished story Blackmur wrote in his twenties, is just right, except that as he got older he developed a compensating paunch. His own ear instructed him that "he declaimed in a voice whose very restraint was sonorous," the voice of the old lion emitting what Blackmur called the hymn in the throat. But the tiny, dime-shaped mouth—Blackmur's early sweetheart thought she heard it saying "piss and prunes"—was too small for the long words that came out of it. Dick, said Wheelwright, "had a mouth so small he had to feed himself with a pin." Above the mouth bristled the dark mustache, the smallest mustache Mark Van Doren ever saw.

Blackmur's appearance, bristling and con-

stricted, reflected the man who took shelter behind it. This man was beleaguered. You meet him in his cramped handwriting, tiny, immaculate, as tight as the phone book. The autograph versions of his two novels so crowd the small quarto pages he used as to make your head spin when you read them. These manuscripts are finished in every detail, and run only half as long as the typewritten copies he prepared for his literary agent. He did not blot a line, but had nothing about him of the poet's fine frenzy. Words, when he composed, came with agonizing slowness, like birdlime from frieze. "It always takes me time to think thought," he wrote apologetically to William Phillips at the *Partisan Review*. This vice (as he saw it) was also a virtue. His best writing fairly breathes deliberation. But the writing, as it is costive, speaks of the man who could never bring himself to throw anything away. The power to discriminate was not part of his power, a strange thing to say of this absolute critic. He suffered, said Eileen Simpson, from paralysis of the will. Merest trivia weighed with him as heavily as heartfelt recollection; and when he died, his house was cluttered with yellowing injunctions like that from the Boston Five Cents Savings Bank, telling how payment of rent was expected for the dwelling at 50 Chambers Street "now occupied by you." It had been twenty-five years since he lived there.

Northrop Frye sensed about him a deep insecurity. He was touched, however, by the fact that Blackmur never tried to conceal this "but made it an integral part of his relationships." Partly this meant a disingenuous candor. He told tales on himself as if he were letting you in on his secret. Mostly, the tales were fictitious. Princeton afflicted him, so did his wife and mother, but he leaned on them all for emotional support. He feared driving a car, Francis Fergusson said. So he never owned one, but took cabs as a gentleman should. He hated to move, and when he ventured out of Princeton to teach at Cambridge University in 1961–1962, he barely made it through the year. Friends who saw him in England wrote how the year away gave him fits. Middle age overtook him before he could bring himself to travel abroad. He did this twice, in 1952–1953 and again four years later. He might have been Marco Polo, the way he went on about his travels.

But the insecure man could fix you with a look wry or quizzical that made you squirm. His eyes were astonishing, not the mad electric eyes of Kenneth Burke or mad Shelley but imperious eyes that danced and flared with pain or malice. "When I start talking too much," said Delmore Schwartz to Blackmur, "let your eyes blaze at me as I have seen them do." Ask him about poetry—a question couched in capital letters—and he looked down his mustache, not deigning to reply. You remembered the twist of his mouth. To those he loved he was often cruel, not loving them less. When the black bile rose in him, he could annihilate a friend. Kingsley Amis, he said, looked at the upper classes through a periscope. In public he flayed the skin from R. W. B. Lewis, another of his speakers at the Christian Gauss Seminars at Princeton. Lewis, he demonstrated, did not know Vergil—the pot calling the kettle black. But the cruelty represented a turning outward on the world of the cruelty he turned mostly on himself.

Blackmur's loyalties were fierce but parochial. People came first with him, then the places they had lived in. He knew that if you put together beauties not human—the stones of Venice, the twin towers of Chartres—they bred beauty into the human. "But where are your holy places in America?" asked the son of Sir Herbert Read. This in its effrontery was typically English, but Blackmur took the point. At dinner after a lecture at the University of Keele, he waited out an attack on his absent friend David Daiches. Then he said to the room: "I like Daiches, I like his wife, and I like his dog."

This intellectual lived much in his blood. He had no country but the country of the mind, and was deeply and instinctively patriotic. As Pearl Harbor came closer, he found his students surprised at the attitude with which he awaited his own involvement—"that as I share the peace I must share the war of my society." He had no brief for government, but the government could have him if it wanted. He did not profess religion. His antecedents were nothing special; he was an American. But piety flamed in him. You imagined him saying, without irony, that his blood had not passed through any huckster's loins. Like Henry Adams, whose avatar he was in his complexity and in his simplicity, he impressed on you "the consciousness that he and his people had a past."

Blackmur was a gentleman, and of course he was a snob. His manners were grave and studied, and he used them like a sword. Henry King in "King Pandar" has these Blackmurian manners. Meeting an obnoxious acquaintance, he "rose and bowed. His bow being unimpeachable where the impeachable was in order, was meant to be the perfect insult." One night when his host made a scurrile remark to a woman, the cheap and easy scurrility that passes for wit, he paled and stiffened, and would not speak. A breezy but affectionate colleague having clapped him on the shoulder and addressed him as Dick, he made his patented stabbed-in-the-back face. He was a great panjandrum—that was what his manner said—and you were wise to keep your distance. Partly the distance between him and others constituted the expense of greatness, and partly in his loneliness he grudged the expense.

When he grew passionate in argument, he used his hands. He was always proud of them, said Darrell, "this well before the larger concern with Gesture became explicit." The hands sought to render speech with a life of their own. Working, they let you see that words and ideas were as palpable for Blackmur as the soil he worked in his gardens. Abstraction was nothing unless, in his phrase, abstraction blooded. He was an expert gardener and he was, until he fell foul of greatness, absolutely concrete in his prose, finding his proper nutriment in "fidelity to the actual."

On this fidelity, as compassion makes it quick, the writing of poetry depends. That is the nub of what Blackmur taught. Alone among the New Critics, he spoke out for Robert Frost. "The fact is the sweetest dream that labor knows"—he thought that line a stroke of genius and, like Frost, he could have written it above his lintel. He knew what Frost was talking about—the reference was to wild orchids that fall before the scythe—and there was, he said, "additional piety in that." He had tried hard to raise wild orchids himself. Sometimes Frost slipped—"everybody slips." He ascribed to his Morgan colt in the poem "The Runaway" a noise like "miniature thunder." But "a colt is not shod. Unshod horses do not make thunderous sounds, especially if they don't weigh above forty or fifty pounds." This kind of prosaic knowledge and piety before it set Blackmur apart from the evacuated world of the university on which he had intruded. The instinct of Professor X—quoting from John Crowe Ransom's poem "Painted Head"—is "to try decapitation and to play truant from the body bush." It made him Blackmur's natural antagonist.

Professor X and colleagues accepted the intrusive presence, at least in the beginning, because they misconceived what he really was. Knowing what they were, they knew what he should be. They bet on his orthodoxy under the skin, and it is true that he valued orthodoxy of the mind—but pragmatically, as "the energy of society in its highest stable form." He understood that it held only as it was capacious, able to absorb the heresies that aspired to orthodoxy themselves. The greatest of these he called the gospel of unity, whether asserted as God or, "as in art, as the mere imposed unity of specious form." The last phrase comes oddly from the crier-up of unity and form. This was Blackmur's gospel. In adopting it for his own, though, he knew it for a heresy.

So he was orthodox and also a skeptic. Like the twelfth-century cleric John of Salisbury, a hero of his, Blackmur preferred doubting to defining rashly what lies hidden. The doubting habit inclined him to accept "ignorance as the humbled form of knowledge." He pursued knowledge in its divers shapes, including the trivial, "to the point where they add to ignorance" rather than confess it. Then, he thought, the best response was silence. This habit and this pursuit made affinities easy but allegiance impossible. His colleagues heard the silences. They had no inkling of the double agent who owed allegiance to no sect or class or theory, and who rejected impartially the Marxism of Malcolm Cowley and the Christianity of T. S. Eliot, disbelieving that "any particular frame of faith, political, moral, or religious, can fit any large body of men at any one time, or even, what is more important, the abler minds among it."

Blackmur's colleagues saw a cicerone like themselves, no doubt more facile and popular than they would wish to be, who could walk their students through the mysteries of modern literature. Allen Tate might have been the man they were looking for. But Tate let them down. When, in the spring of 1940, he was invited to give a talk to the English Club at Princeton, what he gave was "Miss Emily and the Bibliographer." Miss Emily is the gothic heroine who murders her lover and conceals his body in the bedroom in William Faulkner's "A Rose for Emily." This is grim but not so grim, Tate supposed, as what his academic hosts were doing all the time. "Better to pretend with Miss Emily that something dead is living than to pretend with the bibliographer that something living is dead." The pretending explained the phrase, widely current among scholars, "the corpus of

English literature." This phrase was their way "of laying literature out for burial." So Tate prepared his departure two years later from Princeton. "That night," said the secretary of the English Club—he had issued the fateful invitation and the memory of what transpired made him quiver as he spoke—"That night . . . Allen Tate . . . showed himself . . . in all ways . . . a cad."

Blackmur also was a cad in this academic sense of speaking your mind, but never so entangled as Tate in his beliefs nor so aggressive in standing up for them. You do not hear him whistling "Dixie" ("I'll Take My Stand") or challenging H. L. Mencken to a duel. His essays, said Tate, lacked "philosophical background." Partly, that is their virtue. Early on at Princeton, Blackmur recorded how "Tate came in and we talked more of our regular argument, he for hierarchy and absolute order, I for the disponible, non-Euclidean order." "Disponible" is out of Henry James, he of the sensibility so fine as never to have been violated by an idea. The non-Euclidean order works the death of general statement. The order to which Blackmur appealed had its roots in particulars. The exfoliating is particular, too. You feel his bent in laconic remarks by the way, as when he says that "observation is the cumulus of reason." (He might almost have turned that around.) You don't see a man's face—or anything else— "until you have put it into some kind of context." But more than seeing is involved. "To be in a state of life, the details must be freshly observed and aligned with other details." Dante's cosmology is in a state of life, so is the poet who made it. He gave us "the fullest imagined order any single mind in the history of Christendom has ever seen." The verb is decisive. First of all you must see. That is what Dante thought too.

Blackmur talked a lot but you would not call him garrulous. At a guess, Allen Tate, who liked to put his foot in his mouth, was a shade

less offensive to Professor X than this polite fellow who kept tight on what he valued and said only what he saw.

Blackmur the mandarin, who preferred the apothegmatic manner to discursive prose, argued an equivalence between seeing and doing. He said, "You cannot do still life in poetry." This sounds like the old academic confusion, familiar from Sir Philip Sidney and the humanists of the Renaissance, of art and kinesis. What else can it mean, that "poetry moves along a line"? Professor X augments this confusion in proposing to his students that art will make them better men. Blackmur is not so good-natured and enters no such claim. His ultimate claim is more extravagant. He sees how poetry moves along a line—not as it soothes the savage breast or whatever, rather as it confers importance on unimportant things. When you winkle out the sense of what he is saying, you understand how he parts company with the practical stylist like Quintilian or Sir Philip Sidney or President Witherspoon. Blackmur thought art aspires to a condition of tautology where things affect us only for themselves and only as they are themselves. It was another sore spot between him and the academy. This Blackmur stood in a direct line of descent from Wilde and the aestheticians of the Mauve Decade. At his best and most hardhearted he takes you back to their master, John Ruskin, who wrote in the appendix to *Modern Painters:* "Does a man die at your feet, your business is not to help him, but to note the colour of his lips."

Art is for art, and butters no parsnips. "The seal of Princeton University," said Blackmur ironically, "is miraculously good in this respect"—that is, what it says would be miraculous if true. "It says that if you will study hard, you will prosper under the numinous power of God." But prosperity does not turn on diligence, and the connection between poetry and progress or literature and morality is more willed than apparent. Tate, writing to Lincoln Kirstein, objected that Blackmur, for want of a "comprehensive view," took "a schoolmaster's delight in the small differences." The observation is just, if you agree that God lives only in these differences.

Renaissance humanism had asserted hopefully that "a name that is really a name communicates the essence of the thing named." This is to quote Blackmur himself. Unlike his predecessors, though, he is not dealing in magic, and the adverb makes the difference between him and them. What he is telling us underneath the obliquity is that liberty of observation—the only right way to denominate things—is the agent whereby things become most masterfully their own meaning. The becoming suffices. Poetry does not participate in building the New Jerusalem; neither, in Blackmur's view, does it enunciate permanent truths. Poetry partially embodies the truth by the license that is form. It is the deepest version of history.

Sidney, the prince of humanists, in his *Apology for Poetry* exalts poetry above history, and the exalting is hyperbolic and enormously sanguine. Blackmur is more acute and less willing to cosset us. He exalts neither poetry nor history. History is a tissue of "the lies we tell until the meaning of our roles becomes plain." So poetry, step by step, is also mendacious, only "the account we must make of ourselves." We need the mendacity. If it gives a specious color to the reasons the heart has for reshaping life nearer heart's desire, it makes life more tolerable. There is sadness beyond skepticism in the concessive phrase, equability too. Poetry is a game, though played for mortal stakes. "Why not go for fun as far as you can?" The question encapsulates Blackmur's critical perspective. "Art is also play," and in this play or "freedom of movement under control," criticism participates.

Play knows its own rules. "Under control" is the phrase Blackmur uses. But the rules derive from convention. They do not mirror the truth (the definite article being out of place here), only someone's ipse dixit, no doubt approved and hallowed by use and wont. This makes Blackmur a pretty tentative critic. If you look at the criticism of the mid-1930's, you find it saluting, also exemplifying, the man of provisional temper. Shakespeare is admirable as he possessed "a mind full of many provisional faiths." Henry Adams, whose intelligence is "saltatory but serial," is "provisional in every position." The description speaks to Blackmur's own achievement, and in fact you often sense that in writing about Adams he is giving the character of himself. Adams alone did not much engage Wheelwright, but "Henry Adams in relation to Dick Blackmur should be very interesting reading." Saltatory and provisional—these are the binding terms. Blackmur said he rather liked "to work by other people's prescription." This saying denotes the faithful-inspired hack or opportunist. You give him a job to do, and in return he gives value. It teased his mind, in his humility and pride, to work that way. Shakespeare worked that way.

Provisional means hospitable or catholic, also what holds only for this instance or this moment. Like the twelfth-century abbot Suger, another of his heroes, Blackmur saw the moral universe not as a monochrome but as a spectrum of colors that nonetheless make a harmony. It is understood that the harmony may vanish tomorrow. Until the desperation of the later years impelled him to abandon what he called his irregular metaphysics and to fish order from experience—the violent order that is disorder—he was content to take experience as it came. His thought seems turbid partly as shallow clearness, the métier of Professor X, was unavailable to him. Often you feel uncertain in what direction the thought is flowing, "for even a contradiction was to him only a shade of difference, a complementary color." The New Critical Blackmur is not an exegete or moralist or historian of ideas. He is meditating at a remove—art's length—on the mingled yarn of our life.

The life of the criticism is independent, by and large, of formal structures. This, curiously, is what it means to be a formalist. Conceptual thought is for theologians, philosophers, classical scientists, and English professors who are shirking their job. Occam's razor is a very good razor to carry in your pocket and ought to be standard equipment for critics: *Entia non sunt mutiplicanda praeter necessitatem*—don't multiply your concepts beyond necessity, Blackmur told the Japanese. Like a frog, he didn't care much about the systematic organization of the way by which he jumped. Order, he said, taking order tactfully with a dogmatic colleague, is only "the objective form of what you know."

Professor X disagrees. He is the connoisseur of order, but the fictive order he sponsors is imposed from the outside and lives not in things but ideas. Tate gives his character in discriminating precisely the limitation of Edmund Wilson as a literary critic. For Wilson, "the subject matter alone has objective status." The form the work takes is external, only mere technique. So the de-formed substance is correlated with its origin, in the elementary sense with its meaning, and critical thought becomes impossible. How, Tate inquired, does the moral intelligence get into poetry? He answered, "It gets in not as moral abstractions but as form, coherence of image and metaphor, control of tone and of rhythm, the union of these features." This is absolute criticism. To the description of Tate as seduced by ideas, one will want to add Blackmur's more nearly plenary description of Tate as standing at the same time "absurdly outside them" in a violence of uncertainty and conviction.

The sum of the New Criticism—for Black-

mur, Tate, and Ransom the Grail they pursued, for Professor X a gauntlet thrown down in his way—is, in Blackmur's words, "a distrust of rationality as the cumulus and discrimination of skills, and a tendency to make the analyzable features of the forms and techniques of poetry both the means of access to poetry and somehow the equivalent of its content." Each would shy at the description as applying to himself. But this, said Blackmur, is how each of them wrote when he was writing well.

At the time Blackmur entered on his twenty-five-year residence in Princeton, the master critic to the academy was Plato. He spoke not for substantial things but for the de-formed substance or ghostly paradigm of things. Ransom said in 1939, in his Phi Beta Kappa poem at Harvard, "We're in his shadow still." The principal achievement of the New Criticism was to free us of this shadow. The New Critic insists—following Blackmur in a review of Tate's *Reactionary Essays on Poetry and Ideas* (1936)—that what does not transpire cannot be said to have been experienced. Blackmur escapes the Platonic heresy as he holds to the proposition that in poetry and the novel, "in the art of words, every economy and every expense of structure and conception is validated, if at all, in the particular words that render them." This is pious, also provident. "Words verge on flesh"—quoting from an early poem of his—"and so we may, someday, be to ourselves the things we say." Sensibility, Blackmur thinks, consists in "an arduous fealty to facts." A novelist like John Steinbeck, for want of this fealty, will not do. His sensibility was "not *slowed* enough by its subject matter." With the subject matter—not the idea, instead call it matter-of-fact—early Blackmur begins and ends. This does not mean that he is a nominalist among the critics, rather that he is an opportunist, a word meant in praise, willing to follow patiently where the facts take him.

Opportunism and patience come together in

the famous or notorious definition of the dictionary as "that palace of saltatory heuristics." The word he had written was "salutary," Blackmur said. When the printer got it wrong, he thought he would let the printer have his way. It makes a good story. Anyway, the story declares the opportunist or saltatory man whose mind "leaps or jumps from place to place as best it can." Heuristics means learning as well as teaching, and begins with the dictionary as first of all you must honor the word, submitting yourself patiently to the entire range of meaning it discloses. Professor X, here personated by Harry Levin, a model of the academic mind, is impatient of the word, most of all as the word is made flesh. You find him nipping at Blackmur's heels from the beginning, as when in 1940 he reviews *The Expense of Greatness* in the *New Republic* and complains that "Mr. Blackmur has a dictionary." The trouble with the dictionary, from the point of view of Professor X, lies in its solidity and matter-of-factness. What he calls "the rarefactions of New Criticism" start the venom flowing in him exactly as the New Critics are not rarefied but substantial. Tenuity is where he lives; substantiality sticks in his craw. That is why he denounces Blackmur, who cannot live in thin air, for his "distrust of reason." Blackmur thinks "we have not so much of reason that we can afford to lose any of it." Only, in his robustness, he wants to make room for "the quick and very membrane of style." Professor X is Ransom's "Painted Head."

Blackmur fills an ampler role. Dwelling in his palace of saltatory heuristics, he throws back insistently to the words on the page. Adams, for example, is defined by his scruple. "The etymology of the word refreshes the meaning." There is the Latin *scrupulus,* "a small sharp stone, a stone in one's shoe, an uneasiness, difficulty, small trouble, or doubt." The passage goes on like that, and the end is elucidation. No other critic has ever written in English, not from

the beginnings of criticism in the Renaissance, who did his homework with such assiduity. Tick them off on your fingers, the few great critics (they are rarer by far than great poets)—Samuel Johnson, Samuel Taylor Coleridge, T. S. Eliot—each casts a longer shadow than Blackmur. In this respect, however, none of them comes near him. Beyond all others in his trade, he was responsive to the facts. This defines responsibility in criticism—the playing on words is his—and explains how he realizes the ideal to which he aspired, an activity "as objective, indeed almost as anonymous" as any pursued by the Bureau of Standards.

The anonymity makes Blackmur our closest reader of poetry. At the same time, it circumscribes his critical achievement. But the achievement is not of a piece. Anonymity describes the practical critic who wrote to Robert Penn Warren in 1936: "I take it that the final use of criticism is to elucidate the facts." To this Blackmur there succeeds the full-throated and nearly autonomous figure who longs to be freed from poetry, who contends against this longing and makes inspired criticism from the contention. Last of all, there is the "King over the Water"—the title of his essay in dispraise of Ford Madox Ford—who shows what it means to say: "I am myself alone." On one side, in one kind, Blackmur is only litmus paper, instrumental to the job. That is one definition of the critic's job of work. Often in Blackmur's judgments of poets and particular poems, the pH is just right, where in Johnson it comes out all wrong. But Johnson is incomparably the greatest English critic. George Santayana says: "It is the temperament that speaks; we may brush aside as unsubstantial, and even as distorting, the web of arguments and theories which it has spun out of itself." This seems unfair, but accounts for primacy in criticism. Temperament, writ large, is Johnson's possession.

When temperament grew more imperious in Blackmur, the result was not practical criticism, or not chiefly that, like the work of Cleanth Brooks and Robert Penn Warren in their New Critical manifesto to the classroom. The result was a creative meditation worthy to stand with the poetry that affords it a point of departure as much as a reason for being. This Blackmur is the critic as artist. The culmination of his artistry is the book he called, deliberately, *Language As Gesture* (1952), on which his permanent reputation will depend. He thought that "when the language of words most succeeds it *becomes* gesture in its words." In this ultimate work, a pulling together of essays that had first appeared as early as *The Double Agent,* he managed the becoming, so defined the virile man thinking.

One talent, at least, never left him. This was explication. But the best of the book transcends explication and is not as yet crochety, evangelizing, or merely personal. "In the gloom, the gold gathers the light against it"—remembering Pound's line on which Blackmur dwells and builds his own edifice or Adjunct to the Muses' Diadem. Meaning is not to seek, but meaning is elusive. It looms over the horizon and heaves like the sea swell under the bows, and you feel how the critic is also a poet and making a rival construction. The sensibility that declares itself in these essays on poetry partakes of the genius that is its occasion. Intellect has climbed to its highest pitch, is so fastidious, is working with such intensity as to achieve incandescence. Of filler there is hardly any. All that is burned away. Blackmur wanted from his teens to be a true creative artist. After all he did not fail.

His colleagues were not looking for a rival construction, and mostly they liked their poetry under glass. Blackmur's personal tragedy, the kind that waits on the autodidact, was that he came to identify with them. In his own words, harder perhaps than a reader would use, he acquiesced in "the substitution of the authoritarian for the authoritative, of violence for emo-

tion, frenzy for passion." The unrivaled consciousness turned to omnicompetence, the provisional faith to *plenitudo potestatis*. The professor manqué, having no degrees, took to writing learned papers "in solicitude and critique." The critique is poorer for the solicitude. "In these papers, neither is the fog in the fir trees nor is the salt on the briar rose." Ideas, the kind that dance in air, exert their fatal fascination. The validity of the criticism comes increasingly "to depend on the validity of the ideas in that vacuum which is the medium of simple assertion." Increasingly, the voice you hear is the modulated voice of Professor X the belletrist, not Old Rocky Face but a leader-writer in the *New York Times.*

With the ascendancy of this voice and this prescriptive personality—benevolent but not beneficent—Blackmur's professional ascendancy began. The academy acknowledged him as one of its own—always with residual suspicion—as he put away the microscope and began to flourish his optic glass. What things he discovered in it! an equivalent, though still "putative," for the seven parts of the trivium and quadrivium of the Middle Ages—here he is the educational statesman beloved of nice people who deplore the two cultures and want to build a bridge between them—or a modus vivendi inspired by the question (he was false to his genius as he raised it) "What should be done?"— here, God help us, he sounds like Nikolay Chernyshevsky.

Some of this stuff is fun and does really declare the great man before whom, with affection and exasperation, you throw up your hands. For example (Blackmur had been lucubrating, something like that, on a Latin phrase that recurs in the letters of John Quincy Adams): "It is a phrase from, I think, the eighth line of the third ode in the fifth book of the Odes of Horace. I may have that reference not quite right. I speak from memory."

He rifled memory and old books; he made himself a coat out of old mythologies, here the numen, there the *moha*. This outlandish garment he wore in the world's eye. It brought him growing acclaim. In 1944 his patrons made him a fellow of the Institute for Advanced Study, appropriately—for he personified the polymath—in the school of economics. He did not expect to be richly rewarded. He took it for granted that he would be patronized, and was. In time he became a patron himself. He brought John Berryman to Princeton, later Randall Jarrell, Delmore Schwartz, Saul Bellow, others. The National Institute of Arts and Letters, and then the American Academy of Arts and Sciences, elected him a member. The universities belatedly conferred on him the academic credentials he had decided as a young man he did not want or need. Rutgers but not Princeton gave him an honorary degree. Cambridge named him Pitt Professor of American History and Institutions in 1961. He prefigured the peregrine professor of a later time and was sought after constantly on the lecture circuit. His public lectures were mysterious, not more magnificent than dim.

At home in Princeton he hobnobbed with the great and famous. He spent evenings with Oppenheimer and Ben Shahn. When he dined at the Lucius Wilmerdings', he didn't leave until two or three in the morning. Until he left, he didn't stop talking. John O'Hara, whom he met frequently at parties, paid him a particular compliment. "He not only dislikes me," Blackmur said, "but detests me." The detestation was that of one Great Cham for another.

His salary grew and his tastes followed, then exceeded his salary. If you wore a hat, it had better be a Borsalino. You got the best neckwear at that shop on the via Condotti. Sometimes at dinner he served his guests Romanée-Conti. He drank his bourbon in tumblers black almost to the top. "Why are there no second acts in American literature?" someone is supposed to have asked James Thurber, who answered: "Because writers after forty can afford to buy their liquor by the case."

More than any other faculty member, Blackmur made himself familiar with the mysteries of the budget. He could calculate to the penny, from a generalized account of university housing, the amount of rental increase against a colleague's house on Broadmead or Fitzrandolph. Why should he have done this? The answer is buried in his penny-pinching youth. Faculty politics engrossed him, and he blew them up out of all proportion, generally getting them all wrong. On the floor of the faculty he might have been wearing a toga. It would have become him more than most. Now he was Pliny the Younger, a *laudator eloquentissimus*. At Lahiere's, the best restaurant in Princeton, he held court five days a week. He had his own chair against the north wall. And now he was Ben Jonson, inviting a friend to supper. There is a line he used to quote, derisory of famous men: *"What then?" sang Plato's ghost. "What then?"*

For a long time the prophet went unhonored in his own place. The English department did not want to promote him. Then Blackmur's patrons intervened. They were Christian Gauss, the dean of the college at Princeton; John Marshall, associate director of the Rockefeller Foundation and a close friend from early days in Cambridge; the economist Walter Stewart, a Rockefeller Foundation trustee and a permanent member of the Institute for Advanced Study; Lucius Wilmerding, another fellow in the school of economics. In the city he belonged to the Century Club. So did President Dodds. Finally Harold Dodds let it be known that he was for Blackmur. The English department saw that it had no option, and in 1951 the man who never completed high school was promoted to professor.

Did he hear the dirge in the bells of his accession? Like Neil Paraday, the famous writer in Henry James's "The Death of the Lion," perhaps like James, assuredly like Adams, Blackmur shows us in his life how renouncement depends on recognition. The flame that is the life attains its highest point, then the snuff that lives within it abates it. Blackmur had pushed to the point of success. But he had written long before how "success is not the propitious term" for a life, for a work. The propitious term, he said, is failure. Richard Blackmur was a dust-and-ashes man, self-convicted of what he called "that fundamental condition of the mind known as *ennui*." He never permitted himself to taste his honors before they sated, he never omitted to drink to the lees every drop in the cup of his dejection. In an early essay he drew on Pascal, "the great scrupulous mind of the seventeenth century," with whose night thoughts he lived on intimate terms. "We combat obstacles in order to get repose, and, when got, the repose is insupportable; for we think either of the troubles we have, or of those that threaten us; and even if we felt safe on every side, *ennui* would of its own accord spring up from the depths of the heart where it is rooted by nature, and would fill the mind with its venom." Perhaps Blackmur rejoiced in his triumph. Its entail was insupportable to him. In his self-contempt, he took care that it would be.

On his nineteenth birthday, Blackmur had looked back on the years of adolescence when, as he put it, "I stepped out alone"—not rodomontade by a long shot—happy in the awareness of "true genius" in himself, "sure of my victory." His elation did not last. "I'm less sure now," he wrote. "If it turns out that I fail as creative artist, then I shall know I have only a swim for a life ahead of me." In middle age, he supposed it had turned out that way.

By all odds, it should have turned out that way. Disorder and early sorrow mingle their spurs in Blackmur's story, and he conformed in age to the bent imparted in his beginnings. Against this bent or impairment he struggled all his life, but neither as boy nor man could he escape what he called the great grasp of unreason, and failure looked unshunnable for him. His story is exhilarating as he did not fail.

In Blackmur's papers at Princeton, this note in his own hand survives: "The right question to ask about a man of size, once he is dead and all his motion done, all his growth and his deterioration stopped, is always some form of the question: What good was he? What was the goodness in him that he amounted to—the goodness, the very virtue, that he was?" Blackmur in these questions was trying to make sense of the life of Henry Adams. But let the questions address his own life—or better, his achievement, now that the life is done. In the "very virtue" of this achievement, limitation participates. When Blackmur was still in his twenties, he wrote: "Our vices father our virtues, and in intent are indistinguishable." This swapping back and forth is how it was with him. The insecure man had great courage, and the man of many weaknesses was endlessly fertile in discovering new sources of strength. He triumphed as he made his weakness feed his strength.

In the medieval song of Coeur de Lion, the minstrel Blondel de Nesle cries:

O Richard! O mon Roi!

L'univers t'abandonne.

The Mozart sound of André Grétry's opera *Richard Coeur de Lion* only amplifies the pathos of these lines. Blackmur found them in Adams, for whom they conveyed his own suffering in a "pattern of acceptance, rejection, and expression." In this pattern Blackmur also composed the sense of his life. The pattern mirrors the life and distorts it. In his view of himself, the acceptance that he won counted far less than rejection. Only rejection was sure. Also, he considered it just. "I used to say that I had never known above one or two persons who had not at some crucial point let me down. Nothing could be further from the truth. In no instance I can think of among those which used to trouble me had I any right of firmer expectation than to have been—not let down—but let go; and so it was." Everyone with whom he became close let go at some crucial point. Out of rejection, whether real or imagined, came the work by which he lives, also the privation that diminishes the work. There is Blondel's expressive song beneath the prison walls, then there is the prison in which King Richard lies captive. In the trembling jar between, Blackmur's very virtue was engendered.

Perhaps, as his friend Francis Fergusson thought, Blackmur was losing his critical gift about the time he came to Princeton. It seems right to present his artistic career, anyway on one side, as describing a downward curve. This is surprising only as you overlook the imposition he carried with him. The greater surprise consists in the magnitude of what he achieved. The achievement is figured in the image of the gyres, familiar from his master William Butler Yeats. As one source of energy waned in him, another source supervened. He abdicated the life of a free lance, you could say he quit on his talent. But he made himself a great teacher, and his impact on a generation of students, many of whom became famous in the arts and in public affairs, is still perceptible.

Blackmur aspired to the role of lawmaker, and in later years he tried the catechistic manner and the legislating voice. But the ability to conceptualize was beyond him. So he was unlucky but lucky, too. He told the truth but told it slant. This precluded the chance for general statement. Also it predicted the fragmentary nature of his work. He passed judgment on the work in the preface to his *Eleven Essays in the European Novel*—"fragments of an unfinished ruin" was his self-denigrating phrase. The de-

nigrating is just. But the provisional bias you discern in the work gives Blackmur his charter. Debarred from acquaintance with the capital-letter Thing, he dealt almost exclusively in lowercase things. For want of a better, his mode was observation. Looking hard, he said what he saw. In this way he made his small body of permanent poetry.

Blackmur's meticulous temper verged on morbidity and played into the criticism with unexpected results. Out of his impairment, he fashioned an instrument almost preternatural in its acuteness. His essays in criticism—they include the life of Adams—present the man who could not manage a total performance. What he gives you is not an integer but a series of provisional approaches—essays, precisely, in the sense that his hero Michel de Montaigne used the word. Life as he saw it was essentially discrete, and this was impairment too. He missed the Pisgah sight or unified theory. So he lowered his eyes and became our best American critic.

Selected Bibliography

WORKS OF
R. P. BLACKMUR

CRITICISM
The Double Agent; Essays in Craft and Elucidation. New York: Arrow Editions, 1935.
The Expense of Greatness. New York: Arrow Editions, 1940.
Language As Gesture; Essays in Poetry. New York: Harcourt, Brace, 1952.
The Lion and the Honeycomb; Essays in Solicitude and Critique. New York: Harcourt, Brace, 1955.
Anni Mirabiles, 1921–1925: Reason in the Madness of Letters. Washington, D. C.: Library of Congress, 1956.
Form and Value in Modern Poetry. Garden City, N. Y.: Doubleday, 1957.

New Criticism in the United States. Tokyo: Kenkyusha, 1959.

Eleven Essays in the European Novel. New York: Harcourt, Brace, and World, 1964.

A Primer of Ignorance, edited by Joseph Frank. New York: Harcourt, Brace, and World, 1967.

POETRY

From Jordan's Delight. New York: Arrow Editions, 1937.

The Second World. Cummington, Mass.: Cummington Press, 1942.

The Good European and Other Poems. Cummington, Mass.: Cummington Press, 1947.

Poems of R. P. Blackmur. Princeton, N. J.: Princeton University Press, 1977. (With an introduction by Denis Donoghue.)

BIOGRAPHY

Henry Adams, edited by Veronica A. Makowsky. New York: Harcourt Brace Jovanovich, 1980. (With a foreword by Denis Donoghue.)

BIBLIOGRAPHIES

Baker, Carlos. "R. P. Blackmur: A Checklist." *Princeton University Library Chronicle,* 3:99–106 (April 1942).

Pannick, Gerald J. "R. P. Blackmur: A Bibliography." *Bulletin of Bibliography,* 31:165–69 (1974).

Tate, Allen. *Sixty American Poets, 1896–1944.* Washington, D. C.: Library of Congress, 1954.

Thomas, Harry. *An Annotated Bibliography of R. P. Blackmur,* with a critical essay. New York: Garland Press (in progress).

BIOGRAPHICAL AND CRITICAL STUDIES

Foster, Richard Jackson. *The New Romantics.* Bloomington: Indiana University Press, 1962.

Frank, Joseph. *The Widening Gyre.* New Brunswick, N. J.: Rutgers University Press, 1963.

Fraser, Russell. "R. P. Blackmur: The Politics of a New Critic." *Sewanee Review,* 87:557–72 (Fall 1979).

———. *R. P. Blackmur: A Hero's Life.* New York: Harcourt Brace Jovanovich (in press).

Greenbaum, Leonard. *The Hound and Horn.* The Hague: Mouton, 1966.

Hyman, Stanley E. *The Armed Vision.* New York: Knopf, 1948.

Jarrell, Randall. *Poetry and the Age.* New York: Knopf, 1953.

Kenner, Hugh. *Gnomon.* New York: McDowell, Obolensky, 1958.

Pritchard, William H. "R. P. Blackmur and the Criticism of Poetry." *Massachusetts Review,* 8:633–49 (Fall 1967).

Schwartz, Delmore. *Selected Essays,* edited by Donald A. Dike and David H. Zucker. Chicago: University of Chicago Press, 1970.

Sutton, Walter E. *Modern American Criticism.* Englewood Cliffs, N. J.: Prentice-Hall, 1963.

Wain, John. *Essays on Literature and Ideas.* New York: St. Martin's, 1963.

Webster, Grant. *The Republic of Letters: A History of Postwar American Literary Opinion.* Baltimore–London: Johns Hopkins, 1979.

Wellek, Rene. "R. P. Blackmur Re-Examined." *Southern Review,* n.s. 7:825–45 (1971).

—RUSSELL A. FRASER

Pearl S. Buck

1892—1973

PEARL SYDENSTRICKER BUCK's biography is one of the most unusual and varied in the history of American letters. She was born on June 26, 1892, in Hillsboro, West Virginia, while her missionary parents were on a brief furlough from their Chinese pastorate. Taken to China as an infant, she grew up with fundamental Oriental influences, since her parents preferred to live among the natives rather than isolate themselves in missionary compounds. At an early age she was more conversant in Chinese than in English. Her playmates were Chinese, and like the youthful Willa Cather amid the immigrant families of the Midwest, Buck was early attuned to the customs, household activities, and family life of her neighbors. She was a bright, inquisitive child and an excellent student. She grew up on the Bible, Plutarch's *Lives,* the traditional Chinese sagas, and, from about the age of seven, the stories of Charles Dickens. She remarked that she read all of Dickens' novels over and over for at least ten years. Dickens conveyed a "great zest for life" and intensified an interest in people in all their variety. Late in her teens Buck developed a keen interest in the works of Theodore Dreiser and Sinclair Lewis. She delighted in their detailed factual presentations and savored their portrayal of character. From her earliest years she not only enjoyed hearing stories but also wished to tell them.

Her mother's influence was crucial, since Caroline Sydenstricker insisted upon frequent written exercises apart from tutorial or school assignments. She especially emphasized correct grammatical form and clarity, diligently examined each essay her daughter wrote, and made suggestions for revision and improvement. She encouraged her daughter to submit her writings for publication; thus, many of Buck's childhood writings were published in the *Shanghai Mercury.*

In the midst of this educational development, there always lurked the menace of danger. In 1900, Buck, her sister, and her mother had to flee for their lives during the Boxer Rebellion. Numerous white families were murdered during this period, and even small children were not spared. Buck spent a year in Shanghai as a refugee. Later, during the Nationalist uprising of 1926–1927, when Chiang Kai-shek's forces attacked Nanking, more whites were slaughtered. As the soldiers neared the family dwelling and death appeared imminent, a Chinese neighbor guided the Buck family to her home and hid them in a "half room" there. Eventually American and British warships arrived in the Yangtze River and began shelling the revolutionaries. Buck and her family were taken aboard the gunboats and again brought to Shanghai. On another occasion an angry crowd surrounded the family home and threatened to kill her and her sister and mother (the father at this time was away on a missionary journey), since the people blamed the Christians for a drought. Only her mother's persuasiveness and calm friendliness preserved the family from harm. Such a continuing climate of peril would inevitably sharpen a sensitive and perceptive mind, as well as emphasize a sense of dramatic conflict.

At seventeen Buck was sent to the United States to attend Randolph-Macon Woman's College. Not only did she excel in her studies, but she also wrote numerous stories and poems, and even collaborated on a school play. She became president of her class and was elected to Phi Beta Kappa. In her senior year she won two literary prizes. After receiving her degree in 1914, she stayed at the college as a teaching assistant until recalled to China by the serious illness of her mother, whom she nursed back to health. In 1917 she married John Lossing Buck, an American agricultural specialist employed by the Presbyterian Board of Foreign Missions. She and her husband settled in northern China, and Buck became closely involved in her husband's work and familiar with the farmers' lives and customs. Again she became intimately acquainted with native ways, and her command of the Chinese language attracted the people.

In 1921 the Bucks moved to Nanking, where John Lossing Buck secured a post at the university. She also taught classes there, in English literature, and gave literature courses at two other Chinese universities. The students were in ferment because more modern customs and less traditional attitudes were challenging previously accepted standards of behavior and political thinking. These problems gave Buck the opportunity to comment in print, and as early as 1923 her articles began to appear in numerous periodicals, including the *Atlantic Monthly, Trans-Pacific, Living Age,* and the *Nation.*

Her university lecturing, writing, and household activities were burdened by the realization that her first child, Carol, was mentally retarded. She took the child to America for treatment in 1925, and her husband was given a year's leave of absence. While in the United States she decided to join him in advanced study, and therefore enrolled at Cornell to pursue an M.A. in English. She acquired the degree in 1926 and wrote an additional essay that was awarded the Laura Messenger Prize in history, the largest financial prize offered by the university. She had deliberately sought this lucrative award.

Upon returning to China that same year, Buck continued her writing and published essays as well as short stories. In 1930 her first book, *East Wind: West Wind*—which, although considered a novel, really consists of two long short stories—appeared.

This volume, immediately popular with the reading public, focuses on a young Chinese married couple who are caught in the conflict between traditional customs and the new, fashionable Western beliefs. The husband, a physician who has spent many years abroad, wants his wife to be on an equal level, but she has been reared and trained in the ancient manner and wishes to be no more than a total slave. She is particularly distressed when her husband insists that she unbind her feet. She has followed one of the oldest and more frequently practiced Chinese customs, designed to develop tiny and pretty feet. Her husband knows that this binding has done considerable physical damage to her feet. Kwei-lan, the wife, is placed in a quandary. To her, bound feet have always been an essential mark of beauty, and she has undergone much pain and inconvenience while growing up, enduring the soaking of her feet in warm water and the tight bandaging. When Kwei-lan tells her mother of the problem, the mother finds her son-in-law's attitude difficult to understand. Although she is thoroughly rooted in the old ways and disapproves of change, the mother recommends that Kwei-lan please her husband. The conflict is resolved in this way. Husband and wife become more intimate, and Kwei-lan adopts up-to-the-moment Western ways. The contrast between the old and the new is strikingly delineated.

In the second story Kwei-lan's brother, studying in the United States, marries an American girl against his family's wishes, since, according to ancient custom, he has been betrothed by his family to a Chinese girl since childhood. When he brings his wife to China, his parents refuse to acknowledge her status. When, in time, the wife becomes pregnant, the mother-in-law grows even more despondent and dies. Unless one of his parents recognizes the marriage, the son will be unable to obtain his inheritance. When his father insists that the marriage agreement contracted in childhood be observed, Kwei-lan's brother totally rejects his family and has his name officially stricken from the ancestral records. The baby that arrives, though, becomes a bond between East and West; and although much tragedy has been involved in the child's conception, the infant will bring about a knowledge and unity of two different worlds, so that, in time, harmony and understanding may develop out of the present antagonism.

East Wind: West Wind possesses some of the defects of many first works of fiction. It is verbose, uneven, dotted with "purple passages," and rather loosely organized. Yet the characterizations are exceedingly well drawn and convincing. The parents' attitude and veneration of traditional customs and patterns of behavior give many insights into the China of the past. Kwei-lan's amazement at her husband's suggestions and her attempts to adjust to the new modes of Western life are persuasive and arouse considerable sympathy for her plight. The inflexible views of Kwei-lan's brother ring true, and his stubbornness, contrasted with that of

his parents, never appears farfetched or exaggerated. This note adds much verisimilitude to the situation and intensifies the dramatic tension.

Furthermore, *East Wind: West Wind* exemplifies two qualities that became hallmarks of Buck's writing. This novel features a strong narrative drive; it is compelling and agreeable to read. It impels the reader forward and keeps one turning the pages in fascination and suspense. Second, there is an authentic flavor of time and place. We are on the scene, and reality cannot be doubted. The locale, customs, and attitudes of the characters are perceived from a firsthand viewpoint, and this quality furnishes decidedly effective verisimilitude. Some critics have argued that the locale itself is responsible for the story's appeal, that the aura of "faraway places" carries an inherent interest. To some degree this may be true; but no matter how exotic or picturesque setting, atmosphere, and characters are, they still must be presented with a tone and ring recognizably valid, and Buck is obviously tuned to the correct notes. She achieves total mastery over the Chinese material she treats; and although *East Wind: West Wind* contains defects, its author has discovered her métier.

In 1931, *The Good Earth* appeared, one of the most successful books in publishing history. There persists the misconception that this was a novel without an apprenticeship, yet this notion is patently untrue. Besides her youthful appearances in print, and later numerous short stories and articles, Buck had already written a biography of her mother that she had temporarily decided not to publish. She had also completed a novel, but the manuscript was destroyed when her home was looted during the Nationalist revolution of 1926–1927. Thus, including *East Wind: West Wind*, Buck had written three full-length books before the appearance of her most significant novel.

The Good Earth demonstrates that its author had gained a thorough knowledge of Chinese peasant life. This authenticity furnished a universality to the novel that constitutes one of its most vibrant appeals. Carl Van Doren noted that the Chinese family analyzed by Buck seemed to be "as familiar as neighbors." The book incorporates eternal verities: birth, marriage, children, failures and successes, death, a new generation. The ambivalent tension that a wedding can generate, the occasional bouts with illness that all humans experience, the difficulties suffered from inconsiderate relatives, and the intense disappointment caused when children, grown to maturity, turn against their parents' values and wishes are just a few of the universal episodes that ring so true despite the distant setting.

Just as the problems and events create a compelling verisimilitude, so too does Buck's command of the locale. It is evident that she knows her setting thoroughly. When the book achieved instant popularity, some chauvinistic Chinese critics, finding the portrayal of their country and its people unflattering, immediately attacked the novel as inaccurate. One critic claimed that no woman in China ever had premarital intercourse; another insisted that Chinese robber gangs no longer existed, and even faulted the way making tea was described. In rebuttal Buck, as well as Lin Yutang and others, was able to refute such extreme viewpoints. As she remarked in an article in the *Yale Review,* many Chinese intellectuals living in foreign countries feel that they have a mission to protect China. Consequently they propagate the notion that Chinese life centers on spirituality, intellectualism, and the philosophical aspects of Confucianism. In such a romantic, idealistic portrayal the life of the common Chinese farmer is distorted or simply ignored. The *New York Times* felt obliged to editorialize on this debate, defending *The Good Earth* and

expressing appreciation for the portrayal: "Mrs. Buck has enabled us to witness and appreciate the patience, frugality, industry and indomitable good humor of a suffering people, whose homes the governing intellectuals would hide from the sight of the world." Although Buck was easily able to refute every charge made against the novel's authenticity, the notion still lingers in certain circles that her portrayal of Chinese life was inaccurate; this notion even appeared in some of the obituary accounts of her career. This misconception must be laid to rest. A knowledge of Chinese history and studies of the Chinese peasant totally support her portrayals of Chinese life.

Part of the appeal of *The Good Earth* is achieved by the characterization of Wang Lung and his wife, O-lan. Wang Lung is a personification of human nature in all its vagaries. In his early life he works with particular diligence, and his attitudes parallel the qualities of the soil he tends. He bears his burdens with a pragmatic stoicism and opportunistically snatches fortune's favor when it is briefly up for the taking. As he grows more prosperous and successful, the pitfalls of wealth enmesh him in indolence, promiscuity, and cruelly indifferent egoism, especially in areas where poverty and family concerns had prevented such irresponsibility and thoughtlessness. He is a paradigm of mankind's admirable aspects as well as its despicable tendencies, and as such brings forceful reader identification.

O-lan is less complex. She knows and suffers the pain of existence, but her stoicism is much more complete than Wang Lung's. She requires only a husband and family to care for. She gives her family self-sacrificing devotion, and centers all her strength on day-to-day necessities. She endures repression, poverty, neglect, disloyalty, disappointment, and emotional injury, yet she remains undefeated. She is a Hemingway code hero, never exaggerating her plight and accepting every blow of fate with amazing resignation. She receives her one triumph when one of her sons marries and she can confidently look forward to grandchildren. She joys in her role as breeder, as race propagator, as a link between past and future generations. The portraits of the two main characters animate the novel and, to paraphrase Dorothy Canfield Fisher's comment, they engage our sympathies as much as real people whom we daily encounter. But Wang Lung and O-lan so dominate the book that the other characters are diminished: they appear as types rather than as totally convincing people. This is one of the few blemishes of *The Good Earth*.

The style of *The Good Earth* is one of its most appealing qualities. It derives from the mellifluous prose of the King James Version of the Bible intermingled with the technique of the traditional Chinese sagas. In many respects the two style sources are similar. The choice of words is clear, simple, and vivid, and features considerable use of parallelism and balanced sentence structure. The sentences, on the whole, tend to be lengthy as well as solemn and stately. There is an archaic flavoring derived from the choice of words, the repetition, and the natural musical flow of the parallelism. Purple passages and colorful biblical imagery have been omitted, and the style is expertly tuned to the subject matter—simple but forceful, moving but stoic, graceful but never excessive.

Considerable controversy has centered on the question of whether *The Good Earth* is a naturalistic novel. Oscar Cargill has argued the similarity of Pearl Buck's viewpoint to that of Émile Zola, and she has acknowledged that she read and admired Zola's writings. She has confused the issue further by often using the term "naturalism" to describe her early work. It is clear, though, that by "naturalism" she means "realism"—a close, detailed look at life as it really is, rather than a slanted view deliberately

emphasizing the seamier aspects of existence for a sociopolitical purpose.

Although naturalism and *The Good Earth* emphasize a documentary, objective approach to the presentation of material, and focus on people of the lowest economic levels, there is a marked difference between the novels of Zola and Buck: she stresses the importance of free will. Her characters are not overwhelmed in a deterministic world, totally oppressed by the forces of heredity and environment. They realize that through the exercise of choices, through hard work and human initiative, difficulties and problems can be overcome and despair subdued. While it is not in any manner a pronounced message, in the sense of being an obvious preachment, *The Good Earth* possesses an affirmative belief in human nature and in the ability of men and women to rise as high as their ambitions and willingness to strive will carry them. The "message" must be inferred; but industry, common-sense behavior, and a closeness to the soil are extolled, while luxury and idleness are seen as corrupting and destructive.

After the success of *The Good Earth*, Buck decided to proceed with a sequel describing the fortunes of Wang Lung's family. She hoped to keep readers absorbed by involvement in a roman-fleuve as well as by presenting other phases of Chinese life. In *Sons* (1932) the three offspring of Wang Lung are a pleasure-loving, decadent landlord, a shady merchant, and a former military officer turned warlord. The major focus is on the third son, called Wang the Tiger. He becomes a powerful brigand and land baron who exerts control over a large section of a province. Although the warlord was a prominent feature of Chinese life—at least until the Communists came to full control—and many of these brigands were colorful and larger-than-life characters, Wang the Tiger does not have the personality to capture the imagination. His all-consuming passion is his son Yuan. He expects that Yuan will follow in his footsteps and ultimately become an even more puissant leader. But the boy is uninterested in a military life, and his father's disappointment does not arouse sympathy because the Tiger's character is remote and has small appeal.

The same combination of Chinese saga and biblical narrative is used, and in parts of the novel it is handled very competently. Nevertheless, the style cannot really give adequate color when the main character is colorless and so much of the material seems lifeless and unduly distant. Then, too, the universality, so crucial a part of *The Good Earth*, is missing. Although Buck undoubtedly knew real-life counterparts of Wang Lung and O-lan, she was unfamiliar with warlords (except for reading about them). This distancing seriously mars the book.

The saga of Wang Lung's family was carried forward in *A House Divided,* the last segment of what came to be called the *House of Earth* trilogy. In this novel Yuan quarrels with his father and attempts to find direction for his life. For a short time he returns to his grandfather's original farm, but he cannot adjust to that environment. He then goes to live in Shanghai and mingles with the wealthy, fashionable people introduced to him by his elder uncle and other well-to-do relatives. Eventually he travels to America, where he acquires a doctoral degree. But in none of these places is he really at home. He returns to China and encounters new government reforms and revolutionary activities. But he has neither certitude nor real roots. He is too far from his grandfather's farming background to be content on the land, and he is too questioning of modernistic thinking to be at ease in a China that, in the late 1920's, is in turmoil, torn between the old customs and radical, modernistic notions.

A House Divided suffers badly from a lack of unity. The novel moves from the farm to the city, and from China to the United States and back to China. There is almost no cohesiveness as the book constantly scatters its impact. Here begins a defect that was to grow in Buck's fiction and that would damage many of her post-1930's novels: an obsession with overplotting. In her devotion to the traditional Chinese saga, she talks of the "storyteller in a village tent," who by his stories "entices people into his tent." She comes to believe that "Nothing must delay the story. Story was what [was] wanted." As a consequence the story is allowed to run rampant without characterization fully drawn or a scene totally probed. The plot becomes an all-consuming passion, and probability and a sense of verisimilitude—so ascendant in *The Good Earth*—start to decline.

The reader is not allowed to penetrate deeply and logically enough into many of the important characters—Yuan, for instance. We are told a considerable amount about Yuan, but we are not really convinced that we know him or that he is appealing enough to want to know. Whereas Wang Lung and O-lan were absorbing and intriguing individuals, Wang the Tiger and Yuan seem more like puppets who are being manipulated, with the strings of the puppeteer all too obviously on view.

Before the third volume of the *House of Earth* trilogy was published, one of Buck's most memorable novels, *The Mother* (1934), appeared. The protagonist is a young farm wife who, in addition to her household and family chores, works in the fields. After her erratic and indolent husband deserts her, she continues all her previous chores and has to work even harder. One of her children is almost totally blind, and this increases her burdens. This child later dies, and the sorrow of the mother intensifies. Still later, her favorite son becomes involved in political activities and is executed. The mother's suffering is deeply experienced and the reader's empathy engaged. When her first grandchild arrives, the mother's view of life is resuscitated. A joy of hope and purposefulness assuages all her previous heartbreak.

In attempting to draw a portrait of the eternal, universal mother, a saga mingling joy and sorrow, birth and death, despair and hope, Buck has written a book with many effective scenes and many poignantly realized emotions; yet the novel is only partially successful. Its weakness rests in the fact that the mother is not sufficiently individualized. She is, and is intended to be, a type, but the difficulty is that the type dwarfs a necessary individuality. One needs to believe in her as a flesh-and-blood character in her own right, not just as a representative *mater dolorosa.* The typecasting detracts from those qualities needed to render her larger than life.

The year 1936 was distinguished by the publication of two of Buck's finest books: *The Exile,* a biography of her mother, and *Fighting Angel,* a biography of her father.

Caroline Stulting Sydenstricker, Buck's mother, was an effervescent extrovert. She was exceedingly pleasant, outgoing, and lively, but possessed a sensual strain that warred with religious tendencies. The deeply serious and spiritual Absalom Sydenstricker had settled on a missionary calling early in life but was required to work on his father's farm until he was twenty-one. When further schooling was completed, he became a Presbyterian minister; and after he married Caroline Stulting, they set out for China as missionaries. The pair found they were ill-suited. Caroline wanted to share more fully in her husband's work, while he really wanted a housewife. He was almost indifferent to anything not totally directed toward his missionary calling. He was too rigid and too ascetic for a wife who took a more balanced, more all-embracing view of life.

Caroline and Absalom endured much hardship and danger in China. On several occasions they barely escaped death. Both of them gave up many things and sacrificed greatly for their missionary cause, and each in his or her own way—opposite as they were in so many things—lived a heroic life in a period that their daughter recorded in every possible familial, social, political, and historical detail.

The portraits of Buck's parents emerge clearly and fully. Absalom, in particular, is shown in all of his lonely mysticism and otherworldliness. He really did not know his family and was never close to anyone, since only God dominated his thoughts. Because Buck felt her father's remoteness and aloofness, her picture of him is frequently caustic and usually thoughtful. She clearly sees his deficiencies, yet she realizes he was very honorable and totally dedicated. *Fighting Angel* is therefore the stronger book because it is free from sentimentality. The picture of Buck's mother, while equally honest and perceptive, frequently becomes maudlin because the author was very close to her warm, spirited mother and could not help but be emotionally tied to her. Both books, taken as a whole, are remarkable historical recordings of a way of life. When Buck was awarded the Nobel Prize for literature in 1938, the citation of the Nobel committee read: "For rich and generous epic description of Chinese peasant life and masterpieces of biography." It is unfortunate that these biographies are now so seldom read, because the description is reasonably accurate.

Buck settled permanently in the United States in 1934. Her marriage had collapsed, and in the following year she married publisher Richard J. Walsh. She now began to write on American topics as well as continuing to use Chinese subject matter.

This Proud Heart (1938) was Buck's first notable novel using an American setting. Susan Gaylord, the protagonist, is admittedly based on the author. Susan is exceedingly energetic and very intelligent. Although happily married, she is restless and seeks further experiences and fulfillment. She has a special gift for sculpting but refuses to leave her husband and children to pursue the additional study and training needed to perfect her art. Her husband's death gives her the opportunity to travel to France for further study. She falls in love with an avant-garde artist and remarries, but in time realizes that his selfishness and jealousy prevent her from achieving artistic fulfillment. She separates from him and determines single-mindedly to develop her talent for sculpting.

The theme of the woman genius has received relatively little treatment in literature, so *This Proud Heart* focuses on a particularly captivating topic. The autobiographical aspects add further appeal. Buck was aware that she possessed enormous energy and a very fine mind. Although she came into contact with many intellectual men, and Richard Walsh, her second husband, was very bright and talented, she could say late in her life that the Harvard philosopher Ernest Hocking was the only man she ever met who had a better mind than she. The more thoroughly familiar one becomes with Buck, the more one realizes that this remark is doubtless true. Her mind was acute and always intent on intellectual matters, and every conceivable subject was of interest to her. She constantly researched topics that aroused her interest. Yet at the same time she had a strong romantic strain. She wanted to be loved, to know all the joys of marriage and family, and yet to be treated as an absolute equal. This conflict appears more commonplace in recent years because of the women's liberation movement. Nevertheless, for women like Buck the difficulty moves to a higher level because genius is involved. A woman like her who can create, who has an extraordinary talent, must reconcile this gift with wifehood and motherhood, because in Buck's nature both were strong drives.

Although the genius of Susan Gaylord is acknowledged by everyone in the novel, her aptitude is never fully explained. It is simply there. It appears to be an innate combination of intelligence, energy, and talent. Perhaps this is as far as one can reach in explaining genius, but the feeling persists that the reader should be brought more into Susan's mind. She is externalized too much; hence we do not come to know and understand as much as if a more introspective or stream-of-consciousness technique had been employed.

The novel is fascinating thematically, but its impact is considerably reduced by deficiencies in style. Buck is writing a serious novel, for the first time in a new idiom. She leaves behind the mixture of Chinese saga and biblical language that marked her earlier fiction, and attempts an American style that is dominated by clichés and a limited vocabulary. All the freshness and beauty evident in the books on Chinese topics are lost in prose that is incredibly flat and pedestrian. It is evident that Buck had, in a sense, to learn an American idiom. *This Proud Heart* should have been ruthlessly edited for stylistic awkwardness and infelicities, but the success of her earlier books obviously precluded this much-needed task.

Considerable insight may be gained into Buck's philosophy of writing if her major pronouncements on fiction are chronicled. Her first statements appeared in two talks given in Peking, early in 1932. She analyzed the traditional Chinese saga, which she used as the basis for much of her work, and noted that the authors presented the omniscient point of view and stressed external statements of characterization. Internal states of mind were either ignored or treated rather casually. There was no deep probing. Because she adopted this approach, Buck's novels—especially the post-1930's stories—are frequently unconvincing in characterization. We are often told that a character "feels" this or that, but this externalizing prevents a penetrating analysis of state of mind. Without detailed observation of their minds in action, the characters often seem capricious and flimsily motivated, acting only as cardboard cutouts subject to their creator's fancy and manipulations.

Buck also stressed the considerable burden put on the story. The Chinese saga writer wished, above all, to keep his audience interested. Action was paramount, and therefore the writer had to keep adding new episodes, striving for constant suspense. Although Buck claimed that she was more interested in characterization than in story, in reality the story often seizes the predominant role and Buck is caught in the trap of plotting, more plotting, and overplotting. She realizes she must keep narrative interest, and she frequently achieves this by writing a novel of almost pure storytelling without equally rewarding insights into character.

In a later address, "On the Writing of Novels" (1933), Buck insisted that no single form of relating a story was superior to another. She did not believe that the form is more significant than the plot. She indicated that form tends to be a preoccupation of literary critics, and it is evident that she did not possess a high regard for modern schools of criticism or for professional pronouncements on novel writing such as those of E. M. Forster and Percy Lubbock.

In a highly significant passage Buck remarked that didacticism is not looked upon with favor by literary pundits and that she can see the logic and value in this viewpoint. Nevertheless, she was obviously attracted to the didactic aspect of fiction, although in theory she acknowledged that an artistic genius cannot be a moralizer because the material would then be altered or slanted to fit the message and reality would be distorted. She pointed out that in the traditional Chinese sagas "little moral precepts are inserted almost anywhere." A notable con-

flict in Buck's career is here revealed in embryo. She certainly was keenly aware of the pitfalls of turning novels into preachments, yet she was unable, especially in her post-1930's work, to resist the appeal of propagandizing for various causes and attitudes. Perhaps there was a strong subconscious need to "preach" inherited from her missionary father. Although she was not religious in the sense of adhering to an organized church, she certainly felt a mission to convince her readers of worthwhile and humane beliefs. She wanted to eliminate racial prejudice, poverty, oppression, war, and other miseries that prevent people the world over from achieving a sensible mode of behavior in which love, kindness, generosity, common sense, and peace predominate.

When she received the Nobel Prize (1938), Buck gave her address on the development of the Chinese novel and observed that she wanted to write for the many, not the few. She did not intend to write for scholars or literary critics. If the ordinary readers were interested mainly in popular magazines, then she would tailor her stories for those magazines. According to *The Exile's Daughter* (1944), the biography written by her sister, Cornelia Spencer, Buck insisted that

. . . story belongs to the people. They are sounder judges of it than anyone else, for their senses are unspoiled and their emotions are free. No, a novelist must not think of pure literature as his goal. He must not even know this field too well, because people, who are his material, are not there. . . . He must be satisfied if the common people hear him gladly.

As her career progressed, Buck's attempt to reach the largest possible audience intensified. She not only made her novels much more didactic, thereby hoping to inculcate sensible moral values and civilized behavior, but also began to write almost unceasingly for large-circulation magazines, furnishing both stories and articles on numerous contemporary issues. One of her most revealing statements was made in an address before the National Education Association: "One cannot dismiss lightly a magazine bought and read by three million people.... It is a serious thing for literature if three million people read—not literature, but something which gives them greater satisfaction." Spencer elaborated on this attitude:

Underlying her interests and her writing and her other active life there was and there is one unchanging unity.... All she does must work toward mutual understanding between the common peoples of the earth and toward justice for all.... More and more, then, in keeping with her purpose she wrote where she would be read, not only by the student and lover of books but by the workman and the clerk and the stenographer. With deliberate intent she wrote that everyone might read because she wants to write for people.

It is evident that Buck could not resist the lure of reaching the widest audience possible and of preaching to her readers. This attitude may explain, in part, her prolific writing. Although she possessed boundless energy, much of her *furor scribendi* may be explained by her desire to preach her messages in both fictional and nonfictional form. She seemed to believe that she could not lose her audience if she kept up an unceasing flow of material. Producing books and articles at an incredible rate kept her in the limelight, where she could hold the attention of countless readers and constantly enlighten them. Theodore Harris' "official" biography claims several times that Buck's goal was "to entertain." This infinitive needs a partner—"to entertain and to enlighten" is a more precise description of her goal. The missionary spark so strong in her parents did not die with them—in her own special manner Buck carried on their

humanitarian aims independent of sectarian considerations.

Such a philosophy of entertaining, of preaching, of reaching the greatest number of people meant that Buck's aesthetic view of the novel was narrowly prescribed. Her credo was the very opposite of art for art's sake, and it cut her off from the highest possible artistic goals. Perceptive symbolism, finer points of style, and inventive approaches such as the stream-of-consciousness technique are just a few of the most challenging and broadening developments in the novel precluded by such a limited view of fiction.

In her address on the occasion of receiving the Nobel Prize, Buck observed that she had been instructed by the Chinese never to regard the novel as an art form. When she was young, she was taught and much influenced by a Mr. Kung, who was a follower of Confucius. Confucian philosophy denigrated the novel as frivolous and unintellectual. The Chinese saga was, therefore, always related to the common people, and an effective novelist was required to be natural and ordinary in both language and character portrayal. The Chinese novel was supposed to be a representation of life without any of the artifice of pure literature. Also, Buck's family regarded novels as secondary, frivolous, and irreligious. Thus, parental upbringing and Chinese tutoring combined to plant in her mind a jaundiced view of "fiction."

Perhaps realizing, after writing *This Proud Heart,* that she was not yet prepared to deal effectively with contemporary styles, Buck turned her attention back to the Orient and produced *The Patriot* (1939), one of her best books. This novel is a historically accurate portrayal of the late 1920's and 1930's. I-wan, the chief character, is, like so many other young Chinese, filled with enthusiasm for Chiang Kai-shek's new revolutionary movement; but it is soon apparent that Chiang will compromise his ideals and that few efforts will be made to bring about greater freedom and social and economic improvement. Many youthful enthusiasts are eventually hunted down as dangers to the state. I-wan flees to Japan, to escape persecution as a Communist. He marries a Japanese girl and observes Japanese military activity against Manchuria and China. The general view of the Japanese character of that period in history is sharply delineated. Japanese devotion to duty and to country are underscored, while the Japanese militarism and emperor worship that carried the country into World War II are viewed in all their ramifications. I-wan perceives the seeming contradictions in the Japanese character—a tenderness, yet a refusal to shrink from all the emotional appeals and the utter horrors of war.

The Patriot is a well-conceived portrait of two countries caught at a crucial moment in history. Buck also demonstrates that she is an astute observer of Japan. While some events in the story appear improbable, the historical accuracy of the novel gives it a basic validity.

In her next work of fiction, *Other Gods: An American Legend* (1940), Buck takes up an American topic and attempts to avoid the stylistic pitfall of *This Proud Heart* by setting much of the action in the Orient. The protagonist, Bert Holm, captures considerable attention and newspaper headlines by climbing to the top of a mountain in the Himalayas. He projects an image of rugged handsomeness and fearless courage. In reality he is a rather childish, naive, and totally nonthinking individual. He has been raised to the status of a hero, yet does not have concomitant qualities that would make him sensible and balanced. His ascent of a second mountain results in the death of his climbing partner, a death caused by Holm's selfishness and childlike, reckless behavior. Holm later thinks that he might enjoy visiting Hitler and Mussolini, since, like him, although on a much

greater scale, they are idolized by crowds and assume herolike proportions. In an interview at this time, Buck linked Holm with Charles Lindbergh, Douglas "WrongWay" Corrigan, and some of the "prima donnas" of the New Deal.

The novel's themes are significant. The facts that all heroes have feet of clay and that frequently these defects are deliberately hidden from their adoring public (Bert Holm has a public relations agent to keep his image untainted) constitute a lesson that needs emphasis in every generation. Buck sees the hero in the United States as particularly vulnerable because the Americans' love of independence and democracy is so firmly implanted that they are distrustful of subordinating, in a sense, their beings to another person. If the hero does let the American public down, the tide of disillusionment and resentment is particularly overwhelming and remorseless. Bert Holm is kept from this fate by his wife and his public relations agent; but he, like others in his position, walks a very delicate line, and there are always iconoclasts lying in wait to topple the hero from his pedestal.

One begins to notice another specific pattern in Buck's novels after *House of Earth*, a pattern that was to follow for most of her career: she invariably picks an interesting topic to write about. There will be some moral, intellectual, political, social, or historical problem analyzed—at times the topic will blend these various materials. She will rarely pick facile subject matter just to relate an adventure or tell a love story. She may be primarily trying to "entertain," but such "entertainment" is always built around some intellectual issue, some controversial, challenging, or thought-provoking material.

Pursuing her late 1930's–early 1940's policy of veering back and forth between Chinese and American topics, Buck chose as her area of inquiry the Japanese invasion of China and the

Chinese resistance against this atrocity. *Dragon Seed* (1942) had a wide audience and was made into a popular movie, doubtless because it had become timely with America's recent involvement in World War II.

The novel vividly depicts the horrors of Japanese air raids, the effects of the underground resistance movement, and the forceful closing of ranks that an invasion usually entails. Yet Buck carries this material further, intruding an obvious propaganda note. The Japanese are depicted as behaving barbarously, and this constant denunciation is strongly pronounced. There can be no question where sympathy and point of view rest. *Dragon Seed* appears almost to have been written at the behest of the Chinese government, and it became immensely effective propaganda.

Dragon Seed is also damaged by something Buck rarely does: she introduces a romance into the story merely for the sake of adding a love interest. The beauteous Mayli, who is presented almost as a kind of comic strip Wonder Woman, is matched by Lao San, a handsome, courageous fantasy version of the *Übermensch*. This totally incredible romantic element clashes mightily with the realism of the primary material; and although the propagandistic note is not affected, the book's credibility and artistry are weakened.

Encouraged by the favorable reception of *Dragon Seed*, Pearl Buck produced a sequel. *The Promise* (1943) focuses on Chinese efforts to assist their British allies in Burma. Chinese forces go to Burma but are not allowed to enter the military action for many weeks. By that time the Japanese have pushed the British into a chaotic retreat. As the British and Chinese prepare to retreat over the Irrawaddy River, the British prematurely blow up a bridge in order to thwart the Japanese advance. As a result of this precipitous British action, the Chinese troops are trapped without an opportunity to

escape. The British, though, manage to cross the river to safety before destroying the bridge.

It is the thesis of *The Promise* that racial prejudice was the major factor causing the disastrous Chinese campaign in Burma. The British supposedly did not want the Burmese to see Chinese troops led by their own officers, and refused to accept the Chinese as equals. In light of subsequent historical studies, it appears that there is much validity to Buck's argument, although the "official" British view is that poor planning and various strategic errors were the main causes of the defeat. Although the novel is blatant propaganda designed to aid the Chinese efforts and to demonstrate the predicament of being caught between the Japanese on two fronts, the strength of its point of view has reinforced documentary accounts of this phase of World War II. Since propaganda is at the forefront, the characters become stock figures fulfilling their assigned roles in the thesis. Although *The Promise* can in no way be considered a successful novel, it is living history and its thesis remains long after all other aspects of the book are forgotten.

Buck's prolific pen began to overwhelm her publishers. She was writing more books than could be profitably marketed at one time. If she had her way, she would be turning out two or three books a year. To solve this problem, her publishers suggested a pen name. John Sedges was born, and *The Townsman*, the first of five novels published under this pseudonym, appeared in 1945.

Buck felt that she would have an opportunity to reach a new audience and that her American novels might be given more balanced critical treatment if her identity was concealed. She did not like the idea of being considered a writer whose success occurred only when she treated Chinese subject matter. She also felt, not without justification, that male authors were treated more fairly than female writers, and she deliberately chose a "plain English" male pseudonym.

The hero of *The Townsman* is a school-teacher in the early American West. Much of the material was based on Richard Walsh's relatives (indeed, Buck admitted that Jonathan, the protagonist, is based on her husband's Uncle John). She even visited Kansas in order to research material at first hand. She studied local history, traveled extensively, and collected the reminiscences of many of the pioneers and their descendants. Since Richard Walsh had originally come from Kansas, he was able to furnish extensive help with her historical probing.

As a result of considerable research, *The Townsman* furnishes a very well documented portrayal of the settlement and growth of the fictional town of Median, Kansas, from the earliest pioneering days in the nineteenth century. Jonathan Goodliffe, the protagonist, realizes, and cleverly uses, the appeal of a school to the early western immigrants. The land around the town is turned into a thriving farm area, and the community becomes a center of local business activity. The gradual settlement, growth, and stability of the community under the leadership of the Jonathans of the West is handled so well that Ernest Leisy commends the book in *The American Historical Novel*. For once the emphasis has been taken away from the outlaws and sheriffs and dance hall girls, and the real source of the ultimate strength and permanence of a settlement stands on view.

Given the authenticity of the settings and background, it is distressing that the novel is weakened by several stereotyped characters. Only Jonathan emerges as persuasive. The book must also be faulted for a too obvious attempt at propagandizing for racial equality. A black family in the story is treated unfairly by whites; and while the preachment that results is morally valid, it is not under artistic control. Buck

is usually on the side of the angels, but such excessive moralizing is inappropriate. All too often in her post-1930's works she seems to believe that a writer can be an influential polemicist and an artist at the same time. In some of her earlier novels, most notably *The Good Earth*, she was much more detached from her material and presented it with controlled and firm distance that ensured fundamental objectivity.

The remaining John Sedges novels—*The Angry Wife* (1947), *The Long Love* (1949), *Bright Procession* (1952), and *Voices in the House* (1953)—are undistinguished journeyman writings, worthy neither of contempt nor of particular praise. They preach civilized, honorable behavior, put a strong emphasis on romance, and are decidedly sentimental. Their characters are utter stereotypes, lacking flesh-and-blood dimensions. The books read smoothly and quickly, then are immediately forgotten. Nevertheless, the Sedges series did begin with *The Townsman,* a better-than-average work that ranks high among American local-color studies. It will always be valuable for its comprehensive portrayal of aspects usually ignored or overlooked in discussions, books, and movies about the early West.

In the midst of the John Sedges books, Buck did not ignore Chinese topics. The appearance of *Pavilion of Women* (1946) caused best-seller lists again to flash the message of Buck's popularity. Madame Wu, the leading character, and Brother André, the totally unselfish, dedicated scholar, combine to create what is probably Buck's strongest statement of benevolence and humanitarianism within the pages of a novel. In several respects Madame Wu is a fictional counterpart of her originator. Brilliant, energetic, and a capable manager, she is converted to kindliness, generosity, and a loving awareness through André's philosophy and example. The book insists that biblical values (love of neighbor, charity, patience, and beneficence) can solve any problem. It reflects not only Buck's personal statement but also a basic emphasis on values and a search for stability that constituted much of immediate post–World War II fiction, drama, and home-from-the-war films.

It should be stressed that this humanitarianism exists apart from standard religious orthodoxy, since Madame Wu in effect becomes the good pagan of ancient classicism and André is a defrocked priest who has been ostracized because of heretical beliefs.

A new aspect of Buck's thinking is introduced when the death of Brother André intensifies Madame Wu's spirituality. She comes to believe that André's spirit is hovering about and actually guiding her in daily activities. She embraces a belief in life after death because André's divinity watches over and directs the course of her life from beyond the grave.

Buck's talent as a storyteller and her ability to focus on interesting subject matter enabled her to follow *Pavilion of Women* with *Kinfolk* (1949), another best-selling novel. This book underscores a telling and significant point. For hundreds of years many Chinese intellectuals, as well as the upper classes, either ignored the farmers or oppressed them. Snobbishly destructive and scornful attitudes replaced humane, altruistic, and logical concerns. Landlords, political figures, and government bureaucrats were guilty of this oppression, and the seeds for communism were sown. The gradual rise of Mao Tse-tung came to completion in 1949, when his government took full control. This novel furnishes valuable insights into the reasons behind his ascent to power.

The young American-reared physician James Liang works with the impoverished Chinese farmers. He not only aids them medically, but he and his sister help them economically and educationally. James's marriage to a young peasant girl helps to promote the farmers' cooperation. The thesis, although overly logical, is thought-provoking: only through a union of the intellectuals and the peasants will China remedy its deficiencies and take a giant step forward in progress and stability.

From her earliest period of writing to the end of her life, Buck constantly wrote short stories. Indeed, several of her briefer unpublished narratives are being issued posthumously. Buck brought to her shorter fiction the traditional Chinese narrative techniques used in the novels. The omniscient point of view is employed, and characters are revealed mainly by dialogue. Buck does not probe deeply into internal states of mind. There are no penetrating analyses involving poetic emanations or perceptive subtleties of memory. The stories are related directly, in a utilitarian prose that is neither pedestrian nor elevating; the style is pleasantly readable and smooth—really unnoticeable, since the author's and reader's concentration rests on the story being told. Narrative drive is the major concern, and plot interest and energy are effectively maintained. While the shorter narratives are eminently readable, the majority are generally forgettable. They are mostly glossy magazine fiction with a persistent emphasis on romance.

Buck was not above frequent sentimentality and a Pollyanna's view of most situations. In reviewing *Fourteen Stories* (1961), Richard Sullivan remarked:

They have craft, compassion, and admirable goodwill. They are never careless; they deal with meaningful matter; they are seriously intended, generous and hopeful. . . . [but] Everything always gets nicely, neatly, tidily resolved in these pages. . . . [The] stories present human experience . . . as engaging matters to be worked out with just a bit of sound humanitarian . . . good sense, and with most excellent good intentions. Good stories seldom solve problems; they simply pose them in bright words.

Pearl Buck's best short fiction pieces are on Chinese subjects. In "The First Wife" (1931–1932) a young Chinese goes abroad to study. After being away from his homeland for several years, he returns and finds himself opposed to the old ways. He is hired as a government official and moves in intellectual and sophisticated circles. Although his wife is devoted and ready to aid him in every way, he rejects her because she is too old-fashioned and uneducated to fit in with his new friends and his progressive way of life. He divorces his wife, who is shattered by his unwarranted cruelty and indifference. She finally commits suicide. The old China and the new China are thus bitingly juxtaposed, with tragic results. The contrast is effectively presented and thoroughly persuasive. Although the suffering and bewilderment of the young wife are accentuated, Buck manages to hold back undue emotionalism and the maudlin sentimentality that could easily have occurred.

Similar material is treated with equal skill in "The Rainy Day" (1925). A young Chinese student has been educated at an American university, where he has produced an outstanding dissertation and has been regarded as one of the most brilliant scholars ever produced by that school. When he returns to China, to help his country keep pace with new discoveries and developments, he is faced with a perplexing problem. His family wishes him to marry the girl to whom he was betrothed as a child. He is also expected to support several of his relatives. Again the clash between the traditional ways and the more intellectual, sophisticated goals of the new China resounds forcefully. He does not desire a high-salaried position in a field he has no interest in; yet, unlike his counterpart in "The First Wife," he is too honorable, too sensitive, and too conscious of ancestral requirements to reject the old ways. He seeks refuge in opium. This time the old dominates the new, with disastrous results.

The China scene is again handled especially well in "The Angel" (1937), in which the focus is on Miss Barry, a lonely American missionary. Although she has come to a foreign country to spread the message of brotherly love emphasized in the Gospels, she finds herself constantly incensed against Chinese workers and servants who cannot perform any task to her satisfaction. She discovers that in general she cannot relate to the Chinese; this situation intensifies her isolation and alienation, and brings further conflicts with her vocation. Finally she becomes totally irrational and commits suicide in an especially violent way. Although the bare outline of the story may not convey the force and sharpness of the conflict, this is a powerfully realistic saga, totally credible and expertly free of sentimentality or false notes. "The Angel" demonstrates that Buck could compose a commanding narrative when she chose, and it is one of a handful of her stories that can be reread with satisfaction.

"Enough for a Lifetime" (1935) also focuses on the missionary spinster in China. Amy Wiley, although dedicated to a spiritual calling, has found little joy and love in her life. Her superior is particularly harsh and demanding, and her associates in the mission compound succeed only in making the atmosphere more oppressive and gloomy. Eventually she is given the opportunity to play the part of Elizabeth Barrett Browning in an amateur production of *The Barretts of Wimpole Street*. She involves herself completely in the dramatization and imagines that she and her handsome leading man are in love. Although she receives a setback upon discovering that her dramatic partner is romantically attached to someone else, she soon adjusts, being overwhelmed by a realization of what love is and means. The Elizabeth Barrett–Robert Browning relationship has given her a new outlook and purpose. She can now imbue her life and career with new dedication and live with inner strength and conviction. Again the realism without frills—an approach used so well in *The Good Earth*—works effectively to render this short story memorable. It should be noted that this is one of Buck's earlier short stories. As her career progressed, her writing became more romantic and the taut realism diminished.

The later stories are dominated by a cloying optimism and excessive romanticism. For example, in "The Lovers" (published posthumously in 1977) a young couple decide to marry. Their romance and joie de vivre bring the girl's estranged parents back together. In "Miranda" (also published posthumously in 1977) a male and a female physician fall satisfactorily and all too predictably in love. In "John, John Chinaman" the prejudice a young Chinese American faces is diluted when he is chosen as the first recruit in the World War II draft lottery held in his midwestern home town. These later stories indicate how far Buck had strayed from the searing, sharp realism of "The Rainy Day" (1925) and "The Angel" (1937).

When not writing novels and short stories, Buck was publishing magazine articles and works of nonfiction, studies of racial prejudice, discussions about Soviet communism and Nazi Germany, and books for children. During World War II she was intensely involved in promoting the Allied cause. She gave talks, produced radio scripts, and wrote numerous articles and pamphlets. In 1941 she founded the East and West Association, a group designed to bring about closer harmony and understanding between the Orient and the West. Throughout the war she denounced fascistic and totalitarian philosophies, while remaining equally critical of racial prejudice and imperialism. She was responsible for keeping China, the almost forgot-

ten ally of America in World War II, in the public eye, and also managed to bring about the delivery of much-needed food and military supplies to that country.

Later, when she learned that many children had been fathered by American servicemen abroad and that these youngsters were destitute and ill-treated, Buck founded Welcome House, an adoption agency for such children. She and her second husband, Richard Walsh, took the first two unwanted children into their home. Ultimately, Buck established the Pearl S. Buck Foundation, which set up centers in several foreign countries to assist the half-American children fathered in those nations. She was also involved in the Training School in Vineland, New Jersey, which worked to improve the lot of mentally retarded children. She publicized the need for the independence of India from Great Britain and objected to the treatment of those Japanese Americans who were taken from their homes and farms and interned in distant camps.

Buck spoke out on virtually every question involving freedom and human rights. She was active in the American Civil Liberties Union and was especially incensed over the censorship of books. After World War II she also cautioned against what she perceived to be the undue influence of the military in American life. She felt that America might surrender its precious freedoms; and although she did not fear a military dictatorship, she believed that citizens could become so indoctrinated by the military mind that peace and general freedom of thought might be jeopardized.

These activities were carried on while Buck maintained a full writing schedule, usually four hours a day, five days a week, producing both novels and volumes of nonfiction. Her humanitarian endeavors explain part of Buck's popularity with the general reading public. Her audience knew that she was involved in bringing about a better world; and though these efforts hampered her artistry, they placed her in an unusual category. Of all the writers in the history of American literature, Buck was perhaps the most altruistic—not a mere speaker of the word, but a writer devoted to practical action.

Buck's restless and inquiring mind was always fascinated by contemporary events. She became especially interested in questions involving atomic power. Again a novel resulted from her studies; *Command the Morning* (1959) was the product of visits to Los Alamos, New Mexico, and to almost every other atomic study or test area in the United States.

The main focus of this book is the Manhattan Project, from its conception to the first explosion at the New Mexico test site. At this point the novel wrestles with the question of actually using the bomb against the Japanese. Before the defeat of the Germans, the development of the bomb was thought to be a race against the German technical skill that might enable the Nazis to acquire and use the bomb first. Once Germany was defeated, it became obvious that Japan did not have this ability. Many of the experts supported a naval blockade of Japan and the use of conventional weapons; others believed that the lives of many American soldiers would be saved if the bomb were employed. Although arguments were amassed on both sides of the issue, the decision to use the bomb was made. It is immediately evident how Buck feels about this event. Despite seeming attempts at objectivity, she vehemently opposes the dropping of the bomb. She marshals every conceivable argument, including the racial issue. She suggests that the atomic bomb would not have been used against Germany because of a concern for the white race, whereas using it on Orientals would not cause a second thought.

Although most of the characters in *Command the Morning* are stereotypes, the book is a rewarding experience because it was so thoroughly researched. The history of atomic research leading to the dropping of the bomb is presented in considerable detail. The exposition of atomic developments is so lucid that the novel becomes an illuminating textbook as well as a captivating story.

Although Buck continued to write almost a novel a year until her death, only three of these narratives—*The Living Reed, The Time Is Noon,* and *The Goddess Abides*—warrant detailed consideration. *The Living Reed* (1963) is prefaced by a nine-page discussion of the history of Korea. Buck points out that for centuries Russia, China, and Japan had been interested in controlling Korea, which has fertile land and attractive seaports. At one time Russia and Japan had concluded a secret accord in which they agreed to divide Korea at the thirty-eighth parallel. Buck's preface summarizes the most significant aspects of Korean history until shortly before 1883, when a treaty was signed between Korea and the United States. This preface serves as a useful introduction to a book that is not just a novel of Korea but a textbook chronicle.

The first section of this three-part study uses an obvious narrative device. Il-han, the protagonist, receives permission from Queen Min to tour Korea in order to investigate the people's resolve in what promises to be a struggle against Japanese encroachment. Although transparent, the technique neatly accomplishes its purpose, since the reader is taken on an instructive tour of Korea, visiting the mountain settlements, the farms, and the coastal regions. This segment presents a valid cross section of the population, establishes an authentic feeling for time and place, and effectively describes social customs and traditions.

In the second part Buck emphasizes the brutality of Japanese rule after their conquest in 1905. (Although the United States had signed a treaty in 1883 guaranteeing the independence of Korea, America did not intervene, mainly, it is argued, because of political ineptitude.) Some Koreans look to Woodrow Wilson and his "self-determination" statements as a salvation from Japanese oppression. Il-han, in particular, idolizes Wilson and joins the Korean delegation that travels to Paris during the peace conference after World War I. (Such a delegation actually did visit Wilson.) Again disillusionment with American promises and statements results.

The third section follows the wanderings of one of Il-han's sons, who is a rebel leader. The Japanese attack on Pearl Harbor in 1941 arouses new hopes for the Korean independence movement. But after the war America concludes an agreement with the Russians allowing them to occupy Korea from its northern border down to the thirty-eighth parallel. The novel moves to a tense climax as the forces of the incoming American military government land at Inchon, in the south, and, instead of acknowledging the Koreans, defer to the Japanese army of occupation.

Buck builds her indictment of American treatment of the Koreans with devastating power. American incompetence and lack of knowledge of the real importance of Korea and of the political realities in that area of Asia are intensely and vividly demonstrated. The knowledge that all the historical facts are authentic—as Buck makes clear in the prefatory note and in the epilogue—gives the book a striking impact.

Although most of the characters, with the possible exception of Il-han and Yul-han, suffer diminution in contrast with the historical happenings, *The Living Reed* is a book to remember. The characters fade, but the events and the history portrayed linger and render this work one of the most unforgettable of Buck's novels. The book represents her fiction at its thematic best. It makes the history of Korea memorable, and although Buck does not carry the story as far as the war in the 1950's or the later standoff

between North and South Korea at the thirty-eighth parallel, she compels readers to understand what led to these distressing events. *The Living Reed* has gone through numerous printings and deserves such attention because it gives the American reader the background material necessary to understand American involvement in Korea, which from its beginnings has been tainted by inadequate knowledge and illusionary hopes.

The Time Is Noon (1967), one of Buck's most unusual novels, had been written much earlier, but she and Richard Walsh deemed it much too personal to publish, even though the manuscript had been set up in type. Research has now established that the novel was composed over a three-year period (1936–1939) and was begun not long after she divorced John Lossing Buck and married Richard Walsh. (Walsh also had to obtain a divorce in order to marry her.)

Joan Richards, the protagonist of *The Time Is Noon,* has many affinities with Buck. She has a large-boned, heavy figure, yet is facially attractive. Intelligent, college-educated, and with vast energy and strength, she dreams of having a husband and children, and is extremely family-oriented.

Although certain obvious changes were made (for instance, the heroine's father is a minister in the United States during the 1920's rather than in China; her husband is a farmer rather than an agricultural expert; and her married lover is an aviator rather than a talented publisher), the autobiographical parallels are so apparent that it is quite understandable why publication of the book was delayed for almost thirty years: the issue of the two divorces was unquestionably the major factor. Both Buck and Richard Walsh were concerned about the effect of their divorces on her public image and on the sale of her books. When she devotes a section of *Other Gods* to the way in which the hero, Bert Holm, must manage the proper image presented to his adoring public, she is doubtless speaking from personal experience, remembering the risk of scandal during an era when divorce was generally frowned upon.

What is of more consequence is that *The Time Is Noon* contains some of Buck's best writing—writing having the forceful realism characteristic mainly of her books published in the 1930's. There are two particularly powerful segments: the penetrating portrayal of daily life in a minister's family and the depiction of Joan Richards' early period of marriage while living with her husband's family.

In describing Joan's life with her mother and father, Buck transposed material from *The Exile* and *Fighting Angel* onto the pages of the novel. The dialogue and descriptions are so authentic that the reader understands why her biographies fascinated the Nobel committee. The father's God-obsessed remoteness is brilliantly conveyed, and his wife's ambivalent response is equally persuasive. When she becomes terminally ill, Mary Richards does not want to see her husband. The resentment that has been building for years boils over in her last illness. The family situation, with its underlying compromises and tensions, is rendered with excellent verisimilitude.

When Joan Richards marries, she goes to live on the farm of her husband's parents. Again a family is depicted with rare authenticity and power. The Pounder family is completely joyless. Their existence is a perpetual round of work, meals are silent rituals, and the only thing the family shares is a regular Bible-reading session. They want nothing fresh or out-of-the-ordinary to disturb their dull, plodding lives. The mother, in particular, does not wish her ways disturbed. (Even Christmas, in such circumstances, is a dismal experience.) For the mother everything is extra work and trouble. Mrs. Pounder simply does not wish to be both-

ered, to make an effort, to be concerned and involved. When her children were small, she did not want to invite their playmates into her house. Youngsters, like everything else, were a burden. Even her own children are epitomized with the comment that although they were well behaved, they "made work." Though the other members of the household are also genuinely alive, the mother-in-law is splendidly brought to life. This episode echoes in every way Buck's best writing of the 1930's.

The Goddess Abides (1972), published the year before her death, is another novel in which Buck is personally involved. Edith Chardman, the forty-two-year-old heroine, is loved by two men: a twenty-four-year-old scientist and a seventy-six-year-old philosopher. Both men look upon her as a goddess. She furnishes inspiration and adds idealism to their lives. Although a passage from Robert Graves's *The White Goddess* is quoted at the beginning, Buck is not concerned with any of the deeper aspects of myth or theories of primitive concepts evolving into modern beliefs. She is close to the idea of the medieval knight and his ladylove, the courtly love tradition. A woman beloved rests on a pedestal and inspires her knight (in this case her knights) to high-minded thoughts and noble deeds. This notion, Buck believes, can still be valid in the latter part of the twentieth century. At least in the case of Ernest Hocking (the retired Harvard philosopher, who is called Edwin Steadley in the novel), there is documentary proof in his letters that he beheld Buck as a modern goddess. The identity of the young scientist is unknown, but he could be a composite based on several younger men of Buck's acquaintance. A reading of the nonfiction dialogue *For Spacious Skies* (1966), written in collaboration with Theodore F. Harris, illustrates one such case.

The Goddess Abides is fundamentally a paean to love. Certainly for both Buck and Ernest Hocking their experience as friends and correspondents was elevating and invigorating, and buoyed their lives. The themes of the grandeur of love and the glories of giving and self-sacrifice—themes reiterated in several of Buck's books—here reach their most emphatically emotional expression in her fiction. This heavenly love will not cease on an earthly plane, it is clearly implied; it will pass beyond death and, in some form, unite the lovers in a spiritual existence. As the love of the aged philosopher does not terminate with his death, but continues, so Jared Barnow, the young scientist, must use goddess worship for his own development and growth. Love on its proper plane must seek the fulfillment of the lover and the beloved. When Edith arranges the opportunity for Barnow to marry another, her self-sacrifice and encouragement will aid him in the most ennobling way possible. Worship is used constructively and beneficently, for the betterment of all parties concerned. By using the man's worship in this way, the goddess ennobles herself. Individual aspirations, development, and possibilities reach their highest potential and transcendence, and ultimately all of this passes on to a heavenly realm.

Although the themes and philosophy reach for the highest realms, the novel possesses an unreal, flowery aura—and yet there is the evidence of the Hocking letters and *For Spacious Skies*, which indicates that, improbable as it may seem, Buck is relating the situation as it actually was.

Deep personal involvement played a particularly significant role throughout Buck's career. In her early writing, especially in *The Good Earth* and the biographies of her father and mother, she created powerful books that record Chinese peasant life and the American missionary experience with memorable accuracy and feeling. Such works could have been written only from perceptive, sensitive, firsthand knowledge and experience.

Buck eventually decided that she wanted to reach the widest possible audience with her personal philosophy and viewpoints; thus didacticism became the primary concern. While this didacticism was involved with excessive optimism, stereotyped characterization, and overplotting, it could never diminish her spellbinding narrative gift. This ability led to her best-selling status and made her the most widely translated author in the history of American literature. (Only Mark Twain has approached her in this category.)

Buck's personal commitment was also evidenced in her lifelong devotion to social ideals. She worked tirelessly for human rights, racial equality, and understanding between East and West. Even after her death, in Danby, Vermont, her royalties work to aid several humanitarian causes, chiefly the Pearl S. Buck Foundation, which provides Amerasian children with food, clothing, medical supplies, and educational opportunities.

It would appear that Buck's fame will continue into the future on two levels: as author and as humanitarian.

Selected Bibliography

WORKS OF PEARL S. BUCK

NOVELS AND SHORT STORY COLLECTIONS
East Wind: West Wind. New York: John Day, 1930.
The Good Earth. New York: John Day, 1931.
Sons. New York: John Day, 1932.
The First Wife and Other Stories. New York: John Day, 1933.

The Mother. New York: John Day, 1934.

A House Divided. New York: Reynal and Hitchcock, 1935.

House of Earth. New York: Reynal and Hitchcock, 1935. (Trilogy of *The Good Earth, Sons,* and *A House Divided.*)

This Proud Heart. New York: Reynal and Hitchcock, 1938.

The Patriot. New York: John Day, 1939.

Other Gods: An American Legend. New York: John Day, 1940.

Today and Forever. New York: John Day, 1941.

Dragon Seed. New York: John Day, 1942.

The Promise. New York: John Day, 1943.

Portrait of a Marriage. New York: John Day, 1945.

The Townsman. New York: John Day, 1945. (Written under the pseudonym of John Sedges.)

Pavilion of Women. New York: John Day, 1946.

The Angry Wife. New York: John Day, 1947. (Written under the pseudonym of John Sedges.)

Far and Near. New York: John Day, 1947.

Peony. New York: John Day, 1948.

Kinfolk. New York: John Day, 1949.

The Long Love. New York: John Day, 1949. (Written under the pseudonym of John Sedges.)

God's Men. New York: John Day, 1951.

Bright Procession. New York: John Day, 1952. (Written under the pseudonym of John Sedges.)

The Hidden Flower. New York: John Day, 1952.

Voices in the House. New York: John Day, 1953. (Written under the pseudonym of John Sedges.)

Come, My Beloved. New York: John Day, 1953.

Imperial Woman. New York: John Day, 1956.

Letter from Peking. New York: John Day, 1957.

Command the Morning. New York: John Day, 1959.

Fourteen Stories. New York: John Day, 1961.

The Living Reed. New York: John Day, 1963.

The Time Is Noon. New York: John Day, 1967.

The New Year. New York: John Day, 1968.

The Good Deed and Other Stories of Asia, Past and Present. New York: John Day, 1969.

The Three Daughters of Madame Liang. New York: John Day, 1969.

Mandala. New York: John Day, 1970.

The Goddess Abides. New York: John Day, 1972.

All Under Heaven. New York: John Day, 1973.

East and West. New York: John Day, 1975.

Secrets of the Heart. New York: John Day, 1976.

The Lovers and Other Stories. New York: John Day, 1977.

The Woman Who Was Changed and Other Stories. New York: Crowell, 1979.

NONFICTION

East and West and the Novel: Sources of the Early Chinese Novel. Peking: North China Union Language School–California College in China, 1932.

The Exile. New York: Reynal and Hitchcock, 1936.

Fighting Angel. New York: Reynal and Hitchcock, 1936.

The Chinese Novel. New York: John Day, 1939.

Of Men and Women. New York: John Day, 1941; reiss. 1971 with new epilogue.

American Unity and Asia. New York: John Day, 1942.

The Spirit and the Flesh. New York: John Day, 1944. (Combines *The Exile* and *Fighting Angel* in one volume.)

Talk About Russia. New York: John Day, 1945. (With Masha Scott.)

Tell the People. New York: John Day, 1945.

How It Happens. New York: John Day, 1947. (With Erna von Pustau.)

American Argument. New York: John Day, 1949. (With Eslanda Goode Robeson.)

The Child Who Never Grew. New York: John Day, 1950.

My Several Worlds. New York: John Day, 1954.

A Bridge for Passing. New York: John Day, 1962.

Children for Adoption. New York: Random House, 1964.

The Gifts They Bring: Our Debt to the Mentally Retarded. New York: John Day, 1965. (With Gweneth T. Zarfoss.)

Essay on Myself. New York: John Day, 1966. (This is the first part of a two-part pamphlet; the second is by Jason Lindsey, below.)

For Spacious Skies: Journey in Dialogue. New York: John Day, 1966. (With Theodore F. Harris.)

The People of Japan. New York: Simon and Schuster, 1966.

To My Daughters, with Love. New York: John Day, 1967.

China as I See It, edited by Theodore F. Harris. New York: John Day, 1970.

China Past and Present. New York: John Day, 1972.

BIOGRAPHICAL AND CRITICAL STUDIES

Bentley, Phyllis. "The Art of Pearl S. Buck." *English Journal,* 24:791–800 (December 1935).

Birmingham, Frederic A. "Pearl Buck and the Good Earth of Vermont." *Saturday Evening Post,* 244:70–73, 135, 139, 141, 143–44 (Spring 1972).

Block, Irwin. *The Lives of Pearl Buck.* New York: Crowell, 1973.

Canby, Henry Seidel. *"The Good Earth:* Pearl Buck and the Nobel Prize." *Saturday Review of Literature,* 19:8 (November 19, 1938).

Cargill, Oscar. *Intellectual America: Ideas on the March.* New York: Macmillan, 1941; repr. Cooper Square Publishers, 1968. Pp. 146–54.

Carson, E. H. A. "Pearl Buck's Chinese." *Canadian Bookman,* 21:55–59 (June–July 1939).

Cevasco, George A. "Pearl Buck and the Chinese Novel." *Asian Studies,* 5:437–50 (December 1967).

Cowley, Malcolm. "Wang Lung's Children." *New Republic,* 99:24–25 (May 10, 1939).

Dickstein, Lore. "Posthumous Stories." *New York Times Book Review,* March 11, 1979, pp. 20–21.

Doàn-Cao-Lý. *The Image of the Chinese Family in Pearl Buck's Novels.* Saigon: Dúc-Dinh, 1964.

Doyle, Paul A. *Pearl S. Buck.* New York: Twayne, 1965.

——. "Pearl S. Buck's Short Stories: A Survey." *English Journal,* 55:62–68 (January 1966).

Harris, Theodore F. *Pearl S. Buck. A Biography.* 2 vols. New York: John Day, 1969–1971.

Henchoz, Ami. "A Permanent Element in Pearl Buck's Novels." *English Studies,* 25:97–103 (August 1943).

Janeway, Elizabeth. "The Optimistic World of Miss Buck." *New York Times Book Review,* May 25, 1952, p. 4.

Langlois, Walter G. *"The Dream of the Red Chamber, The Good Earth,* and *Man's Fate:* Chronicles of Social Change in China." *Literature East and West,* 11:1–10 (March 1967).

Lask, Thomas. "A Missionary Heritage." *New York Times,* March 7, 1973, p. 40.

Lee, Henry. "Pearl S. Buck—Spiritual Descendant of Tom Paine." *Saturday Review of Literature,* 25:16–18 (December 5, 1942).

Lindsey, Jason. *A Study of Pearl S. Buck.* New York: John Day, 1966. (The second part of a two-part pamphlet; see Buck's *Essay on Myself,* above.)

Shimizu, Mamoru. "On Some Stylistic Features, Chiefly Biblical, of *The Good Earth.*" *Studies in English Literature* (Tokyo), English no. 1964:117–34.

Spencer, Cornelia. *The Exile's Daughter, a Biography of Pearl S. Buck.* New York: Coward-McCann, 1944.

Thompson, Dody Weston. "Pearl Buck." *American Winners of the Nobel Literary Prize,* edited by Warren G. French and Walter E. Kidd. Norman: University of Oklahoma Press, 1968. Pp. 85–110.

Van Doren, Carl. *The American Novel 1789–1939.* Rev. and enl. ed. New York: Macmillan, 1940. Pp. 350, 352–53.

Van Gelder, Robert. "Pearl Buck Talks of Her Work." In his *Writers and Writing.* New York: Scribners, 1946. Pp. 26–28.

Woolf, S. J. "Pearl Buck Talks of Her Life in China." *China Weekly Review,* 62:145–46 (September 24, 1932).

Zinn, Lucille S. "The Works of Pearl S. Buck: A Bibliography." *Bulletin of Bibliography,* 36:194–208 (October–December 1979).

—PAUL A. DOYLE

Malcolm Cowley

1898 —

"WHAT we need are more American classics, not more criticism," Malcolm Cowley remarked in conversation in April 1971, during the time that he was writing *A Second Flowering*. The point, which is misleadingly simple—like many of his shrewd observations—cuts to the heart of the literary situation in the United States, since the masters of the early modern period—William Faulkner, Ernest Hemingway, T. S. Eliot, John Dos Passos, Robert Frost, and others—had completed their major work in the 1940's and early 1950's.

Since about 1950 it has been obvious that this is the Age of Criticism, as Randall Jarrell lamented in an essay of the same title (collected in *Poetry and the Age,* 1953). Jarrell could complain about this situation even as he regularly contributed to the rising flood of criticism with his own reviews and essays. Were Jarrell alive today, one can be certain that he would be outraged by the present state of criticism. Since about 1970 the pyrotechnics of criticism have blinded readers in and out of the academy, and the light, while sometimes dazzling, has been momentary in most cases. The literary landscape has more often than not been thrown into new darkness by the latest critical strategies. The critical hegemony of the 1940's and 1950's, painstakingly established through the triumph of the New Criticism, has been shattered. We now have a criticism—structuralism, phenomenology, deconstructionism, new literary history, and other schools—that is in considerable disarray, largely because the critics involved believe that criticism has parity with literature.

In "The New Age of the Rhetoricians," the opening chapter of *The Literary Situation* (1954), Cowley comes to the same general conclusion as Jarrell, but he does so in an entirely different spirit as he shows the close relation of criticism to contemporary literature:

Unexpectedly, most of the really new developments since 1940 have been in the field of criticism. Even the new creative writing shows a high degree of critical consciousness—so much of it that the novels and poems of the new age sometimes read like themes written to illustrate the best critical principles. Criticism has come to occupy such a central place in the literary world that it is hard to find historical parallels for the situation.

Cowley goes on to observe that "there are indeed clear traces of Alexandrianism in present-day critical writing, but more among the younger disciples than the older critics." He praises Eliot, Kenneth Burke, Yvor Winters, Allen Tate, R. P. Blackmur, I. A. Richards, Lionel Trilling, Edmund Wilson, Newton Arvin, Francis Fergusson, Jarrell, and others, saying that "an atmosphere of lowered creative vitality is not a characteristic of the newer criticism." He hastens to add, however, that the younger critics "of the less original or adventuresome type" are failing to ask the right questions and make the proper judgments, and that they are writing about absurdly narrow "objects of admiration."

Cowley's conclusion is that "criticism has not become autonomous, for all the efforts to make it so, and its future still depends on that of the other literary arts." Since he framed this postulate, matters have gotten considerably worse; and it is probably fair to say that criticism since at least 1965 has contributed more nearly to the exhaustion of literature than to its enrichment, just as Cowley predicted. It would be more accurate to say that the classics have been more nearly submerged by a numbing weight of commentary than exhausted by criticism.

Over the long course of his distinguished career, Cowley has seen the rise and decline of literary modernism, and in response the rise of a subtle (sometimes supersubtle) criticism from the new humanism through structuralism. When he was a student at Harvard in the 1910's, and immediately thereafter, a freelance writer, criticism, with the exception of H. L. Mencken's and that of a few other writers, was in a primitive state. In the academy one found only philology and literary history, and American literature was ignored. But Eliot was beginning to write the masterly essays that went into *The Sacred Wood* (1920), and he was soon followed by I. A. Richards.

These fathers of the *Scrutiny* critics in England and of the New Critics in the United States exercised an immense influence that Cowley has often felt but steadfastly resisted, even though he has been sympathetic to many of the critics involved, especially Kenneth Burke, whom he has called "one of the truly speculative thinkers of his American era," and

who has erected a vast system of interpretation and thought that extends from literature to many other fields. Only a little less complex is R. P. Blackmur, who praised Cowley for his "deliberately plastic intelligence" in his review of *Exile's Return.* Although Cowley has often expressed sympathy not only for Blackmur but also for Ransom, Tate, and others of the New Critics who struck a criticism that could measure and chart the terrain of modernism, he regularly enters caveats about this criticism.

In "The Difficulties of Modernism and the Modernism of Difficulty" (1979) Richard Poirier persuasively argues that modernism depends upon "the phenomenon of grim readings," "the degree of intimidation felt in the act of reading"; he taxes Eliot and James Joyce as the chief proponents of the "promotion . . . of the virtues and necessities of difficulty" and accuses them of forcing the reader to believe "that the act of reading should entail difficulties analogous to those registered in the act of writing." This article of faith, convincingly fobbed off on the reading public by Eliot, Ezra Pound, and others, is that "the difficulty was something only the poet could confront *for* us, and that the reader should be selfless and humble and thankful for the poet's having done this." The modernist therefore often exults in the rituals of technique, in the indirections of the guarded style.

That Edmund Wilson, Philip Rahv, the New Critics, and others propagated the virtues of modernism and rewrote literary history in its shadow is a truism; and, as Poirier argues, these critics were not as severe about the defects of modernism, especially its obscurantism, as they should have been. All the same, this criticism was conducted in a proper spirit, and none of these men were enthusiasts. Unlike many present-day critics they did not attempt to displace literature: they saw criticism (in Rahv's formulation) as a department of letters and viewed it as a "superstructural form of literature, . . . a form of literature about literature." Criticism, Rahv concluded in 1958, "has cognitive value in relation to literature to the degree, no more and no less, that literature can be said to have cognitive value in relation to life."

Hence the critic should perpetually reforge "the unity of the literary mind," and he or she should "recover the role of the participant in the literary event." Instead, unlike Rahv's ideal, which Cowley's work admirably fulfills, we now have a criticism that, more often than not, is an exploration of the critic's self. In this new impressionism, an impressionism that seeks to overthrow history, the text is mere fodder for the critic's ego to engorge and regurgitate. The structuralist would fastidiously recoil from Rahv's axiom that "criticism exhausts itself" in its essential act of assimilation and mediation— mediation between art and life—for the structuralist takes for granted that the bath water should be kept and the baby thrown out.

What is Cowley's role and position in the currents and crosscurrents of criticism? First, it should be emphatically said that he has maintained a remarkably consistent position over the course of his career, even in the 1930's, when he was strongly influenced by Marxism. ("Reviewing his articles between 1932 and 1939, one suspects he only half believed his own adjuration to artists to take part in the class struggle. He believed in it objectively but not religiously," Daniel Aaron has argued in *Writers on the Left,* 1961.) Cowley's fundamental belief, the bedrock on which he has anchored his criticism, is framed in "Adventures of a Book Reviewer" (1967): "Literature is a part of life, not subordinate to other parts, such as politics and economics, but intimately affected by them and sometimes affecting them in turn. All the parts were interwoven . . . in the web of history."

In —*And I Worked at the Writer's Trade* (1978) Cowley says (after complaining about the New Critics' "ignorance of the writing profession" and their neglect of social, economic, historical, and biographical factors):

I too believed that the work itself should be the focus of the critic's attention, but I was also deeply interested in the authors: how they got started, how they kept going, how they pictured themselves, and the myths that they embodied in their work. I was interested in their social backgrounds and in the question of whom they were thinking about when they said "we." I liked to speculate on the relation between an author and his audience.

Cowley's criticism is eclectic and pluralistic, and remains peculiarly his own. The influences, such as that of Van Wyck Brooks, have been thoroughly absorbed. ("I have tried to avoid critical endogamy and inbreeding," he says in "A Many-Windowed House," 1970.) He would agree with John Crowe Ransom's judgment that "the critic must be his own authority." The critic must always depend upon the authority of the text ("I always start and end with the text itself," Cowley writes) and the authority of his response ("I also try to start with a sort of innocence . . . , a lack of preconception," he adds). No school and no method, however sophisticated, will do the critic's job for him.

What Cowley characteristically does is to read the writer's work in the largest possible context—as much of the work as possible, not merely the most important or the most representative. He said of the philosophy underlying the Viking Portables: "The notion revealed here is that a masterpiece, although it can be studied alone, becomes richer when read in relation to an author's whole production, his oeuvre." On criticizing the literary work in "A Many-Windowed House," he said, "a truly innocent search might lead us into studies of the society in which an author lived. . . . [or] the nature of the particular audience for which it was written."

Of his specific field of endeavor, Cowley has written that it is and always has been "the contemporary history of American letters, though I also liked to trace the lines of descent by making incursions into the literary past." Cowley's most important subject is the lost generation, but he has written a great deal on the first flowering of American literature, especially of Nathaniel Hawthorne and Walt Whitman, and of the interrelations between the two periods. Unlike Edmund Wilson he has written as convincingly of poetry as of prose: his essays on Whitman, Edwin Arlington Robinson, Pound, and Frost are among his best, and it is worth noting that his views of Pound and Frost are dissenting—minority reports. He is very much his own man. Why this is so, and how this ruggedly independent man formed his character and vision, may be partly inferred from a biographical sketch of his life and a brief history of his career.

Malcolm Cowley was born during a thunderstorm on August 24, 1898, on a farm near Belsano, Pennsylvania. Belsano is seventy miles east of Pittsburgh, where he attended public school from 1904 through 1911. After leaving the Liberty School, he went to Peabody High School in Pittsburgh, excepting four months in 1912, when he was enrolled at a Swedenborgian school near Philadelphia. Cowley's father, a physician who practiced old-style homeopathic medicine, was a Swedenborgian, a fact to which his son alludes in "Prayer on All Saints' Day" (1978): "Graves played no part in our Swedenborgian family, / with my father's trust in celestial reunions." From the eighth grade through the twelfth, Cowley was in school with Kenneth Burke, his lifelong friend.

In 1915 Cowley matriculated at Harvard, where he ranked second in his class of 700 at the end of his freshman year. In April 1917 he went to France to drive an ambulance for the American Field Service, but ended up driving a munitions truck instead. Early in 1918 he was back at Harvard for the spring semester, but in the fall he went to a training camp for artillery officers. After he was mustered out of the army, Cowley moved to Greenwich Village in New York City, where he married Marguerite Frances Baird in August 1919. In the fall he returned to Harvard for his final semester (officially graduating with the class of 1919 in the winter of 1920). He earned a Phi Beta Kappa key at Harvard as well as a B.A. His formal education, superior to that of most of his literary contemporaries and peers, nurtures some of his many strengths as a writer and editor. In 1920–1921 he became a free-lance writer in Greenwich Village before becoming a copywriter for *Sweet's Architectural Catalogue*.

In 1921, Cowley was awarded an American Field Service Fellowship. He attended the University of Montpellier and earned a diploma in French studies. The fellowship was renewed for 1922–1923. The Cowleys then lived in Giverny, fifty miles west of Paris. Cowley met many of the artists associated with dada, particularly André Breton, Tristan Tzara, and Louis Aragon. During this period, which he has chronicled in *Exile's Return* (1934), he also helped with the editing and publication of two little magazines, *Broom* (1921–1924; edited by Harold Loeb, later in association with William Slater Brown and Matthew Josephson) and *Secession* (1922–1924; edited by Gorham B. Munson with Josephson and Kenneth Burke), which were born in Europe and died in New York. Among the contributors were Conrad Aiken, E. E. Cummings, Marianne Moore, Wallace Stevens, Jean Toomer, and William Carlos Williams.

In 1923 Cowley returned to New York, going back to work for *Sweet's Architectural Catalogue*. Two years later he moved to Staten Island and resigned from the catalogue to return to free-lancing. He was able to make a bare living at it. In 1926 he and his wife moved to Sherman, Connecticut, where they rented a house for ten dollars a month. In 1928 he bought an abandoned farm in upstate New York near Sherman. The seventy-acre farm sold for $2,800. He made the down payment with a prize of $100 from *Poetry,* Harriet Monroe's well-known little magazine. Among the Cowleys' neighbors were Matthew Josephson, Allen Tate and Caroline Gordon, Robert M. Coates, Hart Crane, John Brooks Wheelwright, and Peter Blume.

In October 1929, Cowley went to work for the *New Republic,* beginning an active association with that magazine that lasted until 1948. He joined the magazine's editorial board in 1930 and started a ten-year tenure as its literary (or book) editor, succeeding Edmund Wilson. When he lost that post in 1940 owing to his Communist sympathies, he became the magazine's weekly book reviewer. Cowley resigned from the *New Republic* in 1948, when its offices were moved from New York to Washington, but he continues to write reviews for it on occasion. He has described his years at the *New Republic* in the afterword of *Think Back on Us . . .* (1967) as well as in *—And I Worked at the Writer's Trade* (1978) and *The Dream of the Golden Mountains* (1980). That he was probably the best literary editor in the long history of this magazine one can easily perceive in reading *Literature and Liberalism: An Anthology of Sixty Years of "The New Republic,"* edited by Edward Zwick (1976).

Although Cowley's association with the *New Republic* is the most important of his professional career as an editor, its importance is rivaled by his tenure at the Viking Press, where he has been instrumental in creating one of the best literary lists in English published between the late 1940's and the early 1980's. When the history of the Viking Press is written, Cowley's

role in developing the Portable series will be seen as crucial to its commercial and critical success. As Marshall Best, general editor of the series, has said in correspondence, "his help in selecting other Portables and in suggesting suitable editors and contents has been beyond calculation." As general editor of the Viking Critical Library, Cowley has played another significant role in the evaluation of literary history. But he has accomplished still more at Viking, including the astute copyediting of many texts; and this story has been told only in Best's interview (with Louis Sheaffer) in Columbia University's project in oral history.

In 1931, Peggy Cowley went to Mexico to obtain an uncontested divorce. The agreement was amicable: Cowley deeded the farm to her. In late December 1931 she began an affair with Hart Crane in Mexico that ended with his suicide on April 24. At about the same time in 1932, Cowley became involved in the mining strikes in Pineville and Harlan, Kentucky. These brutal episodes are described in *The Dream of the Golden Mountains.* In June, Cowley married Muriel Maurer. Later that summer he became embroiled in the Communist election campaign. ("For the only time in my life I took part in a political campaign," he has ruefully said; in 1980 he could not bear to listen to the Democratic convention as it was broadcast.)

In 1933, Cowley had an entirely different experience of the South: in the late spring and early summer he stayed with Allen Tate, Caroline Gordon, and her family on the Kentucky-Tennessee border near Clarksville, Tennessee. During this visit he met many of the Nashville Agrarians, especially John Crowe Ransom, Donald Davidson, Robert Penn Warren (to whom he dedicated *The Dream of the Golden Mountains*), and Andrew Lytle. "Listening to the Agrarians," he wrote in 1965, "I felt they were trying to make a Northern convert, and for all my radical opinions I agreed with them on many points. I too had been raised in the country and was never happy for long where I couldn't feel the soil under my feet."

The next year brought the publication of *Exile's Return,* Cowley's most famous book. It was panned in most newspaper reviews when it was first released, especially in Franklin P. Adams' "The Conning Tower"; but John Chamberlain, Clifton Fadiman, Bernard Smith, and R. P. Blackmur praised it. ("For years I couldn't bring myself to write another book," Cowley has admitted.) His first collection of poetry, *Blue Juniata,* had been published in 1929. He later revised and expanded both books—*Exile's Return* in 1951 and *Blue Juniata* in 1968. In December 1934 the Cowleys' son Robert was born.

The family moved to a remodeled barn in Sherman, Connecticut, in 1936; Muriel and Malcolm Cowley still pursue their romance there. ("In the end, after starting with goodwill and $300, I was to find myself possessed of, or by, a seven-room house, a cornfield, a brier patch, a trout brook, and a crazy edifice of debts to be razed stone by stone.")

In the late 1930's Cowley continued to fight various literary and political battles that irrupted from communism in its varying forms—Marxism, Trotskyism, and Stalinism—and that swirled around his roles as literary editor of the *New Republic* and fellow traveler. In 1937 he attended a world congress of writers who met in besieged Madrid. In 1939, after the Nazi-Soviet nonaggression pact and the Russian invasion of Finland, he severed his ties with the Communist party; but in 1942 he was taxed for his connections to the party by the Dies Committee of the U. S. Congress. He was then working for the federal Office of Facts and Figures in Washington. After four months on the job he resigned and returned to Sherman. (In 1949 Cowley testified for the defense at the first and second trials of Alger Hiss. This was his last public connection with communism and those accused of being its adherents.)

Cowley received a five-year fellowship from Mary Mellon in 1943, and he spent most of his time during this period reading American literature while continuing to review for the *New Republic. The Portable Hemingway* (1944) and *The Portable Faulkner* (1946) were early fruits of this period of study. *The Portable Hawthorne* was published by Viking in 1948, the year that Cowley became its literary consultant. He has told the story of this important series in "The Greene-ing of the Portables" (1973). In addition to the Portables Cowley has edited Whitman and F. Scott Fitzgerald, the first series of the *Paris Review* interviews (1958), *Winesburg, Ohio* (1960), and, with Howard E. Hugo, *Lesson of the Masters: An Anthology of the Novel from Cervantes to Hemingway* (1971).

Cowley was elected to the National Institute of Arts and Letters in 1949 and served as its president in 1956–1959 and 1962–1965. He also was elected to the American Academy of Arts and Letters, and was its chancellor in 1967–1976.

Cowley became the first Walker-Ames lecturer at the University of Washington in 1950, his first teaching appointment. Subsequently he taught at Stanford University (four times between 1956 and 1965), the University of Michigan (1957), the University of California at Berkeley (1962), Cornell University (1964), the University of Minnesota (1971), and the University of Warwick (1973). The Warwick stint in Coventry, England, was his last teaching assignment, but he has continued to give public lectures.

In 1954, *The Literary Situation* was published; it was followed by *Black Cargoes: A History of the Atlantic Slave Trade* (with Daniel P. Mannix) in 1962; *The Faulkner-Cowley File* in 1966; *Think Back on Us . . . ,* edited by Henry Dan Piper, in 1967; *Blue Juniata: Collected*

Poems in 1968; *A Many-Windowed House,* also edited by Piper, in 1970; *A Second Flowering* in 1973; *—And I Worked at the Writer's Trade* in 1978; and *The Dream of the Golden Mountains* and *The View from 80* in 1980. More than half of his books were published after his seventieth birthday; of these *A Second Flowering,* his best book, is the most conspicuous. Cowley continues to write at the top of his form, as his new books amply demonstrate.

The View from 80 is a remarkable testament. "Every old person needs a work project if he wants to keep himself more alive," Cowley says. "For all my praise of indolence, which has its place in the old man's day, work has always been the sovereign specific." Cowley now has his work as a writer cut out for him, for he is writing an account of the most trying period of his career, 1935–1942.

Malcolm Cowley's published work falls into many categories. The most obvious modes are the personal essay and the autobiographical memoir, criticism formal and informal, literary history, editorials, poetry, translation. In practice it is difficult to sort out the published work aside from the book reviews, editorials, poems, and translations, putting a given piece in this bin or that. But one can make general distinctions that hold true for the most part. *Exile's Return* and *A Second Flowering* belong together as critical and autobiographical accounts of American literary modernism, especially of the figures of the lost generation. *The Literary Situation* and *—And I Worked at the Writer's Trade* are books about the literary profession and the state of publishing; *—And I Worked . . .* has a more definite critical aspect than does *The Literary Situation,* which Cowley says was not intended to be critical but was conceived as "a social history of literature in our times."

The Dream of the Golden Mountains is chiefly autobiography, a reminiscence about the 1930's that shades into social history at many points. It has much in common with *Exile's Return,* Cowley's best-known and most representative book, a work that not only is essential to the unfolding of his literary career and of his thought but also is crucial to one's understanding of the man and his work. The collections, ably edited by Henry Dan Piper—*Think Back on Us . . .* and *A Many-Windowed House*—show, respectively, Cowley the editorialist and book reviewer and Cowley the critic and literary historian in ways that are different from his characteristic modes of address in his own books. *The Faulkner-Cowley File* is a unique chapter in literary relations as an author and editor respond to each other.

At an early age Cowley learned to write the informal essay, a form more demanding than the review or the formal critical essay. Proof that Cowley had mastered this form by the early 1930's is abundant: one need only read "Connecticut Valley" and "Drought" (from "Transcontinental Highway"), which appeared in the *New Republic* in January and February 1931. "Connecticut Valley" is developed by a series of characterizations—of natives and summer people—who make up the community. Zebulon Trumbull and his wife have sold their farm, which his great-grandfather bought from the Indians, and have moved to town. The Denisons have bought that farm, torn down its barn, and refurbished the house in the most modern way. Denison, "the best advertising copywriter in New York City," is deep into middle age at thirty-five. He drinks too much and worries too much. Other representative characters appear. In a few deft strokes Cowley tells us of the lives of the Casey boys, natives who let their land go untilled, and he etches a sharply generalized picture of the lives of other summer people. As the scene fades, the reader is left with an image: it is October, and the summer people are deserting their houses. Everyone, native and alien, lets the land lie untended, and the orchards are also neglected. The beautiful valley is bereft of stewards.

In this sketch, as in "Drought," "The Meriwether Connection" (1965), and other informal essays, one is struck by Cowley's gift for characterization and narrative, his eye for detail, and his idiomatic voice—traits that a novelist might envy. "Connecticut Valley" is a parable about the modern world that achieves its effects through the author's bold delineations and images. Without the characters and the pictures of their lives we would be left with a cold exposition of a growing fad—New Yorkers buying summer places in Connecticut—and its results, with a shrill emphasis on waste and neglect. Cowley the man, like his friends and acquaintances among the Nashville Agrarians, is a steward of the land who keeps a garden and an orchard, reaping the land's benison. Cowley the writer knows that the best way to develop a theme is through people, not ideas—hence his approach to his subject on this and many other occasions.

Cowley's brilliant use of the informal essay and the personal report reaches its fruition in *The Dream of the Golden Mountains,* in which dozens of scenes of the 1930's, both urban and rural, are memorably depicted. He portrays the rout of the bonus marchers, strikes, meetings of the Communist party, writers' congresses, and other representative events. These are complemented by deeply shaded autobiographical portraits of life at the *New Republic* and in pastoral Tennessee and Connecticut. Cowley alternates picture and scene, again like the good fictionist as well as the good reporter. He knows when to slow the pace of the narrative and present a representative scene. At the same time he is adept at stopping the action and concluding a given sequence with a sharp image. One of the best of these appears at the end of "*The New Republic* Moves Uptown." In the last half of the concluding paragraph, Cowley is describing the cocktail party that was thrown to christen the new offices:

Almost everyone drank the martinis fast, then shouted to be heard by his neighbor. John Dewey got into an argument, made a sweeping gesture with his arm too low, and swept the cloth off the new square table, sending fifty glasses crashing to the floor. More glasses appeared and the din rose higher. A young matron was sitting happily on Stark Young's well-tailored lap, where few women had sat before her. George Soule was beaming through rimless spectacles. Bruce Bliven, a temperate man, looked more and more unhappy. "Why don't you go home?" Otis [Ferguson] said to him, and almost added, "Buster." We missed an artist friend and found him vomiting in the women's toilet with his wife holding his shoulders. A little crowd was waiting for the only elevator that ran after six o'clock. This wasn't Herbert Croly's *New Republic;* it was a midtown office party.

In this part of a sequence of roughly 750 words, Cowley not only describes a cocktail party that is typical and untypical but also creates an image of the end of an era at the *New Republic.* He also conveys the hint that the Great Depression is beginning to ease.

Cowley's reviews fall between his informal essays and his formal critical pieces. In the epilogue to *Think Back on Us . . . ,* "Adventures of a Book Reviewer," he described his experiences writing a regular weekly review for the *New Republic.* He called it "my art form for many years" that "became my blank-verse meditation, my sonnet sequence, my letter to distant friends, my private journal." By joining narration and exposition (or anecdote and analysis) Cowley attempted not only to review the given book but also to "produce a reasoned criticism that could be read like a story." Alfred Kazin thinks that these leading reviews "brought the week to focus" for regular readers who relished the confrontation of "a gifted, uncompromising critical intelligence" with a representative new book. The review was more dramatic than a meditation or letter or journal, and it carried with it not only the tang of literary criticism but also the sense of the great world of affairs. In the English-speaking world few book reviewers in our time have been as good over the long haul, and only Edmund Wilson and V. S. Pritchett have been better. Since 1920, Cowley has reviewed hundreds of books, a large proportion of which has remained significant. And the books have encompassed a wide range of interests—sociology and politics as well as literature.

The formal critical essays appeared almost as regularly as the reviews, and covered American literature from the New England renaissance in the 1830's to the present time. *A Many-Windowed House* presents the best selection of these, but others may be found throughout Cowley's books—in the collection *After the Genteel Tradition*, nearly half of which is by him; in *A Second Flowering;* and occasionally in *—And I Worked at the Writer's Trade.*

Cowley's quintessential critical essay in the formal mode has a strong biographical underpinning, just as his informal essays are built on an autobiographical foundation. The epilogue to *A Many-Windowed House* presents Cowley's credo as a critic: he forswears theory in the pure and rarefied sense; and while he stresses the value of the work under consideration, he prefers to deal with the author's life and work as a whole within the social and historical context in which the life was lived and the work was written, rather than considering a particular phase or a single title. "Judgment is the end of the critical process," he says; "but if the work has been defined and interpreted correctly, then judgment often follows as a matter of course." Cowley typically casts a wide net, and even in a review he is stalking larger quarry than the book under consideration. The characteristic essay tells a story in the same way that Cowley's reviews do—the story of the development of an artist's work against the unfolding of his life. Among his best essays in this mode are "Dos Passos: Poet Against the World" (1937), "Frost: A Dissenting Opinion" (1944), "William Faulkner's Legend of the South" (1944), "The Real Horatio Alger Story" (1945), "Whitman: The Poet and the Mask" (1946–1947), "Hawthorne in Solitude" (1948), "Fitzgerald: The Romance of Money" (1953), "Pound Reweighed" (1961), "Hemingway: The Old Lion" (1973), and "Conrad Aiken: From Savannah to Emerson" (1975).

On occasion Cowley has written articles that are not chiefly literary. These include his political essays, but the best known of the miscellaneous essays concerns language rather than politics. "Sociological Habit Patterns in Linguistic Transmogrification" (1956), which has been anthologized often, criticizes the language of sociologists by both analysis and parody. Here Cowley shows himself a master of language and style who is impatient with cant; in his literary criticism he has more than once inveighed against pretentious and obscure prose that is windy, wandering, repetitious, belletristic, and stuffy. In this minor classic one hears distant echoes of James Thurber, George Orwell, and others who have criticized pompous and viscid language, such as E. B. White, who once remarked editorially, "We would as lief Simonize our grandmother as personalize our writing."

Cowley's plain style affords him a tool that is right for every occasion. Some of his readers, particularly the academic ones inclined to think that tortured syntax, Latinate diction, and a highfalutin tone must be used to express the obscure and complex aspects of literary history and criticism, may underrate him because his expression is always simple and clear. "No American at present writes a more lucid prose than Cowley," Tate said in 1929. The simplicity and clarity he had achieved by then and has since maintained are the result of Cowley's constant effort. The result is that effort to measure a subject without distortion or oversimplification. As Kazin has said, this manner of expression suggests "the Hemingway style of artful plainness that united simplicity of manner with a certain slyness." Nouns and verbs provide the backbone of his prose, as they do in Hemingway's. Cowley is suspicious of adjectives and other modifiers, as he has made clear in *A Second Flowering,* especially in "The Other War," "Hemingway in Paris," and "Wolfe: Homo Scribens." At once homely and unvarnished, concrete and economical, colloquial and persuasive, his style is an admirable vehicle for description, characterization, and judgment. Although Cowley has the poet's feel for language, he never indulges himself and becomes giddy with its possibilities, as did Wolfe, Faulkner, Crane, and many another writer of the lost generation.

The distinctive earmark of Cowley's style, his bold signature, is metaphor. What he has done is to deploy metaphors of all kinds, both condensed and expanded (including similes), to amplify, reinforce, and enrich the texture of his meaning. In the examples that follow, one sees the range and depth of Cowley's metaphoric expression.

Farmhouses curl like horns of plenty, hide scrawny bare shanks against a barn, or crouch empty in the shadow of a mountain. Here there is no house at all—

only the bones of a house. . . .

("Blue Juniata," 1926)

Paris was a great machine for sharpening the nerves and stimulating the senses.

(*Exile's Return,* 1934)

Having taken vows of poverty, chastity and obedience to his art, he could accept donations as if he were a whole monastic order.

("Edwin Arlington Robinson," 1948, in *After the Genteel Tradition*)

Sometimes [the writer] regards himself as a soldier fighting against the unknown and unexpressed; he is like a Roman legionary always serving on the frontier. Sometimes he is an explorer trying to broaden that civilized homeland which is the area of consciousness, by finding the proper words for new experiences.

(*The Literary Situation,* 1954)

Before and after the Toronto venture, Hemingway studied writing in Paris as if he were studying geometry without a textbook and inventing theorems as he went along.

("Hemingway in Paris," 1962, in *A Second Flowering*)

Browder was a gray-faced man in a rumpled gray suit; he had the honest face of a clerk in a Kansas feed-and-grain store.

(*The Dream of the Golden Mountains,* 1980)

To enter the country of age is a new experience. . . . Nobody, man or woman, knows the country until he has lived in it and taken out his citizenship papers. Here is my own report, submitted as a road map and guide to some of the principal monuments.

(*The View from 80,* 1980)

In this series of representative instances we see Cowley's exact use of the language of analogy. In the poem, originally called "Bones of a

House," one is struck by the comparison of houses to the people who own them and live in them. The metaphors in prose that I have chosen reveal Cowley's penchant and gift for drawing out the possibilities of the conceit that he forges. Robinson is not simply a monk but a whole monastic order; the writer is not only a Roman soldier on the frontier of the empire but also an explorer who is trying to expand the frontier. Hemingway studies the geometrical possibilities of prose by inventing his own theorems. Browder, the secretary of the American Communist party, looks like an honest clerk. (Another metaphoric characterization in the same book—that of Sinclair Lewis—is equally effective: Lewis' face is likened to "a rubber mask drawn tight over the skull.") In the last example Cowley returns to the metaphor of exploration, but he develops this analogy in an entirely different way: here the subject is immigrant, citizen, and reporter. In a different but related context, Cowley's metaphors provide the sinews connecting the syntax and idiom of his prose. In them one sees the poet at work. Here Cowley permits himself short lyric flights, but the metaphors are always meant—which is to say functional, not decorative.

"I can't keep my pencil out of a manuscript, especially if it's my own," Cowley has remarked; and the soundness of his revisions—their shrewd idiomatic rightness—may be seen in a comparison of the leading paragraphs of the same essay as it was published in two different versions.

John Dos Passos is in reality two novelists. One of them is a late-Romantic, an individualist, an esthete moving about the world in a portable ivory tower; and the other is a collectivist, a radical historian of the class struggle. These two authors have collaborated in all his books, but the first had the larger share in *Three Soldiers*

and *Manhattan Transfer*. The second, in his more convincing fashion, has written most of *The 42nd Parallel* and almost all of *1919*. The difference between the late-Romantic and the radical Dos Passos is important not only in his career: it also helps to explain the recent course of American fiction.

("The Poet and the World," in *New Republic*, April 27, 1932)

Sometimes in reading Dos Passos you feel that he is two novelists at war with each other. One of them is a late-Romantic, a tender individualist, an esthete traveling about the world in an ivory tower that is mounted on wheels and coupled to the last car of the Orient Express. The other is a hard-minded realist, a collectivist, a radical historian of the class struggle. The two authors have quarreled and collaborated in all his books but the first had the larger share in *Three Soldiers* and *Manhattan Transfer*. The second, in his more convincing fashion, wrote most of *The 42nd Parallel, 1919* and *The Big Money*. Although the conflict between them seems to me rather less definite on reflection than it did at first glance, nevertheless it is real; and it helps to explain several tendencies not only in the work of Dos Passos but in recent American fiction as a whole.

("Dos Passos: Poet Against the World," 1964)

The first version is the more direct and succinct, and it demonstrates the qualities that Kazin praises in *Starting Out in the Thirties*: clarity, concreteness, authority. The second version is superior all the same—and not merely because the writer has more room in which to operate. (The revised essay is only 10 to 15 percent longer than the original two parts that M. D. Zabel reprinted as a single essay in *Literary Opinion in America*.)

What immediately strikes one is that in the revised version Cowley has developed his original thesis by metaphor. Dos Passos is "two novelists at war with each other" whose "portable ivory tower" is now "coupled to the last car of the Orient Express." By such homely and obvious metaphors Cowley often secures or amplifies a point. But he does not allow his prose to accrue the wrong tone or momentum when he deploys such metaphors as "two novelists at war." Late in the revised essay he warns: "But the distinction I have been making . . . could be easily carried too far. The truth is that the art novel and the collective novel as conceived by Dos Passos are in opposition but not in fundamental opposition: they are like two sides of a coin." Again we see the homely metaphor at work. Cowley is not afraid to use such figures of speech. On the other hand his "portable ivory tower" is considerably bolder. The extrapolation of the image in the second version enables him to suggest that Dos Passos has a sentimental and romantic side that the author is powerless to harness and control.

There are other differences in the two passages that need detain us but a moment. Cowley effectively uses the second- and first-person address in the fuller version ("you feel" and "seems to me"); the reader now thinks himself part of a common enterprise. The critic also adds words and phrases to give his formulation a more exact shade of meaning and a less stark tone. Dos Passos is now "a *tender* individualist" who is at the same time *"a hard-minded realist."* These sides of the man have *"quarreled* and collaborated" (italics mine). The parallelism between the romantic and the realist is now more exact; in the first formulation Dos Passos' "collectivist" and "historical" side seems to be a tough political antiquarianism rather than what one expects of the hardheaded political novelist: tough-minded realism. The second version is the more considered and persuasive. Here, as elsewhere in his work, Cowley has

made good use of the opportunity to take another look.

The willingness—almost the compulsion—to take another look and to revise time and again is one of many attitudes and habits that set Cowley apart from the vast majority of literary critics. Most of the other important critics of the twentieth century have tended to assume—often wrongly—that their judgments, once formulated, have the permanence and resilience of the Ten Commandments.

Cowley's willingness to revise not only his prose but also his judgments has been part and parcel of his ability to make books from essays that are seemingly scattered, disparate, and fragmentary. Hence he has been able to bring them into a unified whole. Most critics in the twentieth century have been content to collect essays from time to time within the covers of a book and let it go at that. This practice may be seen from Eliot's *The Sacred Wood* (1920) to Blackmur's *The Double Agent* (1935), Tate's *Reactionary Essays* (1936), Ransom's *The World's Body* (1938), Wilson's *The Triple Thinkers* (1938), Rahv's *Image and Idea* (1949), and Trilling's *The Liberal Imagination* (1950). Of these men only Wilson, Trilling, and Cowley have written book-length critical studies. The emphasis here may seem misplaced, and therefore I hasten to say that I am not in any way dismissing or downplaying the great critical achievement of Eliot, Ransom, Tate, Blackmur, and Rahv; what I am pointing out is that writing a book-length critical study is an order of achievement different from writing a series of independent essays that are wholly disparate or only loosely connected. When Cowley says—as he does, for instance, in *The Literary Situation*—that the book in question is not a collection but a unified whole, he is not whistling in the dark, as most critics do in the same circumstances. Most of Cowley's critical and historical books have this kind of unity—from *Exile's Return* to *—And I Worked at the Writer's Trade.* (In this estimate I obviously would not include *Think Back on Us . . .* and *A Many-Windowed House.*)

Cowley's stature as a literary historian and critic cannot be properly seen until one reads two or three of his books. A handful of essays, read in periodicals or anthologies, will not reveal the full force and effect of his literary and critical acumen. There is a deceiving simplicity about many of his essays: the prose, which always meets Orwell's standard of being as clear as a windowpane; the unpretentious and genial tone; the apparently rambling style; the casual anecdotes—all these earmarks and more make it seem that one is being "led up to the most immense spread of literary tidbits," as Kazin remarks. Yet, taken in concert, Cowley's essays and books constitute considerably more than mere literary small talk and gossip. Cowley has given us the most nearly complete account of modern American literary history. In the foreword to *—And I Worked at the Writer's Trade,* his last critical book, he writes: "Once I set out to write, but never finished, a history of American letters in the twentieth century. Most of the chapters that follow might have found a place in it." In fact *Exile's Return, The Literary Situation, A Second Flowering,* and *—And I Worked at the Writer's Trade* constitute a personal history of American literary modernism.

In the prologue to the second edition of *Exile's Return,* Malcolm Cowley says that what he "wanted to write was less a record of events than a narrative of ideas." Here I want to consider the ideas that signify in the unfolding of his life and the making of his work—those not considered elsewhere in this essay.

R. P. Blackmur's concise synoptic view of Cowley's position (which appears in "The Dan-

gers of Authorship," a review of *Exile's Return* and Eliot's *After Strange Gods*) remains accurate and valuable. Cowley

. . . regards literature as it interprets life rightly or wrongly, with reference to a general, complete view of life as distinguished from the free, uncontrolled, merely literary view. [He] deeply realizes that literature does not ever in fact—at least in the degree that it is serious—escape into thin air without first influencing the moral and spiritual life of its readers.

Therefore literature must be tempered by "a definite intellectual and spiritual discipline." "Cowley suggests a discipline that rises from an honest recognition of the class-struggle and all its implications in economic and political life."

Most of Cowley's leading ideas either are presented and extrapolated in *Exile's Return* or appear there in germinal form. He makes the assumption—daring and prescient at the time, but abundantly clear since about 1950—that the lost generation has produced many of the best American writers of the twentieth century. These writers will be partly remembered as the generation that routed the genteel tradition. This assumption about the lost generation conceals another daring and prophetic judgment that Cowley made in the 1920's—that American literature had come of age, could hold its own with European literature, and was a respectable object of study. As he says in the epilogue, "in 1920 it had been a provincial literature. . . . By 1930 it had come to be valued for itself."

In "Malcolm Cowley and the American Writer" (1976), Lewis P. Simpson has written the most comprehensive account of Cowley's career, showing the integral relation of the poetry and the criticism, the relation of poet to critic. This is the heart of Simpson's interpretation of Cowley's quest. In consequence Allen

Tate perceived that relation and remarked it in conversation and correspondence.

As both a creator and an interpreter of the literature of the lost generation, Cowley is a contributor to one of its leading aspects: a myth or a legend of creativity which is definable as a poetics of exile. He apprehended first the American writer's exile from childhood, second his exile from society, and finally his exile from what may be termed the sense of being in the wholeness of the self.... The deracination of the lost generation was inherent in the condition of American life.

This sense of alienation, Simpson goes on to observe, was sharpened by the lost generation's experience in World War I, during which they developed what Cowley calls the "spectatorial attitude," a sense of detachment and remoteness from life that led to their immersion in the "religion of art," the symbolist discipline of pure consciousness that is founded on the notion that only in art is reality fully and truly apprehended. At its most fanatical, as Cowley points out in *Exile's Return*, the religion of art can lead to extreme forms of exile: to an escape from modern society, a withdrawal to a remote primitive land, or to the "irreligion of art, a state of mind in which the artist deliberately fritters away his talents through contempt for the idiot-public that can never understand."

The life of the artist has a more mundane and even practical side, and no other critic has described the writer's quotidian existence with Cowley's thoroughness and sanity. In discussing the secular side of his vocation in *The Literary Situation* and in *—And I Worked at the Writer's Trade,* Cowley has provided a remarkably thorough account not only of the writer's apprenticeship, his working habits, his attitude toward the ideas of his time, and his relation to the academic community and the publishing world but also of his connection to the reading public and the wider world of society as a whole.

(Flannery O'Connor, who experienced several kinds of exile in her brief life, shrewdly described this complicated series of relations in "The Fiction Writer and His Country" [1957]: "When we talk about the writer's country we are liable to forget that no matter what particular country it is, it is inside as well as outside him. Art requires a delicate adjustment of the outer and inner worlds in such a way that, without changing their nature, they can be seen through each other. To know oneself is to know one's region. It is also to know the world, and it is also, paradoxically, a form of exile from that world.")

In the concluding chapter of *—And I Worked at the Writer's Trade,* Cowley describes the code of the serious modern writer, a code that, he goes on to say, "preaches a curious mixture of extreme self-centeredness with something close to self-abnegation" and that is "dangerously incomplete" as a guide to the moral life. Here is his pentalogue: The artist "must believe in the importance of art, as well as the all-importance in his own life of the particular art to which he is devoted"; "he must believe in his own talent . . . having a universal validity"; "he must honestly express his own vision of the world and his own personality, including his derelictions"; he "must produce grandly, to the limit of his powers"; "the work of art should be so fashioned as to have an organic shape and a life of its own, derived but apart from the life of its maker and capable of outlasting it. Only the work provides the artist's claim on the future, his hope of heaven. . . ."

At the end of *Exile's Return* Cowley proposes a similar set of beliefs, which Simpson discusses in "The Decorum of the Writer" (1978). The essential difference in the earlier pentalogue is Cowley's insistence in *Exile's Re-*

turn that the writer participate in reforming society. Simpson considers the implications of this "comprehensive moral criticism of man and his history," showing how the shrinking of the literary sensibility and its ideals since the 1920's and 1930's has affected Cowley. He obviously believes that few writers of the present time will appear in what he calls Art's hagiography and its Book of Martyrs.

In the essay on Wolfe in *A Second Flowering* Cowley also observes that "the usual author is two persons or personalities working in partnership. One of them says the words to himself, then writes them down; the other listens to the words, or reads them." This dialogue, or "process of inner dialectic," is essential to the working habits of any good writer. Cowley has spoken of the process often, and in "Privatation and Publication" (1975) he relates it to his own writing. "I took long walks, sometimes nine or ten miles in the wet snow, while I dreamed about or mumbled the words I should write the following day." His most thorough account of this inner dialogue appears in the introduction to *The Portable Hawthorne:*

Hawthorne seems to have divided himself into two personalities while dreaming out his stories: one was the storyteller and the other was the audience.... This doubleness in Hawthorne, this division of himself into two persons conversing in solitude, explains one of the paradoxes of his literary character: that he was one of the loneliest authors who ever wrote, ... while at the same time his style was that of a social man eager to make himself clear and intensely conscious of his audience.

Hawthorne, more than any other writer in the American renaissance, created his own legends and his own myth. In this and other ways he is related to Faulkner, the writer to whom Cowley has been most attracted (but whom he slightly underrates, just as he overrates Hem-

ingway). It is Cowley who more than any other critic has revealed the mythic dimensions of Yoknapatawpha County. In the powerful conclusion to *A Second Flowering* he writes that nearly all the writers of the lost generation are "great spinners and weavers of legend." Behind their legendary heroes lie "larger patterns of myth." "Hemingway and Faulkner most of all, but other writers as well, seemed to plunge deep into the past, or into themselves, to recover a prehistoric and prelogical fashion of looking at the world; then they looked in the same fashion at events of their own time and thereby surrounded them with a feeling of primitive magic. . . ." That magic earned for them a place among the great writers of the twentieth century, but not the great writers of all time, as Cowley points out: "They lacked the capacity for renewed growth after middle age that has marked some of the truly great writers." This lack of stamina adversely affects most of the writers of the period from Crane to Hemingway, but not Edmund Wilson or Cowley himself. Cowley's work in the 1970's is more than a simple matter of stamina and persistence, for it brings to his career a special aura and achievement, stamping him not as poet and critic but as man of letters.

In the appendix to *A Second Flowering,* "Years of Birth," Malcolm Cowley lists 385 American authors born from 1891 to 1905. The name of each is followed by a succinct description of his or her literary accomplishment: Faulkner is deemed a novelist; Thurber, a humorist; A. J. Liebling, a journalist. Rarely is the description askew, as in the case of Katherine Anne Porter, who is chiefly a writer of short fiction, not a novelist. The most intriguing category by far is man of letters: Cowley calls John Peale Bishop, Kenneth Burke, Allen Tate, Mark Van Doren, Robert Penn Warren, and Edmund Wilson by this term "as a token of their refusal to specialize." But much more is involved. One might ask why Bernard DeVoto, E. B. White, Yvor Winters, Lionel Trilling, and R. P. Blackmur were not included. One answer is that Cowley puts a low premium on editing, teaching, and journalism when he defines a writer as a man of letters: he shies from academic types (Trilling, Winters) and journalists (DeVoto, White). He is also loath to deem a writer "man of letters" who has written principally in two forms: this applies to Trilling (an indifferent fictionist) and to Winters and Blackmur (who wrote only minor poetry aside from criticism).

We can easily perceive that Cowley greatly admires the writers in this category and that he has deliberately limited its members, for with a less stringent measure he could have included many more. Aside from Trilling and the others, Donald Davidson, Katherine Anne Porter, and Glenway Wescott might have been added. The most important omission is not any of these writers but Cowley himself. Here he calls himself a critic and poet; elsewhere he has referred to himself as a literary historian. He is also an editor, essayist, journalist, memoirist, and translator. (These categories are applied to various writers in the appendix.)

The man of letters devotes himself to the literary life. He is the embodiment of the idea (which many educated people would dismiss as a quaint notion, a singular fiction) that there is a fourth estate. This estate only incidentally comprises journalists, excepting the gifted and perspicacious ones like DeVoto and Liebling; in its true nature this realm of the mind and the imagination constitutes the community of writers that exists irrespective of national boundaries. This republic of letters is based upon a common assumption that can be expressed in Henry James's belief that it is "art that *makes* life, makes interest, makes importance."

The professional writers in this community make up the great majority of its membership, to be sure; but the men of letters are its leaders: they are the heart of this body politic. The man of letters like Edmund Wilson or Robert Penn Warren represents the idea of what literature and the literary life can be at their best. He may not necessarily be a great writer—in fact he seldom is—and on occasion some of his work, such as Wilson's collection of stories *Memoirs of Hecate County,* may be embarrassingly mediocre, as Cowley suggested in a review (*New York Times Book Review,* June 8, 1980). But through his dedication to literature and his unflinching professionalism, the man of letters elevates and upholds the profession of writing.

Such a figure has an important role to play in the United States, for there is a deep and solid vein of anti-intellectualism running through American life to which many authors, no matter how great and how committed to art, have profoundly responded. One part of this response may be seen in Faulkner's absurd pretense that he was a farmer, not a writer. (As his brother John's reminiscence clearly shows, Faulkner was a deliberately casual and hopelessly incompetent farmer.) One cannot imagine Wilson's assuming such a preposterous role: he would have seen it as treasonous. Warren, while doubtless thinking that Faulkner's charade was humorous and probably harmless, could not behave in such a way himself despite his subtleties of self-deflation. It is Tate who bridles at this fiction, saying in his obituary of Faulkner: "The main source of my annoyance with him was his affectation of not being a writer, but a farmer. . . . Being a 'farmer,' he did not 'associate' with writers. . . . Excepting Malcolm Cowley he was not a friend of anybody who could conceivably have been his peer." That Faulkner did not assume the role of the farmer or the country bumpkin or the southern "good ole boy" with Cowley was a mark of his respect and affection.

It is essential for most writers to think of themselves as part of a community and as members of a profession. The writer (the real writer, that is, not the hack—the maker of pulp fiction or the Hollywood scenarist or the sports reporter) ordinarily must see himself as having a real profession with actual standards. This does not require membership in a literary circle or clique (such as the Round Table at the Algonquin Hotel, which produced not a single major writer, only minor wits). What this sense of community does entail is a necessary fiction that enables the writer to see himself or herself as part of the tradition and development of literature and that gives the author a sense of belonging to something that is significant and enduring.

Although the role of the man of letters is much diminished in England, in the United States it remains essential, largely owing to the American writer's strong sense of alienation from society at large. This profound sense, which Louis D. Rubin, Jr., has called the experience of difference, and which Cowley has discussed more thoroughly than any other American critic, partly involves the writer's nervous sense that his or her profession is not quite legitimate and that the writer would be better off living in a friendlier environment, such as Europe, or following a more respectable way of life. The writer of minor talent who is not driven by demons can be an amateur, writing as an avocation; but the writer who is bitten by Art, and who is prey to his or her talent (or, in rare cases, genius) and is driven by commitment and egoism, will continue in that lonely course.

In such circumstances the community of letters often becomes a sustaining force, regardless of whether the given writer regularly sees other writers. As Blackmur has observed in "A Feather-bed for Critics":

Without the profession of writing behind him, . . . the individual writer is reduced to small arms; without society behind it, the profession is impotent and bound to betray itself. A deep collaboration is necessary, a collaboration in which the forces are autonomous and may never consciously co-operate, but which is marked by the unity they make together and by the culture which the individual, by the act of his convicted imagination, brings to light.

Blackmur sees the profession of writing as integral and necessary to the writer. The key figure in the profession is the man of letters: he provides the cement to bind society and the individual writer.

The polity of letters and the publishing community have much in common, and there is a far greater sense of shared purpose among these worlds than there is within the academic profession or between writers and academics. The academic world stands apart from the profession of letters in much the same way that journalism does. There is a sharp difference, even an antagonism, between the university and the fourth estate; workaday journalism and the literary vocation are not so sharply divided, but there are basic dissimilarities. "The man of letters pursues literature as a vocation—seeing no difference between his vocation and his avocation," Tate has shrewdly asserted; on the other hand, as John Gross has argued in *The Rise and Fall of the Man of Letters,* "journalism is a career; literature is, or ought to be, a vocation." Careerism (which embraces commercialism and popularization, among other vices), like philandering, alcoholism, and paranoia, is a constant threat to the writer, who, by succumbing to the impulse to live in the public image of what the writer is, damages himself and his work. The example of Hemingway as careerist overshadows all others in this regard.

The man of letters is committed to the life of the mind, but unlike many intellectuals he has a more specific commitment—to literature and to the health of language and culture. "The true province of the man of letters," as Tate has said, "is nothing less (as it is nothing more) than culture itself." If carried too far, this commitment can become a religion of art—aestheticism. In our day, when secular religions of every kind—from communism to transcendental meditation—threaten the fabric of culture in the West, the religion of art seems relatively harmless. The extreme form of the religion of art, aestheticism, Cowley first detected at Harvard. But he has never succumbed to it, doubtless in part because he saw aestheticism in operation in dada and other forms of modern aestheticism in Europe in the 1920's. Yet at the same time (1921) Cowley met Paul Valéry and saw in him a model for the man of letters. Doubtless Tate thought of Valéry's example when he wrote of Poe: "He was the first committed and perhaps still the greatest American literary journalist on the high French model: a critical tradition represented today by Edmund Wilson and Malcolm Cowley."

Lewis P. Simpson has written in the *Sewanee Review* for spring 1976 that Cowley's

... approach to the literary profession is, like that of William Dean Howells or Van Wyck Brooks, often infused with a poetics of literary community. Through the cultivation of a large personal literary acquaintance, through a gift for friendship, through generosity and compassion ... Cowley has urged upon American writers the image of a community based on both goodwill and discipline.

This approach, which springs from a marked geniality as well as generosity and compassion, sets Cowley in a league by himself. Although he has often defended the writer's deportment, Cowley sympathized with Maxwell Perkins and his difficulties with such perpetual adolescents as Fitzgerald and Wolfe by saying that "this bookish, professorial, modest, upright man has chosen a profession in which he has to deal constantly with writers, who as a class have distin-

guished themselves as barroom brawlers, drawing-room wolves, breakers of engagements, defaulters of debts, crying drunks, and suicidal maniacs." Perkins and Cowley came to maturity in the time during which such boorishness became the expected mode of conduct for the writer to indulge himself in. In our day most writers seem intent on proving Ford Madox Ford's axiom that the artist cannot be a gentleman. Part of the writer's habitual behavior toward fellow authors involves a thinly veiled petulance that often erupts into jealousy, dishonesty, disruption, and even violence. Hemingway is the perfect exemplar of such deplorable behavior, but he by no means cornered the market on it. That Cowley has remained open-handed and amiable—that is, himself—throughout his long life without being in any way a camp follower or toady demonstrates that there are exceptions to Leo Durocher's axiom—"Nice guys finish last."

Cowley's difficulties with writers must often have rivaled those of Perkins, who had many unpleasant experiences with Wolfe (who, Cowley observed, sometimes had the disposition of a morose elephant), Fitzgerald, Hemingway, and others. That he has been a respected poet and critic for the entirety of his professional life has given Cowley a considerable advantage in his relations with authors, whether as editor or writer. The poet is the prima donna of the breed *writer,* and Cowley in his early life must have found Hart Crane the most trying of literary friends. In his later life that dubious honor would probably go to Allen Tate, the man who brought Crane and Cowley together. The problems that both Crane and Tate posed to their friends sprang from sexuality: Crane was bisexual in his habits and had many searing experiences as a homosexual; Tate, who was driven by satyriasis through late middle age, had to cope with its aftermath in his last years, an aftermath that included considerable pain and embarrassment for many of his old friends, Cowley among them.

The impact in each case extended to Cowley's domestic life. Despite what must have been great anguish in many respects, he has maintained his affectionate regard for both men and has continued to write about them with personal sympathy as well as critical detachment and approval (see "Remembering Allen Tate" in the spring 1980 *Georgia Review*). This kind of experience—suffering through Crane's drunken violent rages and Tate's mercurial temperament—would have turned many a lesser man not only against the writers and their work but also against the profession. Cowley has an uncommonly even disposition, a remarkable ability to forgive, and a wise but not uncritical acceptance of human fallibility.

Cowley is one of the rare people who can be counted among the saving remnant of what he has called "the truly good men and women" in the literary world, people who are neither saints nor rascals nor scoundrels. Among his wide literary acquaintance since 1915 he mentions only three people—Van Wyck Brooks, Marianne Moore, and Heywood Broun; to this list I presumptuously add John Crowe Ransom, Robert Penn Warren, E. B. White, and A. J. Liebling. Cowley, who has considerably more faith in the literary mind and its works than in the worldly nature of the writer, is a man whose own character has borne the sharp scrutiny of committees of local vigilantes in Seattle and elsewhere and of U. S. congressmen, and has survived intact. The biographers of the future not only will marvel at his literary idealism (White has called him an intellectual idealist) but also cannot fail to be more impressed with his geniality, urbanity, decency, and goodness. In fact, to the unwary he may seem too good to be true, in much the same way that the clear surfaces of his prose and the neat contours of his arguments are deceptively simple.

In his old age Cowley has avoided a state that he describes in *The View from 80,* a book that springs in part from his long and acute study of generations. He fears declining into a simplified version of himself, "of being reduced from the complexity of adult life into a single characteristic." As ever, his fascination with the self is balanced by his view of the literary world and of society. In the deepening shadows of a distinguished career he is continuing to contemplate the patterns of his life and of life in the twentieth century:

Life in general (or nature, or the history of our times) is a supremely inventive novelist or playwright, but he—she?—is also wasteful beyond belief and her designs are hidden under the . . . rubbish of the years. She needs our help as collaborators. Can we . . . lay bare the outlines of ourselves?

In his case the answer is an emphatic yes. Cowley has lived out of himself, through himself, into himself, both making and chronicling literary history. Here is the story as he tells it in "Prayer on All Saints' Day" (1978):

Mother,
lying there in the old Allegheny Cemetery,
last in the family plot—
I stood there on that overcast November day;
I have never gone back.
Graves played no part in our Swedenborgian
    family,
with my father's trust in celestial reunions
and my oblivious selfishness.
Now after thirty-eight years I go back in
    spirit,
I kneel at the graveside, I offer my testimony:
this I have done, Mother, with your gift;
this I have failed to do.

Your hope, all that was left, you placed in me:
I should outshine the neighbors' children,
grow up to be admired,

have worldly possessions too.
Those were modest aims you gave me,
        Mother;
I have achieved them all.

A wife you might have chosen for me,
but I chose her first;
a son to bear my father's name;
an unmortgaged house and a mowed lawn.
The banker squeezes my hand;
the neighbors beam at me, each knowing
I will not wound his self-esteem.
You would have liked that, Mother.
"Oh, Doctor," you might have said,
"we have a good son."

Good, good. There was a time
I called myself a bad son, but a poet.
"My world has deeper colors than yours,"
I boasted, "and the words will come
to match the colors."
Looking for words as for horses loose in the
        back pasture,
I saddled and bridled them,
rode off with a tight rein at a steady trot,
came back one day and paid my debts,
survived.

Now I am older than you were ever to be,
deaf as a gravestone,
weak knees, a faltering walk;
at night lying awake with borborygmus,
by day farting and fiddling among papers;
I have outlived most of my great coevals;
now I write epitaphs for the dead lions.
Does that make me a jackal?

Sometimes lying awake I think of Ora
        Newton,
an orphan, yellow-skinned, always looking
        half-grown,
who served our family for how many years
and was paid three dollars a week and saved
        all three.
She loved me in a tolerant, half-resentful
        fashion.

Once, long after she was married,
she wrote that the mortgage was being
        foreclosed,
but her little farm might still be saved.
She needed money, not much, but I didn't
        have it then
and I told her so, if warmly and at length.
She didn't answer my letter.
I don't know when Ora died.

I think of that equivocating letter;
it is what I haven't done that tortures me at
        night
—rumbles of gas, rumbles of guilt.
Stephen, that just man who helped me often
—we sat together mornings in the smoking
        car;
he listened, gave sound advice, then turned to
        his crossword puzzle—
Stephen dying of cancer forty miles away;
I went to his house when it was too late.
Is there a circle of thorns around the dying?
a circle of ice around the aged,
ice at the center too?

I can be kind at easier moments.
"Don't be unfair to yourself," I say;
"don't forget the unpaid days, the uncredited
        work
for the craft, for brilliant youngsters, for the
        town,
or the yearlong struggle to make the words
        come right."
Yes, I remember the good things too.
Trust me to be here, not complaining,
not making excuses, not letting my envy
        speak,
not ever slipping a knife in the back.
In other things don't trust me too far.

There in the last grave in the unvisited family
        plot,
smile up at me through the earth, Mother;
be jubilant for what you achieved in me.
Forgive my absences.

Selected Bibliography

WORKS OF
MALCOLM COWLEY

The principal collection of Cowley papers is at the Newberry Library in Chicago.

Blue Juniata. New York: Jonathan Cape and Harrison Smith, 1929. Revised and reissued as *Blue Juniata: Collected Poems.* New York: Viking Press, 1968.

"The Poet and the World." *New Republic* 70:303–05 (April 27, 1932).

Exile's Return: A Narrative of Ideas. New York: W. W. Norton, 1934. Revised and reissued as *Exile's Return: A Literary Odyssey of the Twenties.* New York: Viking Press, 1951.

After the Genteel Tradition: American Writers Since 1910. New York: W. W. Norton, 1937. Revised and reissued as *After the Genteel Tradition: American Writers 1910–1930.* Carbondale: Southern Illinois University Press, 1964. (Cowley's chapters in this book, which includes "Dos Passos: Poet Against the World," constitute nearly half of the text, of which he is editor as a whole; other contributors are Lionel Trilling, Newton Arvin, and John Peale Bishop.)

"Unshaken Friend." *New Yorker* 20:28–32, 35–36 (April 1, 1944); 20:30–34, 36, 39–40 (April 8, 1944).

The Portable Hemingway. New York: Viking Press, 1944. (Edited by Cowley.)

The Portable Faulkner. New York: Viking Press, 1946. Rev. ed., 1967. (Edited by Cowley.)

The Portable Hawthorne. New York: Viking Press, 1948. Rev. ed., 1969. (Edited by Cowley.)

Stories of F. Scott Fitzgerald. New York: Scribners, 1951. (Edited by Cowley.)

The Literary Situation. New York: Viking Press, 1954.

"Sociological Habit Patterns in Linguistic Transmogrification." *Reporter* 15:41–43 (September 20, 1956).

Walt Whitman's Leaves of Grass: The First Edition. New York: Viking Press, 1959. (Edited by Cowley.)

Black Cargoes: A History of the Atlantic Slave Trade. New York: Viking Press, 1962. (With Daniel P. Mannix.)

The Faulkner-Cowley File: Letters and Memories, 1944–1962. New York: Viking Press, 1966.

Think Back on Us: A Contemporary Chronicle of the 1930s, edited by Henry Dan Piper. Carbondale: Southern Illinois University Press, 1967.

A Many-Windowed House: Collected Essays on American Writers and American Writing, edited by Henry Dan Piper. Carbondale: Southern Illinois University Press, 1970.

Lesson of the Masters: An Anthology of the Novel from Cervantes to Hemingway. New York: Scribners, 1971. (Edited by Cowley with Howard E. Hugo.)

A Second Flowering: Works and Days of the Lost Generation. New York: Viking Press, 1973.

"The Greene-ing of the Portables." *Book World (Washington Post)* 7:332–54 (April 29, 1973).

—And I Worked at the Writer's Trade: Chapters of Literary History, 1918–1978. New York: Viking Press, 1978.

"Prayer on All Saints' Day." *Sewanee Review* 86:563–65 (Fall 1978).

"Remembering Allen Tate." *Georgia Review* 34:7–10 (Spring 1980).

The Dream of the Golden Mountains: Remembering the 1930s. New York: Viking Press, 1980.

The View from 80. New York: Viking Press, 1980.

BIBLIOGRAPHY

Bergonzi, Bernard. "Malcolm Cowley." *Contemporary Poets,* edited by James Vinson. 2nd ed. New York: St. Martin's Press, 1975.

Eisenberg, Diane U. *Malcolm Cowley: A Checklist of His Writings, 1916–1973.* Carbondale: Southern Illinois University Press, 1975.

SECONDARY SOURCES

Aaron, Daniel. *Writers on the Left.* New York: Harcourt, Brace and World, 1961.

Aldridge, John W. "The Case of Malcolm Cowley." *The Nation* 180:162–64 (February 19, 1955).

———. "Malcolm Cowley at Eighty." *Michigan Quarterly Review* 18:480–90 (Summer 1979).

Blackmur, R. P. *The Double Agent.* New York: Arrow Editions, 1935.

———. *Language as Gesture.* London: George Allen and Unwin, 1954.

Burke, Kenneth. *The Philosophy of Literary Form.* Baton Rouge: Louisiana State University Press, 1941.

————. "I Dipped My Finger in the Lake and Wrote." *New York Times Book Review,* November 17, 1968, pp. 8, 76.

Guth, Dorothy Lobrano, ed. *Letters of E. B. White.* New York: Harper and Row, 1976.

Hoffman, Frederick, Charles Allen, and Carolyn F. Ulrich. *The Little Magazine.* Princeton: Princeton University Press, 1946.

Jarrell, Randall. *Poetry and the Age.* New York: Alfred A. Knopf, 1953.

Kazin, Alfred. *Starting Out in the Thirties.* Boston: Little, Brown, 1965.

Kriegel, Leonard. "Art and the Book Reviewer." *The Nation* 204:732–33 (June 5, 1967).

O'Connor, Flannery. *Mystery and Manners,* edited by Sally and Robert Fitzgerald. New York: Farrar, Straus and Giroux, 1969. (Includes "The Fiction Writer and His Country.")

Poirier, Richard. "The Difficulties of Modernism and the Modernism of Difficulty." *Images and Ideas in American Culture,* edited by Arthur Edelstein. Waltham, Mass.: Brandeis University Press, 1979.

Rubin, Louis D., Jr. *The Curious Death of the Novel.* Baton Rouge: Louisiana State University Press, 1967.

Sheaffer, Louis. Interview of Marshall A. Best. Columbia University Oral History Interview 6 (April 22, 1976). Pp. 213–18. (Written only; not on tape.)

Sheehy, Carolyn. *Sharing the Literary Feast: A Portrait of Malcolm Cowley.* Chicago: Newberry Library, 1979.

Simpson, Lewis P. "Malcolm Cowley and the American Writer." *Sewanee Review* 84:221–47 (Spring 1976).

————. "The Decorum of the Writer." *Sewanee Review* 86:566–71 (Fall 1978).

Stegner, Wallace. *The Uneasy Chair: A Biography of Bernard De Voto.* New York: Doubleday, 1974.

Styron, William. "That Extraordinary Company of Writers Ironically Known as the Lost Generation." *New York Times Book Review,* May 6, 1973, pp. 8, 10–12.

Tate, Allen. "A Regional Poet." *New Republic* 60:51–52 (August 28, 1929).

————. *Memoirs and Opinions: 1926–1974.* Chicago: Swallow, 1975.

Thorpe, Willard. *American Writing in the Twentieth Century.* Cambridge, Mass.: Harvard University Press, 1960.

Weinstein, Allen. *Perjury: The Hiss-Chambers Case.* New York: Alfred A. Knopf, 1978.

Wilson, Edmund. *Letters on Literature and Politics: 1912–1972,* edited by Elena Wilson. New York: Farrar, Straus and Giroux, 1977.

Young, Philip. "For Malcolm Cowley: Critic, Poet, 1898–." *Southern Review,* n.s. 9:778–95 (Autumn 1973).

Zwick, Edward, ed. *Literature and Liberalism: An Anthology of Sixty Years of "The New Republic."* Washington, D.C.: New Republic Book Company, 1976.

—*GEORGE CORE*

W. E. B. Du Bois

1868–1963

Just as the outstanding black American figure of the nineteenth century was Frederick Douglass, so the outstanding black American figure of the twentieth century was William Edward Burghardt Du Bois. In both lives skin color and racial prejudice were decisive forces. Douglass and Du Bois devoted their strength and brilliance to the termination of racism, which influenced every aspect of American life and much of international affairs.

Du Bois' life began during the presidency of Andrew Johnson and ended during the last days of the vice-presidency of Lyndon Johnson. But astonishing longevity was one of the least remarkable features of his achievement. With his Renaissance sweep, Du Bois was involved in all phases of domestic American life from the 1890's to the 1960's; and when racism, colonialism, and imperialism affected lives in other countries, he was deeply involved there too. The height of his influence lasted from about 1910 (when the power of Booker T. Washington and Tuskegee Institute waned) to about 1934 (when he resigned from the National Association for the Advancement of Colored People [NAACP] and from the editorship of the *Crisis*). During that time no other figure spoke so completely for millions of black Americans; never before or since has such near unanimity existed among blacks for a comparable span of time.

In working to create an egalitarian, humane, abundant, and fruitful life for all people, Du Bois endured conflict, sacrifice, insult, and physical danger. This essay will focus on his voluminous writings, into which he put so much of his energy. But we must remember that they constitute only one part of his life, which falls naturally into six main divisions.

Du Bois' student years began in public school in his native Great Barrington, in southwestern Massachusetts, where he graduated from high school in 1884. After an undergraduate career at Fisk University, in Nashville, Tennessee, where he received a B.A., Du Bois entered Harvard as a junior, on scholarship, in 1888. He graduated with another B.A., cum laude, in 1890 and did postgraduate work at Harvard on a fellowship, receiving his M.A. in history in 1891. He spent the years 1892–1894 at the University of Berlin on a Slater Fund Fellowship; this allowed him to travel through Europe undeterred by racism. In 1895 he received the Ph.D. from Harvard, the first black person in American history to obtain a doctorate in a secular subject. His dissertation, *The Suppression of the African Slave Trade to the United States of America, 1638–1870,* was the first publication of the Harvard Historical Series and marked the beginning of the scientific study of black history.

This first phase of preparation was followed by his early years as a teacher-scholar, from 1894 through 1910. Once he returned, via steerage, from Europe (with some $25 to his name), Du Bois applied for teaching positions, in those days necessarily at black schools only. He received offers from Wilberforce University in Ohio and from Tuskegee Institute in Alabama (where it was suggested that he teach mathematics, a subject not dear to his heart). The offer from Wilberforce arrived first, suggesting that Du Bois teach "the classics," and he accepted. From 1894 through 1896 he was professor of Greek and Latin, at a salary of $800 a year. He offered to teach German and sociology as well, but the first subject was regarded as of doubtful utility and the second as possibly subversive; Du Bois was confined to Vergil and Aristophanes. His agnosticism did not please the administration, nor did his successful opposition to the appointment of the university president's unqualified relative to a professorship.

For Du Bois, the rigidity and remote location of Wilberforce, combined with his diminishing enthusiasm for the subjects he taught and his difficulty in extracting the agreed-upon salary from the administration, led to mounting discontent. One glorious experience sustained him: it was at Wilberforce that Du Bois married Nina Gomer, a student from an Iowa farm and the daughter of a black father and a white, German-born mother. Nina Gomer was to be his companion in struggle for over fifty years (until her death in 1950). They had two children, Burghardt Gomer, who died in infancy, and Nina Yolande.

Soon an offer arrived from the University of Pennsylvania asking Du Bois to undertake— under its auspices and those of the Philadelphia Settlement House—a thorough study of the Philadelphia black community. At a salary of $900 a year, in a large modern city, the work would engage contemporary life and issues, not antique languages. In those days, the university could not offer Du Bois a faculty appointment; but since he held a doctorate from Harvard the title of mere "fellow" was thought inappropriate. As a compromise Du Bois was called "assistant instructor in sociology," but he was not listed in the university catalog and was not assigned to teach any classes. His task was purely research. Out of that in 1899 came Du Bois' second book, *The Philadelphia Negro,* a trailblazing work in what is now called urban sociology.

After the year of work in Philadelphia, Atlanta University (which then taught gradeschool, high-school, and college students) offered Du Bois an appointment as professor of economics and history, at another slight increase in salary. The subjects were congenial, and it was understood that Du Bois would take over a fledgling effort, begun in 1896, to organize annual conferences of specialists on "Negro Problems." From 1897 to 1910, Du Bois served on the faculty, directed the conferences, and edited their proceedings for publication.

The third phase of Du Bois' life, that of organizer and agitator, began when he joined the executive board of the newly launched NAACP and became editor of its organ, the *Crisis.* Du Bois edited the *Crisis* from its first number, November 1910, until the issue of July 1934. When relations within the NAACP became intolerable, he accepted an offer from the president of Atlanta University, his dear friend John Hope, to return to that campus full-time. (Du Bois had already offered a summer course there in 1933 on "Karl Marx and the Negro," perhaps the first course of its kind in an American university.)

Du Bois remained in Atlanta for a decade, and in this fourth phase of his career resumed his scholarly activities with undiminished vigor. He founded and edited the quarterly *Phylon,* served as chairman of the department of sociology, taught a full load of classes, and produced his monumental *Black Reconstruction,* published in 1935. That book was followed by an ambitious effort to convey the essential history of African and African-derived peoples: *Black Folk, Then and Now: An Essay in the History and Sociology of the Negro Race* (1939). At almost the same time he published his first major effort to assess the significance of his own life, *Dusk of Dawn. An Essay Toward an Autobiography of a Race Concept* (1940).

In 1944 Du Bois was asked to return to the NAACP as director of special research, with particular responsibility in the areas of colonialism and Africa. This return to organizational activities marks the fifth phase of his life. Du Bois was then in his mid-seventies, and it is quite likely that the NAACP board considered this appointment a kind of honorific retirement for a founder of the association whose name had been synonymous with it for so many years. If so, they underestimated Du Bois, whose health was excellent and whose vigor was that of a person thirty years younger. He insisted on playing an active role, and in 1948, when differences with the board again arose, he resigned to work for the Council on African Affairs, the Peace Information Center, and political causes—including, when he was eighty-two, his own vigorous campaign for U.S. senator from New York on the Progressive party ticket. He received over 200,000 votes.

Du Bois' last twelve years were devoted mainly to three enterprises. First was a massive historical novel, first conceived in the 1930's, published as a trilogy by Mainstream Publishers. *The Black Flame* (1957–1961) contains some thousand pages and tells, as only Du Bois can, what it meant to be a black man in the United States from 1876 to 1956.

While there was much autobiographical material in the trilogy, Du Bois also worked on a more formal autobiography during the years 1959–1961. In 1966 the manuscript of this work was taken out of Ghana, where he had gone five years earlier at the request of President Kwame Nkrumah, after the coup overthrowing the government, and gotten to the present writer, who edited it. It was published with an introduction in 1968 by International Publishers.

Du Bois' third major undertaking, in his ninth decade, was the production of an encyclopedia of African history and cultures. He had originally projected such a work in 1909, but lack of funding made its realization impossible. When Nkrumah, a devoted follower of Du Bois', became Ghana's first prime minister (1957–1960) and then its president (1960–1966), Du Bois was invited by him to come to Ghana and organize the encyclopedia. For this reason, mainly, Du Bois went to Ghana in 1961, organized an international secretariat, and worked on the project until his death. The effort itself was abruptly terminated with the 1966 coup.

Virtually throughout his life, regardless of his other activities, Du Bois worked as writer, editor, and scholar. He began writing for newspapers while still in high school. In April 1883 he served as western Massachusetts correspondent for the *New York Globe* (later *The Freeman*), an influential black newspaper; at least twenty-seven columns, signed by him and edited by the militant T. Thomas Fortune, were published between April 1883 and May 1885. He wrote not only on the comings and goings of black people in the area but also about literature, social reform, and politics. From 1884 through the summer of 1885, he contributed occasionally to the *Daily Republican* of Springfield, Massachusetts. While at Harvard he wrote articles for the *Boston Courant,* a black weekly newspaper. Early in 1891 the *Courant* published his 8,500-word essay (originally delivered before the National Colored League in Boston in March 1891) entitled "Does Education Pay?" To this question he not only replied with a vigorous yes but also insisted, contrary to the arguments of Booker T. Washington (who had not yet captured a national audience), that black people should have a full academic education. He held that limiting them to vocational education was degrading and that nothing was more fully "practical" than the best academic training. It is here that Du Bois first voiced an idea that was to reappear in his writing for decades: "Never make the mistake of thinking that the object of being a man is to make a carpenter—the object of being a carpenter is to be a man."

Du Bois contributed regularly to newspapers from 1927 to 1961. His columns appeared in the *New York Amsterdam News* from the 1920's to 1944; the *Pittsburgh Courier* in the mid-1930's; the *Chicago Defender* from January 1945 through May 1948; Adam Clayton Powell's *People's Voice* in 1947 and 1948; the *Chicago Globe* in 1950; Paul Robeson and Louis Burnham's *Freedom* from 1951 through 1954; and in the left-wing weekly *National Guardian* from November 1948 until May 1961, shortly before Du Bois left for Ghana. In his columns Du Bois treated a range of national and international affairs, the arts, and current questions in social sciences—notably economics, psychology, and history.

Du Bois also had an impact on the thinking of his time through his work as an editor, which began in 1885, when he worked for a year on the staff of the *Fisk Herald,* the university's monthly magazine. From late 1886 until October 1887, he served as a cultural editor and then as editor in chief from November until his graduation the following June.

Two articles stand out from the rest of his work for the *Fisk Herald.* They describe his experiences in the mountain regions of Tennessee, where he had lived among poor black farming families during the summer of 1886. His intended purpose was that of a teacher, but he became a student as well: "Whatever the pupils have gained, it was little to what I acquired." He was to write of this with great pathos in one of a collection of essays, *The Souls of Black Folk* (1903), where his description of the staunch, lovely Josie, with whose family Du Bois lived that summer, is not easily forgotten. The magazine also published "Tom Brown at Fisk," his first effort at writing a novella. Its significance lies in its autobiographical content rather than in its artistry. In it a young woman student goes off to teach in the mountains of Tennessee. Du Bois writes in the opening paragraph, "It's hard to be a woman, but a black one—!!"

Du Bois' editorials are worth noting as hints of his own growing convictions. In November 1887 he urges that education at Fisk should depend not on the gifts of northern philanthropists but, rather, on the contributions of black people themselves; in the same issue he laments that the United States does not "protect the rights of those we educate!" Du Bois early showed his concern for the rights of women and especially the dignity and equality of women. Commenting in December 1887 on a meeting of women held in Nashville, he writes: "The Age of Woman is surely dawning."

In the *Fisk Herald* of November 1887 he describes Afro-American music as "the strangest, sweetest" in the world and urges "the Negro race ... to build up an American school of music which shall rival the grandest schools of the past." His essay on the spirituals, later published in *The Souls of Black Folk,* is the first serious examination of that remarkable genre. In April 1888, preparing for his own graduation, he asks: "Why isn't there a Fisk student at Leipzig, or a Fisk metaphysician at Berlin?"

In his final editorial for the *Fisk Herald,* in June 1888, Du Bois wrote on behalf of the five graduates (three of whom were women) in his class: "We can look back with grateful hearts and forward with renewed zeal for the great work before us." The gratitude was genuine, and to the end of his days Du Bois remained a fervent partisan of Fisk; the "zeal for the great work" inspired him throughout the next seventy-five years.

The years at Harvard, beginning in the fall of 1888, were marvelously enriching. Du Bois had the good fortune to study under William James, Josiah Royce, and George Santayana in philosophy; Edward Channing and Albert Bushnell Hart in history; Barrett Wendell in English; and Francis Greenwood Peabody in ethics. In political economics he studied with Frank William Taussig, and in the natural sciences with Nathaniel Southgate Shaler. Justin Winsor, the university librarian, and Charles Eliot Norton, professor of art history, influenced the young Du Bois. Of these scholars James and Hart were of the most consequence to him; not only splendid teachers, they became his friends and regularly invited him to their homes. In later years, they followed his work.

Laden with academic honors, Du Bois was chosen a commencement speaker in 1890. A young black man speaking on such an occasion received nationwide notice, especially addressing his chosen topic: "Jefferson Davis as a Representative American." Du Bois' point was that Davis' aggressiveness, physical bravery, and imperious will were human characteristics that could promote either social progress or its opposite. He suggested that Africa had something of a salutary value to offer America: the concept of service—of unselfish help to others. Sacrifice and service were more than words for Du Bois: with his energy and his genius he made them his legacy.

Du Bois now embraced scholarship and under Hart's supervision spent more than two years examining contemporary sources and the few secondary accounts that treated the African slave trade and efforts to suppress it in the United States. In 1891 he presented the results of his work to Hart's seminar and received his M.A. With Hart's support, Du Bois spoke at the annual meeting of the American Historical Association in Washington, D. C., in December 1891. His paper, "The Enforcement of the Slave-Trade Laws," anticipated his dissertation five years later. A young black man reporting on any subject before a group of white scholars in the nation's capital was unprecedented. More extraordinary, he described the realities of the slave trade and the complicity of the highest U.S. government officials in violating the law, and concluded:

If slave labor was an economic god, then the slave trade was its strong right arm; and with Southern planters recognizing this and Northern capital unfettered by a conscience it was almost like legislating against economic laws to attempt to abolish the slave trade by statutes. Northern greed joined to Southern credulity was a combination calculated to circumvent any law, human or divine.

The response of the audience was polite, here and there strained. Two of the leading historians present, Herbert Baxter Adams (the secretary of the association), of the Johns Hopkins University, and Edward G. Bourne, of Adelbert College in Michigan, published discerning and laudatory accounts of Du Bois' paper in national magazines. Adams made no mention of Du Bois' color, referring only to his "scholarly" paper and his Harvard connection; Bourne could not resist asking, "What would Southern teachers of history within the lifetime of many readers . . . have thought of going to Washington to listen, among other things, to a paper on the Enforcement of the Slave-Trade Laws by a colored man, the holder of a fellowship at Harvard University?" Despite the politeness of the assemblage and the appreciative comments, no institution represented at the meeting offered Du Bois a post.

As a book, Du Bois' dissertation on the suppression of the African slave trade was widely and favorably reviewed. Some commentators were disturbed by the author's "use of a few adjectives here and there that characterized the advocate rather than the historian." On this question Du Bois' view was clear and unchanging: history and advocacy were inseparable but not identical. In applying for his fellowship at Harvard he had made plain that he sought to master scholarship to better serve his people; in Berlin, in 1893, he confided to his diary that this was his purpose and that, though it might cost him his life, he would fulfill it.

The commitment to serve his people informed his own approach to history and his judgment of the works of other historians. In the closing chapter of *Black Reconstruction,* Du Bois wrote that in reading Charles A. and Mary R. Beard's *The Rise of American Civilization* one had "the comfortable feeling that nothing right or wrong is involved." Two differing social systems develop in the North and South, and "they clash, as winds and water strive." The Beards' mechanistic interpretation fails because human experience is not mechanistic. Furthermore, in such a presentation

There is no room for the real plot of the story, for the clear mistake and guilt of building a new slavery of the working class in the midst of a fateful experiment in democracy, for the triumph of sheer moral courage and sacrifice in the abolition crusade; and for the hurt and struggle of degraded black millions in their fight for freedom and their attempt to enter democracy. Can all this be omitted or half suppressed in a treatise that calls itself scientific?

The reader of Du Bois' writings—creative or scholarly—cannot mistake that the author's judgment of right and wrong, bringing forth "the hurt and struggle" of his people, is precisely his contribution to human knowledge. In the preface to *The Suppression of the African Slave Trade* the reader is told of the author's hope that the book will represent "a small contribution to the scientific study of slavery and the American Negro." Du Bois thought the absence of such a study bespoke racism and that the publication of his book was part of the struggle to overcome the "hurt." It followed that his book was the first to treat its controversial subject; it has not been supplanted.

Du Bois' pioneering book explores the economics of slavery and the slave trade, and the militancy of the slaves, pointing up the significance of Toussaint L'Ouverture and the Haitian revolution (in which the peasants resisted for several months the French troops under Charles Leclerc). He examines in detail the place of slavery in national politics, especially in the political climate of the revolution (and its effect abroad), and in the formation and adoption of the Constitution. He also provides the first discussion of the movement in the South to legalize the slave trade: the reasons for it, the arguments against it, and the politics of legalization leading up to the Civil War.

Du Bois' analysis of the roots of the Civil War in the tenth chapter of *The Suppression of the African Slave Trade* has not been surpassed by contemporary scholarship. His concept of the war as an attempted "political *coup d'etat*" by a desperate slaveholding oligarchy still has much to teach historians. Du Bois states repeatedly and courageously that acts to inhibit or to outlaw the slave trade "came very near being a dead letter" in Washington, D. C.; that "the execution of the laws within the country exhibits grave defects and even criminal negligence"; and that "the efforts of the executive during this period [the 1850's] were criminally lax and negligent."

One must recall that Du Bois' book appeared

in 1896—when George Bancroft's concept of the divinity of the Founding Fathers and the Constitution held sway—to properly appreciate the daring of his observation that

No American can study the connection of slavery with United States history, and not devoutly pray that his country may never have a similar special problem to solve, until it shows more capacity for such work than it has shown in the past. It is neither profitable nor in accordance with scientific truth to consider that whatever the constitutional fathers did was right, or that slavery was a plague sent from God and fated to be eliminated in time.

Du Bois demonstrates that the enslavement of black people vitiated the quality of life in the United States as a whole. The controversy surrounding enslavement led to a war that threatened the very existence of the republic and that took half a million lives. The practices that sustained slavery have not yet been extirpated, and the question of their elimination "sometime must be fully answered," Du Bois warned.

The second book that Du Bois wrote as a young scholar-teacher was at the request of a newly organized movement to reform the ills of urban slums. The College Settlements Association was formally established in May 1890 by representatives from Wellesley, Vassar, Smith, and Bryn Mawr. Toynbee Hall, founded in London in 1884, had a similar purpose and sponsored studies such as Charles Booth's *Life and Labour of the People in London* (1889–1897). Beatrice Potter (Mrs. Sydney Webb) was one of Booth's closest co-workers and a friend of Jane Addams, who visited the hall and inspected its work during the 1880's. From these visits came some of the inspiration for Addams' own Hull House in Chicago. Others associated in settlement work were such re-markable people as Vida Scudder, Isabel Eaton, Lucy Maynard Salmon, Ellen Gates Starr, Samuel McCune Lindsay, Robert Archey Woods, and Susan P. Wharton.

In the 1890's a reform movement that aimed at ousting political bossism was abroad in Philadelphia. The black ghetto tended to favor the city machine, since it provided some jobs and was responsible for the appointment of the first black policemen in the city. The settlement movement was predominantly the work of wealthy people who thought that a study of the actual conditions in the ghetto might assist both settlement work and the reform effort. The result was Du Bois' *The Philadelphia Negro: A Social Study.* Isabel Eaton, who worked for the settlement, wrote a lengthy appendix on domestic servants and assisted Du Bois in gathering data for the book.

To appreciate *The Philadelphia Negro* one must bear in mind not only the reformist and upper-class auspices under which it was produced, but also the period in which it appeared: lynchings were commonplace, Jim Crow laws were on the rise in the South, and "scientific" racism—in history, psychology, anatomy, and anthropology—was being widely promulgated.

Du Bois' basic argument is that black people are fully human and entitled to all the dignity and benefits of American citizenship. The word "Negro," he says, should be capitalized "because I believe that eight million Americans are entitled to a capital letter."

Du Bois attacks the commonplace idea—still prevalent, if not dominant—that poor people are poor because they are poor, that is, unworthy. He does not deny the deficiencies of black people in Philadelphia and in the nation, but his whole emphasis is on the social, economic, and political causes of their impoverishment. The ghetto is symptomatic of the deficiencies of the society; crime is a social phenomenon, and the idea of "Negro criminality" is a piece of racist slander. The high mortality among blacks is not a racial characteristic but a reflection of socioeconomic hardships. Du Bois' arguments ran counter to those in the dominant literature and to the received ideas about the black American population. As for the privations of immigrants in general, Du Bois points out fundamental differences between the situation of European immigrants and of the blacks coming into the cities and into the North—a point still not grasped by some sociologists.

Du Bois' rejection of social Darwinism—a doctrine then all but unquestioned—is explicit. He insists that "in the realm of social phenomena the law of survival is greatly modified by human choice, whim and prejudice. And consequently no one knows when one sees a social outcast how far this failure is due to deficiencies of the individual, and how far to the accidents or injustice of his environment. This is especially the case with the Negro." Scattered throughout the book are suggestions, some only now being developed, about the black family, children, and the church. Above all, the idea that differences existed among blacks as among any people was new.

In *The Philadelphia Negro* Du Bois fully documents for the first time the realities of racism: its effect on jobs, dignity, and the "sheer question of bread and butter." Racism involves "matters of life and death"; what is at stake for black people are "their homes, their food, their children, their hopes." Although he led struggles for civil rights, Du Bois insisted that they were not the heart of the problem. Unless one understands this position it is not possible to understand Du Bois' differences with the board of the NAACP in later years.

In politics during this turn-of-the-century period, Du Bois rejected the path of radicalism and socialism. But if those who had financed his project hoped it would confirm the idea that Philadelphia's political troubles stemmed from ghetto support of the machine, they obtained no comfort from Du Bois' findings. "How long," he writes in one of several cries from the heart, "can a city teach its black children that the road to success is to have a white face? How long can a city do this and escape the inevitable penalty?" For racism to pervade the city "is morally wrong, politically dangerous, industrially wasteful, and socially silly. It is the duty of the whites to stop it, and to do so primarily for their own sakes." The existing situation, he wrote, "is a disgrace to the city—a disgrace to Christianity, to its spirit of justice, to its common sense."

It is a battle for humanity and human culture. If in the hey-day of the greatest of the world's civilizations, it is possible for one people ruthlessly to steal another, drag them helpless across the water, enslave them, debauch them, and then slowly murder them by economic and social exclusion until they disappear from the face of the earth—if the consummation of such a crime be possible in the twentieth century, then our civilization is vain and the republic is a mockery and a farce.

Du Bois later criticized *The Philadelphia Negro* in the *Crisis* (March 1932) for a certain "provincialism." He had examined the oppression of black people "from the point of view of religion, humanity and sentiment" instead of socioeconomic facts and class alignments. There is validity to his hindsight; yet *The Philadelphia Negro* remains a classic not only for breaking new ground—for the abundance of its data and the scrupulousness of its research—but also because it is a passionate work of humanistic science.

That the University of Pennsylvania turned to Du Bois to undertake the study was natural. He alone among black scholars held a doctorate from a renowned university; his dissertation had been published as an important work of scholarship; and his postgraduate study in Germany was considered valuable for any American scholar. But the collaboration of a black man and a white woman—the black man being the senior author—can be seen as unusual then and now. Its success appears in the work and in the fact that Du Bois and Eaton remained friends until Eaton's death thirty-five years later.

On November 19, 1897, Du Bois delivered a paper in Philadelphia to the forty-fourth meeting of the American Academy of Political and Social Science. He had now finished the research for *The Philadelphia Negro* (the writing was done the next year, at Atlanta University). Speaking on "The Study of the Negro Problems," he urged the establishment in a southern black university of "a centre of sociological research" into these problems, supported by such universities as Harvard, Columbia, Johns Hopkins, and Pennsylvania. He noted that Tuskegee Institute and Hampton Institute sponsored conferences on "practical" matters that touched only rural populations. In 1896 Atlanta University had begun to organize the national center for black research that he described, but support was hard to come by: " . . . it is certainly to be desired that Atlanta University may be enabled to continue this work. . . ." Du Bois concluded:

Finally the necessity must again be emphasized of keeping clearly before students the object of all science, amid the turmoil and intense feeling that cloud the discussion of a burning social question. We live in a day when in spite of the brilliant accomplishments of a remarkable century, there is current much flippant criticism of scientific work; when the truth-seeker is too often pictured as devoid of human sympathy, and careless of human ideals. We are still prone in spite of all our culture to sneer at the heroism of the laboratory while we cheer the swagger of the street broil [brawl]. At such a time true lovers of humanity can only hold higher the pure ideals of science, and continue to insist that if we would solve a problem we must study it, and that there is but one coward on earth, and that is the coward that dare not know.

None of the universities named by Du Bois—nor any other except his own Atlanta University—acted upon his suggestion.

Du Bois was convinced that oppression of black people persisted in the United States because educated, influential people did not know the facts. If the facts could be shown, he thought, racism would be vanquished. This vision powered his exhausting work on the Atlanta University Conferences for the Study of the Negro Problems, which he directed—with a budget that never exceeded $5,000 annually—for the next thirteen years.

The purpose of the conferences, especially as conceived by the university president, Horace Bumstead, and a banker-trustee, George Bradford, was to focus annually on the problems of urban southern blacks. The first such gathering had been held in 1896 and was summarized in *Mortality Among Negroes in Cities* (1896), published as Atlanta University Publication No. 1; the next year, the proceedings of the second conference were issued as *Social and Physical Condition of Negroes in Cities* (1897). When Du Bois was offered an appointment as professor of economics and sociology in 1897, it was understood that he would also be responsible for organizing the annual conferences and supervising publication of the proceedings. From 1897 through 1910 he did both, with Augustus G. Dill of the Atlanta sociology department as his fellow editor of publications.

Under Du Bois' guidance, the conferences were to study many aspects of black urban life, with the assistance of experts throughout the country. Each subject would be reexamined every ten years to see what changes had occurred and why, and what to do about them. (The conference of 1902 investigated "The Negro Artisan"; that of 1912 updated and analyzed findings on the same subject.) Among the speakers who addressed these gatherings were such nationally known figures as Franz Boas, Booker T. Washington, Jane Addams, Mary White Ovington, Monroe Work, Washington Gladden, Franklin B. Sanborn, Florence Kelley, and Walter F. Willcox.

In scope, seriousness, and effect, nothing approached the Atlanta conferences. It was one of Du Bois' keen disappointments that they did not survive after his move to the NAACP. He tried to revive them in the 1940's, after his return to Atlanta as head of the sociology department; the twenty-sixth conference, "Conference of Negro Land Grant Colleges for Coordinating a Program of Cooperative Social Studies," was held in 1943. But in 1944 Du Bois became director of special research for the NAACP, and the conferences once again ceased.

The experience of researching and writing *The Philadelphia Negro* and the persuasion of Willcox brought Du Bois to undertake several studies of the South for the federal government. The first of these was issued as part of the Department of Labor *Bulletin* (January 1898) and entitled "The Negroes of Farmville, Virginia: A Social Study." Du Bois had discovered that many of the migrants to the ghetto of Philadelphia had come from Farmville, and he spent July and August 1897 in the town and "lived with the colored people, joined in their social life, and visited their homes." Three-fifths of the population in this seat of Prince Edward County, Virginia, was black. Du Bois wrote that his study had "but the one object of ascertaining, with as near an approach to scientific accuracy as possible, the real condition of the

Negro." His method was heavily statistical and examined the demography and sociology of the black population, especially education, occupations, and family conditions. He also studied the nearby community of Israel Hill, founded by freed slaves of the John Randolph family; at the time of Du Bois' researches 123 black descendants and one white family lived there.

In his conclusion, Du Bois remarked on "the growing differentiation of classes among Negroes," a phenomenon few others had noticed. He thought Farmville typical of "the condition of the Virginia Negro" at the time, but added that only further study could say for sure. He found in the community of black people "a peculiar hopefulness" and a belief "that one day black people will have all rights they are now striving for."

Another study by Du Bois appeared in the Department of Labor *Bulletin* (May 1899): "The Negro in the Black Belt: Some Social Sketches." These "sketches" were "based mainly on seminary notes made by members of the senior class" (their names were given in a footnote) of Atlanta University. The students were "born and bred" in the areas described, which included one town in Alabama and five in Georgia. The conclusion indicates the limits of Du Bois' analytical scope at the time: he suggests that, among the people studied, those who had managed to acquire some property, married with care, and provided education for their children "represent, so far as they go, a solution of the Negro problem." "In them," Du Bois went on, "lies the hope of the American Negro, and—shall we not say—to a great extent, the hope of the Republic."

A final study by Du Bois for the Department of Labor was published in its *Bulletin* of July 1901. After a brief examination of the policy on land for the landless black people during and just after the Civil War, the task of this study is placed: "To make clear the steps by which 470,000 black freedmen and their children have in one of the former slave States [Georgia] gained possession of over a million acres of land in a generation, the value of this land and its situation, the conditions of ownership, and the proper interpretation of these statistics as social phenomena."

The precise method of the study is explained: examination of printed and manuscript sources and inquiry on the ground. The history of Georgia is sketched; the black population is mapped by county, for each decade since the census of 1790; and the occupations and incomes as of 1900 of Georgia's black people are presented. The history and current conditions of landholding by black people in the state are given in detail with an account of tenant farming, sharecropping, and the role of the merchant. The actual economic conditions of black people in every county are tabulated, and the text often gives salient bits of history; for example, that Liberty County "voted solidly against secession" and why.

The final two studies by Du Bois, done directly for the federal government, were undertaken for the Bureau of the Census. *Bulletin No. 8* included "The Negro Farmer" (1904), a statistical study of every category of black farmer throughout the United States—owners, renters, sharecroppers, and tenants. It offers details on acreage, products, and values, and then shows the percentage of total farm production that comes from black people.

Among the special reports issued by the Bureau of the Census in 1906 was *Supplementary Analysis and Derivative Tables, Twelfth Census of the United States,* with a chapter called, again, "The Negro Farmer." This reprinted the earlier bulletin, but added thirty-seven pages of supplementary analysis containing elaborate tables that compared average expenditures of black and white farmers in 1900 and giving data on Indian and "Mongolian" (meaning Asian American) farmers throughout the country.

During the summer of 1906 Du Bois lived in Lowndes County, Alabama, where, at the request of the Bureau of the Census and at considerable personal risk, he directed a careful study of the working and living conditions of black tenant farmers and sharecroppers. This was duly delivered to the bureau in Washington, but publication was withheld. Years later when Du Bois tried to retrieve the manuscript, he was told that it had been burned. He believed that the study had been suppressed for its unsparing criticism of the atrocious conditions endured by the black farmers.

In connection with Du Bois' detailed studies of the living conditions of southern blacks, the point suggests itself that although he was born in Massachusetts and spent most of his life outside the South, he lived in Tennessee, Alabama, and Georgia for about twenty-eight years and visited the region regularly throughout his life. His extensive personal experience and his studies of the history and conditions of the area gave Du Bois expertise in the sociology of the South. The point is important biographically, for it refutes claims made by his opponents—notably Booker T. Washington—that Du Bois was a northern intellectual who knew very little about black people in general and about southern black people in particular. This is sheer nonsense.

While Du Bois was teaching at Atlanta, directing the Atlanta conferences, and producing government-sponsored studies, he was carrying his crusade into the pages of national magazines. The first such article was "Strivings of the Negro People" in the *Atlantic Monthly* (August 1897). Later included in somewhat revised form in *The Souls of Black Folk,* it is the source of Du Bois' often quoted lines:

... the Negro is a sort of seventh son, born with a veil, and gifted with second-sight in this American world,—a world which yields him no self-consciousness, but only lets him see himself through the revelation of the other world. It is a peculiar sensation, this double-consciousness, this sense of always looking at one's self through the eyes of others, of measuring one's soul by the tape of a world that looks on in amused contempt and pity. One ever feels his two-ness,—an American, a Negro; two souls, two thoughts, two unreconciled strivings; two warring ideals in one dark body, whose dogged strength alone keeps it from being torn asunder.

"A Negro Schoolmaster in the New South," which describes his teaching experience in Tennessee, was also published first in the *Atlantic Monthly* (January 1899) and later in *The Souls of Black Folk.* For the mostly white readers of the magazine, these two essays must have been ennobling—or jarring—experiences. Certainly nothing like them had been published in such a forum before. At about the same time, Du Bois' writings began to appear in the *Independent,* a New York weekly that was widely read among Protestant clergymen; in the *Nation,* later owned by Oswald Garrison Villard (who, in part because of Du Bois, moved away from the Tuskegee movement to become a founder of the NAACP); and in *Harper's Weekly, Collier's, Outlook* (Theodore Roosevelt's favorite magazine), and the Hearst-owned *World Today.* These articles treated questions of black crime, education, struggles, and organizations, and brought what were then the radical views of a black intellectual before hundreds of thousands of white readers. Du Bois continued to contribute scholarly articles to learned journals during this period; his essays and reviews appeared in the *American Historical Review* and the *Annals of the American Academy of Political and Social Science.*

And during these years he continued to write for black publications, notably the 15,000-word study "The Problem of Housing the Negro," which was published in six issues of the Hampton Institute's *Southern Workman* between June 1901 and February 1902. He also wrote for Jesse Max Barber's militant Atlanta-based monthly, *Voice of the Negro,* which in 1905 published his four-part article on the history of serfdom and ancient and modern slavery. The September 1906 pogrom in Atlanta resulted in the destruction of the publication's press and editorial offices, and Barber himself fled to Chicago. Du Bois continued to write for the journal during the year it survived in the North; most important was his writing on the Niagara movement, the all-black predecessor of the NAACP that he founded with William Monroe Trotter.

In this period Du Bois also contributed reviews to the *Dial,* the Chicago literary journal. In the issue of April 16, 1901, he mounted a slashing assault on *The American Negro,* a cynical, hateful attack on black people written by a black author, William Hannibal Thomas. Another of his reviews, "The Southerner's Problem" (May 1, 1905), attacks two books by leading white southern writers of the period: Thomas Nelson Page's *The Negro: The Southerner's Problem* and William Benjamin Smith's *The Color Line.* Page was a kind of benevolent racist; Smith, a brutal and vindictive one. Du Bois took each of them apart. This, too, was new fare in a journal with nationwide circulation and largely white readers.

It was in the *Dial* (July 16, 1901)—not in *The Souls of Black Folk,* as is generally asserted—that Du Bois first publicized his opposition to Booker T. Washington. The essay, in modified form, later provided the basis for the historic chapter "Of Booker T. Washington and Others" in *The Souls of Black Folk.* Written as a review of Washington's autobiography, *Up from Slavery,* the essay dissented from that work with great respect and extreme tact. Du Bois makes the point that Washington is the black leader designated by dominant whites:

Among the Negroes, Mr. Washington is still far from a popular leader. Educated and thoughtful Negroes everywhere are glad to honor him and aid him, but all cannot agree with him. He represents in Negro thought the old attitude of adjustment to environment. . . .

Naming black leaders such as Charles Waddell Chesnutt, Kelly Miller, Paul Laurence Dunbar, and Archibald and Francis Grimké, all of whom spurned the Tuskegee movement, Du Bois added that while they had no common program, all

. . . seek nevertheless that self-development and self-realization in all lines of human endeavor which they believe will eventually place the Negro beside the other races. . . . They believe, therefore, also in the higher education of Fisk and Atlanta Universities; they believe in self-assertion and ambition; and they believe in the right of suffrage for blacks on the same terms with whites.

The single most effective and most widely reproduced essay from this period was Du Bois' "Credo," first published in the *Independent* (October 6, 1904). This 500-word prose poem seeks to bestow on black people peace, justice, equality, endurance, ultimate optimism, and pride. It was reproduced in full in the *Literary Digest* the week after it first appeared, published in poster form and hung on the walls of black homes across the country, and reprinted in most states—including some in the South. At least one periodical, the *British Friend* (published by the Quakers in London), picked it up. With this widespread attention to the "Credo" and the appearance in 1903 of *The Souls of Black Folk,* Du Bois' stature as a black leader, second only to Washington, was established.

Du Bois' speeches and writings became increasingly militant after the explicit break with the Tuskegee movement that *The Souls of Black Folk* represented and also in response to accumulating racist assaults on black people both in the streets and in print (during this time Thomas Dixon, Jr., began his career as author of such best-sellers as *The Clansman,* upon which the film *Birth of a Nation* was based). Typical of the change was his speech "Caste in America," delivered many times in city after city, beginning in February 1904 before the Twentieth Century Club in New York City. This frontal assault on racism, elitism, and class oppression in the United States (Du Bois' words) was printed in full or in substantial part in at least eleven newspapers. Such extensive notice was unusual for any speaker and unprecedented for a black militant. Another speech, "The Negro in Large Cities," which discussed the necessity and propriety of decent education, jobs, and housing for black people, was published in two Brooklyn newspapers and the *New York Herald Tribune* on September 29, 1907, and in the *New York Evening Post* the next day.

Acknowledgment of Du Bois' leadership came when he, not Washington, was asked by the *New York Times* to survey the fifty years since the execution of John Brown in December 1859. This was published as "Fifty Years Among the Black Folk" on December 12, 1909. Du Bois emphasized the need for self-realization on the part of his people: they were "girding themselves to fight in the van of progress" not only for themselves but for "the emancipation of women, universal peace, democratic government, the socialization of wealth, and human brotherhood."

It is not surprising, given only the achievements mentioned here, that the convention in 1909 that organized what was to become the

NAACP unanimously decided to offer Du Bois a position on the NAACP executive board. He was put in charge of the research and publication department and was assigned the central responsibility of editing the *Crisis*.

Before we move to the next phase (1910–1934), that of the activist Du Bois, a look at his masterwork and the other late fruits of the previous, scholarly period is in order. The appearance in 1903 of *The Souls of Black Folk* marked not only a milestone in Du Bois' life but also a landmark in American history and literature. The remarkable book on the black experience in America, received no less remarkably by the public, has been a recurrent phenomenon—one thinks of Harriet Beecher Stowe's *Uncle Tom's Cabin* (1852), Richard Wright's *Native Son* (1940), Lillian Smith's *Strange Fruit* (1944), Ralph Ellison's *Invisible Man* (1952), James Baldwin's *Go Tell It on the Mountain* (1953), and Alex Haley's *Roots* (1976). Indeed, just as one could well use the black experience as the focus for a history of the nation, so one might use its literary expressions to illuminate all American literature. In each case the artistry, the mood, and the historical moment come together to produce not only a book but also a social explosion. *The Souls of Black Folk*—issued by a relatively minor house in Chicago, A. C. McClurg & Co.—was reviewed promptly, widely, and on the whole enthusiastically. A surprising number of reviewers described it as the kind of book that came once in a generation and predicted that it would last—that in fact it was a classic. And surely, after almost a century, it has earned that status.

Several of the fourteen chapters of the book had been published earlier in different form, but five were entirely new: "Of the Wings of Atalanta," "Of the Passing of the First-Born," "Of Alexander Crummell," "Of the Coming of John," and "Of the Sorrow Songs." The book as a whole is redolent of Du Bois' loving pride in his people and his belief that they have an ennobling mission to perform for mankind out of their oppressed condition and their great artistry. The volume affirms the centrality of the so-called Negro question to American history and society. It also reflects a kind of national awareness characteristic of Du Bois' mind and a premonition of the impact upon black Americans of the new turning of the United States toward imperialism—what he called "the recent course of the United States toward weaker and darker peoples in the West Indies, Hawaii, and the Philippines."

Each essay shines, but the ones in which he describes the wonderful Josie, his pioneering study of the spirituals, his loving portrait of Alexander Crummell, and the excruciatingly intense essay on the death of his son, Burghardt Gomer, are examples of magnificent prose. Even the title of the book is important. Just as Du Bois in his study of black Philadelphians was careful to say in his preface that he was writing of blacks as people, so *Souls* proclaimed itself at a time when black people were all too commonly reckoned not merely inferior but subhuman.

The timeliness of the book no less than its impressive content explains the force felt by the more sensitive of Du Bois' white readers, such as Ovington, Gladden (then an influential Christian reformer), and Henry James. At the same time the genius of the work and its militancy (extraordinary in its day) also moved tens of thousands of black people. Eugene Gordon, the black author and journalist, remarked to this writer that when he had been a schoolboy in the South, just before World War I, his teacher read the book to the class and that no other experience had been so inspiring to him. The poet Langston Hughes wrote to Du Bois on May 22, 1956: "I have just read again your *The Souls of the Black Folk*—for perhaps the tenth time—the first time being some forty years ago when I was a child in Kansas. Its beauty and passion and power are as moving and as meaningful as ever."

In general, the period from about 1890 to 1910 has been aptly characterized by Rayford W. Logan as the post–Civil War nadir for blacks in America. In that twenty-year period, disfranchisement was completed—in Mississippi (1890) and in Oklahoma (1910); the Populist movement was crushed; lynching became an established and recurring practice, claiming some 2,000 victims in those two decades; and Jim Crow was legalized in every southern state and in Washington, D. C. With these racist practices went the promulgation of racist ideas—the misuse of intelligence tests, faked experiments that contrasted the brains of black and white people (notably by Robert Bennett Bean at the Johns Hopkins University), the racist anthropology of Madison Grant, and racist historiography (such as the studies by William Archibald Dunning and his disciples at Columbia University, in the early 1900's). The commercial newspapers and magazines were filled with racist stories and "jokes," and runaway best-sellers in fiction were coming from the likes of Thomas Dixon, Jr., who wrote about the "horrors" of Reconstruction as black rabble ruled and ruined the prostrate South.

Illustrating the concern among blacks over racist historiography was a letter of July 12, 1909, to Du Bois from James R. L. Diggs, president of the Virginia Theological Seminary and College in Lynchburg. Diggs proposed that black people write accounts of Reconstruction in each of the southern states. "We must get our views of that period before the public," he wrote. "The series of works by southern writers presents our white brothers' side of the question but I do not find the proper credit given our people for what good they really did in those trying days." In December, Du Bois delivered his sec-

ond (and last) paper before the American Historical Association in New York City. Entitled "Reconstruction and Its Benefits," it was published in the *American Historical Review* in July 1910. Thus began a revision in thought among historians of this crucial subject that was to culminate twenty-five years later in Du Bois' magnum opus, *Black Reconstruction.*

Du Bois had already published his biography of John Brown in 1909, to commemorate the fiftieth anniversary of Brown's martyrdom. The idea originated when Ellis P. Oberholtzer, editor of the American Crisis Biographies series, invited Du Bois to contribute one among some twenty-five volumes planned, each a biography of a leading figure in American history. It was suggested that Du Bois do a biography of Frederick Douglass, and he accepted; but the publisher learned that Booker T. Washington wished to write Douglass' life. Du Bois graciously agreed to do another assignment, proposing at first Nat Turner, a subject declined by the publisher, and finally settling on Brown.

In his preface to the biography, Du Bois observes that "the only excuse for another life of John Brown is an opportunity to lay new emphasis upon the material which they [other biographers] have so carefully collected, and to treat these facts from a different point of view." That he does, and "the man who of all [white] Americans," as he wrote, "has perhaps come nearest to touching the real souls of black folk" is seen anew and with sympathy by one such soul.

The book does contain a number of factual errors—Du Bois tended to be rather careless in such matters—and later research has added significantly to our understanding of Brown and his efforts. But on Brown's overcoming of racism, his identification with black people, and the consequent sacrifice of his own life in an effort to end their enslavement, no book has supplanted Du Bois' and few have approached it.

In *John Brown,* Du Bois insists that "the cost of liberty is less than the price of repression, even though that cost be blood." He emphatically reaffirms that idea in the pages added to the 1962 edition, pointing to the revolutions in Russia and China as confirming his view. He once told this writer that of all his books *John Brown* was his favorite; it was a great joy to him that he lived to see the 1962 edition.

From 1910 to 1934 Du Bois gave himself chiefly to tasks of organization, agitation, and propaganda. By 1910 he had concluded that he had been mistaken in believing that racism persisted because white people of influence and culture did not know enough about it. He and others had devoted many years to putting the truth before the public in works that were fully documented and incontrovertible. But racism had not disappeared, either in ideology or in practice; if anything it seemed more pervasive than it had twenty years earlier. Du Bois decided that, although scholarship was useful in fighting it, collective, organized agitation and propaganda were needed to effect political change.

This transition from scholarship to activism had its roots in many of Du Bois' preoccupations before 1910; the divisions of his life indicated here were not clear-cut but represent gradual changes in emphasis. Thus in the period from 1896 to 1910, working mainly as a scholar-teacher, Du Bois had also been the main organizer of opposition to the Tuskegee movement. In 1905 this opposing group organized the Niagara movement, which was dedicated to the achievement of full equality for black people in the United States and which rejected what its members saw as acceptance of second-class education and employment by the Tuskegee movement.

Also during this period Du Bois founded the *Moon,* an illustrated weekly magazine published in Memphis, Tennessee, from December 1905 to July 1906. Only three issues are known to have survived. Most of its content—brief editorial commentary on matters of direct concern to blacks—came from Du Bois' pen. Then, with Freeman H. M. Murray and Lafayette M. Hershaw, Du Bois produced the *Horizon,* the monthly organ of the Niagara movement, from January 1907 to July 1910. For his part Du Bois called attention to articles and books of interest to black people and expressed brief opinions on politics, the women's movement, and the labor movement. Occasionally he would make his point with a short story such as "Principles," a satire on a white "do-gooder" who urges patience among black people; or "Constructive Work," an attack on the pusillanimous and compromising "race leaders." Both stories appeared in the December 1909 issue.

Du Bois' sheer energy and capacity for work had earlier led him to assume the responsibilities of secretary of the Pan-African Congress meeting in London in 1900. For it he wrote "To the Peoples of the World," which called for some modicum of justice for the darker peoples. This meeting marked the beginning of the Pan-African movement, to be revived by Du Bois in 1919.

The Niagara movement, in its break with the Tuskegee group, merged with white organizations seeking the same ends, resulting in the NAACP. Among them were anti-imperialist groups, notably the American Anti-Imperialist League, whose president was Moorfield Storey, formerly Senator Charles Sumner's secretary and by this time a leading attorney. Storey became the first president of the NAACP. The movement also received support from radicals, many of them active socialists, such as William English Walling, Mary White Ovington, Charles Edward Russell, and Florence Kelley. Others came out of the abolitionist tradition and retained strong progressive outlooks, such as Oswald Garrison Villard, the grandson of William Lloyd Garrison. The socialist component in the founding membership of the

NAACP was not, of course, exclusively white. Du Bois certainly thought of himself as a socialist by 1907 and joined the party in 1911.

The outstanding black figure was Du Bois. He was a distinguished author, a man of uncommon learning, and had been tried and proven as an effective editor and public speaker. Taking their futures into their hands, the Du Boises decided to accept the invitation to move to New York and lead in the publication and research work of the fledgling NAACP. The president and trustees of Atlanta University, though greatly admiring Du Bois, did not raise objections to his leaving, for—as Du Bois understood—his militancy was not helping the university attract funds from wealthy donors. For almost twenty-five years after the move, Du Bois stood at the center of the struggle for the freedom of black Americans and for a loosening of the bonds on colonial peoples throughout the world, especially in Africa and the West Indies.

The first issue of the *Crisis,* dated November 1910, numbered 1,000 copies. Under Du Bois' editorship the circulation soon reached 20,000 and continued to spiral upward until, by the end of World War I, the magazine had 100,000 subscribers. The vast majority of readers, like the membership of the organization, were black. When one recalls that blacks in the United States numbered some ten million in this period, about 75 percent of them functionally illiterate and 80 percent of them living in the South (where receiving the magazine was dangerous), the growth of the *Crisis* from its shoestring beginnings is one of the impressive success stories in the history of American journalism.

Of course, this success corresponded to the growth of the liberation movement among black people as a whole, but the magazine encouraged and to some extent directed the movement. Du Bois was a fine editor, prompt and painstaking, and the *Crisis* boasted attractive layouts, excellent photography, extensive coverage of national and international events, and informed attention to the arts. The editorials were short, direct, and witty; the articles, brief and clear. For years, black families and friends gathered in their homes early each month, and one among them would read the *Crisis,* especially Du Bois' "Along the Color Line" or "Opinion" or "Postscript"; for a generation scores of thousands asked "What did the Doctor say this month?" Du Bois' audience was worldwide. His writings helped educate a generation of Africans, such as Jomo Kenyatta, Kwame Nkrumah, and Benjamin Nnamdi Azikiwe; in Asia, Ho Chi Minh commented on the writings in the *Crisis.*

Du Bois made the magazine a leader in the Black Renaissance of the early 1920's. He ran poetry, short-story, and drama contests, and published the first works of Arna Bontemps, Langston Hughes, and Gwendolyn Brooks. Jessie Fauset served as literary editor, and her own writing often appeared in the magazine, along with that of Countee Cullen, Claude McKay, and Jean Toomer. Aaron Douglas, Richmond Barthé, and Elizabeth Prophet were among the artists Du Bois encouraged. The genius of Paul Robeson, Roland Hayes, and Marian Anderson was first called to the attention of black America in the *Crisis.*

In this same decade, Du Bois founded a theater movement for black writers and performers in Harlem and spoke out for the need of black artists and writers to create honestly—neither hiding nor prettifying their experience. He believed that all literature of any consequence partook of social or moral advocacy, and he urged black artists to use their art to liberate their people.

Du Bois also helped to put Eugene O'Neill, Theodore Dreiser, Sherwood Anderson, Sinclair Lewis, Dorothy Canfield Fisher, and the publishers Alfred Harcourt, Horace Liveright, and Alfred A. Knopf in touch with black artists and the black experience. Through the *Crisis* and through private efforts, he similarly informed Mahatma Gandhi, Jawaharlal Nehru, Albert Einstein, Albert Schweitzer, and Clarence Darrow, while introducing them to readers of his magazine.

Du Bois even started a children's magazine, *The Brownies' Book,* which in its short life (January 1920 to December 1921) carried brief editorials and stories by Du Bois and others, including Effie Lee Newsome.

Throughout his twenty-four years at the *Crisis,* Du Bois was in demand as a lecturer, especially to college and church audiences both black and white. He spoke in every state and in hundreds of cities. His style was restrained; he almost always read from a manuscript; his voice had great resonance; and his appearance was dignified.

One of the subjects Du Bois frequently lectured on was the need for a black university system unfettered by religious, political, or financial obligations—a view he continued to express long after the death of Booker T. Washington in 1915. In action, too, Du Bois was unremitting in his insistence on educational excellence: his effort to cleanse Fisk University of a racist administration forced the resignation of its president in 1926.

Having suggested Du Bois' intense activism as an editor and lecturer during these years, we must defy neat categories and acknowledge his writing of this period. A paper written when he attended the First Universal Races Congress of 1911 in London, "The Economics of Negro Emancipation in the United States," reflected his shift from moralistic to materialistic arguments, in accordance with his deepening socialistic commitment. Du Bois now felt that emancipation would have to come through the economic system, and he viewed the future with confidence on three counts: that the interests of the white working people favored black emancipation; that the dogged "determination" of

the black American could not be thwarted forever; and that courageous white people—he mentioned Jane Addams and John Dewey—were increasingly moving to end racial discrimination. The problem, Du Bois insisted, was worldwide and derived from the determination of those in power "to reduce human labor to the lowest depth in order to derive the greatest personal profit."

In a shorter essay, "The Rural South" (1912), Du Bois analyzed the region's economic plight, calling attention to the existence of peonage on a mass scale (despite its illegality under federal law), the almost total disfranchisement of black people, and the dire effects of all this on the South. Another short essay, "The Negro in Literature and Art" (1913), discussed such literary figures as Paul Laurence Dunbar and Charles Waddell Chesnutt. Du Bois described how racism impoverishes a culture; but he predicted that from the rich "mass of material" by then extant, a veritable renaissance in black art would soon take place, as indeed in the 1920's it did.

As a lifelong advocate of political independence, Du Bois early supported Woodrow Wilson's New Freedom and thus helped to bring about the first substantial departure of the black vote from the Republican party, which aided Wilson's narrow victory over Charles Evans Hughes in 1916. But Du Bois broke bitterly with Wilson over the racism in his administration and over American military intervention in Mexico and Haiti.

Du Bois published two penetrating analyses of the war in Europe shortly before the United States entered it in April 1917. "The African Roots of War" (1915) preceded the writings of both John Hobson and Lenin on imperialism and its part in the origins of that war. The article was one of Du Bois' most influential and was reprinted in many newspapers. It is reformist in nature, appealing for "clean hands and honest hearts." But the view that racism and the colonial system were fundamental to an understanding of what was going on in Europe was new. Du Bois also called attention to the "awakening leaders" of China, India, and Egypt, and suggested that the black American may be duty-bound to help awaken the African continent—a hint at the major Pan-African movement he would soon organize.

In "Of the Culture of White Folk" (1917) Du Bois points to his earlier warnings that persistent racism would so eat away the character of white people that they would descend to massacring each other. He also advances the idea that if colonialism and racism survive World War I, they will induce an even greater slaughter in the future.

Du Bois supported the entry of the United States into World War I. He thought at the time—especially because the February Revolution in Russia in 1917 had forced the czar to abdicate—that the Allied powers represented a less retrogressive force than the Central Powers of Imperial Germany, the Empire of Austria-Hungary, and Turkey. He also accepted Wilson's slogans about self-determination and fighting for democracy. Then too, he thought that resistance to the war by black people—assuming it could be brought about—would prove suicidal. Indeed, realizing its need for black labor and soldiers, the nation perhaps would be moved to concede to blacks a new measure of social equality and dignity. It was one of Du Bois' most bitter disappointments to find that he had been wrong about Wilson's purposes and about the true, imperialist nature of the war. Scarcely was the armistice signed before assaults on black communities were launched from Washington, D. C., to Texas and lynchings increased.

After the war, Du Bois' major project became the building of a strong Pan-African movement, work supported in the early organizing years (1919–1921) by the NAACP and the British Labor party. But that support evaporated as the leadership of the NAACP turned inward and became more conservative. During the war Du Bois had also exposed racism in the armed forces. For that and his Pan-Africanism he came to be considered a seditious influence by federal authorities, and secret orders for his surveillance were issued. The *Crisis* began to have trouble with the Post Office, and Du Bois was denounced by such "patriots" as Congressman James F. Byrnes of South Carolina, who later became governor of South Carolina, U.S. senator, secretary of state, and associate justice of the U.S. Supreme Court.

The Pan-African movement was part of a postwar surge of nationalist organization; Pan-Slavism, the Ataturk movement in Turkey, the growth of the Congress movement in India, and the rise of Zionism are other examples. Du Bois did not think of Pan-Africanism itself as exclusionary; rather, he believed it should seek an end to colonialism not only in Africa but throughout the world and give support to all democratic influences, particularly those directed at raising up the working class. In this respect Du Bois' Pan-Africanism was quite different from Marcus Garvey's movement "for return to Africa." At first the Garvey group had been anti-imperialist and fostered pride in black ability and accomplishment—positions Du Bois had held for decades. But soon he expressed concern about the business methods of the group, and when it became ultranationalistic and irrational, Du Bois became strongly opposed to it. He did not, as is often said, seek Garvey's imprisonment, and he opposed Garvey's deportation following his release.

The change in Du Bois' thought after World War I is signaled by his article "Worlds of Color" (1925), in which he reexamines his statement of twenty-five years earlier that "the problem of the Twentieth Century is the problem of the color line." Now he writes that the problem "is what we call Labor"; but he goes on to say that "England, France, Germany, America and Heaven" are all controlled by one oligarchy, which secures its control by its exploitation of colonial peoples. In this sense, then, "the Color Line" remains central to humanity's problems. Expanding the article for publication in *The New Negro* (1925), a book edited by Alain Locke, Du Bois points out the failure of European unions and labor parties to intervene in the exploitation of colonial workers.

Postwar travel abroad greatly increased Du Bois' firsthand knowledge of black peoples and leaders. In 1923–1924, he attended the third Pan-African Congress. On the same journey, as special envoy with ministerial rank, he represented President Calvin Coolidge at the inauguration of President Charles D. B. King of Liberia in 1924. Du Bois conferred with leading figures on both occasions, but the second afforded his first experience of Africa, specifically West Africa, where he traveled widely. Promptly from this experience came three articles: the ironically titled "The Primitive Black Man," "Britain's Negro Problem in Sierra Leone," and "What Is Civilization? Africa's Answer."

Impressed as he was with the organizational quality of African life and the dignity of the Africans, Du Bois saw too a powerful drive toward self-rule. Indeed, he ended "Britain's Negro Problem" by saying: "Black British West Africa is out for self-rule and in our day is going to get it." In his day—thanks to his longevity—they did.

Du Bois' second trip abroad during this period was a two-month visit in 1926 to the Soviet Union, which was still recovering from the devastations of World War I, the civil war, the attempted Polish conquest of the Ukraine, and the fourteen-nation intervention (Japan had been driven out only two years before). For all the impoverishment he saw about him, Du Bois was deeply impressed with the high morale and the commitment to education and science of so diverse a people. Soviet socialism would, he said, succeed. For the eleventh anniversary of the Bolshevik Revolution he was invited to contribute to the *Labor Defender,* an organ of the International Labor Defense; he hailed the attempts of the new Russia and described it as "a victim of a determined propaganda of lies."

Feeling that he lacked reliable information, Du Bois had initially responded cautiously to the Bolshevik Revolution. But by 1920 he clearly sided with it, although not uncritically. This partisanship was strengthened by his Soviet sojourn in 1926. From then on his support of the Soviet Union—the "most hopeful country in the world," as he was to call it in 1949—never wavered.

Although Du Bois spent the quarter-century from 1910 to 1934 chiefly as a publicist, agitator, and organizer, he also wrote his first novel, albeit a novel designed to influence public policy. The critical and commercial success of *The Souls of Black Folk* had led his publisher to suggest to him in 1906 that a novel dramatizing the "Negro problem" might attract even more readers than *Souls.* Du Bois had agreed but was then deep in work at Atlanta University, directing the Niagara movement, editing the *Horizon,* and writing *John Brown.* It was in 1909 that he turned to the creation of what became *The Quest of the Silver Fleece.* Before the spring of 1910, he had sent the manuscript to the McClurg firm; the book appeared in October 1911.

The climate seemed auspicious for one central theme of Du Bois' novel: the life of the cotton fields and the cotton trade. Extraordinary sales had been achieved by Frank Norris' *The Octopus* (1901) and *The Pit* (1903), novels about the wheat trade; by James Lane Allen's

The Reign of Law, a Tale of the Kentucky Hemp Fields (1900); and by Upton Sinclair's *The Jungle* (1906), about meatpacking. Within this same genre, the muckraking journalist David Graham Phillips had published *The Cost* (1904) and *The Deluge* (1905), which were novelistic exposés of banking, and *Light-Fingered Gentry* (1907), a novel on dishonesty in the insurance industry. Indeed, one of Phillips' novels was called *Golden Fleece* (1903); Du Bois' original title had used that phrase but was changed because of the Phillips novel.

Another hopeful sign: the publishers Dodd Mead and Houghton Mifflin had had success publishing fiction by the black authors Paul Laurence Dunbar and Charles Waddell Chesnutt. But far and away more successful among recent works on the theme of race had been the fiercely racist novel of Thomas Dixon, Jr., *The Leopard's Spots: A Romance of the White Man's Burden* (1902).

The tremendous popular success of Dixon's novel tells much about the American temper at the beginning of the twentieth century and the substance of the novel compares strikingly with that of Du Bois'. Dixon argues for the wholesale removal of the black man—women were not yet in question—from politics and seeks to show that educating black people in what is referred to as a "classical institution" "spoils" them and leads to "open demands for the recognition of the economic, social and political equality of the races"—almost verbatim the position of the Niagara movement as formulated in 1906 by Du Bois and implicit in his own novel.

Dixon's book celebrates the suppression of black people as an occasion for unity among the "best" white people, in the North as well as in the South. Conversely, Du Bois' novel aims to disunite white opponents of black liberation and to promote understanding of the need for black dignity and freedom if the letter of the Declaration of Independence is to be realized. As

Dixon's novel ends, the hero tells the heroine that his strength and wisdom derive entirely from her; but she denies it, insisting that his virtues are his own and that she has no wish but to serve him as a dutiful wife. By contrast, Du Bois ends his novel with the hero praising the heroine's strength and wisdom, qualities that she does not deny at all; whereupon she asks him to marry her.

The heroine, Zora, embodies Du Bois' own powerful pride in being black. She senses "the vast unorganized power in this [black] mass." When a black youngster resists a lashing and fights back, the author writes that it is just such righteous resistance that swells the "crime" statistics in the reports of the so-called experts.

In this novel Du Bois continues his insistence that black people need full education, not just enough to make a living but enough to make a life. Linking real education with true democracy, he even suggests that such education might well be subversive, "too socialistic." Even the urban black defection from the Republican party figures in the novel; the author writes that there are "five hundred thousand or more black voters in pivotal Northern States, you know, and they're in revolt."

So too does the theme of Du Bois' Harvard commencement address appear in the sermon that so transforms Zora. To live for the welfare of others and, if one is black, to work for the liberation of one's own people is to live well and joyfully. "In your dark lives," cries the minister, "*who* is the King of Glory? Sacrifice."

By 1911, when *The Quest of the Silver Fleece* appeared, Du Bois had joined the Socialist party. Accordingly, the novel dramatizes class as well as racial oppression, argues the commonality of interests among all who work, and envisions a unity among workers that will make way for a new social system. A propertied white man is made to say: "This system can't last always—sometimes I think it can't last long. It's wrong, through and through. It's built on ignorance, theft and force." A white woman worker on strike, seeing a manacled black youth brought into court, is moved to exclaim: "Durned if I don't think these white slaves and black slaves had ought ter git together." Du Bois also shows the need for planters and speculators to corrupt leadership, to "separate the leaders, the talented, the pushers, of both races from their masses, and through them rule the rest by money." In making the black Zora the moral beacon of the book, Du Bois showed himself to be an early and ardent advocate of the emancipation of black women—and of all women.

The Quest of the Silver Fleece was not widely reviewed and did not sell well. Nor did Du Bois turn his hand again to the novel form for almost two decades. But he did produce other books in a popular vein with a view to advancing his ideas. The first of these came out of an invitation from the editors of the Home University Library of Modern Knowledge, a series presenting the latest findings by internationally known scholars in diverse areas of world history. Du Bois was asked to provide a 75,000-word account of the history and present condition of the African and African-derived peoples. The result was *The Negro* (1915).

Du Bois had not yet visited Africa but had read widely its literature, visited the West Indies, and at the Universal Races Congress in 1911 met numerous African leaders. He had also studied the work of Franz Boas of the United States, Leo Frobenius of Germany, and Harry H. Johnston of Great Britain. But in his preface Du Bois pointed out that research on the black peoples remained insufficient, that he himself knew no African languages, and that brevity of format precluded definitive treatment. Yet he hoped his attempt would "enable the reader to know as men a sixth or more of the human race."

The Negro is a pioneering effort at depicting the broad history of black peoples, and as such has stood well the test of time, as George Shepperson writes in his introduction to the 1970 edition. The sweep of the work is remarkable. No similar effort was made until 1939, when Du Bois himself published *Black Folk, Then and Now,* a much expanded and revised version.

Toward the end of World War I, the publisher Alfred Harcourt expressed interest in bringing out a new collection of Du Bois' essays and sketches. *Darkwater: Voices from Within the Veil* (1920) consists of previously published, but considerably revised and expanded, material from the *Crisis, Independent, Atlantic Monthly,* and other periodicals. The book received much attention and sold well; most white reviewers in the United States remarked on the author's intensity of feeling, militancy, and hatred of racism. Two of the chapters attracted special attention. "Of the Ruling of Men" speaks of the Soviet Union and condemns the rich who "fly to arms to prevent that greatest experiment in industrial democracy which the world has ever seen." Du Bois closes by saying that "perhaps the finest contribution of current socialism to the world is neither its light nor its dogma, but the idea back of its one mighty word—Comrade!" This chapter and a passionate one on "The Damnation of Women," which excoriates the treatment of black women by whites, led Congressman Byrnes again to denounce Du Bois, calling him a "Bolshevik agent."

Du Bois' next book was written under the surprising sponsorship of the conservative Catholic organization the Knights of Columbus. Alarmed at the growing strength of the Ku Klux Klan and the passage of immigration laws in the 1920's that penalized Irish and southern European peoples as well as "colored" folk, the Knights undertook publication of a series of volumes under the general title "Racial Contribution Series." Three such books were published: one on the Jews, another on Germans, and the third *The Gift of Black Folk: The Negroes in the Making of America* (1924). The first five chapters drew heavily on Du Bois' previously published work, but the last four were fresh, especially "The Freedom of Womanhood," which summarizes the contributions and tribulations of black women. Other chapters treat the work of black people in music, painting, and literature, and the place of religion and the church among black Americans. Here Du Bois returns to his recurrent theme of the compassion and service that characterize an especially tormented people.

From the other end of the political spectrum came the next book offer a few years later. The Kansas publisher Emanuel Haldeman-Julius, who issued generally radical works—the so-called Little Blue Books, costing five cents and selling by the millions—suggested that Du Bois write two booklets on, respectively, the geography and history of Africa. These were published in 1930 as *Africa, Its Geography, People, and Products* and *Africa, Its Place in Modern History.* The former, in addition to detailing the continent's geography and natural resources, also offers an account of its religions and languages. The latter draws much on *The Negro* but concentrates on Africa in the nineteenth and early twentieth centuries. It places Africa within the context of European power politics and imperialism, and pays considerable attention to mounting African resistance and counterinitiative.

During his first period of service with the NAACP, Du Bois wrote two particularly distinguished essays, the first of which was a great favorite of its author: "Georgia: Invisible Empire State" was written as a chapter for the two-volume *These United States* (1924), edited by Ernest Gruening. The essay is a lyrical and profound study of the state, its history, its peoples,

its trials, and its promise. Du Bois takes the occasion to examine Henry Grady's idea of a "New South." He also demonstrates the success of racism in dividing the state's working people, locates the motives for lynching and terrorism, and analyzes the character of the Ku Klux Klan. He ends by envisioning a coming unity among those who labor—black and white.

In December 1928, a National Interracial Conference was held in Washington, D. C., sponsored by sixteen organizations. The purpose was to inquire into the prevailing state of knowledge about black life and the uses that such knowledge might serve. Here Du Bois presented a paper on "The Negro Citizen," later published in *The Negro in American Civilization* (1930), edited by Charles S. Johnson. In this paper Du Bois issues a prophetic call for what became known as black power some thirty-five years later. In the past, he says, the question was whether black people could survive outside of slavery; but that was no longer the question. Then arose the question of whether they could be educated; and that too was no longer the question. Now the question had become whether black people could attain political power, how they should do so, and what use they would make of it. Their lack of it vitiates the quality of life for everyone in the United States. Interracial meetings are well and good, he concludes, but they will prove useful only when they "attack the main problem, which is and has been the question of political power for the Negro citizens of the United States."

But for all the ambition of his didactic writings in the 1920's, an even larger theme—that of world revolution—had gripped Du Bois' imagination. Its promptings arose from the real world, but its embodiment was to be another novel, *Dark Princess: A Romance,* published in April 1928. Its subject is a conspiracy promoting a worldwide uprising of colored peoples in

Asia, Africa, the West Indies, and the United States. Positions ranging from terrorism to pacifism are represented. The leader is a woman, a princess of a state in India; and although the plot moves from continent to continent, most of the action takes place in the United States, in the South, New York City, and Chicago. In a description of the work that Du Bois sent to the publisher for possible use in advertising, he noted that the

. . . deeper aim of the book is to outline the reaction of the difficulties and realities of race prejudice upon many sorts of people—ambitious Black American youth, educated Asiatics, selfish colored politicians, ambitious self-seekers of all races. The book is thus a first-hand frank and sincere study of human characters both sides of the color line.

Du Bois was no stranger to dreams of black revolution and black statehood. At the First Pan-African Congress of 1900 (and the Universal Races Congress of 1911 as well) he had traded ideas with people from every corner of the world. A black seaman, Harry Dean, had told him in 1900 of his plan "to lead a black army across the straits of Gibraltar"; Du Bois could appreciate its motive but doubted its practicality.

In 1899 the novel *Imperium in Imperio,* by the black author Sutton Griggs, took as its theme an elaborate and nationwide black conspiracy to establish a black-ruled state in Texas—a scheme reminiscent of actual movements in the 1890's to carve a black state out of what is today Oklahoma. One of Griggs's main characters, Bernard Belgrave, is a brown-skinned Harvard graduate who has first attracted national attention with a commencement address—surely a fictional portrait of Du Bois.

As for actual advocates and prophets of a liberated Africa, Du Bois knew the ideas of virtually all of them, from Alexander Crummell to Henry M. Turner, Edward W. Blyden, Joseph Booth, Casely Hayford, and, of course, Marcus Garvey. According to George Shepperson and Thomas Price, in 1912 Du Bois had discussed with Booth, during one of Booth's periodic visits to the United States, "the possibility of a native revolt in the South and Central African regions." Du Bois followed with care all the news of strikes and uprisings in Africa and the rest of the colonial world, and after the end of World War I his work with the Pan-African Congress kept him in constant communication with African leaders and peoples. By 1906, in his Niagara movement address, Du Bois had written: "The Slav is rising in his might, the yellow millions are tasting liberty, the black Africans are writhing toward the light, and everywhere the laborer, with ballot in his hand, is voting open the gates of Opportunity and Peace." By the end of World War I he was writing with his own italics in *Darkwater:*

What, then, is this dark world thinking? It is thinking that as wild and awful as this shameful war was, *it is nothing to compare with the fight for freedom which black and brown and yellow men must and will make unless their oppression and humiliation and insult at the hands of the* White World *cease.* The Dark World *is going to submit just as long as it must and not one moment longer.*

By 1924 Du Bois was writing of a "tremendous and sometimes almost fanatic increase of race pride" that "white people do not sense" and suggesting that this is the breeding ground not only for hatred of whites but for open war. He continued, in "The Negro Takes Stock" (1924):

. . . it is impossible for twelve million men to fight a hundred million—but can they not hate the harder for their very impotence? Whether they migrate, die or live, can they not add the red flame of their bitter hatred to all the mounting bill of deviltry which the dark world holds against the white? No—there's no hurry; it will not happen in our day. No. But it will happen.

In words like these one can see the theme of *Dark Princess: A Romance* forming, as well as the character of Pergigua, the fictional terrorist.

Frequently in the *Crisis* Du Bois cataloged quotations from the world press on a single subject. Introducing in the March 1926 issue a collection that he entitled "The Hegemony of Race," he wrote: "It is gradually being borne in upon our whiter brethren that this matter of ruling the colored races is not going to be the same easy parade in the future that it has been in the past." It was followed by an extract from an article by David Lloyd George, the former British prime minister, reading in part:

In Asia the brown and yellow races are seeking to throw off the dominion or domination of the pale-faced foreigner. In India there is undoubted unrest. In Africa a formidable war is even now in process between invading Europeans and the native. . . .

The popular magazine *Liberty* was quoted: "China and India are rising. North Africa is in arms . . . Soviet Russia is the enemy of every white government." Similar reports from the Irish and South African press were quoted along with one from the marquess of Willingdon, formerly governor of Madras: "There can be no question that, for the first time in human history, this cry of the dark against the pretentions of the white is an organized and practical determination. Once it was a mere protest, now it is a crusade."

It was out of this climate that *Dark Princess* was written. Into it Du Bois put such fictionally transformed incidents as the altercations that took place in the United States during and after World War I between Indian immigrants and local authorities, the former agitating for their homeland's independence from Great Britain.

The central role of black Pullman porters in the novel reflects the efforts to unionize those workers that were then going forward under the leadership of A. Philip Randolph. As for the rising political strength of the black urban population in the North, a significant strand in the novel, that was something Du Bois had been reporting in the *Crisis*. The account in the novel of the first black congressman to be elected from Chicago preceded by months the actual election of Oscar DePriest in 1928.

The optimism, the affirmation of rational struggle, and the dream of a decent global society that permeate *Dark Princess* were not the themes of the leading white American novelists and playwrights in the 1920's. The themes of the "lost generation" writers are absent in the work of Du Bois and Langston Hughes, Countee Cullen, and Claude McKay. Despair appears and reappears in literature, and the best of this literature endures. But the need for emancipation persists, and works proclaiming it have a way of remaining always contemporary, however dated in form. Du Bois' view of the role of art is fundamental to an appreciation of his fiction. He expressed this view in "Criteria of Negro Arts," which he delivered at the 1926 annual meeting of the NAACP. The artist, he said, must serve truth; in serving that he serves beauty, and in serving both he also serves justice.

Thus all Art is propaganda and ever must be, despite the wailing of the purists. I stand in utter shamelessness and say that whatever art I have for writing has been used always for propaganda for gaining the right of black folk to love and enjoy. I do not care a damn for any art that is not used for propaganda.

The reviews of *Dark Princess* in the white press were mixed. Those in the *New York Post* and the *New York Times* were hostile and chauvinistic. The anonymous *Times* reviewer regretted that Du Bois did not use "his talent" to portray another Porgy, and the *Post* reviewer—the twenty-two-year-old Tess Slesinger—was surprised that Du Bois thought the "natives of India" were colored people. The southern press, when it noted the book at all, condemned it as fanatical; black commentators liked it. The most thoughtful review came from Alain Locke, who with Du Bois and James Weldon Johnson formed a triumvirate of leadership among the American black intelligentsia. Locke's long review in the *New York Herald Tribune* (May 20, 1928) read in part:

... we must thank the talented author of this book for breaking ground for this skyscraper problem novel of the Negro intellectual and the world radical. Chiefly because of the still latent possibilities of the theme it is to be regretted that, as a novel, "Dark Princess" is not wholly successful. As a document, however, it should be widely read.

Locke concluded that, though "half spoiled by oversophistication, [the novel] will be interesting and revealing reading to the white reader who has yet few ways of looking into the many closed chambers of Negro life or of seeing into the dilemmas of the intellectual Negro mind and heart." For black readers, the novel would be "an intriguing problem study of the cross currents and paradoxes of the thinking Negro who to-day faces the problems of two worlds and two loyalties." *Dark Princess* was, among all his books, one of Du Bois' favorites. It appeared soon after his sixtieth birthday, and conveyed—as its final sentence states—both his "Dream of the Spirit" and "the Pain of the Bone."

In June 1934 Du Bois resigned from the NAACP and returned to his first love, teaching and scholarly enterprise. At Atlanta University he taught graduate students in sociology and economics and headed the sociology department. With some difficulty he persuaded the university authorities to fund a scholarly literary quarterly, which he called *Phylon,* Greek for "race." As the editor he opened its first number, early in 1940, thus:

We seem to see today a new orientation and duty which will call not simply for the internal study of race groups as such, but for a general view of that progress of human beings which takes place through the instrumentality and activity of group culture.... We shall usually proceed from the point of view and the experience of the black folk where we live and work, to the wider world.

Du Bois remained the editor through the second number of the fifth volume (1944) and contributed the department "A Chronicle of Race Relations." He also wrote more than a dozen book reviews and contributed articles on Aleksander Pushkin, Robert Moton of Hampton and Tuskegee, and the slave uprising aboard the *Amistad* in 1841.

His most important work during this second tour at Atlanta was *Black Reconstruction: An Essay Toward a History of the Part Which Black Folk Played in the Attempt to Reconstruct Democracy in America, 1860–1880* (1935). Du Bois had been thinking about this book since the close of the nineteenth century, and in the course of its almost 750 pages he revolutionizes American historiography of the Civil War period. For in this great work he shows in detail the positive, democratic strivings of southern black people in the decade after the surrender at Appomattox—and the terror, propaganda, and fraud with which these efforts were undone. He argues mostly from official documents. His final chapter, "The Propaganda of History," remains a classic condemnation of the white chauvinism of American historiography, a charge not altogether outdated.

Du Bois does acknowledge the earlier and

significant works on Reconstruction by John R. Lynch, Alrutheus A. Taylor, and Carter G. Woodson, as well as those by Frederic Bancroft, John Eaton, Charles Edward Russell, and Augustus F. Beard. He notes that for a variety of reasons—including the fact that at times major southern libraries and archives have been closed to black scholars—there are documentary sources he has not examined. But he states his conviction that the story as he has told it is substantially true. The work of succeeding generations has amply vindicated him.

At the time the leading professional journal, the *American Historical Review,* did not review the book, yet elsewhere it found wide and, on the whole, quite favorable notice. It sold better than Du Bois expected, especially after World War II.

With this considerable success, Du Bois persuaded Henry Holt, publisher of *The Negro,* to bring out the revised and much expanded edition he had hoped for since 1915. This appeared in 1939 under the title *Black Folk, Then and Now: An Essay in the History and Sociology of the Negro Race.* As he writes in the preface, some of *The Negro* has been incorporated, but the later volume "for the most part is an entirely new production." Its 391 pages comprise sixteen chapters and an extensive bibliography. The first nine chapters offer a history of the early African civilizations, of the slave trade and of modern slavery, and of the movements for the abolition of both. Two chapters treat the present conditions of black people in the United States and in Europe; and four chapters deal with modern Africa, examining especially land-ownership, the conditions of the working masses, and systems of education and political control. The final chapter, "The Future of World Democracy," explores little-known African uprisings and a major strike in the first thirty years of the twentieth century. It concludes:

The proletariat of the world consists not simply of white European and American workers but overwhelmingly of the dark workers of Asia, Africa, the islands of the sea, and South and Central America. These are the ones who are supporting a superstructure of wealth, luxury, and extravagance. It is the rise of these people that is the rise of the world. The problem of the twentieth century is the problem of the color line.

With the coming of his seventieth year, Du Bois produced a major autobiographical work. In 1938–1939, with the encouragement of his friend Alfred Harcourt, he worked on *Dusk of Dawn: An Essay Toward an Autobiography of a Race Concept* (1940). As Du Bois says in the "Apology," he wishes to trace the development of his ideas more closely than the unfolding of a life. His *Souls of Black Folk* and *Darkwater,* he remarks, "were written in tears and blood," but this one, though "set down no less determinedly," is written "with wider hope in some more benign fluid." His biographical data are duly set forth, but so too is a kind of spiritual and ideological memoir, often beautifully written. During this same period Du Bois' outlook was generally socialist but antagonistic to the Communist party of the United States; yet his view of the Soviet Union remained warm and hopeful. On the final page there is a particularly self-revealing paragraph:

Perhaps above all I am proud of a straightforward clearness of reason, in part a gift of the gods, but also to no little degree due to scientific training and inner discipline. By means of this I have met life face to face, I have loved a fight and I have realized that Love is God and Work is His prophet; that His ministers are Age and Death.

Reaching one's seventh decade is old age, no doubt, and with that come thoughts of death.

But Du Bois had another two decades remaining to him, and into them he put the equivalent of a lifetime. When he returned to Atlanta University in 1934, at the urging of John Hope, he had expected to end his days there. The reality was otherwise. Within two years of Du Bois' return Hope died, and the new president, Rufus Clement, thirty-two years Du Bois' junior and of rather provincial background and bureaucratic training, proved uncongenial to him. The older man's international stature, his plans for work, and his radicalism led to mounting clashes with Clement and members of the board of trustees. Du Bois was forcibly retired—rather to his surprise—in 1944. At the urging of both Walter White and Arthur Spingarn, he returned to the NAACP as director of special research, with particular responsibility for the subjects of colonialism and African affairs. Quite likely some of those who invited him back thought Du Bois, at seventy-six, would pursue a leisurely course. They were wrong, and his return to agitation and propaganda marked a period of great activity, even for him.

He wrote a weekly column, "The Winds of Time," in the *Chicago Defender* from January 1945 to May 1948; he published articles in many periodicals, especially left-wing journals such as *New Masses;* he made several speaking tours throughout the country; he wrote essays and reviews for the *New York Post,* the *New York Herald Tribune,* the *New York Times,* the *American Journal of Sociology,* the *Nation,* and *Scientific Monthly;* and he took part in cultural and scholarly meetings in Haiti at the invitation of the Haitian government. In 1945 he represented the NAACP at the founding of the United Nations in San Francisco, where he warned that to neglect serious consideration of the problems of colonial peoples would be fatal to the preservation of peace. In 1945 and 1946 he edited a volume documenting the oppression of black Americans, which was to be presented as a petition for redress to the United Nations on behalf of the NAACP. Entitled *An Appeal to the World,* it was published by the NAACP in 1947. It received worldwide attention, but the U. S. delegation to the UN prevented its official consideration in that body.

While with the NAACP, Du Bois also produced two books in his area of special research. In 1945 Harcourt, Brace published *Color and Democracy: Colonies and Peace.* The premise of this volume is that after World War II

. . . the majority of the inhabitants of the earth, who happen for the most part to be colored, must be regarded as having the right and the capacity to share in human progress and to become co-partners in that democracy which alone can ensure peace among men, by the abolition of poverty, the education of the masses, protection from disease and the scientific treatment of crime.

Du Bois observes that "colonies are the slums of the world" and that the slum dwellers are in righteous rebellion. If the slums are not replaced, the rebellions will give way to "recurring wars of envy and greed because of the present inequitable distribution of gain among civilized nations." By their own words, Du Bois observes, the Western allies have shown their indifference to the question of colonialism and liberation: "so long as colonial imperialism exists, there can be neither peace on earth nor good will toward men." Du Bois hails the Soviet Union for having released the energies of the masses and for facing squarely the problem of poverty. "It has not, like most nations, without effort to solve it, declared the insolubility of the problem of the poor, and above all, it has not falsely placed on the poor the blame of their wretched conditions."

The second volume written during his final tenure with the NAACP was *The World and Africa: An Inquiry into the Part Which Africa*

Has Played in World History (1947), published shortly before his seventy-ninth birthday. In the preface Du Bois refers to *The Negro* and *Black Folk, Then and Now,* and observes that the world has so changed in the past decade that it seems useful to attempt "a history of the world written from the African point of view." He pays tribute to related work by Robert Briffault, George Padmore, Anna Graves, E. D. Moore, Rayford Logan, and William Leo Hansberry, and adds: "I have also made bold to repeat the testimony of Karl Marx, whom I regard as the greatest of modern philosophers, and I have not been deterred by the witch-hunting which always follows the mention of his name."

The World and Africa begins with a consideration of World War II, goes on to analyze the effects of two centuries of European colonialism, especially in Africa, and concludes with an essay on "the future of the darker races." Their coming liberation is "indispensable to the fertilizing of the universal soil of mankind." His closing thought: "There can be no perfect democracy curtailed by color, race, or poverty. But with all we accomplish all, even Peace." We glimpse here two determinants of Du Bois' last years: the witch-hunt that dogged him and his dedication to the achievement of peace on earth.

While the U. S. Navy, no less, had purchased copies of Du Bois' *Color and Democracy: Colonies and Peace,* the ideas in this later volume brought about another break with the NAACP leadership, which now endorsed the cold war. In 1948 Du Bois left the NAACP and joined the Council on African Affairs, through which Paul Robeson and W. Alphaeus Hunton were working to end colonialism. From this time on Du Bois identified himself with the worldwide, generally Left-led movement of peace councils in the effort to halt the arms race and the cold war.

It was in this cause that Du Bois joined the presidential campaign of Henry Wallace in 1948 and continued in the ranks of the Progressive party. Under its banner, at the age of eighty-two, he campaigned for U. S. senator from New York in 1950. He also served as director of the Peace Information Center, through whose effort the signatures of some 2.5 million Americans were obtained for the Stockholm Peace Pledge, which asked for an end to atomic weapons. The inevitable result—given the climate of McCarthyism—was the indictment of Du Bois and four codefendants as "unregistered foreign agents" under the McCormick Act. Du Bois was arraigned and fingerprinted in February 1951, tried in November 1951, and acquitted that same month in one of the earliest victories against government witch-hunting. The entire story of this episode was told in detail, with supporting documents, in his *In Battle for Peace: The Story of My 83rd Birthday* (1952). Du Bois' efforts to persuade leading publishers to issue this work were in vain; several did not even answer his letters. The Left's magazine *Masses & Mainstream* published the book in 1952, and 10,000 copies were sold.

In the mid-1950's, with scarcely diminished energy, Du Bois undertook to create a vast fictional work that would try to describe what it had meant to be a black person in the United States from the closing years of the nineteenth down to the middle of the twentieth century. By 1956 he had substantially finished this work, and it was published in three volumes (and running to over 1,000 pages) under the title *The Black Flame: The Ordeal of Mansart* (1957), *Mansart Builds a School* (1959), and *Worlds of Color* (1961). As a survey of black life from 1876 through 1956, there is no more comprehensive single work than this trilogy. As a portrayal of Du Bois' life these volumes are more revealing than his avowed autobiographies. Yet, doubtless for political reasons, the trilogy went unmentioned in the conventional reviewing media. Through word of mouth and the efforts of the Left's periodicals, about 10,000 sets were eventually sold.

Du Bois' last book in his lifetime appeared in July 1963, one month before his death. On a visit to the German Democratic Republic in 1960 he was asked by Gertrude Gelbin, the editor of Seven Seas Books (an English-language publisher in East Berlin), to select some of his very brief published pieces about race. Du Bois did so, but the manuscript that he mailed from New York did not reach Berlin. In 1961 he assembled another selection of his writings and, on his way to Ghana, mailed the manuscript from London; this time it reached its destination. The book, *An ABC of Color: Selections from Over a Half Century of Writings,* had an introduction by Kay Pankey. The selections were mainly from the *Crisis,* with a few of his writings from the 1950's. John Oliver Killens later wrote an introduction to the posthumous American edition of 1969.

To date, three books by Du Bois have been published since his death, all of them edited by the present writer. The first, *The Autobiography of W. E. B. Du Bois: A Soliloquy on Viewing My Life from the Last Decade of Its First Century* (1968), was being written in draft during 1958–1959; Du Bois revised it during the next two years and took it with him to Ghana. After the coup there in 1966, the manuscript finally reached the editor, and it was published two years later. This volume is more fully autobiographical than *Dusk of Dawn,* and the works overlap only slightly. The later book tells much about the period from Du Bois' return to the NAACP to the completion of his journey to the Soviet Union and China. There are also details of his decision in 1961 to join the Communist party of the United States, a step he saw as logical in his political evolution.

The second posthumously published volume is *The Education of Black People* (1973); the bulk of it had been tentatively approved for publication in 1940 by the University of North Carolina Press, which then withdrew, citing lack of funds. On his departure to Ghana in 1961, Du Bois entrusted the manuscript to the present writer, who added three essays on education that Du Bois had written in the 1950's and in 1960.

Prayers for Dark People (1980) began as jottings on scraps of paper in 1909 and 1910, short prayers and sermons to be read to his students at Atlanta University. These writings touch on diverse aspects of life and preach service, work, learning, courtesy, and, above all, dedication to the enhancement of the life of black people in the United States. They are informed by a religious sense that Du Bois never lost. Being agnostic, he detested institutionalized religion and dogma, but an unformulated belief in spirituality stayed with him until his death.

Having chosen to join the Communist party shortly before leaving for Ghana in 1961, Du Bois was liable to unusual restrictions under American law. When he sought to renew his passport at the U. S. consular office in Ghana in 1962, he was told that he was guilty of a crime in having used it to go there and that he should return to the United States forthwith. He and his second wife, Shirley Graham Du Bois (whom he married in 1951), then asked President Kwame Nkrumah if they could become citizens of Ghana; Nkrumah remarked that America's loss was Africa's gain and that Ghana would be honored.

Du Bois died on August 27, 1963, the day before the civil rights march in Washington, D. C., and his death was announced to the assembled multitude by Roy Wilkins (then the executive secretary of the NAACP). All present on that occasion knew that the slogans on their banners had in effect been written years before by Du Bois.

He died without pain and was fully lucid to the last. Characteristically, he had prepared what he called his "last message," dated June 26, 1957. At the state funeral in West Africa—from which centuries before his ancestors had been brought to the New World in chains—Shirley Du Bois read the brief text:

It is much more difficult in theory than actually to say the last good-bye to one's loved ones and friends and to all the familiar things of this life.

I am going to take a long, deep and endless sleep. This is not a punishment but a privilege to which I looked forward for years.

I have loved my work, I have loved people and my play, but always I have been uplifted by the thought that what I have done well will live long and justify my life; that what I have done ill or never finished can now be handed on to others for endless days to be finished, perhaps better than I could have done.

And that peace will be my applause.

One thing alone I charge you. As you live, believe in life! Always human beings will live and progress to greater, broader and fuller life.

The only possible death is to lose belief in this truth simply because the great end comes slowly, because time is long.

Good-bye.

Selected Bibliography

WORKS OF W. E. B. DU BOIS

BOOKS

The Suppression of the African Slave Trade to the United States of America, 1638–1870. New York: Longman, Green, 1896.

The Philadelphia Negro: A Social Study. Philadelphia: University of Pennsylvania Press, 1899. (With Isabel Eaton.)

The Souls of Black Folk: The Negroes in the Making of America. Chicago: A. C. McClurg, 1903.

John Brown. Philadelphia: G. W. Jacobs, 1909. Reprinted New York: International Publishers, 1962.

The Quest of the Silver Fleece. Chicago: A. C. McClurg, 1911.

The Negro. New York: Holt, Rinehart, 1915. Reprinted New York: Oxford University Press, 1970.

Darkwater: Voices from Within the Veil. New York: Harcourt, Brace and Howe, 1920.

The Gift of Black Folk: The Negroes in the Making of America. Boston: Stratford, 1924.

Dark Princess: A Romance. New York: Harcourt, Brace, 1928.

Africa, Its Geography, People, and Products. Girard, Kans.: Haldeman-Julius, 1930. Reprinted in 1 vol. with *Africa, Its Place in Modern History.* Millwood, N. Y.: KTO Press, 1977.

Africa, Its Place in Modern History. Girard, Kans.: Haldeman-Julius, 1930. Reprinted (see above). Millwood, N. Y.: KTO Press, 1977.

Black Reconstruction: An Essay Toward a History of the Part Which Black Folk Played in the Attempt to Reconstruct Democracy in America, 1860–1880. New York: Harcourt, Brace, 1935.

Black Folk, Then and Now: An Essay in the History and Sociology of the Negro Race. New York: Holt, Rinehart, 1939.

Dusk of Dawn. An Essay Toward an Autobiography of a Race Concept. New York: Harcourt, Brace, 1940.

Color and Democracy: Colonies and Peace. New York: Harcourt, Brace, 1945.

The World and Africa: An Inquiry into the Part Which Africa Has Played in World History. New York: Viking, 1947.

In Battle for Peace: The Story of My 83rd Birthday. New York: Masses and Mainstream, 1952.

The Ordeal of Mansart. New York: Mainstream, 1957.

Mansart Builds a School. New York: Mainstream, 1959.

Worlds of Color. New York: Mainstream, 1961.

The Black Flame. New York: Mainstream, 1957–1961. (A trilogy containing the three works immediately above.)

An ABC of Color: Selections from Over a Half Century of Writings. Berlin: Seven Seas, 1963. Reprinted with introduction by John Oliver Killens. New York: International Publishers, 1969.

The Autobiography of W. E. B. Du Bois: A Soliloquy on Viewing My Life from the Last Decade of Its First Century, edited by Herbert Aptheker. New York: International Publishers, 1968.

The Education of Black People, edited by Herbert Aptheker. Amherst: University of Massachusetts Press, 1973.

The Complete Published Works of W. E. B. Du Bois, edited and with introduction by Herbert Aptheker. 40 vols. projected. Millwood, N. Y.: KTO Press, 1973–

The Correspondence of W. E. B. Du Bois, edited by Herbert Aptheker. 3 vols. Amherst: University of Massachusetts Press, 1973–1978.

The Book Reviews of W. E. B. Du Bois, edited by Herbert Aptheker. Millwood, N. Y.: KTO Press, 1977.

Prayers for Dark People, edited by Herbert Aptheker. Amherst: University of Massachusetts Press, 1980.

SELECTED ARTICLES

"Tom Brown at Fisk." *Fisk Herald,* 5, no. 3:5–7 (November 1887); 5, no. 4:6–7 (December 1887); 5, no. 6:5–7 (February 1888).

"The Enforcement of the Slave-Trade Laws." *Annual Report of the American Historical Association for the Year 1891.* Washington, D. C., 1892. Pp. 161–74.

"Strivings of the Negro People." *Atlantic Monthly,* 80:194–98 (August 1897).

"The Study of the Negro Problems." *Annals of the American Academy of Political and Social Science,* 11:1–23 (January 1898).

"The Negroes of Farmville, Virginia: A Social Study." *Bulletin of the Department of Labor,* 3, no. 14:1–38 (January 1898).

"A Negro Schoolmaster in the New South." *Atlantic Monthly,* 83:99–104 (January 1899).

"The Negro in the Black Belt: Some Social Sketches." *Bulletin of the Department of Labor,* 4, no. 22:401–17 (May 1899).

"The Problem of Housing the Negro." *Southern Workman* (June 1901–February 1902).

"The Evolution of Negro Leadership." *Dial,* 31:53–55 (July 16, 1901).

"The Negro Farmer." *Negroes in the United States* (U. S. Bureau of the Census Bulletin no. 8). Washington, D. C., 1904. Pp. 69–98. An expanded version was published in *Supplementary Analysis and Derivative Tables, Twelfth Census of the United States* (Special Report of the U. S. Bureau of the Census). Washington, D. C., 1906. Pp. 511–79.

"Credo." *Independent,* 57:787 (October 6, 1904).

"The Southerner's Problem." *Dial,* 38:315–18 (May 1, 1905).

"Fifty Years Among the Black Folks." *New York Times,* sec. 6 (December 12, 1909), p. 4.

"Reconstruction and Its Benefits." *American Historical Review,* 15:781–99 (July 1910).

"The Economics of Negro Emancipation in the United States." *Sociological Review,* 4:303–13 (October 1911).

"The Rural South." *Publications of the American Statistical Association,* 13:80–84 (March 1912).

"The Negro in Literature and Art." *Annals of the American Academy of Political and Social Science,* 49:233–37 (September 1913).

"The African Roots of War." *Atlantic Monthly,* 115:707–14 (May 1915).

"Of the Culture of White Folk." *Journal of International Relations,* 7:434–47 (April 1917).

"The Negro Takes Stock." *New Republic,* 37:143–45 (January 2, 1924).

"The Primitive Black Man." *Nation,* 119:675–76 (December 17, 1924).

"Britain's Negro Problem in Sierra Leone." *Current History,* 21:690–700 (February 1925).

"What is Civilization? Africa's Answer." *Forum,* 73:178–88 (February 1925).

"Worlds of Color." *Foreign Affairs,* 3:423–44 (April 1925).

"The Negro Citizen." In *The Negro in American Civilization,* edited by Charles S. Johnson. New York: Holt, Rinehart, 1930. Pp. 461–70.

BIBLIOGRAPHIES

Aptheker, Herbert. *Annotated Bibliography of the Published Writings of W. E. B. Du Bois.* Millwood, N. Y.: KTO Press, 1973.

Partington, Paul G. *W. E. B. Du Bois: A Bibliography of His Published Writings.* Whittier, Calif.: Paul G. Partington, 1977.

BIOGRAPHICAL AND CRITICAL STUDIES

Belser, Stephen G. "W. E. B. Du Bois: The Argument on the Immortal Child." M.A. diss., San Jose State University, 1971.

Broderick, Francis L. *W. E. B. Du Bois, Negro Leader in a Time of Crisis.* Stanford, Calif.: Stanford University Press, 1959.

Du Bois, Shirley Graham. *His Day Is Marching On.* Philadelphia: Lippincott, 1971.

Rampersad, Arnold. *The Art and Imagination of W. E. B. Du Bois.* Cambridge, Mass.: Harvard University Press, 1976.

———. "W. E. B. Du Bois as a Man of Literature." *American Literature,* 51:50–68 (March 1979).

Rudwick, Elliott M. *W. E. B. Du Bois: A Study in Minority Group Leadership.* Philadelphia: University of Pennsylvania Press, 1960.

Woodard, Frederic. "W. E. B. Du Bois: The Native Impulse. Notes Toward an Ideological Biography, 1868–1897." Ph.D. diss., University of Iowa, 1976.

—HERBERT APTHEKER

Paul Laurence Dunbar

1872–1906

THE 1890's was a bleak time for the debut of a black poet, as Paul Laurence Dunbar quickly discovered. Indeed, it was a bleak time also for a serious white poet, as Edwin Arlington Robinson eloquently testified in his poems and correspondence. Both poets had something in common. They opposed the pursuit by many Americans of mere "things," material possessions; the corruption of all values by commercialism; and the vulgar displays in housing and in entertainment. Robinson learned his opposition to a crass material culture, in part, from his instruction at Harvard (where he was a special student), from Charles Eliot Norton especially. Dunbar acquired his, no doubt, from the sermons that he heard in a black church in Dayton, Ohio, and from the early development of the instinct of a true poet. Neither Dunbar nor Robinson could express an easy allegiance to romantic idealism and look with great comfort on a world controlled by businessmen and industrial tycoons.

But the genteel tradition, the most powerful force in American letters from 1870 through the 1890's, could. It had adopted a convenient form of romanticism, a truncated and modified version that stressed ornamental devices, precision of form, and exotic and historical references, but deplored any substantial contact with the real world. An older and more vigorous romanticism undertook the impossible task of defining what was real in the world and harshly criticized human behavior that did violence to conscience, ignored the ties that linked people, or displayed ignorance of the potential for spiritual development that existed in everyone. The ideas, shunted aside by genteel critics, made a renaissance in American literature that extended from the 1830's through the 1860's. Robinson, in order to save himself as a poet, and as a man who was early overwhelmed by domestic tragedy, returned to the older romanticism, from which he received the power that flows from his early poems. Dunbar, on the other hand, knew it only superficially and turned, rather, to the tradition of English romantic poets, from Robert Burns and John Keats to Dante Gabriel Rossetti and Algernon Charles Swinburne, which did not inspire him to dig deeply in the matter of his own existence or that of others.

Despite the cultivation of impressive skills, rarely do Dunbar's poems in conventional English triumph over the derivative forms, a rigidly proper poetical language, and a set of ideas that in general passes for poetical pieties. Although nature and the redemption of man never stirred Dunbar deeply, two other subjects did. One was the struggles of the black race; the other, the agony of composition: what to put in a poem, how to write it, and especially how to phrase it so that it would be acceptable to a largely white audience. The constraints sound very genteel. Indeed they are, since such periodicals as *Century, Harper's, Scribner's,* and *Atlantic* applied inflexibly the standards of a limited romanticism in the hope of pleasing a large new audience that technological advances in printing had made it possible to reach since 1870. A case can be made that the true bastions of gentility in American literature from the 1870's to the 1890's were these magazines, with their demands for acceptable, salable material, and not the critics of gentility like Edmund Clarence Stedman, Charles Warren Stoddard, or Thomas Bailey Aldrich. Dunbar made his escape from the prison of gentility in a manner rather different from Robinson's.

There were ways to do this. Robinson, as noted before, became a thoroughgoing idealist, not a halfhearted one, and advanced to the point of treating idealism in dramatic frames that questioned and parodied, through irony, romantic belief. *Captain Craig* (1902) represents fully this development in Robinson's art. George Santayana and Trumbull Stickney relied upon the classical, not the English, tradition. The consequence is an economic art, frequently on enduring classical themes, free of the cant, artificiality, and poetical debris that a century of romanticism, despite its glories, had accumulated. Another form of escape from a stifling poetic influence was more domestic and more immediate. James Whitcomb Riley, Frank L. Stanton, William Henry Irwin, and others turned to dialect verse. The advantage of doing so is quite obvious—a fresh language closer to real speech and the likelihood of discovering a poetic matter of importance and accessibility, not the tired conventional themes inherited from romantic verse.

There were hazards too. By the time that Dunbar discovered dialect verse through Riley,

it already had conventions of its own, among them established comic verbal devices, suggesting that making an audience chuckle rather than accuracy of presentation was the more important consideration. It took a keen ear and a responsible sensibility to winnow a true voice out of the "dese's" and "dose's" of black dialect verse, and the same can be said for excursions into Hoosier and German dialects. Dunbar—not unexpectedly, given his background—brought skill to an accurate recording of both black and white dialects, though the black bears a special resonance from his living in a black community and exposure to black folk and historical traditions. Another danger for the writer employing dialect is sentimentality, not the well-worn apostrophes and clichés of romantic verse, but the equally deplorable, complacent, and simplistic distortions of mundane existence. The proposition that daily life had a sweetness, order, and amusing quaintness was no more satisfying or useful in the 1890's than was the idea of life as concentrated in moments illumined by contacts with the ideal, as far removed as possible from the grubbiness of the real world.

In black dialect verse the simplifying and reductive influence came from the plantation tradition, the southern wing of the genteel, which was nourished in part by the efforts of many southerners, and northerners too, to heal the wounds inflicted by decades of conflict and a devastating Civil War. It is no accident that Joel Chandler Harris, the author of tales about Uncle Remus, was a staff writer on the *Atlanta Constitution,* the strong supporter if not the shaper of the New South. Henry W. Grady journeyed north to convince businessmen that the South was a fertile area for investment, while Harris made a winning appeal to the North and to the South as well, suggesting that slavery was not so bad—indeed, quite charming in some of its aspects. Though he is rather too distant from the clank of chains of the slave coffle or the crack of the overseer's whip, Harris did reveal to the nation in the 1880's the power of the black folk tradition.

Dunbar was saved, in general, from the excesses of the plantation tradition by his deep consciousness of being black, though other black writers of dialect were not so fortunate. One sobering reality was the fact that his parents were ex-slaves. Matilda (Glass) Murphy Dunbar was a slave freed by the Emancipation Proclamation; Joshua Dunbar, a plantation plasterer. He had escaped by the Underground Railroad to Canada and later returned to join the 55th Massachusetts Infantry, the second black regiment to be organized in the Union Army. Dunbar could not avoid hearing in some detail about the repressive and cruel aspects of slavery. Such a young man, born less than a decade after the end of the war, was not likely to accept willingly the saccharine portraits and narratives of the plantation apologists.

The dialect tradition in verse prospered, in part because of its close association with journalism. In addition to Harris, many others, both black and white, had turned their hands to dialect, usually with much less success. The role of the journalist here is not accidental. No doubt, what is involved is a familiarity with the talk of ordinary people, especially those with little education, and a remarkable opportunity to hear stories and verse from provincial regions still untouched by the explosive expansion of the cities. Dunbar was strongly attracted to journalism; and his first published poems, "Our Martyred Soldiers" and "On the River," appeared in the *Dayton Herald* in 1888. "Lager Beer," his first dialect poem, was written in German dialect, not in the broken, colorful language of the southern black, and appeared in December 1890 in the *Dayton Tattler,* which Dunbar published and edited for the black community. "Lager Beer" followed the precedent established in the "Hans Breitmann" dialect

ballads by Charles Leland. Though Dunbar's admiration for Riley sparked a serious commitment to dialect verse, Dunbar, through his early journalistic ambitions, knew of many poems by journalists in a number of different forms of dialect. As dialect was nurtured by journalists in the 1880's and 1890's, so the southwestern humor tradition, with its many forms of dialect, from folk talk in Mississippi and Arkansas to the notorious expression of the pike character (an amoral, profane, comic character best represented by Huck's father) in Missouri and points west, was cultivated by editors, feature writers, and reporters for newspapers. Among these writers was Mark Twain.

The reference to Mark Twain is a reminder that both verse and prose works use dialect. Dunbar's interest was essentially in its application to poetry, though he did employ it in narratives that relied upon the plantation tradition. But it is the verse that reflects his serious experimentation in dialect, marking his work as the most successful achievement in America in dialect verse, surpassing the worthy efforts of both James Russell Lowell and James Whitcomb Riley. Charles Waddell Chesnutt, rather than Dunbar, displayed the power of dialect in narrative in *The Conjure Woman* (1899), and he too was troubled by the restraints of genteel literary principles. Never in *The Conjure Woman* does the full force of the black folklore touch the reader. Always there is a literary frame provided by an educated observer, who tempers and mutes the energy of the wild black tales. Though Dunbar was to make a substantial contribution to fiction, he did so within the contemporary conventions that governed the prose narrative, which, with the emergence of naturalism, were undergoing considerable critical examination in the 1890's. Toward the end of his career, Dunbar was preoccupied with developing his ideas about the novel, particularly evident in *The Sport of the Gods*; and it was this interest, rather than his outstanding work in poetry, that led him into the twentieth century. This work of 1902 foreshadows in theme, point of view, scene, and craft the rich development of the modern black novel that received its next advance in *Autobiography of an Ex-Colored Man,* published by James Weldon Johnson a decade later.

A black writer in the 1890's could hope for little support from the general social climate, not simply from the uninspiring literary context. This was the nadir in the post-Civil War history of blacks, as the distinguished black historian Rayford Logan has said. Southern states completed the process of disfranchising blacks, using devices unheard of before in American politics. Blacks suffered from gross discrimination in education, in money appropriated, and in facilities, and Senator J. K. Vardaman of Mississippi in the early 1890's announced his opposition to the support of vocational instruction for blacks, not to mention any vestige of a liberal education. The same bleak situation existed in public accommodations and transportation. The effect upon the black economy was drastic too, with a loss in the South of jobs traditionally held in barber shops, blacksmith shops, stables, and catering establishments. The North was no easy haven for ambitious blacks since it too acted to eliminate political appointments and restrict employment, public accommodations, and housing. When Dunbar graduated from Central High School in 1891, after acquiring honors of various kinds, he could secure, after a desperate search, only a job as elevator operator in the Callahan Building in Dayton. A coincidence that only hindsight finds significant is the title of his last poem published in the *High School Times*: "Melancholia."

The racial crisis of the 1890's did not inhibit advancement on several fronts by blacks. Black business in the South and the North underwent unprecedented expansion, partly because whites pursuing institutional purity ignored the black market. Insurance companies, retail stores, and real estate agencies emerged and prospered. More pertinent is the fact that the crisis stimulated writers who responded in various ways to the new repression. Not since the 1840's and the 1850's, when slavery provoked the writing of an endless number of slave narratives, sermons, and tracts of protest, had black writers appeared in such abundance.

Thus Dunbar faced a cultural environment that was both hostile and challenging. The 1890's concluded one of the least rewarding periods of American literature, though there were evidences of constructive ferment in the interest in real talk rather than the language of the poetical, in the imaginative interpretation of classical themes without the ornate diction of the late romantics, and in the counterromanticism of Robinson, which involved the use of standard romantic themes as opportunities for irony and parody. Dunbar was born in an age committed to business and industry, and little else, one that cried out for opposition by contemporary artists, as if that mattered. Meanwhile business tycoons raided Europe for paintings, sculpture, furniture, stairways, parts of cathedrals, and designs for town houses in New York and Chicago and summer residences at Newport. In Dayton, Dunbar was hard put to sustain his writing and to support his mother; and the generosity of white friends like James Newton Matthews, Charles Thatcher, and Henry A. Tobey meant much to him. His situation was not unique: Robinson nearly starved to death in New York at the turn of the century, and he too owed his ability to devote his energies totally to poetry to generous benefactors. Dunbar bore bruises from the tide of opposition to blacks in America. When success finally came, he was viewed as the black exception, as a model for his race, or as a primitive whose talent came from instinct alone and not from wide reading or experimentation.

Cultural obstructions for Dunbar should not hide the view of the challenge coming from American society. The most provocative stimulus for Dunbar was the new racial repression emanating, but not confined to, the South, which produced and inspired many black writers. There were two basic ways for a black writer to express his reaction to his hostile environment. He could directly protest the status of blacks, citing the violation of civil law and the Constitution, the denial of human rights, and the betrayal of blacks in light of their support of the Union in both the Civil War and Reconstruction. Or he could make a case for the black cultural tradition, tracing its roots to a noble heritage in Africa; investigating the rich folk background in song, tale, jokes, boasts, and artifacts; providing evidence of a rewarding community life despite the blight of slavery; and celebrating heroes like Frederick Douglass and valuable white associates like John Greenleaf Whittier. Although Dunbar did write some important articles that dealt directly with racial oppression, he tended to restrict his interest in the race problem to exploring and using the black cultural tradition, a more indirect response but equally as important as the frontal attack. There was never any question about Dunbar's commitment to the welfare of black people or his pride in black achievement, though there were persistent rumors in polite black society in Washington and New York that he hated his blackness and sought to achieve a reputation as a writer that was without a racial label. Some truth may exist in the charge, since all great artists seek universal recognition, but none lies in the more personal part of it. It is a comment, rather, on Dunbar's social environment. Its source is complicated, involv-

ing deficiencies in upper-middle-class black society at the turn of the century. In northern cities this society was dominated by mulattoes, some of whom noted with a lack of charity that Dunbar had married a very fair wife, Alice Nelson. Others resented the fact that a "pure" black had been the first of the race to achieve national eminence as a poet, and all knew of Dunbar's growing distaste for the limitations placed on him by publishers and of his deepening conviction after 1896 that he had to write dialect verse in order to be read at all.

Dunbar emerged as a writer in a difficult and demanding time and achieved an important place in American literature. What must be considered now is how he approached his writing and what his art means in terms of a developing Afro-American literary tradition.

An important problem for every writer is finding his own voice. Voice, roughly defined, is a consistent way of speaking and a powerful instrument in giving a work of art unity and intensity. It involves diction, manner of addressing an audience, range of reference, and ultimately values in describing or weighing reality. Voice has significance in both fiction and in nonfiction and is absolutely indispensable in good poetry, in which every phrase must contribute to a developing structure. A writer cannot create a voice out of nothing; it represents, rather, a summary of a life, including the trials of day-to-day experience and reading. Long after he has read a work of genuine artistic merit, a reader will remember the voice that has spoken to him.

The determination is a particularly trying matter for a black writer, principally because of the duality in black life. W. E. B. Du Bois pointed to the reality among blacks of a double consciousness and to the two cultures, one black and one white, existing within a single black body; and he held that the problem for blacks was to integrate the two constructively. This is easier said than done, and many black writers have wasted too much of their energy in resolving this dilemma. Though one black writer may lean more toward the white side of the tradition he shares and another toward the black, some sort of resolution is necessary before a voice emerges to order the confusion and to speak with force. Dunbar's problem in discovering an appropriate voice, one that he was never to solve with total satisfaction, stems from his life. That life exposed him almost equally to the black and white aspects of his southern Ohio culture. Such a double exposure was shared with the same even distribution of experience by a few other blacks at the time, notably Du Bois, whose early years were spent in Great Barrington, Massachusetts.

Dunbar's black credentials are considerable. His parents were black without visible intermixture of white blood, a fact that William Dean Howells was to note about the poet in his influential introduction to *Lyrics of Lowly Life* (1896). Born in 1872, not quite a decade after the Emancipation Proclamation, Dunbar learned about slavery from his parents and their friends. His mother talked to him more than his father, and from her the boy picked up an early exposure to poetry, as well as accounts of happy moments in the slave quarters in addition to its repressive side. From his father Dunbar heard only bitter memories. No doubt in the early years much of his absorption of this background before the Civil War was unconscious. But once Riley, whose poems Dunbar had analyzed with care, had made him aware of the use of dialect, and once Charles Henry Dennis, managing editor of the *Chicago Record,* had suggested that he accept the model provided by the poetry of Robert Burns and apply it to the black experience, the young poet talked with more purpose to his mother's friends and neighbors, probing

them for details of their life in slavery and recording not only their tales but also their manner of telling them. Dunbar could scarcely discover more authentic sources, short of being a slave himself in Ol' Kentuck.

A member of the black community in Dayton, Dunbar attended the Eaker Street Methodist Church, where he gave his first public reading, "An Easter Ode," in 1885. A few years later, as a member of the Knights of Pythias, Gem City Palace Lodge Number Two, he saw an all-black minstrel troupe perform at the Park Theater. He organized his own black dramatic group, the Philodramian, which presented, among other productions, "The Stolen Calf," a play written by him. In his last year of high school, he began publishing a black newspaper, the *Dayton Tattler,* an ambitious effort sustained largely by his own fiction as well as poetry. What began with questionable promise on December 13, 1890, expired after no more than eight issues. The *Tattler* is chiefly useful not for "The Gambler's Wife," a serialized western play, or "His Bride of the Tomb," a romance, but for the demonstration of Dunbar's persistent interest in contributing to the advancement of his race. A mature assertion of his commitment to black culture occurred when Dunbar moved to Chicago in 1893 at the time of the World's Columbian Exposition. There he met black leaders Ida B. Wells, Hallie Q. Brown, Mary Church Terrell, and, most important, Frederick Douglass, who offered him a place in the office of the Haiti Pavilion. Of greater significance was the fact that he met black artists actively involved in creative activities. He discussed the problem of writing dialect verse with James Corrothers, a journalist and the author of *Black Cat Club* (1907), and James Edwin Campbell, coeditor of *Four O'Clock Magazine* and author of *Driftings and Gleanings* (1888) and *Plantation and Elsewhere*

(1895), both of whom were published poets, but rather closer to the tradition as influenced by plantation pieties than was Dunbar. He met the black violinist Joseph Douglass, a grandson of Frederick; Harry Burleigh, the composer and singer; the budding dramatist Richard B. Harrison, who later played De Lawd in *The Green Pastures* (1930); and the composer Will Marion Cook. With Cook's encouragement, Dunbar recited his ode "Colored Americans" at Colored Americans' Day.

All of these associations point to the discovery of a poetic voice that was essentially black. The best evidence of its shaping is to be found in those dialect poems that deal with serious problems, like the lack of freedom or the unequal distribution of the world's goods, and in those that display dramatic complexity, frequently tapping rich folk material in music, dance, and narrative. These developments in art required the presence of an intelligent, sensitive, tolerant, speculative observer or commentator committed to humane values and their universal application. Such a voice need not be confined to dialect verse. It appears, though not in its fully developed state, in "Frederick Douglass," which suffers somewhat from the imposition of eighteenth-century rhetoric. Dunbar's finest volume of poems, *Lyrics of Lowly Life*, which consolidated and confirmed the promise of *Majors and Minors* (1896), contains two poems that display qualities of his developing voice: "Accountability" and "Frederick Douglass." The emerging voice was never to issue forth fully and with an enduring resonance because Dunbar was attracted to many ways of speaking, not simply that which was reinforced by his black experience.

In his early years Dunbar achieved general success in Dayton society, apart from the black community. The focus of his accomplishment is to be found in the schools that he attended, all overwhelmingly white. There were few traumas during these years, according to his biographers, and his progress resembles that of any talented white scholar.

Dunbar attended district schools in Dayton during the elementary years and wrote his first poem at the age of seven. Although he was the only black in his class at intermediate school, he had little difficulty making white friends and race posed no barrier to close association with Orville Wright. Dunbar encountered his first great teacher here, Samuel Wilson, who read poetry to his class. Dunbar entered Central High School in 1886 and accumulated an impressive set of honors. He achieved distinction in debating and composition and published poems in both the *High School Times* and the *Dayton Herald*. Election to the exclusive literary society, the Philomathean, confirmed his high status, and serving as editor in chief of the *High School Times* seemed clearly appropriate for a scholar so distinguished as he.

Though discrimination prevented Dunbar from finding a suitable job after graduation, it did not deter him from pursuing his interest in poetry. Legend has it that the black elevator operator at the Callahan Building always had a book in his hand. Dunbar's primary literary conditioning in high school gave great importance to romantic verse. This is evident in his early poems in proper English where there are echoes of William Wordsworth, John Keats, Alfred Tennyson, and Dante Gabriel Rossetti, as well as of Edgar Allan Poe, James Russell Lowell, and John Greenleaf Whittier. Dunbar studied with particular care the successful white practitioners in dialect: Ella Wheeler Wilcox, Eugene Field, Sam Walter Foss, James Russell Lowell, and James Whitcomb Riley. Riley made such a strong impression that Dunbar imitated him in such early poems in dialect as "The Ol' Tunes," "A Banjo Song," "The Old

Apple-Tree," "The Old Homestead," and "An Old Memory." This collection of "Old's" points directly to Riley. But perhaps the most explicit example of such imitation is "A Drowsy Day," written from the point of view of meditative old age and, indeed, using Riley's Hoosier idiom. Dunbar directly expressed his admiration for Riley in "James Whitcomb Riley (From a Westerner's Point of View)," apparently never published during Dunbar's lifetime.

White literary associations, publishers, benefactors, and authors were major influences in promoting Dunbar's career. Perhaps the first opportunity for him to acquire a reputation, extending then not much beyond the Dayton city limits, was provided by a meeting of the Western Association of Writers. His reading of poems to the convention in June 1892 attracted the attention of James Newton Matthews, who became a much-valued benefactor.

Certain newspapers were especially interested in Dunbar's work, notably the *Chicago News-Record* and the *Toledo Bee*. One of Dunbar's most significant white benefactors was the foreman of the printing department of the Press of the United Brethren, who accepted *Oak and Ivy,* Dunbar's first volume of poems, without any financial guarantee from the author. The volume appeared in December 1892, just in time to be a Christmas present for his mother, to whom it was dedicated. Other committed white supporters included Matthews, who wrote a letter about Dunbar to Riley and sent complimentary letters and notices to newspapers; Charles Thatcher, a lawyer in Toledo, who offered to send Dunbar to college; and Dr. Henry A. Tobey, who did the same, specifying Harvard as the preferred institution, and who with Thatcher sponsored Dunbar's second volume of poems, *Majors and Minors.*

Nor were white writers indifferent to his talent. Riley wrote to him in 1892, "Already you have many friends and can have thousands more by being simple, honest, unaffected, and just to yourself and the high source of your endowment." Riley raised here the problem of voice, though his terms were moral rather than literary. George Washington Cable, the short-story writer and novelist famous for his portrayal of the Creoles in Louisiana, praised Dunbar's work and commented on his pure African descent, which had a special meaning for a Presbyterian surrounded in New Orleans by vestiges of African culture. Robert Green Ingersoll, the well-known orator and essayist, expressed appreciation for Dunbar's poetry, especially for six poems, all written in conventional English. James A. Herne, the author of *Shore Acres* (1892) and other plays exhibiting the first evidences of substantial realism in the American theater, was the channel to Dunbar's most influential white supporter in the world of American letters. This was William Dean Howells, whose review in *Harper's Weekly* gave Dunbar a national reputation. Concerned as well about the problem of voice, Howells sought to define the literary approach that seemed to him to be immensely impressive in Dunbar's verse. The poet, Howells wrote, was "the first man of his color to study his race objectively, to analyze it to himself, and then represent it as art as he felt it and found it to be, to represent it humorously, yet tenderly, and above all so faithfully. . . ." Howells preferred the dialect poems in Dunbar's collection (the "Minors," as Dunbar described them), suggesting problems about the poet's attitude toward the use of dialect that later emerged more fully. Howells was particularly impressed by "The Party," which opened "vistas into the simple, sensuous, joyous nature of his [the Negro] race." One can hardly blame Howells for his choice, but "The Party," though "sensuous," is not "simple," and its dramatic complexity denies that all is joy in Dunbar's heaven of fine food and extraordinary entertainment. Howells offered Dunbar the opportunity that he yearned for and, in addition, some good advice that the poet in subsequent years had difficulty accepting.

The dilemma of one black poet seemed clear in 1896. Dunbar was the product of many experiences, one merging into another, perhaps without great differentiation. But in his creative world he made a sharp distinction between what was black and what was white. Experience determines in large measure voice, and Dunbar's had exposed him to black and white associations, manners, and values. This liberal spread is not of much help in arriving at a unique and memorable way of speaking. Dunbar never understood fully that he had to make a decision, though he did agonize about what seemed to be restrictions imposed by his audience. The choice of voice is finally an act of will, and it requires a sense of where a poet's greatest strength lies. William Butler Yeats turned to Ireland to discover it; T. S. Eliot to a decadent England, full of intimations of cultural collapse, with a few strands of hope resting in vestiges of Christian doctrine; Robinson and Robert Frost to New England. And where would Dunbar turn? His direction was not clear in 1896, possibly because his choices were so many and he felt no pressure really to sort them out.

Dunbar's options were formidable. The black tradition presented two. The first is the poetry of high rhetoric about noble black themes. In *Lyrics of Lowly Life* two excellent examples are "Frederick Douglass" and "Ode to Ethiopia." Such a rhetoric is almost impenetrable to the insertion of anything natural, least of all a voice, but Dunbar deserves credit for bringing his own values to the tribute to Douglass. Then there is dialect verse, more accessible to the creation of a natural voice. But dialect has its unnatural dangers. One is the language itself, the temptation to follow slavishly the minstrel or the plantation traditions. Dunbar offered eloquent testimony on this point, moved, perhaps,

by his own involvement with Will Marion Cook's musical show, *Clorindy* (1898): "The outlandish, twisted mispronunciations of minstrel darky talk had none of the musical cadence of real Negro speech; it kept the Negro character a clown and a scamp." The second part of Dunbar's statement involves the matter of substance as well. The plantation tradition did not give black people minds worth reckoning with. Black characters were loyal servants, obedient to the very end; self-indulgent darkies who longed for corn pone and possum and were not above stealing a pig from the tolerant white man in the big house; clowns delighted to engage in antic routines for the amusement of a white audience; and lifelong children without any age of maturity, who required guidance and assistance, never a corrupting formal education.

Though there were only two black options, many more came from the white tradition. One hears echoes of an ode by Keats in "Ere Sleep Comes Down to Soothe the Weary Eyes," a Wordsworthian exercise in morality in "The Lesson," a tale of mystery within a strangely animate nature by Samuel Taylor Coleridge in "The Rising of the Storm," memories of a sonnet by John Milton, stressing endurance and patience, in "Not They Who Soar." And the list includes poems that also owe much to the late English and American romantics. In this area the opportunity to choose overwhelmed Dunbar, and few poems display any imprint of a personal touch that is special and unique. Those that do are worth noting in *Lyrics of Lowly Life*: "The Poet and His Song," "The Mystery," "Unexpressed," "Religion," "The Dilettante: A Modern Type," and "We Wear the Mask" offer much more than the reverberations of a lament by Poe in "Dirge" and "Ione," or the rhetoric of Lowell in "Ode for Memorial Day" and "Columbian Ode," or the sensuous language of the late romantics in "Song," or the numerous pious expressions of the homeside poets, Whittier and Longfellow, in "The Master Player."

Dunbar in a half dozen poems in the *Lyrics* seeks a more personal way of talking, probes the experience that he knows, and produces finished, sharply focused statements. The search for the natural voice appears easier for Dunbar in dialect verse, and the evidence of successful achievement is far richer. A moment when the natural voice emerges with great clarity and power is in "When Malindy Sings." Here the narrator expresses his appreciation for the talent, the aspirations, and the sensitivity of black people, and demonstrates their unique way of acquiring dignity and spiritual satisfaction. It is a voice grounded in the real experience and speech of blacks, displaying understanding, not condescension; compassion rather than a preoccupation with what is merely amusing:

> Who dat says dat humble praises
>   Wif de Master nevah counts?
> Heish yo' mouf, I hyeah dat music
>   Ez hit rises up an' mounts—
> Floatin' by de hills an' valleys,
>   Way above dis buryin' sod,
> Ez hit makes its way in glory
>   To de very gates of God!

The search is clearly not so easy or productive in conventional English verse, and what appears in the *Lyrics* is largely imitative, well done, and sufficient to establish the reputation of a lesser poet in the genteel tradition, but, in the final analysis, only imitative.

Dunbar did not make the decision that would enhance his stature as a poet. He could not bring himself to perform the act of will, to concentrate upon his strengths and to create the geography, the psychology, and the imagery that must accompany a fundamental artistic decision of this kind. His poetic development ends with *Lyrics of Lowly Life,* though he would continue to write poems and to publish three major volumes of verse.

Dunbar devoted his energy increasingly to fiction after 1896, but the problem of voice, now a narrative voice, still haunted him. *The Uncalled* (1898), his first novel, was begun in England and finished in the home of Professor Kelly Miller, an outstanding black essayist, at Howard University in Washington, D. C. The novel seems promising because it employs the background of southern Ohio, which Dunbar knew, and centers on a young man who rejects the "call," the divine command to become a minister of God, in favor of a more generous and more human form of Christianity without the authority of the cloth. The plot is sufficiently close to incidents in Dunbar's life to capture a few overtones from it, but it is clearly not the story drawn from the author's life, as his wife, Alice Moore Dunbar, once claimed. The conflict is far too simple, the sense of a rich town or city life absent, and the approach to a point of view, uncertain and fuzzy. The novel has only white characters who act from a superficial or pious motivation, suggesting that the proper tradition of the work was to be found in the religious line in sentimental fiction. The novel for Dunbar was only a beginning, and he would move, though sometimes in a wayward fashion, toward the discovery of a more rewarding matter and a more sophisticated way of approaching it. He succeeded in part in *The Sport of the Gods* (1902) in a manner more convincing, perhaps, than is to be found in any of his poems.

Dunbar did not solve the problem of voice in either poetry or fiction, but he nevertheless succeeded in creating a body of work that commands high respect and careful critical attention. What he achieved also requires consideration of the cultural environment of the 1890's from which his work emerged.

Dunbar wrote poems, novels, short stories, articles, dramatic works, and lyrics. Because it is not possible to do justice to all of his talents, it makes sense to concentrate upon those areas of the canon that would establish his reputation as a writer: the poetry and the fiction. The poetry comprises verses written in dialect and a greater number written in conventional English. The fiction includes both novels and short stories, with the burden of experimentation located in the novels. Because the short stories essentially document Dunbar's interest in exploiting the plantation tradition and represent a phase in his general development as a writer of fiction, they do not deserve consideration apart from the novels.

Dialect verse is a topic that still inspires mixed feelings in black intellectuals, despite the black consciousness-raising of the 1960's. The reasons are not hard to find. For years dialect was used to derogate and ridicule black people. The problem now is not simply a matter of the plantation tradition and the minstrel stage but the flow of such characters as Stepin Fechit, Sunshine Sammy, and Al Jolson in black face continuing into the twentieth century, insulting misrepresentations sprung from the nineteenth. This sad history makes a critic doubt that serious art can come from a language so consistently employed for one purpose.

But the black novelist, poet, diplomat, and political activist James Weldon Johnson thought not. Though he had used dialect in song lyrics presented on the musical stage in New York, he refused to use it in his poetry. He insisted that dialect, though colorful and musical as he well knew, had too many limitations because of its unfortunate history. According to Johnson, black dialect invited two well-established reactions, the pathetic and the humorous, and neither was appropriate for serious art. In *God's Trombones* (1927), those artistic renderings of black folk sermons, he did not use dialect; he restricted himself rather to occasional touches of the colloquial and to imitations of the syntax and the imagery of the black exhorter. The result is not wholly reassuring, because Johnson's work lacks the exhortative power and energy of a genuine black folk preacher who had never heard of literary reservations about the language that he used and would care little if he had. His responsibility was to his congregation and to God, to whom he spoke directly in moments of spiritual frenzy. The decision to concentrate upon dialect was not an easy one for Dunbar, given the pressures from black society and interested white readers. Johnson could not make it and Dunbar was reluctant to do so, though his ear for language was much superior. If a decision was hard in the 1920's, it was much harder in the 1890's, when the plantation tradition occupied a central place in contemporary sentimental literature and the minstrel stage was a staple of American entertainment.

Dialect verse first appeared in the work of southern white writers who achieved humorous effects by using it in light verse or in reproductions of folk narratives. Foremost among them were Irwin Russell, whose poems were published posthumously in 1888; Joel Chandler Harris, who achieved fame for the *Uncle Remus* tales; Thomas Nelson Page, author of *In Ole Virginia* (1887), and ambassador to Italy from 1913 to 1919; and Armistead Churchill Gordon, coauthor with Page of *Befo' de War: Echoes in Negro Dialect* (1888). Black writers moved into the field too, though often with feelings of ambivalence.

The truth is that black writers were at the point of making a commitment to dialect at least a decade before the works of white writers appeared. Frances E. Watkins Harper, a black poet, offered the substance and the structure of a typical dialect poem in "Learning to Read" (1872); the only thing lacking is the dialect. The voice is that of an old freed slave, Aunt Chloe, who reminisces about a small triumph; the scene is the "little cabin," the conventional place of happy times on the old plantation. There are the expected references to the southern black cuisine, "pot liquor," for example, and to black character, noting that stealing is an established practice. Aunt Chloe, herself, is excessively pious, and her small triumph is the acquisition of glasses without being able to read. She does so because she wants to read the Bible on her own, and she realizes her ambition. All of the elements of a typical dialect poem are here: the sincere and simple narrator; the locale; the jaundiced, tolerant view toward black character; the sentimental wish that is acted upon; the food; and the pervasive sense of Christian piety—but not the language, except in touches of dialect.

Harper's poem is clearly not high art, nor are almost all of the poems in the dialect tradition. But Johnson was wrong. High art could and did come from black dialect, but only under certain conditions imposed by a sophisticated poetic intelligence. Dunbar made high art from dialect, as did a few of his contemporaries, though most turned to more elaborate versions of the Harper formula. Dunbar, though the master of his special craft, was not alone in practicing it with an amount of distinction.

James Edwin Campbell, a black journalist who had received his education at Miami College (now Miami University of Ohio), had some of Dunbar's ambitions. Much of his dialect verse follows the usual pattern, but "Ol' Doc' Hyar" does not. It is a beast fable that has a strange toughness. Instead of possessing a pervasive sentimentality and an abiding Christian piety, the world of "Ol' Doc' Hyar" is amoral, if not immoral, offering a climate for trickery, if not for downright malevolence. Doc' Hyar

practices a form of quack medicine, and Mistah B'ar is his unfortunate victim. The final stanza expresses Doc' Hyar's attitude toward his inadequacies as a physician:

But de vay naix day Mistah B'ar he daid;
Wen dee tell Doc' Hyar, he des scratch he
    haid;
"Ef pashons git well ur pashons git wu's,
Money got ter come een de Ol' Hyar's pu's;
Not wut folkses does, but fur wut dee know
Does de folkses git paid"—an Hyar larfed
    low,
        Dis sma't Ol' Hyar
        What lib up dar
Een de mighty fine house on de mighty high
    hill!

The lesson that "Ol' Doc' Hyar" teaches the critic is that dialect verse acquires a new power and a distinctive racial energy as it approaches the folk tradition. This is one of the ways by which a routine dialect exercise can become art. Gone are the artificial conventions of the sentimental and the familiar locale with all of its expected associations. Instead there is a fresh, serious view of human behavior (though in beasts) that raises uneasy reservations about the drift and the values of current society.

The energy emanating in the nineteenth century from a black folk culture, infinitely richer than the formal tradition, was not lost upon Dunbar, though he could employ the conventions of ordinary dialect verse with a skill that no other writer of dialect possessed. Johnson maintained that "When De Co'n Pone's Hot" was superior to Riley's "When the Frost Is on the Punkin," and he is unquestionably right. Johnson points to a superior delicacy in handling nuances of sentiment, a more musical lilt, and the use of a more deft and economic technique. But the poem is, nonetheless, thoroughly within the mainstream of conventional dialect verse. The subject is food, good eating southern style. The basic emotion is an excess of sentiment lavished upon a familiar and modest object. The manner is that of high rhetoric: "Tek away yo' sody biscuit," and the overriding atmosphere is that of Christian piety. What gives this ordinary dialect poem distinction is the swing of the heptameter couplets and the economic technique, both mentioned by Johnson. In addition there is imaginative imagery, unusual in dialect verse, based upon incongruous juxtapositions:

> Dey is times in life when Nature
>   Seems to slip a cog an' go,
> Jes' a-rattlin' down creation,
>   Lak an ocean's overflow;
> When de worl' jes' stahts a-spinnin'
>   Lak a picaninny's top,
>   . . .
> When de oven do' is opened,
>   An' de smell comes po'in' out;
> Why, de 'lectric light o' Heaven
>   Seems to settle on de spot. . . .

There is substantial hope for a young poet who can offer such startling images.

"An Ante-Bellum Sermon" is another matter. Dealing with a serious topic, freedom from slavery, it employs the framework of a folk sermon preached to a congregation still enslaved. Dunbar uses his form with great skill, staying close to the traditional movement in such a sermon, which is a progress toward truth-telling and the revelation of the words and wisdom of God. Another characteristic of the folk sermon is the primitive reconstruction of familiar stories in the Bible. In general, what is lost in accuracy is more than compensated for by the awesome power that God has assumed and the crushing consequences of his acts. For a short period the cosmos is located in a shabby cabin a convenient distance from the big house. The substance of the poem is the retelling of the story of the liberation from Egypt of the children of Israel. The complexity of telling is described by the narrator as "a-preachin' ancient" and "talkin' 'bout to-day." The trouble is that one line of discourse keeps slipping into another at strategic intervals, requiring continuing admonition from the minister to his congregation: "Now don't run an' tell yo' mastahs / Dat I's preachin' discontent." At the same time the opportunities for a relationship to "to-day" abound, extending from:

> Dey kin fo'ge yo' chains an' shackles
>   F'om de mountains to de sea;
> But de Lawd will sen' some Moses
>   Fu' to set his chillun free.

to:

> Fu' de Bible says "a servant
>   Is a-worthy of his hire."
> An' you cain't git roun' nor thoo dat,
>   An' you cain't get ovah it,

and:

> We will praise de gracious Mastah
>   Dat has gin us liberty. . . .

The "gracious Mastah" is clearly not the one in the big house, who is not prepared to make slaves "citiz'—," the word that the minister cannot finish since it would place him in great danger. Though he pretends not to, he makes a clear case for a lack of justice in his own day; "preachin'" is more powerful than "talkin'," and ends on a triumphant note with a reference to the inevitable coming of Moses.

A demonstration of how dialect verse can become high art in the hands of a master, "An Ante-Bellum Sermon" has a serious theme treated with dramatic complexity and subtlety. It relies upon the authority of a folk form, using its particular defining characteristics. It has the benefit of a delicate correlation of dramatic and intellectual movements, and it has the advantage of a narrator whose point of view is apparently objective but who speaks naturally and effectively through character, background, and dramatic movement.

"Accountability" is another demonstration of the successful treatment of a serious idea. The subject matter here is contemporary rather than eternal. Determinism was much on the minds of intellectuals in the 1890's, and as Dunbar wrote this poem Frank Norris and others were constructing narratives alleging that a form of natural determinism was the essential reality of existence.

Determinism in "Accountability" is pushed to a humorous and ironic conclusion. The point, in fact, is the irony: a serious world view seen in the perspective of a chicken yard. The poem begins with a tribute to the greatness of God, who does not neglect the "alleys" and displays concern for nature, the city, differences in human nature, and all of the happenings in the world. God's omnipotence must also include the capture by the narrator of "one o' mastah's chickens." Revealed in the poem are the limits of determinism, a reservation of intellectual significance, and a disposition by human beings to rationalize their behavior.

"Accountability" has the qualities of "An Ante-Bellum Sermon": it is serious and humorous; it has a dramatic complexity provided by the presence of two value systems, and it has the advantage once more of an intelligent, speculative narrator who orders naturally and without contrivance the movement in the poem. The result is a dialect poem full of somber implications and informed by a meaning that could come only from the common sense and practical wisdom of an oppressed people.

"A Negro Love Song" is on its face a superficial lyric without the probing of accepted assumptions and the dramatic complexity found elsewhere in the Dunbar canon. It does contain one innovation of Dunbar's that deserves comment, since it enlivens the verse and appears in more highly developed poems. The routine expression of love is placed within the context of what appears to be a dance, and the refrain "Jump back, honey, jump back" reminds the reader of this possibility. This repeated phrase has another use; it serves to cut the sentiment, which would otherwise be cloying. Much to be admired too, but not unusual in Dunbar's poems, is the clarity of structure. It consists of the memory of a man's encounter with a lady, a record of her impression upon him, and a declaration of love followed by an overly economic response. The attempt to limit an excess of sentiment represented by the repetition of "Jump back, honey, jump back" is echoed by a conclusion something less than reassuring for the lover:

> Love me, honey, love me true?
> Love me well ez I love you?
> An' she answe'd, "'Cose I do"—

"When Malindy Sings" is more complex than it appears. Its power comes from the ultimate frame into which Malindy's music fits, and the strength of her talent is enhanced by comparisons and sacrilegious domestic distractions:

> Towsah, stop dat ba'kin', hyeah me!
> Mandy, mek dat chile keep still. . . .

Sacrilege is the correct term for these apparently harmless family activities, for Malindy has the power of the folk preacher, for whom, at high points in his sermon, nothing stands between his voice and God's. The folk tradition of black people once again intrudes here as it does in "An Ante-Bellum Sermon." It affirms that in a special black cosmos, which is both awesome and personal, there can be direct transfers of glory, in word and in song. Not frequently, it is true. But every time Malindy sings, the faithful and the knowing respond, just as they did when God sent Moses to liberate the Israelites, establishing an expectation in the congregation that he will do so again when sufficiently provoked.

Malindy's song transcends earth and provides an intimation of the eternal life, though the channel of connection is not educated or sophisticated but, rather, simple, intense, and touched by otherworldly power:

> Who dat says dat humble praises
>   Wif de Mastah nevah counts?
> Heish yo' mouf, I hyeah dat music,
>   Ez hit rises up an' mounts—
> Floatin' by de hills an' valleys,
>   Way above dis buryin' sod,
> Ez hit makes its way in glory
>   To de very gates of God!

Though the poem's great power rests in the folk connection with God within a clearly defined black cosmos, the poem has other virtues that are dramatic and thought-provoking. What we hear is one side of a conversation, presumably with Mandy, who lacks the narrator's faith, experience, and perception. Though another voice never breaks the flow of the monologue, Mandy—if she hears at all—acquires an education about the organization of the cosmos, learning how close God is to faithful blacks:

> Let me listen, I can hyeah it,
>   Th'oo de bresh of angels' wings,
> Sof' an sweet, "Swing Low, Sweet Chariot,"
>   Ez Malindy sings.

The comparisons have Dunbar's shrewdness in selection, including white Miss Lucy with her music book and devotion to practice. She is the only representative from the world of written notes and polite society. The other comparisons are from nature, and these representatives, more sensitive and more understanding than Miss Lucy, simply stop their music when Mal-

indy sings. Fiddlin' man, robins, la'ks, mockin'-bird, and "Folks a-playin' on de banjo" appear in the poem with a lack of differentiation in nature between what is human and what is not. "When Malindy Sings" calls upon Dunbar's full power: his reliance upon the black folk tradition, his dramatic skill, and, above all, the thoughtful, speculative, humane presence that hovers above the narrator's voice.

Dunbar's virtuoso poem in dialect is "The Party." This may be the most popular poem in black dialect ever written, and an ear attuned to distances can still hear "Dey had a gread big pahty down to Tom's de othah night" floating from high school auditoriums all over America. "The Party" lacks the serious, compelling ideas that inform Dunbar's very best dialect poems, unless one considers the cultivation of envy in an enchanted listener a great idea. Great or not, it has a long tradition, originating, no doubt, with Satan. The poem is an extraordinary collection of all of the technical devices in Dunbar's arsenal, and he would never again display his many skills in black dialect with such brilliance and abundance.

"The Party" contains all of the elements of a typical dialect poem: the good times on the old plantation; the humorous antics of blacks as they imitate their masters; the exaggerated and distorted movements associated with the minstrel stage; the emphasis upon simple emotions of hunger, jealousy, pride—all fallible; the racial vulnerability of the preacher, in regard to food and dancing; the broad rhetoric; and the food: white bread, egg pone, roasted shoat, ham, hot chitterlings, sweet potatoes—the entire southern black cuisine.

More important in generating excitement is the dramatic frame. The narrator tells his story to someone who has not been lucky enough to be at the party. Since he clearly wishes to arouse the appetites and to encourage envy and frustration, he may not be above exaggerating what he has seen, heard, and tasted—perhaps not even above departing from the truth. The reader senses the mounting excitement in the captivated listener and also the narrator's developing involvement in his tale. Excitement, indeed, is not doubly but triply compounded if the reader's reaction is counted.

"The Party" offers Dunbar's most skillful use of the dance in his poetry. The movements of the dance and the lyrics both appear here. Their relationship is curious, since the lyrics come from a high culture not available to the blacks who are dancing and singing. This incongruity is functional, since much of the poem deals with the efforts of the blacks to imitate their white superiors in both dress and manners. The dance routines appear twice; the most revealing sequence is the second, in terms of the basic comparison of white and black societies:

You know when dey gits to singin' an' dey
    comes to dat ere paht:
  "In some lady's new brick house,
  In some lady's gyahden.
    Ef you don't let me out, I will jump out,
  So fa' you well, my dahlin'."
Den dey's got a circle 'roun' you, an' you's got
    to break de line. . . .

This sequence suggests a problem beyond imitation. It is the effort of an outsider to join the circle that has been defined wholly in terms of white gentility. Scott Thomas was so anxious to do so that he "lit head-fo' most in de fiah-place right plump." The suggested moral here is about racial dignity and pride and the temptations to abandon these virtues for immediate success in white terms, but this matter should not be pushed too far.

What has been presented is the range in form, idea, and technique of Dunbar's best dialect poems, works of art that require no condescending introductions. What is the best in dialect verse is the best in Dunbar's whole po-

etic canon. Nowhere else does he display such diversity of technique, subtlety of form, command of folk sources, and sense of authority over poetic movement. The demanding ordering principle that makes all this possible is voice, and the pity is that Dunbar chose to yield to it so infrequently. Although all of Dunbar's poems in dialect have his music and acute sense of what is dramatically appropriate, none has the power or provides the tug on the imagination of these examples of his highest art.

None of the poems in conventional or literary English approaches the magnificence of the great dialect poems, despite Dunbar's mounting reservations after 1896 about the publication of dialect verse. The consequence of the refusal to recognize the sources of his greatest strength appears in *Lyrics of the Hearthside* (1899), Dunbar's first volume after the *Lyrics of Lowly Life*. Though his technical competence is much present, the volume is dominated by poems written in the high romantic style that the poet admired so much. The verses devoted to humor and dialect, which appear at the back of the volume, lack the force of the earlier poems in dialect. Certainly "Little Brown Baby" does. Dunbar appears to have made his decision about where he should place his poetic energies and talents, and it is, for many critics, the wrong one.

The clearest statements of Dunbar's unhappiness about being identified as a dialect poet are in his conversations with Johnson. One exchange occurred in 1901, and Johnson, who had reservations also about the "possibilities of stereotyped dialect," reports:

He said, "You know, of course, that I didn't start as a dialect poet. I simply came to the conclusion that I could write it as well, if not better than anybody else I knew of, and that by doing so I should gain a hearing, and now they don't want me to write anything but dialect."

Johnson also records in his autobiography, *Along This Way* (1933), that five years later Dunbar's attitude remained unchanged and that he commented in the year of his death, "I've kept on doing the same things, and doing them no better. I have never gotten to the things I really want to do." What those things were are unknown, but Johnson guesses that they were long poems, perhaps of epic length, about blacks. This speculation has a relationship, possibly, to *The Sport of the Gods,* which has some of the qualities of a prose epic.

Dunbar's poems in literary English usually have one praiseworthy quality: they are touched by his remarkable skill in metrics and versification. His prosody absorbs with ease complicated metrical structures found in English literature from the sixteenth through the nineteenth centuries.

These poems comprise three categories. What may be called "imitations" is the first. The term is not quite fair, because in the very best of his verses that derive from English and American practice Dunbar has innovations of substance that are his own. Certainly this is true in "Ere Sleep Comes Down to Soothe the Weary Eyes," the first poem in *Lyrics of Lowly Life,* and in "The Haunted Oak," which first appeared in *Century* magazine in December 1900. A second category is a set of heroic poems that are either tributes to the black race or to individual leaders like Douglass or Alexander Crummell. A good example of the formal salutation to the race is "Ode to Ethiopia," an early poem that appears in *Lyrics of Lowly Life.* "Alexander Crummell—Dead" is an eloquent memorial for the black clergyman whose religious endeavors touched America, Europe, and Africa, and it was published by the *Boston Traveler* on March 22, 1899. A third form is the personal account of Dunbar's struggle with writing, acceptance, distortions of meaning, and frustration. These poems have great economy

and make up for their compression by displaying unusual force. These are unquestionably some of the most moving of all his poems. "We Wear the Mask" and "The Poet" fall here, the former from *Lyrics of Lowly Life* and the latter in *Lyrics of Love and Laughter* (1903), where it seems somehow out of place.

"Ere Sleep Comes Down to Soothe the Weary Eyes" has every appearance of being one of Keats's journeys of the imagination to a realm of peace and overwhelming, sensuous beauty, a place of abundance and satisfaction haunted only by the near presence of death. The difference in Dunbar's poem is that the journey is through a form of purgatory, not an adventure carried by the hedonistic impulse alone. Instead of a draft of cool wine from the South, the narrator discovers a "base witch's caldron," and the pilgrim is overwhelmed by "griefs and heartaches we have known" that "Come up like pois'nous vapors that arise / From some base witch's caldron. . . ." As if the memories of the past are not appalling enough, the poet's fancy projects his spirit to a world not known but offering little comfort:

> To lands unspeakable—beyond surmise,
>   Where shapes unknowable to being
> spring. . . .

Neither past nor future offers the balm, satisfaction, and peace that he seeks. He is reduced to his naked, unflattering self in the twilight world:

> But self exposes unto self, a scroll
> Full writ with all life's acts unwise or wise,
>   In characters indelible and known. . . .

Not until the "awful self alone" is viewed does sleep come. It is not a sating of the senses but a relief from "sad world's cries," from probing "th' eternal mystery," and from fretting with frustration and unsuccessful attempts to penetrate the surrounding gloom. Sleep is a release and blessing and a condition more firmly attached to death than what is revealed in an ode by Keats.

Dunbar has drastically altered the substance of the journey of the imagination, though he does not go quite so far as Poe does in "Dream-Land" (1844), in which the narrator finds satisfaction in an underworld less than life, full of distortions and phenomena enduring a minimal existence in a twilight world.

"The Haunted Oak" is equally fascinating with its use of the form of a border ballad to record the lynching of an innocent black man. The oak responds to the hanging from one of its boughs by rejecting life for the blameless bough that has participated in this atrocity:

And never more shall leaves come forth
    On a bough that bears the ban;
I am burned with dread, I am dried and dead,
    From the curse of a guiltless man.

The machinery of the border ballad is abundantly displayed: the familiar metrics, the repetition of phrase, the curse, the ominous and knowing nonhuman phenomena like trees and birds, the violence, and the sense of betrayal. The border ballad is admirably suited to document a lynching; it has done justice to many a violent deed occurring on the boundary between England and Scotland. One innovation in "The Haunted Oak" is the use of a tree to tell the brutal story. It is a witness tree in the true sense, in that it declares that the souls of all of the apparently respectable participants—the judge, the doctor, the minister, and the minister's eldest son—are in mortal danger:

And ever the judge rides by, rides by,
    And goes to hunt the deer,
And ever another rides his soul
    In the guise of a mortal fear.

Like "Ere Sleep Comes Down to Soothe the Weary Eyes," "The Haunted Oak" makes im-

pressive use of derivative forms. Old vessels are filled with new wine, and the new is almost as good as the old.

"Ode to Ethiopia" is one of Dunbar's heroic pieces designed to instill pride and dignity in black people. It employs a pattern of references that comes from the black nationalism of the late nineteenth century, which centered on Ethiopia as the motherland of the race. This form of nationalism, a predecessor in some ways to the New Negro Renaissance, stressed a noble African past and expressed confidence in the continuing rise of the black race within the family of nations. The sole reference to an ancient and noble past is fairly general:

Be proud, my Race, in mind and soul;
Thy name is writ on Glory's scroll
    In characters of fire.

The immediate past was Dunbar's more pressing concern: "When Slavery crushed thee with its heel, / With thy dear blood all gory." He emphasizes the survival of the race during slavery and the display of humanity and tolerance that blacks exhibited after securing their freedom. The final stanza is a rousing affirmation of a glorious future for black people, powerful enough to stir the emotions of all members of the race:

Go on and up! Our souls and eyes
Shall follow thy continuous rise;
    Our ears shall list thy story
From bards who from thy root shall spring,
And proudly tune their lyres to sing
    Of Ethiopia's glory.

"Alexander Crummell—Dead," a moving tribute to a black leader, presents two contrasting attitudes toward his death. The first is the strong statement that Crummell has deserved his rest because of his many services to his fellow man:

Back to the breast of thy mother,
Child of the Earth!
E'en her caress can not smother
What thou has done.

The second is an uncertainty about the leadership for black people as a consequence of Crummell's following "the trail of the westering sun." A set of disturbing questions is posed:

Who shall come after thee, out of the clay—
Learned one and leader to show us the way?
Who shall rise up when the world gives the
        test?

No answer is given to these queries, reflecting a decision about the conclusion, which gives unexpected strength to the poem. An average tribute would point inevitably to the new heroes who are inspired to follow Crummell's inspiration. Here there is only the wise advice to the reader—and amazingly to Crummell:

Think thou no more of this—
Rest!

"Ode to Ethiopia" and "Alexander Crummell—Dead" explore two forms of heroism. One involves assurance that the black race has done well so far and has every reason to be proud of its history and humanity, and it expresses confidence in a bright future and in a sure path to glory. The second is a more subtle performance. "Alexander Crummell—Dead" accepts the death of a great man, as the title implies, and offers questions about the future. What is impressive is the tough-mindedness of the speaker, who points in a general way to Crummell's holiness and his achievements despite opposition, but who offers no assurances about what will follow him. An approach to the future, the poet says, begins with awareness of loss and shouldering responsibility. "Ode to Ethiopia" glorifies the past and future; "Alex-

ander Crummell—Dead" stresses, rather, the challenge of the present day.

It is probably a mistake to describe "We Wear the Mask" and "The Poet" as personal poems, for they are much more. They describe the problems of a black artist, and these may be projected to define a more general condition shared by many aspiring artists in an unfriendly world.

The "mask that grins and lies" is surely, first, the property of an artist, deriving, no doubt, from the use of masks by actors in classical drama. It hides "torn and bleeding hearts" because exposing an artist's inner reality to a world governed by "human guile" would be pointless, perhaps humiliating. The artist has pride and refuses to stoop to test the questionable response of an unsympathetic and unappreciative audience. Christ offers an avenue of last appeal, but the artist fails to receive either hope or balm from divinity. The only sure realities dwindle down to three basic facts: "We sing," because true artists have to, no matter what the world says; "the clay is vile," projecting an unchanged world in which "guile" still governs; "long the mile," suggesting that the time during which this alienated state must be endured is long, very long. But what remains for the artist is his talent and his pride:

But let the world dream otherwise,
    We wear the mask!

The poem applies with special force to Dunbar, dramatizing not only the attachment to dialect verse, which he was just beginning to resent, but his attendant roles as a skilled reader of his own poetry and as a model for the race. The pronoun used in the poem is "we," and the poet conceivably here identifies with all black artists performing in vaudeville or minstrel shows, writing for these theatrical productions, or turning out verse and narratives that are acceptable to a genteel audience.

A second level of meaning suggests the participation of the race. All blacks, to survive in society, must conform to standards of which they do not necessarily approve and learn to play the games and assume the masks that will ensure protection and, occasionally, advancement. A further extension of meaning involves everyone. All people living in a shallow and pretentious society, an expression of gentility in an extreme state, wear masks. No one fully reveals his inner reality to another, for the reasons that Dunbar has stated.

It is no wonder that "We Wear the Mask" is Dunbar's best-known poem in literary English. It is a poignant cry of distress calling attention to a pathological condition for which there is no immediate remedy. It has meanings on many levels, ranging from the definition of a personal problem to the inadequacies of the entire society. The particular dilemma becomes, without strain, the property of all readers.

A comparison of "We Wear the Mask" and "The Poet" is revealing. Both deal with the same general subject matter: the failure of the world to recognize a distortion of talent—a "mask," in short—and its patent disinterest in the whole body of the poet's achievement or, indeed, the life and the psyche of the artist. "The Poet," however, suffers from the contraction of meaning and reference that characterizes so much of Dunbar's verse after 1896. "We Wear the Mask" offers meaning on many levels, but "The Poet" does not. The poem is plainly what it is, with little possibility for extension of reference.

The poet's preferred subject matter is recorded in the poem, though admittedly in terms that are a little vague. All of them bear the imprint of the ideals of nineteenth-century romanticism, with no reference to the contemporary pessimism, which Dunbar's poem "The Mystery" reflects. The subjects listed are " . . . life, serenely sweet, / With, now and then, a deeper note"; " . . . the world's absorbing beat," which

the poet knows, in some mystical way; and " . . . love when earth was young, / And Love, itself, was in his lays." These are general topics—too general, and one cannot blame the public for desiring something more specific, since it was sated with romantic lays about life, the world, and love.

The poet suffers when " . . . the world, it turned to praise / A jingle in a broken tongue." The application to Dunbar could not be more precise, though the poem underestimates his contribution to literary English in order to exaggerate the world's rejection. What is also clear is that Dunbar has come, in the later years of his career, to place a low value upon his dialect verse.

"The Poet" is a specific statement that has intensity and pathos, but its application is limited, primarily to an assessment of Dunbar's own achievement, and not broad with a cluster of implications and rich associations that touch the world.

Dunbar's verse in conventional or literary English, though varied in quality, offers moments of excitement and power surpassed only by the master poems in dialect. The poems examined here suggest the wide range in his literary interests, and though individual poems are memorable and moving, there does not seem to be any focus in the poems in literary English. True, Dunbar did not attain the highest levels possible for him in the area of his greatest strength and in forms making demands upon the full powers of his fertile imagination, but he accomplished a great deal toward destroying stereotypes about black intellectual capacities and appealing to a large audience, both black and white. Dunbar is the first great black poet in America, a fitting pioneer for Langston Hughes, Melvin B. Tolson, Robert Hayden, and Gwendolyn Brooks.

Dunbar's fiction has tended to suffer a form of critical neglect for three reasons. His reputation as a poet has overshadowed his other artistic contributions, and this situation is quite understandable given his career as a poet. Dunbar was somehow considered a less effective writer of fiction than Chesnutt, who emerged with him in the 1890's as the first really professional black artists in America. This second reservation requires qualification. Certainly "One Man's Fortunes," "Mr. Cornelius Johnson, Office-Seeker," and "A Council of State," all in Dunbar's most seminal volume of short pieces, *The Strength of Gideon and Other Stories* (1900), deserve to stand alongside the tales in Chesnutt's *The Wife of His Youth,* published the previous year. The last cause for neglect is unquestionably Dunbar's continuing association with the plantation tradition, an enduring commitment that fictional experimentation in other areas does not support. There may be a simple answer—money, the sustained desire of the contemporary magazines for this always successful and much-tried fictional staple. It is very likely that Dunbar distinguished between plantation breadwinners and the more daring excursions into social realism and the social order in black urban communities. In any event, more than half of his approximately 100 short pieces are tales from the old plantation, more or less furnished with the characters and formulaic plots too well known for repetition. Hugh Gloster, a fine critic of black fiction, can assert with some justification:

In his short stories, . . . Dunbar generally accepts the limitations and circumscriptions of the plantation tradition. Glorifying the good old days in the accepted manner, he sentimentalizes master-slave relationships and implies that freedom brings social misery to the black man. Negro migrants to the North are usually represented as nostalgic misfits. . . .

Gloster is ultimately wrong, partly because he underestimates the value of Dunbar's attempts to explore social problems in the North and the alienation of the outsider there, and partly be-

cause he does not fit together the short stories and the novels to see how they relate to each other.

The fact that Dunbar was working on *The Uncalled* and *Folks from Dixie* during the same period suggests that he was perfectly capable of carrying in his head two quite different structures for fiction. Essentially they represent two sides of the strong sentimental tradition in America. *The Uncalled* (1898) is a novel about a minister, Freddie Brent, an orphan whose foster parent, Hester Prime, forces him to accept a call to undertake divine work that Freddie hears imperfectly, if at all. Freddie ultimately quits the Methodist ministry when his stern superior, Reverend Simpson, asks him to preach a sermon reprimanding a poor fallen woman. Freddie finds an expanded life, joy, and love in Cincinnati, although many critics have said that Dunbar has found nothing to praise in the city:

I have learned to know what pleasure is, and it has been like a stimulant to me. . . . I have come face to face with Christianity without cant, and I respect it for what it is.

The novel falls into a rather special line of sentimental narratives about the troubled minister, though there are touches of realism and few black characters within its structure. *The Uncalled* does not deserve to be classified with the strong realistic novels of midwestern life, *The Hoosier Schoolmaster* (1871) by Edward Eggleston and *The Story of a Country Town* (1883) by Edgar Watson Howe. Dunbar's Dexter, Ohio, has no complex social dimensions and poses to the minister a simple problem of the restricted, as opposed to the expanded, life under the umbrella of Christianity. The questions that really disturbed churchmen at the time—science, the corruption of wealth, and urban alienation—have no place here.

Although *Folks from Dixie* is essentially a collection dealing with plantation life, it is more of a mixed bag than it appears to be. Though several tales are set in northern backgrounds, the genuine surprise in the collection is "At Shaft 11," a story of a miners' strike in West Virginia. Violence occurs when black strike-breakers are introduced into the mine. Blacks battle whites for the possession of the property until the troops arrive and disperse the white strikers. The blacks retain their jobs under the original management of the mine. The significance of the tale is not so much who wins or loses but rather Dunbar's willingness to face the vexing problems of a new era and to provide a glimpse of a larger and more impersonal system of economic distribution and human relations, in which race plays only a part, and possibly not a dominant one. This discovery of what appears to be an external, larger-than-life force is one that Dunbar was not to forget.

A comparison of the two books suggests that Dunbar chose the short fiction for the launching of trial balloons. The novel is the careful, if not cautious, achievement, restricted by the limitations of the sentimental line of narratives of which it is a part. *Folks from Dixie*, despite its unprepossessing title, offers the radical departure in fictional material, vastly different from anything to be found in the novel.

A similar incongruity exists between *The Love of Landry* and *The Strength of Gideon and Other Stories*, both published in 1900. *The Love of Landry* is more a product of the sentimental tradition; both this and *The Uncalled* have as their main actors white characters. *The Uncalled* dealt with a real problem that had a modest appeal for thoughtful readers. *The Love of Landry* has no problem at all, except to promote the alliance between representatives of two upper-class families. A product of Dunbar's stay in Colorado while recuperating from tuberculosis, the novel poses the question of a difference between eastern and western attitudes and realities. (Interest in it extended beyond Dunbar. William Vaughn Moody's play, *The Great Divide,* produced with considerable success in New York in 1906, probed for more substantial distinctions between easterner and westerner.) Landry talks of breathing space and a lack of duplicity in the West, and Mildred, who has suffered from general weakness in her constitution, is rejuvenated by her visit to Colorado. A visit becomes a permanent stay since East and West are to be joined in marriage, with the place of residence for the couple to be apparently in the West. Nothing could be fluffier than this tale, which moves toward seriousness only with the appearance of a black porter.

The Strength of Gideon, on the other hand, contains much more provocative matter. The range of topics is broad indeed. There are plantation stories emphasizing black fidelity to families of former masters ("The Strength of Gideon"); black wisdom in assisting the families of former masters in accommodating to post-Civil War poverty; and black good sense and faithfulness to other blacks, despite temptations offered by freedom and the North. The collection also has plantation anecdotes dealing with familiar characters who enjoy favorable turns of fortune so that a bad case is made good. More innovative are the stories about the corruption of blacks by the cities. Perhaps the most compelling of these is "The Finding of Zach," in which a wild young buck is cleaned up and made respectable by the Banner Club, a black social club patronized by entertainers and other people who have seen much of the world, so that he can greet his father, who has come to New York to see him. Then there are urban anecdotes in which city ways seem either better or more honest than country approaches to life. The most impressive pieces by far are Dunbar's explorations of the forms of discrimination in the urban North.

"One Man's Fortunes" presents the brief legal career of Bertram Halliday, who has returned to his hometown with a college degree and the idealism of Henley. He is determined to study law, despite the objection of his friend H. G. Featherton, a white lawyer who thinks that the time is not ready. He is hired by Featherton to get out the black vote for his election as a "Christian judge" and is fired immediately after the election. Deeply embittered, he decides to teach in the South. Webb Davis, a college graduate as well and a realistic counterpart to Halliday, has prospered by setting up a barber shop and engaging in local politics.

"Mr. Cornelius Johnson, Office-Seeker" records the frustration of a black candidate who arrives in Washington to collect what is due him as a consequence of his efforts in an Alabama election. Optimism is succeeded by doubt and then despair, as Congressman Barker either refuses to see him or delays giving him what he seeks. Johnson is totally crushed by the news that the Senate has refused to confirm his appointment. At the end he is a broken and bitter man.

"A Council of State," the most ambitious tale in the volume, describes the successful attempt of Boss Luther Hamilton to prevent criticism of the administration at the Afro-American Convention. His agent and confederate is Miss Kirkman, an intelligent, hard, near-white woman who "found it more profitable to ally herself to the less important race because she could assume a position among them as a representative woman, which she could never have hoped to gain among the whites." Miss Kirkman packs the convention with proadministration people, tears up the speech of her fiancé, who wishes to complain about administrative neglect, and defeats the progressive forces.

There is much that is new in these stories: black involvement in urban political power struggles, insensitivity to other blacks because of ambition or fear of losing status, and vulnerability to capricious acts of fate, unexpected inconsistencies in character or the attraction of forms of unrealistic idealism. One no longer talks of the innocent, pleasure-loving blacks in

these urban sketches, because innocence has died and the only ambition worth respecting is power.

The Fanatics (1901) is a sentimental novel, set both in Dorbury, Ohio, and on a Virginia plantation. What occurs on the plantation is predictable, following the familiar pattern of the plantation romance. What happens in Dorbury is something else, since there we find actions for the first time that have had the benefit of experimentation and trial in short fiction. This new matter is inserted within a sentimental frame and acquires a life of its own apart from the general pattern of reconciliation in Dorbury between representatives from the North and South—not only long-separated lovers but fathers and sons as well—after the Civil War.

The predictable action is full of emotional crises, declarations of love, denunciations and disowning, transformations, and reconciliations. The matter and manner of the novel achieve a distinction above that of the plantation romance only when blacks appear.

Dorbury does not like or accept blacks, sentiments shared both by northerners, who hold blacks responsible for the war, and southerners, who have accepted them only as slaves. The chapter "The Contrabands" and the one following, "License or Liberty," present an explosion in Dorbury when a group of rootless, shifting blacks, shaken from their home environment by the war, arrives in town. The blacks stand fast in a violent confrontation, and the leader of the mob, a drunkard, rabble-rouser, and defiler of the weak, is killed by a new arrival from the South, whose family suffered insults from Raymond Stothard. The only prominent citizen sympathetic to the blacks is a white ex-Confederate soldier from a prominent family, Stephen Van Doren.

Sympathy does not come from the blacks in Dorbury. They bar the new arrivals from entering their church and are apprehensive about their own status, which might be degraded by an influx of ignorant blacks from the South. The regeneration of Nigger Ed, a forlorn black and the town drunk before the war, who performs heroic services on the battlefield and wins acceptance with respect and love by the whole town when he returns, offers little comfort.

For the first time Dunbar has introduced into the novel unpleasant matter documenting real problems involving blacks. The description of the black upheaval in Dorbury is accomplished with the same clear-eyed, objective perspective that first appears in the short pieces. Blacks and whites are good and bad—perhaps mostly in-between—and they shape ambitions, high and low, and struggle to achieve them. The plantation mythology has no place here.

Though Dunbar published two other collections largely of plantation tales, they do not really figure in his development as a writer of fiction. *In Old Plantation Days* (1903) represents, if anything, regression, since it records in the familiar style the quaint actions of slaves on Colonel Mordaunt's property, over which the Colonel presides with appropriate dignity and tolerance. *The Heart of Happy Hollow* (1904) offers, with the plantation tales, more varied items, and the whole collection is an improvement upon *In Old Plantation Days*. *The Heart of Happy Hollow* includes, for example, a shocking story of violence, "The Lynching of Jube Benson." Both collections may suffer from Dunbar's waning energies and the unfortunate progress of tuberculosis, which would cause his death.

The real culmination of Dunbar's achievement as a writer of fiction is *The Sport of the Gods* (1902). The novel incorporates much of the substance and the style of his finest tales. There are specific points of connection: Dunbar's handling of the problem of a group's ostracism by a town; his knowledge of the many forms of cruel exploitation that can occur in a

city; his evenhanded view of the presence of good and evil in whites and blacks, except that these qualities suffer at times from a certain vagueness; and his skilled portrayal of the mounting frustration—even rage—in the black psyche. These are matters of substance that are new in a Dunbar novel, but not foreign or alien to the short fiction. *The Sport of the Gods* possesses them all.

Equally important is the approach to character and action, the guiding intelligence that organizes and paces the events within a narrative. The narrator is a cultivated observer who displays a detached manner and a disposition to point up ironies in the developing action. His voice is consistent and unforced; it has the natural authority of someone who knows the country and the city and has the historical perspective to make informed commentary when required. In *The Sport of the Gods* Dunbar clearly shapes a form in fiction that suits his purpose, and he does not respond to the demands of traditional structures. His irony, muted in narratives of sentiment, is here in full display. The first sentence suggests to some extent the manner of the whole novel:

Fiction has said so much in regret of the old days when there were plantations and overseers and masters and slaves, that it was good to come upon such a household as Berry Hamilton's, if for no other reason than that it afforded a relief from the monotony of tiresome iteration.

This serves as an introduction to the two large ironic propositions that dominate the novel. The first involves the way of life of the Hamiltons in the years following emancipation. The plantation romance offers a picture of good times before and after the war, and affirmation comes, apparently, from the favorable situation of Berry Hamilton, who is an old and respected retainer of Maurice Oakley's. What seems good turns vicious and offers a demonstration that the relationship between a former master and a former slave amounts to little. There are none of the traditional virtues of trust, kindliness, and benevolence here—just narrowness, vindictiveness, and a lack of charity.

The North does not fare much better. New York, before and after the war, was regarded as a haven of opportunity and freedom for the homeless and oppressed, especially by blacks who made their way in recurrent waves to the city. As Dunbar has destroyed the Hamiltons' "bower of peace and comfort," he systematically demolishes the expectation that New York will be the Hamiltons' salvation:

To the provincial coming to New York for the first time, ignorant and unknown, the city presents a notable mingling of the qualities of cheeriness and gloom.

This mixed beginning is a preface to a reaction on the newcomer's part that is even less encouraging:

. . . after he has passed through the first pangs of strangeness and homesickness, yes, even after he has got beyond the stranger's enthusiasm for the metropolis, the real fever of love for the place will begin to take hold upon him. The subtle, insidious wine of New York will begin to intoxicate him. . . .

And the expected conclusion follows:

Then he is hopeless, and to live elsewhere would be death.

Such a place is clearly not the appropriate home for Mrs. Hamilton and her two children, Joe and Kitty, to seek the comfort and psychic restoration that they require.

The story of the Hamiltons is a tale of two locales, a small southern town and New York City. Berry Hamilton, despite twenty years of faithful service in the Oakley household, is accused of stealing money that has actually been gambled away by the spendthrift, artistic brother of his master, Maurice Oakley. Hamilton is tried and sentenced to ten years in prison; the rest of the family are turned out of their comfortable house on the Oakley grounds and suffer hostility and ostracism by blacks and whites in the town. Fannie Hamilton and her children make their way to New York, where they undergo a spectacular degeneration. Weak, callow, and much pampered by his parents, Joe becomes a drunkard, a parasite, and a murderer. Kitty, "a pretty, cheery little thing" who "could sing like a lark," goes on the stage and tosses aside her moral instruction with almost the same eagerness. With her husband in prison, the faithful, religious, and loving Fannie takes another man, who beats her. He dies violently just in time to avoid being murdered by the newly released Berry. His liberation is a consequence of the good work of a white reporter, Skaggs. A frequenter of the Banner Club, Skaggs encounters Joe and senses from his drunken babbling that a good story exists for the *Universe,* his paper. Skaggs pursues the sordid story to its southern source, where he discovers Maurice Oakley's cruelty, his brother Frank's confession—revealing that the money was squandered, not stolen—and Maurice's refusal to acknowledge the confession. The whole affair finds its way to the pages of the *Universe,* and Berry receives justice and freedom at last, but not in time to do much about his shattered family. The elder Hamiltons return to the South and receive a warm welcome and a home from Mrs. Oakley, now repentant and contrite. Broken, humbled, and sad, the couple live in a peace shattered only by the shrieks of Maurice, who with the public revelation of his shocking behavior and his family's dishonor, has lost his mind.

There is no simple moral for the story. It is certainly not to be found in the general question that the novel poses: "Oh, is there no way to keep these people from rushing away from small villages and country districts of the South up to the cities, where they cannot battle with the terrible force of the strange and unusual environment?" True, the city corrupts, and it is especially hard upon untrained, ill-prepared blacks like Mrs. Hamilton and her children. But there are people of nobility and strength in black New York, to be found especially among the artists. Hattie Sterling, the generous and vulnerable musical comedy singer and dancer, who befriends the weak Joe, looks at her life and future with complete realism. Mr. Martin, "the managing star of 'Martin's Blackbirds,'" impresses his associates by his display of professionalism and integrity. The city, then, does not corrupt everyone, no more, indeed, than the country, where the standards of a depraved gentility still seek to dominate in a changing world.

Some critics claim that *The Sport of the Gods* is a naturalistic novel. But Dunbar's suggestion that powerful, impersonal forces are at work in the city is not really pursued or documented; nor are the vague references to the will scattered throughout the novel. There is no overwhelming influence of setting, since possibilities exist for something other than an inevitable degeneration. The Hamiltons suffer their various calamities because of deficiencies of character, not from an impassive naturalistic fate. There are none of the other trappings of naturalism: the careful documentation of the total environment, the preoccupation with a design imposed by heredity, and the symbolism.

The Sport of the Gods must be accepted for what it is: a fine, ironic, penetrating novel that neither offers easy solutions nor lends itself to classification. Although there are moments of striking realism, especially in the scenes in the Banner Club, Dunbar's structure is too mannered, too dependent at times upon accident and melodramatic reversals to be called realistic. *The Sport of the Gods* is, in fact, a carefully planned narrative designed to sweep away vestiges of old myths and to encourage honesty in looking at and evaluating reality and an acceptance of self, with all of its deficiencies. There are few triumphs in Dunbar's mature, if slightly cynical, world, and that world has not much to do with gods. The gods, if anything, are the symbols of old expectations, unrealistic and without support in fact or possibility, and these creatures of fantasy play havoc with vulnerable mortals. Protection exists in honesty and maturity. Having been deeply wounded by life in the city, the sensible course for the elder Hamiltons is to return home, where they are able to resume their life much wiser than before.

The Sport of the Gods is a splendid demonstration of the power of a controlling voice. The completely informed narrator orders the events with authority and a newly discovered freedom. He is not deterred from using events because they are realistic or melodramatic, nor is he inhibited in his comments on the action or on the characters' motivation. He has chosen to give the novel a large perspective, a wide view of the black experience as it undergoes psychic change in the South and the agonies of migration. Dunbar's sweep is not epic, but it is suggestive of a quality of narration just short of that. The triumph of the novel is the triumph of voice. For once, the mature, speculative, objective narrator appears; and that appearance, more than anything else in the novel, is Dunbar's legacy to the twentieth century.

Dunbar's literary achievement is important for all black artists who follow him. He made an outstanding contribution in poetry, both in dialect verse and in literary English, although he never fully sensed where his greatest strength rested. But all poets who use the spoken language of the people as their medium owe Dunbar a great debt because he stretched dialect to incorporate serious ideas and to achieve new artistic effects. No poet in America has approached his success in this respect. Dunbar also stands as a pioneer in the development of the black novel. The influential *The Sport of the Gods* has sometimes been hailed as the first black novel using at some depth an urban background. Infinitely more important is the fact that this first black novel is ordered by a sophisticated narrator who exercises his freedom to choose and to organize fictional elements from any source. *The Sport of the Gods* is the first well-constructed ironic novel on the black experience with a fictional voice that speaks with authority and without commitment to a cause, on an important and central event in black history, migration to the cities.

Dunbar's life is so close to the model presented by the romantic artist that it is difficult to consider him anything other than a creature totally given over to idealism. Out of a modest home in Dayton, Dunbar quickly rose to fame. He fell in love with Alice Ruth Moore after seeing her picture in a magazine next to a poem of hers. He experienced the hurt of separation from Alice, after accepting their mutual decision to live apart, at a time when he received honors for his literary achievements and more generous payments from publishers. He died of tuberculosis at the age of thirty-three, on February 9, 1906. But the aura of high romanticism is misleading. Dunbar's great accomplishment is pushing beyond romantic restrictions and standards, both in his poetry and his fiction. His doing so makes him the father, in effect, of black poetry and fiction in the twentieth century. What he has done for blacks, he has done for all America, and he will survive as a great, innovative, and brave artist.

Selected Bibliography

WORKS OF PAUL LAURENCE DUNBAR

POEMS

Oak and Ivy. Dayton: United Brethren Publishing House, 1893 [1892].

Majors and Minors. Toledo: Hadley and Hadley, 1895 [1896].

Lyrics of Lowly Life. New York: Dodd, Mead, 1896.

Lyrics of the Hearthside. New York: Dodd, Mead, 1899.

Poems of Cabin and Field. New York: Dodd, Mead, 1899.

Candle-Lightin' Time. New York: Dodd, Mead, 1901.

Lyrics of Love and Laughter. New York: Dodd, Mead, 1903.

When Malindy Sings. New York: Dodd, Mead, 1903.

Li'l' Gal. New York: Dodd, Mead, 1904.

Chris'mus Is A' Comin' and Other Poems. New York: Dodd, Mead, 1905.

Howdy, Honey, Howdy. New York: Dodd, Mead, 1905.

Lyrics of Sunshine and Shadow. New York: Dodd, Mead, 1905.

A Plantation Portrait. New York: Dodd, Mead, 1905.

Joggin' Erlong. New York: Dodd, Mead, 1906.

NOVELS

The Uncalled. New York: Dodd, Mead, 1898.

The Love of Landry. New York: Dodd, Mead, 1900.

The Fanatics. New York: Dodd, Mead, 1901.

The Sport of the Gods. New York: Dodd, Mead, 1902.

SHORT STORIES

Folks from Dixie. New York: Dodd, Mead, 1898.

The Strength of Gideon and Other Stories. New York: Dodd, Mead, 1900.

In Old Plantation Days. New York: Dodd, Mead, 1903.

The Heart of Happy Hollow. New York: Dodd, Mead, 1904.

COLLECTED EDITIONS

The Life and Works of Paul Laurence Dunbar, edited by Lida Keck Wiggins. Naperville, Ill.: J. L. Nichols, 1907.

The Complete Poems of Paul Laurence Dunbar, with the Introduction to Lyrics of Lowly Life by W. D. Howells. New York: Dodd, Mead, 1913.

Speakin' o' Christmas and Other Christmas and Special Poems. New York: Dodd, Mead, 1914.

The Best Stories of Paul Laurence Dunbar, edited by Benjamin Brawley. New York: Dodd, Mead, 1938.

Little Brown Baby, edited by Bertha Rogers. New York: Dodd, Mead, 1940.

The Paul Laurence Dunbar Reader, edited by Jay Martin and Gossie H. Hudson. New York: Dodd, Mead, 1975.

BIBLIOGRAPHIES

Blanck, Jacob N. "Paul Laurence Dunbar, 1872–1906." In *Bibliography of American Literature,* vol. 2. New Haven: Yale University Press, 1957. Pp. 498–505.

Burris, Andrew M. "Bibliography of Works by Paul Laurence Dunbar, Negro Poet and Author, 1872–1906." *American Collector,* 5:69–73 (1927).

Cunningham, Virginia. *Paul Laurence Dunbar and His Song.* New York: Dodd, Mead, 1947. Pp. 267–83.

Fuller, Sara S. *The Paul Laurence Dunbar Collection: An Inventory to the Microfilm Edition.* Columbus: Ohio Historical Society Archives Library, 1972.

Metcalf, E. W., Jr. *Paul Laurence Dunbar: A Bibliography.* Metuchen, N. J.: Scarecrow Press, 1975.

BIOGRAPHICAL AND CRITICAL STUDIES

Achille, Louis T. "Paul Laurence Dunbar, poète nègre." *Revue Anglo-américaine,* 11:504–19 (August 1934).

Allen, Walker M. "Paul Laurence Dunbar: A Study in Genius." *Psychoanalytic Review,* 25:53–82 (1938).

Arnold, Edward F. "Some Personal Reminiscences of Paul Laurence Dunbar." *Journal of Negro History,* 17:400–08 (1932).

Baker, Houston A., Jr. "Paul Laurence Dunbar: An Evaluation." *Black World,* 21:30–37 (November 1971).

Bone, Robert. *Down Home: A History of Afro-American Short Fiction from Its Beginnings to the End of the Harlem Renaissance.* New York: Putnam, 1975.

Brawley, Benjamin. *Paul Laurence Dunbar: Poet of His People.* Chapel Hill: University of North Carolina Press, 1936.

Burch, Charles Eaton. "The Plantation Negro in Dunbar's Poetry." *Southern Workman,* 50:227–29 (May 1921).

Butcher, Philip. "Mutual Appreciation: Dunbar and Cable." *CLA Journal,* 1:101–02 (November 1957).

Candela, Gregory L. "We Wear the Mask: Irony in Dunbar's *The Sport of the Gods.*" *American Literature,* 48:60–72 (March 1976).

Clippinger, Lulu May. "A Visit to Paul Dunbar." *Watchword* (March 6, 1906), pp. 151–52.

Cunningham, Virginia. *Paul Laurence Dunbar and His Song.* New York: Dodd, Mead, 1947.

Daniel, Theodora W. "Paul Laurence Dunbar and the Democratic Ideal." *Negro History Bulletin,* 6:206–08 (June 1943).

Dunbar, Alice Moore. "The Poet and His Song." *A.M.E. Church Review,* 31:121–35 (1914).

Flusche, Michael. "Paul Laurence Dunbar and the Burden of Race." *Southern Humanities Review,* 11:49–61 (Winter 1977).

Fox, Allan B. "Behind the Mask: Paul Laurence Dunbar's Poetry in Literary English." *Texas Quarterly,* 14, no. 2:7–19 (Summer 1971).

Gayle, Addison, Jr. *Oak and Ivy: A Biography of Paul Laurence Dunbar.* Garden City, N. Y.: Doubleday, 1971.

———. *The Way of the World: The Black Novel in America.* Garden City, N. Y.: Doubleday, 1975.

Gloster, Hugh. *Negro Voices in American Fiction.* Chapel Hill: University of North Carolina Press, 1948 Pp. 46–56.

Hudson, Gossie Harold. "A Biography of Paul Laurence Dunbar." Unpublished dissertation, Ohio State University, 1970.

———. "Paul Laurence Dunbar: The Regional Heritage of Dayton's First Black Poet." *Antioch Review,* 34:430–40 (Summer 1976).

Hughes, Langston. *Famous American Negroes.* New York: Dodd, Mead, 1954. Pp. 82–90.

Larson, Charles R. "The Novels of Paul Laurence Dunbar." *Phylon,* 29:257–71 (Fall 1968).

Lawson, Victor. *Dunbar Critically Examined.* Washington, D. C.: Associated Publishers, 1941.

Loggins, Vernon. *The Negro Author: His Development in America.* New York: Columbia University Press, 1931.

Martin, Jay, ed. *A Singer in the Dawn: Reinterpretations of Paul Laurence Dunbar.* New York: Dodd, Mead, 1975.

Phillips, Waldo. "Paul Laurence Dunbar: A New Perspective." *Negro History Bulletin,* 29:7–8 (October 1965).

Redding, Jay Saunders. *To Make a Poet Black.* Chapel Hill: University of North Carolina Press, 1939. Pp. 56–57.

Revell, Peter. *Paul Laurence Dunbar.* Boston: Twayne, 1980.

Stronks, James B. "Paul Laurence Dunbar and William Dean Howells." *Ohio Historical Quarterly,* 67:95–108 (April 1958).

Terrell, Mary Church. "Paul Laurence Dunbar." *Voice of the Negro,* 3:271–78 (April 1906).

Turner, Darwin T. "Paul Laurence Dunbar: The Rejected Symbol." *Journal of Negro History,* 52:1–13 (1967).

———. "Paul Laurence Dunbar: The Poet and the Myths." *CLA Journal,* 18:155–71 (December 1974).

Wagner, Jean. *Black Poets of the United States, from Paul Laurence Dunbar to Langston Hughes.* Urbana: University of Illinois Press, 1973.

Young, Pauline A. "Paul Laurence Dunbar: An Intimate Glimpse." *Freedomways,* 12:319–29 (1972).

—CHARLES T. DAVIS

Ralph Ellison

1914 –

ONE of the "enduring functions of the American novel," Ralph Ellison has written, "is that of defining the national type as it evolves in the turbulence of change, and of giving the American experience, as it unfolds in its diverse parts and regions, imaginative integration and moral continuity. Thus it is bound up with our problem of nationhood." In *Invisible Man* (1952), one of the most significant American novels since World War II, Ellison gives us a terrifying and yet vibrant national metaphor: we are invisible men.

In Ellison's created world, as in American society, the quick pace of change, the caprice, the arrogance alongside the innocence, the newness and the general instability of institutions, and, above all, the impulse to recoil from the awful demands of American democracy—all keep Americans from seeing each other or even themselves. The complexity and diversity of American life, along with the development of the novel as form, has brought forth novels like *Invisible Man:* "picaresque, many-leveled . . . swarming with characters and with varied types and levels of experience." Ellison's novel is more than a "slice of life": it is an attempt at no less than a new definition of the national character, a modern national epic.

Accordingly, the vision in Ellison's novel, and indeed throughout his fiction, is ultimately af-

firmative. Virtually all of his fiction—ten stories before the novel, eleven after—features a young black man stretching toward adulthood. We see in this work the evolution of a central theme: the more conscious a person is of his individual, cultural, and national history, the freer he becomes. As a young writer, Ellison quickly became dissatisfied with the typical naturalistic scenarios in which characters struggling to survive the merciless American environment are eventually overcome by impersonal forces. To Ellison, this documentary fiction was dull—and failed to capture the richness and variety of black life as he knew it. Influenced by a broad range of writers, including Richard Wright, André Malraux, and Ernest Hemingway, Ellison began to focus on the person who, by force of character and will, manages to endure.

Ralph Waldo Ellison was born in Oklahoma City, Oklahoma, on March 1, 1914. Aggressiveness and optimism about life seem to have run in his family. His grandfather, Alfred Ellison, was an illiterate ex-slave who had nonetheless served during Reconstruction as constable, marshal, and magistrate in the Ellison clan's hometown, Abbeville, South Carolina. In the tense and violent post-Reconstruction days, Alfred Ellison lost his political titles and returned to driving a dray and chopping cotton, while his wife, Harriet, worked as a washerwoman. Still, he retained his defiant willingness to assert his rights. Once, after a friend had been lynched, he walked through Abbeville with his hands clasped behind his back, announcing to the whites on the street, "If you're going to kill me, you'll have to kill me right here because I'm not leaving. This is where I have my family, my farm, my friends; and I don't plan to leave." Another time Alfred Ellison talked a white mob out of lynching one of his friends. The old man, said Ralph Ellison many years later, must have talked to the whites in an "unknown tongue."

At four Ralph and his younger brother, Herbert, were taken to South Carolina to see Grandfather Alfred and his brother, the boys' Uncle Jim. A half-century later Ellison still remembered the scene: Uncle Jim in his horse and buggy, the bridge to the homestead, the pecan trees planted by the boys' father, the reaping and gathering of vegetables, the old church that was used as a chicken house, the immense fireplaces inside which he could stand and see light flickering down. In Ellison's words, "it was very important for me to go to South Carolina and to visit and see the old house, to see those fireplaces, to see the forms, to see how fertile things were, to see what my relatives did."

If South Carolina evokes for Ellison sacred memories of places and persons, Oklahoma, his birthplace, does even more so. "I dream constantly of Oklahoma City," he told an interviewer in 1975. "My childhood is there." His parents, Lewis Alfred Ellison and Ida Millsap Ellison, left the Deep South for Oklahoma in 1911, only four years after the territory was granted statehood. At least Oklahoma (a word coined by the Reverend Allen Wright, a Choctaw-speaking Indian, to mean "red man") had no firm tradition of slavery. As it turned out, segregation laws were imported from neighboring Texas and Arkansas; but even so, the blacks who had trekked west in wagon trains to escape southern oppression fought hard for their political rights. The blues lyric "I'm going to the Territory, baby / I'm going to the nation" meant, for blacks heading west during this hopeful period, "I'm going to be free." This determination for freedom, the fighting spirit of the people, and the sense of possibility suggested by the vast expanses of undeveloped land gave Oklahoma a frontierlike aspect. All the same, Oklahoma City was an established place. The capital city, recalls Ellison, "seemed fully articulated with its streetcars and its tall buildings. It appeared to be in the same class with say Kansas City or St. Louis or Chicago—only it was much smaller and very much better."

Especially after the death in 1917 of Lewis Ellison (who had worked as a construction foreman and then as an independent businessman, selling ice and coal), the Ellisons were poor—at times extremely poor. Still, Ralph and Herbert were made to feel that the worlds of the rich and the white were approachable. This confidence had been their father's; Lewis Ellison, an avid reader, named his son after Emerson. It was reinforced by Ida Ellison, a woman of enormous determination, faith, and purpose. A stewardess at the Avery Chapel Afro-Methodist Episcopal Church, who valued action in *this* world, she brought home records, magazines, and books discarded in white homes where she worked as a maid. And she saw to it that her sons had electrical and chemistry sets, a rolltop desk and chair, and a toy typewriter. Her activism extended to politics. "If you young Negroes don't do something about things," she would tell her sons, "I don't know what's going to happen to this race." An ardent supporter of Eugene Debs's Socialist party, she canvased for the party's gubernatorial candidate in 1914. In 1934, after Ralph had gone off to Tuskegee Institute, she was jailed for attempting to rent buildings that Jim Crow laws had declared off limits to blacks.

Usually the family lived in a three-room shotgun house. "We ate poor food," Ellison remembers, "which was generally well-prepared, sometimes not, because my brother and I were taught to take care of ourselves when my mother went out and worked." The Ellisons became so close to their neighbors, the Randolphs, that Ralph considered the families to be extensions of one another. Taylor Randolph recalls that his family would assist Ida Ellison, whom his parents called "Brownie," during this trying period: "I remember one day when it was so cold and snowy that we didn't dream Brownie could have gone out to work. But our mother thought she had better go over and check anyway. And when she got there, she found that Brownie *had* gone out to work. And, sure enough, the fire had gone out, and Ralph and Herbert were huddled up, freezing. My mother took them right back to our house and kept them there until Brownie came home from work. This was a time when there was a great togetherness among families, and when there was a great sympathy for people who had to struggle to bring up their children."

Despite hard times, breaks in the pattern of segregation contributed to the relatively free atmosphere. Indians and blacks had lived side by side in Oklahoma for generations. "There were Negroes who were part Indian," observes Ellison, "and who lived on reservations, and Indians who had children who lived in town as Negroes." The Ellisons had many white friends, and black-white cultural integration, at least, was relatively widespread. Downtown theaters were not segregated until the 1920's. And after blacks were barred from the white theaters, black actors like Richard B. Harrison (who later played De Lawd in Marc Connelly's *The Green Pastures*) continued to perform regularly on "Deep Second" (the blacks' nickname for Second Street, the main strip in Oklahoma City's black neighborhood); Harrison included Shakespearean soliloquies in his repertory. Miss Clark, the maid of the English actress Emma Bunting, used to stay with the Ellisons when Bunting's repertory company came to Oklahoma City, and she brought stories of the professional theater and of England into the Ellison household.

As teen-agers Ellison and his comrades dreamed of being latter-day Renaissance men; they snatched desired symbols along with attitudes and values from blacks, Indians, and whites alike. Ellison wanted to read everything he could at the Paul Laurence Dunbar Library: fairy tales, James Fenimore Cooper, Bernard Shaw, and even a translation of Freud's *Interpretation of Dreams,* which he thought to be a fanciful version of the dream books used by certain "scientific" players of the numbers game. He wanted to play expert "sheenee" (a kind of street hockey played with sticks and tin cans) and varsity football, to imitate the styles of certain "vague and constantly shifting figures"— from his community, from lore and literature, from the movies—figures "sometimes comic but always versatile, picaresque, and self-effacingly heroic." He identified with people he met on odd jobs around town: in private clubs where he waited tables, at buildings where he ran the elevator, on downtown streets where he shined shoes and hawked newspapers. He identified too with the tellers as well as the heroes of the tales that he heard in J. L. Randolph's pharmacy, where he also worked. On rainy or snowy days, local men would pack the store and trade yarns, some of which had been told best, he was informed, years before by his father. J. L. Randolph recalls that Ellison "was always delving into things. He asked about the drugs we sold, and asked about what it felt like to be a druggist. By fifteen or sixteen Ralph was quite a talker. He would sit at the fountain and talk about doing things in a big way. His concern back then was how to get started."

Not all of Ellison's early job experiences were uplifting. The battle-royal scene in *Invisible Man* was suggested not only by similar scenes that he had read about but also by those he had witnessed as a waiter at private clubs. The specific event that ignited his imagination occurred while he was job hunting as a youngster:

One summer when I was still in high school I was looking for a job (and it gets to be 105 to 110 in the shade in Oklahoma City; it used to, anyway). I met a friend and he said, "If you go up to Broadway between Ninth and Tenth there is a car lot there and the man wants someone to help him around the car lot." He said, "I couldn't take it because I got another job, but you better hurry up there." So I turned on the fan, as they say; and by the time I arrived, I was pretty moist. There was this white man sitting out under a tree; and I said, "Sir, I understand you need someone to work here"; and he said, "Yes, sit over here on this box." (He had a crate with a cushion on it.) He said, "Sit over here and tell me about yourself." He began to ask me about my grades, about my parents, and so on; and I began to feel that I was getting this job. And then, at the moment when I was most certain that the job was mine, I felt a charge of electricity in my tail; and I went up in the air and I came down. . . .The whole thing, again, was a ritual of initiation—a practical joke—wherein a Ford coil, a coil from an old Model T Ford, has been hooked up to a battery. . . . Of course, there was no job.

In the music-centered Oklahoma City of the 1920's Ellison heard church performers, marching bands, tent showmen, silent movie accompanists, and those who amused themselves by improvising on ukuleles, kazoos, and C-melody saxophones. With musicians as the heroes most revered, it is small wonder that from age eight through his middle twenties, he wanted to be a musician. Ellison himself wanted to be able to read music as well as to improvise. Thanks to Zelia N. Breaux, supervisor of the music program for the Negro schools in Oklahoma City, Ellison learned music theory at Douglass High School and soon picked up a working knowledge of the soprano saxophone and several brass instruments. As first-chair trumpeter in the Douglass school band, and then as the group's student conductor, Ellison played light classics and marches at church recitals, graduation exercises, football games, lodge and fraternity social functions, and for special productions at the Aldridge Theater, of which Mrs. Breaux was co-owner. Meanwhile, Ludwig Hebestreit, conductor of the Oklahoma City orchestra, taught Ellison privately and invited him to the Little Symphony concerts for children. Ellison recalls being "the only brother of color" permitted to attend these concerts at that time. In return for these favors, young Ellison cut the conductor's lawn.

Ellison admired the elegance, artistic discipline, and seemingly infinite capacity for self-expression that were the hallmarks of jazz musicians. These men and women, some of whom played by ear, some of whom were conservatory-trained, were the heroes of Deep Second. At the Aldridge Theater and at Slaughter's Hall (the public dance hall), Ellison heard Ma Rainey, Ida Cox, and King Oliver as well as the Old Blue Devils band (the nucleus of which became the Count Basie band), with Walter Paige, Oran ("Hot Lips") Page, Eddie Durham, and Jimmy Rushing. As a high school student, Ellison played occasional dance jobs in pickup groups, sat in on rehearsals of the Blue

Devils, and learned the jazz idiom at jam sessions. In Halley Richardson's shoeshine parlor, for instance, Ellison heard Lester Young playing with and against other tenor-sax men, sitting in the shoeshine chair, "his head thrown back, his horn even then outthrust, his feet working on the footrests."

In 1933 Ellison left Oklahoma for Tuskegee Institute, to which he had been accepted as a scholarship student. He wanted to write a symphony encompassing his varied experiences: as a poor black boy who never felt inferior to anyone because of race or class, as a frontier boy with a certain city slickness, and as a classically trained musician steeped in blues and jazz who wanted to capture their rocking power in classical forms.

Tuskegee was a trade and teachers' school, and its founder, Booker T. Washington, was an apostle of intellectual conservatism; still, Ellison developed there as a musician. The dean of the music school was William L. Dawson, best known as a skillful arranger of spirituals and as the composer of the *Negro Folk Symphony*. In the face of deeply entrenched segregation law and custom, Dawson had built Tuskegee into one of the major music centers of the South, with department heads like the pianist Hazel Harrison, who had been one of Ferruccio Busoni's prize pupils in Berlin. As in high school, Ellison played first trumpet in the school orchestra and, on occasion, served as the band's student director.

He also delved into other arts at Tuskegee. He played a leading role in a campus play and in his third year began to test his powers in painting and photography; between school classes he attended an art class to learn watercolor. The instructor, Eva Hamilton, encouraged Ellison to try sculpture. Another favorite teacher, Morteza Drexel Sprague, guided much of his wide reading. But on his own Ellison discovered T. S. Eliot's "The Waste Land," and the poem deeply engaged him: "I was intrigued by its power to move me while eluding my understanding. . . . There was nothing to do but look up the references in the footnotes to the poem." So began Ellison's conscious study of literature. In 1935, as a "reflex" of his reading, Ellison tried his hand at writing poetry. It was at first "an amusing investigation of what seemed at best a secondary talent . . . like dabbling in sculpture."

Because of a mix-up about his scholarship, at the end of his third year Ellison found that he had neither the forty-dollar tuition fee for the coming term nor any money to live on. He decided to venture to New York City, where he thought he could make and save money for the fall more easily than in Alabama. Though she knew that music was his first love, Eva Hamilton was enthusiastic about Ellison's prospects as a sculptor and gave him a letter of introduction to Augusta Savage, a black sculptor in Harlem. Fully intending to return to school, Ellison headed north to New York.

Apart from the winter of 1937, which he spent in Dayton, Ohio, the war years in the merchant marine, and two years (1955–1957) in Rome as a guest of the American Academy of Arts and Letters, Ellison has lived in New York City since his arrival there in 1936. Although he journeyed north specifically to study sculpture and to earn money as a musician, he was also drawn to New York by its glamour and promise of greater freedom. "New York," he has said, "was one of the great cities prominent in the Negro American myth of freedom, a myth which goes back very far into Negro American experience. In our spirituals it was the North Star and places in the North which symbolized Freedom and to that extent I expected certain things from New York." He expected, in fact, a dazzling fulfillment of "an irrepressible belief in some Mecca of equality." Harlem he supposed to be "a glamorous place, a place where wonderful music existed and where there was a great tradition of Negro American style and elegance."

In *Invisible Man,* the protagonist informs the outspoken veteran of the Golden Day brothel that he is on his way to New York, and the vet responds excitedly:

"New York! . . . That's not a place, it's a dream. When I was your age it was Chicago. Now all the little black boys run away to New York. Out of the fire into the melting pot. I can see you after you've lived in Harlem for three months. Your speech will change, you'll talk a lot about 'college,' you'll attend lectures at the Men's House . . . you might even meet a few white folks. And listen," he said, leaning close to whisper, "you might even dance with a white girl!"

The vet recites portions of the southern black myth of New York and tells some of its history to his medical attendant: " . . . think of what this means for the young fellow. He's going free, in the broad daylight and alone. I can remember when young fellows like him had first to commit a crime, or be accused of one, before they tried such a thing. Instead of leaving in the light of morning, they went in the dark of night. And no bus was fast enough. . . ." In fact the Invisible Man has himself been accused by the college president, Bledsoe, of a crime against the "beautiful college": he has allowed a rich, white "friend of the school" to see the nearby black slum and to be hit in the face. Although Ellison had had no climactic run-in himself with the Tuskegee administration, when he headed north he too looked forward to breaking away from southern Jim Crow practices as well as from a certain provincialism that he had confronted at Tuskegee.

Harlem was not exactly the promised land heralded by the folklore. Twelve years after coming north, Ellison wrote: "To live in Harlem is to dwell in the very bowels of the city . . . a ruin . . . overcrowded and exploited politically and economically." Black Manhattan he found the "scene and symbol of the Negro's perpetual alienation in the land of his birth." For when the black southerner moves north, he surrenders vital cultural supports:

He leaves a relatively static social order in which . . . he has developed those techniques of survival to which Faulkner refers as "endurance," and an ease of movement within explosive situations which makes Hemingway's definition of courage, "grace under pressure," appear mere swagger. He surrenders the protection of his peasant cynicism—his refusal to hope for the fulfillment of hopeless hopes—and his sense of being "at home in the world" gained from confronting and accepting (for day-to-day living, at least) the obscene absurdity of his predicament. Further, he leaves a still authoritative religion . . . family . . . and a body of folklore—tested in life-and-death terms against his daily experience with nature and the Southern white man—that serves him as a guide to action.

More than one newcomer has found Harlem and New York City to be a battleground of wills, chaos continually erupting within the orderly pattern of streets and traffic lights. Many of the so-called surreal city scenes in Ellison's fiction derive from his attempt to bring into focus the contradictions and confusions actually observed in Harlem:

. . . the most surreal fantasies are acted out upon the streets of Harlem; a man ducks in and out of traffic shouting and throwing imaginary grenades that actually exploded during World War I; a boy participates in the rape-robbery of his mother; a man beating his wife in a park uses boxing "science" and observes Marquess of Queensberry rules (no rabbit punching, no blows beneath the belt); two men hold a third while a lesbian slashes him to death with a razor blade; boy gangsters wielding homemade pistols (which in the South of their origin are but toy symbols of adolescent yearning for manhood) shoot down their young rivals. Life becomes a masquerade, exotic costumes are worn every day. Those who cannot afford to hire a horse wear riding habits; others who could not afford a hunting trip or who seldom attend sporting events carry shooting sticks.

Yet, if many blacks have been bent and broken by Harlem, if one sees "white-haired adults crawl in the feudal darkness of their childhood," if Harlem "is the scene of the folk-Negro's death agony, it is also the setting of his transcendence." In Harlem "you see the transformation of the Southern idiom into a Northern idiom . . . Harlem is a place where our folklore is preserved and transformed. It is the place where the body of our Negro myth and legend thrives. It is a place where our styles, musical styles, the many styles of Negro life, find continuity and metamorphosis." Like Ellison, millions of blacks have brought their institutions and optimism to the cities of the North; and the emerging northern black culture did provide some sense of continuity for them. In the midst of Harlem's fantasticality and turmoil, opportunities for personal and artistic growth abounded. In 1966 Ellison observed that "Harlem was and still *is* a place where a Southern Negro who has a little luck, and who has a little talent, can actually make himself into the man or woman of his dreams."

In *Invisible Man,* the factory hospital is a metaphor for the modern industrialized city that fractures black folk-consciousness. There the white doctors, with shrieks and electric shocks, endeavor to force the young fellow to learn his place, to forget his history and identity, and to yield to the power of the cold, steely machine. Their intention backfires, however, and the Invisible Man is only purged of his fear of the North and of whites. Emerging from the hospital, he feels transformed and realizes dimly that he is still on the twisting road to freedom.

In 1936, well before World War II (when the police began to warn whites away from that vast black neighborhood) Harlem was evolving into what James Weldon Johnson called the black American cultural capital, beckoning to artists and intellectuals, black and white. In the 1930's and 1940's Ellison could be found browsing at the Schomburg Library and at Lewis Michaux's bookstore, then located on Seventh Avenue at 125th Street. Ellison would save his nickles and dimes to go to the Savoy Ballroom once or twice a week. "The Savoy was thriving and people were coming to Harlem from all over the world. The great European and American composers were coming there to listen to jazz—Igor Stravinsky, Francis Poulenc. The great jazz bands were there. Great dancers were being created there." Twice a week, often with Langston Hughes, Ellison went to Harlem's Apollo Theater. By 1940 Ellison was going to after-hours hangouts where musicians jammed: to Sidney Bechet's place, where Teddy Wilson or Art Tatum held down the house piano, to the Rhythm Club, to Clark Monroe's Uptown House, or to a place where the waiters sang as they served drinks. "Jazz was part of a total culture, at least among Afro-Americans," said Ellison. And as in Oklahoma City, jazzmen were heroes.

During the heyday of the jazz club Minton's, Ellison was among those "who shared, night after night, the mysterious spell created by the talk, the laughter, grease paint, powder, perfume, sweat, alcohol and food—all blended and simmering, like a stew on the restaurant range, and brought to a sustained moment of elusive meaning by the timbres and accents of musical instruments locked in passionate recitative." There Ellison would listen to musicians he had first heard in Oklahoma City: Charles Christian, Lester Young, "Hot Lips" Page, Ben Webster. Also at Minton's he heard the creators of the "bop" idiom: Charlie Parker, Thelonious Monk, Dizzy Gillespie, Bud Powell, and Charles Mingus.

Because he lacked the money for a musicians' union license, and because there was such an abundance of talent in New York, Ellison did not find steady work as a trumpeter. In fact, he performed only once in public, his last engagement as a professional musician, playing the trumpet for a dance recital by Anna Sokolow. But he still wanted to write symphonies and studied for about a year with Wallingford Riegger. In 1936 a friend took him to the Edgecombe Avenue apartment of Duke Ellington, who remembered seeing Ellison at Tuskegee. The bandleader invited the young man to the following day's rehearsal but then had to cancel the invitation. Not wanting to press the point, Ellison said no more about the matter, and it was dropped. By the late 1930's, when he became immersed in writing fiction, Ellison laid down his trumpet forever, refusing even to attend concerts for fear of being diverted.

During the Great Depression finding work of any kind was not easy. At first, still hoping to return to Tuskegee, he worked for almost a year behind the food bar of the Harlem YMCA, where he had a room. Many odd jobs followed, one of the most interesting of which was as substitute receptionist and file clerk for the psychoanalyst Harry Stack Sullivan. That job lasted only a few months, but the experience proved instructive: as he was filing, Ellison would glance through patients' case histories, and what he read spurred him to reconsider the importance of dreams. When he began writing fiction and reading authors who employed dreams in their fiction—especially Dostoevsky, who, as Ellison has said, "taught the novelist how to use the dream"—the young writer realized how much his stint with Sullivan had shown him.

In 1936 and 1937 Ellison also worked in factories around New York. Later he worked as a free-lance photographer and builder of record players and radios. During one series of weeks without work, he slept on the daybed in a friend's living room and on benches in St. Nicholas Park.

The sculptor Augusta Savage explained that her duties on a WPA arts project made it impossible for her to instruct Ellison. Alain Locke and Langston Hughes, impressed with Ellison's sculpture, suggested that he work with another Harlem artist, Richmond Barthé, and Ellison studied with him for about a year before abandoning sculpture.

Ellison's contact with the literary world was already made. He had met Hughes quite by chance on his second day in New York. Through Hughes he met Richard Wright, whose poems "I Have Seen Black Hands" and "Between the World and Me" Ellison considered the best ever written by a black writer; and their friendship blossomed. Although Wright was six years older and on the verge of his first major literary success (*Uncle Tom's Children* in 1938), the two were in basically the same predicament: they were radically inclined black intellectuals with southern backgrounds, trying to survive in New York and struggling to make art in the midst of the Great Depression. They talked endlessly about politics and art, drank, and exchanged jokes and stories.

Wright said candidly that Ellison had started too late to develop into a serious writer, but he was impressed with his friend's ability to discuss literature and urged him to write a short story for *New Challenge,* a leftist literary magazine of which Wright was an editor. Ellison begged off. He was at that time still a musician and lacked writing experience. Wright forced his hand by asking instead for a short review of Waters Edward Turpin's novel *These Low Grounds*. With this review, entitled "Creative and Cultural Lag" (Fall 1937), Ellison took the decisive step toward becoming a writer.

When Wright again asked Ellison to write a short story, for the Winter 1937 issue of *New Challenge*, Ellison agreed. Drawing on his experience of bumming on trains, he wrote "Hymie's Bull," his first short story. Although heavily derivative of Hemingway, it impressed Wright and got as far as galley proofs. But in the end some new poems by Margaret Walker and others superseded "Hymie's Bull" and the story was dropped—as was the Communist party's moral support. Problems between the other editors, Dorothy West and Marion Minus, led to the magazine's suspension and the Winter 1937 number went unpublished.

In February 1937 Ellison's mother died in Dayton, Ohio. In a haunting memoir, "February" (1955), he recalls her death and the awesome Dayton winter during the recession of 1937:

February is a brook, birds, an apple tree—a day spent alone in the country. Unemployed, tired of reading, and weary of grieving the loss of my mother, I'd gone into the woods to forget. So that now all Februarys have the aura of that early morning coldness, the ghost of quail tracks on the snow-powdered brook which I brushed aside as I broke the brook to drink; and how the little quail tracks went up the ice, precise and delicate, into the darker places of the bank-ledge undisturbed.

Ida Ellison's death proved a painful initiation into manhood for her son: ". . . I was in my early twenties then, and I had lived through my mother's death in that strange city, had sur-

vived three months off the fields and woods by my gun; through ice and snow and homelessness. And now in this windless February instant I had crossed over into a new phase of living. Shall I say it was in those February snows that I first became a man?"

Ellison's statement that he survived by his gun through ice, snow, and homelessness is no mere figure of speech. He and his brother both arrived in Dayton almost completely out of money. At night, when the temperature skidded toward zero, they slept in a car parked in a garage open at both ends. They supported themselves by hunting quail, which they either ate or sold to local General Motors executives. Although the Ellison brothers had hunted since childhood, never had it been such a serious enterprise. By reading Hemingway's descriptions of "leading" a bird in flight, Ellison became an excellent hunter during those lean months. Years later he said of Hemingway: "When he describes something in print, believe him . . . he's been there." Ellison returned to New York weary and distraught, but one issue was settled: all of his creative energies would be channeled into becoming a good writer.

In Ohio, Ellison had begun writing in earnest. After hunting all day, he wrote at night and studied Joyce, Dostoevsky, Gertrude Stein, and Hemingway—"especially Hemingway," he recalls. "I read him to learn his sentence structure and how to organize a story." Ellison began to arrange his life so that writing would be his main focus, "to stake my energy against the possibility of failing." Out of money but determined to continue writing, in 1938 Ellison was hired by the Federal Writers' Project.

Ellison's four-year experience on the project provided $103.50 monthly, enough money to live on, and a good deal more. Besides rescuing him from unemployment, the work stocked him with "information and insights about [his] country during a highly formative period of

[his] literary life." It also made Ellison aware of being part of a community of writers, black and white, fledgling and established, all trying to perfect their craft. And it was on the project that Ellison began to find his voice in fiction. He grappled with questions that were to provide the dominant themes in his writing: Who is the American? Who is the black American? How is a man's past related to his identity? What role does folk art play?

Ellison pursued his project assignments with diligence. One of the first, a study of "Famous New York Trials," gave him the opportunity to learn something of the history of New York's political and legal systems. The aspiring writer spent many days at the New York Court of General Sessions, reading crime reports and court transcripts. Even when the research was tedious, the drama and ritual of the courtroom suggested forms to consider as possible material for fiction.

Along with about twenty other black employees of the writers' project, Ellison spent months in the Schomburg Library doing research for a projected book of social history, *The Negro in New York*. As a member of that research team, Ellison wrote a series of short memorandums, several hundred words in length, on prominent black New Yorkers and historical incidents involving the black community. From June 9, 1938, to June 29, 1942—almost his entire tenure on the project—Ellison submitted such papers as "Negro Instructors in New York Institutions of Higher Learning," "Jupiter Hammond," and "Great Riots of New York; Complete Account of the Four Days of the Draft Riot of 1863." These essays were interpretive as well as expository and often prefigured the balance and grandeur of Ellison's later prose, although many of them lacked his characteristic precision and zest.

From 1938 to 1940 Ellison worked also under the supervision of Nicholas Wirth of the New York "Living Lore Unit." This group of twenty-seven writers sought to recount the history of New York City in the words of its inhabitants. The resulting unpublished collection of "urban and industrial folklore," assembled under the working title "Chase the White Horse," testified to their conviction that a vital part of American history lies in the tales, toasts, songs, and boasts of folklore. In this research group, Ellison collected children's game-rhymes, chants, and taunts, some of which turned up later in his fiction. Part of the song "Buckeye the Rabbit," which Ellison heard recited by five Harlem girls while playing, appears in *Invisible Man:*

> I'm riding through Kentucky
> I'm riding through the sea,
> And all I catch behind me
> Is a buckle on my knee.
> Buckeye the Rabbit,
> Shake it
> Shake it
> Shake it
> With a buckle on my knee.
> I swing to the bottom
> I swing to the sea
> And all I catch behind me
> Is a buckle on my knee
> So Buckeye the Rabbit
> Shake it
> Shake it
> With a buckle on my knee

Ellison sometimes recognized a remnant of a saying or rhyme he had heard in the South, reduced to a mumble or nonsense phrase in Harlem. Out of the rural context in which the story or rhyme had originated, the meanings of the folk art changed—and at times appeared to dissolve entirely. Even reduced to mumbles, however, the folklore often retained ritual meanings and signified a tradition, a bridge to the South and to the past. "That's what the people have to work out of," Ellison has said. "This tradition goes way back to the South, and some of it goes back to Africa."

Ellison also visited hundreds of Harlem apartments and public places, where he collected stories from adults. This process of interviewing and transcribing sharpened his ear for idiosyncrasies of language and his mind for getting particular patterns of speech onto paper. He was often able to get a story on paper "by using a kind of Hemingway typography, by using the repetitions . . . I could get some of the patterns and get an idea of what it was like."

On May 10, 1939, Ellison talked to a man in Eddie's Bar in Harlem, described as a modernistic room with green walls, marine designs, red imitation leather upholstery, mirrors, and a nickel phonograph—"all of this in good taste." The unnamed man, who brings to mind Langston Hughes's character Jesse B. Simple, told Ellison:

Ahm in New York, but New York aint in me. You understand? Ahm in New York but New York aint in me. Who do I mean? Listen. Im from Jacksonville, Florida. Been in New York twenty-five years. Im a New Yorker! But Im in New York an New York aint in me. Yuh understand? Naw, naw, yuh dont get me. What do they do; take Lenox Avenue. Take Seventh Avenue; take Sugar Hill! Pimps. Numbers. Cheating these poor people outa whut they got. Shooting, cutting, backbiting, all them things. Yuh see? Yuh see whut Ah mean? *I'M* in New York, but *New York aint* in me! Dont laugh, dont laugh. Ahm laughing but Ah dont mean it; it aint funny. Yuh see. Im on Sugar Hill, but Sugar Hill aint on me.

The man ended his song of himself with a eulogy to "spirits": "Whut did the saint say? He said a little spirits is good for the stomach, good to warm the spirit. Now where did that come from? Yuh dont know, yuh too young. Yuh young Negroes dont know the Bible. Dont laugh, dont laugh. Look here Ahll tell you somethin: Some folks drinks to cut the fool but some folks drinks to think. Ah drinks to think."

Ellison submitted one especially vivid report on June 14, 1938. Standing on 135th Street and Lenox Avenue, Leo Gurley told Ellison about "Sweet-the-monkey." Gurley began his story with what folklorists term a "signature": "I hope to God to kill me if this aint the truth. All you got to do is go down to Florence, South Carolina and ask most anybody you meet and they'll tell you its the truth."

Gurley's "Sweet-the-monkey" in some respects resembles the narrator of *Invisible Man:*

It was this way: Sweet could make hisself invisible. You don't believe it? Well here's how he done it. Sweet-the-monkey cut open a black cat and took out its heart. Climbed a tree backwards and cursed God. After that he could do anything. The white folks would wake up in the morning and find their stuff gone. He cleaned out the stores. He cleaned up the houses. Hell, he even cleaned out the dam bank! He was the the boldest *black* sonofabitch ever been down that way. And couldn't nobody do nothing to him. *Because* they couldn't never see im when he done it. He didn't need the money. Fact is, most of the time he broke into places he wouldn't take nothing. Lots a times he just did it to show 'em he could. Hell, he had everybody in that lil old town scaird as hell; black folks and white folks. . . .He wont let himself be seen.

Many of the verses, jokes, and peculiarities of speech that enrich Ellison's fiction were drawn from his experience in Oklahoma and Alabama; other are based on notes made in Harlem for the Federal Writers' Project. There he refined his sense of the folkloric context: the occasions in which persons were likely to use the stylized speech of folklore. Thus in his fiction, the lore is more than mere "local color"; it is ritualistic and reflective of a whole cultural style. For example, in *Invisible Man* the protagonist tells a black man on the street to "take it easy" and the man replies with an ebullient boast, here serving an initiatory function:

"Oh, I'll do that. All it takes to get along in this here man's town is a little shit, grit, and mother-wit. And man, I was bawn with all three. In fact, I'maseventhsonofaseventhsonbawnwitha cauloverbotheyesandraisedonblackcatbones highjohntheconquerorandgreasygreens ... I'll verse you but I won't curse you—My name is Peter Wheatstraw, I'm the Devil's only son-in-law, so roll 'em! ... My name's Blue and I'm coming at you with a pitchfork. Fe Fi Fo Fum. Who wants to shoot the Devil one, Lord God Stingeroy! ... Look me up sometimes, I'm a piano player and a rounder, a whiskey drinker and a pavement pounder. I'll teach you some good bad habits. You'll need 'em."

On the Federal Writers' Project, writers studied folklore and exercised their literary craft transposing the lore into written literature. Ellison collected lore and studied history by day, but wrote his own fiction by night. The project inspired some writers' rediscovery of the American vernacular in the 1930's, and in those years Ellison applied his new awareness of language and folklore to the past and to human identity. "The character of a people," he has said, "is revealed in their speech." The project's structured examination of language and folklore helped his writing grow beyond the limits of literary realism. If Harlem proved a somewhat tarnished "Mecca of equality," it did offer young Ellison opportunities for artistic growth.

Ellison's increasing maturity as a writer coincided with a gradual shift in his political perspective. During the late 1930's he was an enthusiastic supporter of many Communist party tenets, but by the mid-1940's he was publicly denouncing the party. He was first drawn to left-wing politics by his mother's involvement with the Socialist party in Oklahoma; by his own experience of poverty, segregation, and hard times; and by the impact of such events as the Scottsboro and Herndon cases and the Civil War in Spain. André Malraux's political, critical, and fiction writings also affected Ellison profoundly and further stirred in him the prospect of participating in a concerted effort by—in Malraux's word—"conscious" revolutionary artists, intellectuals and the people to redeem an immoral world torn by war and depression. Ellison recalls that the "swell of events which I plunged into ... the stimulus that existed in New York during the thirties was by no means limited to art; it was also connected with politics; it was part of the *esprit de corps* developed in the country after we had endured the Depression for a few years. It had to do with my discovering New York and the unfamiliar areas of society newly available to me."

Ellison's friends influenced his leftward progress. Wright was an active member of the Communist party when they met. Having been secretary of the John Reed Club in Chicago, he was considered a party spokesman. Hughes was a charter member of the radical American Writers' Congress and had been writing leftist articles, fiction, and poetry for almost ten years. In 1937 Hughes traveled to the Soviet Union, which he described in reports for the *Chicago Defender* as a haven of interracial cooperation. Though never a member of the Communist party, Hughes often wrote and spoke in behalf of party causes.

Fron 1937 to 1944 Ellison wrote over twenty book reviews for such radical periodicals as *New Challenge, Direction,* and the *Negro Quarterly;* in 1940 the *New Masses* printed at least one piece of his every month.

In the 1930's Ellison joined the chorus of critics calling for realism as the literary mode appropriate for the radical writer. Mirroring the Communist party position of the day, Ellison's criticism often described black Americans as members of a state or nation (like a Russian soviet) within the United States. The literature of black Americans (the subject of about half of his reviews of the 1930's and 1940's) was, he believed, an emerging national literature that should serve to heighten the revolutionary consciousness of black people. The black writer should instill in his audience not merely "race consciousness" but awareness of class. Ideally, the revolutionary black writer should inspire black working people to unite with workers of other "nationalities" against the bourgeoisie, white and black.

While the Great Depression years brought tremendous difficulties, they were also, in Ellison's words, "great times for literature," times for "the conscious writer" to study his society's laws and to examine its citizens' emotions "stripped naked." Furthermore, the writer could perceive the great American themes of tomorrow shining "beyond the present chaos." The black writer's particular duty was to overcome the handicap of living in racist, capitalist America and to teach his readers to do likewise. His greatest responsibility, said Ellison, echoing Joyce's phrase, was "to create the consciousness of his oppressed nation."

Toward this nation-building effort, Ellison's first published writing, his review of *These Low Grounds* (1937), called for a greater awareness of literary technique and tradition among what he called "realistic" black writers. He also steadfastly maintained, then and in years to come, that black folklore is one of the richest sources for the black writer.

In 1940 and 1941, Ellison published "Stormy Weather" and "Recent Negro Fiction," his longest and most searching critical essays up to that time. They were pioneering works in establishing the creative use of folklore as a touchstone for evaluating black literature. While reviewing one of Langston Hughes's autobiographies, *The Big Sea,* Ellison proclaims that of the "New Negro movement" in American letters in the 1920's, only Hughes, much of whose poetry had been based on black speech and the blues, transcended the "bourgeois," white-imitating wave of black writing and survived the shattering impact of the Great Crash. Most black writers of the 1920's wrote as if blind to the technical experiments of Hemingway, Gertrude Stein, and Joyce; furthermore, they had ignored what Ellison termed "the folk source of all vital Negro art." Hughes, however, "castigates the Negro bourgeoisie. . . .Declining its ideological world, he gained his artistic soul. . . .Hughes's vision carried him down into the black masses to seek his literary roots. The crystallized folk experience of the blues, spirituals, and folk tales became the stuff of his poetry."

Obviously there is a nationalistic—perhaps a proletarian—note struck here. There is also a point about diction and rhetoric. Ellison explains that the black writer of the 1930's, discovering the path mapped out by Hughes, began to sense that black workers spoke a "language of protest," a black urban idiom, and that "the speech patterns of this new language had long been present in Negro life, recorded in the crystallized protest of American Negro folklore." Hughes's fiction reflected the transformation of rural folk expression into urban folk expression, which, by the 1930's, was fast becoming "the basis of a new proletarian literature." His radical perspective and power as a spokesman for the people derived from Hughes's having followed "the logical development of the national folk sources of his art." In other words, Hughes used the language, tone, and structure of the blues and spirituals in his work; writing from the perspective of the folk, his radicalism glowed with the energy and irony of "the dozens," the boast, the deadpan tale.

The Big Sea, however, is not explicit enough for Ellison in its realism or radicalism. Its use of understatement as a narrative pose was "charming in its simplicity" but risked the possibility of being misunderstood:

Many *New Masses* readers will question whether [understatement] is a style suitable for the autobiography of a Negro writer of Hughes's importance; the national and class position of the writer should guide his selection of techniques and method, should influence his style. In the style of *The Big Sea* too much attention is apt to be given to the esthetic aspects of experience at the expense of its deeper meanings. Nor—this being a world in which few assumptions can be taken for granted—can the writer who depends upon understatement to convey these meanings be certain that they do not escape the reader. To be effective the Negro writer must be explicit; thus realistic; thus dramatic.

Ellison has remained somewhat suspicious of understatement in fiction. In a review in 1946 he attacked his literary hero Hemingway for using understatement as a deceptive mask; beneath his clipped prose, writes Ellison, Hemingway takes reactionary positions. As late as 1953, upon accepting the National Book Award, Ellison explained that he chose not to take the narrative stance of the "'hard-boiled' novel, with its dedication to physical violence, social cynicism, and understatement. Understatement depends, after all, upon commonly held assumptions and my minority status rendered all such assumptions questionable."

Ellison also criticized Hughes's self-portrayal as a picaresque figure rather than a tough-minded hero whose self-awareness deepens with experience. Using Malraux's terminology, Ellison observed that by rendering himself as picaresque, "Hughes avoids analysis and comment, and, in some instances, emotion." Hence "a deeper unity is lost. This is the unity which is formed by the mind's brooding over experience and transforming it into conscious thought. Negro writing needs this unity, through which the writer clarifies the experiences of the reader and allows him to recreate himself." In a proper autobiography, writes Ellison, the black writer is responsible for revealing the process whereby he has gained his artistic consciousness in a world in which "most of the odds are against his doing so." In the South "the attainment of such a consciousness is in itself a revolutionary act." The black writer's duty is to recognize that "the spread of this consciousness, added to the passion and sensitivity of the Negro people . . . will help create a new way of life in the United States."

The desire for a "conscious hero" in American literature has remained a theme of Ellison's. In 1942, reviewing William Attaway's *Blood on the Forge* for the *Negro Quarterly,* Ellison commended the author's presentation of southern "folk" blacks as harried and confused in the concrete mazes of the urban North. He pointed out that the artistic vision is incomplete, however, without the presence of a character whose consciousness is reborn in the North:

Conceptually, Attaway grasped the destruction of the folk, but missed its rebirth on a higher level. The writer did not see that while the folk individual was being liquidated in the crucible of steel, he was also undergoing fusion with new elements. Nor did Attaway see that the individual which emerged, blended of old and new, was better fitted for the problems of the industrial environment. As a result the author is so struck by the despair in his material that he fails to see any ground for hope in his characters. Yet hope is there. . . .

A few years later, in "Flying Home" (1944), "King of the Bingo Game" (1944), and *Invisible Man* (1952), Ellison would present his own black protagonists threatened with liquidation in modern industrial society. His heroes' resiliency, folk memories, and luck, however, help them to "fuse" with "new elements" in their environment; they are "reborn" better able to deal with the churning world of airplanes and factories. In 1948 Ellison described the bemused protagonist of *Invisible Man,* which he was then writing, as "a character who possesses both the eloquence and the insight into the interconnections between his own personality and the world about him to make a judgment about our culture." Ellison's early desire for conscious heroes in American writing foreshadowed his eventual break with many of his literary and political friends, including Wright.

But in his literary essays of the early 1940's Ellison champions Wright as living testimony to the shining possibilities within the black community. Against all odds, Wright had made himself into a highly conscious activist and writer. For Ellison, Wright's early novellas, published as *Uncle Tom's Children* (1938), constituted his best fiction; their protest and existential themes emerged not from overt Marxist or Kierkegaardian theorizing but from the fiction itself, rich in folklore. And in the review "Recent Negro Fiction" (1941), Ellison held up *Native Son* (1940) as "the first philosophical novel by an American Negro. This work possesses an artistry, penetration of thought, and sheer emotional power that places it in the front rank of American fiction." Wright's autobiography, *Black Boy* (1945), prompted Ellison to compare it with works by Joyce and Dostoevsky, and with the blues. Wright's eloquent "song" of trouble and trial is filled "with blues-

tempered echoes of railroad trains, the names of Southern towns and cities, estrangements, fights and flights, deaths and disappointments, charged with physical and spiritual hungers and pain. And like a blues sung by such an artist as Bessie Smith, its lyric prose evokes the paradoxical, almost surreal image of a black boy singing lustily as he probes his own grievous wound."

Despite Ellison's admiration for his mentor, and despite Wright's encouragement (he inscribed a copy of *Uncle Tom's Children* "To Ralph, who I hope will someday write a better book than this"), by 1940 a degree of "anxiety of influence" afflicted the friendship. Ellison's early fiction style so resembled Wright's that Wright protested. Upon seeing one short-story manuscript, Wright exclaimed, "Hey, that's my stuff!" Ellison deliberately left the piece unpublished, like most of his exercises of the period, and afterward he never showed Wright any work in progress. "You might say," Ellison later commented, that in this awkward scene Wright "influenced me *not* to be influenced by him."

That Ellison was finding his own direction in writing is clear from his fiction of the 1940's. And in critical essays of the 1960's he explains his early dissatisfaction with *Native Son* and *Black Boy.* Recognizing that Bigger Thomas in *Native Son* represents black humanity smoldering under the ashes of despair and white oppression, Ellison nevertheless cannot accept Bigger as an adequate portrait of the Afro-American. To him this character is little more than an ideological formulation, a sociological mortar shell fired at the guilty conscience of white America. Blacks themselves know that life in the ghetto is not as dimensionless and dull as Wright paints it. *Native Son* is too deterministic and anchored in Marxist ideology:

In *Native Son* Wright began with the ideological proposition that what whites think of the

Negro's reality is more important than what Negroes themselves know it to be. Hence Bigger Thomas was presented as a near-subhuman indictment of white oppression. He was designed to shock whites out of their apathy and end the circumstances out of which Wright insisted Bigger emerged. Here environment is all—and interestingly enough, environment conceived solely in terms of the physical, the non-conscious. Well, cut off my legs and call me Shorty! Kill my parents and throw me on the mercy of the court as an orphan! Wright could imagine Bigger, but Bigger could not possibly imagine Richard Wright. Wright saw to that.

Black Boy fared little better in Ellison's later criticism. Here again the portrait of black life is too raw and hopeless in Ellison's view. When Wright decided to employ determinist ideology and to dwell upon the crushing power of environment, instead of the individual's ability to overcome it, that, wrote Ellison, was doubtless "the beginning of Wright's exile."

In 1944, when Ellison's disagreement with radical American leftists was already strong, the war policies of the American Communist party impelled Ellison and many other blacks to leave the organized Left entirely. When the party lent what Ellison called its "shamefaced support" to segregation in the armed forces, many blacks became bitterly disillusioned with the radicals' vaunted good will toward minorities.

The party blundered in ignoring the fact that "little Hitlers" (white racists and racist policies) plagued blacks at home; for blacks the war against fascism had to continue on the home front as well as overseas. When the party attacked this position as "narrowly nationalistic," it seemed to Ellison that Soviet foreign policy moved the American Communist party more than did the plight of its local black members. In an interview years later, Ellison said of the Communist party:

They fostered the myth that Communism was twentieth-century Americanism, but to be a twentieth-century American meant, in their thinking, that you had to be more Russian than American and less Negro than either. That's how they lost the Negroes. The Communists recognized no plurality of interests and were really responding to the necessities of Soviet foreign policy, and when the war came, Negroes got caught and were made expedient in the shifting of policy. Just as Negroes today who fool around will get caught in the next turn of the screw.

However radical their politics, American Communist party leaders often suffered from what Gunnar Myrdal called "the American dilemma." In Ellison's words:

the Party had inherited the moral problem centering upon the Negro. . . . For in our culture the problem of the irrational, that blind spot in our knowledge of society where Marx cries out for Freud and Freud for Marx, but where approaching, both grow wary and shout insults lest they actually meet, has taken the form of the Negro problem.

In *Invisible Man,* the protagonist's decision to renounce his wholehearted support for the Brotherhood is based on his discovery that the radical group is racist. The Brotherhood sacrifices Harlem's interests for the sake of "international" goals and tries to mold the Invisible Man into their conception of the Good Negro: one passively willing to use his energy and his art (which is his oratory) exactly as the Party commands. In the novel the Brotherhood stands, to a large extent, for the American Communist party. But Ellison also wanted the Brotherhood to be seen in a larger context: the party was not the only group of white American political activists to betray their black countrymen for narrow political ends.

In 1942 Ellison quit the Federal Writers'

Project to become managing editor of the *Negro Quarterly* and worked on its staff for one year, leaving just before the journal closed. Angelo Herndon, who was just then breaking away from the Communists, was the editor of this radical "Review of Negro Life and Culture," which featured leftist artists and scholars, black and white. Sterling A. Brown, Herbert Aptheker, Richard Wright, Norman McLeod, J. Saunders Redding, E. Franklin Frazier, Owen Dodson, and Stanley Edgar Hyman all contributed to the *Negro Quarterly* during its brief existence (only four issues were published). Besides his review of William Attaway's *Blood on the Forge,* Ellison wrote an unsigned editorial that obliquely criticized the Communist party and urged black leaders to concentrate more on the interests and needs of blacks.

Calling for black unity and self-determination, without mentioning the Communists, he warned that when black leadership is provided from outside the black community,

Negro people [are] exploited by others: either for the good ends of democratic groups or for the bad ends of Fascist groups. And they have the Civil War to teach them that no revolutionary situation in the United States will be carried any farther toward fulfilling the needs of Negroes than Negroes themselves are able, through a strategic application of their own power, to make it go. As long as Negroes fail to centralize their power, they will always play the role of sacrificial goat, they will always be "expendable." Freedom, after all, cannot be imported or acquired through an act of philanthropy, it must be won.

In this comment, as in several of Ellison's early political writings, the artist inadvertently upstages the political analyst. Black leaders, he argues, must realize that the hope of consolidating black power rests on their ability to analyze and use the lore and language of black

Americans. Without understanding Afro-American myths and symbols, no black leader can succeed, regardless of his program's merits:

Much in Negro life remains a mystery; perhaps the zoot suit conceals profound political meaning; perhaps the symmetrical frenzy of the Lindyhop conceals clues to great potential power—if only Negro leaders would solve this riddle. On this knowledge depends the effectiveness of any slogan or tactic.... [American war aims] will be accepted by the Negro masses only to the extent that they are helped to see the bright star of their own hopes through the fog of their daily experiences. The problem is psychological; it will be solved only by a Negro leadership that is aware of the psychological attitudes and incipient forms of action which the black masses reveal in their emotion-charged myths, symbols and wartime folklore.

Ellison calls here for a more efficient propaganda effort by black leaders and for their increased identification with the political interests of the black masses. He also seems to call on the black artist and the student of black culture to express the true values and forms of black life. But it was Ellison himself who went on to explore the mysterious relation of folklore, art, and politics most daringly in his own early stories.

The years 1939 to 1944 were years of apprenticeship for Ellison who, in a *New York Post* feature story of 1943, was identified as "a short story writer." He published eight stories during this period, and his writing grew in eloquence and complexity from one work to the next. He wrote many more stories than he tried to publish, looking upon some as exercises.

As we might expect, his first short stories, "Slick Gonna Learn" (1939) and "The Birthmark" (1940) were in the realistic mode and highlighted the jagged edges of the black-American environment. These stories offer explicitly political resolutions. But as early as 1940, as Ellison began to draw upon his Oklahoma City background, his vision was not so much that of a political realist as of a regionalist: his first Buster and Riley stories, "Afternoon" (1940), "Mister Toussan" (1941), and "That I Had the Wings" (1943), explored the language, folklore, and unique features of a southwestern town as seen by two curious and daring black boys. "It Is a Strange Country" (1944) is a transitional wartime story, important because of its heightened technical complexity. Here too an Ellison protagonist first declares his ineradicable Americanness as well as his blackness.

The final two stories of the early 1940's, "Flying Home" and "King of the Bingo Game," are more than mere apprentice pieces. In these works the young fiction writer discovers his own surrealistic voice and manages to integrate folklore, ritual, politics, history, and an absurdist vision of American experience in a way that may be termed "Ellisonian." These important early stories center on the individual's struggle to cope with a world that has become machine-mad; in both works a black protagonist struggles to confront the question, Who am I?

In 1943 Ellison joined the merchant marine, in part because he had belonged to the National Maritime Union since 1936, when he picketed for them, but mainly because he "wanted to contribute to the war, but didn't want to be in a Jim Crow army." While still in the service, Ellison was awarded a Rosenwald Fellowship to write a novel. In fact, he already had one outlined: a wartime story in which a black pilot is shot down, captured by the Nazis, and placed in a detention camp where he is the highest-ranking officer, and pitted by his Nazi guards against the white prisoners. Ellison continued working on this novel even after he began *Invisible Man* in 1945. But it never achieved

enough unity to satisfy its maker, and only one section, "Flying Home," was published.

Constructed as a story within a story, "Flying Home" deals with two thwarted flights: that of the black pilot Todd, whose plane collides with a buzzard and crashes in a field in Macon County; and that of Jefferson, who comes to Todd's rescue and who in his "tale told for true" sails from heaven back to the hell of Alabama. Jefferson's uproarious folktale, cataloged by collectors as early as 1919, eases the pain of Todd's injured ankle and his wait for a doctor's help. It also serves an initiatory function for this starry-eyed greenhorn, who, like Jefferson's heavenly flier, must eventually confront the evils of Jim Crow Alabama, however high he has flown. In this brilliantly layered story (which nods cordially to the swing instrumental of the same name and period) a variety of other folk motifs directs the young pilot on his looping homeward flight.

The critic Walter Blair has written that comic folklore aids the American's attempts to adjust to "totally new ways of living" as well as to "amazing differences between himself and his neighbors." In a lecture on American humor, Ellison himself has pointed out that funny tales provide not only escape and entertainment but also instruction. "Americans began," he says, "to tell stories which emphasize the uncertain nature of existence in the new world and as we did so, we allowed ourselves some relief from the pain of discovering that our bright hopes were going to be frustrated." Thus we have tall tales about the flintiness of farmland bursting with mile-high cornstalks, corroded buried treasure, and the brutality and sorcery of the Indians. Thus in the land of the free and the brave, we have humorous tales about the hatred and the casual violence of surly white men toward men black and red.

Jefferson's tale, listed by the folklorist Richard Dorson as "Colored Man in Heaven," provides Todd with a perspective for viewing his plight as a black trainee flier whose plane has been knocked down by a buzzard (called a "jimcrow bird" locally) onto the land of a racist white man named Graves. The folkloric lesson also needles the segregated air force of World War II, during which the question was raised of whether black fliers could be trusted in combat. Implied, too, is the more general question of how to face a segregated society that is patrolled by violence—or yet more generally, how to confront a manmade world full of sorrow and death. From Jefferson's tale Todd learns to laugh at the fact that his brightest and loftiest hopes may at last be grounded by jimcrow birds.

Like many Afro-American humorous tales, the "Colored Man in Heaven" joke momentarily accepts as true certain black stereotypes. As Jefferson tells it, the moment he got to heaven he raised such a ruckus by speeding that he scared the white angels and "knocked the tips offa some stars." Some of the heavenly "boys" even claim that Jefferson, flying with just one wing, stirred up a storm in Alabama and caused some lynchings. "Like colored folks will do," he forgets a warning from St. Peter, who finally loses patience with the "flying fool" and sends him back to Alabama. But Jefferson has the last word. "Well," he says, "you done took my wings. And you puttin' me out. You got charge of things so's I can't do nothin' about it. But you got to admit just this: while I was up here I was the flyingest sonofabitch what ever hit heaven!" Far from expressing self-hatred, this tale turns the black stereotype of the unmanageable, forgetful, smart-mouthing black man inside out. As a black in-joke, "Colored Man in Heaven" takes the teeth from racist charges by accepting them as true and then laughing at their foolishness. If he does "act up" in heaven, at least while there Jefferson is the "flyingest" of the heavenly fliers.

This tale also gives historical perspective to the dilemma of living in Jim Crow America. Jefferson finds that black angels do not fly, because they are required to wear heavy harnesses. He himself refuses to be encumbered and discovers that, "smooth as a bird," he can "loop-the-loop," even on one wing. But all this earns him a dressing-down by St. Peter in front of smirking white angels. Jefferson is finally thrown back into segregated Alabama. Similarly, not only were blacks in the "heaven" of America burdened with the harness of slavery, but at the abrupt end of Reconstruction the political freedoms tentatively held out were snatched back. Blacks again found themselves in a society filled with restrictions based on race. By the 1940's black men were trained to fly planes at the Tuskegee airfield, but for a long time black air force pilots (like Todd) were barred from combat duty. Knocked back by "jimcrows," Todd must learn the old survival technique of laughing at—or otherwise distancing himself from—an oppression with deep historical roots.

This tale is also part of a greenhorn's initiation into a complex and violent society. Todd's greenness is reflected in his undue optimism about being allowed to fly in combat. Why does he want to fly? "It's as good a way to fight and die as I know," he tells Jefferson. Asked if he has ever been hindered by whites who don't want blacks to be pilots, Todd tightens up and says, "No one has ever bothered us." To this the older man says, "Well, they'd like to." In Jefferson's tale even St. Peter and God himself seem involved in the conspiracy to keep blacks harnessed. The whole story angers Todd at first, but he relaxes as he sees that symbolically he too has been knocked down from the heaven of his aspiration. In the end he is freer of illusions; he is more shrewd and wary. Like the Invisible Man, Todd has crossed over into the fallen realm of adulthood. As he is carried from the field by Jefferson and Jefferson's son it is "as though he had been lifted out of his isolation, back into the world of men. A new current of communication flowed between the man and boy and himself."

The last story Ellison published before he began to work full-time on *Invisible Man* was "King of the Bingo Game." This compelling story, the first in which he felt he had discovered his own fictive voice, synthesizes much that he had learned as an apprentice and foreshadows certain of the most memorable forms and themes of *Invisible Man.* As in "Slick Gonna Learn," the protagonist is an unemployed young black man whose wife's need for medical care has made him desperate for money. Here again, as in all his previous stories, a young black man fights for freedom in a land tightly gripped by authority figures. In this surrealistic story, however, with its dreamlike shifts of time and levels of consciousness, the struggle is seen in its most abstracted form. In an epiphany the unnamed hero realizes that his battle for freedom and identity must be waged not against individuals or even groups but against no less than history and fate.

The King is Ellison's first character to sense the frightening absurdity of everyday American life. He has seen a woman walking into the bright street with a bedbug on her neck. He dozes in a theater and imagines himself a boy in the South, chased by a train that has jumped the track to pursue him, "and all the white people laughing as he ran screaming." He sees himself as "a long thin black wire that was being stretched and wound upon the bingo wheel." His nose begins to bleed, and he feels "as though the rush of blood to his head would burst out in baseball seams of small red droplets, like a head beaten by police clubs." It is in this wildly imagistic realm, where past and present, dreaming and waking converge, that the King, like the Invisible Man, sees the visions that may spell salvation.

In Ellison's earliest stories, Buster and Riley find that southern folk culture—despite its sudden violence—provides clear and stable definitions of black manhood. Up north, however, the King discovers that the values he had learned in Rocky Mount, North Carolina, do not apply. He is hungry and thirsty but knows better than to ask strangers in a movie theater for food and drink. "Up here it was different. Ask somebody for something, and they'd think you were crazy." When the King stands perplexed on the bingo stage, not only does the white master of ceremonies laugh at him ("So you decided to come down off that mountain to the U.S."), so do the blacks. "Ole Jack thinks he done found the end of the rainbow," someone shouts. As his emotions mount, the audience claps and shouts in mockery:

> Shoot the liquor to him, Jim, boy!
> Clap-clap-clap
> Well a-calla the cop
> He's blowing his top!
> Shoot the liquor to him, Jim, boy!

With no encouraging spiritual or anthem, with no guide like Jefferson to remind him of the way home, this hero must make his way alone. "He felt alone, but that was somehow right." Finding his southern folk consciousness shattered and half-forgotten in the North, the King must rely on his creativity and resilience to win his freedom and identity.

His fate seems to have been irreversibly determined long before his birth. Standing before the bingo wheel, he feels that he has "moved into the spell of some strange mysterious" being and that he is blinded by the wheel's lights and awestruck by its power: "He felt vaguely that his whole life was determined by the bingo wheel; not only that which would happen now . . . but all that had gone before, since his birth, and his mother's birth and the birth of his father. It had always been there, even though he had not been aware of it, handing out the unlucky cards and numbers of his days." Here the King echoes a question posed by the Invisible Man: What if history is a gambler?

If it is, the King feels he must do more than hope his lucky number comes up: he must subvert the process that has left him and his generations luckless. His refusal to stop turning the bingo wheel symbolizes this forthright subversion. By refusing to play a game that he has been fated to lose, he discovers who he is. First he realizes that he has lost the old identity: "somehow he had forgotten his own name. It was a sad, lost feeling to lose your name, and a crazy thing to do . . . 'Who am I?' he screamed." Then "he was reborn. For as long as he pressed the button he was The-man-who-pressed-the-button-who-held-the-prize-who-was-the-King-of-Bingo." Like the Invisible Man, the King frees himself when he discovers that he has been a sleepwalker, a fool, naive enough to accept unquestioningly the judgments handed down by an indifferent bingo wheel of fate, of circumstance, of history. Like the Invisible Man, he sees the cruelty of the culture and society that have shaped his personality; the vision frees him of his illusions. The instant before he is hit by the descending stage curtain, he is in full control of his fate. Moreover, he is symbolically reborn, better able to deal with life's absurd and dreadful turns. Before the curtain is rung down, the King hears the taunts and laughter in the theater but, foreshadowing the steely determination of Jim Trueblood in *Invisible Man,* he says, "Well, let 'em laugh. I'll do what I gotta do."

In 1945, exhausted by hard work and by a grueling merchant marine voyage, and hopeless over the unfinished war novel, Ellison went to recuperate at a friend's farm in Wakesfield, Vermont. Certain ideas seemed to come into focus there. He had been reading Lord Raglan's *The Hero,* a study of historical and mythic heroes, and had been thinking about leadership in the Afro-American community. Why, he wondered, did black leaders so often seem uncommitted to their black constituents? Why did they so often seem dependent not on the will of blacks but on the largesse of white patrons? Along with these questions, Ellison was pondering a number of others—and overall, the persistent problem of finding a literary form flexible enough to contain his vision of the wild and shifting American hodge-podge of cultures and characters. He determined to write a novel about black identity, heroism, and history, and to write it in a style "unburdened by . . . narrow naturalism."

One morning in 1945, still in Vermont, Ellison scribbled the words, "I am an invisible man"—his novel's first sentence. He recalls that he played with the idea and "started to reject it, but it intrigued me, and I began to put other things with it. And pretty soon I had a novel going, and I began to work out of a conceptual outline on it. And as fast as I could work out the concepts, the incidents started flowing in on me." Back in New York, Ellison continued work on the novel in his apartment on St. Nicholas Avenue, but he also went downtown every morning to work like any businessman. Using a friend's Fifth Avenue office, he put in at least eight hours a day writing before returning to his home.

The project was blessed with the support of Ellison's present wife, Fanny McConnell, of whom he has written "my beloved wife . . . has shown, again and again, through her sacrifices, encouragement and love, more faith in the writer and his talent than the writer has shown in himself."

He worked on *Invisible Man* for five years, taking one year off to work on another novel. *Invisible Man* was published in 1952. To many critics the novel seemed like a miraculous first work. But Ellison's first published fiction, "Slick Gonna Learn," had been conceived as part of a novel. By the 1940's, with "Flying Home" and "King of the Bingo Game" he had discovered a voice and a set of questions and concerns that were timeless but were his own. By the mid-1940's he had absorbed the lessons of Mark Twain, Hemingway, Richard Wright, and the social realists; and he had experimented with the narrative devices of many writers, especially Henry James, Faulkner, Dostoevsky, and Joyce. The sentence "I am an invisible man" started him on a work into which he could pour all he had learned as an apprentice perfecting his craft.

With the publication of *Invisible Man,* Ellison moved suddenly into the front ranks of American writers. His novel evokes visions and tensions peculiar to American life as Afro-Americans know it: Ellison's brown-skinned, nameless seeker suffers and scoots, forth and back through a thicket of briars well-known to American blacks. Yet *Invisible Man* is a modern masterpiece that, as Wright Morris has written, "belongs on the shelf with the classical efforts man has made to chart the river Lethe from its mouth to its sources." Expressing richly the meaning of life in Harlem (and the southern background of that life), Ellison manages to describe what he says he finds in the work of the painter Romare Bearden: "the harlemness of the human condition." *Invisible Man* is a deeply comic novel, with moments of terror and tragedy; it is a *Bildungsroman* in which a young man awakens to consciousness by piecing together fragments and symbols from history, myth, folklore, and literature, as well as his own painful experience.

Set in the approximate period 1930–1950, *Invisible Man* is the story of the development of an ambitious black, a young man from the provinces of the South, who goes to college and then to New York in search of advancement. This greenhorn at first wants no more than to walk in the footsteps of Booker T. Washington, whose words he quotes at his high school graduation and at a smoker for the town's leading white citizens. At the smoker he is given a new briefcase and a scholarship, but is first required to fight blindfolded in a "battle royal" with other black youths. That night he dreams that his grandfather tells him to open the briefcase, which contains a document reading: "To Whom It May Concern, Keep This Nigger-Boy Running." But the youngster remains naive. He goes off to college but is expelled when he makes the fatal mistake of taking a visiting white trustee to a section of the local black community (and, metaphorically, to a level of black reality) never included in the college-town tour. Bledsoe, the college president, sends the hero packing to New York, first giving him a set of private letters of introduction that, he finally discovers, also courteously request that he be kept running—and jobless.

Eventually he does find work in New York, first in a paint factory, where he is discharged after being seriously hurt in an explosion—one that ultimately jars him into a new self-awareness and courage. He gives a moving speech at the eviction of an elderly Harlem couple and is hired by a predominantly white radical political organization called the Brotherhood. The group seems to confirm his childhood wish by telling him he will be made the "new Booker T. Washington . . . even greater than he." But the Brotherhood also sets him running. Despite his success in Harlem, the downtown "brothers" withdraw support for his program. A race riot erupts, and, still carrying his briefcase, which now contains, besides his diploma, several other mementoes of his adventures, he falls down a manhole into an abandoned, bricked-up cellar. There he closely examines the papers in his briefcase and realizes how fully he has been betrayed by those who had professed to help him. And yet he discovers too that not only "could you travel upward toward success but you could travel downwards as well." He will remain down there, bathed in stolen light from the power company, and in blues music; he will compose his memoirs in his hole at the edge of Harlem, in hibernation. "Please, a definition: A hibernation is a covert preparation for a more overt action." If others cannot or will not see him, he at least will see himself. His narrative, full of irony, insight, and fury, shows that he has attained full self-awareness—even a certain wisdom—and that he has been able to act, to write this stunning book.

The shape and style of *Invisible Man* bespeak its determination to step toward the universal through "the narrow door of the particular." The novel resounds with black folklore, in which, says Ellison, "we tell what Negro experience really is. We back away from the chaos of experience and from ourselves, and we depict the humor as well as the horror of our living. We project Negro life in a metaphysical perspective, and we have seen it with a complexity of vision that seldom gets into our writing." Blues, spirituals, sermons, tales, boasts, and other black American folk forms influence the characters, plot, and figurative language in this teeming novel. The striving young man is drawn toward the freedom of consciousness and conscience by the magic horns and voices of the folk. Nonetheless, he himself is never so much a blues hero or Bre'r Rabbit as he is like Bre'r Bear, outmaneuvered until the end by Bre'rs Fox and Dog—in his case Bledsoe; Brockway, the factory supervisor; and One-Eyed Jack, who recruits him for the Brotherhood. Like the befuddled butt of many a folktale, this young man seems determined to be somebody's greenhorn, somebody's fool.

The novel is built not only upon the foundation of black lore but also of black literature. It is a benchmark black novel that seems aware of the entire tradition of Afro-American letters. In it one overhears the black and white tricksters (slaves and slaveholders) of slave narrative locked in combat. One senses again the slaves'

desperate yearning for education, mobility, and individual and communal freedom. There are particularly strong echoes of works by W. E. B. Du Bois, James Weldon Johnson, Zora Neale Hurston, and Richard Wright, all of whom wrote fictional portraits of tragicomic characters, "articulate heroes" in search of broader freedom.

But the power of *Invisible Man* is more than that of a repository of black influences. As if in defiance of the single-minded critic, Ellison adapted symbolism and rhetorical strategy from any and every source he felt would enrich the texture and meaning of his work: Sophocles, Homer, Dostoevsky, Malraux, Joyce, and Freud all figure in *Invisible Man*. Some allusions and symbol clusters fade out like wistful jazz riffs; others recur and provide the novel with structure. But no single critical "method" can explain this capacious novel, which owes as much to the symbolist tradition of Melville and Hawthorne as it does to the vernacular tradition of Mark Twain and Hemingway. This is not a "realistic" novel or an understated "hard-boiled" novel, or a symbolist romance (it is not, in any case, to be *only* so categorized); instead, it is an epic novel of many voices, an experimental narrative constructed upon the author's mastery of American language: as he describes it, a

rich babel . . . a language full of imagery and gesture and rhetorical canniness . . . an alive language swirling with over three hundred years of American living, a mixture of the folk, the Biblical, the scientific, and the political. Slangy in one instance, academic in another, loaded poetically with imagery at one moment, mathematically bare of imagery in the next.

The Invisible Man embodies this confluence of traditions. He is a modern Odysseus, a latter-day Candide, a "black boy" comparable to Wright, a black and obscure Jude, a Yankee yokel, a minstrel endman. Of the several secondary characters who also embody a rich mixture of allusions, two stand out: Trueblood and Rinehart. Both are significant influences on the protagonist's growing awareness.

It is Trueblood, the sharecropper, whom the hero encounters when giving Mr. Norton, the white trustee, a tour of the college environs. "Half-consciously" the student drives over a hill into a section of the black community built during slavery and, at Norton's "excited command," stops in front of Trueblood's shack. Trueblood had, in earlier days, been invited to entertain white guests of the school, but no more: he has brought disgrace to the black community by impregnating his own daughter. "You have looked upon chaos and are not destroyed!" says Norton. "No suh! I feels all right," says Trueblood. Not just willingly but "with a kind of satisfaction and no trace of hesitancy or shame," Trueblood recites the exuberant tale of his forbidden act; it is a private performance for the student and Norton, whose face, at story's end, "had drained of color." Shaking, the white man gives the farmer a hundred-dollar banknote: "Please take this and buy the children some toys for me," the northern philanthropist says.

Rinehart enters the narrative late in the novel. To escape two followers of Ras, a black nationalist whose organization rivals the Brotherhood, the Invisible Man puts on glasses with lenses so dark that they appear black; he is immediately mistaken for Rinehart. "But ... where's your new hat I bought you?" a young woman asks. To complete his disguise he buys the widest white hat in stock at a local store and is mistaken for Rinehart all evening: Bliss Rinehart, gambler and pimp; Rine the lover and cool "daddy-o"; Rine the briber and "confidencing sonofabitch"; Rine the numbers runner; Reverend B. P. Rinehart, "Spiritual Technologist ... No Problem Too Hard For God."

The Invisible Man is stunned by Rinehart: "Could he himself be both rind and heart? What is real anyway? ... The world in which we lived was without boundaries. A vast seething, hot world of fluidity, and Rine the rascal was at home."

Trueblood and Rinehart make their homes in quite different worlds. Trueblood has remained in the South, in a log-cabin homestead dusty with slave history. By contrast, while Rinehart may once have preached in Virginia, he has become a master manipulator of a chaos that is distinctively northern in scope. Indeed, what these black men have most in common is that both have stood before teeming chaos and have survived. Rinehart has embraced chaos. Trueblood has faced his crime of incest—the sin associated with confusion, degeneracy, and death, from Sophocles' *Oedipus Rex* to Freud's *Totem and Taboo*.

Both characters bring to mind the Afro-American musical form, the blues. Trueblood has done wrong (but didn't mean to) and is bashed in the head by his wife, who leaves him for a time and spreads the tale of his wrongdoing until even the preacher calls him "the most wicked man" he has ever seen. Yet Trueblood tells his story until it achieves a certain cadence, and it ends with song. "Finally, one night, way early in the mornin', I looks up and sees the stars and I starts singin'. I don't mean to, I didn't think 'bout it, just start singin'. I don't know what it was, some kinda church song, I guess. All I know is I *ends up* singin' the blues. I sings me some blues that might ain't never been sang before, and while I'm singin' them blues I makes up my mind that I ain't nobody but myself and ain't nothin' I can do but let whatever is gonna happen, happen. I made up my mind that I was goin' back home...." Trueblood is what Albert Murray has called a "blues hero": a resilient improviser who confronts the low-down dirtiness of life, the "changes" and the "breaks," and who manages with style and grace to keep on keeping on.

Rinehart is no blues man in this broadly heroic sense. "Rinehart, Rinehart," thinks the Invisible Man, "what kind of man is Rinehart?" His name is a name from a blues song: "Rinehart, Rinehart, / It's so lonesome up here / On Beacon Hill. . . ." But instead of evoking terror or pity, instead of putting confusion into perspective, as does Trueblood, Rinehart personifies confusion. He is the no-good "sweet-back," the evil mistreater that the blues bemoan. Trueblood sings the blues as a cathartic statement to assuage a tragic predicament, but Rinehart dispenses the blues to others: he distributes travail and thrives off it.

Trueblood's classical ancestors include Oedipus the King, but Rinehart's forebears are shape-changers and tricksters. His middle name, Ellison has written, is Proteus.

Yet both characters capture the note and trick of Afro-American life and function in quite specific ways. Trueblood's tale is a lesson and a graphic warning, from which the Invisible Man learns that "there's always an element of crime in freedom." Trueblood's breaking of the incest taboo (even if, as he insists, he was asleep while doing so) suggests that the Invisible Man can also break the law and so extend the definition of what it means to be black and what it means to be human. Rinehart's lesson is that the world is much more ambiguous—and, again, full of possibility—than any narrow-minded, strict, schematic thinkers like the Brotherhood can know. "Underground" in Harlem there are operators undreamed of by One-Eyed Jack and his "brothers." Some, like the unscrupulous Rinehart, prosper in the dark maze. Others, like the "hip" young men the narrator sees in the subway station, have also been ignored by the Brotherhood. "Men out of time, who would soon be gone and forgotten. . . . But who knew but that they were

the saviors, the true leaders, the bearers of something precious? . . . What if history was a gambler, instead of a force in a laboratory experiment, and the boys his ace in the hole?" Rinehart the trickster is a figure of escape and of possibility whose presence suggests that beneath the surface of the American commonplace there burns a bright and raging world.

Invisible Man is a complex, ironic novel in which the hero discovers a great deal about American history and culture. In the end he sees that he has been a fool, that, like Trueblood and Rinehart, he must confront chaos or it will engulf him. When he plunges underground, he vows to stop running the course that Bledsoe and others had set for him and can say with Trueblood: "I ain't nobody but myself . . . I made up my mind that I was goin' back home."

Ellison's only book since *Invisible Man* has been the excellent collection of essays, *Shadow and Act* (1964). Its initial appeal seemed to be that in it the "invisible" author would at last emerge from underground: here, as one reviewer proclaimed, was Ralph Ellison's real autobiography." And *Shadow and Act* does contain autobiographical essays, notably its introduction and "Hidden Name and Complex Fate"; while in the reviews and interviews here collected the author also draws extensively upon his own experience. Because the essays (none retouched) were written over a twenty-two-year period, they reveal certain aspects of his development from the twenty-eight-year-old, Marxist-oriented WPA worker of "The Way It Is" (1942) to the seasoned writer of 1964: by the latter date he is not "primarily concerned with injustice, but with art."

In his introduction Ellison offers a sort of apologia, explaining that the essays "represent, in all their modesty, some of the necessary effort which a writer of my background must make in order to possess the meaning of his experience." When the first essay appeared, he tells us, he regarded himself "in my most secret heart at least [as] a musician," not a writer. "One might say that with these thin essays for wings," he notes, "I was launched full flight into the dark." Thus, "their basic significance, whatever their value as information or speculation, is autobiographical." Nonetheless, the book contains thematic unities that are even more compelling. A good deal of the cumulative power of *Shadow and Act* derives from its contrasting black American life as seen through the lenses of politics, sociology, and popular culture and as observed and lived by one sensitive, questioning man.

Shadow and Act has enduring validity as a unified work of art because of its author's single-minded intention to define Afro-American life. Ellison sometimes gently punctures, sometimes wields an ax against inadequate definitions of black experience. In place of what he detects as false prophecy, usually uttered by social scientists, he chooses as broad a frame of reference as possible to interpret black experience in richly optimistic terms. "Who wills to be a Negro?" he asks, rhetorically. "I do!"

Once Ellison had released the galley proofs for *Invisible Man*, he felt emotionally and artistically spent. But he had begun jotting down ideas for a new novel even before *Invisible Man* was published, so that if it failed he would be too busy to worry. In 1952 he said he had a new novel "on the bench." In 1953, shortly after the National Book Award ceremonies honoring *Invisible Man*, he suggested that his new novel might be an elaboration of the first. "I don't feel that I have exhausted the theme of invisibility," he said. Indeed he felt that he could salvage some material edited out of the several drafts of the novel. "Out of the Hospital and Under the Bar" (1953), an early version of a chapter in *Invisible Man*, works well as a short story, not as a mere clipping from the larger work; "Did You Ever Dream Lucky?" (1954) concerns

Mary Rambo, the novel's Harlem landlady. As early as 1953, however, Ellison had begun laying the structural framework for a totally new novel that he felt sure would be much better and more complex than *Invisible Man*. Since then Ellison has been stoking the fires of this new novel. Its eight published sections, along with sections read on public television and on college campuses, have made the wait for the finished volume—or volumes, as Ellison has tantalizingly suggested—something of a vigil.

In 1965 Ellison told an interviewer that he wanted to publish a book "in the coming year," adding, "so the pressure's on." Where is this long-promised novel? When he is at all willing to discuss its progress, Ellison recites the history of a wayward work, tedious in the initial construction and reconstruction; destroyed, in part, by fire; bedeviling in the re-reconstruction. In 1970 James McPherson noted that tales concerning the awaited novel were plentiful: "One man has heard that he has pulled it back from his publisher again for more revisions; another says that Ellison worries about its being dated; a third man says that Ellison cannot finish it." One explanation was heard from the writer's wife. "She says she heard him in his study at night turning pages and laughing to himself. He enjoys the book so much that he isn't in a hurry to share it with the public." Richard Kostelanetz reports that an old friend of Ellison's has said: "Ralph is insanely ambitious. He actually writes quickly but won't release this book until he is sure it is the greatest American novel ever written." Ellison refuses to publish more selections from the novel's current manuscript not only because he is "not so strapped for money that I have to publish those pieces" but also because he wants "the impact of the total book . . . rather than the published pieces." "Can you say when it will be finished?" an interviewer inquired in 1978. "No," responded Ellison, "I've done that too many times and been wrong."

The writing slowed to a baffled halt, for a time, after the hail of assassinations in the 1960's—President John F. Kennedy, Martin Luther King, Robert Kennedy. With the assassination of a major political figure as the novel's central incident, the eruption of real killings "chilled" Ellison, for "suddenly life was stepping in and imposing himself upon my fiction." Ellison's conviction that his new novel must somehow deal with these real assassinations kept the book in blueprint:

Much of the mood of this book was conceived as comic. Not that the assassination was treated comically, but there is humor involved.... Anyway, I managed to keep going with it . . . I know that it led me to try to give the book a richer structuring, so that the tragic elements could contain the comic and the comic the tragic, without violating our national pieties— if there are any left.

That Ellison was far out of step with the most vocal black ideologists of the 1960's also slowed his writing. When Haki Madhubuti (Don L. Lee), Amiri Baraka (LeRoi Jones), and other black writers and social critics were asserting the national identity and the Africanness of black Americans, Ellison stiffly dissented: "I'm not a separatist. The imagination is integrative. That's how you make the new—by putting something else with what you've got. And I'm unashamedly an American integrationist." At Oberlin in April 1969 Ellison was given a brittle reception by black students, one of whom complained: "His speech was about how American black culture had blended into American white culture." Ellison had noted, for example, that the Afro hairstyle had become "a part of American popular culture" and warned the black students not to be surprised if whites began to adopt it. "The students went out screaming," a young woman recalled. "Who is he to insult what we wear? No honky could wear an Afro.

They're stealing what is ours." At a meeting after the speech, the black students said, "You don't have anything to tell us." One student said of *Invisible Man:* "Your book doesn't mean anything, because in it you're shooting down Ras the Destroyer, a rebel leader of black people." Ellison said that the book was written a long time ago but that he would not apologize for it, to which the student answered, "That just proves you're an Uncle Tom."

At Harvard in December 1973 Ellison spoke about the philosopher Alain Locke as a champion of American pluralism. By then the mood on campus had changed. There were awkward silences when Ellison told the gathering that blacks are not an African people but an American one; yet the final applause was enthusiastic. At that point Ellison appeared to have weathered the radical tempest. By 1980 he could look back on those difficult days with irony, defensive pride, and some anger. Of those who contributed strident attacks to a special Ellison issue of *Black World,* a defunct black journal, Ellison has said.

Safe behind the fence provided by a black capitalist, they had one big "barking-at-the-big-gate" go at me. They even managed to convince a few students that I was the worst disaster that had ever hit Afro-American writing. But for all their attacks I'm still here trying—while if I'm asked where is *Black World* today my answer is: Gone with the snows of yester-year / down the pissoir—Da-Daa, Da-Daaa—and good riddance!

In Richard Kostelanetz's words, "One reason Ellison has not been able to complete his second novel is that all these distractions demand so much of his attention, as much to flush the ideological junk out of his own head as to speak about corruption in the social world." Black writers, Kostelanetz comments, seem to have a harder role to play than do white writers because blacks are cornered into commenting on sociopolitical issues that white writers can avoid.

As if these deflections were not enough, in the late 1960's Ellison's summer home in Massachusetts was destroyed by fire, as were 365 pages of the new novel, an entire year's revisions. "I assure you, that's a most traumatic experience," he recalled, "one of the most traumatic of my life!" The writer Jervis Anderson has noted:

Perhaps nothing more painful occurred in the working life of a well-known writer since Thomas Carlyle lost the manuscript of the first volume of his history of the French Revolution, a servant in the home of John Stuart Mill having used it to help get a fire going. Carlyle is said to have sat down, with astonishing calmness, and reproduced what he had lost. Ellison found it difficult to begin the task of restructuring, rewriting, and recapturing the fluid composition and insights of the first draft. The subtleties and rhythms of a first inspiration are almost impossible to reclaim. But if it is at all possible to overcome these problems, then Ellison, with his belief that difficult circumstances can almost always be made to yield benefits and victories, is the sort of writer to do it.

Like most of his earlier fiction, the new work is experimental: now familiar, focused, compelling; now ill-lit, uncertain, frightening. "The new book's form," explains Ellison, is "a realism extended beyond realism." This is "a crazy book, and I won't pretend to understand what it's about. I do think," he adds, "there are some funny passages in it." The mixture of allusions is characteristic; images and narrative strategies echo Joyce and Faulkner especially, as well as classical and religious myth. And as in *Invisible Man,* popular American sources also energize the narrative: "I use anything from movies to comic strips," he says. "Anything: radio, sermons, practical jokes. In fact anything that suggests new ideas for handling narrative; even jazz riffs." Startling shifts in point of view change the shape of events in sometimes surprising ways: everything depends on whether we view the action through the Reverend Hickman (black blues musician turned evangelist, whose voice and eloquence have earned him the nickname "God's Trombone"); Bliss (Hickman's adopted son, a boy preacher who abandons his calling, disappears, passes for white, and emerges as Senator Sunraider, the venomously antiblack representative from Massachusetts); McIntyre (naive but sincere white reporter); Lee Willie Minifees (jazz musician who, enraged at Sunraider's racism, burns his gleaming Cadillac on the senator's lawn); or Cliofus (stuttering man-child with a terrifyingly clear memory and a way with words). Thrust into the realm of such tales as "And Hickman Arrives," "Night-Talk," "Juneteenth," "Cadillac Flambé," "Backwacking," "The Roof, the Steeple and the People," "It Always Breaks Out," "A Song of Innocence"—stories told as letters, fuzzy musings, tirades, sermons, or lies—the reader is forced to confront questions that Ellison says issue from the heart of America's condition as a nation still unformed. Where, what, who am I? What is illusion, what is real? What is black, what is white, what is American?

This is fiction scored for many voices. In the 1920's, working the southern revival circuit, the Reverend Hickman and the Reverend Bliss deliver the dialogue sermon published as "Juneteenth." Blending with his mentor's trombone voice, Bliss's voice is a clear piccolo. The two trade phrases about the losses sustained by blacks during slavery, and the tragic recital swerves at comedy's edge as Bliss says:

. . . Amen, Daddy Hickman! Abused and without shoes, pounded down and ground like grains

of sand on the shores of the sea ...
... Amen [Hickman answers] And God—
Count it, Rev. Bliss ...
... Left eyeless [Bliss responds] earless, nose-
less, throatless, teethless, tongueless, handless,
feetless, armless, wrongless, rightless, ... motherless, fatherless, sisterless, brotherless, plow-
less, muleless, foodless, mindless—and Godless,
Rev. Hickman, did you say Godless?

Even so, laments Hickman. But in this sermon of redemption, blacks are shown stripped
of African culture—but are reborn as Afro-
Americans, tempered for struggle in this land
of trouble and sacrifice. The trombone enters
Hickman's voice as he says:

Ah, but though divided and scattered, ground
down and battered into the earth like a spike
being pounded by a ten-pound sledge, we were
on the ground and in the earth and the earth
was red and black like the earth of Africa. And
as we moldered underground we were mixed
with this land. We liked it. It fitted us fine. It
was in us and we're in it. And then—praise
God—deep in the ground, deep in the womb of
this land, we began to stir!

Between sermons, Bliss chats with his friend
Body, who swears he has sat in a dark room and
watched white men and "hosses" and an entire
railroad train shine out of a black box and move
around on a glistening screen. The little
preacher, who has never seen a movie, shakes
his head and warns Body about the sin of false
witness; but Body, speaking a broad vernacular,
stings Bliss with a warning of his own:

... dont come preaching me no sermon. Cause
you know I can kick your butt. I dont have to
take no stuff off you. This here aint no Sunday,
no how. Can't nobody make me go to church on
no Friday, cause on a Friday I'm liable to boot
a preacher's behind until his nose bleeds....

That's the truth, Rev, and you know the truth
is what the Lord loves.

In Ellison's new fiction, antagonists include
elementary-school principal Dr. Peter Osgood
Eliot, "who usually looked no more human than
a granite general astride a concrete horse," and
school disciplinarian the Reverend Blue Goose
Samson, "with his well-stropped head," who,
informed of trouble, comes to class "dragging
half a tree limb behind him" to whip the offender along with "all the boys in the first five
rows." The teacher is Miss Mabel Kindly.
"What's the difference," she quizzes her scholars,"between a multplier and a multiplicand?"
On a field trip to view the remains of a whale,
she is ultraproper in manners and enunciation:
"The whale, chill-dreen, is an ani-mule." Small
wonder Cliofus dislikes school and prefers the
easing music and language of distant, highball-
ing trains:

Miss Janey's right, though [he reflects]; those
trains ease me.—Eeeeease me! What I mean is,
they ease my aching mind. When I watch those
engines and boxcars and gondolas I start to
moving up and down in my body's joy and when
I see those drivers start to roll, all those words
go jumping out to them like the swine in the
Bible that leaped off the cliff into the sea—only
they hop on the Katy, the Rock Island and the
Santa Fe.... Space, time and distance, like
they say, I'm a yearning man who has to sit still.
Maybe those trains need those words to help
them find their way across this here wide land
in the dark, I don't know. But for me it's like
casting bread on the water because not only am
I eased in my restless mind, but once in a while,
deep in the night, when everything is quiet and
all those voices and words are resting and all
those things that I've been tumbling and running and bouncing through my mind all day
have got quiet as a ship in a bottle on a shelf,
then I can hear those train whistles talking to

me, just to me, and in those times I know I have all in this world I'll ever need mama and papa and jellyroll. . . .

It is a similarly innocent boy, Severen, who by the 1950's has grown up to stand in the gallery of the Senate and to gun down Sunraider. Bliss/Sunraider is also from the South—his white-black, sacred-secular, revival-sideshow, city-country, downside-up boyhood eventually driving him to insulate himself behind the alabaster walls of jingoism and white-is-rightness. The novelist Leon Forrest has said that Bliss/Sunraider emerges as "something of a brutalized metaphor himself of what happened to the baby democracy, tossed from hand to hand and born out of wedlock (*à la* Fielding's Tom Jones, to say nothing of some of the leading people in the U.S.)." In Ellison's vision, America is a 200-year-old child, a strangely wrinkled baby, a Bliss destined to choose among heritages.

Some of Ellison's detractors charge that he dotes on the complexity of American experience in order to avoid speaking out against simple injustice; that he hides behind the grand banner of high art rather than "telling it like it is." He believes that the American melting pot has in fact melted and that blacks are as American— in some ways more so—as any Johnny Appleseed. This conviction, some critics say, obscures the fact that black Americans constitute a distinctive group with particular strengths as well as special troubles. As for Ellison's "complexity," it is part and parcel of his discipline as a writer. It is the novelist in him that insists on asking such bothersome questions as, "What, by the way, is one to make of a white youngster who, with a transistor radio, screaming a Stevie Wonder tune, glued to his ear, shouts racial epithets at black youngsters trying to swim at a public beach—and this in the name of the ethnic sanctity of what has been declared a neighborhood turf?" Ellison told a Harvard gather-

ing in 1973: "All of us are part white, and all of y'all are part colored." The novelist also insists on the cruel and tragic aspects of American comedy, on the blues side of black religion, on the upper-class elegance of the black poor, on the universality of what Ellison still calls "Negro" experience, and on the "harlemness" of the human condition.

Many of Ellison's critics do not know that he was a left-wing critic and author for the *New Masses* and an advocate of black nationalism who has done his share of political stumping. Even now, Ellison maintains that writing novels is bound up with the process of nation-building: rediscovering, redefining, revitalizing America. The critic Kimberly W. Benston has observed that although their conclusions are often at odds, Ellison and Baraka have much more in common than is usually noticed. Both are concerned with various, crisscrossing lines of tradition that inform peculiarly Afro-American "responses to life"; both have looked upon an American scene marbled with ambiguity and contradiction and have sought "strategies for saving and improving the best aspects of the black self." Both see clearly that in the melting pot are ingredients unmistakably and magnificently black.

In fact, with Baraka and Richard Wright, Ellison has been the most eloquent and influential spokesman for what, "on the lower frequencies" (Ellison's phrase), it means to be black and American. In Ellison's work one finds penetrating and yet lyrical descriptions of black life, insider's rare perceptions of the contour and meaning of a peculiarly American experience. Greater than these other writers is Ellison's sense of America's confusion and of the bleakly tragic barriers (underrated by most conservatives, liberals, and revolutionaries alike) against which we all struggle. Greater, too, is his faith in America's possibility of redemption and his awareness of the difficulty of securing true redemption from that most American sin, vanity. "Remember," he told a graduating class in 1974, "that the antidote to *hubris,* to overweening pride, is irony, that capacity to discover and systematize ideas. Or, as Emerson insisted, the development of consciousness, consciousness, *Consciousness.* And with consciousness, a more refined conscientiousness, and most of all, that tolerance which takes the form of humor." With his unfailing humor and tragic awareness, Ralph Ellison is an important voice in American fiction, a "man of good hope" whose work bespeaks his dedication to artistic craft and to the idea that writers are among America's most vital nation-builders.

Selected Bibliography

WORKS OF RALPH ELLISON

BOOKS
Invisible Man. New York: Random House, 1952.
Shadow and Act. New York: Random House, 1964.

SHORT FICTION
"Slick Gonna Learn." *Direction,* 2:10–11, 14, 16 (September 1939).
"The Birthmark." *New Masses,* 36:16–17 (July 2, 1940).
"Afternoon." In *American Writing,* edited by Hans Otto Storm et al. Prairie City, Ill.: J. A. Decker, 1940. Pp. 28–37.
"Mister Toussan." *New Masses,* 41:19–20 (November 4, 1941).
"That I Had the Wings." *Common Ground,* 3:30–37 (Summer 1943).
"In a Strange Country." *Tomorrow,* 3:41–44 (July 1944).
"King of the Bingo Game." *Tomorrow,* 4:29–33 (November 1944).
"Flying Home." In *Cross Section,* edited by Edwin Seaver. New York: L. B. Fischer, 1944. Pp. 469–485.
"Did You Ever Dream Lucky?" *New World Writing,* 5:134–145 (April 1954).
"February." *Saturday Review,* 38:25 (January 1, 1955).
"A Coupla Scalped Indians." *New World Writing,* 9:225–236 (1956).
"And Hickman Arrives." *Noble Savage,* 1:5–49 (1960).
"The Roof, the Steeple and the People." *Quarterly Review of Literature,* 10:115–128 (1960).
"Out of the Hospital and Under the Bar." In *Soon, One Morning,* edited by Herbert Hill. New York: Knopf, 1963. Pp. 242–290.
"It Always Breaks Out." *Partisan Review,* 30:13–28 (Spring 1963).
"Juneteenth." *Quarterly Review of Literature,* 13:262–276 (1965).
"Night-Talk." *Quarterly Review of Literature,* 16:317–329 (1969).
"A Song of Innocence." *Iowa Review,* 1:30–40 (Spring 1970).
"Cadillac Flambé." *American Review,* 16:249–269 (February 1973).
"Backwacking, a Plea to the Senator." *Massachusetts Review,* 18:411–416 (Autumn 1977).

SELECTED ESSAYS AND REVIEWS
"Creative and Cultural Lag." *New Challenge,* 2:90–91 (Fall 1937).
"Stormy Weather." *New Masses,* 37:20–21 (September 24, 1940).
"Recent Negro Fiction." *New Masses,* 40:22–26 (August 5, 1941).
"Collaborator with His Own Enemy." *New York Times Book Review,* February 19, 1950, p. 4.
"Society, Morality, and the Novel." In *The Living Novel: A Symposium,* edited by Granville Hicks. New York: Macmillan, 1957. Pp. 58–91.
"What These Children Are Like." In Seminar on Education for Culturally Different Youth, *Education of the Deprived and Segregated.* New York: Bank Street College of Education, 1965.
"Tell It Like It Is, Baby." *Nation,* 201: 129–136 (September 20, 1965).
"The Novel as a Function of American Democracy." *Wilson Library Bulletin,* 41:1022–1027 (June 1967).

"What America Would Be Like Without Blacks." *Time,* 95:54–55 (April 6, 1970).

"The Little Man at Chehaw Station." *American Scholar,* 47:25–48 (Winter 1977–1978).

BIOGRAPHICAL AND CRITICAL STUDIES

Anderson, Jervis. "Going to the Territory." *New Yorker,* 52:55–108 (November 22, 1976).

Baker, Houston. *Long Black Song: Essays in Black American Literature and Culture.* Charlottesville: University Press of Virginia, 1972.

Benston, Kimberly W. "Ellison, Baraka, and the Faces of Tradition." *boundary 2,* 6:333–354 (Winter 1978).

Blake, Susan L. "Ritual and Rationalization: Black Folklore in the Works of Ralph Ellison." *PMLA,* 94:121–136 (January 1979).

Callahan, John F. "The Historical Frequencies of Ralph Waldo Ellison." In *Chant of Saints,* edited by Michael S. Harper and Robert B. Stepto. Urbana: University of Illinois Press, 1979. Pp. 33–52.

College Language Association. *CLA Journal,* 13 (March 1970); special Ellison issue.

Covo, Jacqueline. *The Blinking Eye: Ralph Waldo Ellison and His American, French, German and Italian Critics, 1952–1971.* Metuchen, N. J.: Scarecrow Press, 1974.

Davis, Arthur P. *From the Dark Tower.* Washington, D. C.: Howard University Press, 1974.

Gibson, Donald B., ed. *Five Black Writers: Essays on Wright, Ellison, Baldwin, Hughes, and LeRoi Jones.* New York: New York University Press, 1970.

Hersey, John, ed. *Ralph Ellison, a Collection of Critical Essays.* Englewood Cliffs, N. J.: Prentice-Hall, 1974.

Kazin, Alfred. *Bright Book of Life.* New York: Dell, 1971.

Kent, George. *Blackness and the Adventure of American Culture.* Chicago: Third World, 1972.

Kist, E. M. "A Laingian Analysis of Blackness in Ralph Ellison's *Invisible Man.*" *Studies in Black Literature,* 7:19–23 (Spring 1976).

Kostelanetz, Richard. "Ralph Ellison: Novelist as Brown Skinned Aristocrat." *Shenandoah,* 20, no. 4: 56–77 (Summer 1969).

Murray, Albert. *The Omni-Americans.* New York: Outerbridge and Dienstfrey, 1970.

Nash, Russell W. "Stereotypes and Social Types in Ellison's *Invisible Man.*" *Sociological Quarterly,* 6:349–360 (Autumn 1965).

O'Meally, Robert G. *The Craft of Ralph Ellison.* Cambridge, Mass.: Harvard University Press, 1980.

Reilly, John M., ed. *Twentieth Century Interpretations of Invisible Man: A Collection of Essays.* Englewood Cliffs, N. J.: Prentice-Hall, 1970.

Scott, Nathan A., Jr. "Black Literature." In *Harvard Guide to Contemporary American Writing,* edited by Daniel Hoffman. Cambridge, Mass.: Harvard University Press, 1979. Pp. 287–341.

Stepto, Robert B. *From Behind the Veil: A Study of Afro-American Narrative.* Urbana: University of Illinois Press, 1979.

Tischler, Nancy M. "Negro Literature and Classic Form." *Contemporary Literature,* 10:352–365 (Summer 1969).

—ROBERT O'MEALLY

Philip Freneau

1752—1832

*P*HILIP FRENEAU'S friends and enemies recognized him as the spokesman for some of the dominant impulses of their age. In 1771, while a student at the College of New Jersey (now Princeton University), he spoke for the cultural aspirations of his fellow students in "The Rising Glory of America," a poem written with Hugh Henry Brackenridge that predicted that leadership in the arts would someday come to America. During the war, Freneau was the "poet of the American Revolution" to his contemporaries. His poems of battles on land and sea commemorated American heroism and memorialized the dead. After the Revolution, Freneau spoke for the disillusion of many Americans, warning in his poetry and prose that the principles of the Revolution could be lost in ambition, avarice, and corruption. "That rascal Freneau," as George Washington called him, outspokenly attacked entrenched power and defended the common man, opposing privilege of every sort.

Despite his influence, Freneau's readers did not consider him a great writer, and history has not redeemed his reputation. His contemporaries did not value romantic poems like "The Wild Honey Suckle," which is now considered his best work. Modern readers dismiss most of the satires and poems of action that Freneau's audience liked. Even Moses Coit Tyler, Harry Hayden Clark, and Fred Lewis Pattee, who attempted to gain recognition for Freneau's "true merit," did not rate him very highly; and Lewis Leary's assessment in *That Rascal Freneau* (1941), that the poet's life and work are a study in "literary failure," has endured. Most of Freneau's work remains the concern only of literary historians and antiquarians.

But the contemporary reader should not dismiss Freneau too hastily. He introduced much that is central to the development of American letters. He wrote during a period in the nation's intellectual life when it had begun to establish its cultural as well as political independence. For Freneau, cultural independence meant the creation of a new kind of artist and a new literature: a "democratic" artist who was both an ordinary member of society and a spokesman for it; and an "American" literature that focused on native materials and had an independent aesthetic—one that could give expression to the ideals of the new republic. In short, when Freneau began writing he envisioned no less than the creation of a literary New Jerusalem in America.

Not surprisingly, Freneau's life and work have the excitement, but also the lack of finish, of the innovator and the experimenter. He was in and out of a dozen careers as he tried to find his place as a man of letters. He experimented with innumerable forms of expression—from the lyric poem to the journalistic essay—as he attempted to speak for the new society. In the midst of his many failures, he produced much that was successful: important poems and essays that are part of the shape of American literature. His work also is of historical importance, capturing the changing tones of the Revolutionary period. He is, in sum, a writer whose life and work reflect the ideas and sense of mission of his time, and one who moved American letters firmly in the direction of independence.

Philip Morin Fresneau (the "s" was dropped at the death of his father) was born on January 2, 1752, in New York City, the first child of Pierre and Agnes Watson Fresneau. He grew up with two sisters and a younger brother in comfortable circumstances, the family having established itself in commerce and land investment in New York and New Jersey after the arrival from France in 1707 of André Fresneau, Philip's grandfather. Freneau's boyhood was spent in school in New York City and on the family estate at Mount Pleasant, near Middletown Point, in Monmouth County, New Jersey. He studied Latin and Greek and read widely in the family's large library. In addition, he had numerous opportunities to meet leaders of commerce and culture who were friends of his father. But his father's death, in October 1767, marked the end of this period of relative peace and of the family's financial security.

In November 1768, intending to prepare for the ministry, Freneau entered Princeton, where John Witherspoon, a moderate Calvinist of the Scottish commonsense school of philosophy, was president. Witherspoon believed that educated men should lead society to improvement through appeals to "the simple perceptions of common sense," the ability to "sense" the truth that all people, to some degree, share and that is "the foundation of all reasoning." Students learned leadership and trained in the methods of commonsense reasoning through daily exercises in declamation. At these sessions students expounded on many topics, but most frequently they discussed the political issues related to American independence. Freneau soon found himself deeply involved in these exercises and in political activity, declaring himself staunchly in favor of Americans' rights as free men. He especially admired the Reverend John Livingston's essays dealing with the "inestimable value of liberty." Inspired by Livingston's views, Freneau, together with his friends James Madison, Hugh Henry Brackenridge, and William Bradford, and using Livingston's "American Whig" pseudonym, formed the American Whig Society. Its purpose was to rival the Tory Cliosophic Society.

In the ensuing quarrel between the American Whigs and the Tory Cliosophics, Freneau discovered an interest in political writing and a talent for invective and partisan debate. He threw himself into the quarrel with the Cliosophics, writing satires designed to "dash the proud Tory in his gilded car." His efforts culminated in a jumbled satiric novel, *Father Bombo's Pilgrimage to Mecca* (completed in 1770, but not published until 1975), written jointly with Brackenridge. Satirizing the Tories at the college and burlesquing the intellectual pretension, inhumanity, and social instability of American society, the work—coarse, crude, and unfocused as it was—did capture the antiauthoritarianism, quarrelsomeness, and insecurity of the age.

Under Witherspoon's influence at Princeton, Freneau also took up the study of belles lettres. He learned that the cultivation of "taste" was important to the moral and social improvement of individuals and societies. Literature made an immediate "impression on the mind" and so raised the moral and intellectual sensibility of the audience. The classics were fundamental and he read Xenephon, Homer, Cicero, Vergil, and Horace—many of whose poems he later translated. He also read the English writers, concentrating on William Shakespeare, John Milton, John Dryden, Samuel Butler, Joseph Addison, Jonathan Swift, and Alexander Pope.

Freneau was impressed with what he read. But in the climate of Princeton with its debates on "independence," he believed that America could develop a literature of its own. As he and his fellow Whigs perceived it, culture was on the move westward. It had traveled from Greece and Rome through Europe and Britain and would soon find a home in the New World. The literature growing out of this cultural movement would deal with American values and material and would express America's commitment to reason, liberty, and the rights of man. It would also capture the great moments in American history, moments that in drama and significance had as much to offer the writer as any events in Europe's past.

Freneau's first attempt to translate the idea of an "American" literature into a poem was "Columbus to Ferdinand" (1770), a very imaginative evocation of Columbus' mood as he prepared to set sail for the New World. Freneau was fascinated with the discovery of America and with Columbus' venture into the unknown. In Freneau's mind, it was the great demonstration of the power of reason to bring about human progress. Columbus was the hero of this enterprise, and Freneau believed that he had never been given due credit for his explorations. (In recognition of Columbus' achievement, Freneau regularly used the term "Columbia" in referring to his country, rather than the more common "America.") In this poem Columbus, led by his desire to know something more of "this huge globe," begs Ferdinand to let him sail west. He knows that reason (which in Freneau's poetry is usually associated with responsibility, discovery, society, and philosophy) will

protect him from danger: he "dreads no tempests on the untravell'd deep, / Reason shall steer, and shall disarm the gale." Reason also leads the way, finally, to America "the mighty land."

Even as he focused on American themes, however, Freneau recognized that before America could have its own belles lettres, it had to appreciate the power of the beautiful and the legitimacy of the merely fanciful. As Freneau well knew, most Americans had a deep distrust of any writing that lacked a purpose or a moral, believing it to be frivolous and even immoral. A Protestant by training who appreciated Witherspoon's form of Calvinism with its highly moral and socially committed view of life, and also a follower of Enlightenment philosophy, with its belief in the power of reason to resolve problems, Freneau was aware that there was little in either of these practical systems of thought that left room or toleration for the purely sensual, strange, or beautiful—qualities that for Freneau were the essence of poetry.

Although he never developed an argument defending the purely aesthetic in poetry, Freneau showed his perception of the problem in "The Power of Fancy," the most skillful of his college poems and the first of its kind in American literature. Reflecting the "graveyard school" of the English poets Edward Young, Thomas Gray, and Mark Akenside in its macabre depiction of night life, the poem is nevertheless original in portraying Fancy as that quality of the Divine Mind which allowed it to create the universe, "this globe, these lands, and seas." Fancy is also one of the products of Divine Reason, although it has a will of its own. It is a "wakeful, vagrant, restless thing" that leads the speaker to the far reaches of the sun and stars, to the "prison of the fiends," and to "good and fair" Belinda's tomb. With its associations of escape, illusion, isolation, and death, Fancy is a powerful, attractive force, responsible, the speaker asserts, for "half my happiness below."

Freneau, with his interests in politics and writing, had a productive and satisfying life at Princeton, and despite the threat of impending war, he and his classmates were for the most part optimistic. Witherspoon and the Princeton faculty had imbued them with an idealism toward America and its mission as the beacon of liberty and the land of free and equal men, and they fully expected to contribute to its future. Freneau and Brackenridge captured this spirit in "The Rising Glory of America," a poem written for the 1771 commencement. Expressing the Scottish moral-philosophical view that the human race was progressing toward a "millenium" where "Paradise anew shall flourish, by no second Adam lost," the poets hail America as "the best of climes," where the arts and science would thrive. Here would be a land "by freedom blest and richly stor'd with all the luxuries." It was a hope that—for Freneau at least—never quite fulfilled its promise.

Freneau graduated from Princeton in 1771 with a love of poetry and politics but with little idea of what he was going to do with his life. The family circumstances were straitened, and he needed to earn his living. In April 1772 he began to teach school at "Flatbush on Long Island," but was so unhappy and unsuccessful that he left after two weeks, arousing the anger of his students' fathers, who, he wrote to Madison, "swore that if I was caught in New York they would either Trounce or maim me." He also contemplated turning "quack," or entering the ministry, which at one point he described as the "study of nothing." Indeed, little would satisfy him but the writing of poetry, and in 1772 he tried to establish himself as a poet with the publication of *The American Village,* a short collection of four poems. The publication was not successful. Describing the experience to Madison, Freneau wrote, "as to the main poem,

it is damned by all good and judicious judges and my name is on the title page, this is called Vanity by some—but 'who is so fond as youthful bards of fame?'"

But Freneau's expression of failure was ill-founded and premature. Indeed, his writing was at a definitive and formative stage. During this period, which lasted from approximately 1771 to 1776, he remained faithful to his desire to form an American literature made out of American materials, giving expression in his poetry to the emotional, political, and philosophical currents of his age. *The American Village* was one such attempt. In these poems he had tried to show aspects of the life of the ordinary American, whose common sense and independence were to form the backbone of the new nation. With his almost Puritan recognition of human evil and weakness, the picture Freneau gave was not overly idealistic. It was, rather, a varied and often a humorous one.

Most important, the volume contains "The American Village," which, despite its dependence on Oliver Goldsmith's *The Deserted Village* (1770) and Alexander Pope's *Windsor Forest* (1713), is noteworthy in its expression of American feelings about primitive life, nature, and the rural tradition. This 450-line adaptation of pastoralism to the American scene sounds the note of conflict between the requirements of peace and contemplation and "cities and the noisy throng" that still resounds in American writing. It also expresses longings for simplicity and escape from care (the same vein that Longfellow was to tap so successfully a century later), which Freneau believed could be found in the rural life. Thus, unlike Goldsmith's poem, which laments the passing of the country village with the coming of industry to England, Freneau's poem celebrates the presence of the rural tradition in America. The country village provides peace and solid comfort, reflecting the prosperity of a predominantly agricultural land.

It is a place where a man might pass "the slow circle of a harmless life." But this pastoralism is not unqualified. Perfect peace exists only in the imagination because men spoil everything with which they come into contact. Echoing Pope, the speaker remarks that "Men are more fierce, more terrible" than beasts of prey. Realizing this, he longs to be rid of his "distressful years" with "not one comfort left but poetry." Nevertheless, the poem ends with the speaker accepting his life, but turning away from the pastoral in search of "new scenes" to occupy his mind.

In his poetry Freneau also gave expression to the political developments of the period. A libertarian with a hatred of monarchy, special privilege, organized religion, and any other means by which, he believed, the few sought to control the behavior of the many, he violently opposed the British, who, with their "vile despotic sway" employed all these methods of tyranny. In Freneau's view, they supported pride and privilege, vaunted their culture, manners, and religious institutions, while heartlessly destroying American liberty and peace. In particular, they had betrayed the American colonies by refusing to grant them the rights accorded to Englishmen.

In July 1775, when the British began the siege of Boston, Freneau responded with a series of patriotic poems supporting American resistance. In these poems he is the "modern poet," not the pastoral one, and his angry tone is full of righteous indignation. After furiously cataloguing British offenses in the earliest of these poems, "A Political Litany," he concludes that Britain may "be damned" for all he cares. More somberly, in "American Liberty," his anger is compounded with the awareness that British treachery will cost American lives. Even as he is shocked that "Britons of old renown'd" can descend to "enslave their brethren in a foreign land," he calls for brave men to "warm in the cause of Boston's hapless town" and "shew the world America can bleed."

Although the patriotic verses are blunt efforts in a propaganda war rather than distinguished poetry, they establish Freneau as one of the most capable satirists of the pre-Revolutionary period, and they convey vividly the outrage and anger of the Americans. Three of the most effective poems are "General Gage's Soliloquy," "The Midnight Consultations," and "General Gage's Confession," which satirize the British through techniques of ridicule and irony that Pope had made famous in *The Rape of the Lock* (1712) and *The Dunciad* (1728). John Burgoyne, whose plays and verse ridiculing the Americans were so dislikable in their assumption of British cultural superiority, receives special attention in "The Midnight Consultations":

Is he to conquer—he subdue our land?—
This buckram hero, with his lady's hand?
By Cesars to be vanquished is a curse,
But by a scribbling fop—by heaven, is worse!

As in *The Dunciad,* the British and Tory speakers in these poems reveal their own vileness. They confess that they act out of "ambition," "thirst for power," and desire for "a place in fame's proud temple." But they are cowards who let the common soldiers take the responsibility for the murder of Americans. Thomas Gage, responsible for the siege of Boston, has finally had enough. In "General Gage's Confession," which deals with his recall to Britain, he confesses to a friar who absolves him of his sins, saying "hell, you know, is only for the poor." Gage, his conscience finally awakened, dismisses the friar's "holy whining" and rejects the absolution. He compares himself to Pontius Pilate: "Tho' he confess'd and wash'd his hands beside, / His heart condemn'd him and the monster dy'd."

In addition to *The American Village* and his

political verses, Freneau wrote many other poems during this period, most of which he did not publish until after the war. In their imaginativeness, use of American materials, and concentrated expression of the emotions of the revolutionary period, these poems represent his most significant contribution to pre-Revolutionary American letters. For the most part they express the negative feelings about the upcoming war that a jingoistic nation moving inexorably toward revolution was reluctant to recognize. The poems also are personal, reflecting Freneau's knowledge that the war meant inevitable sacrifice and suffering, and the possible interruption of his career. Such a poem is "The Dying Elm," which, as Richard Vitzthum has shown, indirectly expresses in restrained, melancholy tones, the sense that the heat of the world can destroy the poet's creativity. The elm, "companion of unsocial care," provides the speaker with "shades and love-sick whispers." If it fades "like angry Jonah's gourd at Nineveh" the speaker "thro' vehemence of heat" might, "like Jonah, wish to die." The same theme and mood inform "The Vernal Ague," in which the speaker complains that his traditional escapes into the "groves of half distinguish'd light" have "lost their charms." He prays for renewal "o'er the features of the mind" before "endless winter chills the soul."

Other poems examine the premises on which the nation was founded and show that there was something tainted in the very source of its life. The nation started in violence, and that seems to be its heritage. In "Discovery," Columbus and his men keep looking for "new seas to vanquish, and new worlds to find"; but also "rove to conquer what remains unknown," spreading corruption and war, the "sad records of our world's disgrace." In "The Pictures of Columbus, the Genoese," Columbus—with the best of motives—nevertheless brings tragedy to the New World. He travels to understand "Nature's bold design," to find "worlds yet unthought of," and to sail "far away beyond the reach of men," but his sponsors and fellow travelers are corrupt and greedy. Columbus realizes this when he lands at Cat Island, where he sees at first "sweet sylvan scenes of innocence and ease." Here "God and nature reign; / Their works unsullied by the hands of men." But soon he comes upon the body of a native who has been murdered by the sailors for what they thought was gold in his teeth. Columbus, disillusioned, cries, "Is this the fruit of my discovery! / If the first scene is murder, what shall follow / But havock, slaughter, chains and devastation. . . ." Sorrowfully, Columbus continues his explorations and ultimately returns to Spain, where he meets disgrace and oblivion, hoping that "freedom" will someday rise on the "plains" that he has discovered—he who "lived to find new worlds for thankless kings."

In other poems Freneau questions the idealism of the Americans. Are they any different or better than other people? The answer is pessimistic in two poems written in the fall of 1775, "The Distrest Shepherdess" and "Female Frailty" (later entitled "Mars and Hymen"). Lacking in patriotic sentiment or moral indignation, these cold-blooded portraits of women's faithlessness make clear that some Americans had not become moral or heroic simply by virtue of being at war with the British. In both poems women lament the deaths of their soldier-lovers, who have been fighting the British in Canada. Mariana, the distressed shepherdess, is angry about her lover's "madness" in leaving her and, after reciting her grievances, concludes "Here's Billy O'Bluster—I love him as well." Lucinda, in "Female Frailty," is angry that her Damon, "with his soldiers, went strutting away." Thyrsis, who is not in uniform, successfully talks her out of her grief and wins her hand; he has, she notes, "all I wish for, but the *lace*."

Like his fellow Americans, Freneau knew that war would bring death and devastation to the land and, like them, he did not express his fear of suffering and death openly. However, he indirectly made his feelings clear in "The House of Night," which could have been written only by someone who had suffered through deep conflict about the war. Although influenced by the poems of the English "graveyard school," particularly Young's *The Complaint, or Night Thoughts on Life, Death, and Immortality* (1742–1745), the poem is very much an American product, imaginatively exploring the impulses and fears that beset Freneau and his fellow countrymen as war impended. The poem, which Lewis Leary calls "certainly the finest poem written and published by an American during the time of the Revolution, and probably the finest written and published anywhere during these years," is a dream vision that ingeniously reverses the pastoral tradition. At midnight, on the Chesapeake, the speaker, a poet "by fancy led," is blind to "the woods, in fairest vernal bloom." For him each "childless tree" seems to stand naked. To the howls of wolves, he approaches dark buildings where he finds no peace but hears talk of coffins, shrouds, and a tomb. He enters a building and confronts Death, who talks of "broad mouth'd cannon and the thunder-bolt" and seems to sneer at poets, like the speaker, "who by the laurel o'er him did aspire." A young man attending him accuses Death of being warlike and of looking forward to the Revolution, remarking, "Even now, to glut thy savage rage, I see / From eastern shores a bloody army rise ... / Rejoice, O fiend, Britannia's tyrant sends / From German plains his myriads to our shore." Death refuses to accept the blame: "Even Death abhors such woe to see / I'll quit the world while decently I can." Death dies, and the speaker, having imagined the worst and noting that "Dreams are perhaps forebodings of the soul," awakens from his nightmare and is back in the pastoral world on a "bloomy morn." He is resigned to fate: "Content to die, just as it be decreed / At four score years, or now at twenty-three."

Thus, as the war fever rose, and even as he poured forth patriotic verse for the New York newspapers, Freneau needed to distance himself from the battle. "MacSwiggen," published in November 1775, indicates that this was indeed the case. In this poem the speaker attacks a Tory poet whom he calls MacSwiggen, "patron of dunces and thyself the same." After angrily summing up the Tory writer's sins, the speaker suddenly pulls out of the fight: "Sick of all feuds, to Reason I appeal / From wars of *paper,* and from wars of *steel,* / Let others *here* their hopes and wishes end, / I to the sea with weary steps descend...." Shortly thereafter, Freneau left New Jersey for the West Indies.

From 1776 to 1778 Freneau lived on a plantation in St. Croix, employed in various capacities and making numerous trading expeditions among the islands. Although his life was superficially comfortable, his real experience must have been something like a nightmare come true. As he had envisioned in so many poems, here was a natural paradise, offering him beautiful scenery, fine weather, and an untroubled life. But his own country was at war and he was no help; and on St. Croix beauty coexisted with evil. Slavery, exercised even more cruelly than in America, poisoned the atmosphere, brutalizing slaves and owners. What Freneau had suspected and imagined in his poetry was all too real: man corrupted and destroyed whatever he touched.

During this period Freneau wrote two major poems that reflected what must have been his sense of uneasiness about the war and his own absence from it. In "The Hermit of Saba" he deals with the impossibility of escape from evil, a familiar theme that had concerned him since "The American Village" and that must have had additional significance now that he himself was trying to find peace in a world at war. The message is stark and unqualified, the language moving. A hermit, living on a deserted island to escape the corruption of civilization, rescues three shipwrecked sailors. Believing that the hermit has hidden real wealth on the island rather than the "spiritual" riches that he talks about, the sailors murder him. The poem ends with an explosive interjection from one of the sailors: "Perdition on these fiends from Europe." Their great greed and malice "unpeoples isles, and lays the world in ruin." Clearly, Freneau was frustrated: slavery on the islands and war at home. Was there no "safe" place for a poet?

The other major poem to come out of this two-year experience in the West Indies is "The Beauties of Santa Cruz." Replete with lush images of tropical flowers and suffused with melancholy, the poem shows corruption to be at the heart of life on the island. In many aspects an imaginative recreation of Freneau's experience, it opens with a speaker encouraging a shepherd from the "northern glooms" to seek "more equal climes, and a serener sky." Yet, with growing insistence, the speaker reveals the island's dangers and evil. One must be careful of what one eats and drinks. Some of the fruit of the sugarcane can cause the drinker to quit "his friends, his country and his all." One might be lured to his death through enchantment with the beautiful "animal" flower. Finally, evil people inhabit the island, and their lust for gold leads their "murderous hands" to oppress others with brutal slavery. Recognizing these dangers, the speaker still intends to remain but understands that his brother might stay in the North and "repel the *tyrant*, who thy peace invades."

In July 1778 Freneau returned to New Jersey, where he found the land ravaged from the recent Battle of Monmouth. He enlisted in the First Regiment of the New Jersey Militia and was a "scout and guard along the shore." A few

months later he became a sea privateer, serving on board the *Indian Delaware,* the *John Coustor,* and the *Rebecca.* He had several skirmishes with the British and sustained a minor bullet wound. On May 25, 1780, his journal recalls, the ship he was aboard was captured. He was put on the British prison ship *Scorpion,* which was moored in the Hudson. Three weeks later, when he became ill, he was transferred to the hospital ship *Hunter,* in the East River. There he remained, feverish for six weeks until his friends secured his release. As he wrote in his journal, he returned home by the back roads, so debilitated that he feared his "ghastly" looks would frighten the neighbors. Though the war continued, Freneau's days of direct confrontation with the British were over.

In addition to his military service, Freneau continued to pursue his interest in belles lettres. His work was welcomed in the *United States Magazine,* published in Philadelphia by Brackenridge and Francis Bailey. Attempting to establish a national magazine that would reflect the cultural as well as political aspirations of the country, they published Freneau's romantic poems such as "The Beauties of Santa Cruz" and "The House of Night" to appreciative responses from readers. Freneau also tried his hand at a play, *The Spy,* a treatment of Benedict Arnold's desertion to the British, but he never completed the project.

Freneau also became caught up in the politics of the war and developed an interest in journalism as well as other kinds of political writing. He published editorials and satires of the British in the *United States Magazine* until that journal failed in December 1779; and, in August 1781, he accepted the editorship of its replacement, the *Freeman's Journal,* also published by Bailey. This periodical was far more political than its predecessor, involving itself in national and local politics as well as in anti-British activity. Freneau was drawn into the battles and soon gained a reputation as a splenetic, vituperative writer, harsh not only on the British but also on his American political foes.

During his editorship, Freneau used his versifying skills to attack his enemies, and he wrote approximately fifty poems like "On the Fall of General Earl Cornwallis":

> What pen can write, what human tongue
>   can tell
> The endless murders of this man of hell!
> Nature in him disgrac'd the form divine;
> Nature mistook, she meant him for a—swine.

Typical also is "Rivington's Last Will and Testament," which was only one salvo of many in a war that the *Freeman's Journal* was waging against James Rivington's Tory *Royal Gazette*:

> IMPRIMIS, my carcase I give and devise
> To be made into cakes of a moderate size,
> To nourish those tories whose spirits may
>   droop,
> And serve the king's army with Portable
>   Soup.

Perhaps disturbed by the violence of these quarrels, Freneau abruptly resigned his editorship in September 1782 and accepted a post as "Clerk, Postmaster General of the United States." He held this position for almost two years while contributing frequently to the *Freeman's Journal*. In 1784 he began a career on the sea, sailing regularly to Jamaica; and in 1785 he became master of the *Monmouth*, his brother Peter's sloop, and later captain of the schooner *Columbia*, also his brother's. He traded on the east coast, stopping often at Philadelphia but spending most of his shore time in Charleston, South Carolina, where his brother lived.

During this period Freneau continued to write poetry and also developed as an essayist, publishing his work in the *Freeman's Journal* and other periodicals. By this time his poems, especially those attacking the British or celebrating American victories, were widely known,

and he had earned the reputation as "the poet of the American Revolution." In 1786, he capitalized on this reputation and published *The Poems of Philip Freneau, Written Chiefly During the Late War*. The edition, more or less chronologically arranged, contained 111 poems, many previously published, and covered Freneau's output since his college days. The collection shows his overwhelming involvement with his country: only thirteen poems do not have explicitly "American" themes. Mostly satires attacking the enemy within and without, the poems demonstrate the breadth of Freneau's activity in the propaganda war of the Revolution.

The work also demonstrates Freneau's skill as a poet. While many of the satiric and propagandist poems appear merely to be verse in an angry war of words, others—notably what might be called "battle poems"—recount American suffering and bravery against the British and are worth reading today. Among these are the bellicose and bitter "America Independent," the jaunty "Song on Captain Barney's Victory," the thoughtful and controlled "Captain Jones's Invitation," and the heroic "The British Prison Ship." At their best, these poems convey the drama of Revolutionary events and an appreciation of the human selflessness and courage that made them significant. "A Poem on the Memorable Victory Obtained by the Gallant Captain Paul Jones" records Jones's victory over the British ship *Seraphis*. It expresses Freneau's admiration for and fascination with Jones, and also shows the excitement and vitality that Freneau associated with the sea:

> 'Twas Jones, brave Jones, to battle led
> As bold a crew as ever bled
>   Upon the sky surrounded main;
> The standards of the Western World
> Were to the willing winds unfurl'd,
>   Denying Britain's tyrant reign.

"To the Memory of the Brave Americans" commemorates General Nathanael Greene's victory at Eutaw Springs, South Carolina, on September 8, 1781. Devoid of bitterness and restrained in tone, the elegy elevates the battle and its dead from the immediate cause to a commentary on the tragedy of the Revolution:

> They saw their injur'd country's woe;
> The flaming town, the wasted field. . . .

It is also a fitting reflection on the American soldier: "None griev'd, in such a cause to die—". And it rises above the partisanship of the war:

> Now rest in peace, our patriot band;
>   Though far from nature's limits thrown,
> We trust they find a happier land,
>   A brighter sunshine of their own.

Other memorable poems in the collection, mostly meditative and lyrical, deal with the tone or "spirit" of the nation as the war ended. As his earlier poems had expressed the dark side of war—the fear, violence, and sense of betrayal existing in America during the Revolution—these later poems express the dark side of victory, capturing the sense of disappointment and failed expectations even as the nation looked forward to peace and to the great experiment in republican government. Indeed, Freneau shared this disappointment. An idealist and dreamer whose "Rising Glory" had predicted a period of political and cultural independence, Freneau in the 1780's was frustrated when the great experiment in free government seemed to be bogged down in political maneuvering; and cultural freedom seemed as remote as ever with the British continuing to dominate American literature.

"A Moral Thought" (later entitled "The Vanity of Existence") captures this sense of disillusionment and introduces the melancholy tone that characterizes much of the later poetry in this edition. The poem observes that "vain pursuits, and joys as vain / Convince us life is but a dream" made up of disappointed expectations. The observer, after watching the splendid show of light on the sea at night, remarks:

> But when the tide had ebb'd away,
>   The scene fantastic with it fled,
> A bank of mud around me lay,
>   And sea-weed on the river's bed.

"The Dying Indian" also deals with disappointment through its evocation of an alternative view of life—the primitive. It was an appealing view in a nation that occasionally wanted to forget its uncertain struggle to establish a rational, republican government and to escape its troubles through nostalgia for an ideal past or through romantic idealization of the primitive life. To some degree Freneau also indulged in this desire to escape the increasingly complicated demands of civilization, but even as he wrote sympathetically about the Indians' faith in primitive customs and ideas, he recognized that there was no turning back. Thus, while "The Dying Indian" evokes nostalgia for the simplicity of the natural life, it also suggests that it is based on illusion. The dying Indian might try to imagine what life after death might be like in terms of his hunting grounds: "What solitary streams, / In dull and dreary dreams, / All melancholy, must I rove along!" He also might convince himself that death will bring "some new born mansion for the immortal mind!" But an observer does not share the Indian's fantasies and, as the Indian dies, remarks matter-of-factly: "He spoke . . . / Then clos'd his eyes, and sunk to endless sleep."

"Verses Made at Sea in a Heavy Gale" (later entitled "The Hurricane") is perhaps the most pessimistic and powerful poem in this collection. Based on his reaction to a storm at sea while he was on a trip to Jamaica, the poem describes Freneau's feelings of helplessness in the face of nature's overwhelming power. Also, in its call for a new "Columbus" and for a "Pilot" to guide the ship as "tempests rage with lawless power," the poem symbolically suggests America with its lack of leadership, and it captures an underlying mood in the nation—the sense that fate and the future were somehow beyond human control. Finally, with its broad references to "death and darkness," to "a strange, uncoasted strand . . . where fate permits no day" and to "uncharted territory" with "no compass to direct the way," the poem comments on the human condition and on the futility of human endeavor, concluding that a ship in a hurricane must grope alone:

> While mountains burst on either side—
> Thus, skill and science both must fall;
> And ruin is the lot of all.

Although *The Poems* of 1786 sold well and established Freneau's reputation as a poet of the Revolution, he did not seem especially pleased with the book, which he said Francis Bailey had put together in a "strange way" while he had been at sea. Perhaps he thought that the collection did not represent his mature abilities as a thinker and poet. By this time, he was less concerned with American achievements in the war, which had been the focus of *The Poems,* and more preoccupied with the nation's readjustment to peace. This critical period was an opportunity for the country to establish itself according to the ideals for which the war had been fought. As far as Freneau could see, however, America seemed far from interested in forming either a just government or an independent culture. People seemed, rather, to be concentrating on getting ahead, taking care of themselves, and making money.

These attitudes were discouraging to Freneau, who suffered from them on many levels. Politically, he was out of tune with the swing toward conservatism in government and self-aggrandizement in society. Personally, he suffered from misunderstanding and lack of recognition. *The Poems* had established him as a patriot and writer of occasional verse, but he certainly had not achieved recognition as a serious or major poet. The public praised his satires and light verse but ignored the lyrics, which in Freneau's opinion were his true poems.

In 1788 Freneau published *The Miscellaneous Works of Mr. Philip Freneau, Containing His Essays and Additional Poems,* which in many respects served as a correction of, and complement to, *The Poems*. Here Freneau was the serious thinker and artist as well as the satirist and patriot; here he expressed his views on American life and values. Thus, *The Miscellaneous Works* is more revealing than is *The Poems* of the complexity of thought and the range of expression that Freneau had achieved by the mid-1780's. It balances poems and essays about urban life and society with those about rural retreats, primitivism, and isolation; poems about travel and the sea with those about poetry and the writer's life. There is also a consistency of view. Lighthearted or serious, melancholic or satiric, the majority of poems and essays convey a pessimistic view of the individual and his world, and show the degree to which Freneau had become critical of his society and skeptical of its optimistic reliance on "progress" and "reason" to solve its problems.

A number of the pieces, for example, are about poetry and the poet's life in America, and reflect Freneau's sense that American society had failed to support its artists. Writers were certainly not the central and respected figures, the "new bards," whom he had envisioned populating America in "The Rising Glory of America" fifteen years before. As "On the Folly of Writing Poetry" reports, they were the least respected members of society and the most deserving of sympathy: "Of all the fools that haunt our coast / The scribbling tribe I pity most." In part, the poems and essays point out, American authors suffer because of their nation's dependence on Britain. "Literary Importation" asks: "Can we never be thought to have learning or grace / Unless it be brought from that damnable place?" But in America critics and readers ignore poets, and moreover the Revolutionary climate is hostile to them. "An Author's Soliloquy" complains: "An age employ'd in pointing steel / Can no poetic raptures feel." Only satire is popular:

> Her visage stern, severe her stile
> A clouded brow, a cruel smile
> A mind on murder'd victims plac'd—
> She, only she can suit the taste.

Other poems—some of them the best that Freneau ever wrote—express more general views of the human condition. In "The Indian Student," "The Indian Burying Ground," and "Lines Written at Port Royal," Freneau writes with lyric intensity and in a straightforward language well advanced from the neoclassical imitativeness that still characterized his satires, to show his awareness of the chaos, fragility, and irrationality of human life and of mankind's helplessness in the face of the overwhelming forces of nature. In particular, many of these poems deal with the sea, which as Richard Vitzthum has shown, had become for Freneau a symbol for the unknown and of the irrational power of nature. In "The Departure" a trip out to sea symbolically expresses the speaker's sense of failed creativity and knowledge of approaching death. In "The Lost Sailor" the sea represents loss, uncertainty, and death. "Poor Ralph," attracted by "masts so trim, and sails as white as snow," wants to leave his friend and go to sea, even though he knows:

'Tis folly all—for who can truly tell
What streams disturb the bosom of the main,
What ugly fish in those dark climates dwell
That feast on men. . . .

Nevertheless, Ralph goes, his "black ship" never to be seen again.

The best and most famous poem in this volume is "The Wild Honey Suckle." It is quintessentially American, demonstrating for the first time in poetry how closely nature and the American process of thinking about life were intertwined. Since their arrival in the New World, the "settlers" had had to order their lives in terms of the natural forces that surrounded them, and by the pre-Revolutionary era they knew as well that their culture and values were tied to the land. As Michel-Guillaume Jean de Crèvecoeur and others had shown, the new land had shaped an "American" character. Going even further, Witherspoon, lecturing at Princeton when Freneau was a student, had reflected Lockean thinking and commonsense philosophy, and had emphasized the connection between the natural world and the human. A knowledge of nature led to a knowledge of human life—from its morality to its art.

"The Wild Honey Suckle," deriving from this tradition and demonstrating Freneau's capacity to use nature symbolically to express his sense of the meaning of life, draws its power from the restrained depiction of a "fair" American flower, which in its life and death demonstrates the transiency of beauty and of life—and the apparent purposelessness of both. This "comely" flower in its "silent, dull retreat" far from "the vulgar eye" is shattered with its exposure to "unpitying frosts, and Autumn's power." But the death of this "little being" is pointless:

> If nothing once, you nothing lose,
> For when you die you are the same;
> The space between is but an hour,
> The mere idea of a flower.

(In a later edition, Freneau refined the last line to: "The frail duration of a flower.")

Most of the essays in *The Miscellaneous Works* had been published previously in the

Freeman's Journal, in which Freneau expressed broad-ranging criticism of American society. Some of these focus on American manners and values. Written in the personae of such characters as Christopher Clodhopper, Priscilla Tripstreet, and Robert Slender, the essays accuse Americans of being poorly educated, boorish, materialistic, status-seeking, and power-hungry. Witty and urbane, the essays are a tribute to Freneau's ability to expose the materialistic side of American life with deftness and grace.

Others of the essays are very serious and deal with more profound reservations about American life than those that have to do with its poor manners and grasping, provincial ways. They are concerned with a philosophy of life and with human nature, asking whether man indeed has the capacity to shape a free and peaceful society. Perhaps he is so depraved that he would convert any system, no matter how benevolent initially, into despotism.

In these essays the observations are made through the eyes of the Philosopher of the Forest (originally the Pilgrim in the *Freeman's Journal*), a figure new to American letters and one whose creation established Freneau among America's leading post-Revolutionary essayists. Something of a pre-Thoreauvian character who lives alone in the forest outside of Philadelphia, spending his time commenting "on political, moral, philosophical, or religious subjects," the Philosopher is a dreamer and a skeptic. In an age of rationalism, he emphasizes mankind's irrational impulses—the power of dreams and visions to bring to the surface some of the hidden truths about the human character. At a time when faith is placed in "progress" and human perfectibility, he broods on the imbedded evil in human character. While deists are arguing that the universe is mechanistic and ordered, the Philosopher sees chance and barely concealed chaos.

In one imaginative group of essays the Phi-

losopher dreams about the beginning of creation and is led by Genius to Nature, who holds before him "a just, disinterested, benevolent, upright, and honest man." After showing off her creation, Nature takes the mold for this man to the Deity for his admiration. But the scene shifts, and the Philosopher sees "Nature's journeymen" trying to achieve her perfect creation. One journeyman, Firando, does very well, making two superb Africans, but his apprentices fail to do as well. One creates "a thief, another a bully and a wrangler, a third a dunce, a fourth an idiot, a fifth a monster of avarice or envy; a sixth a sycophant—and so on, almost without end." Because the handiwork is so bad, threatening to bring disorder to the universe, Firando and his apprentices create numerous snakes, "severe and perpetual labor," "extremities of hot and cold," and other hardships that will keep the new beings too busy surviving to cause trouble.

Other essays of the Philosopher reflect on the manifestations of man's character in his dealings with others. With the exception of a benevolent clergyman who, like the Philosopher, lives in the woods away from the everyday bustle, the Philosopher finds only greed, ambition, selfishness, and other hateful qualities among men. He recalls, for example, a Swiftian-style trip in 1765 to Snatchaway (England), where he landed penniless after a shipwreck. Here the "people at large are the slaves of the rich and great; are saddled with kings, royal families, [and] lords spiritual and temporal." People in this city "are so miserable" that even their females "hanged, drowned, or strangled themselves." They were "intolerably proud, and ambitious"; they ignored the Philosopher; and he left as soon as possible.

The Philosopher series ends with essays on America, the nature of fame, and the meaning of life. The essays point out man's history of injustice, his desire to get ahead, and his disposition to war. Perhaps "the bold and manly sentiments" combined with the wealth of America will help her to produce a nation where men will no longer "treat each other as savages and monsters." But such is the evidence that the Philosopher is skeptical about the future and closes the essays with the observation:

> ... I am really in doubt whether a man that is constitutionally a lover of fighting ... is an emanation from the all perfect Spirit ... or, on the contrary, a mere mass of those vexatious, discordant, chaotic atoms which are doomed to be everlastingly at enmity with each other, till the *soul of the universe,* the great principle of harmony and beauty, shall again move upon the superficies of these troubled waters, and bring light out of darkness, beauty and regularity from confusion, darkness, and disorder.

Despite the pessimism of so many of the pieces, *The Miscellaneous Works* was received, as the 1786 collection had been, as an example of Freneau's "humor, wit, and satire." His reputation for these qualities grew as "The Wild Honey Suckle" and "The Indian Burying Ground" were largely ignored in favor of reprintings of his lighter, satiric verse. From Boston to Charleston, Freneau became known as a satirist and writer of patriotic verse; an American "bard," the "genuine son of Neptune and Clio."

What Freneau thought of this reception is not known, but from this time on he became less concerned with romantic poetry and more involved with political writing. Soon after the publication of *The Miscellaneous Works* he retired from the sea and in April 1790 married Eleanor Forman, the daughter of a New Jersey neighbor. He returned to journalism, accepting a job with the *Daily Advertiser* in New York City.

It was a critical time for the nation and for Freneau, who soon found himself deeply immersed in politics again. The problem, as he saw it, was that in the move to establish a strong central government—which had culminated in the Constitution and in the election of George Washington—the forces of conservatism had gained the upper hand. The nation, increasingly under the domination of the powerful and the rich, was in danger of losing the rights it had fought for. While the poor were struggling for survival, the privileged, joined together in the Federalist party, were consolidating their gains.

But the *Daily Advertiser* did not provide Freneau with enough opportunity to express his opposition to the new government's policies. While liberal in its politics, the newspaper avoided controversy. Becoming impatient, Freneau considered starting a newspaper of his own. His plans changed when he was approached by his old Princeton friend, James Madison, to found a newspaper in Philadelphia, where the new capital was to be moved. Madison, who by this time was a leader among the Republicans. spoke on behalf of Thomas Jefferson and others, to urge that Freneau begin a Republican newspaper to counteract the Federalist organ, the *Gazette of the United States,* which was published by John Fenno, a staunch supporter of Alexander Hamilton. When Jefferson offered him an appointment as a "clerk for foreign languages in the office of Secretary of State" for $250 a year, a stipend that provided some financial help, Freneau agreed to the move. In October 1791, he established the *National Gazette* in Philadelphia.

For the next two years, Freneau edited the *National Gazette,* becoming one of America's most outspoken and vituperative journalists. He threw himself into the fight against the Federalists, attacking them in editorial after editorial and criticizing both their politics and their characters. Identifying Alexander Hamilton as his special villain, Freneau opposed his proposal for a central bank and his system of funding the national debt—changes in the economic system that, in his view, would make the rich richer and defraud the poor.

Freneau soon paid the price for his vehemence. He was drawn into personal and spiteful exchanges with his opponents, who did not hesitate to attack his character as well as his arguments. The lowest point in the quarreling occurred when the *Gazette of the United States* accused Freneau of being Jefferson's mouthpiece and in his pay. In July 1792 a letter, probably written by Hamilton, pointed out that: "The Editor of the 'National Gazette' receives a salary from government." It asked whether the salary was paid "for *translations;* or for *publications*" and whether he was paid "to oppose the measures of government, and, by false insinuations, to disturb the public peace?" Indignant, Freneau denied the charges, signing an affidavit to the effect that in conducting his newspaper he was "free—unfettered—and uninfluenced." He also responded in kind to his attackers, accusing Fenno and his followers of being in the pay of the Federalists and calling Hamilton and others names in verse. In "Addressed to a Political Shrimp, or, Fly upon the Wheel," he implied that Hamilton and the Federalists were "rats and mice" and that Hamilton was a "reptile" whose "venom ever spits in vain." He concluded that "they that on no Treasury lean, despise your venal pen—your canker'd heart." In a series of poems to "Shylock Ap-Shenkin" (John Fenno), he accused Fenno and others of lying, harrassment, "knavery," and corruption. The tone of the accusation is angry, the language crude:

Because some treasury-luncheons you have
    gnaw'd,
  Like rats, that prey upon the public store:
Must you, for that, your crude stuff belch
    abroad,
    And vomit lies on all that pass your door!

One bright spot amid these adverse political developments, however, was the political revolution in France. To Freneau, the French Revolution was the first sign since the American war that the forces of tyranny might be stopped and that a new period of freedom might yet be in store for mankind. America was not alone in the fight for freedom, and while it struggled to preserve its principles, the French were offering an example and an inspiration. As Freneau wrote in December 1791 in the *National Gazette:* "As a friend of humanity, I rejoice in the French Revolution, but as a citizen of America the significance is greatly heightened. . . . The fate of the two governments has appeared to be intimately linked together, and that of either dependent on the other."

The great spokesman for this revolution was Thomas Paine, whose *Rights of Man* Freneau reprinted in full in the *Gazette*. For Freneau, Paine articulated the ideals of this new age, showing that reason and virtue operating in harmony with an ordered universe might produce a world where mankind could live in freedom. As he wrote in "To a Republican, with Mr. Paine's Rights of Man":

Rouse'd by the REASON of his manly page,
Once more shall PAINE a listening world
    engage:
From Reason's source, a bold reform he
    brings,
In raising up *mankind,* he pulls down *kings.*

Freneau used the *National Gazette* to support the Revolution, even after Louis XVI and Marie Antoinette had been executed and the excesses of the revolutionaries were becoming known in America. He also opposed Washington's policy of neutrality when France and Britain went to war, arguing that the British had a long history of tyranny and opposition to freedom. Moreover, he effusively welcomed the new French ambassador, Edmond Charles Édouard Genêt, to America in 1793 with "God Save the

Rights of Man," a poem written in his honor. When it became clear that Genêt was violating American neutrality by outfitting privateers in American ports, and that Washington wanted to disassociate the American government from him, Freneau wrote a series of articles under the pseudonym "Veritas," criticizing Washington and his policies and accusing him of being the dupe of "British emissaries" and "mushroom lordlings."

Washington reacted angrily to Freneau's opposition. He had never liked the fact that the *National Gazette* had served as a place to voice disagreements within the administration between the Hamiltonians and the Jeffersonians, and now he asked Jefferson if Freneau could not be curbed. Jefferson declined to act, noting that Freneau's paper "has saved our constitution which was galloping fast into monarchy." Far from being subdued, Freneau continued to criticize the leadership and so angered the president that Washington referred to him in a cabinet meeting as "that rascal Freneau."

By 1793, Freneau had become one of the nation's most powerful spokesmen for Jeffersonian republicanism and French egalitarian philosophy. He had effectively argued for the rights of the common man and opposed the forces of "special privilege," giving encouragement to "the friends of civil liberty" from Boston to Charleston. In the process, however, he had earned the reputation of being a partisan, angry political journalist—"a mere incendiary," as Timothy Dwight called him. His readers considered him a political writer, not a serious poet. Whatever respect was accorded American poets was reserved for the "Hartford Wits": Dwight, John Trumbull, Joel Barlow, and David Humphreys.

But Freneau had not stopped writing poetry, nor had he lost his commitment to an independent American literature. Bitterly resentful of the dominance of belles lettres by the Hartford Wits—those "moulded pedants from the East," as he called them—with their servile acquiescence to British forms and style, he concentrated on verse that was determinedly "republican" and American: straightforward, plainspoken, and "democratic." Lacking the intensity and imaginative power of his earlier verse, these new poems reflect Freneau's social and philosophical views, in particular his growing acceptance of deism, with its emphasis on an ordered universe governed by benevolent laws of nature, and of reason, with its faith in man's rationality to improve the human condition. The poetry also reflects the influence of Paine and the French *philosophes,* especially in its emphasis on egalitarianism and its attacks on privilege and vested interest.

This poetry is not Freneau's best, much of it being simply occasional verse celebrating some special event such as the arrival in America of Paine's *Rights of Man* or the anniversary of American independence; yet some poems do bear rereading. Among those written at this time are the ones that explore the life of the common man in America. They come close for the first time in American letters to a picture of the ordinary man that is neither romantically idealistic nor patronizingly satiric. Typical is the small landowner in "The Pennsylvania Planter," who farms independently of "party," "new-made 'squires," or "Mammon." Statesmen and legislators have nothing to gain from him and shun his "homely door." In "humble hope his little fields were sown, / A trifle, in your eye—but all his own." Typical also is the character in "To Crispin O'Conner," an immigrant settled in the west on a spot of land "that no man envied, and that no man owned." With hard work he prospers. But what a different fate he would have met had he remained in Europe: "Nine pence a day, coarse fare, a bed of boards, / . . . Slave to dull squires, kings' brats, and huffish lords."

Others of the more interesting poems are character sketches of humble Americans who are suffering under the new administration. Among them are the soldiers of the Revolution whom the nation has apparently forgotten. In "The American Soldier" the patriot is destitute and alone, "too poor to shine in courts, too proud to beg." With battle scars and a wooden leg, he is lost in "the abyss of want." All that freedom has left him is "famine and a name!" Similarly ignored, the village newspaperman who gave his best years to the support of the Revolution slowly goes out of business. As described in "The Country Printer" he is the "guardian" of his country and its laws, and the speaker pleads that he not be allowed to fade away:

From this pure source, let streams unsullied
    flow;
Hence, a new order grows on reason's plan,
And turns the fierce barbarian into—man.

These poems appeared regularly in the *National Gazette,* where they did not make much of an impression in the midst of the lively political exchanges that filled the newspaper. But Freneau soon lost his entire audience. Widely read as it was, the *National Gazette* could barely support itself, and when the yellow fever epidemic descended on Philadelphia in 1793, Freneau reluctantly stopped publication, in October, and left for his home in Monmouth to reassess his career.

Freneau's return to Monmouth, where his mother and sister were still living, gave him the chance to settle his family, which now included a new baby, Agnes, in addition to a two-year-old daughter, Helena. Though he smarted from the political battles of Philadelphia, worried about the debts contracted from the failed newspaper, and vowed, as he informed Madison, to pass his days in peace "on a couple hundred acres of sandy patrimony," he was

soon immersed in his chief pleasures, writing and politics. With type brought with him from Philadelphia, he set up his own printing press and published *The Monmouth Almanac for the Year M, DCC, XCV.* He also published a new collection, *Poems Written Between the Years 1768 and 1794.*

For Freneau, this collection must have been a way of putting the last few turbulent years into perspective and of giving a retrospective view of his achievement as a poet. Containing 289 poems that span his career, this edition shows his steady movement away from "fancy" and toward the political and philosophical. *The Poems* also emphasize his humanitarian concerns with cruelty and oppression. Included, for example, are two previously uncollected poems from the early 1780's. "To the Keeper of the King's Water Works" tells of Freneau's experience in the port of Jamaica, where an official had refused his sailors water "while hogs, and dogs, and keepers drink their fill." The sharply worded "To Sir Toby" tells about the owner of a sugar plantation in Jamaica who enjoys his wealth while creating a living hell for his slaves. Emphasizing the need for reason, and espousing the tenets of deism, the majority of the poems in the collection deal with social and political issues—even the treatment accorded Louis XVI and Marie Antoinette ("Folly's sad victims, fortune's bitter sport"). Although the volume does not provide much new in the way of insight into Freneau the poet, it is the only edition of his works that he supervised from beginning to end, and for many of his poems, therefore, it must be considered authoritative. It was also one of his least popular publications and soon after its appearance in 1795 ceased to be advertised in the New York newspapers.

In addition to the almanac and the edition of his poems, Freneau tried to support himself with a bookstore and with the publication of a newspaper, the *Jersey Chronicle.* Published weekly from May 2, 1795, to April 30, 1796, the paper was "intended to review foreign and domestic politics of the times, and mark the general character of the age and country." Far from the center of political activity, the newspaper could do little but carry extracts from other newspapers, both national and international. But it was distinguished by Freneau's editorials espousing the rights of man, opposing monarchy, articulating the principles of American republicanism, and attacking Britain and supporting France on every issue.

In particular, the paper was enlivened by a series of essays by "Tomo Cheeki," one of Freneau's most imaginative creations, who gives a sharply focused indictment of American life and values in some of the most trenchant prose of the post-Revolutionary period. With the simplicity and asceticism of the primitive and the reason and detachment of the philosopher, Tomo Cheeki, a Creek Indian who is in Philadelphia with thirty other chiefs to "settle a treaty of amity with the republican government of this country," observes the habits of the white men and concludes that they have "ever proved proud, cruel, base and treacherous enemies of what they call the uncivilized life." Selfishness, greed, and irrationality appear to be at the root of their actions. As a deist, who takes "the whole of this stupendous system to be a great machine answering some prodigious purpose, of which the white men, any more than ourselves, have not the least idea," Tomo Cheeki is impatient with those who believe that the machine was "designed solely for their use and benefit." But, stoical and witty, he does not yield to despair. There is some hope for the future. Enough trust still exists so that a man can submit to the barber's razor "without danger of having his weazon cut!" Bemused, critical, poetical, Tomo Cheeki closes his essays looking forward to his retirement to the forest to pass his days "at a distance from men."

Although the *Jersey Chronicle,* with the

Tomo Cheeki essays, was popular in New Jersey, Freneau could not earn enough from it to support his family. Hoping to find a more profitable publishing venture with "the spirit of the *National Gazette,*" he looked about New York City for a situation. In March 1797 he formed an association with the printer Alexander Menut and founded a new periodical, *The Time-Piece; and Literary Companion.* Perhaps in deference to his partner, the paper at first concentrated on the cultural life of the city, opening itself up, as it declared, to "political, moral, or other interesting discussion." It was sprinkled liberally with sentimental poems and letters mostly from women readers and contained essays of Freneau's explaining the principles of republicanism. But there was little political controversy. When the French Directory snubbed Charles Cotesworth Pinckney, the new ambassador, because it believed American policy had become pro-British, Freneau remained silent.

In September 1797, Freneau took on a new partner, Matthew L. Davis, and the tenor of the newspaper changed. It became active in politics and soon attracted the attention of the Federalist Noah Webster, editor of the *Minerva* in New York City, and of William Cobbett, a Federalist who wrote under the pseudonym "Peter Porcupine," for his *Porcupine's Gazette* in Philadelphia. Soon the vituperation that had marked Freneau's *National Gazette* period reappeared. When Cobbett called him "a tool, a toad-eater, a lick spittle" for his past connection with Jefferson, Freneau said he was a blackguard and derided him in the *Time-Piece:*

Ah—Peter!—Thou, poor lousy numps
Who loadest little horses' rumps,
    And mak'st them trot and sweat,
        On sandy road
        Beneath the load
Of trash call'd *Peter Porcupine's Gazette.*

Unfortunately for Freneau, with the Federalists firmly entrenched in New York and Philadelphia, he was at a disadvantage. He complained that merchants were afraid to advertise in his paper for fear of the controversy. Others failed to pay for their subscriptions, and still others dropped them. He was convinced that the habits of greed and opportunism had destroyed the spirit of republicanism and that people did not want to be reminded of their lapse from the high standards of the past. As he wrote in "To the Americans of the United States":

> The coming age will be an age of prose:
> When sordid cares will break the muses'
>   dream,
> And Common Sense be ranked in seat
>   supreme.

Calling his newspaper venture "the wrongest step I could possibly have taken," Freneau admitted failure, and stopped editing the *Time-Piece* in December.

Discouraged and financially hard-pressed, Freneau traveled to Charleston, staying with his brother Peter for a while before settling once again at Monmouth with a family now increased by the arrival of a third daughter, Catherine. It must have been a difficult time for him, not only because he was short of funds and had to mortgage and sell property to meet his bills, but also because he was without a public platform during a time when issues that he felt strongly about were at the forefront of national debate. John Adams, the new president, was determined to muzzle the press that had harassed him throughout his vice-presidency and had made his election so problematic. Congress supported him in his efforts and in 1798 passed the Alien and Sedition Acts, which, among other restrictions, subjected to fine and imprisonment any person who should "write, print, utter or publish . . . any false, scandalous, and malicious writing or writings against the government of the United States" or its officers. Twenty-four Republican editors were soon arrested, including Freneau's colleague Benjamin Bache of the Philadelphia *Aurora,* and John Daly Burk, who had taken over the *Time-Piece.*

Freneau also was at odds with American policy toward France. He believed that the Americans were being duped by the British and the Federalists into an unwarranted hostility toward France. In his view, the Federalists wanted to assist the British in the defeat of France because they distrusted that country's dangerous faith in democratic values and in the common man. In 1795, he had vehemently criticized Jay's Treaty of Commerce with Britain on the ground that it discriminated against the French; and when the French responded to the treaty by snubbing the Americans, declaring the American alliance of 1778 at an end, and harassing American shipping, Freneau defended the French policy. He also stood uneasily by in April 1798, when Americans learned that three French officials, referred to in dispatches as Mr. X, Mr. Y, and Mr. Z, had solicited bribes from Adams' envoys. With the slogan "Millions for defense, but not one cent for tribute," the nation prepared for war with France. To Freneau, the war fever was more evidence of unprincipled Federalist manipulation and of that party's desire to crush the egalitarian spirit engendered by the French Revolution.

Isolated, but certainly not wishing to be imprisoned for expressing his views, Freneau nevertheless found a way to make his opposition to the government clear. He resurrected one of his old literary characters, Robert Slender, from his *Freeman's Journal* days. In those days Slender had been a writer and a weaver; in his reincarnation he is a humble, honest, timorous "mechanic," who goes "unnoticed among the swinish herd, as the poor are generally called by the great and well-born." Wanting peace and quiet, he spent the Revolution "snug out of the fight." If anything, his sympathies are with the Federalists who promise leadership and order.

But he is led to question their principles when he reads an essay in the Philadelphia *Aurora* signed by a "Monarchist" (but written by Freneau), defending the imprisonment of Congressman Matthew Lyon, a captain in the Revolution who has opposed the sedition acts. The Monarchist argues that his "imprisonment and fine did more good to America, by inculcating a proper submission to our rulers, than anything that could be devised, short of cutting off his head: which indeed would have been *wrong* in itself, but would have been right nevertheless, for great advantages would have sprung from it." Unhappy with the Monarchist's extreme position, which nevertheless seems to be compatible with the Federalists', Slender writes a series of letters to the *Aurora* in which he records his simple quest for the truth. He tells of discussing his worries with his neighbors, clergymen, his cousin Simon, and especially his friend the Latinist, who with his classical learning might be knowledgeable enough to explain Federalist policies to him. Slender gradually realizes that the Federalists put some men, those whom the "President delighteth to honour," above the law, while others are denied due process. Being a "little fellow" whose "dependence for protection is on society," he "loves the law" and is afraid of the Federalist abuse of it. He also sees that he might have gotten himself into trouble by writing to the *Aurora*. Perhaps his innocent "questions" will be considered seditious. "God be praised" that at least he is not "an *alien!*"

In a series of forty-four letters Robert Slender wonders about and queries Federalist policies, always overhearing or putting into the mouths of others views that might be considered seditious. For example, he manages through indirection to take up the issue of organized Calvinist support of the Federalists and opposition to the current French government. At other times he is humorously obtuse. While having "a pint of ale at a tavern," he hears talk of an "aristocratic Beast let loose in the country," where it can do all the harm it wants because it has "put itself under the protection of the Society of the Cincinatti," the hereditary society of officers of the American Revolution and their descendants. He hurries home "looking on this side and that" for fear the Beast "would leap upon me from some of its lurking places."

As he debates with his friends and neighbors, Slender becomes less fearful and more outspoken, finally becoming angry at Federalist toleration of the impressment of American seamen and its surrender to the British of Jonathan Robbins, an impressed seaman who had jumped a British ship. Although he has been warned by his neighbors that the Federalists will "do all they can to *intimidate* weak minded people, *keep back* returns, *forge votes,* and *bribe* voters," Slender decides to oppose the Federalists in the next gubernatorial election in Pennsylvania and to support the Republican candidate, Thomas McKean. In a stirring essay beginning "Oyez, Oyez," he calls upon the voters to come "under the banners of freedom, and once more conquer—let the word be LIBERTY and M'Kean." Robert Slender had finally become a free, principled Republican.

Dramatic and lively, the Slender letters appeared regularly in the *Aurora*. In response to popular demand, Freneau collected twenty-four of them in a volume entitled *Letters on Various Interesting and Important Subjects; . . . by Robert Slender, O.S.M* [One of the Swinish Multitude] (1799), which Slender dedicated "to the Freemen, the Lovers of Liberty, the Asserters, Maintainers and Supporters of Independence Throughout the United States." The edition was very successful, going through several printings, but a promised second volume never appeared. This volume, for all intents and purposes, marked the end of Freneau's journalistic career—a charming, witty testament to his skill as a political writer, satirist, and prose stylist.

After the publication of the Slender letters,

Freneau virtually retired from politics. When the presidential campaign of 1800 got under way and his old enemy John Adams opposed Thomas Jefferson, Freneau remained on the sidelines. He was caught up in farming, his fourth and last daughter, Margaret, had just been born, and he was in financial difficulties and evidently was sensitive about having his situation exposed. In a letter to Madison, the South Carolina jurist Aedanus Burke noted that "Freneau is still in embarrassed circumstances. He is an honest man, and an undeviating Republican; yet utterly incapable of soliciting for himself." Mary Austin, in her biography, says that Freneau turned down an offer for a position in Jefferson's new administration, instructing the intermediary to "tell Thomas Jefferson that he knows where Philip Freneau lives, and if he has important business with him, let him come to Philip Freneau's house and transact it."

Although he would not accept a post in the administration, Freneau was pleased with Jefferson's victory and the defeat of Adams, whom he called "the Duke of Braintree." Approaching fifty, he maintained a private life, farming and looking for opportunities in shipping. From 1802 to 1804 he was captain of his brother's trading vessels, traveling between New York and Charleston and to the Canary Islands. From 1804 to 1809 he farmed, occasionally mortgaging or selling portions of his property to pay his bills. Throughout these years he "scribbled verses" and in the fall of 1804 probably contributed letters under the pseudonym "Joe Bunker" to the support of William Penrose, Democratic candidate from Pennsylvania for Congress.

He briefly returned to publishing in 1809, when he prepared a two-volume edition of his works for the benefit of Lydia Bailey, the widowed daughter-in-law of Francis Bailey, publisher of Freneau's earlier volumes. Entitled *Poems Written and Published During the American Revolutionary War,* the edition contained most of the poems of the 1795 collection with the notable omission of many of the poems about the French Revolution. (With the ascent of Napoleon, Freneau may have thought that the promise of the Revolution had not been fulfilled and had decided to keep silent.) With its emphasis on "poems originating from the temporary events of the American War," as the advertisement declared, the edition clinched Freneau's reputation as the poet of the American Revolution and sold very well. He was, according to Joseph Lloyd, editor of the *Pennsylvania Democrat,* entitled to respect as "a man, as a poet, and as a patriot." For Lloyd, Freneau was, "in the true sense of the word, a useful poet."

Despite this judgment, which for all its flattery perpetuated Freneau's reputation as a political poet, the edition was not exclusively political. In particular, there are thirty-seven previously uncollected poems written between 1795 and 1809 that show that Freneau's best work in those years was either lightheartedly satiric or philosophical—certainly not "useful" in the political sense. There are also seventeen poems, some older and some new, pseudonymously attributed to Hezekiah Salem. This fictional character, a poor clergyman who farmed pumpkins in Connecticut, first appeared in the *Time-Piece.* He was, Lewis Leary believes, the final butt of the poet's long quarrel with New England, on whom Freneau "purposely sluffed off" the poems of which he "was least proud." But, in addition, Freneau gave him some of his most entertaining, such as "The New England Sabbath-Day Chace" and "The Parting Glass." Hezekiah is also "responsible" for "On a Honey Bee, Drinking from a Glass and Drowned Therein." In this graceful, mock-heroic poem, the speaker wonders what draws the bee to the fatal glass: "Did storms harass or foes perplex, / Did wasps or king-birds bring dismay— ...?" Bemused, the speaker bids the bee enjoy itself and drink, even if it means death: "Go, take your seat in Charon's boat, / We'll tell the hive, you died afloat."

Poems Written and Published During the American Revolutionary War also contains eloquent and restrained philosophical poems that express Freneau's deistic beliefs and are indeed the most compressed, intense statements of deistic ideas in American literature. Moreover, the poems reveal the extent to which Freneau had been able by this time to reconcile the evil and irrational in human nature with the deistic belief that the universe is ordered, reasonable, and good. In "Science Favorable to Virtue," "Reflections on the Constitution of Nature," and "On the Powers of the Human Understanding," the poet shows that reason gradually controls the passions, and he predicts that man will ultimately fit into "the eternal scheme." Thus, as "The Powers of the Human Understanding" argues, "To slow perfection moves the mind / And *may* at last attain / A nearer rank with that first cause. . . ."

After the publication of this book, Freneau lived quietly at Monmouth, farming, keeping up with political developments, and writing verse inspired by special occasions such as the death of Thomas Paine or the celebration of the Fourth of July. He watched the activities of Napoleon and increasing American involvement in European affairs. When Congress declared war on Britain in 1812, Freneau approved. It was the familiar story: British tyranny threatening American independence. As the public anticipated war, he saw many of his Revolutionary poems such as "To the Memory of the Brave Americans Under General Greene" reappear in print. When the war was under way, he wrote some new verses commemorating American battles on Lake Erie and on the high seas. He also wrote about the British invasion of Washington and satiric verse about the ineptitude of both the British and the American leadership. In substance, the verses repeated the themes that Freneau had sounded in the Revolution, the need to resist oppression and to preserve the freedom of the common man. A few of the poems appeared in print. Most did not.

After the war, enough interest remained in his work for the bookseller David Longworth to plan an edition of these later poems. Freneau's reaction to the proposition was cautious. As he wrote to Madison on January 12, 1815: "With some reluctance I consented to gratify his wish, altho' I think after the age of fifty, or thereabouts, the vanity of authorship ought to cease, at least it has been the case with myself." In a subsequent letter he informed Madison that the edition was ready, again disavowing any merit for his work: "I consider my poetry and poems as mere trifles." But clearly he was excited by the project and looked forward to the publication of the book.

To his disappointment, *A Collection of Poems, on American Affairs, and A Variety of Other Subjects, Chiefly Moral and Political,* appearing in two volumes in the spring of 1815, was the least successful of Freneau's editions, "falling," he admitted, "nearly dead born from the press." Although he attributed the failure to "party men" and to his political enemies, the truth was that "this veteran bard," as Washington Irving's *Analectic Magazine* called him, had little new to offer. Most of the volume contained the patriotic and satiric verses that the public had come to expect from him, but much of it now seemed old-fashioned and dated. The *Analectic Magazine* summed up his predicament:

With full applause, in honour to his age
Dismiss the veteran poet from the stage;
Crown his last exit with distinguished praise,
And kindly hide his baldness with the bays.

As with all of Freneau's collections, this edition contains solid new poems mixed in with the conventional political verse. There is the graceful "To a Caty-Did, the Precursor of Winter," thought to be written for his daughter Catherine. In gentle, childlike couplets the poem explores Freneau's favorite subject, the transiency of life. Listening to the song of "the evening Caty-did," the speaker wants to know whether it utters "joy or grief—?":

> Did you only mean to say,
> I have had my summer's day,
> And am passing, soon, away. . . .

Playfully, the speaker acknowledges nature's power over the Caty-did:

> Nature, when she form'd you, said,
> "Independent you are made,
> My dear little Caty-did:
> Soon yourself must disappear
> With the verdure of the year,"—
> And to go, we know not where,
> With your song of Caty-did

A number of poems are restrained expressions of Freneau's deism, demonstrating his capacity to use simple, measured language to put forth his sense of reconciliation with nature and his faith in the inherent goodness of the universal order. Moreover, these poems, among them "On the Uniformity and Perfection of Nature," "On the Universality and Other Attributes of the God of Nature," and "On the Religion of Nature," are the final and perhaps most powerful summations of eighteenth-century deism and rationalism before they faded into romanticism; and they are, in addition, eloquent testaments to Freneau's acceptance before his death of a natural, benevolent order in the universe. As he wrote in "On the Uniformity and Perfection of Nature": "All, nature made, in reason's sight / Is order all, and *all is right*."

Although Freneau subsequently continued to write verse and occasionally contributed to periodicals, he was, as he himself admitted, "out of the Literary World." He lived out his remaining seventeen years in obscurity and poverty, facing increasing financial difficulties and selling every year or two another tract from the Monmouth farm. On October 18, 1818, his Mount Pleasant home was completely destroyed in a fire, which took with it his books, papers, and according to Freneau "some" of his "best poems." Although he soon moved into a new house, he was beset by poverty. He worked on the public roads of Monmouth to pay his taxes, and legend has it that he went from door to door in the neighborhood doing odd jobs. In August 1832, at the age of eighty, he applied for a pension for his service in the Revolution, but he did not survive to receive the thirty-five-dollar annual stipend. On December 18, 1832, he was caught in a blizzard on his return home from a visit to the village of Freehold. He was found dead in the snow the following morning.

Freneau's death did not bring about any radical reassessment of his achievements. His contemporaries still remembered him as a "revolutionary bard" with an "acrimonious" pen, but few recalled many of his poems. In the busy time of the Revolution he had contributed where he could, and the nation had absorbed his work before moving beyond him. Nevertheless, he had made a lasting contribution to American culture. He had set a course for an "American" literature, one that recognized the place in its culture of the plain, the natural, and the humble. His call for independence in art as in life did not go unheeded in America. In the same month that Freneau died, Ralph Waldo Emerson resigned from the ministry of the Second Church of Boston and later wrote in his journal:

> I would be free; I cannot be
> While I take things as others please to rate
> them.

It was a statement that heralded a new era in American belles lettres: it was a view that Freneau would have understood.

Selected Bibliography

WORKS OF PHILIP FRENEAU

A Poem on the Rising Glory of America. Philadelphia: printed by Joseph Crukshank for R. Aitken, 1772.

The American Village, A Poem. To Which Are Added Several Other Original Pieces in Verse. New York: Inslee and Car, 1772. Facsimile reprint with introduction and biographical data by H. Koopman and V. Paltsits. New York: Burt Franklin, 1968.

The British Prison-Ship: A Poem. Philadelphia: Francis Bailey, 1781.

The Poems of Philip Freneau, Written Chiefly During the Late War. Philadelphia: Francis Bailey, 1786. Facsimile reprint in *The Poems (1786) and Miscellaneous Works (1788) of Philip Freneau*, edited by Lewis Leary. Delmar, N.Y.: Scholars' Facsimiles and Reprints, 1975.

A Journey from Philadelphia to New-York, . . . by Robert Slender, Stocking Weaver. Philadelphia: Francis Bailey, 1787.

The Miscellaneous Works of Mr. Philip Freneau, Containing His Essays and Additional Poems. Philadelphia: Francis Bailey, 1788. Facsimile reprint in *The Poems (1786) and Miscellaneous Works (1788) of Philip Freneau*, edited by Lewis Leary. Delmar, N.Y.: Scholars' Facsimiles and Reprints, 1975.

The Monmouth Almanac for the Year M,DDC,XCV. Middletown-Point, N.J.: Philip Freneau, 1794.

Poems Written Between the Years 1768 and 1794, by Philip Freneau. Monmouth, N.J.: Philip Freneau, 1795. Facsimile reprint with introduction by Lewis Leary. New York: Scholars' Facsimiles and Reprints, 1976.

Letters on Various Interesting and Important Subjects; . . . by Robert Slender, O.S.M. Philadelphia: D. Hogan, 1799. Facsimile reprint with introduction and biographical note by Harry Hayden Clark. New York: Scholars' Facsimiles and Reprints, 1943.

Poems Written and Published During the American Revolutionary War. 2 vols. Philadelphia: Lydia R. Bailey, 1809. Facsimile reprint with introduction by Lewis Leary. New York: Scholars' Facsimiles and Reprints, 1976.

A Collection of Poems, on American Affairs, and A Variety of Other Subjects, Chiefly Moral and Political. 2 vols. New York: David Longworth, 1815. Facsimile reprint with introduction by Lewis Leary. New York: Scholars' Facsimiles and Reprints, 1976.

Some Account of the Capture of the Ship "Aurora." Introduction by Jay Milles. New York: M. F. Mansfield and A. Wessels, 1899.

The Poems of Philip Freneau, Poet of the American Revolution, edited with biography and critical evaluation by Fred Lewis Pattee. 3 vols. Princeton, N.J.: The University Library, 1902–1907.

Unpublished Freneauana, edited by Charles F. Heartman. New York: [C. F. Heartman], 1918.

Poems of Freneau, selected and edited with an introduction by Harry Hayden Clark. New York: Harcourt, Brace, 1929.

The Last Poems of Philip Freneau, edited with an introduction by Lewis Leary. New Brunswick, N.J.: Rutgers University Press, 1945.

The Prose of Philip Freneau, selected and edited by Philip M. Marsh. New Brunswick, N.J.: Scarecrow Press, 1955.

Father Bombo's Pilgrimage to Mecca, 1770, by Hugh Henry Brackenridge and Philip Freneau, edited with an introduction by Michael Davitt Bell. Princeton, N.J.: Princeton University Library, 1975.

The Writings in Prose and Verse of Hezekiah Salem, Late of New England: To Which Is Added An Account of His Last Yankee Venture, edited with an introduction by Lewis Leary. Delmar, N.Y.: Scholars' Facsimiles and Reprints, 1975.

BIBLIOGRAPHIES

The most complete bibliography of Freneau's published works is in Lewis Leary, *That Rascal Freneau*, pp. 418–80.

Marsh, Philip. *Freneau's Published Prose: A Bibliography*. Metuchen, N.J.: Scarecrow Press, 1970.

Miller, Ann. "Checklist of Freneau Material in The Monmouth Historical Association, Freehold, N.J." *Monmouth County Historical Association Bulletin*, 1:49–57 (1948).

Spiller, Robert E. et al. *Literary History of the United States: Bibliography*, 4th ed. 2 vols. New York: Macmillan, 1974.

BIOGRAPHICAL AND CRITICAL STUDIES

Adkins, Nelson F. *Philip Freneau and the Cosmic Enigma*. New York: New York University Press, 1949.

Andrews, William L. "Freneau's 'A Political Litany': A Note on Interpretation." *Early American Literature*, 12:193–96 (Fall 1977).

——. "Goldsmith and Freneau in the 'American Village.'" *Early American Literature*, 5:14–23 (Fall 1970).

Arner, Robert D. "Neoclassicism and Romanticism: A Reading of Freneau's 'The Wild Honey Suckle.'" *Early American Literature*, 9:53–61 (Spring 1974).

Austin, Mary S. *Philip Freneau: The Poet of the Revolution*. New York: A. Wessels, 1901.

Axelrad, Jacob. *Philip Freneau: Champion of Democracy*. Austin: University of Texas Press, 1967.

Bowden, Mary Weatherspoon. "In Search of Freneau's Prison Ships." *Early American Literature*, 14:174–92 (Fall 1979).

——. *Philip Freneau*. Boston: Twayne, 1976.

Cady, Edwin H. "Philip Freneau as Archetypal American Poet." In *Literature and Ideas in America: Essays in Memory of Harry Hayden Clark*, edited by Robert Falk. Athens, Ohio: Ohio University Press, 1975.

Clark, Harry Hayden. "The Literary Influences of Philip Freneau." *Studies in Philology*, 22:1–33 (1925).

——. "What Made Freneau the Father of American Poetry?" *Studies in Philology*, 26:1–22 (1929).

——. "What Made Freneau the Father of American Prose?" *Transactions of the Wisconsin Academy of Sciences, Arts, and Letters*, 25:39–50 (1930).

Eberwein, Jane Donahue. "Freneau's 'The Beauties of Santa Cruz.'" *Early American Literature*, 12:271–76 (Winter 1977–1978).

Forman, Samuel E. *The Political Activities of Philip Freneau*. In *Johns Hopkins University Studies in Historical and Political Science*, Series XX, nos. 9–10. Baltimore: Johns Hopkins Press, 1902. Reprinted New York: Arno Press, 1970.

Kyle, Carol A. "That Poet Freneau: A Study of the Imagistic Successes of *The Pictures of Columbus*." *Early American Literature*, 9:62–70 (Spring 1974).

Leary, Lewis G. "The Dream Visions of Philip Freneau." *Early American Literature*, 11:156–82 (Fall 1976).

——. "Philip Freneau." In *Major Writers of Early American Literature*, edited by Everett H. Emerson. Madison: University of Wisconsin Press, 1972.

——. *That Rascal Freneau: A Study in Literary Failure*. New Brunswick, N.J.: Rutgers University Press, 1941. Reprinted New York: Octagon Books, 1964.

Marsh, Philip M. *Philip Freneau: Poet and Journalist*. Minneapolis: Dillon Press, 1967.

——. *The Works of Philip Freneau: A Critical Study*. Metuchen, N.J.: Scarecrow Press, 1968.

Vitzthum, Richard C. *Land and Sea: The Lyric Poetry of Philip Freneau*. Minneapolis: University of Minnesota Press, 1978.

SUPPLEMENTARY STUDIES

Davidson, Philip G. *Propaganda and the American Revolution, 1763–1783*. Chapel Hill: University of North Carolina Press, 1941.

Kolodny, Annette. *The Lay of the Land: Metaphor as Experience and History in American Life and Letters*. Chapel Hill: University of North Carolina Press, 1975.

Martin, Terence. *The Instructed Vision: Scottish Common Sense Philosophy and the Origins of American Fiction*. Bloomington: Indiana University Press, 1961.

May, Henry F. *The Enlightenment in America*. New York: Oxford University Press, 1976.

Nye, Russell B. *The Cultural Life of the New Nation, 1776–1830*. New York: Harper, 1960.

Pearce, Roy Harvey. *The Continuity of American Poetry*. Princeton, N.J.: Princeton University Press, 1961.

Silverman, Kenneth. *A Cultural History of the American Revolution*. New York: Thomas Y. Crowell, 1976.

Tyler, Moses Coit. *The Literary History of the American Revolution, 1763–1783*. 2 vols. New York: G. P. Putnam, 1897. Reprinted New York: Barnes and Noble, 1941.

—MAUREEN GOLDMAN

Margaret Fuller

1810–1850

AFTER Margaret Fuller's death, Elizabeth Barrett Browning wrote, "If I wished anyone to do her justice, I should say ... 'Never read what she has written.'" And although Ralph Waldo Emerson judged her conversation "the most entertaining in America," he also said, "Her pen was a non-conductor." Countless others testify that her writing never matched the vividness of her talk, her presence, and above all, her story.

Certainly the barest recitation of the facts of her life commands attention. She was born on May 23, 1810. From the age of six, Fuller was tutored so rigorously by her father that in her mid-teens she could match wits with the brightest men at Harvard. She is supposed to have said, "I now know all the people worth knowing in America and I find no intellect comparable to my own." She was no beauty, but her conversation was so clever and eloquent that her plainness was forgotten. Called "an exotic in New England," she defended and interpreted Johann Wolfgang von Goethe in a community scandalized by him. A plan to go to Europe when she was twenty-five was deferred for eleven years by her father's death and the need to act as head of the family.

An intimate of the transcendentalists, especially of Emerson, Fuller edited their journal, the *Dial,* and taught at Bronson Alcott's con-troversial school. For five winters, beginning in 1839, she offered "conversations" for the leading women of Boston, a series of meetings at which they were induced to think aloud. In 1845 she published *Woman in the Nineteenth Century,* one of the first American books analyzing the situation of women in her time. *Summer on the Lakes in 1843* (1844), on her travels in the West, won Fuller a position as the first woman member of the working press at Horace Greeley's *New York Tribune.* She produced articles on social questions and a body of literary criticism rivaled in America at the time only by that of Edgar Allan Poe.

While writing dispatches from Europe, Fuller came to know Thomas Carlyle and George Sand, and was close to Giuseppe Mazzini and Adam Mickiewicz. She became one of the first war correspondents when the revolutions of 1848 broke out. In Rome she was the secret lover of an Italian revolutionary, whose child she bore and kept hidden in the Abruzzi mountains. She remained in Rome for the brief days of the Roman Republic and directed a hospital when the French held the city in siege. After the fall of Rome, Fuller claimed she was married, but offered no details; and after moving to Florence with her family, she continued work on a book on the Italian revolution.

Her political radicalism made Elizabeth Barrett Browning, her friend in Florence, call Fuller "an out and out Red" and imagine that her book was drenched in "the blood colours of Socialistic views, which would have drawn the wolves on her . . . both in England and America." On July 19, 1850, the wolves were cheated by shipwreck within sight of the American shore. Henry David Thoreau spent days on Fire Island, New York, searching for her body and her manuscript, to no avail.

Such a life would compete for our notice with the work of a much more talented writer than Fuller. But more than the patent drama and originality of her life, the sense that it was at once enigmatic and paradigmatic has kept her legend alive—tantalizing, infuriating, elusive. Henry James, who heard of her death as a boy of seven, wrote of the "haunting Margaret-ghost" that would not be laid to rest, and indeed she stalks the houses of his fiction. Alger Hiss recalled in the 1970's how, when he clerked for Oliver Wendell Holmes in 1930, the justice retold his father's accounts of discussions of Margaret Fuller, long after her death, in the Saturday Club; Holmes summed up: "She stuck in their craw."

Fuller was famous for her appetite ("Such a predetermination to *eat* this big Universe as her oyster or her egg," Carlyle wrote, "I have not before seen in any human soul") but was herself apparently indigestible. Hence more ink—from pens great and small—was spilled about Fuller than about any other American woman of her time. The elder Holmes may have drawn on Fuller for his novel *Elsie Venner,* and James probably modeled both the predatory and the mesmerizing feminists in *The Bostonians* on her. Fuller's best-known fictional disguise is, of course, the Zenobia who so richly displays Nathaniel Hawthorne's ambivalence toward passionate and intellectual women in his *Blithedale Romance.*

The first direct reading of Fuller, the two-volume *Memoirs of Margaret Fuller Ossoli* (1852), which intercalates her informal writings with the recollections of friends, resembles a rush to judgment. In this labor of love, the editors—Emerson, James Freeman Clarke, and William Henry Channing—came to praise Fuller, but also to bury her. For however rebellious they had been as clergymen, the duty of protecting a lady's reputation revitalized all their orthodoxy. (Emerson confessed, tellingly, that the project "might turn out to be a work above our courage.") These gentlemen quelled their doubts (while forgetting to destroy records of them) to announce that Fuller was safely married before her child was conceived, ignored her growing radicalism, and excised all indiscretions. But, with pencil and even scissors, they did further damage. Channing was probably the worst offender; as Emerson shrewdly discerned, Channing was "too much her friend to leave him quite free enough." In his hands Fuller's adjective in "It will be terrible for me to leave Italy" becomes "sad," and "I . . . am happy, yes I *am* happy here" becomes the sedate "I am contented." By the addition of domestic and religious pieties to her sentences, she is locked for posterity in a posture against which she had rebelled.

Thomas Wentworth Higginson began reinterpretation of Fuller in 1884 with his exhumation of the woman of action. In 1903 the startling publication of the long-suppressed love letters to the previously unknown James Nathan generated new readings, chief among them Katharine Anthony's oedipal one in 1920. In 1942, Emma Detti introduced the friendship with Mickiewicz and fleshed out the background of Italian political life. Drawing on these and similar materials, Joseph Jay Deiss in 1969 offered a portrait of a sexual and political renegade. In 1977, Ann Douglas found, in

Fuller's rejection of fiction for history, the exception that proved the rule of feminization of American culture.

From our perspective it is tempting to read Fuller's story as a myth of a woman who lived two lives or who died in the early nineteenth century and returned a few generations later to complete her life with a modern critical sensibility. But when did the first life end and the second begin? With the crisis in her relations with Emerson, her feminist activities, her trip west, her move to New York, or her passage to Europe? All these were decisive turning points. It is perhaps more accurate to see Fuller as a woman of the nineteenth century nurturing a modern woman within.

This helps us to think about her problematic writing. Sometimes this modern woman, wary of being trapped in her time by use of its language, pushed away from all texts, including her own. But intermittently the modern woman sought expression. Fuller's failures were marked by a belated romantic rhetoric, or an outlandish, semicoherent jargon of her own. Although it was often strained, her writing was also a straining toward a future, altered society, a culture that would mirror and validate her reality as her America could not do. Sometimes she saw lucidly that the language of modern feeling had to be invented and that deep cultural change must accompany such speech. Increasingly, as Fuller approached such change in her last years, she found words—and her writing became easy, eloquent, and forceful. In a defense of the excesses of her style of living, she once implied a related explanation of her writing style: "In an environment like mine, what may have seemed too lofty or ambitious in my character was absolutely needed to keep the heart from breaking and enthusiasm from extinction." A woman seeking free action in nineteenth-century America must overdo to do

at all, she argues, and that may be the best justification of her early writing. Our sense of rhetorical extravagance in the sentence diminishes in proportion to the credence we lend to her thought.

More useful to us than Elizabeth Barrett Browning's warning is Poe's observation: "Her acts are bookish, and her books are less thoughts than acts." Both Fuller's life and her writings were a series of rough drafts, hurried experiments of a woman who knew the time was late or early—in any case short—for the place was wrong, or the people narrow; but perhaps, if she could imagine another way of saying or doing it, the world around would change to be capable of receiving it. Because "it" was there—the ability, the courage, the energy, the hunger, and the conviction that the self had more to know and feel and do than was given. Read together, her life and work then make a single text, an unfinished text, or better, a potential one—and certainly a criticism of the canon of existing texts, because the canon gave Fuller no help. She spoke, at her best, in another tongue.

Although the criticism for which Fuller was most valued in her time was of literature, we now profit most from the critical light that her life and work cast on the situation of American women and on the underlying social assumptions of her time. As Alexis de Tocqueville saw better than any American, the two were intimately connected. Visiting the United States in the 1830's, de Tocqueville noted that, as a "puritanical people and a commercial nation," Americans had a double motive for binding women in conventional marriages: ensuring the purity of their morals and securing order and prosperity in the home. But as a democratic nation, placing high value on individual independence, they believed "They had little chance of repressing in women the most vehement passions of the human heart." The only sure way "was to teach her the art of combating those passions for herself," by placing "more reliance . . . on the free vigor of her will," by arming reason as well as virtue.

So reared, the young unmarried woman revealed a freedom of mind and action unmatched in Europe. But as a wife she was more submissive, dependent, dutiful, and conformist than her European counterpart. What wrought this change? The young woman herself, who, in the culminating exercise of her virtue, reason, and free will, chose such marriage. De Tocqueville further noted that American women "attach a sort of pride to the voluntary surrender of their own will, and make it their boast to bend themselves to the yoke, not to shake it off." Although he observed that this system might produce in young women alarming forwardness and in wives a cold virtue, he admired what he took to be their freedom of choice. He seems to have been seduced by the very sophistry he describes, which dresses up conditioning as freedom. On her visit Harriet Martineau was not deceived for a moment: "While woman's intellect is confined, her morals crushed, her health ruined, her weaknesses encouraged, and her strength punished, she is told that her lot is cast in the paradise of women."

While these Europeans were noting these contradictions, Margaret Fuller, then in her twenties and without benefit of their analyses, was suffering them. Her problem was that of all American women who wanted to realize in their adult lives a concept of freedom that was intended to be simply a plaything of their youth. As de Tocqueville had seen, the puritanical and economic objectives that defined the American nation defined woman as well—as a creature destined for marriage, and fulfilled and useful only in the family circle. To conceive of women differently was tantamount to challenging the assumptions on which the nation was built. Ultimately Fuller did this, implicitly challenging puritanical assumptions by her sexual behavior, explicitly questioning the economic assumptions, and especially their social and political corollaries, in her writing from Italy.

Fuller's apprenticeship to this critical lucidity abroad was her willingness to be a freak in America. Poe's version is the most succinct; he said, according to Perry Miller, that humanity is divided into three classes: men, women, and Margaret Fuller. But many others, and she herself as well, saw her as a hybrid, a union—sometimes happy, sometimes not—of two usually exclusive tendencies: more often than not, these tendencies were "masculine" and "feminine." Both de Tocqueville and Martineau were struck by an American insistence, unknown in Europe, on differences between men and women. De Tocqueville noted that "The women of America, who often exhibit a masculine strength of understanding and a manly energy, generally preserve great delicacy of personal appearance and always retain the manners of women." Martineau judged sharply that "the prevalent persuasion that there are virtues which are peculiarly masculine, and others which are peculiarly feminine" effectively crushed the morals of both sexes.

By their natures Fuller's parents reinforced the sexual stereotypes, and by their method of rearing her they contributed to her sense of being hopelessly divided between these stereotypes. Her mother, Margarett Crane Fuller, seems to have followed without effort the model of the "true woman" esteemed at the time. Although as a teenage schoolmistress she could keep rough boys in line, she seems as a wife to have submitted serenely to her husband's domination, to illness, to the bearing of nine children and the death of two of them in infancy.

Her steady faith and confident acceptance of her lot seem to have instilled idealism in her children.

Individuality and strong, even controversial, behavior seem to have been constant traits of the Fullers, who had been in Massachusetts since 1629. Timothy Fuller, Margaret's father, worked his way through Harvard, where he was demoted to second place in his class because of his participation in a student rebellion. Serving two terms in Congress before becoming Speaker of the Massachusetts House of Representatives, he opposed the expatriation of the Seminoles and the Missouri Compromise. In his love for literature of the French Revolution and his Jeffersonian principles, and in his loyal and unpolitic support of John Quincy Adams for president as late as 1832, he showed his political independence. These political stances, his Unitarian faith, and his abrasive personality made him something of a renegade in Cambridge until political discouragement drove him to the country to pursue farming, as his father had done.

When, at the introspective age of thirty, Fuller came to write an autobiographical romance (later printed in the *Memoirs*), she gave an ideal and generalized account of her parents that connects the woman with physical nature, emotionality, spirituality, and idealism, and the man with the social world, intellectual discipline, and practicality. The tendency of the daughter to learn to follow the mother was distorted in Fuller's case by the unusually great influence of her father and the unusually retiring role of her mother. Though the two women grew closer after Timothy Fuller's death, the mother appears to have been a loving but somewhat distant figure on the child's landscape.

Timothy, a scholar who "grudged the hours nature demands for sleep," was spurred by the precocity of his eldest child to initiate a rigorous program of classical education when she was six. The curriculum was not unusual for the sons of professors, but was unknown for girls in this age of sentimental education, and—except in cases like John Stuart Mill's—it was rarely administered by fathers. He quizzed Margaret in Latin and English grammar until long past her bedtime; he rejected apology, hesitation, qualification, or circumlocution in her performance, effectively cutting her off from prevailing styles of female discourse. A few years later, as Paula Blanchard has demonstrated, he realized the cost in social terms of his one-sided nurture, and urged her to be less bold in speech, less obsessed with books, and more concerned with posture and decorous manners. It was too late; taking stock of her assets at the age of twelve, this daughter had resolved to be "bright and ugly."

The intellectual and psychological effects of an education so odd, so strenuous, and so tied to paternal approval and love are incalculable. Fuller herself repeatedly revised her estimate. At thirty she wrote that the paternal influence whetted her appetite for heroic action and realism, for meeting the challenges of the actual world with disciplined will—all the values she associated with the Romans, whose literature and culture Timothy, as a true son of the American Revolution, chiefly stressed. But her expression of her relation to the Romans was problematic. "I kept their statues as belonging to the hall of my ancestors, and loved to conquer obstacles, and fed my youth and strength for their sake," she wrote, quite as if a New England girl might grow up to be a Roman hero.

On the negative side Fuller felt that her father's nocturnal drills caused her to suffer as a child from terrifying nightmares and later from "continual headache, weakness, and nervous affections, of all kinds." A deeper distortion stemmed from his imposing the values of intellect, will, and action completely at the expense of those related to feeling—imagination, passion, and receptivity to nature. "The child fed with meat instead of milk becomes too soon mature," she observed sententiously. "With me, much of life was devoured in the bud."

The rigid perfectionism of the Romans and of Timothy Fuller's nurture was later counterbalanced in some measure by Margaret's discovery of the Greeks' love of beauty and of the moral and psychological realism of Molière, Miguel de Cervantes, and especially William Shakespeare. Of the Greeks, she wrote in her autobiographical romance that she "loved to creep from amid the Roman pikes to lie beneath this great vine, and see the smiling and serene shapes go by. . . . I loved to get away from the hum of the forum, and mailed clang of Roman speech, to these shifting shows of nature, these Gods and Nymphs born of the sunbeam, the wave, the shadows on the hill." It is striking that, in Fuller's imagery, the classical world is bisected by gender into male Rome (vertical pikes, "mail," the forum) and female Greece (horizontal vine, nymphs, nature). But it is hardly surprising, for by the same account her earliest refuge from the father's books was the seclusion of the garden, her mother's cherished work place. There she would indulge all afternoon in childish and passionate dreaminess.

Understandably, then, Fuller came to feel divided into separate selves. But she turns inside out the model for female complexity, noted by de Tocqueville, in which the "masculine" gifts and impulses hide within a conventionally "feminine" exterior. For Fuller, as the side nurtured by her father came to be public, that associated with her mother became private, even invisible:

His influence on me was great, and opposed to the natural unfolding of my character, which was fervent, of strong grasp and disposed to infatuation, and self-forgetfulness. He made the common prose world so present to me, that my natural bias was controlled. . . . My own world sank deep within. . . . But my true life was only the dearer that it was secluded and veiled over by a thick curtain of available intellect, and that coarse but wearable stuff worn by the ages— Common Sense.

Well into her thirties, Fuller remained ambivalent about this dividing and repressive curtain knit in childhood. Finding her vocation and finding herself would depend on her tearing down the curtain. In addition, she would have to learn to reject the notions of masculine and feminine that were locked into the culture, for as long as she described her problem in these terms, she conspired in delaying her progress to selfhood and freedom.

By 1824, Timothy Fuller was anxious enough about Margaret to send her, against her will, to acquire "female propriety" at the Misses Prescott's School in Groton, Massachusetts. The intimacy Fuller developed with the headmistress, Susan Prescott, had the desired effect of making her want—sometimes—womanly "tact and polish" to complement the genius she took for granted. But back at home in 1825 she found that intellectual ability was always her steadiest resource. She noted that the study she pursued on her own filled her with a "gladiatorial disposition" that prevented her enjoying casual society.

Society came late and not casually to this lonely adolescent. Yet in the yeasty Cambridge of the late 1820's, full of brilliant talkers and dedicated to the romantic cult of friendship, Margaret Fuller's arrival was a spectacular event. It was only by approaching people as a gladiator that she could, paradoxically, win them and lower her own guard. Many were initially repelled by this long-necked, robust young woman with eyes alternately squinting and dilating, by her dominating erudition and scathing wit. William Henry Channing confessed that he avoided one "so armed from head to foot in saucy sprightliness," and Emerson underscored the martial image: "The men thought she carried too many guns." For an extraordinary number of men and women, though, closer acquaintance with her, especially tête-à-tête, broke down their resistance. Thus, Sarah Freeman Clarke wrote: "Though she spoke rudely searching words, and told you startling truths, though she broke down your little shams and defenses, you felt exhilarated by the compliment of being found out." Women like Sarah Clarke felt Fuller's assault on their reserves and pretenses, but some of the men apparently were wounded in their vanity and in their sense of what was proper to the "gentler sex."

Once Fuller as warrior had broken through the shields of privacy or prejudice, she could lay down arms and disclose her unusual talent for empathic understanding. Doubtless she was exacting and often difficult in this second phase. But her friendship was rare and original, for it drew on the provinces, as then understood, of both sexes; they were united for her in Goethe's phrase that she inscribed in a friend's journal: "extraordinary generous seeking." With precocious psychological understanding, she seemed to know that the secret, even shameful, aspects of the personality had to be exposed and accepted for the integrated—the word then was "ideal"—self to flourish. Sarah's brother, James Freeman Clarke, recalled that Fuller's conversation could uniquely "make an epoch in one's life." He wrote to her, "What should I ever have been but for you? . . . You gave me to myself."

"She was, indeed, the Friend. This was her vocation," pronounced Channing in the *Memoirs,* with all the finality of an epitaph. (Indeed,

it was on Fuller as friend that the three editors of the *Memoirs* wrote most comfortably and extensively.) Could friendship have been the vocation she sought? Certainly friendship was for her an object of most intense study, and character and destiny were as worthy of analysis as great literature. "Her wit, her insight into characters," Elizabeth Hoar wrote to a friend, are "such that she seems to read them aloud to you as if they were printed books." Sometimes the critique needed revision, as when Fuller thought in 1839 that she had underrated Bronson Alcott: "I will begin him again and read by faith awhile." Certainly she tried to make of friendship an art that would exploit all her resources. But as friendship approached vocation for Fuller, it had to meet so many conditions and needs—it had almost to feed on crisis—that both friendship and Fuller were endangered. This was a hard lesson, and in her thirties she would have to study it twice.

It is small wonder that women who welcomed her intimacy often did so with the quality of reasoned courage disclosed by the odd locution of Sarah Shaw nearly four decades after Fuller's death: "I feel proud that I had the sense to love and venerate her as I did." To be Fuller's friend took a certain daring. The volatile young poet William Ellery Channing (William Henry's cousin, who married Fuller's sister, Ellen) made the shrewdest complaint. "I feel strongly attracted towards you, but there is a drawback in my mind," he told her, as she recorded it. "You will always be wanting to grow forward, now I like to grow backward too. You are too ideal. Ideal people anticipate their lives, and they make themselves and every body around them restless, by always being beforehand with themselves." He also accused her of lacking spontaneity in group conversation, of being "disciplined, artificial."

Touching Fuller's weakness, Ellery also touched her strength. Fuller had not only to resist models of American women, she had also to invent herself. It is tempting to think of her poised on a threshold, projecting into a room an image of what woman should be, then walking in and entering the image. Invention can be creation only if the atmosphere is receptive, the ground fertile; on barren land it is artifice. Whether Fuller's inventions were creative or artificial depended partly on the society she met and partly on her ability to transform it. Like the enthusiastic thinkers who surrounded her, she put too much stock for too long in the personal power of transformation.

Fuller welcomed Ellery's objections, feeling that she must "learn from them all," but added, "I must not let them disturb me." She was more willing to be ridiculous than to abandon her quest: "I will bear the pain of imperfection, but not of doubt." But she found no one who could do for her what she had done for James Clarke—give her to herself. Friendship could not be her vocation; to identify what could, she needed a mentor and a guide.

By the age of twenty, Fuller no longer cut such an outlandish figure. Eliza Farrar, the Cambridge matron who later wrote *The Young Lady's Friend,* had taken her in hand and taught her to lose weight and master the manners, coiffure, and dress of a young lady. Fuller seems not to have minded, but she had little expectation of the fate meant to accompany the fashion. She had left the Prescotts' School, as Blanchard points out, expecting to enter a "life of letters." Granted, she could feel brokenhearted when a delightful cousin failed to notice her passion and married someone else. And doubtless she smarted when James Clarke confided to her his attraction to one deferential young woman after another. (In a journal she confesses: "Of a disposition that requires the most refined, the most exalted tenderness, without charms to inspire it. Poor Mignon!") Al-

though she wanted love, she may not have wanted marriage. She thought the curse of loneliness "nothing compared with that of those who have entered into relations but not made them real."

In her late teens Fuller enjoyed a rich "life of letters" with a small circle of friends, some from the Harvard class of 1829. Together they read Charles Lamb, William Wordsworth, Samuel Taylor Coleridge, and Carlyle. Influenced by the last two and by Henry Hedge's enthusiastic invitations to share his unique collection of books from Germany, Clarke and Fuller read Friedrich von Schiller and Goethe together. At twenty-one she wrote that, feeling oppressed by emotional disappointments, family cares, and social obligations, "I took up the study of German, and my progress was like the rebound of a string pressed almost to bursting."

The prospect of reading, translating, and interpreting German literature came to Fuller's rescue at a time when her circle was breaking up and the young graduates were beginning their careers. She would soon have to draw heavily on Goethe's creed of self-sufficiency, for in 1833, disillusioned with political life, her father resolved to retire from her beloved Cambridge to a farm in her detested Groton. There she had the tutoring, five to eight hours daily, of her four youngest siblings added to an unusually onerous share of women's work—for her mother, grandmother, and brothers were often ill, and an infant brother died in her arms. In her "spare" time Fuller read at a prodigious rate in German, French, and English romanticism, European and American history, architecture, and astronomy—and discussed what she had read in her growing correspondence.

In Groton, Fuller conceived the bold idea of writing a life of Goethe, who had died in 1832 and was not merely unread in America but shouted down for his monstrous worldliness by most of the enlightened men she knew. For

Fuller, Goethe expressed as no one else did her desire for knowledge gained through passionate, broad, and subtle experience; and the wisdom of his female characters inspired her. At the age of twenty-two, she wrote: "How often I have thought, if I could see Goethe, and tell him my state of mind, he would support and guide me." Her dream of a biography was thus at once generous and self-validating. She felt that only she could write it. Ironically, she thought she would have to go to Europe to learn the details of the private life of the writer who had so liberated her spirit, for no American scholar who had met Goethe would share them with a lady.

That problem was flanked by another that became acute when Fuller tried to write. If American men would not supply the matter, American women of course could not provide the model for Fuller as writer. The learned women of New England could not help a woman inspired by Aspasia, the courtesan who was the mistress of Pericles, noted for bold will and intellect; her description of Aspasia's portrait as marked by "the voluptuousness of intellect" would surely have jarred their still puritanical imaginations. Fuller noted wryly that no Muse came to her, a woman, and yet she was dogged by migraine; "It is but a bad head—as bad as if I were a great man!" But she was not a man, and only the confirming example of a woman of letters could help to free her from the psychosomatic part of her symptoms.

All the examples were in Europe, for there the institution of the salon in particular had long given women of intelligence, wit, and sympathy an influential role with men of letters and politics, a role unknown in America. In her sixteenth year Fuller had been attracted to Madame de Staël, not by her political audacity but by her large spirit; the brilliance of her conversation, her intense friendships, and the writing that captured the imagination of a generation amply compensated for her plain appearance.

In a few years Fuller's contemporaries would compare her with Germaine de Staël and also with the heroine of the Frenchwoman's popular romance, *Corinne, or Italy,* for Fuller too was given to rushes of magnetic, extemporaneous speech. Actually, Corinne's rejection of England for Italy—that is, for genius, self-expression freed of convention—provides a strong and prophetic link to Fuller. Corinne's inability to sustain her independence must have disappointed Fuller, and she outgrew de Staël and eventually disparaged her vanity and sentimentality: "She could not forget the Woman in the thought; while she was instructing you as a mind, she wished to be admired as a Woman; sentimental tears often dimmed the eagle glance." The passage recalls Fuller's careful concealing in childhood of the "true" or emotional life behind the curtain of intellect.

In the 1830's George Sand's social novels gave Fuller the courage to want to tear down the curtain, to try to rejoin her divided selves through fiction: "I have always thought that I would not [write of human nature], that I would keep all that behind the curtain, that I would not write, like a woman, of love and hope and disappointment, but like a man of the world of intellect and action." But her fiction-writing ventures failed, and, as with de Staël, Fuller was quick to discern Sand's "womanish" failings: "She has genius and a manly heart! Will there never be a being to combine a man's mind and woman's heart, and who yet finds life too rich to weep over?"

Though she would later write more warmly of Sand's courage, Fuller's anxiety about female weakness was too great in her younger years to let her choose Sand as a model. The heroic "common sense" instilled in her by her father was doing its work, making her disparage in women artists the emotionality she had come to cherish in her friends and leading her to discern egoism or inadequacy when they sought to transcend the emotional sphere. In writing she continued for years to feel that she was committed to one part of herself while betraying another. "It is a mockery thus to play the artist with life, and dip the brush in one's own heart's blood," she wrote. And again:

For all the tides of life that flow within me, I am dumb and ineffectual, when it comes to casting my thought into a form. No old one suits me. If I could invent one, it seems to me the pleasure of creation would make it possible for me to write. . . . I love best to be a woman; but womanhood is at present too straitly-bounded to give me scope. At hours, I live truly as a woman; at others I should stifle; as, on the other hand, I should palsy, when I would play the artist.

Plainly the "form" Fuller sought was not only literary; it would enlarge woman's role while including her gifts, and consequently would expand existing notions of artist and art. "Conversation is my natural element," she wrote, putting it another way. "I need to be called out, and never think alone, without imagining some companion." (This explains her frequent adoption of the dialogue form in her work.) Although she felt that this habit betrayed "a second-rate mind," it also marked a dialectical one. Fuller may justly have feared that the isolation of writing, compounded by the isolation of her position, could lead only to solipsism. In any case she wanted writing to be more a matter of relationship.

In the same summer (1835) that she realized her inability to write fiction, Fuller met Harriet Martineau, who had fought illness, poverty, and disapproval to publish, on her own, her *Illustrations of Political Economy*. Still longing for a confirming mirror, Fuller hoped her new friend would "comprehend me wholly, mentally, and morally, and enable me better to comprehend myself"; still hungry for criticism, she rejoiced that "There are no strong intellectual sympathies between us, such as would blind her to my defects."

When Martineau offered to take Fuller with her to England, and her father consented, thus rewarding her for tutoring in rural exile, it seemed too good to be true—and it was. Timothy Fuller's sudden death from cholera in the fall of 1835 had the effect of detaining her for eleven years in her country, years that would totally alter the meaning a European trip would hold for her.

Her father's death forced Fuller to become, in effect, head of the household (a position for which her mother was even less prepared than she), to learn how to disentangle his financial affairs, to fight against her narrow-minded and domineering uncle Abraham Fuller for her siblings' right to education, and later to guide them to work, to a profession, even to lodgings. Her father's death also left her emotionally orphaned, and for some years she searched for a father as well as a mentor.

Curiously, it was Harriet Martineau, from whom, as a European woman, Fuller had hoped for so much, who introduced her to that American father, Ralph Waldo Emerson. He was a man she had longed to meet for years before she managed it, and she continued to regard him with love and reverence long after she discerned how little he could directly help or understand her. Each became for the other a touchstone for values attractively alien, and their friendship did much to clarify for both the bounds their temperaments set for them. Seven years older than Fuller, Emerson must have first drawn her by his likeness to her father in reserve and intellectual earnestness. More important, he seemed to offer what Timothy Fuller could not, an end to her anomalous social status—if not something to do, at least a way to be. For, though a man, he had found it necessary to invent his vocation.

Thus, when Emerson read *Nature* aloud to her, Fuller might have drawn hope and support from its closing exhortation, "Build therefore your own world." As an alternative to the inhospitable social world, Emerson's vision sanctioned a world fashioned after her idiosyncratic individuality, not resistant to it. Her "own world" would become simultaneously the sedulously cultivated circle of high-minded intimates and the infinite expanse of the private self. "From him I first learned what is meant by the inward life," she wrote gratefully.

In the beginning there was a pleasing reciprocity. When they met in 1836, Emerson, like Fuller, was grieving; and the death of his brother Charles had brought such a sense of loss that the "very sober joy" in his second wife, Lidian—one of the most pious, frail, and self-sacrificing of the transcendentalists—could not compensate for it. While he inducted Fuller into the worlds of solitude and natural harmony, she offered him the best of real society. Sometimes Emerson was exuberantly grateful for the company of Fuller and her young friends ("Your poor hermit . . . will yet come to know the world through your eyes"). But just as she eventually felt constrained by Emerson's ahistorical and solipsistic "inwardness," so did he resist breaking out of his inveterate reserve. A tension grew with their friendship for which both would use the same striking word. Emerson's adoption of Michel Eyquem de Montaigne's phrase, "Oh, *my friends,* there are no friends," was for Fuller "a paralyzing conviction," while Emerson confided in his journal after one of her visits, "Life too near paralyzes art." What they had to offer each other was great, but given the ascetic basis of his craft and her need for dynamic relation, the threat of mutual paralysis was always near.

There were also more covert confusions. Teaching self-reliance, Emerson instilled expectations, even dependencies, for which he was unable to take responsibility. His belief that each person should follow his inner convictions conflicted with his wish that those convictions should take on the coloration of his own. And Fuller could not separate her desire to forge an independent, richly integrated self from a desire to have that self accepted, even sanctioned, by a person of Emerson's stature.

These tensions came to a head in 1840, when both moved to deepen their friendship, but from fatally diverse motivations. Emerson contemplated writing an essay on friendship, though to Fuller he confessed to being "perplexed lately with a droll experience of limitation as if our faculties set a limit on our affections." With Fuller as his guide, he sought to identify his limits; by contrast Fuller wanted through this engagement to arrive at her greatest potential. (In such a contest the conservative objective prevails.) Of course, this very verbal exercise afforded them the pleasurable opportunity to make metaphors and to dramatize—to the verge of caricature—their differing stances.

In mid-August, Fuller challenged Emerson to enlarge the grounds of their friendship, which, he wrote, she "stigmatized" as "commercial." Although their correspondence on this subject was bold enough, their private thoughts of course reveal more. She wrote:

I am bent on being his only friend myself. There is enough of me would I but reveal it. Enough of woman to sympathize with all his feelings, enough of man to appreciate all thoughts[.] I could be a perfect friend and it would make me a nobler person. I would never indulge towards him that need of devotion which lies at the depth of my being. He measures too much, he is too reasonable. I could not be my truest child-like self. But I might be my truest manlike self.

The contradictions run rampant. Though Emerson draws on both her "masculine" and "feminine" qualities, Fuller feels she can openly be only "manlike." And the bald possessiveness of the first sentence belies the noble self-sacrifice. It is as if she wanted in this relation to replace both marriage and vocation. Here was a lust for the kind of power that comes only through dependency; had she had her way, she might have remained a satellite of Emerson's forever.

Fortunately for the future of Fuller's independence and self-awareness, Emerson refused her experiment. In a journal entry he upbraids her as he never could directly:

You would have me love you. What shall I love? Your body? The supposition disgusts you. What you have thought and said? Well, whilst you were thinking and saying them, but not now. I see no possibility of loving anything but what now is, and is becoming; your courage, your enterprise, your budding affection, your opening thought, your prayer, I can love, but what else.

As Fuller sought an exclusive, mutual, and total comprehension, Emerson wanted from her and others only what was potential, suggestive, and fleeting—what, in short, could be absorbed into his own system. The persistent challenging otherness of a friend called up no response in him.

Emerson's behavior was consistent with his developed theory of friendship. When Fuller, angered by his insistence that she was alien to him, threw in his face virtual quotations from his essay "Friendship"—writing, "But did you not ask for a foe in your friend? Did you not ask for a 'large formidable nature?'"—she was fixing on only part of that theory, for in the same essay he rationalized his retreat. (If he did not mean all that he said, he tried to say all that he meant.) "Though I prize my friends I cannot afford to talk with them and study their vision, lest I lose my own," he wrote, and "The soul environs itself with friends that it may enter into a grander self-acquaintance or solitude."

Thus, as he had encouraged intense relations with Fuller in order to pursue his understanding of friendship, so, when the essay was done, did he follow his own analysis and withdraw. "I see very dimly in writing on this topic," he wrote to her on October 14, 1840. "Do not expect it of me for a very long time."

Fuller accepted his plea to return with good-will to their old footing, and they remained friends throughout her life. But beyond the emotional obfuscation, their crisis had exposed differences in value that had intellectual and ideological implications. She touched on them when, in her last visit with the Emersons in 1844, she teased him lightly about how Concord lacked "the animating influences of Discord."

Before Fuller discovered her own path, she drew heavily on the stimulating and steadying influence of Concord and the transcendentalists. Her intellectual commerce with Emerson was brisk. He helped her to fill the gaps in her knowledge of English literature, and she shared Continental literature, finally breaking down his resistance to George Sand and Goethe. Moreover, he led her to Bronson Alcott, who offered her her first job, at his Temple School. Teaching was the most conventional of female occupations—and one she had long shunned—but Alcott's pedagogy was so original for its time as to be scandalous. Following Wordsworth's conviction that children are nearer their celestial origins than adults are, he directed their education inward—and was charged with heresy, blasphemy, and obscenity. Fuller preferred Alcott's self-culture to her father's forced march, and defended him; but privately she noted that Alcott's spirituality lacked robust vitality and excluded the material and the complex. She went on to spend two restless years teaching at the Greene Street School in Providence, Rhode Island, a less radical and more lucrative school.

After resigning her teaching post, Fuller wrote her translation of Johann Peter Eckermann's *Conversations with Goethe,* which George Ripley, the versatile cofounder of Brook Farm, published in 1839. Goethe was under regular and vehement attack in New England, and Fuller's introduction was tartly polemical:

The objections, so far as I know them, may be resolved into these classes—
He is not a Christian;
He is not an idealist;
He is not a democrat;
He is not Schiller.

She then took them one by one, becoming for that time one of Goethe's most balanced readers anywhere, and the only American in her circle who distinguished art from idealism. Her enthusiasm for Continental literature now sharpened her interest in the evolution of an authentic American literature.

Early in 1840, Fuller undertook the most demanding of her transcendentalist enterprises, the editing of the *Dial.* Members of the "Transcendental Club" wanted a journal to compete with the conservative or theological or stridently partisan ones in New England that failed either to publish or to appeal to them. Initiating "a protest against usage, and a search for principles," the first editorial in the *Dial* proposed "not to multiply books, but to report life." Although "the portfolios which friendship had opened to us" were promised to fill its pages, Fuller had to beg contributors for them; and for one issue of 136 pages had hastily to provide 85 pages from her own notebooks. As editor she tried to be impartial, and later defended her practice of publishing representative pieces, even when she did not like them, against Emerson's preference for satisfying his own taste: "I wish my tastes and sympathies still more expansive than they are, instead of more severe. Here we differ." Apparently her tolerance was no-

where shared. "I hope our Dial will get to be a little *bad,*" Emerson complained early; and Theodore Parker was not abashed to say that the *Dial* needed a beard. These rivaling calls for virile boldness seemed to drive Fuller into an uncharacteristically "feminine" neutrality, and made the *Dial* she edited for two years less challenging than any of her later work.

Fuller's poems, stories, and art and music criticism are too subjective to interest us now, but in her literary criticism she undertook the first systematic examination of criticism in America. She argued that criticism should go beyond the impressionism that chiefly characterized the critic; it should combine empathic elucidation of literary works on their own terms with judgment by objective and external standards.

In her twenty months in New York, Fuller wrote two literary pieces a week for the *New York Tribune,* thus outstripping all in her New England circle in practical criticism. ("The Muses have feet to be sure," Emerson remarked doubtfully, "but it is an odd arrangement that selects them for the treadmill.") But Fuller was satisfied to "aid in the great work of popular education." She was uniquely able to mediate between timid Americans and the variously threatening Goethe, Lord George Byron, and Sand. Placing Goethe's worldliness, Byron's morbidity, and Sand's free passion in the contexts of their ages and their options, she made them accessible, even enlightening. Her perspective made her want to encourage an American literature that was individual but not provincial.

Fuller leveled her judgments without regard for fashion. She found the lionized Henry Wadsworth Longfellow "artificial and imitative," and deplored James Russell Lowell's "want of vitality." Though his "great facility at versification" generates "a copious stream of pleasant sound," she concluded that "his verse is stereotyped; his thought sounds no depth; and posterity will not remember him." By contrast, she admired Frederick Douglass, praised Poe—though not enough for his liking—found the early Hawthorne the most promising writer of fiction, tried to rescue Charles Brockden Brown (a feminist, as she read him) from oblivion, and gave a friendly notice to *Typee,* by an unknown Herman Melville. As for Emerson, though she generally praised his second volume of essays, she also found fault with his uncomplicated spirituality: "We doubt this friend raised himself too early to the perpendicular and did not lie along the ground long enough to hear the secret whispers of our parent life. We could wish he might be thrown by conflicts on the lap of mother earth, to see if he would not rise again with added powers."

Privately and publicly Poe and Lowell satirized this "authoress," but in the *Brooklyn Daily Eagle,* young Walt Whitman welcomed "right heartily" her *Papers on Literature and Art,* published in 1846. Deploring the "tone of supercilious contempt" with which serious writing by women was often greeted, he felt that the book demonstrated women's ability to "enter into the discussion of high questions of morals, taste, etc."

Ultimately Emerson's influence was important for Fuller—and later for Whitman and Thoreau—as a springboard from which to leap to her quite separate fate. To understand her leap, we must remember that for Emerson the notion of the "inward" life turned on a pair of propositions. One was that the self (more precisely *his* self) was inherently "representative" both of his countrymen and of America. The other was that this representative self could evolve only through quiescent isolation. If the individual's "latent conviction" expressed the "universal sense," that person could best pursue that conviction and become a "representative"

American by self-insulation from compromising contact.

The America that Emerson chose to represent was of course that creation unique in the experience of mankind that had analogues in the apocalyptic visions of John Winthrop and Thomas Jefferson and George Bancroft. For Winthrop, Jefferson, and Bancroft, the Author of this idea was God, while for Emerson, the author was the self—or, more accurately, Emerson. "His method of self-renewal," writes Sacvan Bercovitch, "consisted in arrogating the meaning of America to himself." America thus became an idea that sprang from no religious, political, or social institution, but from "the purest minds" only. Given this secularization, internalization, and intellectualization of the myth of American destiny, that destiny and individual integrity were to be secured by identical means: by isolation and abjuration of all action except that of the mind.

Fuller had studied Jefferson with her father on the Groton farm, and in her New England years had no quarrel with the notion of the unique historical mission of America. But she never really believed that her self was representative or that it held any meaningful connection to America except in active participation. After rereading *Nature,* she confessed to Emerson that she delighted "more in thought-living than in living thought."

Underlying her resistance to Emerson and representativeness was Fuller's sense of her irreducible otherness. Her ideological break with Emerson was initiated in what was, ironically, one of her most transcendentalist works. In her *Dial* essay "The Great Lawsuit," later expanded into *Woman in the Nineteenth Century,* she applied transcendentalist tenets to women, particularly the universal sacred right and duty to develop one's nature fully. That Fuller felt impelled to argue woman's humanity proves that however warmly she had been received by transcendentalist gentlemen, she experienced herself, next to them, as "other."

Probably the earliest source of Fuller's feminism was her feeling for her mother. She wrote that after her father's nocturnal drills she often had nightmares of following her mother's corpse to the grave, just as she had followed her infant sister's body. In her biography Katharine Anthony made this dream the keystone of her oedipal reading of Fuller's career. But a fragmentary manuscript, in which Fuller fictionalizes her parents' marriage, suggests other readings. In this fragment she takes two stunning liberties with fact. She disguises herself, the narrator, as a *son,* and tells how the mother— weakened by the husband's neglect of her inner life and destroyed by grief over her second child's death—*dies.* (In actuality Fuller's mother survived her daughter by several years.) The narrator speculates: "Had she lived there was enough in me corresponding with her unconscious wants to have aroused her intellect and occupied her affections. Perhaps her son might have made up to her for want of that full development of feeling which youth demands from love."

Fuller's fiction gives her real, recurrent nightmare of her mother's death a range of meanings: guilt over the father's greater attention to herself than to the mother; the death-in-life she saw in conventional wifery; the mother's real passivity and relative absence from the child's rearing; the mother's inability to provide a model for the growing girl to emulate; the killing of the internalized female in the child by the refusal of both parents to value and nurture it. In this way the dream captures Fuller's anger and sense of loss. The son's fantasized rescue then expresses variously the desires to atone for the father's perceived greater attention to herself, to take the father's place with the mother, to regain a lost closeness, to repair the deficiencies in her mother's life so that she would be able in turn to mother the child more deeply and richly—or, internally, to create a mothering self who would provide acceptance for "this Margaret Fuller" that she could not find elsewhere.

Fuller was aware of the way in which her anomalous life made her fictionalize and internalize the whole range of human relationships: "I was always to return to myself, to be my own priest, pupil, parent, child, husband, and wife." As her mother was, spiritually, no predecessor, so society offered no precedent for Fuller; she would feel impelled to mold her "precedents" belatedly from the material at hand.

Her friendships with other women were marked by these needs to transform the other in order to be loved and accepted. The fervency of the language of these friendships may in part be attributed to the cult of romanticism (much of it echoes the extravagant exchanges in the correspondence between Bettina von Arnim and her friend Karoline von Günderode that Fuller translated and published in 1842 in *Günderode; A Translation from the German*). It may also be partly understood as a consequence of the rigorous separation of human qualities by gender that would encourage women to believe that only they could understand one another. But we should not explain away the intensity in Fuller's love of women, which came from a need to heal a wound sustained in childhood, and to enlarge women's mutual understanding and, hence, their capacities. "It is so true that a woman may be in love with a woman and a man with a man," she wrote of a friend whom she loved in youth, "with as much passion as I was then strong enough to feel." Looking back, Elizabeth Hoar of Concord said, "Had she been a man, any one of those fine girls of sixteen, who surrounded her here, would have married her: they were all in love with her, she understood them so well."

Understanding women was not the same as endorsing them or their sphere. "Plain sewing is decidedly immoral," Fuller once put it succinctly. Although her sense of her own exceptionality was a habitual defense, gradually a desire to work for women—and thus for herself—replaced it. Her "conversations" for women, likely inspired by the heady sessions of the "Transcendental Club," nourished a sense of herself and of possible vocations that eventually led her far beyond the Concord circle and its aims.

In a letter of 1839, Fuller proposed to assemble a circle of "well-educated and thinking women"; her object was to help them "systematize thought and give a precision and clearness in which our sex are so deficient, chiefly, I think, because they have so few inducements." Thus employing her father's standards, she aimed to answer the questions he could not. She felt confident of success if the women would abjure "coterie criticism" and "that sort of vanity in them which wears the garb of modesty." Her first series of "conversations" was on Greek mythology; in five winters she also treated fine arts, ethics, education, and women, especially their influence on family, school, church, society, and literature. Paying a small fee, about twenty-five women—eventually more than forty appeared—gathered at noon once a week for two hours in Elizabeth Peabody's bookstore. The participants were almost all from eminent families or accomplished in their own right or prominent later in the abolitionist and feminist struggles.

For them the experience was plainly instructive and exhilarating. Yet Harriet Martineau's terse dismissal of these "gorgeous pedants" whose leader refused to discuss abolition is better remembered than their enthusiasm. From a short-range feminist perspective or a radical political one, one might agree with Martineau and find that this Yankee version of the salon both overindulged the women and mystified the real issues of their lives. Contrasted with Angelina Grimké's speaking tour, which culminated in 1838 with an antislavery appeal before the Massachusetts state legislature, Fuller's "parlatorio," as Emerson styled it, was mild amusement indeed.

But from a liberal or a long-range feminist point of view, Fuller's premise that women should nurture their serious responses to each other, as well as their obligations to family and society, was trailblazing. The "vindication of woman's right to think" that Elizabeth Cady Stanton later found in the "conversations" was subtly subversive; for thinking women the precincts of love stretched beyond the hearth, and morality was reinformed with free choice and personal responsibility.

For Fuller the "conversations" were alternately gratifying and inadequate: "Oh that it gave me more pleasure to do *a little* good, and give *a little* happiness. But there is no modesty or moderation in me." Yet, in contrast with her tortured relationship with Emerson in 1840, Fuller was here actively fusing her enthusiastic feeling with disciplined thought. Triggered by her intimate experience of unused and directionless energy, her sympathetic work with the women began to show her the way to wholeness, the free exercise of her power. She would become whole, and her power real, in her intelligent and committed action for those who lacked such power.

The "conversations" also helped Fuller with her peculiar writing problem. She had created a setting for "thought-living"—in which texts were acts and words were a matter of relationship—and, drawing on it, wrote her *Dial* essay on women. Thoreau precisely named her triumph when he praised the essay as "rich extempore writing, talking with pen in hand." To expand the essay into *Woman in the Nineteenth Century,* Fuller had further to give up the old intoxication, much of it self-induced, that came from straining for a unique, unprecedented form of expression. She had, in her words, to abandon her aspiration for "the sceptre or the lyre," with which, in her pose of sibyl or Corinne, she had loved to "mould many to one purpose," and to take up "the slow pen."

Fuller understood better that ideas are not autonomous, that only massive cultural changes could permit the conception and articulation of some: ("We have not language . . . to express such ideas with precision"). Meanwhile, she could use the pen merely to point to "something new" in "the life of man," for "hearts crave, if minds do not know how to ask it." Supported by this clarity, she wrote fast, and completed the book in mid-November 1844: "It kept spinning out beneath my hand." She felt her achievement with eloquent simplicity: "I had put a good deal of my true life in it . . . should I go away now, the measure of my foot-print would be left on the earth."

Fuller wrote this book at Fishkill, New York. She was about to start work for the *New York Tribune,* a job Horace Greeley had offered her after reading her *Summer on the Lakes in 1843.* The trip to the Great Lakes and Wisconsin had done much to wean her from the thought of New England; and her *Woman* reflects these changes in her quickened sense of independence and psychological integrity and in a new attention to the claims of society and politics.

A measure of Fuller's psychological confidence is the relative ease of her treatment of the vexed question of whether female nature is distinct from male nature. Although she concurs with the cultural conviction that woman's nature is distinct, she insists that this female essence never appears unmixed: "two sides of the great radical dualism," male and female, "are perpetually passing into one another"; and "there is no wholly masculine man, no purely feminine woman." Another measure is her por-

trait of her "friend" Miranda—really an idealized self-portrait—who seeks to dispose of once and for all these paralyzing classifications: "Let it not be said, wherever there is energy or creative genius, 'She has a masculine mind.'"

Moreover, in Miranda's story Fuller reevaluates her father's training, and the contrast is sharp. In the 1840 autobiographical romance she had called it his "great mistake," but now she says it stems from "a firm belief in the equality of the sexes." Where previously she argued that she was cheated of her female nature, now she sees that he addressed her "as a living mind," not a plaything. Where the effect earlier was of a life "devoured in the bud," now it is of "a dignified sense of self-dependence." Although both versions are surely polemical exaggerations, the healing experience of the "conversations" that intervened between them must help to explain the change from despair to pride.

The independence that Fuller stresses is a combination of the transcendentalist virtue of self-reliance and the activist virtue of "self-impulse." She means that, believing woman was made for man, man disqualifies himself from representing woman, and that, until she represents herself, woman is "only an overgrown child." She means that celibacy among women is honorable and solidarity is essential.

In analyzing society—the effects it has on women, the role women should take in society—*Woman in the Nineteenth Century* is curiously hybrid. Calls for various social reforms and even for militant action sound through the old music of pure transcendentalist individualism. Grafted onto the philosophy of romantic self-culture is the homely democratic faith of the Declaration of Independence. The latter leads Fuller to praise the abolitionist movement she had chosen to ignore in her "conversations" and to admire its activists, Angelina Grimké and Abby Kelley. In her revision she also calls upon women to respond en masse to the threatened annexation of Texas; and she heralds public speaking and petition carrying by women, widely censored as immodest and offensive, as the exercise of "moral power" that men have abjured. She also writes with a candor remarkable for the time on the double standard in marriage and on women's need to understand sexuality and prostitution.

In the context of feminist thought, *Woman* presented a broader but much less single-minded attack on the question of woman than its chief predecessors had done. It represented an advance beyond Mary Wollstonecraft's *Vindication of the Rights of Woman* chiefly in its insistence that women must take responsibility for their own liberation. In America, Catharine Beecher and the Grimké sisters had very recently written with a political urgency that Fuller was only beginning to feel.

The political difference between Beecher and Sarah and Angelina Grimké was polar. Enemies of the clergy and the vested interests of the nation, the abolitionist Grimkés argued for absolute equality and were the first to give the lie so clearly to de Tocqueville's fancy of the woman whose mature freedom lies in self-repression. By contrast, Beecher endorsed and even extended de Tocqueville's reasoning. For her the emergency was the imminent dissolution of the nation, witnessed daily in the microcosm of the family. Only a firmly differentiated character in women and the discipline of deference could save the day, for such willed submission was the mark of a superior moral sensibility, the influence of which would spread irresistibly beyond the home to the nation at large.

As conservatism bound Beecher to sexual stereotypes, so political radicalism freed the Grimkés from them. Fuller at moments echoes the thoughts of both, though she is closer to the Grimkés, especially when she shows acid scorn for those who feel that women must be sheltered in an inner circle: "Those who think the physical circumstances of Woman would make a part in the affairs of national government unsuitable, are by no means those who think it impossible for negresses to endure field-work, even during pregnancy, or for sempstresses to go through their killing labors." At such moments, and with the calls to action, Fuller moves for the first time toward radicalism, though she appears not yet aware of its cost.

Active feminism worked to clarify for Fuller the ways in which pure transcendentalism was inadequate for her: it showed her that there were vocations that drew on all her qualities and initiated her career of activist journalism; it was leading her into fuller engagement with the world. She never lost her feminist perspective, but it triggered a process of political analysis and action that carried her beyond the struggle for women alone. She never ceased caring for women, but the distancing, altruistic mode disappeared. At the same time, in her own life she at last recognized and claimed the freedom she needed for herself. In a sense, only by ceasing to be a leader of women could Margaret Fuller become—for those who could see the meaning of her life in its last years—a model.

Fuller's intuitive identification of herself as "other" drew her increasingly to those who could not readily be subsumed under universals, let alone be represented by Emerson. In *Summer on the Lakes,* Fuller's preoccupation with the degradation of the contemporary Indians seems to derive sometimes from an inability to break through their discomforting otherness, sometimes from a kindred sense of oppression. Whatever their source, her shame and indignation at the crimes of her own race were genuine, and made her keen to find in books on Indians and in the whites she met the psycho-history of racism, the inevitable "aversion of the injurer for him he had degraded." As for the white settlers, to whom she looked for a "new order," they generally revealed far too little otherness.

Fuller deplored the importation of Yankee narrowness and calculation in the men and of European standards of culture in the unhappy women, who usually had been dragged unwilling and unprepared into the West. But by the end of this voyage—during which she had made her bed on a barroom floor and with aplomb shot the rapids in an Indian canoe—she called it "pleasant" to hear "rough men tell pieces out of their own common lives, in place of the frippery talk of some fine circle with its conventional sentiment, and timid, second-hand criticism." Perhaps such experiences helped make her style more lean and pointed. Surely they educated her tastes and readied her for the diversity of New York.

Before Fuller left New England, Emerson had written to her from New York that the "endless rustle of newspapers" made him appreciate "not the value of their classes but of my own class—the supreme need of the few worshippers of the Muse—wild and sacred—as counteractions to this world of material and ephemeral interest." Her bias was the reverse. She celebrated this refuge of immigrants of all classes with its great harbor embraced by the "wood of masts" that she found better than any poem. Standing in the city, she felt "the life blood rushing from an entire continent to swell her heart." She liked living in New York, and wrote, "I don't dislike wickedness and wretchedness more than pettiness and coldness."

Horace Greeley resisted Fuller's famous influence, and was therefore the first man in a long while who could "teach" her many things. In her weekly column on social issues, she supported his causes—the Irish, Fourierism, anti-slavery, and opposition to the Mexican War—as well as generating some of her own. She attacked capital punishment; she welcomed the persecuted immigrant Jews and Germans; she sought more enlightened education and broader employment for the poor and for women. No longer preoccupied with ideal friendship or restricted to acquaintance in her class, Fuller's concern for women in trouble could flourish, and her feminism grew with her social awareness. She frequently visited the women in Sing Sing Prison at Ossining, New York; and with Isaac Hopper, an intrepid activist of the Underground Railway, planned the first halfway house for female convicts. Liberal as her reportage was for the time and revolutionary as it was in its familiarity with worlds hitherto closed to a woman of her class, it was still eminently genteel muckraking, and it should be read as apprentice work. She compared her visits with the prisoners with "my Boston classes," but she was beginning to see that self-culture was no longer adequate to solve the vast problems of New York.

When the advent of an aggressive foreign policy was added to these experiences of social inequity, Fuller became increasingly doubtful about the myth of the special destiny of America. After the annexation of Texas and on the eve of war with Mexico, she wrote that the national eagle, in the coming time, "will lead the van, but whether to soar upward to the sun or to stoop for the helpless prey, who now dares promise?" She took an interest in the many varieties of nascent socialism, and she even published her translation from a German immigrant newspaper of one of the earliest discussions of Karl Marx and Friedrich Engels in the United States. But no alternative ideology, no critical method, could replace the myth of moral destiny; and had Fuller not left the country in August 1846, to write about Europe for the *Tribune,* her perspective might simply have soured.

In her *Tribune* column she took farewell of New York, "where twenty months have presented me with a richer and more varied exercise for thought and life than twenty years could in any other part of these United States." She sailed for England as one of the first American correspondents of either sex, and as companion to the philanthropist Marcus Spring, his wife Rebecca, and their young son Eddie. In Great Britain exploration of social conditions and new tendencies crowded out most of the time Fuller would earlier have spent with culture and "genius." She gave the British Museum one day, and the memory of Robert Burns's rebuke to the aristocracy carned more space than her visit to once-cherished Wordsworth. She regretted that Wordsworth's "habits of seclusion" deafened him "to the voice which cries loudly from other parts of England, and will not be stilled by sweet poetic suasion or philosophy, for it is the cry of men in the jaws of destruction." She listened with interest to British reformers, and she wrote enthusiastically about the public baths of Edinburgh and public laundries of London, as well as the new educational institutions for working people created by British women.

Galvanizing Fuller's attention to reform was the omnipresent shock of poverty in England. Dogging her progress through all the celebrated cities was the unforgettable sight of the industrial slums—"the underside of Europe's costly tapestry"—especially their worn female victims "too dull to carouse" and their children fed on opium. "Poverty in England has terrors of which I never dreamed at home," she wrote, yet we know she had toured the slums of Five Points in New York City with Channing. What

her unconscious adherence to the democratic rhetoric of America made her miss at home, the tradition abroad of critical political rhetoric laid bare. What Fuller had perceived as inequity in America began to look like hopeless class division, though like most of her contemporaries and all of her class, she could barely frame the problem in these terms. Then she visited France on the eve of the 1848 revolution. The life of the salons and the streets was crackling with rival socialist theories, heightening her sense of the urgency of action.

An illuminating series of private events had kept pace with this stimulating public tour. As Europe heated up for revolution, experiences and encounters prepared Fuller for fundamental and irrevocable change in her personal life. In New York a troubling romance with an opportunistic aesthete and businessman, James Nathan, had tempted her to express, for the first and last time in her life, a longing for the vicarious existence then deemed woman's natural fate. When the relationship became too demanding or convoluted, Nathan, of German Jewish descent, retreated to Europe. If Fuller had come to Europe still hoping to join him, that hope was effectively killed when she received a letter announcing his engagement to a German woman.

Shortly afterward, descending from Ben Lomond in Scotland after a four-mile climb, Fuller was separated from her hiking companion, failed to find the path, and was forced to spend a dangerous night alone on a narrow ledge, keeping in constant motion to survive the cold mist that mounted in visionary shapes. She resisted the lures of fatal passivity and was found in the morning by a rescue party. Her "mental experience," she wrote in her dispatch, was "most precious and profound," a "presentation of stern, serene realities"; and it is tempting to think it was cathartic. She not only relinquished pursuit of Nathan, but also effectively quit all longing for misty embraces, whether of man or of idea.

At the same time Europeans who had admired her *Woman* and her newly issued *Papers on Literature and Art* were receiving Fuller handsomely and apparently were more comfortable with her in intellectual discourse than many had been at home. "I find myself in my element in European society," she wrote to Emerson. "It does not, indeed, come up to my ideal, but so many of the encumbrances are cleared away that used to weary me in America, that I can enjoy a freer play of faculty and feel, if not like a bird in the air, at least as easy as a fish in the water." Europe did not come up to her ideal, but made her freer: she all but confesses that idealism confined her. For Europe was offering Fuller two crucial sensations that America never did: the shock of class consciousness and the warm bath of personal (and implicitly physical) acceptance. De Tocqueville's knot was coming undone. She was more than ready for the liberating influences of Mazzini in London and of Sand and Mickiewicz in Paris, who would help her discover how to move against the two pressures, social and religious, that bound American women in place.

Fuller's meeting with Giuseppe Mazzini during her last month in England helped to channel the powerful indignation that the tour of Britain had stirred. In exile, Mazzini was organizing for a war to oust the Austrian rulers and unite Italy's eight separate states in a democratic republic. If Emerson's goal of the inward transformation of man by spiritual example still held Fuller in its spell, Mazzini snapped that spell. He later wrote to her that he feared that Emerson would "lead man too much to contemplation." For all his soaring idealism, Mazzini understood that revolution was a matter of concrete and violent action. For all his personal charisma, he understood that it had to be the work of a mass of people, and he inveighed against individualism in the interests of the "collective thought" he had adopted from the Saint-Simonians. Fuller did not give herself over to hero worship. Even in her first account of Mazzini ("the most beauteous person I have seen"), she remarked subtly, "He is one in whom holiness has purified, but somewhat dwarfed the man." Yet before she left England, she had enlisted in his cause and he had provided her with the addresses of his secret agents on the Continent.

In France, Fuller met George Sand, whose work she had boldly defended in America, though always with parenthetical regret for her lapses in private virtue ("Would indeed the surgeon had come with quite clean hands!"). In the liberating atmosphere of France, Fuller was fired by Sand's personal freedom, a consequence of her happy fusion of mind, body, and spirit. "I never liked a woman better," she wrote to the Concord circle. "She needs no defence, but only to be understood, for she has bravely acted out her nature, and always with good intentions." Acted out her nature—it was a moment of prophetic self-recognition, and Fuller was later to use almost the same words in explaining her liaison with Giovanni Angelo Ossoli.

Also in Paris, the poet and revolutionary Adam Mickiewicz linked the influences of Sand and Mazzini. Lecturing on Emerson, Mickiewicz had ultimately found that the American "isolates us too much, not taking into account epoch, nation or earth. Emerson's man dangles one knows not where." Sharing many of Mazzini's political goals, Mickiewicz was also a modern feminist who exhorted Fuller to free herself of the bondage of celibacy. Pointedly she described him to Emerson as "the man I had long wished to see with the intellect and passions in due proportion." Sand's and Mickiewicz's inspiration to give herself to physical and emotional intimacy, and Mazzini's to dedicate herself politically, combined to propel her to the land and the city that her earliest study had taught her to love. In Rome historical events would join with Fuller's unleashed capacity for growth and change to undercut and alter the influence of transcendentalism, and to offer the most comprehensive definition of self and her most satisfying work.

In the spring of 1847, when Fuller arrived in Italy, a state of optimistic excitement prevailed. The liberal Pope Pius IX, elected a year earlier, had proclaimed a universal amnesty for political prisoners, admitted laymen into a council of state, and authorized a civic guard. These measures both undermined the pope's temporal power and stimulated pressure for reform in the seven other states of Italy. The intellectuals whom Fuller met generally favored the moderate program of the exiled priest Vincenzo Gioberti, in which a reformed papacy would preside over a loose federation of Italian kingdoms and duchies protected by King Charles Albert of Piedmont. Armed with her own democratic convictions and Mazzini's vision of republican union, Fuller saw through the moderate scheme.

Her journalistic commitments helped her to clarify her analysis. Most of her twenty-one dispatches from Italy have more concentrated force and shapeliness than anything else she wrote. She paints a European panorama: her quick sketches of conditions in Germany, Austria, and France include shrewd predictions of the political and social evolution to be expected in those countries; denser drawings of the mounting struggles throughout Italy reveal the interlocking dynamics of these situations; finally she concentrates on a changing series of detailed portraits of the pope and the people of Rome. She is especially absorbed by the pope's gradual decline in leadership and by the growth of consciousness in the people—their awaken-

ing need for autonomy and their learning to invest trust and responsibility in themselves, not in princes or divine destiny. Sometimes these dispatches are crabbed or obscure when her involvement was too intense or the departure of a steamer too imminent to permit leisurely exposition, but the old defensive attitudinizing is absent. More partisan than anything she did before, her writing in this last period is more intimately a part of her action and her feeling, and in no way expresses a choice in which something else is sacrificed. In these dispatches all her values are intact, and are so focused and actualized that they make her accounts of hopefulness, restlessness, political suspense, and battle riveting even now. Caught up in Mazzini's vision and the dazzle of events, she tends to overestimate the real limitations on Charles Albert's options and, for a while, the value of Giuseppe Garibaldi. But she is otherwise perspicacious. Urgency drives the old wishfulness out of her social analysis. And in her assessments of the motives of rulers and priests, she draws on a fund of skeptical insight wholly new in her writing. Something of the bite and flash said to characterize her conversation at last dominates her work.

Although her friends included staunch Giobertians, Fuller sought out radicals in Genoa, Milan, Florence, and Rome. One of these, met by chance, was Giovanni Angelo Ossoli, a Roman nobleman of meager means who had received from the priests only the education necessary to fit him to follow his father and three older brothers into the pope's service. But, disapproving the pope's exercise of temporal power, Ossoli was a nascent Mazzinian when he met Fuller, now thirty-seven, ten years older than he. Moved by his tenderness and his intimate appreciation of nature, she was stirred also by his courageous defiance of his family in rejecting the only livelihood for which he had been prepared.

Late in 1847, at about the same time that Ossoli joined the civic guard, the organization in which the radicals readied themselves for struggle, he became Fuller's lover. Their differences satisfied old needs of both. Ossoli, the youngest of six children and still grieving for the mother who had died when he was six, needed a confident, even authoritative, woman. And Fuller cherished in him, as she had in several men, the way he defeated "masculine" stereotyping. The surmise of an American acquaintance, W. H. Hurlbut, who found Ossoli an "underdeveloped and uninteresting Italian," though unsympathetic, is sound: "She probably married him as a representative of an imagined possibility in the Italian character which I have not yet been able to believe in." All her life Fuller had committed herself to "imagined possibilities"—in herself, her friends, the Indians, her students, the ladies of Boston, and the prostitutes of New York—but in Italy she gambled her all on possibility. "I acted upon a strong impulse," she later wrote to her sister. "I neither rejoice nor grieve, for bad or good. I acted out my character."

The character thus discovered was neither that of the "true woman," the quintessential Victorian wife celebrated by her biographers in the nineteenth century, nor the prophet of modern sexual freedom celebrated by some in the twentieth century. It was, rather, a character existing but undisclosed before 1847 because, in its compound of passionate feeling, ardent thought, and thirst for action, it had not found the people and the occasion to release it whole. Fuller was eloquent on her opportunity. "It was no false instinct that said I might here find an atmosphere to develop me in ways I need. Had I only come ten years earlier!" she wrote, adding, "So much strength has been wasted on abstractions, which only came because I grew not in the right soil."

The change in Fuller emerged sharply in her transformation of a word indispensable to the transcendentalists. To Channing she wrote that "famous people" and "magnificent shows and places are only to me an illuminated margin on this text of my inward life." As the "inward life" was earlier implicitly transcendent, so now it was implicitly immanent, rooted in the material and the actual. This inward life required Fuller to turn from American idealism to the realities that Italy proffered: to respond to simple intimacy, to master the language of the "common people," to learn to economize, Roman style, and to discover as a participant the "great future" of Italy.

In this rejection of art for the people of Rome, and in her wish to grow with them in making a revolution, Fuller stood on its head the bias characteristic of almost all American visitors. They distinguished between "eternal Rome," the temple of art, and its apparently unrelated and unworthy race of custodians and tenants, renowned for theft, beggary, and voluble lying. When this ideal and static Rome erupted in revolution in 1848, these pilgrims were devastated and their reflexes were conservative. The Italian crowd—in which Fuller now loved to mingle, scenting in it the stuff of heroic struggle—became for them a frightening rabble.

Consequently she confided to Greeley, "I suffer more than ever from all that is peculiarly American and English." It seems paradoxical that she longed for a "divorce" from the language itself at the very time that she was pouring it out in exhortations to her countrymen. The paradox dissolves when we see that her experience in Italy clarified for Fuller the source of her frustrations with America. At home she now saw none to honor but the abolitionists, to whom she apologized in the *Tribune* for having found them "rabid and exaggerated" in tone. Except for them, she felt that the "spirit of America flares no more" in America, but had leaped the ocean to blaze in Italy. So, until 1850, she refused the entreaties of Emerson and her family to repatriate because she had most to say to Americans from Italy.

This refusal speaks for the ways in which Fuller now repudiated Emerson's perspective. At stake was more than the rejection of the life of the mind for the life of action. She and Emerson now differed over nothing less than the relation of the individual to American destiny, the autonomy of that destiny, and their understanding of national growth. Emerson's identification of the individual's convictions with the "universal sense" of Americans, of the private dream with the national dream, despite the excitement it generated, could pose no critical cutting edge to established society. Fuller's rapport with the Italian revolutionaries signified the fundamental abandonment of her attempt to be a "representative" American in Emerson's sense, her acceptance of her otherness, and her wish to use that otherness to rescue an American essence that was being betrayed at home.

For Emerson the greatness of America depended on her extracting "this tapeworm of Europe from the brain of our countrymen," on the achievement of an autonomy that was tantamount to national isolation. Fuller now denied the mythic specialness and autonomy of American destiny; she offered the actual struggle of a foreign people as a guide to completing the American Revolution and entering a brotherhood of nations. For Emerson growth of the nation, like that of the self-reliant individual, derived from a beneficent American nature. For Fuller it derived pragmatically from many dynamic processes; nations change under the pressure of challenges posed by other societies.

So Fuller remained in Italy, held there by personal as well as political exigencies. In January 1848, when uprisings began to flare like a string of firecrackers lacing Europe, Fuller, nearly thirty-eight and chronically ill, discovered that she was pregnant. The prospect of survival was scarcely less fearsome than death, for Ossoli's marriage to a foreign Protestant radical would be illegal, and probably would be impossible without much more money than they had; moreover, Fuller had by then great reservations about marriage. She turned with relief from the impasse of the private struggle to the exhilaration of the public one. She devoured the news of the February revolution in Paris, the March rising in Vienna, and especially the "Five Glorious Days" in Milan when the Austrian garrison was expelled. "It is a time such as I always dreamed of," she wrote, and she began to contemplate becoming its historian.

Meanwhile, for the *Tribune* she wrote acidly of the folly of a nationalist pope and a republican king. The behavior of Pius IX and Charles Albert bore out Fuller's predictions. The Italian in Pius IX blessed the troops marching to Milan from the papal states, and a month later the pope in him disavowed war against the Austrian Catholics. Charles Albert, or "Re Tentenna" ("King Wobbly"), refused to trust Giuseppe Garibaldi and his gaudy legion, and went to defeat. By summer it was over, and counterrevolution ruled Europe.

Seeking seclusion, ostensibly to write her history, Fuller was then in the Abruzzi mountains. She awaited with equal anxiety the birth of her child and news of her radical friends in reconquered Milan. (Thus a letter to Ossoli begins by raging, "Oh! how unworthy the Pope is! . . . And this traitor of a Carlo Alberto! they'll be damned for all the centuries to come," and ends "I love you in these important days better than ever. The moon has been so beautiful these last nights, it has pained me not to have your company.")

Angelo Eugenio Filippo Ossoli was born September 5, 1848, in the village of Rieti. Though her joy in motherhood was unforeseen and overwhelming, Fuller's need actively to support the revolution made her leave the child two months later with a wet nurse in the hills. She rejoined

Ossoli in Rome just in time to celebrate in the pages of the *Tribune* the murder of the pope's dictatorial minister Pellegrino Rossi, the ensuing flight to Naples of the terrified pope, and the noble behavior of the Romans in the first flush of self-determination.

On the eve of the declaration of the Roman Republic in February 1849, Fuller begged America—through the *Tribune*—to send a sensitive and statesmanlike ambassador, adding, "Another century and I might ask to be made Ambassador myself." Even after Mazzini returned to Rome as one of the presiding triumvirs of the new republic, the cautious United States sent only a chargé d'affaires. Then France, in the full sway of reaction, sent its army to defeat the isolated Rome. "We will wait, whisper the nations, and see if they can bear it," wrote Fuller scornfully. "*If they can do without us,* we will help them."

During the long siege of June, while news about her child was cut off and the last Americans fled Rome, Fuller stayed with Ossoli, who now commanded a battery. The sight of Rome under bombardment, Mazzini's suffering, and the wounded made her "forget the great ideas" and confess that she was not of the heroic "mould." But she insisted on spending what she thought would be the last night of the Roman Republic with Ossoli at his post, and she worked long hours to organize one of the hospitals in Rome. In this role she subverted the official detachment of her country and acted as ambassador for the potential America that she kept urging to life in her dispatches.

In all this she was a faithful supporter of Mazzini and heir to an American revolution that few others, despite their rhetoric, saw as a living force in the world. But there was a moment in 1848 when she went beyond both these sources and the utopian socialists as well. She saw in the February revolution in Paris the struggle of classes, and welcomed the merging of social with political revolution though it would "break many a bank, many a heart, in Europe." She held up this ominous model to her American readers, urging them to "learn in time for a preventative wisdom" how to forge a "true democracy" by guarding the "true aristocracy of a nation," the "laboring classes."

That spring even Mazzini failed Fuller. She wrote that his vision of political liberation, unaccompanied by broader social transformations, was inadequate. Then, in the need to defend the beleaguered Roman Republic, she suspended all criticism. But after Rome fell—when Fuller, Ossoli, and their child moved in the autumn of 1849 to exile in Florence—she seems to have picked up the threads of a broader social critique. In Florence she returned mentally to Paris. "There is the cream of all the milk," she had written. Now she studied what had happened in its more critical revolution, examining both its liberal sources in Alphonse de Lamartine and its socialist roots in Louis Blanc. This work suggests that she was preparing to write something more broadly historical and possibly more theoretical than her impressions of the Italian struggle.

Fuller's private experience also fed her thinking. There is no minimizing her loss. "Private hopes of mine are fallen with the hopes of Italy. I have played for a new stake and lost it," she wrote. Had the Roman Republic triumphed, work for Fuller and Ossoli might have emerged and continued to give form to their lives. But even defeated and living in a Florence again in despotic hands, facing a future emptied of promise, Fuller and Ossoli tasted a happiness that probably neither had known since childhood. Fuller wrote of the "power and sweetness" of Ossoli's presence, and rejoiced in the "unimpassioned" love of the child: "It does not idealize," she wrote with hard-won wisdom, "and cannot be daunted by the faults of its object." Nothing but a child "can take the worst bitterness out of life."

Ossoli's love also freed Fuller for self-acceptance, from the curse of "anticipating" her life. Writing to Channing, she distinguished between those like him, who "loved me with a mixture of fancy and enthusiasm, excited by my talent at embellishing life," and Ossoli, who "loves me from simple affinity." Most illuminatingly she compares the tenderness of Ossoli's love for her with that of her mother, and expresses confidence that those two, in particular, will love each other when they meet.

Yet there were problems surrounding Fuller's proudly laconic announcement of her marriage and motherhood in the summer of 1849. Her friends begged her for details but to no avail; others were gossiping about "a Fourierist or Socialist marriage, without the external ceremony." In his notebook for the *Memoirs,* Emerson wrote "1847 . . . married perhaps in Oct., Nov, or Dec," then canceled the "perhaps." No document or reliable account survives. Fuller was either lying and avoiding embroidery as much as possible, or telling the truth in such a way as to signal the unorthodox view she held of her union and to fend off the stifling initiation into "true womanhood." Ossoli's lack of intellectuality did not bother her, but she knew that "to many of my friends, Mr. Emerson for one, he will be nothing." She held advanced notions of freedom: "Our relation covers only a part of my life," but "I do not feel constrained or limited." She thought that Ossoli, being younger, might come to love another; in such a case "I shall do all that this false state of society permits to give him what freedom he may need. I have thought a great deal about this."

Intrigued but not convinced by Brook Farm during her American years, Fuller had shown increasing interest in Fourierism in Europe. Her inquiries during her last year about the North American Phalanx in Red Bank, New Jersey—where the "relation of the sexes" was a question freely to be settled "by woman herself"—suggest that she might have considered

living there to correct in some measure this "false state of society." In the 1840's two notions of socialism—organization of the working class and reorganization of the family—lay, as it were, side by side in the cradle. It is barely possible that Fuller meant to bring both notions together in her book, in which case its loss is greater than generally imagined and Mrs. Browning's fear about wolves quite justified.

As it was, the little family was dogged by fear of police surveillance and poverty; and Fuller, the breadwinner, felt she could no longer rely on presents and loans. Her work for the *Tribune* had, inexplicably, stopped. She had played out her hand. She believed that her book was the most important project she had undertaken, and that it would best be sold by her in America. She knew they would face "the social inquisition of the United States"; that she was too tired for the "pain of conquest"; and that Ossoli, like her, had a superstitious dread of sea travel. Moreover, on the eve of her departure in May, her most forward-looking friends, the Springs—in consultation with Emerson and Channing—urged her to remain in Italy.

All the signals were clear: the person Fuller had become could not return to America. The long trajectory of her short life was not circular. To respect herself, she had first had to use what was at hand in America, to go the route of idealism, transcendence of the material aspects of her condition. When this had made her strong enough, Fuller left New England and in New York began to apply her energy more directly to the material reality of her self and her world. But her repressed or diverted sexuality and her dependence on notions of divinely ordained national destiny show that she was still subject to American limitations of mind. Only in Italy did Fuller learn that love, made of generous commitment to the autonomy of both persons, had been obscured by her obsession with ideal passion, and that the need to recast relations between sexes and between classes had been obscured by the proud idealism of her country. Only now could she come to understand the meaning of her most intimate prayer, "Give me truth: cheat me by no illusion."

Even Fuller's death still calls out for interpretation. We know that during the twelve hours between the time the ship struck the sands off Fire Island and the time it was submerged, she was on deck watching some swim safely to shore and others drown. We know that she repeatedly refused to save herself. We know that she saw the lifeboat brought to the beach by people unwilling to risk a rescue. We may imagine that they reminded her sharply that none in America had run the risks she had run. We know that she said to the ship's cook, "I see nothing but death before me." We cannot know if she was speaking of her immediate extremity or her larger condition. Reports conflict, and we do not know whether at the last she tried to swim ashore, clinging to a board. We know that Emerson wrote in his journal, on receiving news of her death, "I have lost in her my audience," failing thus to know how many years earlier he had suffered that loss. As for her audience, it remained to be created.

Selected Bibliography

WORKS OF MARGARET FULLER

SEPARATE WORKS

Conversations with Goethe in the Last Years of His Life, Translated from the German of Eckermann. Boston: Hilliard, Gray, 1839.

Günderode; A Translation from the German. Boston: E. P. Peabody, 1842.

Summer on the Lakes in 1843. Boston: Charles C. Little and James Brown, 1844. Reprinted Nieuwkoup: B. De Graaf, 1972.

Woman in the Nineteenth Century and Kindred Papers Relating to the Sphere, Condition and Duties of Woman, edited by Arthur B. Fuller. Boston: John P. Jewett, 1845. Reprinted Freeport, N.Y.: Books for Libraries Press, 1972. *Woman in the Nineteenth Century* reprinted separately New York: W. W. Norton, 1971.

Papers on Literature and Art. New York: Wiley and Putnam, 1846. Reprinted New York: AMS Press, 1972.

At Home and Abroad, or Things and Thoughts in America and Europe, edited by Arthur B. Fuller. Boston: Crosby, Nichols, 1856. Reprinted Port Washington, N.Y.: Kennikat Press, 1971.

Life Without and Life Within, edited by Arthur B. Fuller. Boston: Brown, Taggard, and Chase, 1860.

Love-Letters of Margaret Fuller, 1845–46. Introduction by Julia Ward Howe. New York: D. Appleton, 1903. Reprinted Westport, Conn.: Greenwood Press, 1969.

The Dial: A Magazine for Literature, Philosophy, and Religion. 4 vols. New York: Russell and Russell, 1961. (Contains many of Fuller's writings.)

ANTHOLOGIES

Chevigny, Bell Gale. *The Woman and the Myth: Margaret Fuller's Life and Writings.* Old Westbury, N.Y.: Feminist Press, 1976. (Also contains six critical biographical essays and writings on Fuller by her contemporaries.)

Miller, Perry. *Margaret Fuller: American Romantic.* New York: Doubleday, 1963. Reprinted Ithaca, N.Y.: Cornell University Press, 1970.

Wade, Mason, ed. *The Writings of Margaret Fuller.* New York: Viking Press, 1941.

BIBLIOGRAPHIES

Myerson, Joel. *Margaret Fuller: A Secondary Bibliography.* New York: Burt Franklin, 1977.

———. *Margaret Fuller: A Descriptive Bibliography.* Pittsburgh: University of Pittsburgh Press, 1978.

BIOGRAPHICAL AND CRITICAL STUDIES

Allen, Margaret V. *The Achievement of Margaret Fuller.* University Park: Penn State University Press, 1979.

Anthony, Katharine. *Margaret Fuller: A Psychological Biography.* New York: Harcourt, Brace, and Howe, 1920. Reprinted Folcroft, Pa.: Folcroft Press, 1969.

Blanchard, Paula. *Margaret Fuller: From Transcendentalism to Revolution.* New York: Delacorte/Seymour Lawrence, 1978.

Braun, Frederick A. *Margaret Fuller and Goethe.* New York: Henry Holt, 1910.

Brown, Arthur W. *Margaret Fuller.* United States Authors series. New York: Twayne, 1964.

Cargill, Oscar. "Nemesis and Nathaniel Hawthorne." *PMLA,* 52:848–62 (Summer 1937).

Chevigny, Bell. "The Long Arm of Censorship: Mythmaking in Margaret Fuller's Time and Our Own." *Signs,* 2:450–60 (Winter 1976).

Conrad, Susan Phinney. *Perish the Thought: Intellectual Women in Romantic America, 1830–1860.* New York: Oxford University Press, 1976.

Dall, Caroline Healey. *Margaret and Her Friends, or Ten Conversations with Margaret Fuller upon the Mythology of the Greeks.* Boston: Roberts Bros., 1895.

Deiss, Joseph Jay. *The Roman Years of Margaret Fuller.* New York: Thomas Y. Crowell, 1969.

Detti, Emma. *Margaret Fuller Ossoli e i suoi correspondenti.* Florence: Le Monnier, 1942.

Douglas, Ann. *The Feminization of American Culture.* New York: Alfred A. Knopf, 1977.

Memoirs of Margaret Fuller Ossoli., edited by R. W. Emerson, W. H. Channing, and J. F. Clarke. 2 vols. Boston: Philips, Sampson, 1852. Reprinted New York: Burt Franklin, 1972.

Higginson, Thomas Wentworth. *Margaret Fuller Ossoli.* American Men of Letters series. Boston: Houghton Mifflin, 1884.

Howe, Julia Ward. *Margaret Fuller.* Boston: Roberts Bros., 1883.

James, Henry. *William Wetmore Story and His Friends.* Boston: Houghton Mifflin, 1903.

Jones, Alexander. "Margaret Fuller's Attempt to Write Fiction." *Boston Public Library Quarterly,* 6:67–73 (April 1954).

Kearns, Francis E. "Margaret Fuller and the Abolition Movement." *Journal of the History of Ideas,* 25:120–27 (January–March 1964).

McMaster, Helen Neill. "Margaret Fuller as Literary Critic." *University of Buffalo Studies,* 7:35–100 (December 1928).

Myerson, Joel. "Margaret Fuller's 1842 Journal: At Concord with the Emersons." *Harvard Library Bulletin,* 21:320–40 (July 1973).

Randel, W. P. "Hawthorne, Channing, and Margaret Fuller." *American Literature,* 10:472–79 (January 1939).

Rostenberg, Leona. "Margaret Fuller's Italian Diary." *Journal of Modern History,* 12:209–20 (June 1940).

Stern, Madeleine B. *The Life of Margaret Fuller.* New York: E. P. Dutton, 1942.

Strauch, Carl F. "Hatred's Swift Repulsions: Emerson, Margaret Fuller, and Others." *Studies in Romanticism,* 7:65–103 (Winter 1968).

Wade, Mason. *Margaret Fuller: Whetstone of Genius.* New York: Viking Press, 1940.

Warfel, Harry R. "Margaret Fuller and Ralph Waldo Emerson." *PMLA,* 50:576–94 (June 1935).

Welliscz, Leopold. *The Friendship of Margaret Fuller d'Ossoli and Adam Mickiewicz.* New York: Polish Book Importing Co., 1947.

Welter, Barbara. *Dimity Convictions: The American Woman in the Nineteenth Century.* Athens: Ohio University Press, 1976.

—BELL GALE CHEVIGNY

Allen Ginsberg
1926–

In 1855 in "Song of Myself," Walt Whitman promised he would "become undisguised and naked" and "permit to speak at every hazard, / Nature without check with original energy." Almost exactly 100 years after Whitman's startling personal declaration of independence, Allen Ginsberg stood before a lively crowd of friends at the Six Gallery in San Francisco and passionately declaimed a new song of the self, a poem that had to be howled instead of sung, about a self that had to be retrieved from madness before it could be celebrated. Whereas Whitman could proclaim and celebrate a transcendent self in a healthy universe ("Clear and sweet is my soul, and clear and sweet is all that is not my soul"), Ginsberg had first to confess and reclaim a perverted and nearly annihilated self from the ravages of an insane world: "I saw the best minds of my generation destroyed by madness, starving hysterical naked, / dragging themselves through the negro streets at dawn looking for an angry fix, / angelheaded hipsters burning for the ancient heavenly connection to the starry dynamo in the machinery of night. . . ." "Howl" created a shock wave in American poetry and culture, but it was only a first noisy step in Allen Ginsberg's lifelong struggle to "become undisguised and naked" and to "permit to speak at every hazard" his own nature, however strange.

"Ginsberg, this poem 'Howl' will make you famous in San Francisco," shouted Jack Kerouac after that historic first reading in 1955. "No," corrected San Francisco poet-patriarch Kenneth Rexroth, "this poem will make you famous from bridge to bridge." But "Howl" made Ginsberg famous around the world. Without "Howl" and the notoriety it received when it was ill-advisedly seized and prosecuted as an obscene book by U. S. Customs and San Francisco police in 1956, Ginsberg's other poems might never have been published. Almost surely Ginsberg would never have burgeoned so grandly as public personality–guru–prophet–paterfamilias–spokesman for several generations of beats, hippies, war protestors, environmentalists, and counterculturists of various sorts.

"Howl" is a volcanic eruption, a breakthrough in the cultural crust, a turning point in the life of the poet and American poetry. It is an "eli eli lamma lamma sabactahani saxophone cry" of the "suffering of America's naked mind for love" and a passionate throwing-off of the guilt and self-hatred imposed by a culture whose proper image is Moloch, that ancient Hebrew deity who demanded blood sacrifices of the young.

But while "Howl" purports to speak for a mid-1950's generation of American youth suffering in a "lacklove" nightmare of "robot apartments" and "demonic industries," such a generation did not actually emerge until the Vietnam war years in the middle 1960's. If poets are, as Ezra Pound claimed, "the antennae of the race," then Ginsberg's antennae need not have been uncommonly long to have described the '60's *zeitgeist* a mere ten years early; but in fact "Howl" is a uniquely personal poem dealing primarily with the poet's own past. While a few of the relative clauses of the single long sentence of part I do refer to a narrow circle of friends (Peter Orlovsky, Jack Kerouac, Carl Solomon, Herbert Huncke, Lucien Carr, William Burroughs, and Neal Cassady), most are thinly veiled autobiography. It is Ginsberg himself

> who passed through universities with radiant
> cool eyes hallucinating Arkansas and
> Blake-light tragedy among the scholars
> of war,
> who were [was] expelled from the academies
> [Columbia] for crazy & publishing
> obscene odes on the windows of the skull,

> . . .

> who studied Plotinus Poe St. John of the
> Cross telepathy and bop kaballa because
> the cosmos instinctively vibrated at their
> [his] feet in Kansas, . . .
> who thought they were [he was] only mad
> when Baltimore [Harlem] gleamed in
> supernatural ecstasy,

> . . .

> who lost their [his] loveboys to the three old
> shrews of fate . . .

> . . .

> who were [was] burned alive in their [his]
> innocent flannel suits on Madison avenue
> amid blasts of leaden verse . . .

> . . .

> who journeyed to Denver, who died in Denver,
> who came back to Denver & waited in
> vain, . . .

> . . .

> who dreamt and made incarnate gaps in Time
> & Space through images juxtaposed, . . .
> to recreate the syntax and measure of poor
> human prose and stand before you
> speechless and intelligent and shaking
> with shame, rejected yet confessing out
> the soul. . . .

"Howl" is not, then, about the best minds of a generation but about the "majestic flaws" of Ginsberg's own mind. "Howl" is a poem of pathology, and the pathology was at least as much private as public. Assuredly, there was madness enough in the complacent 1950's, but it was usually corked tight. The tongue tied in our mouth began to be loosened in Ginsberg's primarily because Moloch had visited him more terribly.

In separate prefaces to *Howl and Other Poems* (1956) and *Empty Mirror, Early Poems* (1961), William Carlos Williams speaks of Ginsberg's poetry as a trip through hell and marvels that Ginsberg ever survived to write a book of poems. If we are ever adequately to understand a poetry so unabashedly confessional and obsessed, we will have to look unblinkingly at the private hell that Ginsberg has had to live through.

Allen Ginsberg was born in Paterson, New Jersey, the son of Louis and Naomi Ginsberg, on June 3, 1926. His father, a high school English teacher with modest poetic talents in the tradition of Longfellow and Whittier, was a man of fairly orthodox and limited mind. His mother, a Russian emigrée and a political activist in her youth, became irrevocably insane during Ginsberg's formative years. According to his own frank and compassionate portrait of her in *Kaddish and Other Poems, 1958–1960* (1961), she was a paranoid schizophrenic who believed she was in danger from assassins and was spied upon and plotted against by Stalinists, Hitlerians, and members of her own family:

'Allen, you don't understand—it's—ever since those 3 big sticks up my back—they did something to me in Hospital, they poisoned me, they want to see me dead—3 big sticks, 3 big sticks—

'The Bitch! Old Grandma! Last week I saw her, dressed in pants like an old man, with a sack on her back, climbing up the brick side of the apartment

'On the fire escape, with poison germs, to throw on me—at night—maybe Louis is helping her—he's under her power—'

In the home, her careless nakedness and seemingly seductive conduct became a source of severe conflict and obsession for her son:

One time I thought she was trying to make me come lay her—flirting to herself at sink— lay back on huge bed that filled most of the room, dress up round her hips, big slash of hair, scars of operations, pancreas, belly wounds, abortions, appendix, stitching of incisions pulling down in the fat like hideous thick zippers— ragged long lips between her legs—

The boy is "revolted a little, not much— seemed perhaps a good idea to try—know the Monster of the Beginning Womb—Perhaps— that way. Would she care? She needs a lover." Numerous poems connect Ginsberg's fear of women with obsessive memories of his mother—"I can't stand these women all over me / smell of Naomi," he writes in "Mescaline"—and the only set of asterisks in "Howl"

("With mother finally ******,") almost implores the reader to infer actual incest.

At age twelve Ginsberg had the traumatic experience of escorting his screaming, hallucinating mother on a five-hour bus trip to a Lakewood, New Jersey, rest home. Returning to Paterson alone late at night, Ginsberg "Went to bed exhausted, wanting to leave the world (probably that year / newly in love with R—— my high school mind hero. . . ."

Ginsberg later followed "R——" to Manhattan and Columbia University, where he met and confessed his love for Jack Kerouac. The heterosexual Kerouac, who was playing on the Columbia football team at the time,

. . . was very handsome, very beautiful, and mellow—mellow in the sense of infinitely tolerant, like Shakespeare or Tolstoy or Dostoevsky, infinitely understanding. . . . his tolerance gave me *permission* to open up and talk. . . . He wasn't going to hit me. He wasn't going to reject me, really, he was going to accept my soul with all its throbbings and sweetness and worries and dark woes and sorrows and heartaches and joys and glees and mad understanding of mortality. . . .

But, if we are to believe the myth that Ginsberg builds everywhere in his supposedly naked poetry, it was with Neal Cassady that Ginsberg began an exuberant odyssey of heroic love.

However, it is not heroic love that the early Cassady–Ginsberg correspondence reveals but a tense and often brutal symbiosis. Cassady, the irrepressible, fun-loving, fast-moving "cocksman and Adonis of Denver" in Ginsberg's poems and Kerouac's novels, is here quite out of his element—self-conscious, nervous, defensive, and clearly not telling the whole truth. He is troubled that he doesn't feel for Allen the genuine love that Ginsberg so desperately needs; he fears that he may be unable to love anyone; he tries to talk himself into believing this "objectivity of emotionality" has enabled him "to move freely in each groove as it came" and thus proves he is not dangerously and parasitically dependent on Allen: "I've brought this out so you can see an example of my lack of compulsive, emotional need for anyone." Ginsberg is the soul-genius who will educate and sensitize Neal's spirit; but the more experienced Cassady is in the driver's seat physically and is scarcely able to conceal a patronizing attitude toward the tortured young man who "trembles" for love ("Love & Kisses, my boy, opps!, excuse, I'm not Santa Claus am I? Well then, just— Love & Kisses").

When the inevitable break finally came at the end of 1947 (after Ginsberg had "journeyed to Denver," "died in Denver," and come "back to Denver & waited in vain"), Allen abjectly begged Neal for the love he so desperately believed in and needed:

You know you are the only one who gave me love that I wanted and never had. . . . What must I do for you to get you back? I will do anything. Any indecencies any revelations any creation, any miseries, will they please you. . . . I mean to bend my mind that knows it can destroy you to any base sordid level of adoration and masochistic abnegation that you desire or taunt me with. . . . I hate & fear you so much that I will do anything to win your protection again, and your mercy.

I am lonely, Neal, alone, and always I am frightened. I need someone to love me and kiss me & sleep with me; I am only a child and have the mind of a child. . . . I have always been obedient & respectful, I have adjusted my plans to yours, my desires to your own pattern, and now I do ask—I pray—please neal, my neal, come back to me, don't waste me, don't leave me. I don't want to suffer any more, I have had my mind broken open over and over before, I have been isolate and loveless always. I have not slept with anyone since I saw you not because I was

faithful but because I am afraid and I know no one. I will always be afraid I will always be worthless, I will always be alone till I die and I will be tormented long after you leave me.

Such letters illuminate Ginsberg's poetry more than any number of interviews and critical analyses. This isolation, fear, self-disgust, and extraordinary hunger for love lie everywhere at the heart of his work.

After the break with Cassady, Ginsberg endured long months of severe depression and isolation alone in a Harlem apartment. His friends were all temporarily out of touch—Burroughs was in Mexico, Huncke in jail, Kerouac holed up on Long Island writing a novel, and Cassady in California about to get married. Ginsberg's mother had once again been incarcerated in a mental hospital. In the midst of this dark night of the soul, unable to act, near catatonia or suicide, Ginsberg was masturbating in his bed one afternoon, idly looking over William Blake's "Sick Rose" and "Ah, Sunflower," when he suddenly began to understand the poems and simultaneously "heard a very deep earthen grave voice in the room," which he immediately assumed was Blake's own voice. It was as if God spoke tenderly to his son: Ginsberg's body "felt *light,* and a sense of cosmic consciousness, vibrations, understanding, awe, and wonder and surprise." Looking out the window, he "saw into the depths of the universe, by looking simply into the ancient sky. The sky suddenly seemed very *ancient.* And this was the very ancient place that he [Blake] was talking about, the sweet golden clime, I suddenly realized that *this* existence was *it!*" Ginsberg saw the "living hand" in the blue of the sky and the craftsmanship of the carved cornices of Harlem, and understood that "existence itself was God." This was the initiation into consciousness that he was born for, and he vowed that he would "never forget, never renig [sic], never deny. Never deny the voice—no, never *forget* it, don't get lost mentally wandering in other spirit worlds or American or job worlds or advertising worlds or war worlds or earth worlds."

But Ginsberg does seem to forget, or at least repeatedly to mistranslate and misapply the Blakean message that this world is the "sweet golden clime." Instead of turning to love of the world, Ginsberg turned to the quest of the mystical experience itself and to the use of drugs as "obviously a technique for experimenting with consciousness." In an early poem (1948–1952) of *Empty Mirror* ("The Terms in Which I Think of Reality"), Ginsberg reminds himself that "Time is Eternity" and that a first step toward adjusting to "Reality" is "realizing how real / the world is already." But although he can view the flux and variety of the world as marvelous and will in time learn to be its skillful cataloger (never with Whitman's expansive joy), the world is so full of unpleasant detail that he is "overwhelmed" and turns to "dream again of Heaven." The inescapable fact for Ginsberg is that "the world is a mountain / of shit" and the human predicament is unfortunate at best:

> Man lives like the unhappy
> whore on River Street who
> in her Eternity gets only
>
> a couple of bucks and a lot
> of snide remarks in return
> for seeking physical love
>
> the best way she knows how,
> never really heard of a glad
> job or joyous marriage or
>
> a difference in the heart:
> or thinks it isn't for her,
> which is her worst misery.

Among Ginsberg's special miseries was his arrest and prosecution in 1948 as an accomplice to Huncke, drug addict and thief, who had moved in with the hospitable student and used his New York apartment to stash stolen goods. Ginsberg managed to escape a jail sentence by pleading insanity (he had talked to Blake and seen God!) and spending eight months in the Columbia Psychiatric Institute.

The poems of Ginsberg's troubled early years (1948–1952) are gathered in *Empty Mirror* (1961) and *The Gates of Wrath; Rhymed Poems* (1972). The rhymed poems of the latter show us not the wild madman–prophet–orgiast of "Howl" and later poetry, but the Columbia honor student and English major, the clean-shaven, youthful Dr. Jekyll desperately busy keeping Mr. Hyde locked in the basement with meter and rhyme. They are neither very honest nor very good poems.

Among them are several written to Neal Cassady. Carefully avoiding gender pronouns and explicit sexuality, they speak in all-too-familiar love-poem abstractions and clichés—"my heart was broken in your care; / I never suffered love so fair" ("A Western Ballad"). When they do deal in particulars, as in "Do We Understand Each Other?" they reveal a twenty-two-year-old poet who is as silly as a thirteen-year-old:

> My love was at the wheel,
> And in and out we drove.
> My own eyes were mild.
> How my love merrily
> Dared the other cars to rove:

Sexual content is disguised and anesthetized by polysyllabic abstraction and contorted syntax, as in "A Lover's Garden":

> As seconds on the clock do move,
> Each marks another thought of love;
> Thought follows thought, and we devise
> Each minute to antithesize,
> Till, as the hour chimes its tune,
> Dialectic, we commune.
>
> The argument our minds create
> We do, abed, substantiate. . . .

Considering the repression and dishonesty of such poems, it is easy to understand Ginsberg's subsequent turn to a spontaneous poetics that refuses revision and seeks to record the "naked activity" of the mind. "Now if you are thinking of 'form' or even the 'well made poem' or a sonnet when you're lying on the couch, you'll never say what you have on your mind."

In a few poems truth threatens to break through as a "shroudy stranger" or "shadow." According to Carl Jung, there is in each of us an archetypal "darker brother" who must be recognized and embraced if we are to achieve psychic health and wholeness. In contemporary Western culture, that shadow or repressed self is almost always associated with the body and the libido; the "bright self" or public persona is usually associated with the head and rational faculties. The shadow figures in Ginsberg's poems are beyond his understanding and control, and seem full of unconscious contents relating to his ambivalent feelings about his own body.

Ginsberg consciously connects the "stranger" who haunts his dreams with the voice of the Blake visions, with the presence of God, and with his own desire to die. Thus the Blake of the auditory hallucinations sometimes seems to be Ginsberg's alter ego, one who asks the young poet in "Psalm" to convert the energy of his Harlem pentecost into substance or "bone."

> I saw it here,
> The Miracle, which no man knows entire,
> Nor I myself. But shadow is my prophet,
> I cast a shadow that surpasses me,
> And I write, shadow changes into bone....

Sometimes the shadow seems to be the Divine One hiding inside Ginsberg and looking out through his eyes: "What a sweet dream! to be some incorruptible / Divinity, corporeal without a name, / Suffering metamorphosis of flesh" ("Psalm"). While both of these interpretations of the dream shadow point Ginsberg toward the need to accept his life in the real world, he characteristically strays into longing for death because he "cannot go be wild / or harken back to shape of child" ("Ode: My 24th Year"). Though the Harlem vision told him *this* was *it,* he persists in "Psalm" in wanting the *it* without the *this:*

> Ah, but to have seen the Dove of still
> Divinity come down in silken light of summer
>   sun
> In ignorance of the body and bone's madness.

Given Ginsberg's desire to pass from the world into pure vision or pure voice, and given his desperate and frustrated hunger for physical tenderness and love, it is perhaps inevitable that the dream figures should suggest the homoerotic attractiveness of death. The dream stranger in "A Dream" is sometimes a pale boy with beautiful hair and eyes "Walking in a winding sheet, / As fair as was my own disguise" who invites the dreamer to follow him safely "through the grave":

> "And we will walk the double door
> That breaks upon the ageless night,
> Where I have come, and must once more
> Return, and so forsake the light."

> The darkness that is half disguised
> In the Zodiac of my dream
> Gazed on me in his bleak eyes....

Ginsberg is both attracted and frightened, tempted and repulsed by those bleak eyes. Either suicide or homosexuality means death; death by one is but a means of avoiding death by the other. Ginsberg would rather die than live with that dark self, but death and that self already seem inextricably fused. Sometimes, as in "The Shrouded Stranger," it appears as a nightstalker with reddened eye who follows old men and young boys and peeps in at windows

ready to take with him anyone who would suc-
cumb to his strange attraction:

> Maid or dowd or athlete proud
> May wanton with me in the shroud
>
> Who'll come lay down in the dark with me
> Belly to belly and knee to knee
> Who'll look into my hooded eye
> Who'll lay down under my darkened thigh?

Ginsberg's dreams are haunted because he cannot accept the dark self that his unfortunate childhood created in him but which society will not bless. As late as 1963, in "The Change: Kyoto-Tokyo Express," he admits that he has always denied his "own shape's loveliness" and felt his sexual desire "to be horrible instead of Him." Thus despite the dream stranger's attractive connection to Blake or God, or death, Ginsberg wrestled with him as a fearful adversary who "holds me in his keep / and seeks the bones that he must find"; who "cries out in my name; / he struggles for my writhing frame" ("The Voice of Rock").

If the early rhymed poems conceal Ginsberg, the more prosaic journal jottings of *Empty Mirror* reveal him. These are not poems so much as desperate notes to the self:

> I feel as if I am at a dead
> end and so I am finished.
> All spiritual facts I realize
> are true but I never escape
> the feeling of being closed in
> and the sordidness of self,
> the futility of all that I
> have seen and done and said.
> Maybe if I continued things
> would please me more but now
> I have no hope and I am tired.

In these last lines and elsewhere Ginsberg urges himself to adjust and "make a home in wilderness" ("A Desolation"), but he can experience life only as "A Meaningless Institution" wherein he has been given "a bunk in an enormous ward / surrounded by hundreds of weeping, / decaying men and women," and abandoned without friends or instructions. No matter how much he lectures himself as he does in "Metaphysics" ("This is the one and only / firmament; therefore / it is the absolute world. / There is no other world. / The circle is complete. / I am living in Eternity. / The ways of this world / are the ways of Heaven"), he cannot make his peace with "ruinous, vile, dirty Time." In "Walking home at night" he thinks of himself

> in company with obscure
> Bartlebys and Judes,
>   cadaverous men,
> shrouded men, soft white
> fleshed failures creeping
> in and out of rooms like
>   myself. Remembering
>   my attic, I reached
> my hands to my head and hissed
> "Oh, God how horrible!"

Oppressed by his sense of how ill he is, Ginsberg wonders in "Marijuana Notation" "Is it this strange / for everybody?" In "I Have Increased Power" he sees that his illness comes from having "no active life / in realworld"; his "dreamworld and realworld / become more and more / distinct and apart," but the real world contains no "consummation forseeable / in ideal joy or passion." "Tonite all is well" shows Ginsberg at the verge of breakdown:

> . . .I am ill,
> I have become physically and
> spiritually impotent in my madness this
>   month.
> I suddenly realized that my head
> is severed from my body. . . .

For Ginsberg and for all of us, this is a key perception. Ginsberg's may be a private pathology bordering on clinical hebephrenic schizophrenia, but it is shared to a greater or lesser degree by nearly everyone living in a highly systematized technological urban culture. It is closely related to the "dissociation of sensibility" that T. S. Eliot described in Western culture a half-century earlier, and which has become an increasingly important subject for a multitude of poets as widely different as John Crowe Ransom ("Painted Head"), Gary Snyder ("Milton by Firelight"), and Robert Bly ("A Man Writes to Part of Himself" and all of his work).

Ginsberg's head has been severed from his body. The result, inevitably, is both spiritual and physical impotence, because all potency or power requires a yin-yang admixture or dynamic interchange. Moreover, such a "horizontal" cleavage does not occur without a "vertical," or lateral, bifurcation of the self as well. The "head" in Ginsberg is split between his consuming focus on intuitive mystical experience (Blake, God, eternity—"the ancient heavenly connection to the starry dynamo") and his rigidly patterned superego posing as the rational, thinking self (the machinery in "the machinery of night"); the "body" is torn between the seething shadow of repressed feeling and its nearly catatonic shell, the practical self paralyzed in an empty, meaningless life. The dismembered Ginsberg cannot translate or convert his direct intuitive knowledge from the Blake visions into action or affection in the real world; his reason tells him "all spiritual facts are true," but they are inert and without mana; his feelings are condemned by his superego and fill him with disgust; and his sensations and practical abilities are numbed by the falseness of his life in the nine-to-five world. These mutilated, alienated "selves" roughly correspond to the four functions of the Jungian mandala (intuition, thinking, feeling, sensation); but the unifying fifth or "transcendent function," the Self at the center, is missing. That is the Self that Whitman sang, joining body and soul, outer and inner, good and evil, male and female, animal and angel, in an erotic and mystical union.

Ginsberg is "at a dead end," torn apart, one of the hollow men. He has no Self, and thus it is that the *Empty Mirror* is empty. The gods of his head and the daemons of his body are in conflict: the Old Testament, judging Father struggles against the benevolent "living hand" of the Blake visions; the dionysiac shadow is "burned alive" in the "flannel suit" of the market-research analyst. The superego and the id, the visionary and the "responsible" citizen are all in arms against one another. It should be no surprise, then, that "war" emerges as the primary metaphor of all of Ginsberg's poetry and that his poetry can best be understood as a life-long search for the missing center, for the Self or Soul or Sacred Heart that bridges the gaps between mind and body, Eternity and Time. It is of course the classic work of poetry to put the severed self together again, to show that the Self and the world are the body of God, the Incarnate Word, and that the Self is not separate from but coextensive with the natural world. That precisely was Whitman's glorious achievement in "Song of Myself."

In only one of Ginsberg's early "East Coast" poems does he find enough strength or enough self to confront and challenge the "realworld." In "Paterson" (1949) the line lengthens and the breath deepens. The poem moves as if the poet is at last on his feet, pacing his tenement room in anger, choosing for a change to condemn marketplace America rather than himself. Why should he try to fit in? What, after all, does he "want in these rooms papered with visions of money?" Why should he enter that "war" for such a "prize! the dead prick of commonplace obsession, / harridan vision of electricity at night and daylight misery of thumb-sucking rage" (a rather unpleasant portrait not only of the business world but of married life). He would rather go mad, take drugs, suffer any kind of crucifixion, "rather crawl on my naked belly over the tincans of Cincinnati; / rather drag a rotten railroad tie to a Golgotha in the Rockies." Here at last is the first tentative sound of the angry "Hebraic-Melvillean bardic" voice that will break forth in fury in "Howl." It is also the moment when Ginsberg begins to embrace the "beatness" and "beatitude" that comes from accepting one's failure to fit in and "make it" within the acceptable patterns and values of the dominant culture. Ginsberg has tried mightily to be straight and "normal" ("to tame the hart / and wear the bear"), but he has not succeeded. For more than twenty years he has blamed himself, introjecting the guilt for his unhappiness. In "Paterson" he looks outside himself to notice the enemy in the culture at large.

In 1953 Ginsberg abandoned the emotionally dark environs of New York and New Jersey to travel, via Cuba and Yucatan, to a fresh beginning in San Francisco. Within the next year several important events radically altered his life. The first of these was his meeting with Peter Orlovsky, who is the subject of "Malest Cornifici Tuo Catullo" *(Reality Sandwiches, 1953–60)* and who would become his life companion:

I'm happy, Kerouac, your madman Allen's finally made it: discovered a new young cat, and my imagination of an eternal boy walks on the streets of San Francisco, handsome, and meets me in cafeterias and loves me. Ah don't think I'm sickening. You're angry at me. For all of my lovers? It's hard to eat shit, without having visions; when they have eyes for me it's like Heaven.

Ginsberg is still perhaps not equal to love (Peter is too easily lost in the "they" of the last line), but he is clearly in love with being loved, and the physical tenderness and attention seem to validate and energize him. Nevertheless, he continues to seek escape from the everyday world (which he perceives as "eating shit") through visions and sex, and he fears and assumes the negative judgment of Kerouac. Ginsberg cannot accept the world or himself. In his own mind he is still really "meat-creephood." If the Moloch of "Howl," part II, is a "heavy judger of men," then Moloch exists as much inside Ginsberg as outside him. He is not only the reification of "mind" in the nation, but is also the disapproving father, Louis Ginsberg in Paterson, New Jersey, and the superego of Allen Ginsberg himself. But the relationship with Peter Orlovsky is the beginning of Moloch's overthrow.

The second event that freed Ginsberg to write "Howl" is the session with a psychiatrist who, Ginsberg claims, "gave me the authority, so to speak, to be myself." (As James Breslin has noted, Ginsberg had not been able to give himself that permission.) He had previously consulted with a long procession of analysts, Freudians, Reichians, Jungians, Adlerians, and Sullivanians. After multiple sessions exploring Ginsberg's unhappiness, this psychiatrist asked simply, "What would you like to do? What is your desire really?" Ginsberg was almost too embarrassed to say. What he wanted to do was quit his job and never work again, to keep living with someone, "maybe even a man," and give himself completely to exploring visions and relationships. (In other words, to be lazy, immoral, and a failure in the eyes of the Father.) The psychiatrist's answer was simply, "Well, why don't you?" Ginsberg did. The result was "Howl."

Ginsberg arranged to be fired from his job so that he could collect unemployment, moved into an apartment with Orlovsky, and one long weekend, with the aid of amphetamines and peyote, began to wail. "Howl" cannot be imitated. It has to be lived and suffered. It is not a creation of art but an *event* in the life of a man. It is a therapeutic disburdening, a shucking off and breaking free of guilt and self-hatred, an attempt to retrieve and affirm a self that had all but disappeared. It is a personal "confessing out the soul" and a cultural cleansing as well, because it named and to a degree exorcised some of the madness growing in everyone since the Industrial Revolution.

In part II of "Howl" Ginsberg turns on his accuser; in open rebellion against the Father, he names and confronts the monster–God–machine who bashes open the skulls and eats up the brains and imagination of its children:

Moloch whose mind is pure machinery!
Moloch whose blood is running money!
Moloch whose fingers are ten armies!
Moloch whose breast is a cannibal
dynamo! Moloch whose ear is a smoking
tomb!
Moloch whose eyes are a thousand blind
windows! Moloch whose skyscrapers
stand in the long streets like endless
Jehovahs! Moloch whose factories dream
and croak in the fog! Moloch whose
smokestacks and antennae crown the
cities!
Moloch whose love is endless oil and stone!
Moloch whose soul is electricity and
banks! Moloch whose poverty is the
specter of genius! Moloch whose fate is a
cloud of sexless hydrogen! Moloch whose
name is the Mind!

In the face of such a vicious God, the first and perhaps only act of affirmation available to us is to commit ourselves in friendship and sympathy to a fellow victim. This Ginsberg does in part III in a litany of assurances to Carl Solomon, who had been his fellow inmate at Rockland State Mental Hospital:

I'm with you in Rockland
where we hug and kiss the United States
under our bedsheets   the United States that
coughs all night and won't let us sleep
I'm with you in Rockland
where we wake up electrified out of the
coma by our own souls' airplanes roaring
over the roof they've come to drop angelic
bombs the hospital illuminates itself
imaginary walls collapse   O skinny legions
run outside   O starry-spangled shock of
mercy the eternal war is here   O victory
forget your underwear we're free

In the love of these madmen-victims for each other, there is even a little tenderness left over for the body of Moloch himself, for the United States who is otherwise a rather sickly lay. And once the war against desire and the Self has been abandoned, the soul's weapons can be turned outward to the war against "walls" and repressions, and the Self can forget its underwear and be innocently naked. (It is as if the emaciated legions of Buchenwald and Auschwitz were suddenly liberated by Ginsberg's poetic air raid against der Führer.)

In "Footnote to Howl" (functionally "Howl," part IV), Ginsberg celebrates his escape from the concentration camps of Moloch and sings a long litany of praise proclaiming the holiness of all things: "Holy time in eternity holy eternity in time holy the clocks in space holy the fourth dimension holy the fifth International holy the Angel in Moloch!" Ginsberg's embrace of "time in eternity . . . eternity in time" seems genuine here, as if for the moment his life with Orlovsky and his permission to be himself have lifted him to new self-acceptance and a sense of well-being. The poem and "Footnote" form a kind of *Divine Comedy* in which Ginsberg descends through the agonies of hell to face and name the satanic God wedged at the center of the vortex, before ascending the holy mountain of purgatory through his healing sympathy with Carl Solomon. The "Footnote" is the *Paradiso* of the piece, where Ginsberg seems to have achieved a new level of at-one-ment.

"Howl" is easily Ginsberg's most important, passionate, and unified poem. Likewise, the nine shorter poems in *Howl and Other Poems* (1956) are generally superior to his later work.

In "Sunflower Sutra" for example, Ginsberg is able to forget himself long enough to see with clear eyes "the gray Sunflower poised against the sunset, crackly bleak and dusty with the smut and smog and smoke of olden locomotives in its eye— / corolla of bleary spikes pushed down and broken like a battered crown, seed fallen out of its face, soon-to-be-toothless mouth of sunny air, . . ." and can recognize its besmutted but beautiful blossom as an image of his own soul, which had once thought it was "an impotent dirty old locomotive" instead of a flower. "—We're not our skin of grime, we're not our dread bleak dusty imageless locomotive, we're all beautiful golden sunflowers inside. . . ." This is for the poet not a trite preachment but an exciting discovery; there is a becoming innocence and boyish fascination caught in the spontaneous spill of language that names the trash and litter of urban ash heaps and finds an inextinguishable truth growing adamantly among it.

In "America" too, the poet has gained enough emotional distance to attack the country's faults with humor, mimicking the foolishness of the public and the government and recognizing himself as a strange outsider with considerably different thoughts and "national resources": "My national resources consist of two joints of marijuana millions of genitals an unpublishable private literature that goes 1400 miles an hour and twentyfive-thousand mental institutions." Ginsberg faults his country for its greed, mechanization, xenophobia, gullibility, exaggerated seriousness, puritanical morality, and enslavement to *Time* magazine, but pretends to take the country's fears and programs seriously and vows that he, too, had "better get right down to the job" and put his "queer shoulder to the wheel." Anyone who can thus attack evil is no longer so helplessly its victim.

Even the insatiable hunger and preoccupation with physical love seem quieted and disciplined in this volume. In contrast to his later work, "Song" is almost understated:

> The warm bodies
>   shine together
> in the darkness,
>   the hand moves
> to the center
>   of the flesh,
> the skin trembles
>   in happiness
> and the soul comes
>   joyful to the eye—
>
> yes, yes,
>   that's what
> I wanted,
>   I always wanted,
> I always wanted,
>   to return
> to the body
>   where I was born.

Whereas the "return to the body" that seems to be sought in other volumes is a retreat to infancy and the womb, an escape from life, here it seems almost a Whitmanesque realization of the body electric.

The long lines of *Howl and Other Poems* mark a second major shift in Ginsberg's poetics. Beginning before Columbia and continuing into the early 1950's, Ginsberg had been fascinated with formally rhymed and metered poetry imitative of Donne, Marvell, Shakespeare, and others. As a boy he had accompanied his father to meetings of the Poetry Society of America and heard "mostly old ladies and second-rate poets" praise Longfellow while denouncing Pound, Eliot, and Williams. "*Their* highwater mark was, I guess, Edwin Arlington Robinson, 'Eros Turannos' was considered, I guess, the great highwater mark of twentieth-century poetry." According to Ginsberg, his poetic education did not fare much better at Columbia. There the "supreme literary touchstones" were John Crowe Ransom and Allen Tate. The values were those defined by the New Criticism. Whitman "was considered like a creep." Pound was taught only as a "freak-out," and William Carlos Williams, who lived a few miles away from Ginsberg, was almost completely unknown.

Williams was known to his fellow townsman, however. Ginsberg showed him his rhymed poems and was told that "in this mode perfection is basic" and these were not perfect. Williams advised the young poet to become a more careful and detailed observer and to record what he saw more simply and honestly. Looking back over his journals, Ginsberg discovered that there were such poems hidden in his jottings. The best of these discoveries is "The Brick Layer's Lunch Hour" (*Empty Mirror*), describing a young workman whom Ginsberg had watched from his apartment window. The poem shows Ginsberg's talents of observation and is refreshingly clean of the self-consciousness and concern of his other early poems. But all of the prosy short-line poems in *Empty Mirror* also show that Ginsberg had very little feel for "the variable foot" and poetic line of Williams. Moreover, while these clumsily divided short lines might contain the feelings of the moribund East Coast poet, they could not contain the volatile emotions of the more robust Ginsberg of the West Coast.

Although the more expansive, confessional impulse had always been strong in Ginsberg, he had never felt free to indulge it: "The beginning of the fear in me was, you know, what would my father say to something I would write." The spill of long lines in "Howl" was possible because Ginsberg never intended his father or any other judgers to see it ("I wouldn't want my daddy to see what was in there. About my sex life. . . ."): "I suddenly turned aside in San Francisco, unemployment compensation leisure, to follow my romantic inspiration—Hebraic-Melvillean bardic breath. I thought I wouldn't write a *poem,* but just write what I wanted to without fear, let my imagination go, open secrecy, and scribble magic lines from my real mind—sum up my life—something I wouldn't be able to show anybody, write for my own soul's ear and a few other golden ears."

One of the "few other golden ears" he was writing for was Jack Kerouac, who Ginsberg knew would hear "the long saxophone-like chorus lines . . . taking off from his own inspired prose line really a new poetry." Ginsberg was also shaping his sounds to ear echoes of Illinois Jacquet's "Can't Get Started," Lester Young's "89 choruses of *Lady Be Good,*" as described by Kerouac, and "an extreme rhapsodic wail I once heard in a madhouse."

The long line of "Howl" and Ginsberg's later poetry has its literary origins in William Blake's "Marriage of Heaven and Hell," Christopher Smart's "Jubilate Agno," and Whitman's *Leaves of Grass*; but it is also explained in part by physiology—the "neural impulses" and "the breathing and the belly and the lungs" of a poet whose "movement" and "feeling is for a big long clanky statement"; and perhaps in part by abnormal psychology—the oral and anal erotic's enjoyment of explosive purgations (see Edmund Wilson's "Morose Ben Jonson").

Subsequent volumes of poetry indicate that the wholeness or at-one-ment of *Howl and Other Poems* is at best only temporary and at worst perhaps more illusory than real. The seemingly unified self that speaks in these poems may be only a more simplified self, one in which the warring elements have suddenly been reduced from four to two. By abandoning his market research job and "straight" lifestyle, and by repudiating the mental Moloch, Ginsberg has cut away one half of the fragmented self ("sensation" and "thinking"), leaving only the mystic and the "darker brother" ("intuition" and "feeling"). Ginsberg has rejected the systematized moral world of mind and the organized practical world of work. What is left in too much of his later poetry is a Ginsberg who is interested in pure consciousness or pure meat, sainthood or sex, vision or venery. In this he is no different than in *The Gates of Wrath* or *Empty Mirror,* except that there his energy level is down, his movement slow, and his ambience small; after *Howl and Other Poems* his energy is high, his speed rocketing, and his orbit is the world. While I cannot agree with Reed Whittemore that the "Howl" stage of Ginsberg's career is calamitous, or anything other than healthy for poetry and American culture, it is easy to share some of his other concern that

. . . this second stage in the Ginsberg saga has been even more calamitous than the "Howl" stage. The first had the genuineness of anger and despair about it—it was home grown and home felt—but the second has been clouded by great expectations, expectations that Ginsberg himself sometimes manages to temper with solid observations and with his striking death-obsession, but that his devotees infallibly leave raw: nirvana in the pad, nightly, forever. There

is terror for me in their misconceptions of what inner fantasy-life can make of the stony world; and Ginsberg is one of the breeders of that terror. Saintly he may indeed be as a private sinner—I do not question his private credentials—but he has also been a most influential loudmouth, an eccentric evangelist for an apocalyptic faith (and aesthetic) that has in my opinion competed pretty well with Moloch in mind-destroying.

Only twice again in a long, prolific career does Ginsberg approach the power and significance of "Howl," and in each case—"Kaddish" and "Wichita Vortex Sutra"—he is pushed to powerful utterance by overwhelming emotions. Ginsberg's genius lies not in his craft (of which he claims to have none) but in the authenticity of his feelings.

In the title poem of *Kaddish and Other Poems* the poet who had still felt a need to camouflage his biography behind the "best minds" of his generation in "Howl" confronts himself and his subject with an honesty that is at once brutal and compassionate. The first two long sections of "Kaddish" are meditations on death (and life) as well as stream-of-memory narrative detailings of his mother's madness and death. Death is "that remedy all singers dream of," a release from the dream where we are all trapped "sighing, screaming . . . buying and selling pieces of phantom. . . ."

Ai! ai! we do worse! We are in a fix! And
    you're out, Death let you out, Death had
    the Mercy, you're done with your
    century, done with God, done with the
    path through it—Done with yourself at
    last—Pure—Back to the Babe dark
    before your Father, before us all— . . ."

But in spite of "all the accumulations of life, that wear us out," our tortured existences are significant, almost even beautiful, when seen with the intensity of Ginsberg's love for his mother:

> to have been here, and changed, like a tree,
> broken, or flower—fed to the ground—
> but mad, with its petals, colored, thinking
> Great Universe, shaken, cut in the head,
> leaf stript, hid in an egg crate hospital,
> cloth wrapped, sore—freaked in the
> moon brain, Naughtless.
> No flower like that flower, which knew itself
> in the garden, and fought the knife—
> lost. . . .

A pivotal image in the poem (and for Ginsberg's life) lies in a letter written by his mother just before her death: "—2 days after her death I got her letter— / Strange Prophecies anew! She wrote—'The key is in the window, the key is in the sunlight at the window—I have the key—Get married Allen don't take drugs—the key is in the bars, in the sunlight in the window.'" Paradoxically, Ginsberg's mad mother may indeed have had the key for him, a symbolical insight going well beyond the advice to give up drugs and homosexuality. The key is not in the bright sky or the darkness of the room but at the threshold where light enters the material house. But for Ginsberg the bars that stripe and pattern the light have become Moloch, bars that imprison and separate the visionary and erotic self.

"The Lion for Real" offers a humorous account of Ginsberg's predicament after the Blake visions—the difficulty of telling his analyst and friends about the divine lion in his Harlem room. "To Aunt Rose" is a sympathetic identification with another lonely, buried self. The short-lined "Europe! Europe!" and the prophetic long-lined "Death to Van Gogh's Ear!" build on the war metaphor and continue the attack on Moloch. Most of the remaining poems of *Kaddish and Other Poems* are written under the influence of drugs—nitrous oxide, aya-

hausco, LSD, mescaline. Though their message may be (as Ginsberg claims) to "widen the area of consciousness," they do little to widen the reader's.

"Scribbled secret notebooks, and wild typewritten pages, for yr own joy" promises the subtitle-epigraph of *Reality Sandwiches, 1953–60* (1963), a book more interesting as autobiography than as poetry. It reveals both the before "Howl" and after "Howl" Ginsberg—the former a love-starved, death-obsessed businessman pondering escape in death or "the total isolation of the bum" ("Over Kansas," 1954), the latter a nostalgic isolatee walking "in the timeless sadness of existence," looking at his "own face streaked with tears in the mirror / of some window," feeling a "tenderness" toward everything but cut off from ordinary people and ordinary life by his lack of desire to own the bonbons and dresses and "Japanese lampshades of intellection" that are at the busy but empty heart of American culture ("My Sad Self," 1958).

"On Burroughs' Work" is an important early statement of Ginsberg's developing poetics, an insistence (influenced by both Burroughs and Kerouac) that poetry become an honest and spontaneous transcript of consciousness, "purest meat and no symbolic dressing," a naked lunch of reality sandwiches without any kind of lettuce to "hide the madness."

"My Alba" (1953) also contains an early and brilliant example of image juxtaposition that Ginsberg had learned from the paintings of Paul Cézanne. Studying Cézanne in 1949, Ginsberg "suddenly got a strange shuddering impression looking at his canvases, partly the effect when someone pulls a venetian blind, reverses the venetian—there's a sudden shift, a flashing that you see in Cézanne's canvases." The flash was a moment when the two-dimensional plane of the canvas seemed to shift into three dimensions and the juxtaposed planes of color suddenly became solid-space objects; in that flash Ginsberg could see through the canvas into cosmic space and feel a sensation like that of his Blake hallucinations. He later discovered that Cézanne had spoken about his attempt to "*reconstitute* the *petites sensations*" or flashes of perception that he got from nature after his senses had become so refined that he could stand on a hill and merely by moving his head half an inch "the composition of the landscape was totally changed." For Cézanne, this *petite sensation* was the experience of *pater omnipotens aeterna Deus.*

Just as Cézanne worked in two-dimensional planes and trusted to the perceptual leap of the viewer to create the deep space of the painting and the experience of *pater omnipotens aeterna Deus,* so Ginsberg hoped that by simple juxtaposition of disparate images, he might prompt the reader's perception to leap the gap between words and see through the poem to God. Such an intention is behind the "hydrogen jukebox" and "winter midnight smalltown street-light rain" in "Howl," and the "mad locomotive riverbank sunset Frisco hilly tincan evening sitdown vision" of "Sunflower Sutra." But the technique also seems to justify "the unexplainable, unexplained nonperspective line," Ginsberg's jamming together of longer bits, disconnected phrases, glimpses, fragments, subjects in a single poem, separating or joining them only by dashes, line breaks, or open spaces instead of the usual grammatical and logical connections. For all its other virtues, the technique does not work as Ginsberg intended. His poetry seems to have very little success at this mystical flicking of venetian blinds or opening the reader's senses to the immediate apprehension of God. But the technique is a marvelously effective shorthand and can flash the mind with brilliant cultural silhouettes. The "hydrogen jukebox" of "Howl," for example, is a wonderfully radioactive image, throwing off a frenzy of implication and backlighting a huge moral, political,

and emotional landscape reaching from the Pentagon to the Six Gallery.

But an earlier and perhaps even stronger example of this Cézanne technique is found in "My Alba," where Ginsberg regrets the five years he wasted in Manhattan as advertising copyist and market researcher with "mental / sliderule and number / machine" deceiving "multitudes / in vast conspiracies / deodorant battleships." The multiple resonances of "deodorant battleships" are too rich for exploration here, but the startling juxtaposition compresses volumes of commentary on the connections between Madison Avenue, war, deception, greed, prudery, fear and hatred of the body, and national paranoia. It also carries the intensity of Ginsberg's repugnance for a world he experienced primarily as an attack on his own flesh.

Planet News: 1961–1967 (1968) contains "Wichita Vortex Sutra," a poem comparable in power to "Howl" and "Kaddish." It is a vehement protest against the war in Vietnam and a concentration of Ginsberg's continuing poetic attack on Western culture's perpetual war against the flesh. The war that Ginsberg finds most intolerable is the "war on Man, the war on Woman," the war of "cold" more destructive than the international cold war, the mentality that would freeze the blood and desire: "the imposition of a vast mental barrier on everybody, a vast antinatural psyche. A hardening, a shutting off of the perception of desire and tenderness which everybody *knows* and which is the very structure of . . . the atom!" The perception of this "imposition" is not new, nor is the war against it. It is essentially the battleground defined by Blake and the romantics, broadened beautifully by Whitman, D. H. Lawrence, E. E. Cummings, and others. But Ginsberg's outcry is more anguished, his anger more personal, his own foot caught in the trap most painfully.

As early as "Paterson" (1949) and "My Alba," Ginsberg had described the Madison

Avenue–Wall Street world as a "war." He expanded the metaphor in "Howl," where those stalking-horse "best minds" were "burned alive in their innocent flannel suits on Madison Avenue amid blasts of leaden verse & the tanked-up clatter of the iron regiments of fashion & the nitroglycerine shrieks of the fairies of advertising & the mustard gas of sinister intelligent editors. . . ." Ginsberg sees society as a vast, violent conspiracy of greed, repression, and control that sears the soul and mutilates the flesh as surely as flamethrowers and fragmentation bombs.

In "Death to Van Gogh's Ear!" (1958) Ginsberg shouts like Cassandra against an unhearing "war-creating Whore of Babylon bellowing over Capitols and Academies! / Money! Money! Money!" The moans of the poet's soul go unheard because "they" are too busy "fighting in fiery offices, on carpets of heartfailure, screaming and bargaining with Destiny / fighting the Skeleton with sabres, muskets, buck teeth, indigestion, bombs of larceny, whoredom, rockets, pederasty, / back to the wall to build up their wives and apartments, lawns, suburbs, fairydoms. . . ." Other poems, such as "Europe! Europe!" (1958), depict this "war" as one overwhelming international industry, cowing everyone into meek underground crowds of creeps and perishing saints, mistreated lacklove whores, neglected spouses, hardened children with calcified senses:

> electricity scares downtown
> radio screams for money
> police light on TV screens
> laughs at dim lamps in
> empty rooms tanks crash
> thru bombshell no dream
> of man's joy is made movie
> think factory pushes junk
> autos tin dreams of Eros
> mind eats its flesh in

> geekish starvation and no
> man's fuck is holy for
> man's work is most war

Here as everywhere where war is the subject or the metaphor, the lines rush the reader with the noisy broken rhythms of armed attack. The conspiracy is obviously to stun and annihilate all genuine Eros and sell it back to the mutilated self as think-factory junk and tin dreams.

In Western culture the "mind eats its flesh in / geekish starvation," and despite Ginsberg's claim in "The Green Automobile" (1953) that he had "cashed a great check in my skull bank / to found a miraculous college of the body," he has been among the most terribly wounded casualties of the "war." Ginsberg's body-hatred is visible everywhere in the poems, both where he confesses it and where he professes its opposite. "Oh how wounded, how wounded" exclaimed a holy man the first time he saw Ginsberg. The idiopathic hunger for tenderness and love in Ginsberg's poems is so extreme because Ginsberg has found it difficult to grant himself that love; and the persistent virulence of his attack against the warmakers is a projection of his unfinished struggle to excise the cruel Moloch from his own head.

Just as Ginsberg's "darker brother" rose in rebellion against Moloch in "Howl," so does the god of orgy, Dionysus, frequently overthrow the god of war in Ginsberg's dreams and poems. Thus in "To an Old Poet in Peru" (1960) Ginsberg prophesies the dying man a reward "Brighter than a mask of hammered gold / Sweeter than the joy of armies naked / fucking on the battlefield." In other poems, the warfear-law-moneymakers (the U. S. Congress, President Lyndon Johnson, J. Edgar Hoover, Francis Cardinal Spellman) are accused of not sleeping with their wives, having shriveled testicles or shamefully tiny penises, while favored revolutionaries like Chairman Mao are cited for their genital blessings ("*Che Guevara has a big cock / Castro's balls are pink—*").

"Who Be Kind To" (1965) is both a childlike plea and a Buddhalike benevolence that urges us all to "be kind to" the "lackloves of Capitals & Congresses" and the "Statue destroyers & tank captains, unhappy / murderers in Mekong & Stanleyville" so that a "new kind of man" might "come to his bliss" and "end the cold war he has borne / against his own kind flesh / since the days of the snake." The days of the snake are not merely the days after the Fall in Eden (the birthday of good and evil, judgment, reason, polarity, righteousness, schizophrenia, dyads, and binary computers), but especially the days since the culture has become dominated by science, industry, and abstraction ("Moloch whose name is the Mind"), by the "mind-snake" that threatens to engulf the Buddha of Mercy like those snaky banyan roots in *Ankor Wat* (1968) that enclose the sacred temple in an inexorable death grip. The mind abstracts, forgets the realities of suffering and desiring flesh: "Man cannot long endure the hunger of the cannibal abstract" ("Death to Van Gogh's Ear!").

In "Wichita Vortex Sutra" the abstractions and lies of language are as much a target as is America's participation in the Vietnam conflict. The poem, like so much of Ginsberg's later work, is "composed" by speaking into a tape recorder while traveling cross-country. But unlike so many "Poems of These States" in *The Fall of America: 1965–1971* (1972) that randomly notate the passing phenomena almost as if a videotape camera were mounted on the car fender, Ginsberg is selective, noticing primarily the examples of language that swirl before his senses here in the heart of the nation—language from television, newspapers, magazines, radios, billboards, railway boxcars, grain elevators, department stores, street signs, songs, news conferences, and "N–B–C–B–S–U–P–

A–P–I–N–S–L–I–F–E." Words are the poet's tool, his magic, but the words that swirl around Ginsberg are meant not to reveal truth but to manipulate and conceal it. It is language that has designs on its audience, language originating in greed, smug pride, blind patriotism, chamber of commerce boosterism, political and military dishonesty. He enters this vortex of language as a poet and prophet, as representative of the living Word, but language has been so abused that he is "almost in tears to know / how to speak the right language—." He sees himself almost as a Christ, as the savior longing to speak a healing language of forgiveness and love. "Joy, I am I / the lone One singing to myself / God come true—." His call is to come back out of the wars of money and power and language to the erotic, ecstatic body:

> Come lovers of Lincoln and Omaha,
>   hear my soft voice at last
> As Babes need the chemical touch of flesh
>   in pink infancy
>   lest they die Idiot returning to Inhuman—
>   Nothing—
> So, tender lipt adolescent girl, pale youth,
>   give me back my soft kiss
>   Hold me in your innocent arms,
>   accept my tears as yours to harvest
>
>   . . .
>
> No more fear of tenderness, much delight in
>   weeping, ecstasy
> in singing, laughter rises that confounds
>   staring Idiot mayors
>   and stony politicians eyeing
>   Thy breast,
>   O Man of America, be born!

The antiword or opposite language is the language of news headlines that claim "*Vietnam War Brings Prosperity*" and "*Rusk Says Toughness / Essential for Peace*"; of Senator John Stennis, who urges "Bomb China's 200,000,000"; of General Maxwell Taylor and newscasts that repeat "Vietcong losses leveling up three five zero zero / per month" like "the latest quotation in the human meat market—"; of Secretary of Defense Robert S. McNamara who made "A bad guess" about the number of troops that would be needed to handle the war. Ginsberg builds the tide of incoming language to a rhythmic, hysterical chant: "Put it this way on the radio / Put it this way in television language / Use the words / language, language: / 'A bad guess.'" Ginsberg's extraordinary success in capturing the insanity of such language makes painfully clear what most American poets were discovering about Vietnam: that it was a war on language, as all wars inevitably are. As far back as the Peloponnesian War, Thucydides had noticed how war corrupted language because the ordinary meanings of words were changed to fit man's actions: when man's actions were noble, so was *his* language; when ignoble, his language was prostituted to lie and ennoble his actions. Ginsberg's poem makes us feel the tragedy of language once used for alchemy and transformation, for sacrament and atonement, now used for greed and power by mad and inept sorcerers:

Communion of bum magicians
     congress of failures from Kansas &
       Missouri
  working with the wrong equations
  Sorcerer's Apprentices who lost control
     of the simplest broomstick in the
      world:
           Language

Both the Vietnam war and the language war are part of the larger war of Apollo and Dionysus in America's lopsided culture. In a brilliant visual and historical metaphor, Ginsberg imagines a spreading tornado of violence spiral-ing outward from the symbolic and geographical heart of the nation, Wichita's Hotel Eaton:

Carry Nation began the war on Vietnam here
        with an angry smashing axe
           attacking Wine—
Here fifty years ago, by her violence
began a vortex of hatred that defoliated the
   Mekong Delta—
  Proud Wichita! vain Wichita
  cast the first stone!—

The allusion to the Hebrews who were about to stone the woman taken in adultery suggests once more that war and most human misery flow from *judgment* (Moloch the heavy judger of men), from the blind righteousness of those who have forgotten or denied their own flesh. Ginsberg writes as one who has himself cringed and trembled before such stones of judgment all his life.

If the black-magic language of politicians and generals can create war, then an opposite language of love spoken fervently enough by a sufficient poet ought to have power to bring the war to a halt. Thus Ginsberg is not indulging in literary or symbolic gesture when he declares an end to the war but is raising a prophetic voice in the linguistic wilderness, calling on "all powers of the imagination," all Gods, Seraphim, Prophets, shamans, and holy men of all time and space, and invoking the magic power of the Word: "I lift my voice aloud, / make Mantra of American language now, / pronounce the words beginning my own millennium, / I here declare the end of the War!" Though Ginsberg's serious act of language was largely smiled at by both supporters and detractors at the time, it is perhaps his one act of extraordinary genius. In a time and place where no one believed in such powers (but where they were nevertheless negatively at work), Ginsberg possessed the single imagination remaining in Moloch that was "crazy" enough to take language and poetry seriously.

The long series of cross-country car–plane–bus–train tape-recorder compositions, "Poems of These States," constitutes the bulk of *The Fall of America: 1965–1971* (1972), winner of the National Book Award. As a tribute to Ginsberg's life and work, the award is well deserved; as witness to the excellence of the poetry in *The Fall of America,* the award is of less certain probity. The poems are largely transcripts of the "movie of the mind" and the passing show outside the window. Ginsberg's notations are precise but undiscriminating; he gives us the face of the nation but as an ant crawling across Mt. Rushmore might give us the face of Washington, with every pebble, pimple, and scar: cornstalks standing in the fields, smoking factories, dead rabbits on the highway, road signs, junkyards, hamburger stands, polluted streams, tail-lights, hogs in the sun. And interspersed with these objects of the passing landscape are the myriad "objects" of the media-mind-body-scape: radio evangelists, ax murders in Cleveland, Sunday comics, leg pains, sexual reminiscences, self-congratulations on having given up smoking, Vatican pronouncements, bits of myth, racial tensions, newscasts, international politics, Bob Dylan songs, vomiting, the war in Southeast Asia, assassinations, depleted natural resources, and everything that a man of Ginsberg's mind and history might think, feel, hear, see, taste, touch, remember, and imagine.

These notations become random lists rather than Whitmanesque catalogs. There is no recognition that the phenomenal world and the self are one and the same thing. Ginsberg does not "assume" the world or put it on like flesh as Whitman does. He is "out of the game," not "both in and out of the game watching and wondering at it" like his predecessor. The window does not connect but cuts him off, insulates him from a world that is bulging with insane clutter. Ginsberg is Isaiah as a nonparticipant, and steadily losing energy.

That Ginsberg should relate to the self and the world differently than Whitman is not a criticism of Ginsberg but a revelation of his time and culture. Both poets are representative—I want to say symptomatic—of the human possibility and human circumstance in their time. Ginsberg cannot participate or enter in, because the "game" has begun to have such devastating implications. Whereas Whitman could put the Self together by naming the particulars of the world, for Ginsberg too much of the self is already fragmented and lost in those multitudinous crowdings of things outside the window and inside the head, as if the self needed to be defended from, rather than joined with, the world. Where Whitman could reach out to touch the Oversoul, Ginsberg's reach touches everywhere the stony face of the monster god.

Most of the last half of *The Fall of America* is a section titled "Ecologues of These States 1969–1971." The poems are both "ecologues" (bucolic and shepherdly meditations centered at Ginsberg's farm in Cherry Valley, New York) and "eco-logues," words for the ecology and the mother that is earth. They show a tiring poet withdrawing from the world, wondering "Who can prophesy Peace, or vow Futurity for any but armed insects." The Molochians seem unstoppable in their power and greed, their killing of whales and polluting of streams: "murder of great & little fish same as self besmirchment short hair thought control, / mace-repression of gnostic street boys identical with DDT extinction of Bald Eagle—." (Again the underlying implication is that the self and the world ought to be One, but because we are severed from our own bodies we are cut off from the world; hatred of self equals the abuse of nature.)

The calmest and sanest poem in *The Fall of America* is "Ecologue," where the details of the road are replaced by those of the farm—heifer, billy goat, windmill, moon,

> & last week one Chill night
> > summer disappeared—
> little apples in old trees red,
> > tomatoes red & green on vines,
> green squash huge under leafspread,
> > corn thick in light green husks,
> sleepingbag wet with dawn dews
> > & that one tree red at woods' edge!

Sanity grows in Ginsberg and in the poem because there is genuine work for the hands and the mind, things to be done, participated in: "Shelf the garage! / Where stack lumber handy to eye? / Electric generator money? Where keep mops in Wintertime?"

If *The Fall of America* saw "Death on All Fronts," *Mind Breaths: Poems 1972–1977* (1977) also carries titles like "Yes and It's Hopeless." Ginsberg seems a second time to have been defeated by the "world," as he was in 1954; he is not twice-born, but twice-beat, and this time he is left even more humble, gentle, and "beatific" than before. Although we have come to like the man behind them, most of these poems are so poor they will not bear discussion. They are written by a man who has given up his prophetic and messianic role and does not believe he can change anything. The fervor has fled. Mostly he is writing because it has become a habit.

One of the few good poems of *Mind Breaths* is the title poem, where Ginsberg sits in his newly discovered *vipasyana* meditation, paying attention to the space into which his breath flows. In a manner evocative of Whitman's grand, slow flights of the imagination across the national landscape, Ginsberg follows his moving breath out into the world. This too is a notation poem, but it is an imagined and much less bumpy ride than the car–plane–bus–train compositions—the lines flow even and slow like the calm breathing of the poet. The moving breath does not merely pass by but surrounds and laves and participates with its objects; and the poem and self seem whole and unified because the breath circles the globe and returns to the breather, who is thus encompassed with a single breath/world.

A second worthy poem of *Mind Breaths,* "Sad Dust Glories," is separately published with six additional poems in *Sad Dust Glories: Poems Written Work Summer in Sierra Woods* (1975). In these, as in "Ecologue," Ginsberg gathers grace from the work of his hands, through the physical labor that has been missing in his life. He is helping to build a cabin in the Sierras on land near Gary Snyder's home and relishes the new pleasure of being

> virtuous tired
> glasses slipping off
> > my blurry nose
> hitting the shining steel
> > mushroom head
> First time a chisel
> > in my hand—

He feels a new sense of self, wonders who he is "wandering / in this forest building / a house," he who has never worked or planted—"Words my seeds." But now he is caught up in the new body rhythms and sensations: "Work! Work! Work! This / inspiration / proves I have dreamed" ("Energy Vampire"). The Sierras and the work tie Ginsberg at last to the here and now, to the "realworld":

> Could you be here?
> Really be here
> > and forget the void?
> I am, it's peaceful, empty,
> filled with green Ponderosa
> > swaying parallel tops

fan like needle circles
glittering haloed
in sun that moves slowly
lights up my hammock
heats my face skin
and knees.

Ginsberg's best poems succeed brilliantly and his worst fail utterly because of his poetics of "First Thought, Best Thought" and "Mind is Shapely, Art is Shapely." Because he sought self-revelation instead of poem-as-made-object, Ginsberg stopped revising poems or making clear discriminations between poems and other kinds of language jotted in journals, spoken into tape recorders, written in letters to friends, or hallucinated on drugs. Following the lead of Kerouac, Ginsberg "got into" the "existential thing of writing conceived of as an irreversible action or statement, that's unrevisable and unchangeable once it's made." This finally leads to the rejection of distinctions between life and art, and to the idea that "everything we do is art." Because there can be no craft in the usual sense, no working over of the poems, the poem's quality depends indeed on how shapely the poet's mind happens to be at the moment the poem gets made. Shapely mind usually coincides with authentic passion, as in Ginsberg's best work—"Howl," "Kaddish," "Wichita Vortex Sutra," and a few others where strong feelings lift him above his obsessive ego concerns and psychological debilities; but the great bulk of his work is neither shapely nor impassioned.

Ginsberg believes that the proper subject of poetry is the "action of the mind," and the only craft is in learning to observe the mind and "flashlight" its activity. If the poetic rendering is faithful to the motions and rhythms of the poet's mind and body, it should stir similar motion and feeling in the reader. Ginsberg admits that when such rendering is truly spontaneous,

"I don't know whether it even makes sense sometimes. Sometimes I do know it makes complete sense, and I start crying." His desire is to "write during a prophetic illuminative seizure" where he would be in a "state of such complete blissful consciousness that any language emanating from that state will strike a responsive chord of blissful consciousness from any other body into which the words enter and vibrate." Ginsberg is obviously not a poet of ideas but of emotional states; one who sees poetry as "a form of meditation or introspective yoga," a sacrament where one pays complete attention and tries to record and communicate moments of "high epiphanous Mind." But as with his ideas about Cézanne, Ginsberg's theory does not work in practice (readers report few "high epiphanous" moments); instead, Ginsberg's spontaneous compositions communicate not the mystical experience but the naked man, sometimes profound, sometimes beatific, often boring and silly, often obsessed and polymorphously perverse. Ginsberg admits that he is only rarely blessed with "the heat of some truthful tears" and that usually he is "just diddling away."

Ginsberg was greatly excited by Kerouac's idea that future literature would consist of what people actually wrote rather than what they deceived people into thinking they wrote after they revised later on: "And I saw opening up this whole universe where people wouldn't be able to lie any more!" But, as is too often the case, Ginsberg's enthusiasm is exaggerated and illogical. One can tell lies all day without ever revising a word. Honesty has to come at some deeper level. What is logically implied, however, is that Ginsberg believes any control over the mind is dishonest, that thinking is not something a man does but that does him; he is not a thinker but a vehicle for thoughts that think through him like ticker tape. Thus to insist on art as an unedited "actual movie of the mind" is to insist that the active thinker step aside from the task of sorting and discriminating among the images of half-formed thoughts that stream through him, and to embrace and record them all as of equal validity. This apparently carries over, too, into one's life—all actions are equally significant so long as they are spontaneous, not controlled by that Moloch whose name is the mind. In "Today" (1964) Ginsberg tells of such "significant" actions: "I rode in a taxi! / I rode a bus, ate hot Italian Sausages, Coca Cola, a chiliburger, Kool-Aid I drank—/ All day I did things!" And after various and random thoughts of fascism, Buster Keaton, Samuel Beckett, pink shirts, Kali-Ma, "vaginal jelly rubber instruments" discovered in his parents' closet, and the note—"Also today bit by a mosquito (to be precise, toward dawn)"—the poem swells to its climax for Ginsberg: "I took a crap once this day—How extraordinary it all goes! recollected, a lifetime! / Imagine writing autobiography what a wealth of Detail to enlist! / I see the contents of future magazines—..." Unbelievable as it may seem, this is more serious than ironic, more program than parody. The literature of the future, then, is to be autobiography—and autobiography that refuses to make discriminatory judgments among the events of our lives. But again, the logical result of such thinking is not a new literature but the end of literature. Where art and literature exactly duplicate life and are identical with it, they are no longer necessary. It is not merely that everyone could write his own book, but that there would be no use for books at all; and where all thinking and utterance is a "transcript of consciousness" as ticker tape, there is no longer a need for language at all. Such a literature is ultimately a literature of silence. That is one way to silence Moloch, but it is an extravagant one.

At the very least Ginsberg's poetics lead toward a literature of "om," the universal sound containing all possible sounds that, by containing all particulars, erases all particulars. Ginsberg's poetry includes everything and, except for a few great poems, fades in the reader's memory to a great blur of static or background hum.

Ginsberg's poetics are another aspect of his reluctance to deal with the exigencies of time and the responsibilities of his own humanness (which is not at all to say that he is not among the most generous and decent of men). Anything less than a completely open, spontaneous poetics requires the imposition of order and the making of judgments. Not only is judgment an attribute of Moloch, but the imposition of order slows down the motion of the mind and threatens to bring it to a dead stop. A fear of stasis, of ossification, obviously haunted all of the "Dharma Bums" and "On the Roaders" of the 1950's and 1960's who sought to keep constantly on the move and at high speed. As Randall Patrick McMurphy (R. P. M.) of Ken Kesey's *One Flew Over the Cuckoo's Nest* (1962) knew so well, the moment a person stands still Big Nurse and The Combine (additional aliases for Moloch) are at him with their institutional thermometers. William Burroughs, too, had written Ginsberg that "The most dangerous thing to do is to stand still." The defining quality in Kerouac's prose style ("how you decide to 'rush' yr statement determines the rhythm") and Ginsberg's poetics is speed. (In his essay on projective verse, Charles Olson had also advised "get on with it, keep moving, keep in, speed," and his motives, too, were to escape the drying cement of the rational mind.) But random perpetual motion, whether physical or mental, is not conducive to wholeness or humanness. Randall Patrick McMurphy finally has to accept "commitment" and confront Big Nurse. But Ginsberg has not wanted to deal with this complex "real world" inside or outside of the head. He sees that world of patterns and judgments as a threat of death by ossification, and usually seeks to escape it by climbing into a cloud or diving into bed, seeking the patternless purities of disembodied vision or mindless sexuality. He avoids what Joseph Campbell would call the "death of petrifact" by fleeing to the opposite "death of chaos." These very choices seem embodied in the images of "Paterson" where Ginsberg refuses the paralysis of Madison Avenue and opts for a death of chaos (in eros, ecstasy, and motion), "rolling over the pavements and highways / by the bayoux and forests and derricks leaving my flesh and my bones hanging on the trees."

Ginsberg clearly has a problem focusing his energies on the "world between." His attention characteristically slips to either side of the rich world of daily human interchange and work. When asked if he ever contemplated writing an epic poem, his first reactions take the familiar leap and dive: "Yeah, but it's just . . . ideas, that I've been carrying around for a long time. One thing which I'd like to do sooner or later is write a long poem which is a narrative and description of all the visions I've ever had. . . . And another idea I had was to write a big long poem about everybody I ever fucked or slept with." In another interview, while discussing his theories of spontaneous composition and the importance of telling the truth no matter what archetypal thought comes into our minds, Ginsberg's first example of an "archetypal thought" is "I want to fuck my mother." A few minutes later he realizes his example might be shocking enough to "wave a red flag in front of understanding" so he substitutes another: "I want to go to heaven." (Is this another of the child-man's ways of saying I want to be touched and held by my mother or by my father?)

What this adds up to is a poetry with four basic contents: the poetry of vision (almost always involving drug use); the poetry of sex (usually frenzied and obsessive); the poetry of

the "world between" as mind-movie or passing show; and the poetry of prophecy against Moloch. And running through all of these, but most especially in the last, is the reiterated plea for tenderness and love. But only in Ginsberg's most recent and new poetry of physical work do these four isolated poetries draw together in a more satisfying and stable harmony.

At Cherry Valley and in the Sierras, Ginsberg has at last found some measure of the Soul or Sacred Heart or Self that he has searched for and misunderstood most of his life. He found it not in drugs or sex but in the physical body and the physical world of work that combines intuition and sensation and tames the darker brother into quiet thoughtfulness.

In a tiny poem of *Empty Mirror* Ginsberg had claimed "I made love to myself / in the mirror, kissing my own lips, / saying, 'I love myself, / I love you more than anybody.'" And in the neurotic dis-ease of "Sather Gate Illumination" in 1956, he urgently reiterated his self love ("I believe you are lovely, my soul, soul of Allen, Allen— / and you so beloved, so sweetened, so recalled to your true loveliness, / your original nude breathing Allen"). Methinks he doth protest too much. Years later, after an obsessive search for vision through drugs, and after traveling around the world and consulting holy men who urged him to emphasize the human and to "let your own heart be your guru," Ginsberg became a devotee of the Sacred Heart and announced that he had at last "Come sweetly / now back to my Self as I was—" ("The Change: Kyoto–Tokyo Express," 1963). However, Ginsberg persisted in understanding the "pure delight" and "very lovely doctrine" of the Sacred Heart as teaching that the way to wholeness and bliss "is to give yourself, completely, to your heart's desire," an interpretation that once again dismissed every kind of control and rational discipline. But of course the doctrine of the Sacred

Heart has no such easy implications and is much more closely allied to the idea of a difficult struggle to mediate and to love the freckled Incarnation of the Divine in the material world.

Immediately after his Blakean hallucinations in Harlem in 1948, Ginsberg had rushed to his bookcase with a suddenly doubled comprehension to reread St. John of the Cross and Plato and "Plotinus on the Alone." But Ginsberg admitted, "The Plotinus I found more difficult to interpret." A central doctrine in Plotinus is, I believe, that the Soul or Heart is the intermediary between pure spirit and pure matter, between *eidos* and sensation. For Plato, too, the Heart related to the warrior class that stood between the philosopher-kings (head) and the laborers, women, and children (body/genitals). Soul reaches upward toward intellect and divine forms to bring them more surely into embodiment and influence in matter, and reaches downward into the variety and massiveness of matter to lift it upward toward the *nous* and unity. Soul is not lost in the Many, nor does it reside in the One. It is mediator, operating at the level of discursive thought, exerting a rigorous self-discipline by which we awake from the alienation of our lower state and rise again to a knowledge of our true selves. But because in our time Moloch has invaded and occupied the whole area of rigorous moral and intellectual self-discipline and changed the heart (the *cour*-age) of the warrior into the metal of tanks and money, he has in a very literal way robbed Ginsberg of his Heart and Soul, his Selfhood. The "world between" matter and spirit belongs to the monster god, who allows modern men only two possibilities—to become mechanical hollow men who have forgotten the ecstasies of vision and sex; or to become crazy, schizophrenic, head-and-body-severed poets who have "consciousness without a body," "millions of genitals," and "an unpublishable private literature that goes 1400 miles an hour and twenty-five-thousand mental institutions."

Ginsberg was the first of the crowd of writers who emerged in the 1950's and 1960's as "confessional poets"—Sylvia Plath, Anne Sexton, Robert Lowell, John Berryman, Dianne Wakoski, and others—who to a surprising degree share similar backgrounds and psychological problems involving an eroded self-image, compulsive behavior and imagery, death obsession, attempted or actual suicide, time spent in rehabilitative alcoholic and mental institutions, a splitting or doubling of the self in poetic figures, and the traumatic early loss of a parent through madness, abandonment, suicide, or death. These common characteristics should make it clear that "confessional poetry" is not after all merely another movement or school, like the Black Mountain, New York, or Deep Imagist, but an efflorescence of decay, the growing shine of the perishing republic.

There has been a tremendous surface complexity and activity in Ginsberg's life, and indeed he has been more important as an active public figure than as a maker of poems. By the general public he has perhaps been variously viewed as dangerous, obscene, quixotic, or silly; as an advocate and user of drugs; as a leader in the Vietnam war protest; as a mantra-chanting peacemaker, riot-calmer, and holy man; but for a large segment of the aroused population he has stood as a representative of poetry as an art that will not be put to sleep or truckle under to the dull viciousness of "business as usual."

Ginsberg has never been a poet of idea or of craft. His only craft has been emotional honesty; his single "idea" has been tenderness—its scarcity, denial, necessity, beauty, and blessedness. He has crisscrossed the United States, traveled the world, organized the Human Be-In at Berkeley, swallowed peyote and LSD, testified before congressional committees, quieted the rioters at the Democratic National Convention in 1968, "om"'d the judge at the Chicago Seven trial, led the movement of resistance to the Vietnam war, read and taught in colleges, consulted with holy men, adopted Eastern philosophies, chanted mantras, sat in meditation (he has "pried through strata, . . . counsel'd with doctors and calculated close"; he has "wept and fasted, wept and prayed"); and after all this his one wisdom is honesty, his one virtue is compassion.

As a poet his voice has been prophetic and loud (and finally ignored by those most in need of prophecy). His greatest power has come from the magnitude of his own suffering and his own psychological infirmities. These infirmities are multiple and severe, and can be documented everywhere in his poetry. They make him seem "a deliberately shocking, bourgeois-baiting celebrator of a kind of sexuality which the most enlightened post-Freudian man-of-the-world finds it difficult to condone" (Leslie Fiedler); and account for an imagery of sexual behavior that is "hysterically frenzied, suggesting a compulsive search for love and acceptance through ceaselessly self-defeating, external, almost automatic activity" (M. L. Rosenthal). What Rosenthal sees as "a childishly aggressive vocabulary of obscenity" sometimes seems almost a case of pathological coprolalia or Tourette's Syndrome.

But while these sexual obsessions are a recurring infection in the poems, it is paradoxically just this extraordinary and insatiable hollowness and compulsive hunger for love that makes Ginsberg such a formidable opponent to Moloch, and makes us realize how "lacklove" and devoid of tenderness the culture has become. In the war between Moloch and the flesh, Ginsberg is no loudmouth-know-it-all-stateside-civilian but a veteran of the trenches with a gaping stomach wound. His power is what he shows us about the truth of that war. It is hardly a sufficient response to dismiss Ginsberg's poetry as a poetry of neurosis without looking to the neurotic ambience or understanding that a neurotic poetry is the most telling criticism of the culture. The pathology is personal, but not merely personal. Ginsberg is in this sense truly "the biographer of his time" (Helen Vendler).

Like Whitman, when Ginsberg gives us his book of poems, he gives us not a book but a man. Not a pretty man, but a man. Ginsberg may be Whitman as Quasimodo, but he is a modern-day Whitman nonetheless. His song is the Song of the Modern Self, twisted to the point of perversion, eroded almost to the point of invisibility. Ginsberg's great contribution as poet and man has been to confess for us his own need and to raise for us his own uniquely personal *eli eli lamma lamma sabactahani* cry of the naked mind for love.

Selected Bibliography

WORKS OF ALLEN GINSBERG

POETRY

Howl and Other Poems. San Francisco: City Lights Books, 1956.

Kaddish and Other Poems, 1958–1960. San Francisco: City Lights Books, 1961.

Empty Mirror, Early Poems. New York: Totem Press/Corinth Books, 1961.

Reality Sandwiches, 1953–60. San Francisco: City Lights Books, 1963.

Wichita Vortex Sutra. San Francisco: Coyote Books, 1967.

T. V. Baby Poems. New York: Grossman/Orion Press, 1968.

Ankor Wat. London: Fulcrum Press, 1968.

Airplane Dreams; Compositions from Journals. Toronto: Anansi, 1968; San Francisco: City Lights Books, 1969.

Planet News: 1961–1967. San Francisco: City Lights Books, 1968.

The Gates of Wrath; Rhymed Poems: 1948–1952. Bolinas, Calif.: Grey Fox Press, 1972.

The Fall of America; Poems of These States, 1965–1971. San Francisco: City Lights Books, 1972.

Iron Horse. Toronto: Coach House Press, 1972; San Francisco: City Lights Books, 1974.

Sad Dust Glories: Poems Written Work Summer in Sierra Woods. Berkeley, Calif.: Workingman's Press, 1975.

Mind Breaths: Poems 1972–1977. San Francisco: City Lights Books, 1977.

PROSE JOURNALS, INTERVIEWS, CORRESPONDENCE

"Notes for *Howl and Other Poems*." In *The New American Poetry, 1945–1960*, edited by Donald M. Allen. New York: Grove Press, 1960. Pp. 414–18.

The Yage Letters. San Francisco: City Lights Books, 1963. Written with William S. Burroughs.

"The Art of Poetry VIII." *Paris Review*, no. 37:13–55 (Spring 1966).

Indian Journals: March 1962–May 1963. San Francisco: Dave Haselwood/City Lights Books, 1970.

"A Talk with Allen Ginsberg." *Partisan Review*, 38, no. 3:289–309 (1971).

Allen Verbatim: Lectures on Poetry, Politics, Consciousness, edited by Gordon Ball. New York: McGraw-Hill, 1974.

As Ever: The Collected Correspondence of Allen Ginsberg and Neal Cassady. Berkeley, Calif.: Creative Book Arts, 1974.

"Craft Interview with Allen Ginsberg." In *The Craft of Poetry*, edited by William Packard. Garden City, N. Y.: Doubleday, 1974. Pp. 53–78.

Gay Sunshine Interview. Bolinas, Calif.: Grey Fox Press, 1974.

The Visions of the Great Rememberer. Amherst, Mass.: Mulch Press, 1974.

Chicago Trial Testimony. San Francisco: City Lights Books, 1975.

Journals: Early Fifties Early Sixties, edited by Gordon Ball. New York: Grove Press, 1977.

BIOGRAPHICAL AND CRITICAL STUDIES

Breslin, James. "Allen Ginsberg: The Origins of 'Howl' and 'Kaddish.'" *Iowa Review*, 8, no. 2:82–107 (Spring 1977).

Carroll, Paul. *The Poem in Its Skin*. Chicago: Follett, 1968. Pp. 81–108.

Dowden, George. *A Bibliography of Works by Allen Ginsberg: October, 1943 to July 1, 1967*. San Francisco: City Lights Books, 1971.

Davie, Donald. "On Sincerity: From Wordsworth to Ginsberg." *Encounter*, 31, no. 4:61–66 (October 1968).

Fiedler, Leslie. "Master of Dreams: The Jew in a Gentile World." *Partisan Review*, 34:339–56 (Summer 1967).

Hahn, Stephen. "The Prophetic Voice of Allen Ginsberg." *Prospects: Annual of American Cultural Studies*, 2:527–67 (1976).

Heffernan, James A. "Politics and Freedom: Refractions of Blake in Joyce Cary and Allen Ginsberg." In *Romantic and Modern: Revaluations of Literary Tradition*, edited by George Bornstein. Pittsburgh: Pittsburgh University Press, 1977. Pp. 177–95.

Hoffman, Steven K. "Lowell, Berryman, Roethke, and Ginsberg: Communal Poetry." *Literary Review*, 22, no. 3:329–41 (Spring 1979).

Howard, Richard. *Alone With America*. New York: Atheneum, 1969. Pp. 145–52.

Hunsberger, Bruce. "Kit Smart's Howl." *Wisconsin Studies in Contemporary Literature*, 6:34–44 (Winter 1965).

Kramer, Jane. *Allen Ginsberg in America*. New York: Random House, 1969.

Kramer, Jane. "Paterfamilias." 2 pts. *New Yorker* (August 17, 1968), pp. 32–73; (August 24, 1968), pp. 38–91.

Merrill, Thomas F. *Allen Ginsberg*. New York: Twayne, 1969.

Mersmann, James F. *Out of the Vietnam Vortex: A Study of Poets and Poetry Against the War*. Lawrence: University Press of Kansas, 1974. Pp. 31–75.

Parkinson, Thomas F., ed. *A Casebook on the Beat*. New York: Crowell, 1961.

Portugés, Paul. *The Visionary Poetics of Allen Ginsberg*. Santa Barbara, Calif.: Ross-Erikson, 1978.

Rosenthal, Macha L. *The New Poets: American and British Poetry Since World War II.* New York: Oxford University Press, 1967. Pp. 89–112.

——*The Modern Poets: A Critical Introduction.* New York: Oxford University Press, 1960.

Simpson, Louis. *A Revolution of Taste.* New York: Macmillan, 1978. Pp. 43–82.

Tytell, John. *Naked Angels: The Lives and Literature of the Beat Generation.* New York: McGraw-Hill, 1976.

Vendler, Helen. Review of *Planet News. New York Times Book Review,* August 31, 1969, p. 8.

Whittemore, Reed. "From 'Howl' to OM." *New Republic,* July 25, 1970, pp. 17–18.

—*JAMES MERSMANN*

Bret Harte

1836–1902

*T*HE birth of Tommy Luck in Bret Harte's short story "The Luck of Roaring Camp" (1868) was more than the birth of an illegitimate baby in a California mining camp. In a very real sense it was the birth of a new genre in American letters—the local-color genre, with which the name Bret Harte has become synonymous over the years. While some may debate the assertion that "The Luck of Roaring Camp" represents the beginning of the local-color movement, no one can deny that through his voluminous literary output Bret Harte made a strong contribution to local-color writing. Countless readers, both American and foreign, have obtained their first impressions of the California gold-rush days from his stories, and there is little doubt that such a pattern will continue.

Whetted by a curiosity regarding the manners, speech, customs, and habits of thought of the diverse regions of America, reader appetite for local-color stories in the later nineteenth century was virtually insatiable. And no region stirred more interest than the West. Although not a child of the West, Harte made a timely move to California on the heels of the gold rush of 1849 that proved to be a fortunate "union of the man and the hour." Combining the sketch technique of Washington Irving and the gargoyled characters and romantic sentiment of

Charles Dickens with his own wide-open receptivity to the boiling surface of life in the California gold camps, Harte produced a series of stories and poems that during the late 1860's and early 1870's attracted a large number of adoring readers.

The contrast between the social and cultural environment from which Harte came and that about which he wrote is striking. Born Francis Brett Harte on August 25, 1836, in Albany, New York, he was descended on his mother's side from among the first settlers in America—and his pride in that descent never dimmed. His father, Henry Harte, was a teacher at the Albany Female Academy and also operated his own private school. After the panic of 1837 and the failure of his school, Henry Harte became a wandering schoolmaster, moving from city to city. While such wandering made young Frank's (he did not use his middle name until the publication of his first story) formal education rather chaotic and brought it to a close after his thirteenth year, his precocity was well-nourished in the Harte home, where there was a small but excellent library. Beginning at age six, the youngster read his way through William Shakespeare, Charles Dickens, Daniel Defoe, Henry Fielding, Tobias Smollett, Oliver Goldsmith, Miguel de Cervantes, Washington Irving, and Alexandre Dumas the elder.

Henry Harte's death in 1845 forced Elizabeth Rebecca Ostrander Harte to appeal to both sides of the family for support for her and the four children. Richard O'Connor describes their attempt to maintain their self-respect:

They were conscious of a necessity to maintain the standards of gentle birth and lineage. In the process, undoubtedly, Bret acquired those slightly haughty traits which afterward caused people less conscious of the demands of breeding to call him a snob; they were a defense against the shabbiness of his boyhood and the suspicion that people would look down on him unless he looked down on them first.

Young Harte's first literary accomplishment came when he was eleven, with the publication of a poem titled "Autumn Musings" in the *New York Sunday Morning Atlas.* Unfortunately, the poem brought ridicule rather than praise from the family. Harte never forgot that unhappy experience, commenting later that he sometimes wondered "that I ever wrote another line of verse." O'Connor writes that the hurt felt by the youngster was deeper because his mother joined in the derision: "He and his mother were never particularly close, possibly because of her subsequent remarriage and also her disapproval of the woman Bret married. In none of his work was there any warm appreciation for motherhood, though he could wax sentimental enough about whores and madams."

In 1853, Elizabeth Harte and Colonel Andrew Williams, a college friend of her late husband's, announced their engagement, and a short time later she journeyed to San Francisco for the marriage. Harte and his sister Margaret were left behind. Several months later they followed her to California, making the journey by boat via Nicaragua and Mexico. It was an exciting trip, marked by storms that threatened disaster to the ship and by a Mexican revolution. The experience provided the impressionable Harte with background that he would use years later for a long story titled "The Crusade of the Excelsior," a tale of revolution and intrigue in Mexico.

The first three years that Harte spent in California have been the subject of much speculation by biographers. The absence of sound documentation has given rise to various legends and counterlegends—the former, according to George Stewart, viewing Harte as "the two-gun hero of a Western epic," and the latter calling him "an effeminate young 'squirt' who never even entered the mining country." Like most legends and counterlegends, neither view represents the truth. Stewart builds a strong case for Harte's having spent time as a schoolteacher, probably near La Grange, California. Certainly Harte used a schoolmaster character a number of times in stories.

As to Harte's mining experiences, the story "How I Went to the Mines" might be assumed to have some autobiographical base. The main character is a jobless young schoolmaster who decides to try his luck in the mines. He sets out to find an acquaintance in a certain mining district. After a hard two-day journey he reaches a mining camp and goes into a bar to ask about his friend. While drinking a glass of whiskey that he doesn't really want, he finds himself in the middle of a gunfight. Not wanting to show his greenness, he simply stands where he is. After the shooting is over, he discovers that a bullet has shattered his glass, and he calmly asks for another whiskey. At this point he meets his friend's partners, who take him in with them for luck. The story closes thus: "Then we worked at the claim daily, dutifully, and regularly for three weeks. We sometimes got 'the color,' we sometimes didn't, but we nearly always got enough for our daily 'grub.' We laughed, joked, told stories, 'spouted poetry,' and enjoyed ourselves as in a perpetual picnic."

Stewart points to two other stories—"A

Treasure of the Redwoods" and "Captain Jim's Friend"—as further corroboration for Harte's engaging in at least some amateurish mining. These stories, he suggests,

... mutually support one another, and all together gain support from their consistency with Harte's character and from their own unheroic nature. This was scarcely a sort of experience which one would take the trouble to invent once, much less to invent and then repeat twice after ten years and claim as one's own.

Moreover, Harte's own youthful enthusiasm would no doubt have driven him to thrust himself—even if only briefly—into the vital and scenic turbulence of the mining camps.

Although the gold-rush days of 1849 were over and San Francisco and the Bay area were becoming commercialized, life in the mining areas was still raw and close to the surface. In the introduction to *Tales of the Argonauts* (volume II of the standard edition), Harte describes early California:

It is a country unlike any other. Nature here is as rude, as inchoate, as unfinished, as the life. The people seem to have come here a thousand years too soon, and before the great hostess was ready to receive them. The forests, vast, silent, damp with their undergrowth of gigantic ferns, recall a remote carboniferous epoch. The trees are monstrous, sombre, and monotonously alike. Everything is new, crude, and strange. The grass blades are enormous and far apart, there is no carpet to the soil; even the few Alpine flowers are odorless and bizarre. There is nothing soft, tender, or pastoral in the landscape. Nature affects the heroics rather than the bucolics. Theocritus himself could scarcely have given melody to the utterance of these Aetnean herdsmen, with their brierwood pipes, and their revolvers slung at their backs. There are vast spaces of rock and cliff, long intervals

of ravine and cañon, and sudden and awful lapses of precipice. The lights and shadows are Rembrandtish, and against this background the faintest outline of a human figure stands out starkly.

It was to this setting that the Forty-Niners—or Argonauts, as Harte called them—came from every part of America. Fur trappers, well-bred easterners, chivalric southerners—all joined the mad search for gold, leaving, according to Harte,

... families, creditors, and in some instances even officers of justice, perplexed and lamenting. There were husbands who had deserted their own wives,—and in some extreme cases even the wives of others,—for this haven of refuge. Nor was it possible to tell from their superficial exterior, or even their daily walk and action, whether they were or were not named in the counts of this general indictment. Some of the best men had the worst antecedents, some of the worst rejoiced in a spotless puritan pedigree.

Social distinctions gave way easily enough to a pragmatic frontier democracy that judged a man on his conduct and not on his ancestry or background. Loyalty, generosity, and practical sagacity were among the most noticeable traits of the Argonauts. To be sure, they were not all the dashingly romantic types that have flickered across countless movie and television screens, but, as Harte once said, the "faith, courage, vigor, youth, and capacity for adventure necessary to this migration produced a body of men as strongly distinctive as were the companions of Jason." From this life Harte was to select the material that he would fashion into stories good enough to capture the popular imagination and to establish a tradition for the western story that continues undiminished today.

Before he turned his literary talent to such material, Harte tried several other endeavors, ranging from tax collector to Wells Fargo messenger to assistant editor of the *Northern Californian,* a newspaper in the small town of Union. In this latter position he came face to face with the potential for violence in early California. The editor, Colonel S. G. Whipple, made a trip to San Francisco at the end of February 1860, leaving Harte in charge of the paper. During Whipple's absence a small group of white men massacred some sixty Indians, mostly women and children. Harte was incensed and wrote a scathing editorial condemning the atrocity, saying in part:

Little children and old women were mercilessly stabbed and their skulls crushed with axes. When the bodies were landed at Union, a more shocking and revolting spectacle never was exhibited to the eyes of a Christian and civilized people. Old women, wrinkled and decrepit, lay weltering in blood, their brains dashed out and dabbled with their long gray hair. Infants scarce a span long, with their faces cloven with hatchets and their bodies ghastly with wounds.

No resistance was made, it is said, to the butchers who did the work, but as they ran or huddled together for protection like sheep, they were struck down with hatchets.

Because feeling against the Indians ran high in the area, Harte was none too popular. Henry Merwin describes a long evening during which Harte, armed with two pistols, awaited the coming of a mob fired up to do him great bodily harm. Only the timely arrival of a few members of the United States Cavalry calmed the dangerous situation. Although the scene as described may be somewhat exaggerated, Harte left Union within a month.

Throughout his life—and in his writings— Harte was sensitive to the wrongs done to animals, children, and oppressed races. And, as Stewart points out, "Sometimes his feelings were to spoil his art by making him picture these creatures *too* pathetically." In "Three Vagabonds of Trinidad," set in the Union, California, area, Harte depicts the struggle of the oppressed—in this case a dog, an Indian, and a Chinese boy—as they face a man named Skinner, who at one point in the story gives vent to his views of those not of the white race:

. . . but I kin tell you, gentlemen, that this is a white man's country! Yes, sir, you can't get over it! The nigger of every description—yeller, brown, or black, call him "Chinese," "Injin," or "Kanaka," or what you like—hez to clar off of God's footstool when the Anglo-Saxon gets started! It stands to reason that they can't live alongside o' printin' presses, M'Cormick's reapers, and the Bible!

At the end of the story the Indian and the Chinese boy are shot, but the dog gains some revenge by fastening his jaws on the throat of the man who shot them.

After the incident at Union, Harte ended his wandering. Returning to San Francisco, he felt that "the great mass of primary impressions" on his mind had become "sufficiently clarified for literary use." He took a position as typesetter with the *Golden Era,* one of the most highly respected newspapers in the West. Before long he was promoted to the editorial staff, and he had his springboard into the world of letters.

Harte at this period was fortunate to be introduced to Jessie Benton Frémont, daughter of a famous senator and wife of a popular hero. Interested in literature, she was taken with the lonely and sensitive young writer. Soon Harte was dining weekly with the Frémonts. There he met Thomas Starr King, a highly cultured Unitarian minister. At every chance Harte would read his manuscripts to Mrs. Frémont and King, who were both keen critics. Mrs. Frémont exerted a strong positive influence on Harte and was instrumental in getting his story "The Legend of Monte del Diablo" published in the *Atlantic Monthly* in 1863. He once wrote to her: "I shall no longer disquiet myself about changes in residence or anything else, for I believe that if I were cast upon a desolate island, a savage would come to me next morning and hand me a three-cornered note to say that I have been appointed Governor at Mrs. Frémont's request."

In 1860–1861 Harte wrote a weekly column on current events under the pen name "The Bohemian"—one of several pseudonyms he used in his early career. His first story, "My Metamorphosis," was published in the *Golden Era* on April 29, 1860, and was signed Bret Harte. A clever little piece, the story tells of a young man just out of school who, while walking by a lake near a private mansion whose residents seem to be away, decides to take a nude swim. As he is swimming, floating, and diving in carefree abandon, he hears voices and realizes that he is about to be discovered. With the daring and aplomb of youth, he leaves the water and leaps to a pyramidal pedestal of statues and poses as one of them. All goes well except that one young lady, though she says nothing, apparently realizes that one of the statues is alive. Years later the two accidentally meet again and fall in love. Although not a major accomplishment, "My Metamorphosis" was nevertheless a start.

Harte's first published story using the California setting was "The Man of No Account," which appeared in the *Golden Era* in 1860. The story—really a sketch—is about a young man who, with a group of gold seekers, goes to California in 1852. His dull demeanor makes him the butt of the group's jokes, and when they arrive in California, they forget him. But in two years he has struck it rich. Competing with one of the group (who really is of no account) for the affections of a young lady, he aids the man financially and then steps out of the romantic triangle to return to the East. Even though he drowns in a shipwreck, he has proved that he was a man of some account.

The first significant story that Harte published was "The Work on Red Mountain," more commonly known as "M'liss." It originally appeared in the *Golden Era* in 1860, but was revised and republished in the same newspaper three years later under the title "M'liss: An Idyl of Red Mountain." Harte always preferred the first version, writing in a letter to James Osgood, one of the owners of the *Atlantic Monthly,* in 1873 that "at the request of the proprietor, Colonel Lawrence, I attempted to create a longer story or novel of it, but after writing nine or ten chapters I wound it up in disgust. As I always preferred my first conception, I adopted *that* when I put it in 'The Luck.'" In the same letter Harte angrily complained that the *Golden Era* was printing a third version of the story, lengthened by fifty chapters and completed by someone else. He was furious: "I regret to say that they are quite capable of doing either in California, and, as I have received no notice from them, I expect the worst."

The main character in "M'liss" is a young schoolmaster from the East who, armed with a carpetbag, umbrella, and *Harper's* magazine, arrives in California looking for Smith's Pocket, a small settlement where he is to be master of the school. Smith's Pocket was founded by a veritable Smith, who discovered a pocket of gold that yielded $5,000 worth in less than an hour, then gave out. Search as he might, Smith found no more gold. His money soon gone, he turned to quartz mining, then to quartz milling, then to hydraulics and ditching, then to saloon keeping—ending up a drunkard with nothing but a miserable cabin and a motherless child. But Smith's Pocket, unlike its namesake, prospered.

One evening, as the new schoolmaster is working in the school, a dirty and shabbily dressed young girl enters. It is Melissa Smith—old Smith's motherless child. Just as her father is categorized by all as a no-good drunk, M'liss is categorized as an incorrigible urchin. She makes a pitiful plea: "I come here to-night because I knew you was alone. I would n't come here when them gals was here. I hate 'em and they hates me. That's why. You keep school, don't you? I want to be teached!" Had her plea been extended with tears, the master would have offered nothing but pity. But he is touched by her boldness, and feels "that respect which all original natures pay unconsciously to one another in any grade." After warmly encouraging her, he watches her bent little figure stagger down the path.

M'liss does come to school, and the master begins to draw her "out of the shadow of her past life, as though it were but her natural progress down the narrow path on which he had set her feet the moonlit night of their first meeting." The relationship between master and student grows stronger as the months go by; and when old Smith dies, the master arranges for M'liss to stay with a Mrs. Morpher, a kind-hearted woman who in her youth was known as "Per-rairie Rose," but who "by a long series of self-sacrifices and struggles, had at last subjugated her naturally careless disposition to principles of 'order,' which she considered, in common with Mr. Pope, as 'Heaven's first law.'" Among her children is fifteen-year-old Clytemnestra, a neat, orderly, and dull child. It is she whom Mrs. Morpher sees as a model for M'liss. It is also she who competes with M'liss for the attention of the young master.

As M'liss continues in school, the master is struck by her restless and vigorous perception and the audacity with which she gives answers. But he is concerned that in spite of her sincerity, she is revengeful, irreverent, and willful. The master decides to call on the Reverend McSnagley for advice, even though the two of them are hardly friends. But McSnagley can only talk of the great attributes of Clytemnestra—thus causing M'liss to suffer by comparison.

At examination time, when "the savants and professionals . . . were gathered to witness that time-honored custom of placing timid children in a constrained position, and bullying them as in a witness box," M'liss and Clytemnestra are preeminent and share public attention equally—the former with her clearness of material perception and self-reliance, and the latter with her self-esteem and correctness of deportment. The Reverend McSnagley interrupts M'liss as she is talking about the revolution of the earth around the sun: "Meelissy! ye were speaking of the revolutions of this yere yearth and the move-*ments* of the sun, and I think ye said it had been a doing of it since the creashun, eh?" When M'liss agrees, McSnagley turns to Clytemnestra, who responds, "Joshua commanded the sun to stand still, and it obeyed him!" In the face of McSnagley's triumphant look, M'liss slams her fist on the table and retorts, "It's a d—n lie. I don't believe it!"

When a traveling dramatic company visits Smith's Pocket, M'liss is inclined to run away with the group. The master, attempting to discourage one of the group from enticing M'liss away, becomes involved in a brawl and is almost shot. When he faces M'liss afterward, he asks her to go away with him that very night. She agrees.

And, hand in hand, they passed into the road,—the narrow road that had once brought her weary feet to the master's door, and which it seemed she should not tread again alone. The stars glittered brightly above them. For good or ill the lesson had been learned, and behind them the school of Red Mountain closed upon them forever.

In the longer version of the story, M'liss does not go off with the schoolmaster, but remains in Smith's Pocket. A mysterious stranger named Waters appears, and secretly works old Smith's claim. He shoots the Reverend McSnagley and is about to be lynched when M'liss helps him to escape. From him she learns that she has inherited a valuable mine. At this point, in another twist of the plot, M'liss's mother returns. She is a strikingly attractive woman whose "eyes, which were dark and singularly brilliant, were half closed, either from some peculiar conformation of the lids, or an habitual effort to conceal expression." M'liss goes to live with her mother, and becomes less wayward and more conventional in her demeanor.

Harte was correct in preferring the first version of the story. The second one is obviously flawed by the attempt to lengthen it. What was a tightly knit and fairly moving plot becomes in the longer version a loosely structured series of episodes and character intrusions, with the result that the character M'liss, sharply and poignantly drawn in the first version, is considerably diminished. But the second version of the story did become quite popular, and was the basis of four dramatizations and three motion pictures—one with Mary Pickford playing the role of M'liss. An artist of the Royal Academy even painted a portrait of the imaginary M'liss.

Out of his friendship for Starr King, Harte had begun attending the Unitarian church where King was minister. There he met, and became attracted to, Anna Griswold, a singer in the choir. She was a few years his senior and had already established a musical career. Neither family approved of the match, but both

Harte and Anna were determined to wed. On August 11, 1862, they did so.

Because of Harte's meager salary and the inflationary pressures brought on by the war, setting up a new home was not easy. To complicate matters, a baby was soon on the way, and it was not long before Anna Harte began to complain bitterly to her friends about the family's financial condition.

Never one to mingle much in San Francisco society, Harte continued to follow a quiet, studious life after his marriage. Even so, he was establishing friendships and associations with people who would be quite instrumental in furthering his literary career. Among these were Charles Henry Webb, literary editor of the *San Francisco Bulletin;* Charles Warren Stoddard, a twenty-year-old writer who was to become Harte's most intimate friend; and Ina Coolbrith, a young woman with whom Harte developed a close platonic relationship.

O'Connor sees this attachment to Ina Coolbrith as an indication that Anna Harte did not supply whatever it was that Harte desired from a woman. Most of Harte's acquaintances probably could understand his inclination to spend much time at Coolbrith's flat on Russian Hill. Few had anything good to say about Anna. Josephine Clifford McCrackin, another friend of Harte's, described Anna as one who "never seemed a lovable woman. . . . There was a morose, stubborn expression on her face which invited neither cordiality nor sympathy; and when she put her foot down her husband had to 'toe the mark.'" Harte, in O'Connor's view, may have been lordly outside his home, but in it he was indeed a henpecked husband "who increasingly sought refuge from domestic tyranny at his office, in the Mercantile Library or Miss Coolbrith's cozy flat overlooking the Bay. . . ."

While with the *Golden Era* Harte published several other stories in that paper and also began his "condensed novels," some eighteen stylistic parodies of such writers as Victor Hugo, Charles Dickens, James Fenimore Cooper, Charlotte Brontë, Alexandre Dumas, and Edward George Bulwer-Lytton. These were written between 1863 and 1865. The first two were published in the *Golden Era* and most of the others in the *Californian,* a newspaper for which Harte worked for about a year after leaving the *Golden Era.* In 1867, Harte put these "condensed novels" together and published them as *Condensed Novels and Other Papers.*

The "condensed novels" are really sketches, running only a few pages each, but they are true gems of parody—so much so that, as Patrick Morrow points out, "they are not only humorous in their own right but they also constitute a dimension of literary criticism." The *North American Review,* in commenting on Harte's parodies in 1866, called him "a parodist of such genius that he seems a mirror into which novelists may look and be warned." Unlike many other parodists Harte did not choose to parody only novelists he did not like. Dickens and Dumas, for instance, were two of his favorite writers.

Harte's parody of Cooper's *The Pioneers,* titled "Muck-A-Muck," although not as smugly scathing as Mark Twain's "Fenimore Cooper's Literary Offences," nevertheless reflects his distaste for the type of romance that Cooper wrote. Although Harte was not a true westerner, he could not, for example, accept Cooper's penchant for superimposing the accoutrements of civilization on the frontier. Genevra Octavia Tompkins, the heroine of "Muck-A-Muck," on one occasion fears for her father's safety and, after playing (on a piano) and singing an old Irish ballad, sets out after him:

But as the ravishing notes of her sweet voice died upon the air, her hands sank listlessly to her side. Music could not chase away the mysterious shadow from her heart. Again she rose.

Putting on a white crape bonnet, and carefully drawing a pair of lemon-colored gloves over her taper fingers, she seized her parasol and plunged into the depths of the pine forest.

On her journey Genevra is threatened by a grizzly bear, a California lion, a wildcat, a buffalo, and a Spanish bull—all coming at her in single file. As she is preparing to faint, Natty Bumpo arrives on the scene and dispatches these predators with a single shot:

Five animals bounded into the air and five lifeless bodies lay upon the plain. The well-aimed bullet had done its work. Entering the open throat of the grizzly, it had traversed his body only to enter the throat of the California lion, and in like manner the catamount, until it passed through into the respective foreheads of the bull and the buffalo. . . .

While parody is hardly a major literary form, it is not an easy one to master. The "condensed novels" show that Harte had the insight and critical acumen to produce a number of parodies that economically dissect an author without resorting to the high level of ridicule that so many practitioners of that form reach. Stewart is correct when he says that even today the "condensed novels" are excellent reading.

The Civil War, though fought a long way from California, was nevertheless a matter of great concern in that area. Starr King, according to Merwin, deserved much credit for holding California in the Union. Southern sentiment was strong on the Pacific slope, stimulating a movement to divide California into two states, one free and the other slave. After the firing on Fort Sumter, King called upon Harte to write a poem to be read at a mass meeting in San Francisco, on the question of California's remaining in the Union. The poem, "The Reveille," was a stirring call for loyalty to the nation, closing with

Thus they answered,—hoping, fearing,
  Some in faith, and doubting some,
Till a trumpet-voice proclaiming,
  Said, "My chosen people, come!"
    Then the drum,
    Lo! was dumb,
For the great heart of the nation, throbbing,
  answered,
    "Lord, we come!"

After "The Reveille" Harte wrote a number of other patriotic poems that reflect his views of the war—from "John Burns of Gettysburg," who put aside his farm chores to stand steadfast in a white hat with the Union troops, to a poem in commemoration of the fourteenth anniversary of the admission of California to the Union (September 9, 1864). These poems were published in various California newspapers, including the *Golden Era* and later the *Californian.*

In May 1864, Charles Webb had finally raised enough money to begin a new magazine—the *Californian,* the chief contributors to which were Webb himself, Ina Coolbrith, Mark Twain, Charles Stoddard, and Harte. The magazine was larger than the *Golden Era* and had a much more urban and cosmopolitan air. "These ingenuous young men," said William Dean Howells, referring to the contributors named above, "with the fatuity of gifted people, had established a literary newspaper in San Francisco, and they brilliantly cooperated to its early extinction." The *Californian* died on February 1, 1868. Harte had stopped contributing to it two years earlier.

In December 1865, Harte became involved in an incident that in some ways bordered on the ridiculous. Anton Roman, a bookseller, had been urging him to edit an anthology of California poems. Roman had a large collection of verse that he had obtained from Mary Tingley, a young Oakland woman who over the years had assiduously clipped poems from newspapers and magazines. In "My First Book" Harte recalls that he and Roman "settled to our work with fatuous self-complacency and no suspicion of the trouble in store for us, or the storm that was presently to hurtle around our devoted heads."

The title of the anthology was *Outcroppings,* and the storm that broke upon Harte and Roman came from poets who had not been included in the book. The December 9, 1865, *News Letter* mentioned the publication and the rumor that a delegation of 300 or 400 unanthologized poets was descending on San Francisco, seeking "dire vengeance against Harte." A number of reviews—some pro and many con—kept the California literary circle occupied for some time. By Christmas the book had nearly sold out, and the affair faded away.

About this time a miner in Calaveras County discovered a skull 250 feet down a mine shaft. The skull found its way into the hands of Professor J. D. Whitney, who promptly concluded that it was the skull of a human being who died before the lava flowed over northern California. Whitney read a paper to the California Academy of Natural Sciences, theorizing that the skull might change the accepted notions of man's development. Harte, who could not let such pomposity pass, published a poem two weeks later titled "To the Pliocene Skull," in which, figuratively speaking, he reburied the skull. After nine stanzas in which he exhorts the skull to speak and identify itself, he closes with

Even as I gazed, a thrill of the maxilla,
And a lateral movement of the condyloid
    process,
With post-pliocene sounds of healthy
    mastication,
  Ground the teeth together.

And from that imperfect dental exhibition,
Stained with express juices of the weed
    nicotian,

Came these hollow accents, blent with softer
   murmurs
  Of expectoration:

"Which my name is Bowers, and my crust
   was busted
Falling down a shaft in Calaveras County;
But I'd take it kindly if you'd send the
   pieces
  Home to old Missouri!"

Also during this period Harte was secretary of the United States Mint in San Francisco, a position arranged for him by Robert B. Swain, superintendent of the Mint and a benefactor of Harte's. The duties were anything but demanding, and did not interfere with Harte's literary endeavors. Harte met Mark Twain at the Mint. The men were equally impressed with each other, and a month later Twain visited Harte again at the Mint. Harte described that meeting thus:

In the course of conversation he remarked that the unearthly laziness that prevailed in the town he had been visiting was beyond anything in his previous experience. He said the men did nothing all day long but sit around the barroom stove, spit, and "swop lies." He spoke in a slow, rather satirical drawl, which was in itself irresistible. He went on to tell one of those extravagant stories, and half unconsciously dropped into the lazy tone and manner of the original narrator. I asked him to tell it again to a friend who came in, and then asked him to write it out for "The Californian." He did so, and when published it was an emphatic success. It was the first work of his that had attracted general attention, and it crossed the Sierra for an Eastern reading. The story was "The Jumping Frog of Calaveras." It is now known and laughed over, I suppose, wherever the English language is spoken; but it will never be as funny to any one

in print as it was to me, told for the first time by the unknown Twain himself on that morning in the San Francisco Mint.

Later, in a letter to Thomas Bailey Aldrich, Twain paid tribute to Harte, saying, "Bret Harte trimmed and trained and schooled me patiently until he changed me from an awkward utterer of coarse grotesqueness to a writer of paragraphs and chapters that have found a certain favor in the eyes of even some of the very decentest people in the land." The relationship between Harte and Twain, unfortunately, was not to remain on such a friendly basis over the years.

The year after his first collection of poems—*The Lost Galleon and Other Tales* (1867)—was published, Harte joined the *Overland Monthly,* a new magazine founded by Anton Roman. Not only was Harte the first editor, but he also selected the name of the magazine and designed its cover logo—a bear standing on a railroad track. This illustration, wrote Mark Twain, was "the ancient symbol of California savagery snarling at the approaching type of high and progressive Civilization, the first Overland locomotive!"

Because he felt that the *Overland* needed a romance of California on its pages, Harte wrote for the second number the story that eventually won him wide acclaim—"The Luck of Roaring Camp." The story, though, was not to make a smooth entry into print. The printer, shocked at its frank content, sent proofs directly to Anton Roman, with the comment that the story was indecent and irreligious.

Harte, after much discussion, persuaded Roman to let the story appear as written. It received a cool reception from the secular press of California and a very hostile one from the religious press, causing Harte to remark later, "It had secured an entrance into the world, but like its own hero, it was born with an evil reputation, and to a community that had yet to learn to love it."

It is true that if the life and reputation of the story had depended on its reception in California, it would have died then and there. Fortunately for Harte, the *Overland* was widely distributed around the country; and Fields, Osgood, and Company, publishers of the *Atlantic Monthly,* were impressed enough to ask Harte for a similar story for their own publication. Harte felt that he had proved himself and was not content to follow the advice of some of his friends that he not "tempt criticism again." On the contrary, in describing himself in the introduction to the standard edition of his works, he says that with

... reinvigorated confidence in himself and some conscientious industry, he managed to get together in a year six or eight of these sketches, which, in a volume called "The Luck of Roaring Camp and Other Sketches," gave him that encouragement in America and England that has since seemed to justify him in swelling these records of a picturesque passing of civilization into the compass of the present edition.

Included among the six works of the volume Harte mentioned were three of his best short stories: "The Luck of Roaring Camp," "The Outcasts of Poker Flat," and "Tennessee's Partner." All three merit discussion.

The setting of "The Luck of Roaring Camp" is one of both stark isolation and natural beauty. Roaring Camp lies in a triangular valley, between two hills and a river—and in the opening scene is focused upon by a rising moon. It is indeed a world unto itself. On this particular evening in 1850, the camp stirs with a commotion that could not have been caused by a fight, because fights are so common that they arouse little if any notice.

The entire population of the settlement stands like a Greek chorus before the rude cabin of Cherokee Sal, the only woman in Roaring Camp. Although it is never stated explicitly, Cherokee Sal is undoubtedly a prostitute, and at this moment is in an awkward situation for one of her profession. "Dissolute, abandoned, and irreclaimable," she is "suffering a martyrdom hard enough to bear even when veiled by sympathizing womanhood, but now terrible in her loneliness." Cherokee Sal is giving birth.

The men assembled before the cabin are like those of so many of Harte's stories. Living for the present in a crude and reckless fashion, they "exhibited no indication of their past lives and character. The greatest scamp had a Raphael face, with a profusion of blond hair; Oakhurst, a gambler, had the melancholy air and intellectual abstraction of a Hamlet; the coolest and most courageous man was scarcely over five feet in height, with a soft voice and an embarrassed, timid manner."

But as they stand before the cabin, they are nonplussed at what is occurring inside. Cherokee Sal, who no doubt often opened her legs to the men of Roaring Camp in paid-for love, now opens them to bring new life into the world. And the men do not know how to react to this new set of circumstances. Although they are not aware of it, the "sharp, querulous cry,—a cry unlike anything heard before in the camp," sets in motion a change in Roaring Camp that will in some way touch them all. Cherokee Sal dies, but her baby is born.

A miner named Stumpy is more or less appointed custodian of the new arrival, and he takes his responsibility in the most sober way. Stumpy places the child in a candle box on a table beside the bunk where Cherokee Sal lies dead, and invites all to "pass in at the front door, round the table, and out at the back door. Them as wishes to contribute anything toward the orphan will find a hat handy." The gifts range from a revolver to a Bible to $200 in loose coin. As the curious procession files by, an incident occurs that touches one of the group deeply. Kentuck, one of the least sentimental of the miners, bends over the candle box, and the baby reaches up and grabs his groping finger, whereupon Kentuck held "that finger a little apart from its fellows as he went out, and examined it curiously. . . . 'He rastled with my finger,' he remarked to Tipton, holding up the member, 'the d——d little cuss!'" And a relationship is cemented between man and child that lasts until death.

Since there is no woman to nurse the baby, Stumpy decides that Jinny, a jackass, will serve just as well. And so she does. The baby thrives—perhaps because in

. . . that rare atmosphere of the Sierra foothills,—that air pungent with balsamic odor, that ethereal cordial at once bracing and exhilarating,—he may have found food and nourishment, or a subtle chemistry that transmuted asses' milk to lime and phosphorus. Stumpy inclined to the belief that it was the latter and good nursing. "Me and that ass," he would say, "has been father and mother to him! Don't you," he would add, apostrophizing the helpless bundle before him, "never go back on us."

A month later Oakhurst the gambler says during a discussion of a name for the child, "It's better to take a fresh deal all round. Call him Luck, and start him fair." And Tommy Luck—in a very real sense the son of the whole camp—is "christened as seriously as he would have been under a Christian roof, and cried and was comforted in as orthodox fashion."

The Luck, as the miners call him, is given his own cabin that, under the watchful eye of Stumpy, is kept scrupulously clean and whitewashed. His cradle is a rosewood casket, packed eighty miles by mule. The regeneration of

Roaring Camp has begun. The whole camp takes on stricter habits of personal cleanliness—even Kentuck, who "in the carelessness of a large nature and the habits of frontier life, had begun to regard all garments as a second cuticle, which, like a snake's, only sloughed off through decay." Hard and crude as they may seem, the men of Roaring Camp are all touched by the subtle influence of the Luck as his presence awakens their finer sentiments. On summer days, for example, they take him with them to the diggings and spread a blanket for him on pine boughs. And through the day flowers and sweet-smelling shrubs appear as decorations for his bower.

Tractable and quiet, the Luck appears securely happy, even though "there was an infantine gravity about him—a contemplative light in his round gray eyes—that sometimes worried Stumpy." A true child of nature, the Luck is sung to and chattered to by birds and squirrels—and, as Kentuck attests, he even seems able to talk back to them. The Luck becomes a kind of god to the men of Roaring Camp.

Less than a year later, Roaring Camp is inundated by floodwaters and literally swept away. After a frantic search the survivors find the Luck dead in the arms of Kentuck, who is also dying. His last words are "'He's a taking me with him,—tell the boys I've got the Luck with me now'; and the strong man, clinging to the frail babe as a drowning man is said to cling to a straw, drifted away into the shadowy river that flows forever to the unknown sea."

The challenge that Harte faced in writing "The Luck of Roaring Camp" was to take a rather trite plot—that of the lowly prostitute giving birth to a baby who may be seen as the son of man (in this case the son of all the men of Roaring Camp)—with a sentimental ending, and to rescue it from itself. He accomplishes the rescue in two ways. First, by not allowing a single event or a single character—not even the

Luck—to dominate the story, he gives himself the freedom to focus clearly on the specific setting and on the general characteristics of the miners, so that the reader has the feeling that only at this given place, at this given time, and with these given people could the events occur. Second, by deftly blending humor and sentiment so that each either undercuts or highlights the other at just the right moments, he keeps the story from falling into cheap sentimentality or low comedy. Artistic restraint, humor, and sentiment, then, may be said to be the ingredients of "The Luck of Roaring Camp"—ingredients that combine to present the theme of the story: the universal regenerative power of human love in a world where nothing can be assumed.

Despite the degree to which he often extolled the pioneers of California, Harte knew that in reality they, like most human beings, could take moral stances that were often hypocritical and bigoted. And in many of his stories he attacked such stances and the people who took them. Although the theme of "The Outcasts of Poker Flat" is not an iconoclastic attack on moral hypocrisy and bigotry, it is an ironic contrasting of pseudo morality and true morality.

The main character in the story is John Oakhurst, the gentleman gambler who appears in several Harte stories. As he steps into the main street of Poker Flat on a November morning in 1850, he notes a "Sabbath lull in the air, which, in a settlement unused to Sabbath influences, looked ominous." The community has lately experienced some thefts and a killing; and in the righteous indignation that such acts have aroused, a secret committee has decided to drive all improper persons from Poker Flat. That he is one of these neither surprises nor dismays Oakhurst. Too much the gambler to question fate, he philosophically accepts his excommunication. He and three companions are escorted to the outskirts of the settlement. The companions are the Duchess and Mother Shipton, obviously prostitutes, and Uncle Billy, a confirmed drunkard.

As these violators of the fresh moral sanctity of Poker Flat leave their escort, "their pent-up feelings found vent in a few hysterical tears from the Duchess, some bad language from Mother Shipton, and a Parthian volley of expletives from Uncle Billy." Only Oakhurst maintains a stoic silence. They head for Sandy Bar, a settlement that has not yet felt the need for regeneration. The road lies over a steep mountain range. By noon the Duchess refuses to go further, and the party stops well up in the mountains and away from Poker Flat but less than halfway to Sandy Bar.

Oakhurst cannot convince the others of the folly of stopping so soon—and "Uncle Billy passed rapidly from a bellicose state into one of stupor, the Duchess became maudlin, and Mother Shipton snored." Oakhurst leans against a tree, calmly surveying his weaker companions, and "the loneliness begotten of his pariah-trade, his habits of life, his very vices, for the first time seriously oppressed him." Upon this scene come Tom Simson (the Innocent) and Piney Woods, his fiancée, who are running away to get married. Against Oakhurst's advice the two lovers decide to camp with the outcasts. And so the stage is set for the tragedy that follows.

The women take refuge in a ruined cabin nearby, while the men sleep on the ground. Oakhurst awakens early, only to discover that a heavy snow is falling and that Uncle Billy has run off with the horse and mules. The group is now stranded with only the supplies that the Innocent and Piney brought with them, enough for no more than ten days. A week passes, and the snow continues to build up. Singing and storytelling are the only pastimes the group has, with Piney and the Innocent doing most of the honors. The Duchess becomes more cheerful and takes over the care of Piney. Mother Shipton, though, begins to fade, and on the tenth day tells Oakhurst that she is dying. She asks him to take the small bundle from under her head. When he does so, he finds that it contains her rations for the past week. She points to Piney and asks Oakhurst to give them to her. With that she dies.

At Oakhurst's insistence the Innocent heads back to Poker Flat for help. Piling up enough firewood for a few days more, Oakhurst, too, leaves the cabin. The Duchess and Piney are left alone. The former asks Piney if she can pray. When Piney answers no, the Duchess seems relieved, putting her head on Piney's shoulder. "And so reclining, the younger and purer pillowing the head of her soiled sister upon her virgin breast, they fell asleep." And they are found that way—dead—when the Innocent returns with help. Oakhurst is found not far from the cabin, with his gun in his hand and a bullet through the heart—"who was at once the strongest and yet the weakest of the outcasts of Poker Flat."

Interestingly, one of the items that the Innocent has with him is Alexander Pope's translation of the *Iliad,* and the outcasts spend one night listening as he retells the tale for them. One of Pope's poems has a comment that is perhaps appropriate for the predicament in which the outcasts find themselves: "Act well your part for there all honor lies." That all the outcasts except Uncle Billy, in contrast with the "moral" residents of Poker Flat, act their parts well is a point made obvious in the story. Seen by some as the lowest elements in Poker Flat society, Oakhurst, the Duchess, and Mother Shipton succeed, along with the Innocent and Piney, in setting up a community, temporary though it is, that is based not on hypocrisy and pseudo morality, but on love and respect.

Just as the miners in Roaring Camp are regenerated by the Luck, so the outcasts of Poker Flat are regenerated by the beauty of innocence and love in the face of death. If Ernest Hemingway was correct in his belief that morality is something you feel good after, then the unselfish acts of the outcasts in this story should have, in their last moments, made them feel very good indeed.

In the introduction to *Tales of the Argonauts,* Harte speaks of the loyalty of friendship found among the men of the California mining camps. "To be a man's 'partner,'" he says, "signified something more than a pecuniary or business interest; it was to be his friend through good or ill report, in adversity or fortune, to cleave to him and none other. . . . The heroic possibilities of a Damon and a Pythias were always present."

"Tennessee's Partner" is the story of a partnership that, at least on one side, reflects the kind of loyalty delineated above. The main character in this story has no name other than Tennessee's Partner, almost as if his identity is submerged within that of Tennessee. Such is not really the case. Early on, Harte says about Tennessee's Partner, "That he had ever existed as a separate and distinct individuality we only learned later." Since the story is told in retrospect, "later" is not really relevant. What is relevant is the premium that Tennessee's Partner places on the second half of his name—Partner. He is a true partner, who, if given the chance, might well play the role of the fourth-century B.C. Damon.

Tennessee's loyalty to his partner, on the other hand, is questionable, though in one sense one could say it is not really tested. Tennessee's Partner returns to Sandy Bar with a wife, and Tennessee "one day took occasion to say something to the bride on his own account, at which, it is said, she smiled not unkindly and chastely retreated,—this time as far as Marysville, where Tennessee followed." Tennessee's Partner takes the loss of his new wife "simply and seriously," and evidently somewhat philosophically. When the errant wife retreats with someone else, Tennessee returns to Sandy Bar and, to the dismay and disappointment of many, is welcomed with great affection by his partner.

Tennessee, though, soon gets into trouble by stealing things other than wives. At his trial his partner comes to speak in his behalf. Tennessee's Partner's comments are almost eloquent in their utter simplicity:

I come yar as Tennessee's pardner,—knowing him nigh on four year, off and on, wet and dry, in luck and out o' luck. His ways ain't allers my ways, but thar ain't any p'ints in that young man, thar ain't any liveliness as he's been up to, as I don't know. And you sez to me, sez you,—confidential-like, and between man and man,—sez you, "Do you know anything in his behalf?" and I sez to you, sez I,—confidential-like, as between man and man,—"What should a man know of his pardner?"

His defense and his subsequent offer of $1,700 to make amends for Tennessee's actions fail to sway opinion, and Tennessee is hanged.

Apparently unmoved, Tennessee's Partner arranges a primitive funeral for Tennessee, inviting all who are interested to join him. Reflecting the sense of humor common in Sandy Bar, a large number accept the invitation. After depositing Tennessee in the ground, Tennessee's Partner speaks:

"When a man," began Tennessee's Partner, slowly, "has been running free all day, what's the natural thing for him to do? Why, to come home. And if he ain't in a condition to go home, what can his best friend do? Why, bring him home! And here's Tennessee has been running free, and we brings him home from his wandering." He paused, and picked up a fragment of quartz, rubbed it thoughtfully on his sleeve, and went on: "It ain't the first time that I've packed him on my back, as you see'd me now. It ain't the first time that I brought him to this yer cabin when he couldn't help himself; it ain't the first time that I and 'Jinny' have waited for him on yon hill, and picked him up and so fetched him home, when he couldn't speak, and didn't know me. And now that it's the last time, why—" he paused, and rubbed the quartz gently on his sleeve—"you see it's sort of rough on his pardner. And now, gentlemen," he added, abruptly, picking up his long-handled shovel, "the fun'l's over; and my thanks, and Tennessee's thanks, to you for your trouble."

The story, if written today, might have ended there, but Harte continued it to include Tennessee's Partner's death and his last words: "Thar—I told you so!—thar he is,—coming this way, too,—all by himself, sober, and his face a-shining. Tennessee! Pardner!"

Cleanth Brooks and Robert Penn Warren have accused Harte of ignoring the psychological implications of the wife-stealing episode and not bringing it into real focus—thus making the whole story seem anticlimactic and illogical. What Brooks and Warren miss, though, is that Tennessee's Partner defines his role as partner on his own terms. It is, moreover, those terms that give him his individuality. In his mind the partnership has nothing to do with his wife, errant or not. Nor is it dependent on any reciprocation by Tennessee.

A grave man, Tennessee's Partner applies himself steadily to detail, according to Harte, and his partnership is the greatest detail in his life. Thus he applies himself to that partnership until his death. Illogical? Perhaps—though if Harte is to be believed in his comments about the loyalty of partners, logic is irrelevant. Anticlimactic? No. The story hinges on Tennessee's Partner's maintaining his loyalty to the very end, for he is really symbolic of the very nature of partnership as the Argonauts conceived of it—or at least as Bret Harte says they conceived of it.

"The Luck of Roaring Camp" may have given Harte a literary reputation, but it was a sixty-line poem titled "Plain Language from Truthful James," or "The Heathen Chinee," as it came to be called, that really made him famous. The poem was one of those pieces a writer never seriously intends to publish. But when an issue of the *Overland* was short of material, Harte pulled out his poem and sent it to the printer.

Copied by newspapers in America and England, the poem increased the circulation of the *Overland* to the point that one New York news company sold 1,200 copies. The *New York Globe* reported that "Nothing like this has ever been seen on Broadway. . . . We have been obliged to produce it twice in the *Globe* to answer the demands of the public, and we venture to say there is not a secular paper in the United States which has not copied it."

Why was the poem such a popular success? Not even Harte could answer that question. Perhaps Merwin is right when he says that the poem came "at a fortunate moment when the people of this country were just awakening to the fact that there was a 'Chinese problem,' and when interest in the race was becoming universal in the East as well as the West." Or perhaps it was just one of those quirks of literary history that touches a common chord among readers—and nonreaders—of all kinds.

The poem is a parody. Truthful James, the narrator, and Bill Nye start a card game with Ah Sin, a Chinese man, with the idea of cheating him. Pensive and childlike and supposedly ignorant of the game of euchre, Ah Sin overcomes the cards up Nye's sleeve with his own trickery:

But the hands that were played
  By that heathen Chinee,

And the points that he made,
  Were quite frightful to see,—
Till at last he put down a right bower,
  Which the same Nye had dealt unto me.

At this turn of events Nye goes for Ah Sin with the shout, "We are ruined by Chinese cheap labor." In the struggle that follows, nothing is said regarding the fate of Ah Sin. The poem closes with

Which is why I remark,
  And my language is plain,
That for ways that are dark
  And for tricks that are vain,
The heathen Chinee is peculiar,—
  Which the same I am free to maintain.

In his monograph on Harte, Patrick Morrow sees the poem as an effort at social criticism: "In a comic instead of didactic way, Harte showed that Ah Sin quite literally played the American game and beat the masters. That the clever Chinese is run out of the game shows the hypocrisy . . . that formed the basic beliefs of men such as Bill Nye and Truthful James." Thus, Morrow categorizes the poem as a powerful statement against injustice.

If Harte had an attack against injustice in mind when he wrote the poem, his feeling after it made such an auspicious entry into the world of letters was something less than overjoyed. He was concerned that the poem was being read as a justification for cheating Chinese, or worse. "The worst of it was," says Stewart, "that he seems never to have liked the poem or to have seen why people made such a fuss about it, and to his dying day he was a little embarrassed when people referred to him as the author of the famous *Heathen Chinee* or talked about it in his presence."

Vigorously opposed to racial injustice in general and to its application to the Chinese in particular, Harte struck out at such injustice on numerous occasions. In the introduction to *Tales of the Argonauts,* he eulogizes the virtues of the Chinese:

He claimed no civil right; he wanted no franchise. He took his regular beatings calmly; he submitted to scandalous extortion from state and individual with tranquillity; he bore robbery and even murder with stoical fortitude. Perhaps it was well that he did. Christian civilization, which declared by statute that his testimony was valueless; which intimated by its practice that the same vices in a pagan were worse than in a Christian; which regarded the frailty of his women as being especially abominable and his own gambling propensities as something originally bad, taught him at least the Christian virtues of patience and resignation.

One of the best of Harte's stories dealing with the Chinese is "Wan Lee, the Pagan." Published in *Scribner's* magazine in 1874, it is about a Chinese boy, Wan Lee, who at the age of ten is sent to the narrator by one Hop Sing, a respected friend. The boy is to work as a printer's devil on the narrator's newspaper. Good-natured and mischievous, Wan Lee is both a trial and a pleasure to the narrator. After two years he is sent to a missionary school for Chinese children in San Francisco. Staying with a widow and her young daughter, Wan Lee becomes good friends with the latter. The two of them get "along very well together—this little Christian girl with her shining cross hanging around her plump, white, little neck, and this dark little pagan, with his hideous porcelain god hidden away in his blouse."

But Wan Lee's happiness is short-lived. He is stoned to death in the street "by a mob of half-grown boys and Christian schoolchildren!" As the narrator looks upon the battered body of Wan Lee, he puts his hand on the boy's chest and feels something crumble beneath his shirt:

"It was Wan Lee's porcelain god, crushed by a stone from the hands of those Christian iconoclasts."

Harte, while establishing a reputation with his writing, was carefully and patiently performing his editorial duties on the *Overland.* Though frank in his critical estimates, he was ever kind in his remarks to contributors. One of many aspiring writers that Harte aided, his friend Charles Stoddard, was deeply appreciative of his help: "Fortunately for me he took an interest in me at a time when I was most in need of advice, and to his criticism and his encouragement I feel that I owe all that is best in my literary efforts." On March 22, 1869, Harte wrote to Stoddard regarding some material the latter had submitted to the *Overland:* "I have used the best you have sent me, Charley; you would not have thanked me for publishing some which was not so good.... You do not want my advice; I should give you more than I should take myself." Another time Joaquin Miller, who also won fame writing about the West, submitted two poems to Harte for the *Overland.* Harte rejected both with the following comment:

Although I shall not be able to use either of your poems, I think that I fairly appreciate the merit of their performance and promise. I cannot say that I greatly admire your choice of subjects, which seems to me to foster and develop a certain theatrical tendency and feverish exaltation, which would be better under restraint, just now. I see nothing in you worse than faults of excess, which you can easily check by selecting less emotional themes for your muse. You are on your way to become a poet, and will, by and by, learn how much strength as well as beauty lies in repose.

His duties on the *Overland* and at the Mint provided him with a fairly respectable income but, as was true through most of his life, financial problems haunted him. These problems, combined with friction between himself and John H. Carmany, the new publisher of the *Overland,* and a general dissatisfaction with the lack of interest in art and literature exhibited by the inhabitants of San Francisco, made Harte discontented with his life in California. With a lucrative offer of $10,000 from the *Atlantic Monthly* for a year's output of stories, he decided that he would return to the East. Merwin comments on this decision:

No wonder, then, that, with tempting offers from the East, harassed with debts, disputes, cares and anxieties, disgusted with the atmosphere in which he was living,—no wonder Bret Harte felt that the hour for his departure had struck. Had he remained longer, his art would probably have suffered. A nature so impressionable as Bret Harte's, so responsive, would insensibly have been affected by his surroundings, and the more so because he had in himself no strong, intellectual basis. His life was ruled by taste, rather than by conviction; and taste is a harder matter than conviction to preserve unimpaired. Of all the criticisms passed upon Bret Harte there has been nothing more true than Madame Van de Velde's observations upon this point: "It was decidedly fortunate that he left California when he did, never to return to it; for his quick instinctive perceptions would have assimilated the new order of things to the detriment of his talent. As it was, his singularly retentive memory remained unbiassed by the transformation of the centres whence he drew his inspiration. California remained to him the Mecca of the Argonauts."

In February 1871, Harte and his family left San Francisco for New York. The journey was interrupted by a brief stop in Chicago, where Harte was to meet with some prominent men interested in his becoming editor of the *Lakeside Monthly*. He failed to appear at a dinner where the possibilities of his editorship would be discussed because, he said, no one called for him to escort him to the dinner. Whatever the cause of his failure to attend, the men involved lost interest in Harte as an editor. He later wrote to a friend in California that "The childishness and provincial character of a few of the principal citizens of Chicago spoiled the project." And so the Hartes moved on to New York.

Because of the fame his stories and the poem "The Heathen Chinee" had brought him, Harte's progress eastward was, according to Merwin, "detailed by the newspapers with almost as much particularity as were the movements of Admiral Dewey upon his return to the United States after the capture of Manilla." The *New York Tribune* reported that the verdict of the popular mind regarding Harte's writings "only anticipated the voice of sound criticism."

Following his arrival in New York, Harte journeyed to Boston to dine with the famous Saturday Club and to visit with the publishers of the *Atlantic Monthly*. James Russell Lowell was then editor of the magazine, and William Dean Howells, assistant editor. The latter was Harte's host. Howells described his impression of Harte in his "Literary Friends and Acquaintances":

Of course, people were glad to have him on his own terms.... There was never a more charming companion, an easier or more delightful guest. It was not from what he said, for he was not much of a talker, and almost nothing of a story-teller; but he could now and then drop the fittest word, and with a glance or smile of friendly intelligence express the appreciation of another's word which goes far to establish for a man the character of born humorist.

Howells' comments on Harte are an interesting contrast with the comments that Mark Twain was to make a bit later.

Harte, for the most part, made a good

impression on the literary lions of the East, and he himself enjoyed meeting such personages as Howells, Lowell, Ralph Waldo Emerson, Louis Agassiz, Oliver Wendell Holmes, and Henry Wadsworth Longfellow. He was particularly taken with Longfellow. Stewart describes a walk the two took in Cambridge:

A fine contrast they were—the younger man black-haired, dressed to the line of foppery, with that walk which some called mincing; the elder, patriarchal, hair silvery as the winter night, a voice of deep baritone, his whole presence mellowed by age and long-enjoyed honors into a gentle and modest dignity. For once, Harte bowed down in reverence; he offered no satire of Longfellow to Howells [as he did of some others]; on the contrary, the memory of the midnight walk through the snowy streets of Cambridge remained one of his cherished recollections.

With the $10,000 from the *Atlantic Monthly,* Harte was free from his usual financial worries for a while. During the spring and summer of 1871, he did little work, causing some to label him lazy. Whether his lack of production came from a concern that he might not be able to maintain his previous level of quality is a question only Harte could have answered. But he was enjoying his reputation and the role in which it cast him. His contributions to the *Atlantic Monthly* numbered seven—more than the number with which Howells later credited him, but fewer than the minimum of twelve called for in the contract. This failure, says Stewart, "was a real blow to Harte, the first he had received since he had founded the *Overland* and begun his career of greatness."

Despite his strong antipathy toward public speaking, Harte agreed to a lecture tour in order to stabilize his financial position. He prepared a lecture called "The Argonauts of '49, California's Golden Age." It proved a success when he presented it in Boston on December 13,

1871—while, according to O'Connor and Stewart, a sheriff was waiting in the wings with a writ of attachment on the proceeds. Mrs. Thomas Bailey Aldrich reported that the lecture had to be lengthened until Harte's friends could arrange a rescue. Just how he was rescued has never been explained.

In the next three years Harte presented the Argonaut lecture some 150 times, from Canada to Nebraska to the Deep South. His letters to his wife during this time reflect his dislike of the lecture business and bemoan the lack of financial success of the tour. On March 25, 1873, he wrote to her from Ottawa, Canada, saying in part:

I did not want to write this disappointment to you as long as there was some prospect of better things. You can imagine, however, how I feel at this cruel loss of time and money—to say nothing of my health, which is still so poor. I had almost recovered from my cold, but in lecturing in Ottawa at the Skating Rink, a hideous, dismal, damp barn—the only available place in town—I caught a fresh cold and have been coughing badly ever since. And you can imagine that my business annoyances do not add greatly to my sleep or appetite.

While Harte maintained a gracious home for his family in Morristown, New Jersey, he spent much time in a small New York City apartment. The reasons for his extended absences from his family can be explained on several grounds: the need to provide for the family, a desire for tranquillity, and an escape from creditors. "His talent for eluding creditors," says O'Connor, "was matched only by his quicksilver quality as a husband."

The year 1874 was fairly productive for Harte; half a dozen stories made their way into print. The best of these, "A Passage in the Life of Mr. John Oakhurst," resurrects the gentleman gambler who committed suicide in "The

Outcasts of Poker Flat." Unlike so many of Harte's other stories, this one does not have a sentimental ending. The ending in this instance is marked by a note of cynicism.

Oakhurst befriends a man and his rheumatoid wife, Elsie, and arranges a place for them in a resort area, where the man prospers as a carpenter and the woman regains her health and her beauty. Oakhurst falls in love with the woman, not realizing that she is using him to get rid of another suitor, his friend Jack Hamilton. Oakhurst forces Hamilton into a duel and mortally wounds him. As he is dying, Hamilton gives Oakhurst two love letters he has received from Elsie. Oakhurst confronts Elsie with the letters, saying that he has come to kill her. With feminine aplomb she admits her guilt and urges him to shoot her. This gesture unnerves the gambler, and he leaves. The story closes with him back at his faro table in Sacramento.

Also in 1874, Harte, perhaps wanting to prove that he could write something more sustained than short stories, began work on a novel, *Gabriel Conroy*. Such earlier stories as "Cressy," "In a Hollow of the Hills," "A Waif of the Plains," and "The Crusade of the Excelsior" are long enough to be called novelettes rather than short stories. But in *Gabriel Conroy* Harte let out all stops. It was to be a novel that covered all that California had to offer. In Stewart's words, it "would be a colossal painting, a synthesis of innumerable sketches, the representation of a whole historical episode." Too complex to summarize here, the novel centers on the adventures of its hero, Gabriel Conroy. Among the numerous side plots are those dealing with the trials and tribulations of Grace Conroy, Gabriel's sister, and the doings of Jack Hamlin, the gambler who appears in several other of Harte's stories.

Most critics agree that *Gabriel Conroy* proved that Harte was no novelist. Much too ambitious a venture, the novel—really a long string of brief narratives—sinks under its own weight. Harte himself admitted that he had difficulty in moving his characters in and out of the complex plot. Usually a fast writer, he also found both the beginning and the end of the book slow going—writing to his friend Elisha Bliss that "the book winds up slowly. It requires as much care—even more—in *ending* than in beginning." In spite of the weak story line the novel does have some graphic scenes and strong narrative passages that stand out in their own right. Perhaps the best part of the whole book is the prologue, which depicts a group of emigrants trapped by deep snow high in the Sierras.

Having tried novel writing, Harte next turned to play writing. With an earlier story, "Mr. Thompson's Prodigal," as a basis, he built the plot of his play around two of his most successful characters, John Oakhurst and Colonel Starbottle, and a new character named Hop Sing, a Chinese laundryman. *Two Men of Sandy Bar* opened in Chicago, and came to New York on August 28, 1876. The critics ripped the play to shreds, one calling it "the worst failure witnessed on the boards of our theatres for years."

Undaunted, Harte planned another play, this time in collaboration with Mark Twain, who had said earlier that *Two Men of Sandy Bar* "would have succeeded if anyone else had written it. Bret killed off his own chances in New York by having charged loudly and publicly before the opening that the newspaper critics never said a favorable thing about a new play except when the favorable thing was bought and paid for beforehand."

The new play was to be called *Ah Sin,* with each author initially working on his own contribution. When Harte visited Twain so that they could finish the play, the latter reportedly became angry at Harte's sarcastic remarks about the Twain home. Thirty years later, in his *Autobiography,* Twain quoted his scolding of Harte for his behavior:

. . . you are barred from these criticisms by your situation and circumstances; you have a talent and a reputation which would enable you to support your family most respectably and independently if you were not a born bummer and a tramp; you are a loafer and an idler and you go clothed in rags, with not a whole shred on you except your inflamed red tie, and *it* isn't paid for; nine tenths of your income is borrowed money—money which, in fact, is stolen, since you never intended to repay any of it. . . .

Ah Sin opened in Washington on May 7, 1877, and was well received by the audience. The critics were a different story. Although Twain worked on revisions during the ensuing summer, Harte apparently lost interest in the project and had nothing more to do with it. When the play opened in New York, Twain was there but Harte was not.

Harte's career, and Harte himself, were at a precariously low point. Money problems and lack of literary success combined to make good writing almost impossible. He did turn out a number of potboilers for the *New York Sun* but not much else. What he hoped would be a turning point—the editorship of the *Capitol,* a Washington magazine—came to naught when that publication was seized by its creditors.

Through the influence of friends and his own efforts with governmental bureaucracy, Harte obtained an appointment as United States consul in Crefeld, Germany; and in June 1878 he sailed for England, never to return to his homeland. Not surprisingly, his wife and children did not accompany him. The break with Anna was virtually complete as far as any real husband-wife relationship was concerned. Harte did write often, and he apparently sent money whenever he could.

Crefeld was not at all to Harte's liking, and he got away from it whenever possible. He knew almost no German and made little effort to learn any. His letters to Anna during this period reflect his dissatisfaction with the post and his concerns for his financial situation and his health. His hopes, he knew, lay in England; and in January 1879 he went there on a lecture tour—dragging out the "Argonauts of '49" lecture.

The lecture tour was generally a failure from Harte's standpoint. "I came here a week ago to begin my lecture tour," he wrote to Anna, "but my agent has blundered so in the beginning that my friends think it better for me to postpone the tour until later in the season." He followed the advice to postpone, finishing the tour in the spring, again to his financial disappointment. But he did establish social contacts in England that greatly pleased him.

As for his writing, Harte tried unsuccessfully to use the German background in "A Legend of Sammtstadt." He tried in other stories to picture Californians in Europe—again unsuccessfully. With "The Twins of Table Mountain" and "Jeff Briggs's Love Story" he fell back on the California setting. He obviously was not satisfied with his efforts, writing to Anna that "I grind out the old tunes on the old organ and gather up the coppers."

In June 1880, Harte left Germany for a new consular post in Glasgow, Scotland. Not only did the move represent a promotion; it also enabled him to continue his associations in England. The most significant of these was with Marguerite Van de Velde, whose husband, Arthur, was chancellor of the Belgian legation in London. She had read and admired Harte's stories, and it was not long before a room at the Van de Veldes' was set aside for him. She not only translated some of his stories into French, but she also proved an astute critic. With her encouragement Harte began to write with more regularity and fervor.

When Grover Cleveland was elected president in 1884, Harte lost his position. He nevertheless decided to remain in England and reside with the Van de Veldes rather than return to

America. Artistically speaking—and regardless of Twain's accusations that he had deserted his family—this decision was a good one. Harte was free now to write, and what he wrote was of good quality, resembling his earlier work. "Snow Bound at Eagle's," which opens with what is probably the archetypal stagecoach holdup of western fiction, is an example, as is "An Apostle of the Tules."

In the latter story Harte tells the moving tale of Gideon Deane, a neophyte preacher who offers to risk his life to save an outlaw about to be hanged illegally by a group of vigilantes. Because of this action he wins the respect of the gambler Jack Hamlin and others of the town of Martinez. They offer to build him a new church if he will stay there to preach. He declines, in order to go back to Tasajara to take care of a widow and her small children. That, he feels, is the work to which God has called him. In a letter to Anna, Harte said of the story that it was "in my old shorter and more condensed style."

During these years Harte worked steadily at his writing, becoming, according to Stewart, "a factory to produce stories, to meet the factory's financial obligations, to buy supplies of food and clothing, so that the factory might produce more stories to buy more food, and so to grind on in the circle until the factory eventually wore out." And on May 5, 1902, the factory did wear out; Bret Harte died of a severe hemorrhage—at his writing table.

Many modern scholars and critics of literature would probably agree with the view that Bret Harte is an example of how far a writer of limited talent can go—a view that has been held about numerous writers who have captured the imagination of the reading public. In Harte's case the view is applicable at least to some degree, depending on how one defines talent. Not a Herman Melville, a Nathaniel Hawthorne, or a William Faulkner, Harte nevertheless wrote a place for himself in the American literary chronicle by turning his talent for developing narrative, creating scene and incident, and depicting character to the raw material he found in the mining camps of California.

Following a formula that was based on the contrast between appearance and reality, that utilized stock characters, and that spiced sentimental plots with irony and humor, Harte showed, as John Erskine put it, "that the romance of the coast was not in outward things, but in the curious mixture of characters and races, brought together for the moment into the sudden whirlpool of the mining towns." And in so doing, he made the characters of those towns come to life for readers in the East and in Europe.

The medium in which he worked—the short story—was the best for capturing that transient, kaleidoscopic life of the mining camps. It enabled Harte to focus clearly on incidents and characters and to catch their foibles, their eccentricities, and their dreams. Whenever he tried another medium, the novel or the play, he failed. Part of the reason for this failure surely lay within Harte's own abilities, but another part of it lay within the very nature of the subject matter that he chose for his stories. Even his longer stories—"Cressy" is an example—are often based on, and developed from, a single incident.

It is ironic that some of his own contemporaries castigated Harte for his "vulgarity, obscenity, and harsh realism," while critics and scholars today tend to see his work as excessively romantic and sentimental. The irony is underscored in terms of the latter view when one remembers that Harte was vehemently opposed to extreme romanticism and cheap sentimentality. He did have a tendency to idealize his characters—probably because he saw the Argonauts in a grander light than they perhaps deserved—and he certainly used his share of sentimental endings for his stories. But his tonal perspective, at least in his best work, more often than not saved a given story from becoming an exercise in mere melodramatic sentimentality. His sense of parody and his recognition that humor and deep feeling often are closely related also played a significant role in this regard.

Perhaps, as Erskine suggests, if Bret Harte could have turned his gallery of portraits and incidents in the direction of longer compositions, he might have produced not only novels but also an epic of California. Since he could not, the world must be content—and well it should be—with what he did do, as G. K. Chesterton so aptly described it in *Varied Types* (1903):

He discovered the intense sensibility of the primitive man. To him we owe the realization of the fact that while modern barbarians of genius like Mr. [William Ernest] Henley, and in his weaker moments Mr. Rudyard Kipling, delight in describing the coarseness and crude cynicism and fierce humor of the unlettered classes, the unlettered classes are in reality highly sentimental and religious, and not in the least like the creations of Mr. Henley and Mr. Kipling. Bret Harte tells the truth about the wildest, the grossest, the most rapacious of all the districts of the earth—the truth that, while it is very rare indeed in the world to find a thoroughly good man, it is rarer still, rare to the point of monstrosity, to find a man who does not either desire to be one, or imagine that he is one already.

Selected Bibliography

WORKS OF BRET HARTE

FICTION

Condensed Novels and Other Papers. New York: G. W. Carleton and Co., 1867.

The Luck of Roaring Camp and Other Stories. Boston: James R. Osgood and Co., 1870.

An Idyl of Red Mountain. New York: Robert M. De Witt, 1873.

Mrs. Skagg's Husbands and Other Sketches. Boston: James R. Osgood and Co., 1873.

Idyls of the Foothills. Boston: James R. Osgood and Co., 1875.

Tales of the Argonauts and Other Sketches. Boston: James R. Osgood and Co., 1875.

Gabriel Conroy. Hartford, Conn.: American Publishing Co., 1876.

Thankful Blossom, a Romance of the Jerseys, 1779. Boston: James R. Osgood and Co., 1877.

Drift from Two Shores. Boston: Houghton, Osgood and Co., 1878.

Story of a Mine. Boston: James R. Osgood and Co., 1878.

The Twins of Table Mountain and Other Stories. Boston: Houghton, Osgood and Co., 1879.

Jeff Briggs's Love Story and Other Tales. Leipzig: Tauchnitz, 1880.

Flip and Found at Blazing Star. Boston: Houghton Mifflin, 1882.

In the Carquinez Woods. Boston: Houghton Mifflin, 1884.

On the Frontier. Boston: Houghton Mifflin, 1884.

Maruja. Boston: Houghton Mifflin, 1885.

By Shore and Sedge. Boston: Houghton Mifflin, 1885.

Snow Bound at Eagle's. Boston: Houghton Mifflin, 1886.

The Crusade of the Excelsior. Boston: Houghton Mifflin, 1887.

Frontier Stories. Boston: Houghton Mifflin, 1887.

A Millionaire of Rough and Ready and Devil's Ford. Boston: Houghton Mifflin, 1887.

Argonauts of North Liberty. Boston: Houghton Mifflin, 1888.

A Phyllis of the Sierras. Boston: Houghton Mifflin, 1888.

Cressy and Other Tales. Boston: Houghton Mifflin, 1889.

The Heritage of Dedlow Marsh and Other Tales. Boston: Houghton Mifflin, 1889.

A Waif of the Plains. Boston: Houghton Mifflin, 1890.

A Ward of the Golden Gate. Boston: Houghton Mifflin, 1890.

A Sappho of Green Springs and Other Stories. Boston: Houghton Mifflin, 1891.

Colonel Starbottle's Client and Some Other People. Boston: Houghton Mifflin, 1892.

Sally Downs and Other Stories. Boston: Houghton Mifflin, 1893.

Susy, a Story of the Plains. Boston: Houghton Mifflin, 1893.

The Bell-Ringer of Angel's and Other Stories. Boston: Houghton Mifflin, 1894.

A Protégé of Jack Hamlin's and Other Stories. Boston: Houghton Mifflin, 1894.

Clarence. Boston: Houghton Mifflin, 1895.

In a Hollow of the Hills. Boston: Houghton Mifflin, 1895.

Baker's Luck and Other Stories. Boston: Houghton Mifflin, 1896.

Three Partners or The Big Strike on Heavy Tree Hill. Boston: Houghton Mifflin, 1897.

Stories in Light and Shadow. Boston: Houghton Mifflin, 1898.

Tales of Trail and Town. Boston: Houghton Mifflin, 1898.

Mr. Jack Hamlin's Meditation and Other Stories. Boston: Houghton Mifflin, 1899.

From Sand Hill to Pine. Boston: Houghton Mifflin, 1900.

Under the Redwoods. Boston: Houghton Mifflin, 1901.

Openings in the Old Trail. Boston: Houghton Mifflin, 1902.

POETRY

The Lost Galleon and Other Tales. San Francisco: Towne and Bacon, 1867.

East and West. Boston: James R. Osgood and Co., 1871.

Poems. Boston: James R. Osgood and Co., 1871.

That Heathen Chinee and Other Poems. Melbourne: George Robertson, 1871.

Echoes of the Foot-Hills. Boston: James R. Osgood and Co., 1874.

Her Letter, His Answer, and Her Last Letter. Boston: Houghton Mifflin, 1905.

Poems and Stories. Boston: Houghton Mifflin, 1912.

NONFICTION

The Lectures of Bret Harte. Brooklyn: C. M. Kozlay, 1909.

The Letters of Bret Harte, edited by Geoffrey Harte. Boston: Houghton Mifflin, 1926.

Sketches of the Sixties. San Francisco: J. Howell, 1926.

COLLECTED EDITIONS

The Writings of Bret Harte. 20 vols. Boston: Houghton Mifflin, 1896–1914. The Riverside and Overland editions are basically the same as this, the standard edition.

Bret Harte's Collected Works. Argonaut edition. 25 vols. New York: P. F. Collier and Sons, 1906.

BIBLIOGRAPHIES

Gaer, Joseph, ed. *Bret Harte: Bibliography and Biographical Data.* New York: Burt Franklin, 1935.

Stewart, George R. *A Bibliography of the Writings of Bret Harte in the Magazines and Newspapers of California.* Berkeley: University of California Press, 1933.

BIOGRAPHIES

Merwin, Henry Childs. *The Life of Bret Harte.* Boston: Houghton Mifflin, 1911.

O'Connor, Richard. *Bret Harte, a Biography.* Boston: Little, Brown, 1966.

Pemberton, T. Edgar. *Life of Bret Harte.* New York: Dodd, Mead, 1903.

Stewart, George R. *Bret Harte: Argonaut and Exile.* Port Washington, N.Y.: Kennikat Press, 1935.

CRITICAL STUDIES

Beasley, Thomas D. *A Tramp Through Bret Harte Country.* San Francisco: Paul Elder, 1914.

Booth, Bradford. "Unpublished Letters of Bret Harte." *American Literature,* 16:131–42 (May 1944).

———. "Bret Harte Goes East: Some Unpublished Letters." *American Literature,* 19:318–35 (January 1948).

———. "Mark Twain's Comments on Bret Harte's Stories." *American Literature,* 25:492–95 (January 1954).

Duckett, Margaret. "Bret Harte's Portrayal of Half Breeds." *American Literature,* 25:193–212 (May 1953).

———. "The Crusade of a Nineteenth Century Liberal." *Tennessee Studies in Literature,* 4:109–20 (1959).

————. *Mark Twain and Bret Harte*. Norman: University of Oklahoma Press, 1964.

————. "Plain Language from Bret Harte." *Nineteenth Century Fiction*, 11:241–60 (March 1957).

Erskine, John. *Leading American Novelists*. Freeport, N.Y.: Books for Libraries Press, 1910.

Gardner, Joseph H. "Bret Harte and the Dickensian Circle in America." *Canadian Review of American Studies*, 2:89–101 (1971).

Loomis, C. Grant. "Bret Harte's Folklore." *Western Folklore*, 15:19–22 (January 1956).

May, Ernest R. "Bret Harte and the *Overland Monthly*." *American Literature*, 22:260–71 (November 1950).

Morrow, Patrick. "The Predicament of Bret Harte." *American Literary Realism*, 5:181–88 (Summer 1972).

Nadal, E. S. "Bret Harte." *North American Review*, 124:81–90 (January 1877).

Pattee, Fred Lewis. *The Development of the American Short Story*. New York: Harper and Brothers, 1923.

Quinn, Arthur H. *American Fiction: An Historical and Critical Survey*. New York: Appleton–Century Crofts, 1936.

Walker, Franklin. *San Francisco's Literary Frontier*. Seattle: University of Washington Press, 1969.

— *WILTON ECKLEY*

Robert Hayden

1913–1980

*F*ROM 1940 until shortly before his death on February 25, 1980, Robert Hayden published poems of unusual diversity and breadth of experience. A range of modern poetry from the dialect poems of Langston Hughes to the Byzantium poems of William Butler Yeats figured in his development. In broadest terms his verse deals with the tensions between the conditional realities of men's lives and their human aspirations, between a tragic and irredeemable world and the possibilities for transcendence that exist in sensory delight, art, and religion.

As a black American, Hayden is also concerned with history. The relationship between harsh empirical facts—especially the realities of American slavery—and the moral and imaginative use of these facts is an important element of his verse. Although at times his poems rise above the evil of the world, most often history and a hostile universe limit the possibilities of the present. In "Locus" (*Words in the Mourning Time*, 1970), a poem about the undying presences and deadly nature of the southern landscape, Hayden writes:

Here violent metamorphosis,
   with every blossom turning
deadly. . . . Here wound-red earth
   and blinding cottonfields,
rock hills where sachems counseled,
where scouts gazed stealthily

upon the glittering death march
of De Soto through Indian wilderness.
   Here mockingbird and
cottonmouth, fury of rivers.

    . . .

   Here spareness, rankness, harsh
brilliances; beauty of what's hardbitten,
knotted, stinted, flourishing
   in despite, on thorny meagerness
thriving, twisting into grace.

In "Locus" past and present, shade and brilliance, beauty and violent undergrowth twist into qualified "grace." Embodiment of the violent history of the South, the landscape thwarts the ample blossoming of beauty or the poet's transcendent contemplation. By contrast, in the same volume the poet is able, briefly, in "Monet's 'Waterlilies'" to escape history through the contemplation of art:

Today as the news from Selma and Saigon
poisons the air like fallout,
   I come again to see
the serene great picture that I love.

    . . .

Here space and time exist in light
the eye like the eye of faith believes.
   The seen, the known
dissolve in irridescence, become
illusive flesh of light
   that was not, was, forever is.

In these poems we see a manifestation of what Wilburn Williams, Jr., calls Hayden's "bipolar" imagination. Both poems emerge out of the conflict between man's imaginative-spiritual nature and the immitigable aspects of existence. In "Locus" the evil in man and nature condemns the transcendental impulse to unending terrestrial struggle. In "Monet's 'Waterlilies'" the poet is able for a short while to rise beyond "the seen, the known" to a sphere of iridescent serenity. Williams says of Hayden's verse: "The realities of imagination and the actualities of history are bound together in an intimate symbiotic alliance that makes neither thinkable without the other." Michael S. Harper observes similarly that "Hayden has always been a symbolist poet struggling with historical fact, his rigorous portraits of people and places providing the synaptic leap into the interior landscape of the soul. . . ."

Hayden himself suggested to John O'Brien, only partly in jest, that perhaps he was a "romantic realist." Acknowledging elements of romanticism, symbolism, and realism in his poetry, Hayden often underscored in interviews his mistrust of the commonplace sense of "reality" and his belief in the reality of the subjective. (The word he preferred is "fantasy.") He said to Dennis Joseph Gendron: " . . . we live so much of our lives in our own minds. What we consider fantasy and unreality—these things are so much a part of us and determine so much of us. I have always been fascinated by this. The line between the real and the fanciful is a very thin line. . . ."

Unquestionably the reality of "fantasy" or what we shall call "subjectivity" exerted a persistent influence on Hayden's verse. Yet if this attitude placed him squarely in the mainstream of modern poetry, it did not always win him approval or even attention. "There is a chronic American belief," Lionel Trilling observes in "Reality in America" (1940). "that there exists

an opposition between reality and mind and that one must enlist oneself in the party of reality." This tendency to view reality as "material reality," "wholly external" and "always easily to be known," emerges particularly in economically depressed times and amid economically oppressed groups. Sometimes it leads to a complete subordination of art and intellectual life to economic and political "realities." At other times, as was common during the 1960's and 1970's among radical blacks, mind—but only "black" mind—is admitted as part of reality. Stephen Henderson, for example, in *Understanding the New Black Poetry* (1973), defines contemporary black verse exclusively in terms of black themes, black feeling for life (Henderson's term is "saturation"), and structural effects arising from black speech and music as "poetic references." Other themes, feelings, or references are not important in understanding black poetry.

Although it made Hayden the subject of occasional attack, he always opposed such ethnocentric attitudes. Their fault lay for him in their defining the boundaries of reality for the artist and establishing ethnic or political criteria upon which to judge a writer's selection and treatment of material. In the controversy over William Styron's *The Confessions of Nat Turner* (1966), which was attacked by a group of black artists for its misrepresentations, Hayden's sympathies were with Styron and his freedom to write about whomever he chose: " . . . the attack on Styron, the extremely harsh criticism leveled against him, should give all writers pause," Hayden said to Paul McCluskey.

Hayden believed that craft and universality are the criteria upon which a work ought to be judged. Responding to real or anticipated pressure from black quarters, he described himself in his own anthology of black poetry as "opposed to the chauvinistic and the doctrinaire." Significantly, he went on to say that he "sees no reason why a Negro poet should be limited to 'racial utterance' or to having his writing judged by standards different from those applied to the work of other poets"; here he also seemed to be addressing himself to white readers, editors, and critics.

Coercion from this second group did not assume any overt form; it manifested itself as neglect. Until 1975, Hayden had not been published by a large American publishing house. His works were issued in limited editions by small foreign and domestic presses. Even in terms of poetry anthologies, only "Middle Passage," a historical poem about the slave trade, and his sonnet "Frederick Douglass" have appeared in the major anthologies used regularly in college classrooms. "Yet do I marvel at this curious thing: / To make a poet black, and bid him sing!" Countee Cullen wrote in 1925, commenting on the irony of the black lyric poet's vocation in a world scored with evil. At the present time too few people are acquainted with the marvelous richness of Hayden's verse. That it does not always embody the anticipated attributes of black poetry, such as ethnicity and anger, has something to do with this.

Robert Earl Hayden was born in Detroit, Michigan, on August 4, 1913. He grew up in a poor neighborhood, later affectionately, though not without irony, named Paradise Valley by its inhabitants. In the 1920's, blacks, Jews, Germans, Italians, and some southern whites lived there; by the 1930's, with the black migration to the North, the neighborhood was inhabited solely by blacks. Hayden's memories of a huge old synagogue on Montcalm Street becoming the Mount Olive Baptist Church grew out of this transitional period and figure in a poem about the loss of Jewish friends called "The Rabbi" (*Selected Poems*, 1966). "Free Fantasia: Tiger Flowers" (*Angle of Ascent*, 1975) describes the "sporting people / along St. Antoine" and how "I was a boy then, running . . .

errands for Miss Jackie / and Stack-o'-Diamonds' Eula Mae." In "Elegies for Paradise Valley" (*American Journal*, 1978), neighborhood characters return to the poet's mind as if from a region of the dead. These resurrections are stirred by the memory of a storefront gypsy whose séances he attended with his mother and aunt in order to contact a dead uncle.

The quality of life in Paradise Valley is best evoked in "'Summertime and the Living . . .'" (*Selected Poems*). In contrast with the languid environs of George and Ira Gershwin's *Porgy and Bess* hit, the living, according to the poem, was anything but easy. The adult speaker recalls how "sunflowers gangled there sometimes / tough-stalked and bold / and like the vivid children there unplanned." He also remembers how, as a child, there were never any roses

. . . except when people died—
and no vacations for his elders,
so harshened after each unrelenting day
that they were shouting-angry.
But summer was, they said, the poor
    folks' time
of year. And he remembers
how they would sit on broken steps amid

The fevered tossings of the dusk, the
    dark,
wafting hearsay with funeral-parlor fans
or making evening solemn by
their quietness. . . .

Hayden's family life was riddled with emotional complication and trauma more than with poverty. His parents' marriage ended when he was still young. His mother placed him in the care of a childless neighborhood couple, then went to Buffalo, New York, in search of work. Robert remained with William and Sue Ellen Hayden permanently. He assumed their name, and they reared him with the love of actual parents. "All through my childhood my mother was a kind of vision, a kind of imaginary person," Hayden said, trying to describe the impression the visits of his real mother left on him. When he was a teenager, she returned, not merely to Detroit but to live with the Haydens; and then, when jealous conflict with Sue Ellen Hayden made that impossible, to the house next door.

Hayden described his foster mother (the source for "The Ballad of Sue Ellen Westerfield," *Selected Poems*) as extremely neurotic, tortured by a facial "neuralgia" that he suspected was psychosomatic. Her intense love for him was irrationally possessive. She beat him, subjected him to verbal abuse about his real mother, and became violently jealous about the time he spent with her. If this was not enough, William Hayden, Robert's foster father, had "terrible rows" with Sue Ellen's daughter by her first marriage. "I lived in the midst of so much turmoil all the time that I didn't know if I loved or hated," he told Gendron. Still, he felt compelled to add that "while cruel and dreadful things happened and I was exposed to all kinds of really dreadful things, really soul-shattering experiences in the home and all around me, they [his foster family] could be really self-sacrificing on top of all that."

Until Hayden was forty, he thought that he had been legally adopted by the Haydens, and that his original name was Robert Sheffey. He learned when applying for a passport that there never had been a legal adoption, although the "old ones" had told him so; his legal name was Asa Bundy Sheffey. "You know, I am in many respects a divided person," Hayden told Gendron. Hayden's tendency to think of both sets of adults as parents and his prolonged living with divided loyalties and ambivalent feelings help one to understand the man. It also offers valuable insight into the sources of the dogged courage he displayed during his long career as a poet.

Learning to live amid violently contending demands as a youth may, ultimately, have helped Hayden to resist the pressures he faced as an adult from black nationalists to be a "black poet" and from white liberals to be a "spokesman for his race." Also, Gendron suggests that, from the circumstances of his youth, certain themes manifested themselves in his work: "the search for and definition of what constitutes identity, the significance of names, and the dilemma of a man caught between two worlds." Furthermore, rather than immobilizing his sense of self (though for periods this evidently occurred), his struggle with identity seems finally to have given him a penetrating and coherent sense of character. One wonders, after reading his poems about Malcolm X and Nat Turner, what sort of novelist he might have made.

Hayden was always extremely nearsighted. Limited to indoor play because of this and turned inward by the tensions at home, he spent most of his early years in solitary activity. Recalling the summer in late adolescence when he discovered modern poetry, he told Paul McCluskey: "Instead of playing baseball ... or taking part in the other so-called 'normal' activities of the boys in my neighborhood, I would spend hours reading poetry and struggling to get my words down on paper. From that summer on, I continued working at poetry, hoping someday to be known as a poet." By the age of eighteen, he had taken the first step. A poem imitating Cullen's "Heritage" appeared in *Abbott's Monthly*, a Chicago magazine.

Hayden attended Detroit City College (now Wayne State University) from 1932 to 1936 and majored in foreign languages. After college he joined the Federal Writers' Project of the Works Progress Administration (WPA) and until 1938 did research on the Underground Railroad in Michigan and the antislavery movement. He probably acquired his appetite for historical research from this stint with the WPA. In the 1940's, Hayden continued to read about the slave trade, plantation life, slave revolts, and the Underground Railroad; and this material, both as general background and as documentary detail, made the composition of his historical poems possible.

During his college years and afterward, Hayden also acted in Detroit and wrote for the stage. A play of his about Harriet Tubman, *Go Down, Moses*, was produced several times. He served as an arts critic for a black weekly, the *Michigan Chronicle;* and he was also tangentially involved in left-wing labor organizing in Detroit. At one mass meeting he was voted "the people's poet." "These Are My People" (*Heart-Shape in the Dust*, 1940), a long protest poem describing the poverty and idleness of blacks in America during the Great Depression, was "a great thing . . . in Chicago and Detroit" and was performed by groups.

From 1941 to 1946 Hayden did graduate work in English at the University of Michigan, where he studied with and was befriended by W. H. Auden. He received an M.A. in 1944. He had married Erma Morris, a musician and teacher, in 1940; and they had a child, Maia, two years later. In 1946 Hayden moved his family to Nashville, Tennessee, to teach at Fisk University. He spent twenty-two years at Fisk. Although the faculty was racially mixed, socialized together, and lived in an integrated enclave, he described (in his interview with Richard Layman) feeling limited in "the kind of experience we could have . . . the kind of things we could do." His daughter had to attend a segregated school. Also, there was a "provincialism in the South," frustrating to his and Erma's interest in avant-garde painting and dance.

Thus, although Fisk was a "pretty sophisticated place" and he felt he "could be of some service to the young people there," Hayden would have liked to return to the North. But it

was impossible to find a position. In the years when he might have been at the height of his productive powers, he found his stamina drained away in "earning a living." The writer and poet Julius Lester, a student of Hayden's, offers this recollection of him at Fisk:

When I entered Fisk University in the fall of 1956, he had already been there 10 years. . . . On campus, he was regarded as just another instructor in the English department, teaching 15 hours of classes a week. . . . No one at Fisk had the vaguest notion of what a poet's function was, not that they gave it any thought. Yet, somehow, Hayden continued to believe—in himself and poetry—though no one except his wife and a few students and friends in New York ever cared.

Although Hayden worked in relative obscurity, without significant popular or critical recognition, he did have his share of awards and honors, some of major importance. He won the Avery Hopwood Award for poetry at the University of Michigan in 1938 and 1942, and received a Rosenwald Fellowship in 1947 and a Ford Foundation grant to write and travel in Mexico in 1954. In 1966—the same year that Julius Lester recalls his being attacked as an Uncle Tom by students and writers at a writers' conference at Fisk—Hayden received a major international honor, the Grand Prize for Poetry in English at the First World Festival of Negro Arts; he was personally awarded the prize for *A Ballad of Remembrance* by Leopold Senghor, the president of Senegal. In 1975 he was elected a fellow of the American Academy of Poets and in 1976 he became the first Afro-American to be appointed poetry consultant to the Library of Congress. From 1968 until his death Hayden was a professor of English at the University of Michigan at Ann Arbor.

Kaleidoscope, the word used by Hayden as the title of his anthology of black poetry, can be used in its adjectival form to describe Hayden's body of work. In terms of subjects and styles, his poetry is kaleidoscopic. While there are, of course, representative traits in his various styles and representative patterns of thought, the impression his work gives is of relative freedom from thematic or stylistic obsession. His poetic treatments convey a sensibility able to interact with new material in a fresh and inquisitive manner. In his poems Hayden moved through subjectivity and private anguish to a plane where the possibilities for objectivity, clarity, imaginative freedom, and artistic realization lay. Art for him involved language and design cleansed of the egocentric.

Hayden's philosophy of poetry was that it must not be limited by the personal or ethnic identity of the poet. Though inescapably rooted in these elements, poetry must rise to an order of creation that is broadly human and universally communicative. Yeats is the figure Hayden admired and pointed to in his effort to articulate his own goals. This is because Yeats was able to reconcile his private self with both his common humanity and the folk culture and myths of his ethnic group. "I think I always wanted to be a Negro poet . . . the same way Yeats is an Irish poet," Hayden said to Gendron. He then went on to speak of his intense response to Yeats's "Easter 1916" (in which Yeats speaks of "All changed, changed utterly: . . .") in the aftermath of the Detroit riots: ". . . that is the kind of poetry I want to write. Yes, it may reflect a certain kind of experience, a certain kind of awareness, but it's human rather than racial. It speaks to other human beings and it's not limited by time and place and not limited by the ethnic."

The manner in which these goals manifest themselves most prominently in Hayden's verse is the movement of his imagination away from the autobiographical and toward the imper-sonal. In "'Summertime and the Living . . . ,'" for instance, Hayden referred to himself in the third person in order to obtain perspective and objectivity about his childhood. In "'The Burly Fading One'" *(Selected Poems)* he took the early work history of William Hayden and the experience of seeing an early photograph of his foster father, and then enlarged the characterization to mythic outlines about a hard-living, hard-dying "bullyboy" American, Uncle Jed.

Hayden's poems are not necessarily factual. There is no reason, for example, to assume from the lines quoted previously from "Free Fantasia: Tiger Flowers" that Hayden ran errands for St. Antoine Street prostitutes. Given the spirit of the poem, it is more reasonable to assume that it expresses an unchecked wish, an old man's fantasy drawn from the materials of childhood. Similarly, in "'Mystery Boy' Looks for Kin in Nashville'" *(Words in the Mourning Time)* it would be unfortunate for a reader to stop at the identification of Hayden's own conundrum about parentage. Far better if the projected emotions that visit and torment the boy from within trees and behind walls are perceived as universal to a parentless condition. And better still to view the boy as the man-child in any individual, so that the real subject of the poem can be seen as the psychic grotesquerie beneath the cliché "search for identity."

Hayden's commitment, then, was to a truth deeper than realism can provide; it was to a dimension of mind and cultural truth beyond naturalistic fact. And because, for him, that realistic surface was the means to a deeper end, he was a symbolist; and heavy reliance on autobiographical material will not carry a reader to the essence of his poems.

Swinging from a hazy romantic and proletarian vantage point in *Heart-Shape in the Dust* (1940) to an aesthetic allied with dense linguistic and formal effects in *The Lion and the*

Archer (1948), Hayden's mature work did not appear in significant quantity until *A Ballad of Remembrance* in 1962. *A Ballad*, retaining and revising some of the poems from *The Lion and the Archer* and *Figures of Time* (1955), and abandoning all the apprentice work of *Heart-Shape*, presents the first consolidated view of Hayden's protean subjects and styles, as well as his rare devotion to craft. *Selected Poems* (1966) extends this impression with some new poems as well as a thoughtful grouping of his previous work.

After *Selected Poems*, Hayden continued to evolve, responding both to the times and to his internal rhythms, the former tendency somewhat more prominent in his volume of writings from the 1960's, *Words in the Mourning Time* (1970), which contains a poem about Malcolm X and the long title poem responding to the war, riot, assassination, and racial militance of that decade. Hayden's volumes since then—*The Night-Blooming Cereus* (1972), the eight new poems in *Angle of Ascent* (1975), and *American Journal* (1978)—reflect a poet entering his seventh decade and coming to terms with his deeply aesthetic nature and his love of art and beauty for their own sake. They are roughly comparable with Yeats's devotion to "monuments of unaging intellect" in his Byzantium poems in *The Tower* (1928).

Chronological development is not the soundest basis on which to discuss Hayden's work. There is neither the set of philosophical preoccupations nor the persistent subject matter to warrant serial study. Because he was ever responsive to new subjects and to the truths intrinsic to these subjects, it is in terms of style and technique—and then only in terms of limited clusters of subjects and themes—that the kaleidoscopic Hayden yields to broad generalization. In "Kodachromes of the Island" *(Words in the Mourning Time)*, Hayden con-cludes a descriptive poem about a Mexican island with the following lines:

> Alien, at home—as always
> everywhere—I roamed
> the cobbled island,
>
> and thought of Yeats,
> his passionate search for
> a theme. Sought mine.

The roving quality, "alien, at home . . . / everywhere," reveals a basic quality of Hayden's nature: he was a peripatetic modern with a lingering sense of the past, but ever open to the new, to the flow of the contemporary.

Hayden wrote in a spectrum of styles that range from the severely economical to the highly decorative. Toward one end of the spectrum his work is typified by the qualities of concreteness, conciseness, and clarity of effect. Hayden wrote in the concrete and was not usually in agreement with Wallace Stevens that "Life consists of propositions about life." Hayden's lines may rise to the reflective and the abstract, but abstractive lyricism is not the plane on which he usually created. At times, in fact, Hayden gravitated toward the poetics of imagism: "dry," "hard" lines without sentiment or generalization; total dependence on image for emotional and intellectual content; haiku-like concentration. "The Moose Wallow," "Smelt Fishing," "Kodachromes of the Island," and "Gulls" fall into this category. More commonly, though, Hayden's brief lines and clear effects have a sensuous and rhythmic litheness, such as in the opening stanzas of "The Night-Blooming Cereus":

> And so for nights
> we waited, hoping to see
> the heavy bud
> break into flower.

On its neck-like tube
hooking down from the edge
of the leaf-branch
    nearly to the floor,

    the bud packed
tight with its miracle swayed
stiffly on breaths
    of air, moved

    as though impelled
by stirrings within itself.

Another of his styles relied on a heavier application of language in order to achieve the effect of dense, sensuous imagery. This is Hayden's tropical side, reflecting acute sensory equipment and a love of rare, colorful language. "I must confess that I like the exotic, and I go in for exoticism," he told Gendron. Always he had to "tone it down" because he loved to "deal in exotic textures" and "atmospheric words." Yet in "The Diver" *(Selected Poems)* and "Market" *(A Ballad of Remembrance)* he does not tone it down; he lavishes it on like a painter going from paintbrush to palette knife; and the result, especially in the latter, Mexican poem, is a virtuoso performance. The poet becomes utterer, namer, creator of reality:

        Ragged boys
    lift sweets, haggle
    for venomgreen
    and scarlet gelatins.
    A broken smile
    dandles its weedy
    cigarette
    over papayas too ripe
    and pyramids
    of rotting oranges.
    Turkeys like feather-
    duster flowers
    lie trussed in bunchy smother.
    The barefoot cripple

    foraging crawls
    among rinds, orts,
    chewed butts, trampled
    peony droppings—
    his hunger litany
    and suppliant before
    altars of mamey,
    pineapple, mango.

Occasionally Hayden wrote in a style that was still more elaborately ornamented, which he liked to describe as "baroque." This decorative, denser style was used when he treated disturbing material; it served both to reflect and to explore the tension between an ornamental surface and a dark problem, between an embellished defense and a private or social pathology. It appears in "Witch Doctor" *(A Ballad of Remembrance)*. It is present also in "A Ballad of Remembrance," in which Hayden described the Zulu parade of blacks that was a feature of the Mardi Gras and tried to convey the tension of their lives, balanced between gaudy spectacle and underlying racial nightmare.

In the 1960's and 1970's Hayden's poems showed less attraction to ornate diction and elaborate effects. The spirit of imagism prevailed over the rococo temptation. His verse became sinuous, colloquial. Colorful subjects—objects of art or beautiful flowers—satisfied the need for "exoticism" that was formerly satisfied by densely wrought presentations.

Hayden often wrote poems about people—ballads or character poems such as "Unidentified Flying Object," "Aunt Jemima of the Ocean Waves," and "The Dream" (all in *Words in the Mourning Time*). The need in these poems to render the speech or thoughts of his characters led him to refine a technique that is of special interest. Widespread throughout Hayden's verse, this technique is the careful blending of a narrator's voice with a folk character. The narrator's voice in these instances carefully avoids learned diction, so as to blend imperceptibly with the speech or consciousness of the character. The poet is able to enlarge his control over mood, setting, or narrative point of view without overshadowing the protagonist. In "Night, Death, Mississippi" *(Selected Poems)*, an old redneck, retired from the Ku Klux Klan, thinks about his son, who has replaced him in the ranks. (I have italicized the narrator's voice.)

> A quavering cry. Screech-owl?
> Or one of them?
> *The old man in his reek*
> *and gauntness laughs—*
>
> One of them, I bet—
> *and turns out the kitchen lamp,*
> *limping to the porch to listen*
> *in the windowless night.*
>
> Be there with Boy and the rest
> if I was well again.
> Time was. Time was.
> *White robes like moonlight*
>
> *In the sweetgum dark.*
> Unbucked that one then
> And him squealing bloody Jesus
> as we cut it off.

Sterling Brown, also writing from an urbane and educated standpoint, has used dialect successfully in many poems, such as in the "Slim Greer" series. But Brown, in a poem like "Slim in Hell," uses dialect in the narrated portions as well. Hayden pursued a different course, best expressed by James Weldon Johnson in the preface to *The Book of American Negro Poetry* (1922), where he says that a Negro poet needs "a form that is freer and larger than dialect, but which will still hold the racial flavor. . . ." If we add "regional" to "racial," we can see how Hayden, by means of this technique, enlarged the field of his materials and was able to write about folk culture and local color anywhere. In "Market" he follows the descriptive portion quoted earlier with three different voices:

> Turistas pass.
> Por caridad, por caridad.
> Lord, how they stride
> on the hard good legs
> money has made them.

The first voice ("Turistas pass.") suggests the speaker's detachment from tourists and his identification with the Mexican point of view; the second voice ("Por caridad . . .") is the beggar's supplication for charity; and the third ("Lord . . .") is the speaker's anglicized and empathic rendering of the point of view of the crawling beggar. By including the beggar's perspective, Hayden is able to reveal the underside of the bright tropical reality of fruit and fowl.

Wilburn Williams, Jr., has written nicely about Hayden's "multivocal talents" in "The Rabbi." Derogatory terms for blacks and Jews ("schwartze" and "Jew Baby") are used to suggest succinctly the cultural and economic antipathies of Hayden's old neighborhood. The black speaker remembers his youthful closeness with Jewish friends. His feeling of harmony with them is contrasted with the antagonisms of the adults:

> Mazuzah, Pesach, Chanukah—
> these were timbred words I learned,
> were things I knew by glimpses.
> And I learned schwartze too
>
> And schnapps, which schwartzes bought
> on credit from "Jew Baby."
> Tippling ironists laughed and said
> he'd soon be rich as Rothschild
>
> From their swinish Saturdays.
> Hirschel and Molly and I meanwhile
> divvied halveh, polly seeds,
> were spies and owls and Fu Manchu.

Occasionally Hayden was not able to bring his sophisticated consciousness and his folk materials together in a happy alliance. We see instances of this incomplete coalescence in "Electrical Storm" *(Selected Poems)*, where the poem originates not from folk materials but from philosophical ruminations of the educated poet about chance and cosmic design. A similarly unsatisfying result appears in "Full Moon" *(Selected Poems)*, as Hayden contrasted the folk and scientific-technological views of the moon but failed to find a diction that can encompass both points of view.

An unusual philosophical influence on Hayden should be examined before discussing his themes and subjects. This is Hayden's Bahai faith and his allusions to the prophet Bahaullah in some of his poems. Hayden and his wife became Bahaists in the early 1940's, when Hayden was attending the University of Michigan. He was the poetry editor for the Bahai magazine, *World Order*. Some of his poems—for example, "Full Moon" and "'From the Corpse Woodpiles, From the Ashes'"—contain references to Bahaullah as "Him" or "The Glorious One" or the "exiled One." "Words in the Mourning Time," part III, in *Angle of Ascent*, contains the most explicit treatment of Bahaullah as a reconciling and redeeming figure for our age:

I bear Him witness now—
mystery Whose major clues are the heart of
    man,
    the mystery of God:

Bahá'u'lláh:
Logos, poet, cosmic hero, surgeon, architect
    of our hope of peace,

    wronged, exiled One,
chosen to endure what agonies of
    knowledge, what
    auroral dark

bestowals of truth
vision power anguish for our future's sake.

"Bahá'u'lláh in the Garden of Ridwan" *(Selected Poems)* treats the prophet's declaration of his mission on his way to prison and exile in 1863, and "Dawnbreaker" *(Selected Poems)* treats the experience of a martyr; its title refers to early Persian martyrs and is taken from Nabíl's narrative, *The Dawn-Breakers*. Both of these poems play down the identities of the figures with which they deal and are excellent poems about universal religious experiences.

As a Bahaist, Hayden obtained important—perhaps crucial—spiritual resources: for one, a belief in "the essential oneness of all people" and the "basic unity of all religions," and, for another, a belief that "the work of the artist is ... a form of service to mankind" and "a kind of worship." He discussed his religious needs with Richard Layman:

I think that today when so often one gets the feeling that everything is going downhill, that we're really on the brink of the abyss and what good is anything, I find myself sustained in my attempts to be a poet and my endeavor to write because I have the assurance of my faith that this is of spiritual value and it is a way of performing some kind of service. . . . I have the feeling that by holding on to these beliefs and giving them expression in my work, not always directly—most of the time not directly—at least I'm doing something to prepare, maybe, for a new time, for a new world.

In trying to make a critical judgment about Hayden's incorporation of elements from his Bahai faith into his poetry, this last comment hints at the criterion appropriate to the question. So long as Hayden's beliefs inform his work indirectly and his allusions to Bahaullah are in archetypal terms that Western readers can relate to, Hayden's private faith and his interest in its historical material do not stand in the way of effective poetry. On the other hand, when, as in "Words in the Mourning Time," he bears witness to Bahaullah as a figure to redeem our age, a lapse of judgment occurs. Since the general audience does not share Hayden's sentiments about this prophet, his faith seems undemonstrated in the poem, an imposition on the reader. Hayden's immersion in the universalist content of Bahaullah's message may have obscured from him the fact that to Western readers it seems not so much humane and unifying as strange and sectarian. This involved Hayden in at least the appearance of a contradictory stance, since he conceived and described his poetry as "opposed to the chauvinistic and the doctrinaire."

Although his Bahai faith provided Hayden stable ideals to live by, his poetry itself deals with fluctuations of viewpoint, ambivalences explored, uncertainties succumbed to, despair lived to the bottom. In his poetry the self lives in conflict. Finite identity and material reality strain against imagination and transcendental longing. Resolution is never more than partial, respite never more than temporary, equilibrium attainable only by maintaining the terms of the struggle. When pursued directly, the dream of unity brings dissolution of the self. At the same time, resignation to the prison of the self and the material realm is a denial of one's spiritual-imaginative nature. One's ultimate responsibility is to keep one's powers alive through the struggle with self and God.

In "Veracruz" (*A Ballad of Remembrance*) the terms of the struggle are "reality" and "dream." Under the term "reality" are allusions to the finiteness of the self and to poverty, history, power; under the term "dream" are the pleasures of the senses and the flesh, the impulse to merge with the boundless natural world, and the problem of romantic illusion. The setting is the Veracruz harbor. The speaker

is on a breakwater, hit by "bickering spray." As he stands at the seaward end, the shore, with its "inward-falling slum" and old Spanish fort, appears hidden in the color and light thrown up by the intervening waves: " . . . only the sea is real—" and the sea is envisioned as a "barbarous multifoliate" sea of life,

> with its rustling of leaves,
> fire, garments, wind;
> its clashing of phantasmal jewels,
> its lunar thunder,
> animal and human sighing.

This visionary sea is alluring. "Leap now / and cease from error. / Escape," runs through the speaker's mind. Instead, he accepts the shoreward alternative, the common fate,

> the losses and farewells,
> the long warfare with self,
> with God.

The shoreward, repetitive motion of the waves breaking on the rocks at the close of part I defines the concerns of part II. Part II explores the consequences of a romantic poet's trying to channel the "dream," symbolized by the sea, back to "reality," symbolized by the town life. Can the dream transform a recalcitrant reality? Can the poet, refusing suicide, merge imaginatively with the universal forces beyond the self and provide renewal of the actual world?

For the most part the answer is negative. At first, " . . . bedizened in the . . . colors / of a dream," the arcade of the town becomes "ornate with music and / the sea." The poet achieves a temporary fulfillment of his sensuous needs. But then the dream further "beckons / out of reach in flyblown streets / of lapsing rose and purple, dying / blue." As the colors of the dream fade, a quest in "marimba'd night" for a sensual key has no more success. In the end the speaker finds himself in "phantasmal / space." The light of a star is a symbol of his unanswered needs: "one farewell image / burns and fades and burns." Unable to achieve wholeness by identifying with the universal forces beyond the self, the speaker falls back into incompleteness. Remote light replaces boundless sea. Dream thins to illusion.

In "The Diver" *(Selected Poems)* the impulse to yield to death, to slough off the will, is at first irresistible. Through the diver's descent, egoless drift and languid merging with nature are simulated. Echoing John Keats's "Ode to a Nightingale," the diver-poet finds release for his imagination as he sinks "through easeful / azure." At once chill and floridly delicious, his descent—his death wish—opens a private psychological realm that is disorienting but has its own subaqueous logic. Reminiscent of "'Mystery Boy' Looks for Kin in Nashville," the diver imagines a "hide and / seek of laughing / faces." He then declares:

> I yearned to
> find those hidden
> ones, to fling aside
> the mask and call to them,
> yield to rapturous
> whisperings. . . .

The "hidden ones" (dead family members?) draw him into their deathly circle. He yearns to "have / done with self and / every dinning / vain complexity." Yet regression is not in the service of the ego if the "hidden ones" prevail and he succumbs. He flees "the numbing / kisses" that he craves. "Reflex of life-wish" reasserts itself. A "measured rise" begins.

The subject of "A Ballad of Remembrance" is not the desire for unity either with nature or with the past. Rather, it is a descent into the nightmare of southern racism and the perversion of imagination that such a milieu exacts. Social institutions, reaching back into the "shadow" and "blood" of the past, shape the highly charged, subjective setting, a Walpurgis Night of hysteria, menace, confusion, and hallucination. The poet is overwhelmed by a Mardi Gras spectacle. The parade floats, costumes, and tawdry shops possess him as though the boundaries of his ego were shattered, and events move through rather than past him. Unable to separate subject from object, he is victimized by monstrous choices, threatened with monstrous metamorphoses.

The New Orleans imagery ("Tight streets unfolding to the eye / like fans of corrosion and elegiac lace . . .") convey the city's antiquated elegance. In the third stanza the saleswoman's inquiry, "What will you have?" conveys the commercialization, the "prepared tarnishes," of the old South for tourists. The "sallow vendeuse" pushing jewelry with veneers of "nacre" and "ormolu" represents the faded remains of the antebellum culture, with its "oldrose graces" and "manners like scented gloves." Surface is stressed, not substance; nostalgia, not living truth. It is a world of "contrived ghosts," of deadly fantasy.

Meanwhile, "masked Negroes wearing chameleon / satins" pass down the street. If the imagination of an old, artistic culture has been reduced to gift-shop materialism (and for the poet, in its sway, to a decorative view of language), the imaginative life of blacks without freedom has also been perverted. The city's atmosphere is a "switchblade" on which they balance, making spectacles of themselves as Zulus, mermaids, angels, priestesses—a "fortune-teller's / dream of disaster." Out of the phantasmagoria three stances within the racist environment are articulated. The Zulu king says, "Accommodate." The mermaids, angels, and saints say, "Love." The "gunmetal priestess" says, "Hate." In "spiked bellcollar curved like a fleur-de-lys" the villainous priestess is the most compelling:

As well have a talon as a finger, a muzzle as
    a mouth,
as well have a hollow as a heart. And she
    pinwheeled
away in coruscations of laughter, scattering
those others before her like foil stars.

The inexorable sway of the festival over the poet's perceptions continues in the seventh stanza. He walks through various shops. "Metaphorical doors," "coffeecups," "decors of illusion," and "mazurka dolls" dance past him with the same surrealistic fragmentary rhythm as the parade. Finally, in the eighth stanza, the poet is "released from the hoodoo"—the black magic—"of that dance" by the arrival of a friend who is "meditative, ironic, / richly human." (The friend is identified as Mark Van Doren.) The terrifying metamorphoses cease; integrated selfhood returns. The poem rises from the vortex of contrivances as the one authentic thing, a "remembrance, a gift, a souvenir" that has sorted through fantasy and reality, exorcised evil, and found the tones of love with which to say "thank you."

Two minor poems published subsequently take the position that the subjective descents explored in "Veracruz," "The Diver," and "A Ballad of Remembrance" are man's only reality. The speaker in "The Mirages" *(Words in the Mourning Time)* knows that the mirages he sees in a symbolic desert landscape are illusions; but he follows them anyway, for it is "less lonely to do so." In "Sphinx," another poem in the same volume, a sphinx tells the protagonist that it is his fate " . . . to endure / my riddling. / . . . which, in truth, / is only a kind / of psychic joke."

In "The Islands" (*American Journal*), the same categories of experience and the same chafing relations seen in "Veracruz" recur: dream and reality, sensuous freedom and conditional limitation. Here, though, there is weariness with the insoluble evils of the world, and a willingness to accept the subjective and the transcendental as a temporary relief, an island holiday:

. . . I am tired today

of history, its patina'd clichés
of endless evil. Flame trees.
The intricate sheen of waters flowing into sun.

I wake and see
the morning like a god
in peacock-flower mantle dancing

on opalescent waves—
and can believe my furies have
abandoned for a time their long pursuit.

His "furies" are associated with social and economic institutions, with history, race, the "vain complexity" of self; his freedom to pursue "the morning like a god," with release from the conditional.

The transience of subjective "dreams"—indeed, the transient and dreamlike nature of life—begins to emerge with more prominence in the poems Hayden published in the 1970's. Many of these poems respond to the passage of time and may be usefully thought of as the art of old age. The title poem in *The Night-Blooming Cereus*, by describing the ephemeral beauty of the nocturnal cactus flower, evokes the terrible poignancy and "plangency" of life itself. "The Point" (*American Journal*) speaks of "land's end," where "sound and river come / together, flowing to the sea." In golden elegiac light the poet contemplates "all for a moment . . . inscribed / on brightness" "like memories in the mind of God." Hayden's principal means of dealing with the flow of time and the ebbing away of life is art, even if, as with Yeats, it is art "of what is past, or passing, or to come."

Richard Hunt's sculpture of Arachne (a Lydian woman of classical mythology who is turned into an arachnid—or spider—for her presumption in challenging Athena to a weaving contest) becomes the subject of a Hayden poem, with inevitable parallels to Keats's lovers in "Ode on a Grecian Urn." Arachne's mouth "shaping a cry it cannot utter" and her "goggling terror / fleeing powerless to flee" suggest our own metamorphosis into something less than human in this century of Guernica and Auschwitz ("Richard Hunt's 'Arachne,'" *The Night-Blooming Cereus*).

The high point of Hayden's verse about art as a means of redemption from time is "The Peacock Room," in the same volume. An old man visits a historical room exhibited in a museum. Personal and historical associations flood his mind. He is filled with a sense of loss and a heightened awareness of time; but there is also stirred within him an uncanny appreciation of the survival of the room. The room becomes a symbol of art. It generates meditations about time, history, art, imagination, and the nature of reality. Yeats's "Among School Children" is an influence, especially in the stanzas in which a woman's anecdote about her youth is recalled. Yet this in no way diminishes the level of achievement of the poem, nor the sense that Hayden is able, with some frequency, to compose poems of major or near-major rank.

The Peacock Room was a room commissioned by Frederick R. Leyland, a rich English shipowner, to set off a James Whistler painting. The work of Henry Jeckyll, the young decorator who designed the room, was redone by Whistler, who was displeased with the setting for his painting. He painted an extravagant peacock motif throughout the room, destroying priceless leather panels and infuriating the wealthy owner with a demand for 2,000 guineas. The decorator whose work he defaced was shattered. In 1904 the Peacock Room was purchased by

Charles L. Freer and brought to Detroit. In 1919 it was placed in the Freer Gallery at the Smithsonian Institution. Hayden was told about the room by Betsy Graves Reyneau, a painter he met and became friendly with a number of years before her death in 1964. When Reyneau was a child in Detroit, her family was friendly with the Freers, and the party for her twelfth birthday was held in the famous room.

The poem begins with a statement that art is long and life is short, and follows with the question "Which is crueller / life or art?" The cruelty of life is obvious, but the cruelty of art is that it mocks man's impermanence. This is one of the major themes of the poem.

In the second stanza the Peacock Room is described as a "triste metaphor" for the "beautiful" but "unreal" nature of art. Contrasted with it are some of the imponderable nightmares of modern history—Hiroshima, Watts, My Lai. Although the room ("Exotic, fin de siècle") affirms the opulence of the imagination, it also reveals the potential dichotomy between art and life, a dichotomy that broadens the more art views the world as a playground for the imagination or, as the poem puts it, views "environment as ornament." Yet the stanza ends with a counterassertion, a qualified defense of the imagination. History may "rebuke" the "vision chambered in gold / and Spanish leather" for its excess and moral laxity; but the ability of artifacts to recapture the past and redeem men from time is something history "cannot give the lie / to. . . ."

Impersonal history, personal history, and poetic vision are awakened in the poet by the room. Whistler's peacocks become both symbol and agent for the ruthless pride and power of the artist. In the third stanza Whistler's birds express the artist's antagonism to his employer and to the acquisitive capitalist culture on which art depends; in the fourth the peacocks become part of the young rival's nightmare; and in the fifth there is the horrible vision that follows the speaker's memory of Betsy Reyneau. The birds embody the fusion of imagination with death:

> With shadow cries
>
> the peacocks flutter down,
> their spread tails concealing her,
>   then folding, drooping to reveal
> her eyeless, old—Med School
> cadaver, flesh-object
>   pickled in formaldehyde. . . .

The hostility toward the wealthy connoisseur, the frightening manner in which the master's egoism is experienced by the young rival, the union of imagination with the impersonal forces of life—all these suggest the aggressive world that underlies artistic activity. All are antithetical to the effete unreality attributed to the room. "Reality" and "art," even when they move in opposite directions, are never entirely disparate. Even an ornamental art has some of the savagery of the real.

The vision withdraws in the final stanza. The room regains its former repose, but all is not the same. Whistler is dead. Betsy Reyneau is dead. Only the room remains—the room, and the questions posed about the nature of art and life. The perspective of stanza 2 that the room is "unreal" is now reversed. Art is the only reality. Life is but phantom. As for the Peacock Room, it *is* life, history, reality, all that remains of a time that is past. It is living artifact, the perpetuation of man. Even the aestheticism manifested by the room is excusable, for each period of history is precious only for its uniqueness.

Balancing the warring urgencies of life and art, the poet closes with a cluster of Eastern metaphors that speak of the transcendence of temporal viewpoints. "Rose-leaves" and "ashes," symbolizing beauty and sadness, life

and death, gather together the sum of man's temporal existence, then spin gently toward a wisdom figure with detached and "ancient smile." This figure, a "bronze Bodhisattva," like Yeats's Byzantine bronze bird, is a symbol for the poet and for the poem. It symbolizes the poet's enlightened detachment from the illusions of time, and it also symbolizes the commemoration in the poem of Betsy Reyneau, as the Peacock Room memorializes Whistler. Feeding on flesh, beauty, and man's temporal struggles, art alone survives.

Hayden is best known for his historical poems. In 1941, while reading Stephen Vincent Benét's *John Brown's Body* (1928), he was strongly affected by a passage in which Benét confesses his limitations:

> Oh, black-skinned epic, epic with the black
>   spear,
> I cannot sing you, having too white a
>   heart,
> And yet, some day, a poet will rise to sing
>   you
> And sing you with such truth and
>   mellowness. . . .

At this time Hayden, nearly thirty, conceived the ambition to be the poet to sing the history of black Americans—to end the neglect of their past, correct the stereotypes, and bring the inextinguishable urge of black men and women for freedom into current consciousness. He planned to write poems about slavery and the Civil War and a sonnet series about outstanding antislavery figures. Regrettably, only part of this plan was carried out. By 1942 enough poems were finished for him to submit them under the title *The Black Spear* and to win the Hopwood competition at the University of Michigan for the second time.

The finest of these poems is "Middle Passage," published in various periodicals in the mid-1940's and appearing in final form in *A*

Ballad of Remembrance in 1962. The primary historical sources for the poem are Brantz Mayer's *Adventures of an African Slaver* (1928) and the second chapter of Muriel Rukeyser's biography *Willard Gibbs* (1942), in which the story of the *Amistad* mutiny and the legal battle that followed it are narrated. The literary influence is Benét's *John Brown's Body*.

The marvel of "Middle Passage" is its ability to evoke the entire period of the Atlantic slave trade, yet achieve a highly unified effect. From research into actual documents, Hayden creates log entries, court depositions, and trial testimony, all of which give the work its air of historical truth. Careful coordination of this "documentary" material to sustain the themes of inhumanity, greed, moral disease, and blindness is one of the sources of the unity of the poem; the other is the consistent manner in which this material is handled. The moral bankruptcy of the white "Christians" is allowed to reveal itself. Although the poet selects what they say, he does not comment actively. Documentary objectivity, with a reliance on dramatic irony, is his major strategy.

The first part comprises a mosaic of the physical and spiritual torments endemic to the slave trade. The conditions described support the opening assertion that the middle passage is a "voyage through death" or, in spiritual and literary terms, a descent into hell. Illness, confinement, squalor, and suicidal despair afflict the Africans; fear of disease and rebellion, guilt, desperate prayer, and sexual degeneracy beset the whites. The names of ships that the poet intersperses between sections of the poem suggest the pervasiveness of these conditions.

Multiple voices are employed to yield both scope and immediacy. First there is the narrator's omniscient voice, which frames the narrative and offers a moral vision of the action; then the alarmed journal notations—concrete, concise, yet rich in psychological atmosphere—of an officer or crew member; the narrator's ad-

aptation of a disembodied voice of conscience follows next (other italicized passages differ from this one); then the hymns, double-spaced, so that they seem to drift mournfully over the scene as they drift across the page; and last the deluded prayers of crew members asking "safe passage to our vessels bringing / heathen souls unto Thy chastening." The first part concludes with a court deposition revealing the disintegration of authority and the brutal lusts aboard the *Bella J.* The fire that envelops the ship symbolizes the fires of sinfulness much as the ophthalmia on another ship has overtones of the traders' moral blindness.

The second part, using the reminiscences of a retired slaver, enlarges the canvas to include the complicity of African kings. Showing no compunction, enjoying the vivid memories of his adventures, a Conradian profiteer speaks of "wealth aplenty to be harvested / from those black fields." He describes how "for tin crowns that shone with paste, / red calico and German-silver trinkets" a king sent his warriors to "kill the sick and old and lead the young / in coffles to our factories." The simplicity of the second part provides respite from the complex structure of part I. Part II also conveys the moral imperturbability of the whites, even when privileged with hindsight about their "adventures in the slave trade."

Having begun by describing the middle passage as a "voyage through death / to life upon these shores," the poem in part III reaches for some sustaining actuality, some affirmative human basis, upon which life on these shores will be possible—not only for the survivors of the crossing but also for succeeding generations. Here the moral imagination of the poet exerts a more pronounced influence. Although the use of testimony from the trial of the *Amistad* mutineers returns to the documentary method, the narrator's shaping moral vision obtrudes more strongly both in the opening section, which speaks of the "dark ships" as "shuttles in the rocking loom of history," and in the portrayal of the leader of the *Amistad* mutiny as a symbol or icon for the "immortal human wish, / the timeless will" of men to be free.

Charles T. Davis writes about the "mystical emergence of freedom from circumstances that appall and degrade" in Hayden's history poems; and it is this very mystical sense of the inevitable assertion of manhood that Hayden tries to compress into his few words about the leader of the rebellion. In the poem Cinquez is not developed as an individual. He is a "life that transfigures many lives"; and with his efforts to gain freedom, life on the "actual shore" can begin.

In "Runagate Runagate" *(Selected Poems)* Harriet Tubman rises like Cinquez from the "anguish" and "power" of her people. "Runagate" is conceived also as a historical panorama, in this case of the Underground Railroad. As a collage of slave voices and verse, snippets of song, ads for runaways, and wanted posters for Tubman, it is somewhat reminiscent of John Dos Passos' sketches of prominent Americans in *U.S.A.* (1937). The title "Runagate" derives from an archaic form of the word "runaway."

Unfortunately, "Runagate" fails to come together in the way that "Middle Passage" does. The first part is self-consciously literary, unable to escape the rhythms of an "inspired" tone. Richest and most memorable are the instances of folk idiom and imagination in part II, in which the "freedom train" of the spirituals becomes fused with the idea of crossing over to the North:

> *Midnight Special on a sabre track movering movering,*
> *first stop Mercy and the last Hallelujah.*

We see this also in the final lines:

> Come ride-a my train
> Mean mean mean to be free.

One passage captures beautifully the whispered tensions of nocturnal flight:

And this was the way of it, brethren brethren, way we journeyed from Can't to Can. Moon so bright and no place to hide, the cry up and the patterollers riding, hound dogs belling in bladed air. And fear starts a-murbling. Never make it, we'll never make it. *Hush that now,* and she's turned upon us, levelled pistol glinting in the moonlight: Dead folks can't jaybird talk, she says; you keep on going now or die. . . .

Less ambitious but more successful than "Runagate" is "The Dream (1863)" *(Words in the Mourning Time)*. "The Dream" complements the central importance given to heroic leadership and spiritual vision in the two previously discussed poems by illustrating the negative consequences when a dream of freedom has existed unrealized for too long. Sinda, an old slave, is unable to reconcile fantasy and reality when her emancipation finally comes. She had dreamed of "great big soldiers marching out of gunburst, / their faces" those of her menfolk. When instead "Marse Lincum's soldier boys" reach her plantation, she refuses to go:

> . . . those
> Buckras with their ornery
>   funning, cussed commands, oh they were
>   not were not
> the hosts the dream had promised her.

Sinda cannot accept the imperfect arrival of freedom from strange whites, or the everyday burden it will bring. She is too old. By contrast, her son (or grandson) reveals through his letters from the front that it will take youth to face the mud-and-guts struggle and still dream of "ficety gals down here in Dixieland" and how he "mite jus go ahead an jump over the broomstick with one / and bring her home."

"O Daedalus, Fly Away Home" *(A Ballad of Remembrance)* also deals with the wafting dream of freedom. Here it is a dream of escape from the New World; atavistic memories are still vivid among the African-American slaves. In his interview with McCluskey, Hayden described the poem as "developed contrapuntally," with "sadness and nostalgia" counterpointing "gaiety and dancing." The poem links the classical myth of Daedalus and Icarus, who escape the Cretan labyrinth, with a legend among Georgia Sea Island blacks about Africans with the magical power to "fly away home." Lighthearted lyrics of Paul Laurence Dunbar and motifs from Jean Toomer's *Cane* poems (especially "Georgia Dusk") are recognizable influences:

> Drifting night in the Georgia pines,
> coonskin drum and jubilee banjo.
>   Pretty Malinda, dance with me.
>
> Night is juba, night is conjo
>   Pretty Malinda, dance with me.
>
> Night is an African juju man
> weaving a wish and a weariness together
>   to make two wings.
>
> *O fly away home fly away.*

Words such as "juju" (African for magic) and "conjo" (probably short for conjurer) appear frequently in Hayden's folk material. Davis believes that the metrics of "O Daedalus" "suggest the rhythm of a folk dance called 'juba,' widely performed by slaves in the antebellum South." In fact, the poem has been performed with dance accompaniment.

Because it is about the leader of the 1831 slave revolt in Virginia, "The Ballad of Nat Turner" *(A Ballad of Remembrance)* was grouped by Hayden with his other historical poems; yet it might just as appropriately be grouped with poems about religious experience, such as "Bahá'u'lláh in the Garden of Ridwan." Narrated in the first person, it is a character poem in which Turner describes his quest in the

Dismal Swamp of Virginia for a vision of divine approval. At first, visions of death visit the tormented wanderer:

> And came at length to livid trees
>   where Ibo warriors
> hung shadowless, turning in wind
>   that moaned like Africa,
>
> their belltongue bodies dead, their eyes
>   alive with the anger deep
> in my own heart.

As he wanders further,

> . . . wild things gasped and scuffled in
>   the seething night; shapes
> of evil writhed upon the air.

Finally Turner experiences an Old Testament vision of a war of angels, patterned on Ezekiel. With Miltonic detail he sees "angels at war / with one another, angels in dazzling / battle." He describes "the shock of wing on wing and sword / on sword," and how he saw

> . . . many of
> those mighty beings waver,
> waver and fall, go streaking down
>   into swamp water, and the water
> hissed and steamed and bubbled. . . .

In the end "the conqueror faces . . . were like mine." Free of his burden of doubt, reassured of his divine mission, he returns to the "blazing fields, to the humbleness," and bides his time.

Williams observes that "although . . . Hayden's mind ventures backward over time" in his history poems, they "invariably close with a statement or action that points forward." Cinquez makes life upon these shores possible. Harriet Tubman's poem reverberates with the unceasing sounds of the freedom train: "Mean mean mean to be free." Nat Turner has his revolt still before him. And in the one as-yet-unmentioned poem of this group, the sonnet commemorating Frederick Douglass, the great fighter is envisioned as a living influence that flows into the present. Williams puts it well: "The poet emphasizes that the dead hero is still a vital force, and the reality his poem ostensibly commemorates has its full realization in the future.... In the final analysis the poem celebrates not a man who has been but a man still coming into being."

Besides poems about nineteenth-century antislavery figures, Hayden wrote other character poems. About known figures of the modern world (Bessie Smith, Malcolm X) and unknown figures from strange corners of black life (a religious charlatan, a circus Aunt Jemima), these poems exemplify the fertile conceptions and high degree of realization of Hayden's work. Tone is the quintessential ingredient, the crowning grace, of some; in others a bold use of syntax or unusual verbal texture is the facilitating technique.

Dramatic or narrative elements also figure in some poems. A dialogue in "Aunt Jemima of the Ocean Waves" *(Words in the Mourning Time)*, between the low-key speaker and "Aunt Jemima," brings out the pathos in the downhill life of the "Sepia High Stepper" of the 1920's. In "El-Hajj Malik El-Shabazz" *(Words in the Mourning Time)*, the phases or "masks" of Malcolm's development from "Home Boy" and "Dee-troit Red" to his "final metamorphosis" in Mecca are narrated with a brevity that captures his abbreviated lifespan.

"Homage to the Empress of the Blues" *(The Lion and the Archer)* employs a particular syntactic structure to describe the origin of Bessie Smith's blues and the ironic splendor of her stage presentation. Each sentence begins with a "because" clause that is long and highly descriptive of the background of black life or the blues tradition that has risen from it; and each sentence ends with an independent clause that gives the result, the triumphant éclat with which Bessie comes out on stage:

Because somewhere there was a man in a
    candystripe silk shirt
gracile and dangerous as a jaguar and
    because some woman moaned
for him in sixty-watt gloom and mourned
    him Faithless Love
TwoTiming Love Oh Love Oh Careless
    Aggravating Love;

She came out on the stage in yards of
    pearls, emerging like
a favorite scenic view, flashed her golden
    teeth, and sang.

In the first sentence old blues, such as W. C. Handy's "Careless Love Blues," and in the second sentence poverty, persecution, and fantasy are defined as the formative elements of her art. This art, the poem goes on to say, involves a shared sense of experience with her audience and a communal celebration of the triumph of the self over circumstance.

The promiscuous woman who is, at the same time, an inspired singer in the church choir is the subject of "Mourning Poem for the Queen of Sunday" *(A Ballad of Remembrance)*. Spoken in the idiom of the black church, as if by a chorus of mourners, the poem approaches the circumstances of the singer's death (she was murdered, presumably for two-timing) with a high ironic tone, half mock-lament, half genuine dismay. Infinitely wry, the poem pivots teasingly on the refrain, "Who would have thought / she'd end that way?" Yet the void in spiritual terms is real, even if the adulation of church members has always contained lurking suspicions about her. The righteous and the sinner alike are losers:

Oh who and oh who will sing Jesus down
to help with struggling and doing without and
    being colored
all through blue Monday?
Till way next Sunday?

With "four holes in the heart," "the gold works wrecked," her life has conformed to the pattern of the gangster era or a tragic love ballad; yet to her admirers, who cannot do without her,

> . . . she looks so natural in her big
>   bronze coffin
> among the Broken Hearts and Gates-
>   Ajar,
> it's as if any moment she'd lift her
>   head
> from its pillow of chill gardenias
> and turn this quiet into shouting
>   Sunday
> and make folks forget what she did on
>   Monday.

Bewitching artifice is the theme of "Witch Doctor" *(A Ballad of Remembrance)*, a poem that describes a day in the life of a religious charlatan. Included is all the drapery of his mystique—the chic surfaces of his style of life, the tailored movements and calculated effects on his congregation. Not only does his mystique answer the hunger of his followers for some fantasied Being who is opulent, erotic, and unreal, but it also feeds the preacher's own "outrageous" narcissism. Mutual fantasy, Hayden seems to say, is the basis for the rapport; manipulation, the unspoken formula that yields "euphoria" for the members and "mystery and lucre" for their leader.

A poetry that moves toward the conjurer's art captures this obscure pact. Present-tense verbs and participles usher the "prophet" through the decadent textures of his day. Exotic belongings fill his artificial world—mirrors everywhere, a cinquecento stair, a lilac limousine with black leopard-skin interior, the smoke of Egyptian cigarettes. Though it is repellent and luridly funny, the spell on the reader (like the spell on the congregation) is seductive. It taps some

deep vein of delusional need and is as suggestive about the poet's temptation by the magical powers of language as it is about the magnetism of the prophet of Israel Temple. "Witch Doctor," like "Mourning Poem for the Queen of Sunday," is among Hayden's perfect poems.

As Hayden's interest was aroused by a variety of people, so, too, did diverse places engage him as poetic subjects. Earlier a set of lines from "Kodachromes of the Island" ("Alien, at home—as always / everywhere—") was introduced to suggest the breadth of his subject matter. In discussing a final group of poems about places, a perspective intrinsic to these lines can now be brought into greater definition. Sometimes alienation defines the quality of an experience for Hayden; more often estrangement and "at homeness" coexist.

On the one hand Hayden confronted a changing and frightening world as a lonely modern; on the other hand he was able to perceive emotional and intellectual connections with a new environment. This ability to discern meaningful relations in ostensibly alien places derived from his sense of continuity between past and present.

In "Zeus over Redeye" *(Words in the Mourning Time)*, a poem about a visit to the Redstone Arsenal in Alabama, a sense of alienation and dread predominates; yet even here the past offers a reference point for his fears. Myths of the Greek gods (for whom the rockets are named) are the only analogue for the "new mythologies," the new powers and gods breeding in the desert. The rockets are "totems of our firebreathing age" and the grounds of the arsenal are "terra guarded like / a sacred phallic grove."

In another poem in the same volume, "On Lookout Mountain," the poet visits a Civil War battleground in Tennessee. He thinks of "Union soldiers struggling up / the crackling mountainside," where now "Sunday alpinists / pick views and souvenirs." "A world away," he remarks, "scions" of that earlier climb are falling—in Vietnam. And because of Vietnam and the racial warfare at home, he refers to the Civil War battle as "dubious victory."

In the best of these poems in which the past contributes to the imaginative rendering of the present, it is the poet's psychic refraction of the past that colors the present, not formal history or intellectual tradition. The speaker, in "On the Coast of Maine" *(A Ballad of Remembrance),* stalks at twilight

> Past stone walls that keep
> the restless from
> old granite-weary farmers' sleep.

He passes between "Puritan shadow" and "Indian dark," "moving in a hush of time"; ". . . ghostly thunders," like the grumblings of ancestral dead, "are remotely near."

In "Locus" and "Tour 5" *(A Ballad of Remembrance)* this Hawthornean aspect of Hayden's imagination achieves its highest expression. The southern landscape, with its psychic subsoil of Indians, slaves, bloody war, and aristocratic dreams, becomes a "soulscape . . . of warring shades" that lacerates the bright present.

Having quoted at the outset from "Locus," let me conclude with "Tour 5," a poem emblematic of the nature of the poetic intelligence I have been trying to suggest: roving yet not deracinated; alive to the luminous present yet inescapably haunted by, caught up with, the harsh chromatics and shadowy phantoms of the past. The title derives from a guidebook description of a contemporary route to Jackson, Mississippi. The poem itself includes references to the "old Natchez Trace," which Hayden described (in the McCluskey interview) as "originally an Indian trail going from Nashville . . .

down through Mississippi and beyond," "a dangerous and sinister road, used by escaped criminals, highwaymen, murderers." More than simply informational, this background emerges in the poem as a group of associations that is symbolic of a dangerously angry state.

The speaker and his party are on an auto trip through the autumn "blazonry of farewell scarlet / and recessional gold." Past the car window scenes move—"cedar groves," "static villages" with Indian names. But with an inevitability linked with the tragic history of the South, the holiday mood is dampened. As they "buy gas and ask directions of a rawboned man," his eyes "revile" them "as the enemy." Suddenly there is internal difference. Physical journey becomes mental journey; the festive enjoyment ends:

> . . . Shrill gorgon
> silence breathes behind his taut civility
>
> and in the ever-tautening
> air that's dark for us despite the Indian
> summer glow. We drive on, following
> the route of phantoms, highwaymen, of slaves
>   and armies.
>
> Children, wordless and remote,
> wave at us from kindling porches.

Ancestral wounds have begun to bleed. An everyday event has punctured the most human of pleasures. The cruel southern past seeps into a final vision of the present:

> . . . And now
> the land is flat for miles, the landscape lush,
> metallic, flayed; its brightness harsh as
>   bloodstained swords.

Descriptive, symbolic, human—this is vintage Hayden. A surface is beautifully rendered; an internal anguish is subtly conveyed; a vision of the inner nature of things emerges with detached and passionate intensity. Hayden has brought us more fully and humanly into the world. That was his purpose, his calling.

Selected Bibliography

WORKS OF ROBERT HAYDEN

POETRY

Heart-Shape in the Dust. Detroit: Falcon Press, 1940.

With Myron O'Higgins. *The Lion and the Archer.* Counterpoise series, no. 1. Nashville, Tenn.: Hemphill Press, 1948.

Figures of Time. Counterpoise series, no. 3. Nashville, Tenn.: Hemphill Press, 1955.

A Ballad of Remembrance. London: Paul Breman, 1962.

Selected Poems. New York: October House, 1966.

Words in the Mourning Time. New York: October House, 1970.

The Night-Blooming Cereus. Heritage series, vol. 20. London: Paul Breman, 1972.

Angle of Ascent: New and Selected Poems. New York: Liveright, 1975. (Contains poems Hayden wished to collect from previous volumes.)

American Journal. Taunton, Mass.: Effendi Press, 1978.

EDITED VOLUMES

Kaleidoscope: Poems by American Negro Poets. New York: Harcourt, Brace, and World, 1967.

With David J. Burrows and Frederick R. Lapides, *Afro-American Literature: An Introduction.* New York: Harcourt, Brace, Jovanovich, 1971.

CRITICAL STUDIES AND REVIEWS

Davis, Charles T. "Robert Hayden's Use of History." In *Modern Black Poets: A Collection of Critical Essays*, edited by Donald B. Gibson. En-glewood Cliffs, N.J.: Prentice-Hall, 1973. Pp. 96–111.

Faulkner, Howard. "'Transformed by Steeps of Flight': The Poetry of Robert Hayden." *CLA Journal*, 21:282–91 (September 1977).

Fetrow, Fred M. "Robert Hayden's 'Frederick Douglass': Form and Meaning in a Modern Sonnet." *CLA Journal*, 17:79–84 (September 1973).

Galler, David. "Three Recent Volumes." *Poetry*, 110:267–69 (July 1967).

Gendron, Dennis Joseph. "Robert Hayden: A View of His Life and Development as a Poet." Ph.D. diss., University of North Carolina at Chapel Hill, 1975. (A pioneering dissertation on Hayden's life and development; includes the transcript of a four-day interview Gendron conducted with the poet in March 1974.)

Harper, Michael S. "Angle of Ascent." *New York Times Book Review*, February 22, 1976, pp. 34–35.

Jones, LeRoi. "A Dark Bag." *Poetry*, 103:394–401 (March 1964).

Lester, Julius. "Words in the Mourning Time." *New York Times Book Review*, January 24, 1971, pp. 4–5, 22.

Lewis, Richard O. "A Literary-Psychoanalytic Interpretation of Robert Hayden's 'Market.'" *Negro American Literature Forum*, 9:21–24 (Spring 1975).

Novak, Michael P. "Meditative, Ironic, Richly Human: The Poetry of Robert Hayden." *Midwest Quarterly*, 15:276–85 (Spring 1974).

O'Sullivan, Maurice J. "The Mask of Allusion in Robert Hayden's 'The Diver.'" *CLA Journal*, 17:85–92 (September 1973).

Pool, Rosey. "Robert Hayden: Poet Laureate." *Negro Digest*, 15:39–43 (June 1966).

Post, Constance J. "Image and Idea in the Poetry of Robert Hayden." *CLA Journal*, 20:164–75 (December 1976).

Rodman, Selden. "Negro Poets." *New York Times Book Review*, October 10, 1948, p. 27.

Turco, Lewis. "*Angle of Ascent:* The Poetry of Robert Hayden." *Michigan Quarterly Review*, 16:199–219 (Spring 1977).

Williams, Wilburn, Jr. "Covenant of Timelessness and Time: Symbolism & History in Robert Hayden's *Angle of Ascent.*" *Massachusetts Review*, 18:731–49 (Winter 1979).

INTERVIEWS

Gendron, Dennis Joseph. "Robert Hayden: A View of His Life and Development as a Poet." Ph.D. diss., University of North Carolina at Chapel Hill, 1975. Pp. 150–234.

Layman, Richard. "Robert Hayden." In *Conversations with Writers*, edited by Matthew Bruccoli, E. Frazier Clark, Jr., et al. Vol. 1. Detroit: Gale Research Co., 1977. Pp. 156–79.

McCluskey, Paul. "Robert Hayden, The Poet and His Art: A Conversation." In Judson Philips and Lawson Carter, *How I Write / 1*. New York: Harcourt, Brace, Jovanovich, 1972. Pp. 133–213.

O'Brien, John. "Robert Hayden." In *Interviews with Black Writers*, edited by John O'Brien. New York: Liveright, 1973. Pp. 106–23.

—ROBERT M. GREENBERG

O. Henry
1862—1910

O. HENRY and Mark Twain are the most famous pen names in American literary history. O. Henry and Edgar Allan Poe continue to be the chief totem figures of popular fiction: Every year the "best" mystery stories are initiated into the tribe of "Edgars" by the Mystery Writers Association of America; every year the "best" short stories are gathered into *The O. Henry Memorial Award Prize Stories.* Sober, knowledgeable men have compared O. Henry favorably with William Shakespeare, Charles Dickens, François Villon, Laurence Sterne, and the great Russian storytellers. Collections of his stories are found all over the world, translated into nearly all the great modern literary tongues and into many of the less widely spoken as well.

In view of all this fame, it might seem impertinent to ask, "Why should we read O. Henry?" Yet the question is very pertinent, for unlike Twain and Poe, O. Henry attracts few American readers these days and still fewer are interested in writing or talking about him. When asked about the possibility of spiritual afterlife, O. Henry recited the American jump-rope rhyme:

> I had a little dog
> And his name was Rover,
> And when he died
> He died all over.

O. Henry's literary reputation, however it is measured, now seems as conclusively dead as Rover.

It might be revived, though. That is one important difference between a dead dog and a literary corpus. The questions to be asked are whether it should be revived, and if so, how. Literary reputations die, more often than not, because we have lost (or consciously rejected) a way of reading or seeing or hearing: The letter is dead, the eye is blank, the ear is stopped with wax. When our ancestors seem remote, when their tastes seem quaint or primitive, it is hard not to consider ourselves their superiors, and harder yet not to consider their works superfluous. To be sure, we can cultivate a taste for the quaint or primitive, but to think and feel so is akin to necrophilia.

Dead artists can live again only if we somehow see that their ways of feeling and thinking are akin to our own, perhaps closer than the perceptions of our parents and even many of our contemporaries—whose views may seem stodgily, even dangerously, old-fashioned. Then we can recognize these artists as ancestors in spirit as well as in name. They may even come to seem more important than the recently dead or the dying, the artistic parents whose reputations have begun to seem overblown even if they have not yet burst. The phenomenon has long been noticed by psychologists. At issue here is whether O. Henry is such an ancestor, whether by reading him thoughtfully we can recognize his kinship to us and evoke a living and useful presence from his words.

Such a revived O. Henry may well seem different from the one familiar to his contemporaries. Indeed, that result is probably inevitable, for the shock of recognition that Herman Melville felt unites contemporaries, and the electric current that runs through both the modern reader and an ancestor presumed dead but now galvanized into new life, come from perceiving what had been hidden by inherited ways of seeing. These inherited ways belong to our ancestors, the men and women who found O. Henry so familiar and liked what they saw—as they saw it. To restore O. Henry to life may be to disclose what those ancestors did not see in him, or, if they saw it, valued differently. Reviving an artist means less restoring him than discovering him to be our contemporary, a person who sees and feels as we do, or, more likely, as we are coming to feel. It is in the becoming that we seek allies, that we create new historical explanations for how we are coming to see, to hear, to feel, to think.

In 1850, Nathaniel Hawthorne did just that. Meditating on why he had written *The Scarlet Letter* and suggesting, very subtly, to his contemporaries how they might best read it and learn new ways of feeling and thinking, Hawthorne receives a small shock of recognition, a "sensation not altogether physical, yet almost so, as of burning heat" from the scarlet letter he claims to have discovered in the attic of the Salem customhouse during his tenure there as surveyor of customs. (How accidentally apt the title for many writers, for O. Henry as well as for Hawthorne.)

Hawthorne then administers a small shock to his readers, most of whom believed in the "official" history or myth of American origins. According to that history Americans are the spiritual heirs of the Pilgrim and Puritan "fathers." Looking back to those ancestors, Hawthorne finds that in matters of art, at least, and in important moral questions as well, he has less in common with his biological ancestors (old Puritans all) than with his "official ancestor" in the customhouse, Mr. Surveyor Pue.

Pue had been a Royalist, stalwart in his loyalties and foppishly elegant in his tastes, as unsympathetic to Puritan manners and morals as it was possible to be. Yet it was he, at least as Hawthorne tells the story, who sympathized with the already legendary Hester Prynne, he who cared enough to gather her story, he who rises from the grave to visit Hawthorne in the empty attic chamber and galvanize him into retelling that story for Hawthorne's generation.

The implication is clear: If Hawthorne's readers are to read well, see well, and be truly sympathetic, they must reject their supposed heritage and find its alternative, one as new as the day, yet also one with some historical claim to being theirs. So it usually is in times of great change: so it was in Hawthorne's time, so it was in O. Henry's day, so it is today.

That "day" began with O. Henry's birth during the Civil War. It extended through his death in 1910 and into a glorious evening that darkened during the 1920's. Night falls unevenly over so wide and various a country as the United States, but for Cleanth Brooks and Robert Penn Warren it had fallen on O. Henry well before 1943, the year in which they brought out the first edition of *Understanding Fiction*. This text, a companion to their successful *Understanding Poetry* (1938), codified the principles of reading that they and many teachers of literature found to be self-evident. O. Henry figures in *Understanding Fiction,* but to the then new generations of readers he was exhibited as a writer who did not understand fiction. One of his most famous stories, "The Furnished

Room," is given as an example of a badly plotted story. Since O. Henry's fame, especially among those who know him by only a few stories, rests in large part on the supposed excellence of his plots, the strategy of Brooks and Warren is clearly a frontal attack on what seemed to them to be the enemy, the deadening taste in literature and the arts acquired by many of their students from parents and schoolteachers alike.

Brooks and Warren were more crusaders than vandals, partisans of the "modern" art that they had grown to love and that was still being created as they wrote. They sought to create a taste for what they valued, to open the eyes of one generation, to lay in the grave the dead weight of another that had found O. Henry such lively reading. They were the able spokesmen for a minority soon to become a majority, at least among educated readers. "Their" prose writers, those anthologized in their textbook, include Sherwood Anderson, Anton Chekhov, William Faulkner, Ernest Hemingway, James Joyce, Franz Kafka, Katherine Mansfield, Luigi Pirandello, Katherine Anne Porter, Eudora Welty. Warren's name might be added, as could those of other distinguished writers of modernist fiction in the years to come. O. Henry indeed does not belong with these writers. But that is not to say that he does not belong with others of great interest today.

The man known as O. Henry came into the world as William Sidney Porter. When he was born in Greensboro, North Carolina, on September 11, 1862, the omnipresent war was providing much work but little income for his physician father, who seems on all counts to have been a bad manager. Porter's mother died when he was three, leaving her husband the additional burden of three sons (soon lightened to two).

Doctor Porter retreated with his children to his mother's home, then further retreated into drink. The boys were left to their grandmother's care and the tutelage of Aunt Lina, whose primary school made enough money to keep the family in food and clothing. Will learned from her to love reading and writing and sketching cartoons; he learned from his father to be ashamed. He probably also learned how to evade responsibility, how to plead for tolerance of his shortcomings, how to ingratiate, how to make light of the truth. Ashamed, he learned shameful behavior. Most ominous of all, he seems to have learned to play the role called for by his company, so that throughout his life he was an amusing companion but loyal to nobody.

By his own account Porter read widely between the ages of thirteen and nineteen. Robert Burton's *Anatomy of Melancholy* and Edward William Lane's translation of *The Arabian Nights' Entertainment: or, The Thousand and One Nights* were his favorites, he said; and if he remembered accurately, the combination did much to form his literary tastes, nicely divided as they are between playfully moody manner of execution and clever narration that gives the illusion of the world's plenty of invention always at hand. If he elevated these books to the status of favorites only in maturity, as is quite likely, his choice of texts shows how well he understood the nature of his genius. He learned such self-consciousness early.

His grammar-school studies under his aunt gave Porter enough Latin to play with and to sharpen his sense of how Latin roots and stems are transformable into English. Linguistic and narrative transformation thereafter fascinated him, especially, it seems, the backward pull of tradition on the thing transformed. He learned his science practically, as assistant to his pharmacist uncle between the ages of fifteen and nineteen. The drugstore was of the familiar sort: part pharmacy, part soda fountain, part newsstand and tobacco shop, and, for the "boys in the back room," secret and genteel saloon. It encouraged small talk and tale-telling, the convivial arts of male society that both comfort and constrict with their conventions of discourse. The drugstore provided another school of dissimulation, if another was needed; and Porter was at the top of the class, a popular entertainer with his quips and cartoons. It also opened a larger window upon the world, although the reality thus framed was filled mostly with men who might well have drifted away, were it not for the moorings provided by the drugstore.

When Porter's chance came, he cut himself free. At the age of nineteen he was invited by Dr. and Mrs. James Hall to go with them to Texas, to visit their sons. In the American fashion the boys had "westered" and, as hoped, prospered. Porter, facing a dead end in the drugstore, was happy to follow, and except for brief trips when his grandmother and father died, he never returned to Greensboro. For a long time Porter lived the life of a guest, first with Richard Hall and later, starting in 1884, with the Joseph Harrell family in Austin. He learned the ways of cattle and sheep ranching, but largely as an observer. Otherwise he read as much as possible, learned Spanish, and, for his supper, talked charmingly, wrote comic sketches, or drew amusing pictures. When the ranch was between cooks, he cooked—as a member of the family would. Porter's social pleasures were simple and few, but he made the best of them. At other times he sought the company of words—in the dictionary that he perused for hours on end. In Austin he went out when he could, worked briefly in a pharmacy, then retired again to the life of leisured guest.

By the age of twenty-four Porter was so involved in the social life of Austin that earning money once again seemed important. He returned to the daily grind, first as a bookkeeper in a real estate firm, then as a draftsman at the Texas Land Office, which had recently come to be directed by his former host, Richard Hall.

He prepared himself diligently for each of these jobs, studying with the purposeful concentration that he later gave to his stories.

The salary of $100 a month at the land office, together with kindnesses from friends, enabled Porter to marry in July 1887. The groom was twenty-four; the bride, Athol Estes, was nineteen. An elopement overcame her mother's and stepfather's objection, which in part was that both had a history of tuberculosis. Porter did a little newspaper work to augment his salary, and thus began his career as a writer. He was a "stringer," his material for the most part skits and jokes.

In 1891, Porter was once again behind a counter, this time as clerk at a bank, his salary still $100 a month. His wife had borne two children, the first of whom died within hours of birth; she herself survived each time only with difficulty. Tuberculosis was beginning to waste her; medical bills were as common as newspapers in the house; the Porters often took money from her parents to meet these and other expenses. Porter's patron lost his post as land commissioner after being defeated in the Democratic gubernatorial primary (the other candidate, James Hogg, proving to be a sore winner); Porter lost his job in turn. Charles Anderson, who got him work at the bank, was another Greensboro man who had helped him before and whose help proved once again that charm and connections are invaluable aids, but are not in themselves enough to ensure success. Porter therefore rushed to the door when what seemed to be opportunity knocked in the form of a defunct monthly paper, an idle printing press, and a willing partner, James P. Crane. In 1894 he started his own newspaper of sorts, a humorous weekly that he called *The Rolling Stone*. He wrote and drew most of the material himself, at the beginning still holding down his job at the bank.

The Rolling Stone rolled for one year. It was

remarkably good, filled with material that his publisher later mined and sold as O. Henry's. There was considerable political satire (Austin was the state capital), ethnic humor generally of a good-natured sort (although some German families took offense on occasion), a regular parody of small-town newspapers in the form of "Plunkville Patriot" (appealing to the common backgrounds of most Texans, indeed most Americans in those days), and the like. In the "Patriot," Porter comically played with printing conventions, creating "errors" by running together "news" items and "advertisements." News articles and stories generally parodied reportorial and narrative conventions—strategies he later practiced as a storyteller.

Although popular, the paper lost money, which Porter made up by borrowing from his father-in-law and friends. Eventually he seems to have tried his inventive powers on the books at the bank—so, at least, the examiners charged. His friends agreed to repay most of the more than $5,000; but although the bank officers were satisfied, the examiners were not, and a grand jury agreed that there was probable cause for a trial. Despite Porter's best efforts *The Rolling Stone* rolled to a dead stop in April 1895, and for six months the Porters were dependent on Athol's family. Under these circumstances it was easy for Porter to absent himself, his wife, and his daughter from Austin for a while, to write and draw for the *Houston Post* as occasional feature writer and regular author of "Some Postscripts," otherwise known as "the Post Man."

Facing the trial proved to be harder; and when the time came, in the summer of 1896, Porter turned tail, going first to New Orleans for a few weeks and then to Honduras, where he holed up in the shallow-water port of Trujillo. He later compared himself to Joseph Conrad's Lord Jim, victim of a "fateful mistake" at the "supreme crisis" of his life; but as Gerald

Langford points out, "An action can hardly be called a mistake if it is the most characteristic action of one's life—the logical outcome of all that has gone before."

If this brief sketch has failed to convince that, given his character, Porter's flight was inevitable, Langford's definitive biography will be more persuasive. Porter's wit and charm could not win the indulgence of the law, nor were his patrons powerful enough to turn the law aside. Under these circumstances he apparently planned to remain in exile until he would be free from prosecution under the statute of limitations.

Less than a year later, on January 23, 1897, Porter returned to Austin and his dying wife. After her death he was tried and convicted of embezzlement and of flight to escape prosecution. His sentence of five years was the lightest that could be imposed. Although he maintained that he was innocent, and many believed him, it seems likely that he did embezzle at least some of the money to keep the *Stone* rolling. And he was undeniably guilty of flight.

Just before the trial Porter had sold his first story to a large publisher, the S. S. McClure Company, which brought it out on September 18, 1898, in newspapers associated with its syndicate. By this time he was in prison. "The Miracle of Lava Canyon," as the story was called, was the only one of his ever to be published nationally over the name W. S. Porter. Nearly all the rest were to be over pen names, the most famous of which is O. Henry.

That was the name Porter used most often to market his stories while in the Ohio Penitentiary. He sold poems under the name John Arbuthnott, and later some poems and stories as S. H. Peters. *Ainslee's* magazine, simplemindedly unwilling to let a cipher stand in place of a first name, got him to call himself Olivier Henry, and he went so far as to sign six of his stories (at least one of them written in prison) as Sydney Porter, the name he used "legally" after his release. But it was O. Henry who caught on and became a mysterious figure of mythical proportions, identified with his characters (cowboys, conmen, consuls, boulevardiers, actors, writers, merchants, rubes both rustic and slick, lovers of elegant ladies and shopgirls, confidants of the wealthy and the hobo) because no other personality existed in association with the name.

Unlike Samuel Clemens, who paraded himself as his alter ego, Porter used his other identity to shield himself. But the two men are alike in at least one way besides the initial popularity of their literary personas: Both were able to precipitate, by this indirection, a purer self. Both, too, characteristically keep even this self hidden from the casual reader; but to the careful reader go the surprise and pleasure of discovering a clear, tough mind, a self usually free of self-deception, who is the true originator of the words they are reading. This O. Henry seems to have been born between the flight to Honduras and Porter's release from the federal penitentiary in 1901, after serving three years with "good behavior." The Porter who refused to testify at his own trial may already have been this O. Henry.

Porter's three years in prison were as easy as they could have been. He was assigned immediately to the prison hospital because of his experience as a pharmacist. He ate and slept there until he had gained a trusty's job as bookkeeper in the steward's office, "entirely outside and separate from the rest of the institution," as he wrote to his mother-in-law. Porter was thus, by and large, segregated from the other prisoners, freer than most from molestation by them or by the guards, and often in the company of educated men. When he needed company, he sought it out, preferring westerners and conmen. He also had many hours free for reading and writing.

Yet Porter threatened suicide shortly after he arrived; and Dr. John M. Thomas, chief physician at the prison, who knew and liked him well—well enough to recommend that Porter be made the steward's bookkeeper even though it meant that he would lose his best pharmacist—remarked that in eight years as prison doctor, he had "never known a man who was so deeply humiliated by his prison experience."

In his earliest encounter with shame, young Porter learned the behavior that led to his imprisonment. This time he varied his response somewhat by creating a "new life," as prison stories have long taught us to think of it, as a writer. In this way he once again played a role, but he separated himself analytically from that role. As Porter he kept up a correspondence with his dead wife's parents and, through them, with his daughter, who knew only that he had to "be away" for a while. As a writer he turned his attention to analyzing what worked with audiences and why it worked. Already a master of the persiflage of journalistic humor, he sought the secrets of popular fiction. Porter rewrote "The Miracle of Lava Canyon," making it more marketable and more nearly profound—then sold it as "An Afternoon Miracle" to *Everybody's*. He entered the Christmas market by placing "Whistling Dick's Christmas Stocking" with *McClure's*, adjusting the sentiment of the season to the muckraking interests of that magazine by "exposing" the migratory habits of hoboes as well. (It was the first story to be printed as O. Henry's.)

Such calculated manipulation of popular literary conventions, such direct satisfaction of popular and editorial taste, went beyond what had been possible for the editor, chief reporter, and typesetter of *The Rolling Stone*. Prison life provided, ironically, the leisure for such analysis, but the humiliation of living that life provided the energy.

One aspect of prison life opened another perspective on the nature of things, particularly on social relations. Again, as in the Greensboro drugstore, the view was limited in scope, but this time it was much more profound. As prison pharmacist Porter saw and knew many men, could choose whom to talk with, for the most part; but in his dealings with the sick and injured this was not so. They forced him to look closely at what he otherwise could avoid. Here, in an extract from a letter to his father-in-law, written early in his imprisonment, is what he saw and how he saw it:

There are four doctors and about twenty-five other men in the hospital force. The hospital is a separate building and is one of the finest equipped institutions in the country. It is large and finely furnished and has every appliance of medicine and surgery.... The doctor goes to bed about ten o'clock and from then on during the night I prescribe for the patients myself and go out and attend calls that come in. If I find anyone seriously ill I have them brought to the hospital and attended to by the doctor. I never imagined human life was held as cheap as it is here. The men are regarded as animals without soul or feeling. They carry on all kinds of work here; there are foundries and all kinds of manufacturing is done, and everybody works and works twice as hard as men in the same employment outside do. They work thirteen hours a day and each man must do a certain amount of work or be punished. Some few strong ones stand the work, but it is simply slow death to the majority. If a man gets sick and can't work they take him into a cellar and turn a powerful stream of water on him from a hose that knocks the breath out of him. Then a doctor revives him and they hang him up by his hands with his feet off the floor for an hour or two. This generally makes him go to work again, and when he gives out and can't stand up they bring him on a stretcher to the hospital to get well or die as the case may be.... Twice a day they have a sick call at the hospital, and from two hundred to three hundred men are marched in each day suffering from various disorders. They march in single file past the doctor and he prescribes for each one "on the fly." The procession passes the drug counter and the medicines are handed out to each one as they march without stopping the line.

A society builds one of the "finest equipped" hospitals in the country, then staffs it with only four doctors; every day at sick call one doctor prescribes "on the fly" for 200 to 300 men; often a doctor revives a prisoner tortured into insensibility so that he can be tortured some more. It is no wonder that, after having this long look at the conditions around him, Porter threatened suicide. His ostensible reason was that he "never imagined that human life was held as cheap" as in the prison, but the weight of the details suggests another perception, associated but even more disturbing. It is that the systematic brutality takes place under the pretense of care.

Although the hospital seems a monument to social concern, provides "every appliance" to repair the health of the prisoners, in reality it is a sham. The doctors bring no substance to the role of healer. They exist so that the state cannot be charged with inhumanity, and fulfill that role most fully when they are present to see that corporal punishment hurts as much as possible but does not cause a death. Suicide might follow, but the hands of the institution are clean on that account. It does not slit the throat, fashion the noose, or seal the cell and turn on the gas—the common methods noted by Porter. At least for the record, all humane measures have been taken. Porter was part of those measures.

Once safely "outside" and living a "new life" as O. Henry to his readers and as Syd Porter to his new acquaintances, Porter never said a word directly about these horrors and the realization they had forced upon him. He is supposed to have told a fellow prisoner, "I will forget that I ever breathed behind these walls." But Porter's imagination touched again and again upon the routine playing of roles, much as the tongue touches a sore tooth. He seems never to have gotten the systematic pretense of the prison out of his system. To a large extent the humiliation felt at being assigned the roles of thief and prisoner is responsible for his obsession; but his realization that society, at least in its institutional forms, cares more for the role than for the substance completes the reasons for the recurring examination of role and routine in O. Henry's works.

The stories usually have a comic tone, to be sure, but distinctly uncomic possibilities often exist just at the fringes of his ostensible narrative. Sometimes, as though to call attention to his own role as entertainer, O. Henry almost visibly whisks his protagonists away from the brutality awaiting them by obviously superimposing a happy ending.

Two variations on a theme demonstrate how important this direct disclosure of his role was to become. O. Henry's first work to be published, as noted earlier, had been a Christmas story, "Whistling Dick's Christmas Stocking." As a subgenre of sorts (with Dickens' "A Christmas Carol" its best-known example), the Christmas story had to be both appropriately seasonal and happy in its outcome. "Whistlen" Dick, a hobo escaping the cold of winter and the New Orleans police, saves a plantation household from robbery and worse by warning them

of his fellow hoboes' plans. He is rewarded with a Christmas Eve feast and bed, as well as a promise "that the way would be heartily smoothed for him to rise to as high places of emolument and trust as the plantation afforded."

The predictable ending is not long in coming. In the morning Dick hears "certain dread and ominous sounds" as "the mighty din of the ogre Labor shook the earth," sounds so threatening that "the poor tattered and forever disguised Prince in search of his fortune held tight to the window-sill even in the enchanted castle, and trembled." In an instant he is gone, whistling in company with the birds, if one reads for that sentiment, or unable to cease being the poor tattered thing he has become, if one reads for another. Either interpretation can be derived directly from the story that O. Henry has told and from the conventions governing the portrayal of such "knights of the road" as Dick. One might smile at O. Henry's insinuation of the second reading under the first, but there is no surprise to either. O. Henry delivers the expected goods. His role remains secondary to the story he has to tell.

In 1906, seven years later, the Christmas story that O. Henry sold to *Ainslee's* also concerns a hobo, but the more "mature" O. Henry is manifest in the role, even roles, that he assumes in his story. At the outset of "Compliments of the Season," he appears as an essayist (a favorite gambit):

There are no more Christmas stories to write. Fiction is exhausted; and newspaper items, the next best, are manufactured by clever young journalists who have married early and have an engagingly pessimistic view of life. Therefore, for seasonable diversion, we are reduced to two very questionable sources—facts and philosophy. We will begin with—whichever you choose to call it.

The "beginning" that follows this beginning does seem to mix fact and philosophy: "Children are pestilential little animals with which we have to cope under a bewildering variety of conditions."

Another story mixes them even more sardonically. Fuzzy, a "soldier of misfortune," finds the pestilentially insistent poor little rich girl's lost rag doll, which he returns for the $100 reward. Unknown to him, Black Riley, "Pigeon" McCarthy, and "One-ear" Mike are waiting, "fingering under their coats the inevitably fatal weapons that were to make the reward of the rag-doll theirs." But Fuzzy, remembering a long-forgotten role, drunkenly will not leave without "'exchangin comp'ments sheason with lady th'house. 'Gainst princ'ples gen'leman do sho.'" In return he is chauffeured out of harm's way in the family's Mercedes.

The efficacy of seasonal ritual and almost forgotten social status and role is thus asserted against the menacingly and criminally brutal streets, but it is clearly all a sham. O. Henry's role in it is to provide the narcotic of the season for those who need it, but unlike the doctor or pharmacist on sick call back at the Ohio Penitentiary, he openly mocks his role.

It is easy, too, to see him eye the reader in need of a fix. In place of the "engagingly pessimistic" view provided by the young journalists who compete with him by dispensing "the next best" form of the narcotic of print, he pessimistically points to a world of violence from which Fuzzy has been saved only by the storyteller's power. The Fuzzies of society rarely fare so well. "One-ear" Mike's "brass knucks" are well broken in—they are "an heirloom in the family"—he is well socialized in his role, and he re-mains at large. O. Henry is also well socialized in the role he plays within the social ritual at hand. Throughout he has been engaging, often wittily cynical, sometimes as brilliantly inventive as a modernist poet ("Though the dusk of twilight was hardly yet apparent, lights were beginning to spangle the city like pop-corn bursting in a deep skillet").

Unlike the young journalists, O. Henry avoids the single role of being engagingly pessimistic. Both engagement of the reader and pessimism are too important to him to be carelessly mixed. Like the journalist—like Stephen Crane, say, reporting on the Spanish-American war—he is present in the familiar role of storyteller, entertaining with his wit and artful dressing of the "facts," even asserting his personality, as in the opening paragraph—the story, after all, is told from his point of view. Contemporary journalism had "stars," reporters whose personalities infused extra appeal into their dispatches. Among them was O. Henry's contemporary rival for popular fame as a short-story writer, Richard Harding Davis. But O. Henry cannot be summed up as the personality present in his works. Unlike Davis, though quite like Crane when he turned his great talents to fiction, O. Henry transcends the role he fills so obtrusively in his fiction. His pessimism resonates from depths undefined by social role and not to be measured by it.

Porter lived only nine years after leaving prison, nearly all of the period in New York. He stayed briefly in Pittsburgh, rejoining his wife's family and getting to know his daughter again, but New York clearly was where the money was to be made. By 1902 he was there. For a while he sent money for his daughter's care. Then, in 1907, Porter married a childhood sweetheart, Sara Lindsay Coleman, and brought both his wife and his daughter to live with him in New York. When the marriage did not work out, the three went their separate ways—his daughter off to school, for he was determined that she should have the college education he felt had been denied him.

However significant these matters were in O. Henry's personal life, the signal event of his professional career occurred in 1903, when he signed a contract with the *New York Sunday World* to write a weekly feature story, to be syndicated throughout the country. He wrote 113 of these, as well as the generally longer pieces for magazines such as *Ainslee's, Collier's, Cosmopolitan, Everybody's, McClure's, Munsey's, Red Book, Saturday Evening Post,* and *Smart Set.*

In 1904, O. Henry brought out his first book, *Cabbages and Kings,* in which he wove stories about Honduras into a book-length fiction—not a novel but not simply a collection of stories. *The Four Million,* published in 1906, established his reputation. Reprinting, for the most part, stories from the *Sunday World,* pieces already known to the millions who had read them there or in the papers buying the syndicated material, this volume did not range outside New York for its subjects, yet caught the attention of readers everywhere. Its title refers to the entire population of that metropolis, not to the "Four Hundred" for which Ward McAllister had claimed exclusive importance (this being the number that could be fitted into Mrs. William Astor's ballroom).

Some of O. Henry's stories in *The Four Million* touch on that golden circle: in "Mammon and the Archer" the mansion of the wealthy soap baron, Anthony Rockwall, borders on that of "the aristocratic clubman, G. Van Schuylight Suffolk-Jones," and Rockwall's son marries into the set that excludes his father and wants to exclude him. But the even more famous stories "The Gift of the Magi" and "The Furnished Room," like the majority of O.

Henry's tales from the *Sunday World,* keep so close to the experience of the working and shopkeeping classes as to make these pseudonymously penned, essentially anonymous stories a democratic answer to McAllister's self- and class-aggrandizing *Society as I Have Found It,* written in the preceding decade (1890). Society as the otherwise identityless O. Henry found it was quite a different thing.

From 1906 until his death in New York on June 5, 1910, O. Henry was able to bring out two volumes of short stories a year. After his death his publishers put together five more volumes. Nearly all his tales were twice-told, once in newsprint, once again between book covers. Such publication did wonders for his income, but even so he usually spent more money than he made. New York delighted O. Henry, and he moved about Bagdad-on-the-Subway, as he called it, as though he were a caliph in disguise—that, at least, is one of the literary masks he came to use. (In his rooms, sweating in his underwear over his weekly story for the *Sunday World,* he must have felt himself more genuinely to be a modern Scheherazade, spinning yarns because his life depended upon it.)

As soon as possible O. Henry moved from furnished rooms to more spacious lodgings on Irving Place, where the associations with Washington Irving delighted him. When he married, he took a house on Long Island and an apartment in Manhattan. He did his writing in an apartment at the Caledonia Hotel, where he could be reached only by those knowing the password. Nevertheless, acquaintances always could touch him for a loan, and beggars who approached him sometimes found themselves holding coins or bills of large denomination, so fully did he play the caliph in modern business suit. O. Henry stood countless men on the skids to a meal and a bed; he dressed expensively and ate well; and he drank ever more whiskey. By the time he died of diabetes and cirrhosis of the liver, he was drinking two bottles a day. He owed thousands of dollars to his first wife's parents and to people who had befriended him in Texas and elsewhere, and thousands more that had been advanced to him by publishers.

When he died, it was known that Sydney Porter had been O. Henry, but it was not generally known what else he had been. Some acquaintances had known his secret but had not felt free to discuss it with him. When it became known that he had spent three years in prison, his stories became even more popular, as any publicist could have told him would happen. But the role of ex-convict was one he remained unwilling to act.

Just as O. Henry was settling in New York, Frank Norris was proclaiming the death of the short story because the public had fed to satiety on the supply provided by the cheap magazines and Sunday supplements. O. Henry's success proved Norris' diagnosis to be wrong, but before long it was claimed that O. Henry himself had helped to kill the story as a form of art.

Praise found him incomparable and beyond criticism. Shakespeare was most often summoned up as a confrere, the common links being "a flashing wit, abundant humor and quick observation"—thus Henry James Forman, writing in that organ of American gentility, the *North American Review* (May 1908).

Carl Van Doren characterized the profusion of discovery and invention in O. Henry's work, the unique flavor and aftertaste of O. Henry's fiction, thus: "He is gay, irresponsible, impudent, hoaxing; no writer in the language seems clever immediately after one has been reading O. Henry." To this praise he added a shrewd observation: O. Henry was the raconteur of his literary generation, nearer to the actor than to the historian in his modus operandi, which, Van Doren remarked, "must be swift and easy, not too subtle." He also placed O. Henry's matter firmly within the tradition of romance. ("The true adventurer," O. Henry writes in "The Green Door," "goes forth aimless and uncalculating to meet and greet unknown fate.") O. Henry's tales, like those in that great "fountain head of romance," *The Arabian Nights,* attract popular attention because of "a certain popular quality in the plots, as if not a man but a generation had invented them." Implicitly, Van Doren made O. Henry the artful manipulator of already popular material, which is indeed true. He invented new ways of using old material, not new material itself.

Like many others, Van Doren objected to O. Henry's slang, though less understandably, since that practice would seem of a piece with the commonness of his plots and his role as raconteur. Curiously, O. Henry's slang today can seem a fresh discovery; it is the plots that now often seem tawdry. There is good reason to believe that they seemed so to O. Henry as well.

Van Doren's essay appeared as part of the flurry precipitated by the publication, in 1916, of C. Alphonso Smith's *O. Henry Biography.* Smith, who had grown up with O. Henry, renewed interest among readers with his carefully researched biography. It revealed what had taken place during the "shadowed years" in the Ohio Penitentiary, in this way inadvertently adding to O. Henry's legendary status growing out of earlier publicity and his own decision to remain faceless before his public. Smith's position as Poe professor of English at the University of Virginia, a title displayed prominently on the title page, doubtless lent his work added weight with that public.

Not all professors were impressed. The most tenacious and cogent of O. Henry's professorial critics was Fred Lewis Pattee. His fullest assessment came in *The Development of the American Short Story* (1923). Pattee granted that O. Henry was "the greatest short-story writer of his generation," but that conceded greatness—what he called O. Henry's "undoubted powers"—was "debauched" because O. Henry served the god Momus rather than the truth, because he had put his art at the service of "the swift ephemeral press" and produced a "narcotic effect" on demand for the "jaded and *blasé* and sensation-surfeited readers of Sunday papers."

Such criticism is a cultural event. O. Henry obviously had come to stand for the enemy, the mindless hordes of what H. L. Mencken called the "booboisie." (Mencken too found O. Henry to be anathema.) Worse, the boobs had forced the citadels of the universities, so that writing the short story (as "journalized" most successfully by O. Henry) had become the corrupt subject taught by corrupted professors. C. Alphonso Smith, "while exchange professor," had even "lectured on the short-story form in a German university."

Clearly Pattee was distressed by what the Germans must think of us now. He made it amply clear what *he* thought. The final chapter bears the title "O. Henry and the Handbooks"—so he styled those publications of the professors who "advertised their courses by statistics of the number of stories sold by the class the preceding year." Pattee's final criticism of O. Henry can easily apply to his colleagues and their courses: "He worked without truth, without moral consciousness, and without a philosophy of life."

Although Pattee was partisan, he was an honest man. One could place the blame on O. Henry for the emphasis everywhere, by the 1920's, "upon the mechanistic, upon manner, upon a technique that one might learn from books"; but Pattee conceded that, however amoral and unphilosophic O. Henry may have been, he had risen on the wings of pure originality. In contracting with the *Sunday World*

for a story a week, in placing his art at the level of a sweatshop pieceworker's shirt or shirtwaist dress (the examples are not Pattee's), he yet "had shaken off all trace of models and conformity to standards." His stories "were pure O. Henry." Their results were what Pattee regretted.

The record of the "handbooks" makes manifest the justice of Pattee's cause—the times did indeed seem derivative and bad, unless one looked in the direction of the modernist writers already at work. Even then it would have been apparent that no taste (including Pattee's) had developed for them, so that for one regretting the sins of the fathers, which gave every sign of having been visited upon their children in one's own generation, no consolation was in sight.

One writer saw O. Henry's works, their virtues and shortcomings, with even greater acuity than Van Doren had. Oliver W. Firkins placed himself between the middle class, which viewed O. Henry "as the impersonation of vigor and brilliancy," and that "part of the higher criticism" (into which we can justly fit Pattee) that "sees in him little but sensation and persiflage." Firkins paid for his right to hold judiciously to a middle position by removing himself from the field of combat: "Between these views there is a natural relation; the gods of the heathen are *ipso facto* the demons of Christianity." Firkins found O. Henry to be, like himself, a partisan of neither persuasion. Curiously, like Pattee he faulted O. Henry because he did not love the truth, because too often his stories ask the reader to "imagine the unimaginable."

But in one literary trait O. Henry must be ranked supreme: "the designing of stories." Firkins did not mean "the primary intuition" of them, the discovery of a new story. Nor did he mean "skill in development," the intricate designing of plot and accretive building of character. Rather, he meant "the disposition of masses," the "blocking-out of plots." In creating this almost visual effect, which cannot be subtle (at least on first impression) but can have great power, O. Henry has no superiors.

Here is how Firkins blocked out "The Furnished Room" for his readers:

Through the wilderness of apartments on the lower West Side a man trails a woman. Chance leads him to the very room in which the woman ended her life the week before. Between him and the truth the avarice of a sordid landlady interposes the curtain of a lie. In the bed in which the girl slept and died, the man sleeps and dies, and the entrance of the deadly fumes into his nostrils shuts the sinister and mournful coincidence forever from the knowledge of mankind.

The melodramatic nature of such a story, its lack of characterization, its reliance upon chance and coincidence instead of upon psychological motivation, is not the issue. The effect comes from treating these commonplaces almost abstractly, as though they were blocks of color.

Firkins does not put the matter this way, to be sure. In his formulation, "O. Henry's speciality is the enlistment of original method in the service of traditional appeals." Traditional appeal and original method highlight each other. They are the antitheses necessary to his successful synthesizing of them into a story uniquely his and giving a sensation beyond that expected of a story. "O. Henry transports us by aeroplane to the old homestead." So it seems to the reader who can find his or her way to the coign of vantage that Firkins builds above the warfare of the literary heathens and Christians. We may well find that ascent less difficult than our warring ancestors did.

"The Furnished Room," as we have seen, is the story that Brooks and Warren singled out when they prepared to do battle. They display their colors at the outset. Formally, we are told,

the story has two parts. The first tells of the man's final search and suicide; the second is the conversation between the landladies, from which we discover that the girl had indeed lived in the room and died there—by her own hand, as the young man is dying by his own hand at that moment. "What holds the two parts of the story together?" ask Brooks and Warren, and the answer they expect is clearly "Nothing very much." At least nothing very honest. For the ending, the conversation between the landladies, is there only to shock the reader. It has nothing to do with the story, which is about the young man.

That story could have been improved had O. Henry taken more pains to motivate the man's suicide by characterizing him more carefully. But even in an improved story the appended second part would remain "a trick played on the reader" rather than "a trick which fate has played on the young man." After all, even had he known that the girl had killed herself, even had he been motivated by being made aware of her fate, the young man might still have committed suicide.

Brooks and Warren concede that a conclusion motivated in this way "would seem very tame and flat." They use its probable tameness as evidence that O. Henry is practicing his wiles on the reader by writing the story as he does. To use their terminology, the conclusion to the revised version would be "meaningful" but not effective. O. Henry has chosen to create an effect (chills generated by "the sinister and mournful coincidence," as Firkins puts it) instead of generating meaning. To make the ending meaningful in Brooks and Warren's terms would be to destroy O. Henry's effect.

It is possible to defend the story pretty much on the grounds chosen by Brooks and Warren. For example, they single out for criticism the "sweet odor of mignonette" that reminds the young man of the girl and with which O. Henry apparently motivates the young man's suicide. To Brooks and Warren this motivation is insufficient: The "handling of this detail is confused," they write, although "the whole effect of the story depends on the incident of the odor." So it does, which is why O. Henry dwells on it. But if we assume that suicide is an action often imprecisely motivated, that the suicide's mind is often tired and confused; if we assume that no plot is likely to catch in its makeshift intricacy the lightning shifts in circumstance and feeling that convince the suicide there is no other way (even though tomorrow may bring several)—if we make these rather reasonable assumptions, then O. Henry's "motivation" becomes more satisfyingly realistic and the ending more nearly meaningful. Such a reading may not make the story rival one of Shakespeare's plays; but even if we are modest in our comparisons, it might be well to remember that confusion about the motivation of his characters has sometimes plagued that greater writer's critics.

Brooks and Warren do not make these saving assumptions, for they are out to murder, not to create; and in O. Henry's story they see the enemy. Why else begin with a question about form ("What holds the two parts of the story together?") and then move immediately to a discussion of motivation? There are, after all, other possible grounds besides characterization and motivation for perceiving a formal unity in the work at hand. Brooks and Warren, it would seem, choose a ground from which one cannot easily perceive a unity in O. Henry's story. Formalist criticism should be subtler and more generous. So, at least, Samuel Taylor Coleridge advised.

But Brooks and Warren can be forgiven. The enemy was real—the "booboisie," that is—and they were doing the good work of teaching how to read the modernist fiction derived from realism. If their work at times took on the pre-scriptive strategy of the handbook for criticism, it had the virtue of encouraging the reading of a new and inventive literature rather than, as with the earlier handbooks of short-story writing, the derivative multiplication of stories according to fixed formulas. If we now find the strictures of Brooks and Warren too confining, we can still thank them for having been among the literary fathers who taught the value of freedom.

The most useful critic for a reader of O. Henry today is less an ancestor who can head a countertradition than a foreign ally who can suggest untraditional ways of reading. (So it seems at first glance, at least.) Boris Eikhenbaum, writing in 1925, gave the answer to all those critics who had complained that O. Henry stressed manner at the expense of matter, that he loved effect too much and the truth too little. (In essence that is also Brooks and Warren's charge, though they draw it in New Critical fashion.) Inside the Soviet Union, far from the literary wars of the United States, though deeply involved in those of Russian literature and the Bolshevik Revolution, Eikhenbaum saw that "the laws of the short story dictated" that O. Henry "distort reality over and over again." In other words, it is true that O. Henry elevates manner over matter, but it is also true that to do so is essential to writing good stories. A formalist of a different persuasion, Eikhenbaum found O. Henry to be an instructive example in the evolution of literary forms, an artist whose work had much to teach Russian writers of his generation.

O. Henry's reputation among readers throughout the Soviet Union was considerable, another fact that Eikhenbaum took to be instructive. His reasons would seem to be of little interest to Americans, whose concern is with O. Henry and American readers of today, but such a conclusion would be mistaken: Eikhenbaum's argument proceeds on the premise that O.

Henry's is a peculiarly transitional form of literature, and transitional forms are much in evidence and demand today. At least in the history of Russian literature, we are told, short fiction had generally prepared the way for the novel, which Russians generally think (and apparently Eikhenbaum agreed) is a higher form. In Eikhenbaum's present, and under the conditions then prevailing, both short and long fiction stood in need of revival. Historical precedent showed that short fiction had first to be restored if long fiction were to be revived. O. Henry had shown the way, and Eikhenbaum set out to show the way O. Henry had marked. He seized upon O. Henry's popularity to show Russian writers how they might succeed.

O. Henry had revealed his own awareness of what the historical moment demanded. (Consider again the opening paragraph of "Compliments of the Season," in which O. Henry declares, long before John Barth was to come to a similar conclusion, "Fiction is exhausted.") His advantage over Russian writers was considerable, for instead of writing within a tradition dominated by long fictional forms, he wrote at the end of a tradition of short fiction, headed by Irving and Poe, and in which he benefited from a century of experiment and achievement.

Even long fiction in America is "manifestly oriented toward the story," we are told. (Eikhenbaum instances *The Scarlet Letter,* which indeed has a unity of "time, place, and action" similar to that of most short stories. But he says nothing of *Moby Dick* or *Sister Carrie.*) O. Henry is the last in a line of self-conscious practitioners of an art, all master craftsmen well initiated into its mysteries. He can thus deconstruct, in the fashionable phrase of our day, the dead and dying forms surrounding him. Out of that deconstruction, that corrosive dissolution of the dead flesh, he supplies his own boneyard of material for the creation of new formal possibilities in literary art.

The strategy of such an artist is parody. It is through parody that "the regeneration of a genre comes about—a transition from one set of possibilities and forms to another." The nature of short fiction, its source in folklore and anecdote rather than in syncretic forms such as history and travel writing (usually pointed to as sources for the novel), "amasses its whole weight *toward the ending.*" (American writers of O. Henry's time called such endings "the snapper." For a while actors called the "snapper" speech in a play constructed along similar lines "the O. Henry.") Furthermore, as Poe had argued long before, the manner of telling a short story is structurally essential to its success. It prepares for the ending.

O. Henry parodies both ending and manner. Others before him (Bret Harte, Frank Norris) had begun the parody of serious, longer forms, always reducing them in the process to story length. O. Henry concentrates on parodying the story itself. He frequently takes problems in literary practice as the subjects of his stories, such as the problems of finding authentic dialogue ("The Dog and the Playlet," "A Little Local Color") or material for a good story ("'Next to Reading Matter'"). He constructs beginnings that call attention to the teller rather than to the story (one of Mark Twain's tricks). He makes light of the intrigue that is the ostensible subject of his tale ("Tommy's Burglar"). He often gives away the apparent ending of the story well before he ends it—concluding instead with another and more "effective" ending than mere plot would provide (as in "The Furnished Room," one could note). He raises dialogue to a high tension, not to advance the story but to impede it by calling attention to the manner of narration. He interjects commentary for the same reason, and invents the most improbable metaphors, ironies, and the like.

This summary is not Eikhenbaum's, but in using such strategies as these O. Henry's stories are, we are told, "so far from any psychology, any ambition to foster in the reader an illusion of reality and bring him into contact with his heroes as people, that the very categories of comic and tragic can be said to be inapplicable to his works." Their true subject is literature. Their truest readers are the few who see the game for what it is, who enjoy meeting "the parodist almost overcome by his own wittiness and by the irony of his position vis à vis the reader and even vis à vis the craft of fiction itself."

But "parody is a road that leads to something else." According to Eikhenbaum, O. Henry had died before it led him there, but his roadbuilding efforts led in America to Theodore Dreiser, Sherwood Anderson, Waldo Frank, Ben Hecht—to a regenerated literature in which once again choice of material could take precedence over construction. (Had Eikhenbaum written a few years later, he might have pointed out that Ernest Hemingway began his career as a novelist by writing a parody of Anderson.) In Russian literature, though, a new self-consciousness about construction was a precondition to any regeneration. It needed its own O. Henry—or to take a close look at the example of O. Henry.

One cannot say that American literature needs the example of O. Henry. As though, in response to a request for a sample, a malfunctioning computer had thrown up a profusion of names in alphabetical proximity, our literary journals and magazines, our publishers of contemporary serious fiction, our times have given us John Barth, Donald Barthelme, Jorge Luis Borges, Michel Butor, and Richard Brautigan, then thrown in Robert Coover and Thomas Pynchon and a few others to keep the list of accomplished users of parody from beta dominance. It is commonplace to remark on the exhaustion of fiction, and engaging the reader in literary games and gamesmanship is the order of the day.

Yet O. Henry can add variety to these games, and to discover a literary ancestor may give almost as much pleasure as to find another interesting contemporary. His thematic material is different, not only in the literal sense of his parodying forms other than the more common subjects today but also because he approaches from a different angle the shared subjects of sham, convention, role, and identity.

The experience of prison life lent an urgency to O. Henry's themes that contradicts both Eikhenbaum's assessment of him as playful litterateur and Pattee's scornful dismissal of him as "a harlequin Poe with modern laughter in place of gloom." Less philosophical than Borges or Butor, less savvy about the weight of history than Pynchon, he nevertheless shares their gloom. As for self-asserting treatment of old themes in new ways, Barth looks elephantine in comparison, Barthelme almost commonplace. O. Henry has Brautigan's impudence and fascination with the power of narrative convention, yet had to please a wider audience and so worked more closely to the conventions at hand and under his eye. In short, he is worth reading as a literary ancestor who, with some accommodation on our part, can seem a contemporary. Like Laurence Sterne, who is a greater but also less accommodating English cousin, he can be made to live and even to cut capers.

O. Henry's art grows out of anecdote and is rooted in the folk tradition of short oral narrative, but it connects that tradition with the popular press and its "traditional" products for the readers of modern times. In the opening to "The Girl and the Graft"—"graft" being a term frequently used in O. Henry's time and tales to mean "confidence game"—the popular writer sets up a tale to be told by a narrator. The writer's hyperbolic playfulness, though, is hard to tell from the tale spinner's traditional hyperbole:

> The other day I ran across my old friend Ferguson Pogue. Pogue is a conscientious grafter of the highest type. His headquarters is the Western Hemisphere, and his line of business is anything from speculating in town lots on the Great Staked Plains to selling wooden toys in Connecticut, made by hydraulic pressure from nutmegs ground to a pulp.

The parody here is respectful, "parodic" only for lack of a better word. The audacity of a graft based on the recycled product of an earlier graft (the legendary Yankee peddler's bogus nutmegs) that is in turn passed off onto the grafter's descendants is delicious. With this opening paragraph the story writer indicates his awareness both of the sources of his story (the rogue peddler) and the telling of such stories (the oral tradition). He also defines the teller's diction, very respectfully, by measuring it against the parody of elevated diction so important to the story writer's art:

> I sat on his trunk while Ferguson Pogue talked. No one could be franker or more candid in his conversation. Beside his expression the cry of Henry James for lacteal nourishment at the age of one month would have seemed like a Chaldean cryptogram.

Pogue may be a grafter, Pogue's artful storytelling may be the art of a grafter, and O. Henry's composite written story may be the grafter's graft on a grafter's graft; but once these facts are acknowledged by sly glances of the eye or linotype, all is on the up and up.

(What's that, breathless reader?—or, as O. Henry once addressed his overeager audience, "bumptious reader"? The girl's graft is marriage, so that the professional grafter's graft is defeated by the more socially acceptable con of

the golden band and the tie that binds. Thus O. Henry sends us up on two of the game's oldest formulas, the guller gulled and the comic power of marriage.)

O. Henry's readers were more accustomed to journalistic fiction of a sentimental, bathetic sort, perhaps disguised with a well-cut coat of sophisticated banter but with the real bogus goods underneath. His parody of this fiction has a quite different flavor. Some is so close to its original as to be distinguishable only by a bitter aftertaste.

"Blind Man's Holiday" winds together love, suspicion, and a wise and knowing priest, present both for legal and religious reasons and to oversee the sentimental denouement. In this story the new husband is much relieved to discover that his bride has been a night-shift seamstress in a sweatshop rather than the prostitute he suddenly (and belatedly) suspected her of being. O. Henry only suggests sotto voce that her "virtuous" employment may have been nearly as exploitative as her presumedly vicious one—to have done more would have moved his story uncomfortably near the cliché of the virtuous woman of the streets. So he contents himself with planting ambiguities in the plot (the girl's eagerness to leave her employment and her shame at revealing its nature—signs her new husband reads with a conventionally "dirty" mind) and rich layers of literary textures in the ending. The priest's language moves about from the stage bombastic to the wittily jocular ("spying upon the mysteries of midnight millinery") to gruff brogue. Only on reflection does the parody come through, aided by these small signs.

Often, though, O. Henry's parody is open, especially when the target is sentimental or pretentious or both. In "Tommy's Burglar" the burglar "got into the house without much difficulty; because we must have action and not too much description in a 2,000-word story." But before he can bore the lock of the silver closet, he is engaged in conversation by young Tommy about how a burglar ought to behave in such a story and what clichés of plot and characterization it must contain. "A Dinner at ——" involves the story writer in disputes with his protagonist, Hudson Van Sweller, about what he as a "metropolitan type" should say and do— most of all, about whether he should "dine at ——." (To fill the blank, O. Henry's footnotes tell us, we should "See advertising column, 'Where to Dine Well,' in the daily newspapers.")

Such mocking self-consciousness about what writer and reader are up to can erupt at any time. "And now must come swift action, for we have here some four thousand words and not a tear shed and never a pistol, joke, safe, nor bottle cracked," cracks O. Henry in "A Night in New Arabia." The requisite action is taken care of in one sentence, followed by several more of delightfully pertinent impertinence:

Get the point? Of course I know as well as you do that Thomas is going to be the heir. I might have concealed the name; but why always hold back your mystery till the end? I say, let it come near the middle so people can stop reading there if they want to.

That the revelation is essential to O. Henry's plot is overlooked by a reader delighted with this playful attention to the medium. The art of parody in this way conceals the narrative art it is supposed to reveal.

As sensitive as O. Henry was to narrative convention and cliché, he was even more so to these matters in language. As one of his loquacious narrators remarks about a bug collector, "He was an etymologist, or words to that effect." He was attentive both to sources and to contemporary taxonomies of diction, so that he could fix Bulwer-Lyttonese in a cruelly accurate

parody of one sentence's length (see "The World and the Door"). One sketch, "Sound and Fury," is built entirely upon a stenographer's mistaken understanding and proposed corrections of a novelist's dictation. The easy joke is on Miss Lore (she corrects "rows" to "had risen," for example), but the bigger is on the utter banality of what Mr. Penne dictates— hence the title.

Yet the taxonomist does not crowd out the psychologist and metaphysician. O. Henry wrote over and over again about the need for such stock vocabularies of stock emotions. They give definition to the self in trying circumstances, lend shape—although borrowed—to emotions. "The World and the Door" again:

Dear me! in such scenes how the talk runs into artificial prose. But it can't be helped. It's the subconscious smell of the footlights' smoke that's in all of us. Stir the depths of your cook's soul sufficiently and she will discourse in Bulwer-Lyttonese.

Only taxonomists can pun so. Only metaphysicians, however rudimentary their philosophy, can speculate with any precision on epistemology.

O. Henry's speculations along these lines led him to conclude that the imagination, however banally, constantly shapes perception, more often narcotizing it, but always asserting its presence in what we experience. Imagination most often makes itself felt in the words chosen. An old man wanting to give away money proposes charity to a young man browsing in a secondhand bookstall and holding *Sartor Resartus* in one hand and *A Mad Marriage* in another ("'What You Want'"). Neither person understands the other, nor would the authors of the two books, but the old man's mistaking comes as much from stereotyping as the young man's does. In an empty boast that captures, in its ironic echoes of Mike Fink and Davy Crockett, the essence of American popular scorn for the literary imagination, old Tom Crowley the soap baron declares: "'I come from the West, where we imagine nothing but facts.'" The young object of his proposed charity may be addicted to Clark Russell's sea yarns, but he is on the side of truth and beauty when he refuses to buy *that* soap.

The language of the press concerned O. Henry the most. He understood the function of the press and of the journalese that was written, and his understanding flatters neither except in granting both extraordinary power. In "The Unprofitable Servant," which he left unfinished, he considers the art of journalism in tandem with the art of dancing. The dancer who "shall inherit Broadway" is one in "125,000 living creatures training for the stage." Besides talent, that one successful dancer needs training, drilling in the right moves by a master of them. It is an art the craft of which is highly conventional and difficult. Success comes more from submission to its rules than from original genius.

Journalism too is a craft bound by rules. One rule is to be only slightly different from other reporters and newspapers; another rule is to be predictably different. Given some "print-worthy incident," O. Henry claims, four reporters will read differently the shadows on the wall of the cave or process different phenomenal interpretations of the input from the Great Out There. (The examples and diction are not O. Henry's; his are entertainingly journalistic.) In such circumstances a wise man needs only one newspaper. Surely that "is enough for any man to prop against his morning water-bottle to fend off the smiling hatred of his wife's glances."

Newsprint exists, then, to erect thought- and ego-conserving and entertaining fictions between reader and reality. The narrator of "The Head-Hunter" had been a "bush-whacker correspondent" covering what a later generation of military and journalistic dope pushers would call "counter-insurgency action" directed at those natives of the Philippine Islands who were ungrateful for the protecting presence of their new and good friends and brothers from the United States. He resigned because his managing editor had notified him "that an eight-hundred-word cablegram describing the grief of a pet carabao over the death of an infant Moro was not considered by the office to be war news."

Expecting one genre of fiction, the public would not know what to do with a truth cast in a genre other than the one anticipated. On the other hand it might, or at least a part of that public might; but even O. Henry's disgruntled narrator does what he can to suppress the full power of the truth, leaving as he does the cause of the baby's death politely unspecified. He is not yet, it seems, a headhunter who can deposit "the severed, gory head" of his victim "with pardonable pride in the basket at the side of the door." Nor is his editor, no matter how cosmetically retouched that face in the basket. They are civilized. To differing degrees they cannot countenance expecting their readers to prop a severed head against the morning water bottle. (The masses of the story are so disposed as to show that civilized men will drop civilized pretense when a woman is at stake.)

Very rarely the conventions of newspaper stories and journals can be used to cook that rare bird, truth. "The New York *Enterprise* sent H. B. Calloway as special correspondent to the Russo-Japanese-Portsmouth war." But since the Japanese "were not ready for the readers of the *Enterprise* to season their breakfast bacon and eggs with the battles of the descendants of the gods," this companion of Richard Harding Davis had to cool his heels. He could have sent home fictions—other correspondents did—but he had not been sent to write "literature instead of news." His was an honest paper, as papers go. When his story went out, it cleared the censors as innocuous cable talk and scored a scoop.

"Calloway's Code," as the story is called, consisted of the following message: "Foregone preconcerted rash witching goes muffled rumor mine dark silent unfortunate richmond existing great hotly brute select mooted parlous beggars ye angel incontrovertible." The youngest reporter—the one most recently initiated into the mysteries, that is, so the one most aware of the silent rules by which they function—cracks the impromptu code. "'It's simply newspaper English,'" he explains. Much of it is still current: foregone conclusion, dark horse, silent majority, existing conditions, hotly contested, brute force, select few.

"'Old Calloway gives us the cue word, and we use the word that naturally follows it just as we use 'em in the paper.'" Naturally indeed! Yet sometimes second nature can be made to tell the truth. At other times what it tells is as close to the truth as we can get. And of course, so far as the "truth" about being killed or wounded or surviving a battle is concerned, Calloway's dispatch is as far from it as a map is from the terrain it signifies.

But to reason so perhaps puts too fine a point on O. Henry's slight story. Sometimes his tone encourages further probing of this sort; at other times it seems not to. The curious reader might look at the ending of "Calloway's Code" to see how much reflection it encourages, how extensively present the code it uses.

So it often is with parodies, whether full-blown or partial. Some are obvious, some are subtle. Some bite, some kiss, some bite in kissing. O. Henry was not alone among Americans in writing parodically at the turn of the century, but his tone, his attitude, are among the most complex. To measure them adequately and to define their special characteristics, it is probably best to range abroad, comparing him with other masters at satisfying the public's taste, yet mocking it to gratify part of that public or even part of a reader—even, perhaps, moving some to think and feel unconventionally. The examples of Robert Louis Stevenson and the operettas of W. S. Gilbert and Arthur Sullivan establish standards for O. Henry's popular art and provide as well a rough calculus for measuring how nearly unique his use of parody is.

As the master of adventure clearly and stirringly told and as a literary stylist of grace endowed with a wondrously popular imagination, Stevenson has a great deal in common with O. Henry. Adventure is an encounter with the unknown and, like Stevenson, O. Henry often sends his protagonist up against unknown and unknowable "fate," for want of a better word. Stevenson's tales and romances for children also provide a curiously complicated experience for their adult readers, one akin to parody done with a kiss. They are transparently directed at two audiences, the child consumer of the adventure and the occasional parent or adult performer of the text—who is often the bootleg consumer of the same adventure, yet enjoyer of the child's enjoyment. Like parodies, these texts address different audiences in the same words but with different signals. In company with much of the other popular literature for children, they remind us that literary pieces must often gratify quite diverse tastes within society, even within the reader.

But they are not parodies. If the author winks, it is not to question the materials at hand or even to celebrate them. On the other hand, the stories in Stevenson's *New Arabian Nights* are parodies, and O. Henry seems to refer to them in proposing his own revival of "the late Mr. H. A. Rashid." (Scribners had just brought out an American edition of *New Arabian Nights* in 1905, the year O. Henry began to locate some of his tales of adventure in "Bagdad-on-the-Subway.") Stevenson's tales are literary curiosities that corrode the literary and social conventions they lay bare. The adventurer must place himself at hazard willingly, for example, as O. Henry's does in "The Green Door," which in its protosurrealism resembles Stevenson's parodies. But Prince Florizel of Bohemia, Stevenson's modern Haroun al-Rashid, binds himself by his honor to accepting the criminal conduct of the Suicide Club, so that when the cards (or their sinister dealer) mark him as the next victim, he feels that as a gentleman he can do nothing to save himself. Because his companion is not so honor-bound, the tale can be concluded "happily" by his intervention. The resolution effected in this way is as hollow as the hazard of suicide by lot is disgusting, and throughout the tales of the *New Arabian Nights* equally disturbing situations and stratagems denigrate hero and circumstances alike. The princely adventurer, who is first introduced wearing false eyebrows and whiskers (so "to represent a person connected with the Press in reduced circumstances"), is finally reduced by a Bohemian revolution to being "the handsomest tobacconist in London." So much for the hero. In another tale an adventuresome young officer observes servants carrying off what amounts to the stage scenery for his enlistment on the prince's behalf. The whole ethos of adventure is simultaneously being dismantled by Stevenson.

It is hard to say whether youthful high spirits or barely controlled hysteria is responsible for Stevenson's wholesale parody, but there is no mistaking his intention to bite. Perhaps he had first to kill contemporary absurdities of plotting and characterization in order to create his own more nearly realistic adventures. Parody thus would have been a necessary condition for achieving the apparently serene awareness of a multiple readership that plays over such works as *Kidnapped* (1886).

O. Henry, on the other hand, never moves beyond parody, incorporating it instead as an essential element of his art and vision. Adventure erupts into the life of John Hopkins when, after doing inglorious battle with the keeper of the corner cigar store and "the inevitable cop," he is whisked away to do battle for a fair lady in what turns out to be a silly, recurring domestic disagreement. The husband "irresistibly" overpowers the recent champion of the street battle and returns him to his element. The glory of it all lies in the sketch of Hopkins' routine life that encapsulates the brief adventures. "John Hopkins sat, after a compressed dinner, in his glove-fitting straight-front flat." In sentences like this O. Henry represents "The Complete Life of John Hopkins." It, like his conversation, is empty, even of adventure—although his willingness along that line indicates a spark of "romance," as O. Henry calls it, that the modern world has not totally extinguished. The parody of adventure curiously confirms its value. O. Henry bites and kisses.

The example of Gilbert and Sullivan likewise demonstrates that parody can confirm value. In *The Pirates of Penzance* (1879) they kiss the sources that they plunder for their musical material. They further dispose these piracies so brazenly as to call attention to their origins on the operatic stage and in the popular music hall. Ruth's simpleminded "When Frederic was a Little Lad" helps to set up Mabel's later coloratura warblings, just as the Pirate King's utterly empty opening aria with chorus ("'I am a Pirate King'—'He is, he is a pirate king!'") sets off Major General Stanley's patter song, "I am the Very Model of a Modern Major General."

Their sources so openly admitted, Gilbert and Sullivan can call attention to how they dispose the masses of these contrasting materials throughout, for few stage pieces are so effectively blocked out as theirs. Like O. Henry they are masters of design, and the secondary, parodically derivative nature of their music and verses serves them in exercising that mastery.

They too are masters of manner, both of phrase and of total composition. O. Henry's stories, because short, are generally simpler in pattern, but his uncharacteristically long "A Municipal Report" declares its unity in this fashion, with especially interesting results in how the stereotype of the former slave is confirmed and then exploded.

The Pirates of Penzance is concluded by the most obvious sleight-of-hand, the most conventional of signals that the entertainment is over. The pirates are discovered to be "noblemen who have gone wrong"; and since "peers will be peers," they can be reformed, like any other boys, simply by uttering mother's name—in this instance, Queen Victoria's. O. Henry's endings also consist of the most conventional of signals, but at their best they set convention against convention in the service of truth. They bite as they kiss.

Endings are the most obvious structural element of short stories, the place where the writer's hand makes itself the most strongly felt. Consequently, they are the most useful part of the story for declaring and perceiving the artist's interest in parody. *New Arabian Nights* and *The Pirates of Penzance* are disparate but confirming cases in point. If O. Henry's interests lie in that direction, his famous endings should suggest the lay of the literary land. They also should illustrate the uses of parody, for it can indeed lead beyond itself. It can, for instance, fasten us tightly to reality, or it can awaken us to how fully mediated by conventional form all awareness of reality must be. Parody in such instances ceases to be simply the indulgent or satirical mocking of literary or other art forms. It becomes a passkey to the world of forms, and perhaps as well an instrument for registering the pressures exerted upon those forms by the realities of the contiguous but directly unknown realms of natural, social, psychological, and perhaps even spiritual force.

O. Henry is famous for the "snappers" that conclude his brief narratives, but he is by no means unique in using these. Eugene Current-Garcia provides a convenient summary of the surprise endings available to O. Henry: "the hoax and the practical joke, the anti-conventional or distorted revelation of events, the paradoxical or antithetical disclosure, the manipulation of psychological concepts, the double reversal, the problem close—all of which had been worked with varying success by O. Henry's predecessors and contemporaries." That O. Henry uses all should not be surprising. The question is how he uses them. Sometimes he simply closes definitively. The silly "October and June" is a practical joke of sorts and never can be anything more; the famous "The Gift of the Magi" exploits the double reversal for maximum effect but gives no prospect from which to reconsider the story.

To be sure, in the course of telling the latter story O. Henry indicates how aware he is of his role by asking the reader to "Forget the hashed metaphor." The metaphor in question, though, defines the recently shorn Stella's delighted ransacking of the stores for her husband's present. O. Henry merely uses his self-consciousness to validate the pleasure she takes in self-abandonment. At such times convention rules the heart; the self-conscious artist intrudes upon its precincts. O. Henry, consequently, will risk bathos but not irony when he comes to putting an end to his Christmas story.

Often, O. Henry's endings set convention against convention. As a result truth will be heard, even if it proves to be banal. That is why the elements of O. Henry's surprises so often cancel or undercut each other. Nor are they simply unresolved paradoxes or antitheses. They point toward a common ground in experience or a synthesis of meaning, but such a "truth" cannot be offered as O. Henry's ending. The reader must derive it from the story by means of the ending. "The Furnished Room" ends by directing attention away from the suicide's motivation to the larger question of motives, their sources and etiologies. "A Municipal Report" concludes by making murder a socially useful tool, thus so shocking conventional expectations as to bring back into question the social roles and special dictions parodied throughout the story.

Perhaps "The Country of Elusion" most clearly shows the artist enlisting his reader in backward revision. For the most part the narrative is a sketch of New York's Bohemia, ostensibly even an essay rather than a tale: "The cunning writer will choose an indefinable subject; for he can then set down his theory of what it is; and next, at length, his conception of what it is not—and lo! his paper is covered."

But the narrative that emerges, although rudimentary, seems to develop differently. Bohemian Mary Adrian enjoys her Saturday night of spaghetti, wine, and repartee; but, as the narrator remarks of the Bohemians, "Freedom is the tyrant that holds them in slavery." Consequently, Mary escapes for her Sunday to the home and religion of her parents, where, "out of the clutch of the tyrant, Freedom," she feels her soul fill "with a delicious, almost a fanatic joy." When she returns to the city, she can declare "'I have been away in Bohemia'" because, as O. Henry tells us, that is "nothing more than the little country in which you do not live."

Mary's declaration has "spoiled" O. Henry's climax. But not his ending, which coincides with the end put to Sunday night's Bohemian revel by the efficacious slap that Mary administers to Kappelman when he tries to kiss her. Upon this ending is superadded yet another, an "anticlimax" that turns out to be *the* ending, the judgment by Minnie, another native of Mary's hometown that "'if she had stayed there a week,'" instead of the day she did, Kappelman "'would have got his kiss.'"

Initially these shifts are bewildering. The indefinable subject, "Bohemia," is twice defined explicitly. It is both that society in which free-

dom rather than convention enslaves (where the conventions of laissez-faire hold sway, that is) and that unknown place where convention seems not to rule. Between these definitions is a third, Mary's implication that it is the place where one can freely yield to convention because one is otherwise free from it—one is only a temporary resident.

Mary's definition and the one O. Henry extrapolates from it differ in one important principle. Mary can visit her Bohemia and enjoy it because she knows its conventions, whereas the person who conceives of Bohemia as free of convention is merely ignorant—no such place exists, it is only the "hillside that you turn your head to peer at from the windows of the Through Express." In slapping Kappelman, Mary violates the conventions of New York's "sham-Bohemia" by applying those of Crocusville, which by her definition ought not to apply. The glow of Kappelman's cheek shows that they do. So too does the general exodus: The Bohemians hear in the slap "the sound of the ax of the fly cop, Conscience," so they vacate the premises before the raid can get under way. The cop may have been born in Crocusville or whatever the name of the town, but he lives on in New York. Habit, another of O. Henry's terms for convention, thus would seem to tyrannize whether it is called freedom or the straight and narrow way.

But this is to reason without Minnie's conclusion, O. Henry's anticlimax. Her worldly wisdom, gleaned from a life in Crocusville and a short vacation in New York's Bohemia, concludes that a few days of real suffering at the ancestral homestead would have stilled Mary's conscience. Instead of the easy conclusion that all living is conventional and all conventions essentially the same, Minnie sees that some conventions are to be preferred over others. New York is not simply an urban Crocusville.

O. Henry offers this conclusion as one of those from the great vault in which are stored "the anticlimaxes that should have been tagged to all the stories that have been told in the world." All, that is, lie in their endings; all need their conclusions qualified. Endings are too definite. So too, consequently, would be the suppressed anticlimaxes. To be truthful, stories need both. Yet conventionally they come with only one—even when it is a "surprise." The wise reader, for whom Minnie stands in as O. Henry reads her his manuscript story, must supply the other ending, then reject its imperial claim to being the real truth. The wise reader must both be Minnie and take over from her.

"Mammon and the Archer" does not invite so openly the reader's revision, yet it conceals in its ending a fact that brings that ending into doubt. It seems to end in an unambiguous double reversal. At first Aunt Ellen announces her nephew's engagement and attributes his success to true love rather than to her brother's money: "'Money is dross compared with true love, Anthony.'" Then Anthony pays off the man who organized the traffic jam that gave his son the time he needed to press the engagement. Incorrigible Anthony takes delight in asking if his henchman had seen "'a kind of a fat boy without any clothes on shooting arrows around with a bow.'" Kelly's mystified but negative answer confirms the old man's belief in the power of money, while the exchange between the two ends the story with what seems a conclusive exhibition of that power.

Yet part of Kelly's report opens ample room for doubt. "'The boys was on time to the fraction of a second.'" The cab, though, would have been nearly a minute early—would have been, that is, except that it had stopped that little time for young Richard to retrieve the dropped ring, the "little emblem of true love" that his aunt had referred to in singing the power of love. Had it not been for that delay, organized by love or chance or fate, the traffic jam organized by Anthony's money would have been several seconds late, and the sentimental cyni-

cism with which the story seems to end would have been openly punctured.

As it is, it would seem that both Aunt Ellen and brother Anthony are right, but it is left to the reader to see that the story is about Mammon *and* the Archer, not—as the apparent reversal in the ending suggests—Mammon *over* the Archer.

O. Henry located this story precisely in the middle of his second volume of stories, *The Four Million* (1906). Around it and its evenly balanced conclusion he distributed a number of other, somewhat larger, symmetries such as paired stories of similar theme or treatment. The whole is then enclosed within a frame of four stories, a kind of prologue followed by "The Gift of the Magi" to open the collection, and "The Furnished Room" followed by a kind of epilogue to close it. The three famous pieces are thus related to each other almost geometrically in a pattern identical to that of *The Scarlet Letter,* in which the second, middle, and penultimate chapters provide the "scaffolding" for the whole.

O. Henry's prologue, "Tobin's Palm," reunites separated lovers through the fortunate and kindly intercession of a writer; the epilogue, "The Brief Début of Tildy," is about a plain waitress briefly elevated to the ranks of the interesting because a customer kisses her. After the suicides in "The Furnished Room," though, a happy ending is not in order, and the fellow apologizes for having done "tanked up" what he never would have done sober. The consolation offered to Tildy by her beautiful colleague is, under the circumstances, of little worth to Tildy, though it provides a wry conclusion to the collection as well as to the story: "'He ain't anything of a gentleman or he wouldn't ever of apologized.'"

Sometimes writers can be matchmakers, as O. Henry begins the collection by showing us, but too much of such intervention denies reality. On the other hand, to deny that the writer may intervene is to close one's eyes to the obvious fact that the writer makes the story, that whatever "reality" it has is derivative or formative, not primary. O. Henry's volume is organized, like his best stories, to keep these realities before us. It is also organized so as to encourage reading between the lines, between the stories, for matter and insight that lie beneath or transcend the stories themselves.

O. Henry's first volume of stories is organized in quite different fashion. *Cabbages and Kings* (1904) begins with "The Proem: By the Carpenter," tuning what follows to the nonsense of Lewis Carroll's "The Walrus and the Carpenter." The setting is not nonsense but the Trujillo, Honduras, that O. Henry had known during his brief exile. On the other hand, the stories are all either operetta stage shows concerning love and revolutionary misfiring or vaudeville dialect acts or elaborated tall tales and other forms still close to oral tradition. In order to sell shoes, for example, a character imports cockleburs into the near paradise of Anchuria, O. Henry's fictional Honduras. Then, to make the tale of "Shoes" taller, in "Ships" the enterprising exporter of the original barrel of cockleburs shows up with two ships full of the no longer necessary seeds, expecting to sell them to the "factory" he imagines must somehow use them. This foolishness has its points: Such petty graft mimics the devastating, larger machinations of the Vesuvius Fruit Company, and the variety-show aimlessness of the different stories makes taking the whole seriously both difficult and important. In one way O. Henry tries to make a whole out of them: he provides a complicated plot that, in a few stories revised or written for this purpose, lends a sort of coherence to the whole.

But despite all the care expended on providing this plot, O. Henry leaves enough rough inconsistencies to torment the careful reader. At the outset we are told that scarcely anybody has ever seen the president, for he is never there, yet within a few stories it turns out that Coralio, the Trujillo of the book, becomes the "Newport of Anchuria" for five months of every year, with the entire government in residence. What should a reader do with such apparent nonsense?

The ending smooths only a few of the prickly spots. It solves several mysteries but not the mystery of the book's form. Of course O. Henry wrote short stories, not novels; and he wove some together into this book that might seem for a while a novel to those who prefer that form of entertainment, but that is likely to disappoint devotees of either form. The book is perhaps a failed experiment, and it is true that it did not bring the fame and royalties O. Henry had hoped for. But the apparent shortcomings of the stories still invite the reader's inventive intervention, while O. Henry's resolution of the mysteries in the plot may hint at other kinds of resolution not so bound to the conventions of storytelling. Eikhenbaum was drawn to the volume because of its "cyclical" structure, its movement toward the narrative form of so many novels. He might better and more consistently have liked it because of its manifest failure to take the forms of its parts and whole seriously—so that, perhaps, the reader must correct that failure and remanipulate them.

The plot, for instance, reveals who lies beneath the headstone marking a grave as that of President Miraflores. Needless to say, it is not Miraflores' grave. Throughout *Cabbages and Kings* choice as well as chance or fate has cast other identities into different roles, so that name and role (the disguises of conmen and revolutionary agitators alike) dissolve as signs of reality. O. Henry's great themes—the arbitrariness of all convention, the nameless forces that he calls fate (imaged in part by the Vesuvius Fruit Company), the consequently artificial character of personal identity—are all roughly suggested by the meandering plot and shifting identities of *Cabbages and Kings*. These can be analyzed more subtly and fully by a reader who takes the near nonsense of them as a sign of seriousness.

The other volumes are rarely as carefully ordered as these. In 1907, O. Henry brought out *The Trimmed Lamp,* a collection of city stories mostly from the *Sunday World,* and *Heart of the West,* stories written, by and large, before he had signed the contract with the *World.* The next year he kept the same pattern. *The Voice of the City* collects more stories from the *World,* while *The Gentle Grafter* concerns confidence men working mostly in the South and West, though visiting New York on occasion. All but two of the stories are narrated by Jeff Peters, who "in the line of unillegal graft" is "a reducer of surplusage" rather than a man "to be dreaded by widows and orphans." All but three (the two narrated by others and the final story) were written for this volume, which consequently is the most nearly unified in tone and subject of all O. Henry's books. Perhaps creating a narrator freed his inventive powers; perhaps it was the sophisticated use of folk-narrative situations and material. Although Eikhenbaum liked these stories for their picaresqueness, they leave curiously little opportunity for the reader's creativity to gain a purchase.

In 1909, O. Henry published *Roads of Destiny* and *Options,* both miscellanies but the latter comprised recent work with one exception. *Strictly Business* (1910) was the last collection supervised by O. Henry. The businesses are many (yet most often love and marriage), the strictness occasionally lax; but it contains some of the most interesting late stories, the central one of which, "A Ramble in Aphasia" (amnesia, as we now say), is a comic treatment of identity, role, and repression that obliquely reduces conflict in social roles to a proposed reform in the shelving habits of druggists.

A few stories in the posthumously published collections make reading the wholes worthwhile. *Rolling Stones,* for example, contains what O. Henry justly thought the best of his Jeff Peters stories, "The Atavism of John Tom Little Bear." Behind its stereotyping of sex and race roles one can find just the opposite in the self-knowledge of the deracinated American Indian of the title. It is easy to see why O. Henry left it out of *The Gentle Grafter,* for it is unusually open to the less gentle reader's imagination.

Such readers will find much of O. Henry fascinating. But they must meet him more than halfway sometimes, and even so they will not always find him there. Poe, who like O. Henry sought a popular audience, counseled against trying to make the "suggested meaning" of a story anything more obvious than a *"very* profound undercurrent, so as never to interfere with its upper one without our own volition, so as never to show itself unless called to the surface." Poe was writing about allegory; O. Henry's "suggested meaning" is something quite other. Yet the two judged the demands of popular taste identically. Most readers do not want to hear the author talking over their heads to other readers—it spoils the effect that they find entertaining. Knowing this O. Henry keeps his suggested meanings well hidden by making their subject the conventions he manages so entertainingly.

There are several ways of thinking about works of art that only partly reveal themselves. Hemingway described these creations as icebergs, three-fifths hidden. One can think, less metaphorically, of the larger set of facts and circumstances that must exist in order for the fragmentary form that we call a story to have claims to existence outside itself. Sometimes these circumstances can be told narratively, are even hinted at in the narration of the story. Sometimes they cannot be told, only touched through the mediation of the story. Such are the icebergs that Hemingway tried to create, that

Sherwood Anderson created, that so much of Romantic and modern literature evokes as its melting and shifting ground. Ernst Theodor Amadeus (E.T.A.) Hoffmann, Poe, Hawthorne, Ivan Turgenev, Chekhov, Anderson, Hemingway—all in different ways call into relation with their stories a reality that cannot be expressed directly. It is frequently called fate, and it often impresses itself as horror or wonder or a mixture of the two. Stories otherwise as different as Turgenev's "Bezhin Lea" and Anderson's "Death in the Woods" have its evocation in common.

O. Henry's stories rarely seem to evoke it. The narrative conventions that adorn their surfaces glitter so charmingly as to satisfy more commonplace responses. Their creator is even more careful than Poe not to compromise his role as popular entertainer. His icebergs are shrouded in a mist on which the sunshine plays. Yet mist must come from somewhere, and the skilled navigator will intuit the shape of the melting mass that, underneath, gives rise to the mist. To change the metaphor, O. Henry's is an art of surfaces delightfully played with, surfaces rearranged by their manipulator in performances immediately recognizable as his. Most readers stay seated in the audience, taking it all in as they would a vaudeville show; the best will be pricked by his performance to try their hand at the game. They will apprentice themselves to a man narrowly obsessed by the terror and beauty of man's role as manipulator of surfaces, a wizard of elusion and aphasia rather than of Oz, a man who has looked too closely for comfort at the social lies of convenience that we call civilization.

When O. Henry was about to be checked into the hospital to die, he was asked what name should be entered on the records. "Call me Dennis," he is supposed to have said. "My name will be Dennis in the morning." The derivation of "Dennis" from "Dionysius" may be ascertained from most dictionaries, and O. Henry may indeed have been playing with an especially deep-rooted surface. There is another possibility. "My name will be Dennis" seems to have been a slang idiom. When William Sidney Porter was about to be indicted for embezzlement, he is supposed to have remarked to an old friend that if the bank examiner should find his error, "'my name will be Dennis.'" So, apparently, it was.

Yet the man lived on, privately as Syd Porter, publicly as O. Henry. He came to know the underworld from the inside and to see the upper world from the underside. It seems likely, then, that he had long before also seen the connection between the casual slang and its mythic rightness. It was ever his method, at his best, to take what is mindlessly uttered or enjoyed and make it significant to the diligent initiate.

In one mystery O. Henry was the only initiate—his name. Scholarship may one day sift out the competing explanations, but it is unlikely. It is also unnecessary. For a man so obsessed with the power of social role, convention, and other sources of social conditioning, what better name than a mysterious one, what better sign than one pointing at once to the commonplace and the unknown?

Selected Bibliography

WORKS OF O. HENRY

Cabbages and Kings. New York: McClure, Phillips, 1904.
The Four Million. New York: McClure, Phillips, 1906.
The Trimmed Lamp. New York: McClure, Phillips, 1907.

Heart of the West. New York: McClure, 1907.

The Gentle Grafter. New York: McClure, 1908.

The Voice of the City. New York: McClure, 1908.

Options. New York: Harper, 1909.

Roads of Destiny. Garden City, N.Y.: Doubleday, Page, 1909.

Strictly Business. Garden City, N.Y.: Doubleday, Page, 1910.

Whirligigs. Garden City, N.Y.: Doubleday, Page, 1910.

Sixes and Sevens. Garden City, N.Y.: Doubleday, Page, 1911.

Rolling Stones. Garden City, N.Y.: Doubleday, Page, 1912.

Waifs and Strays. Garden City, N.Y.: Doubleday, Page, 1917. (In addition to twelve stories, this volume collects critical and appreciative essays, none of which is listed below.)

O. Henryana. Garden City, N.Y.: Doubleday, Page, 1920.

Postscripts, edited and with an introduction by Florence Stratton. New York: Harper, 1923.

O. Henry Encore, edited and with an introduction by Mary S. Harrell. Garden City, N.Y.: Doubleday, 1939.

The Complete Works of O. Henry. Garden City, N.Y.: Doubleday, 1953. (Earlier editions, nearly all issued by Doubleday, are numerous. Only those published after 1917 can be considered complete.)

Collected Stories of O. Henry, edited by Paul J. Horowitz. New York: Avenel, 1979.

BIBLIOGRAPHIES

Clarkson, Paul S. *A Bibliography of William Sydney Porter (O. Henry).* Caldwell, Ida.: Caxton, 1938.

Long, E. Hudson. "O. Henry (William Sidney Porter) (1862–1910)." *American Literary Realism,* 1:93–99 (Fall 1967).

BIOGRAPHICAL AND CRITICAL STUDIES

Abrams, Fred. "The Pseudonym 'O. Henry': A New Perspective." *Studies in Short Fiction,* 15:327–29 (Summer 1978).

Arnett, Ethel Stephens. *O. Henry from Polecat Creek.* Greensboro, N.C.: Piedmont Press, 1962.

Brooks, Cleanth, and Robert Penn Warren. *Understanding Fiction.* New York: Holt, 1943.

Clarkson, Paul S. "A Decomposition of *Cabbages and Kings.*" *American Literature,* 7:195–202 (May 1935).

Current-Garcia, Eugene. *O. Henry (William Sydney Porter).* New York: Twayne, 1965. (Contains selected, annotated bibliography.)

Davis, Robert H., and Arthur B. Maurice. *The Caliph of Bagdad.* New York: D. Appleton, 1931.

Firkins, O[liver]. W. "O. Henry." In *Modern Essays,* edited by Christopher Morley. New York: Harcourt, Brace, 1921. Pp. 100–12.

Gallegly, Joseph. *From Alamo Plaza to Jack Harris's Saloon: O. Henry and the Southwest He Knew.* The Hague: Mouton, 1970.

Jennings, Al. *Through the Shadows with O. Henry.* London: Duckworth, 1923.

Langford, Gerald. *Alias O. Henry: A Biography of William Sidney Porter.* New York: Macmillan, 1957.

Long, E. Hudson. *O. Henry: American Regionalist.* Austin, Tex.: Steck Vaughn, 1969.

———. *O. Henry, the Man and His Work.* Philadelphia: University of Pennsylvania Press, 1949.

McLean, Malcolm D. "O. Henry in Honduras." *American Literary Realism,* 1, no. 3:39–46 (Summer 1968).

O'Connor, Richard. *O. Henry: The Legendary Life of William S. Porter.* New York: Doubleday, 1970.

Pattee, Fred Lewis. "O. Henry and the Handbooks." In his *The Development of the American Short Story.* New York: Harper, 1923. Pp. 357–64.

Peck, H. T. "The American Story Teller." *Bookman,* 31:131–37 (April 1910).

Smith, C. Alphonso. Introduction to *The Trimmed Lamp.* In *The Biographical Edition of the Complete Works of O. Henry.* Garden City, N. Y.: Doubleday, Page, 1925.

———. *The O. Henry Biography.* Garden City, N.Y.: Doubleday, Page, 1916.

Van Doren, Carl. "O. Henry." *Texas Review* (later *Southwest Review),* 2:248–59 (January 1917).

Williams, William Wash. *The Quiet Lodger of Irving Place.* New York: E. P. Dutton, 1936.

—*KENT BALES*